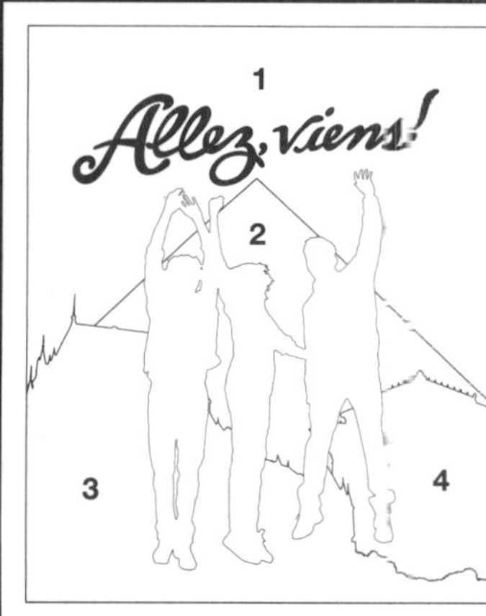

Front cover:

1 Pattern from a 17th century textile from Lyons which features a stylized pineapple – first brought to Europe from the West Indies, it was a favorite fruit of European royalty

2 Pyramid of glass designed by I.M. Pei as part of President François Mitterrand's renovation of the Louvre museum in Paris in the 1980s

3 The majestic Château Frontenac in Quebec City, a world-renowned hotel built in 1893

4 The famous Fort-de-France landmark Bibliothèque Schœlcher, named for the man who abolished slavery in Martinique in 1848

Back cover:
Young woman in traditional costume of Brittany, an area of France known for its intricate lacework

Holt French Level 1

Allez, viens!®

With Integrated Multimedia

John DeMado
Emmanuel Rongiéras d'Usseau

HOLT, RINEHART AND WINSTON
Harcourt Brace & Company
Austin • New York • Orlando • Atlanta • San Francisco • Boston • Dallas • Toronto • London

Portions of this work were published in previous editions.

COVER PHOTOGRAPHY CREDITS

FRONT COVER: (br), Schœlcher Library, Fort-de-France, Martinique, HRW Photo/Marty Granger; (bl), Château Frontenac, Quebec City, Canada, Miwako Ikeda/International Stock; (c), Louvre, Paris, France, Photo AKG London; (c), students jumping, Telegraph Colour Library/FPG International Corp.

BACK COVER: France, Brittany, young woman in regional costume, Steve Vidler/Leo de Wys, Inc.

FRONT AND BACK COVER: (bckgd pattern), Copyright © 1992 by Dover Publications, Inc.

Acknowledgments appear on page R83, which is an extension of the copyright page.

Printed in the United States of America

ISBN 0-03-052079-7

2 3 4 5 6 7 061 02 01 00 99

AUTHORS

John DeMado
Washington, CT

Mr. DeMado helped form the general philosophy of the French program and wrote activities to practice basic material, functions, grammar, and vocabulary.

Emmanuel Rongiéras d'Usseau
Le Kremlin-Bicêtre, France

Mr. Rongiéras d'Usseau contributed to the development of the scope and sequence, created the basic material and listening scripts, selected realia, and wrote activities.

CONTRIBUTING WRITERS

Jayne Abrate
The University of Missouri
Rolla Campus
Rolla, MO

Sally Adamson Taylor
Publishers Weekly
San Francisco, CA

Linda Bistodeau
Saint Mary's University
Halifax, Nova Scotia

Betty Peltier
Consultant
Batz-sur-Mer, France

REVIEWERS

Dominique Bach
Rio Linda Senior High School
Rio Linda, CA

Jeannette Caviness
Mount Tabor High School
Winston-Salem, NC

Jennie Bowser Chao
Consultant
Oak Park, IL

Pierre F. Cintas
Penn State University
Abington College
Abington, PA

Donna Clementi
Appleton West High School
Appleton, WI

Cathy Cramer
Homewood High School
Birmingham, AL

Robert H. Didsbury
Consultant
Raleigh, NC

Jennifer Jones
U.S. Peace Corps volunteer
Côte d'Ivoire 1991–1993
Austin, TX

Joan H. Manley
The University of Texas at El Paso
El Paso, TX

Jill Markert
Pflugerville High School
Pflugerville, TX

Inge McCoy
Southwest Texas State University
San Marcos, TX

Gail Montgomery
Foreign Language Program
Administrator
Greenwich, CT Public Schools

Agathe Norman
Consultant
Austin, TX

Audrey O'Keefe
Jordan High School
Los Angeles, CA

Sherry Parker
Selvidge Middle School
Ballwin, MO

Sherron N. Porter
Robert E. Lee High School
Baton Rouge, LA

Marc Prévost
Austin Community College
Austin, TX

Norbert Rouquet
Consultant
La Roche-sur-Yon, France

Michèle Shockey
Gunn High School
Palo Alto, CA

Ashley Shumaker
Central High School West
Tuscaloosa, AL

Antonia Stergiades
Washington High School
Massillon, OH

Frederic L. Toner
Texas Christian University
Fort Worth, TX

Jeannine Waters
Harrisonburg High School
Harrisonburg, VA

Jo Anne S. Wilson
Consultant
Glen Arbor, MI

FIELD TEST PARTICIPANTS

Marie Allison
New Hanover High School
Wilmington, NC

Gabrielle Applequist
Capital High School
Boise, ID

Jana Brinton
Bingham High School
Riverton, UT

Nancy J. Cook
Sam Houston High School
Lake Charles, LA

Rachael Gray
Williams High School
Plano, TX

Katherine Kohler
Nathan Hale Middle School
Norwalk, CT

Nancy Mirsky
Museum Junior High School
Yonkers, NY

Myrna S. Nie
Whetstone High School
Columbus, OH

Jacqueline Reid
Union High School
Tulsa, OK

Judith Ryser
San Marcos High School
San Marcos, TX

Erin Hahn Sass
Lincoln Southeast High School
Lincoln, NE

Linda Sherwin
Sandy Creek High School
Tyrone, GA

Norma Joplin Sivers
Arlington Heights High School
Fort Worth, TX

Lorabeth Stroup
Lovejoy High School
Lovejoy, GA

Robert Vizena
W.W. Lewis Middle School
Sulphur, LA

Gladys Wade
New Hanover High School
Wilmington, NC

Kathy White
Grimsley High School
Greensboro, NC

To the Student

Some people have the opportunity to learn a new language by living in another country. Most of us, however, begin learning another language and getting acquainted with a foreign culture in a classroom with the help of a teacher, classmates, and a textbook. To use your book effectively, you need to know how it works.

Allez, viens! *(Come along!)* is organized to help you learn French and become familiar with the cultures of people who speak French. The Preliminary Chapter presents basic concepts in French and strategies for learning a new language. This chapter is followed by six Location Openers and twelve chapters.

Location Opener You'll find six four–page photo essays called Location Openers that introduce different French-speaking places.

Chapter Opener The Chapter Opener pages tell you the chapter theme and goals, and outline what you learn to do in each section of the chapter.

Mise en train *(Getting started)* This illustrated story, which is also on video, shows you French-speaking people in real-life situations, using the language you'll learn in the chapter.

Première, Deuxième, and **Troisième étape** *(First, Second, Third Part)* After the **Mise en train,** the chapter is divided into three sections called **étapes.** At the beginning of each **étape**, there is a reminder of the goals for this part of the chapter. Within the **étape,** are **Comment dit-on... ?** *(How do you say . . . ?)* boxes that contain the French expressions you'll need to communicate and **Vocabulaire** and **Grammaire/Note de Grammaire** boxes that give you the French words and grammatical structures you'll need to know. Activities in each **étape** enable you to practice the new expressions, vocabulary, and structures and thereby develop your skills in listening, reading, speaking, and writing.

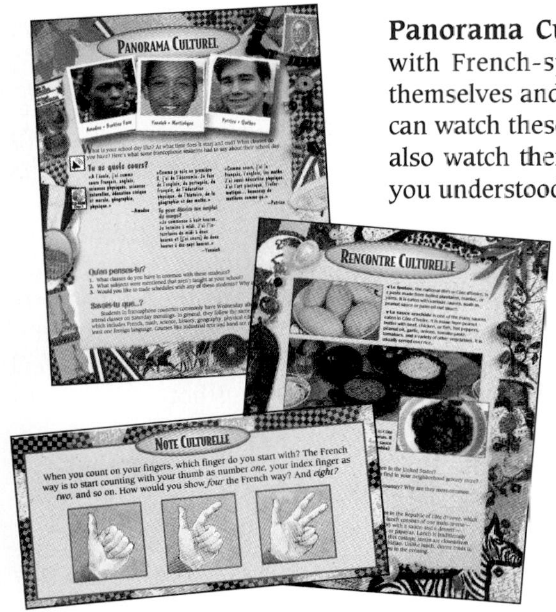

Panorama Culturel *(Cultural Panorama)* On this page are interviews with French-speaking people from around the world. They talk about themselves and their lives, and you can compare their culture to yours. You can watch these interviews on video or listen to them on audio CD. You can also watch them using the CD-ROM program, then check to see how well you understood by answering some questions about what the people say.

Rencontre Culturelle *(Cultural Encounter)* This section, found in six of the chapters, gives you a firsthand encounter with some aspect of a French-speaking culture.

Note Culturelle *(Culture Note)* In each chapter, there are notes with more information about the cultures of French-speaking people. These notes might tell you interesting facts, describe common customs, or offer other information that will help you learn more about the French-speaking world.

Lisons! *(Let's read!)* The reading section follows the three **étapes.** The selections are related to the chapter themes and help you develop your reading skills in French. The **De bons conseils** *(Helpful advice)* boxes in this section are strategies to improve your reading comprehension.

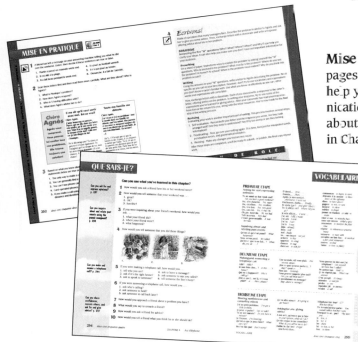

Mise en pratique *(Review)* The activities on these pages practice what you've learned in the chapter and help you improve your listening, reading, and communication skills. You'll also review what you've learned about culture. A section called **Ecrivons!** *(Let's write!)* in Chapters 3–12 will help develop your writing skills.

Que sais-je? *(Let's see if I can . . .)* This page at the end of each chapter contains a series of questions and short activities to help you see if you've achieved the chapter goals. Page numbers beside each section will tell you where to go for help if you need it.

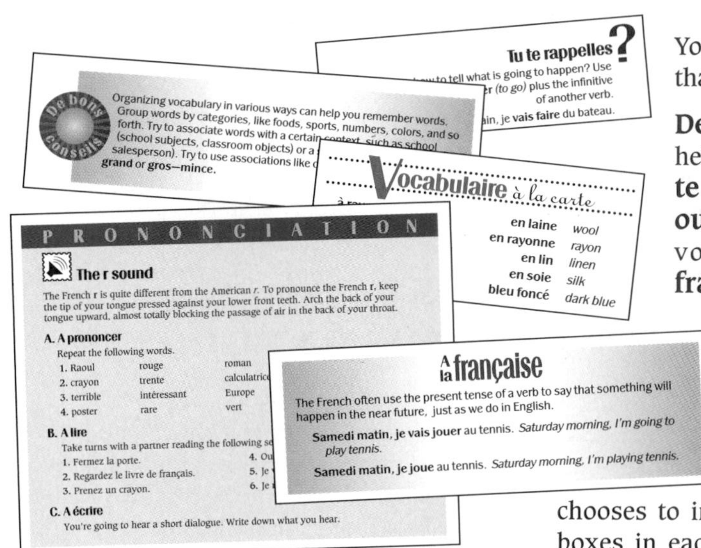

You'll also find special features in each chapter that provide extra tips and reminders.

De bons conseils *(advice)* offers study hints to help you succeed in a foreign language class. **Tu te rappelles?** *(Do you remember?)* and **Si tu as oublié** remind you of expressions, grammar, and vocabulary you may have forgotten. **A la française** *(The French way)* gives you additional expressions to add more color to your speech. **Vocabulaire à la carte** *(Additional Vocabulary)* lists extra words you might find helpful. These words will not appear on the quizzes and tests unless your teacher chooses to include them. **Prononciation** boxes in each chapter will help your pronunciation in French.

Si tu as oublié
the verb aller
va à la page 154.

Vocabulaire *(Vocabulary)* On the French-English vocabulary list on the last page of the chapter, the words are grouped by **étape.** These words and expressions will be on the quizzes and tests.

You'll also find French-English and English-French vocabulary lists at the end of the book. The words you'll need to know for the quizzes and tests are in boldface type.

At the end of your book, you'll find more helpful material, such as:

- a summary of the expressions you'll learn in the **Comment dit-on... ?** boxes
- additional vocabulary words you might want to use
- a summary of the grammar you'll study
- a section of additional activities to practice the structures you'll learn
- a grammar index to help you find where structures are presented

Allez, viens! Come along on an exciting trip to new cultures and a new language!

Bon voyage!

Explanation of Icons in *Allez, viens!*

Throughout ***Allez, viens!,*** you'll see these symbols, or icons, next to activities. They'll tell you what you'll do with that activity. Here's a key to help you understand the icons.

Listening Activities This icon indicates a listening activity. You'll need to listen to the CD or your teacher to complete the activity.

CD-ROM Activities Whenever this icon appears, you know there's a related activity on the *Allez, viens! Interactive CD-ROM Program.*

Writing Activities You'll see this icon next to writing activities. The directions may ask you to write words, sentences, paragraphs, or a whole composition.

Pair Work Activities Activities with this icon are to be done with a partner. Both you and your partner are responsible for completing the activity.

Group Work Activities If an activity has this icon next to it, you'll complete it with a small group of classmates. Each person in the group is responsible for a share of the work.

Come along—to a world of new experiences!

Allez, viens! offers you the opportunity to learn the language spoken by millions of people in countries in Europe, Africa, Asia, and around the world. Let's find out what those countries are.

CHAPITRE PRELIMINAIRE

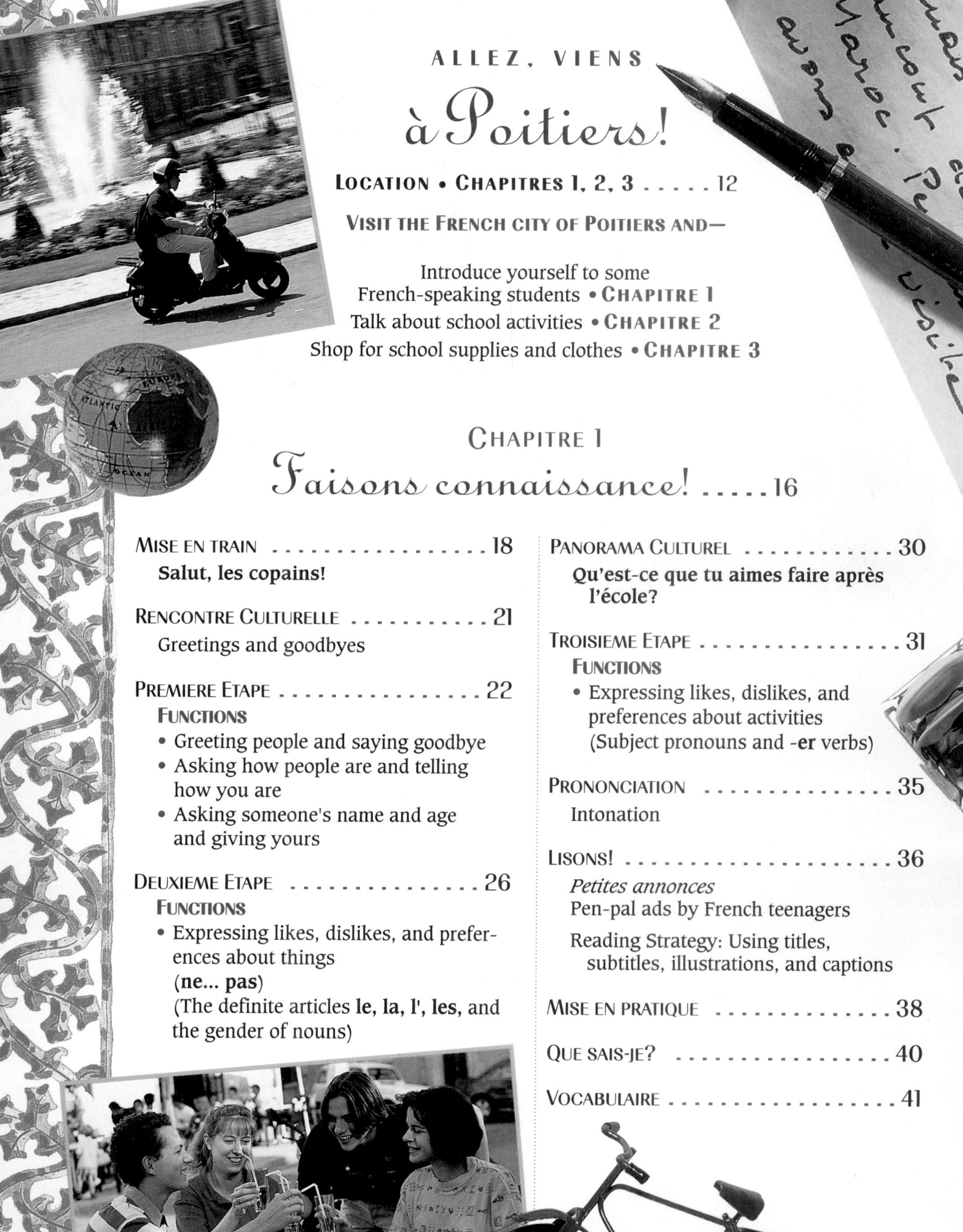

ALLEZ, VIENS

à Poitiers!

CHAPITRE 1

Faisons connaissance! 16

CHAPITRE 2
Vive l'école! 42

Chapitre 3

Tout pour la rentrée.....66

ALLEZ, VIENS

à Québec!

CHAPITRE 4

Sports et passe-temps 94

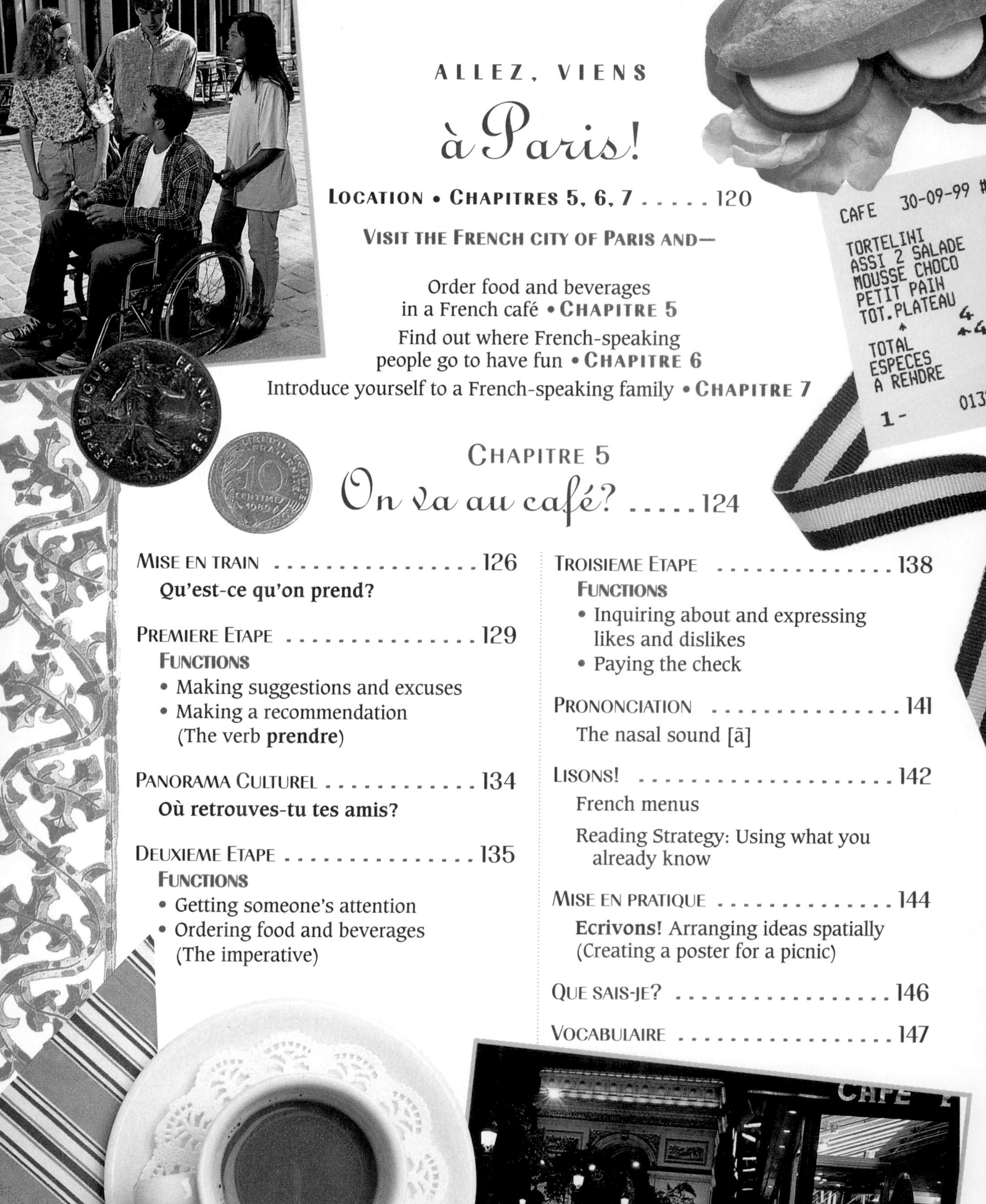

ALLEZ, VIENS

à Paris!

VISIT THE FRENCH CITY OF PARIS AND—

Order food and beverages in a French café • **CHAPITRE 5**

Find out where French-speaking people go to have fun • **CHAPITRE 6**

Introduce yourself to a French-speaking family • **CHAPITRE 7**

CHAPITRE 5
On va au café? 124

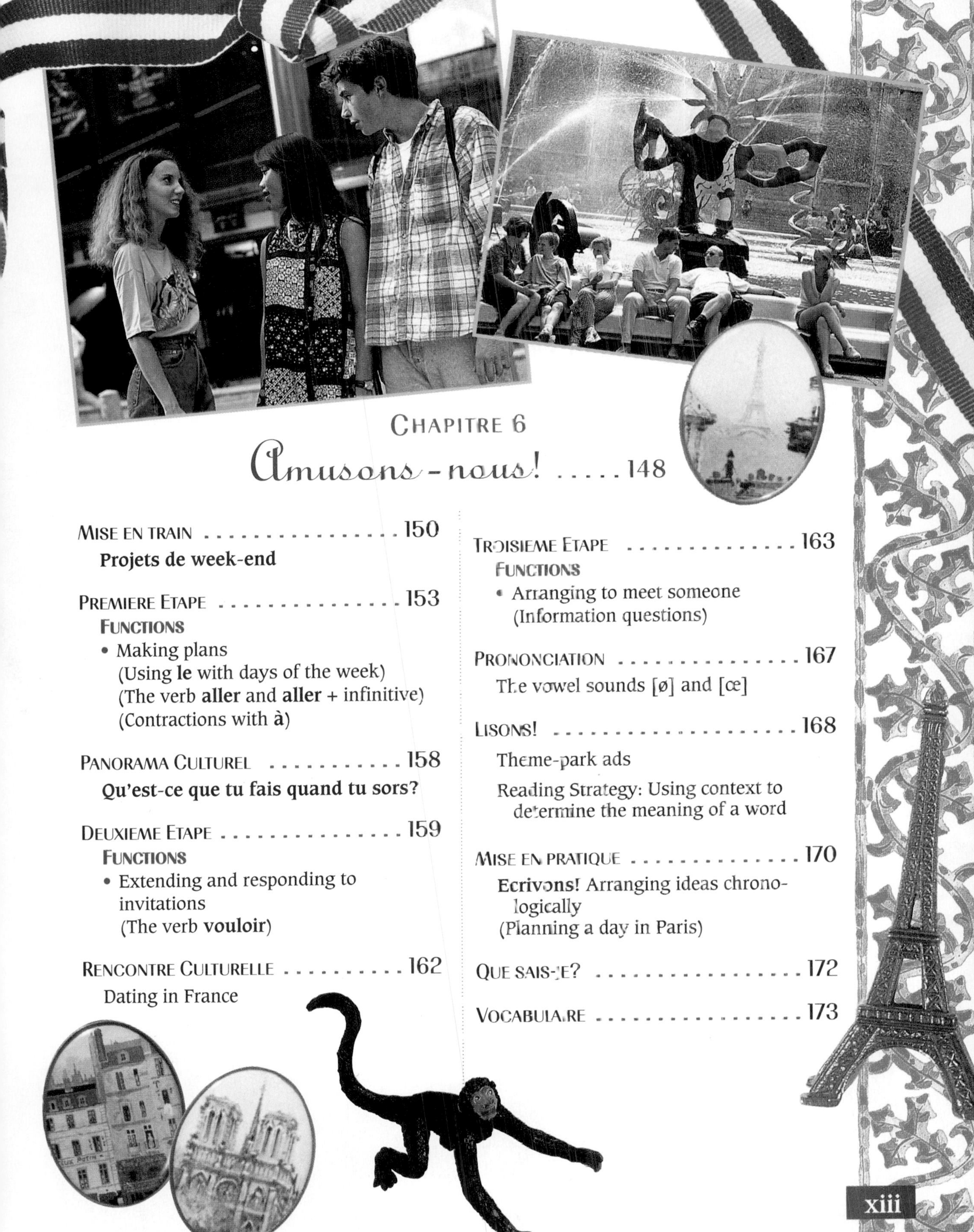

CHAPITRE 6

Amusons-nous! 148

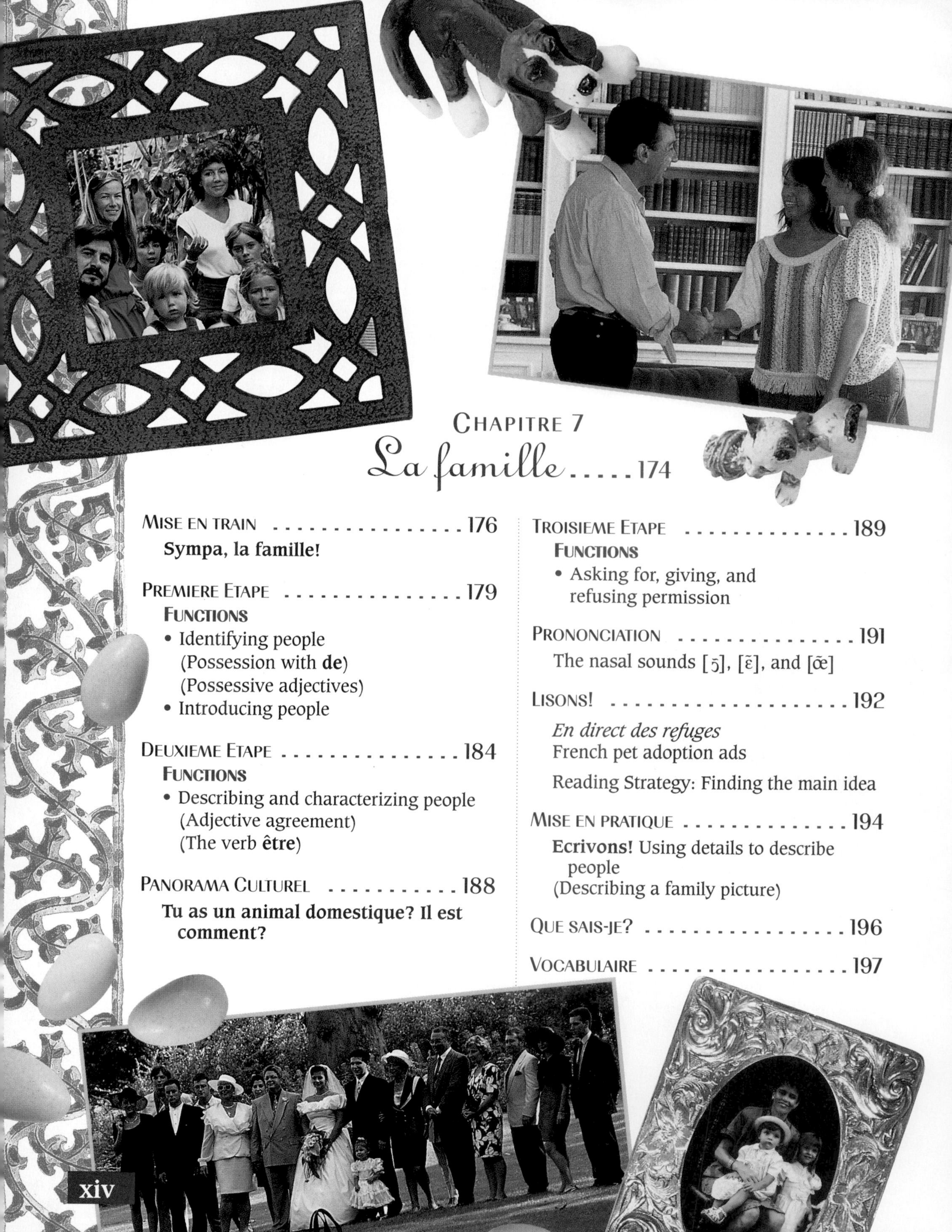

CHAPITRE 7
La famille.....174

ALLEZ, VIENS

à Abidjan!

CHAPITRE 8

Au marché 202

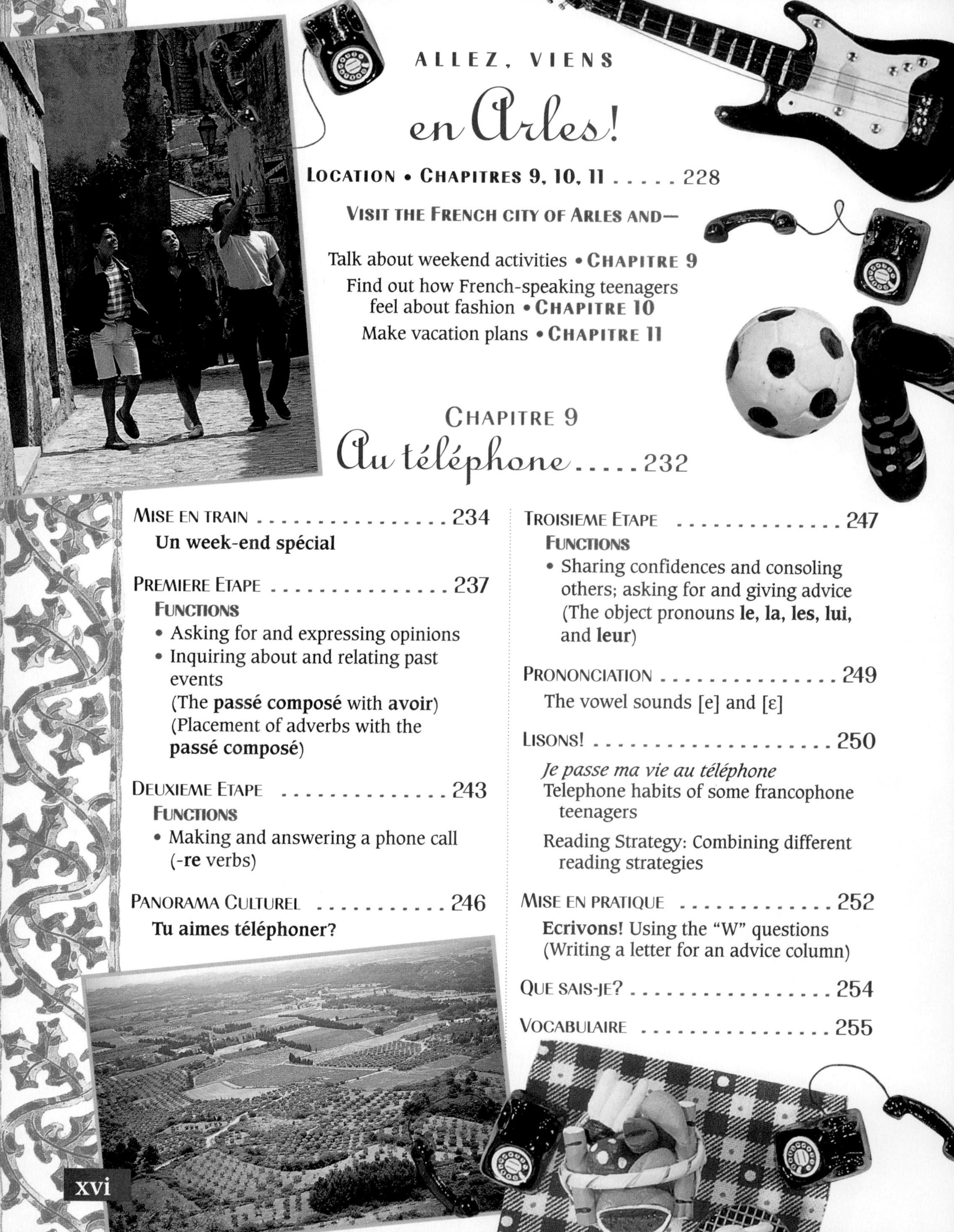

ALLEZ, VIENS

en Arles!

CHAPITRE 9

Au téléphone 232

CHAPITRE 10

Dans un magasin de vêtements 256

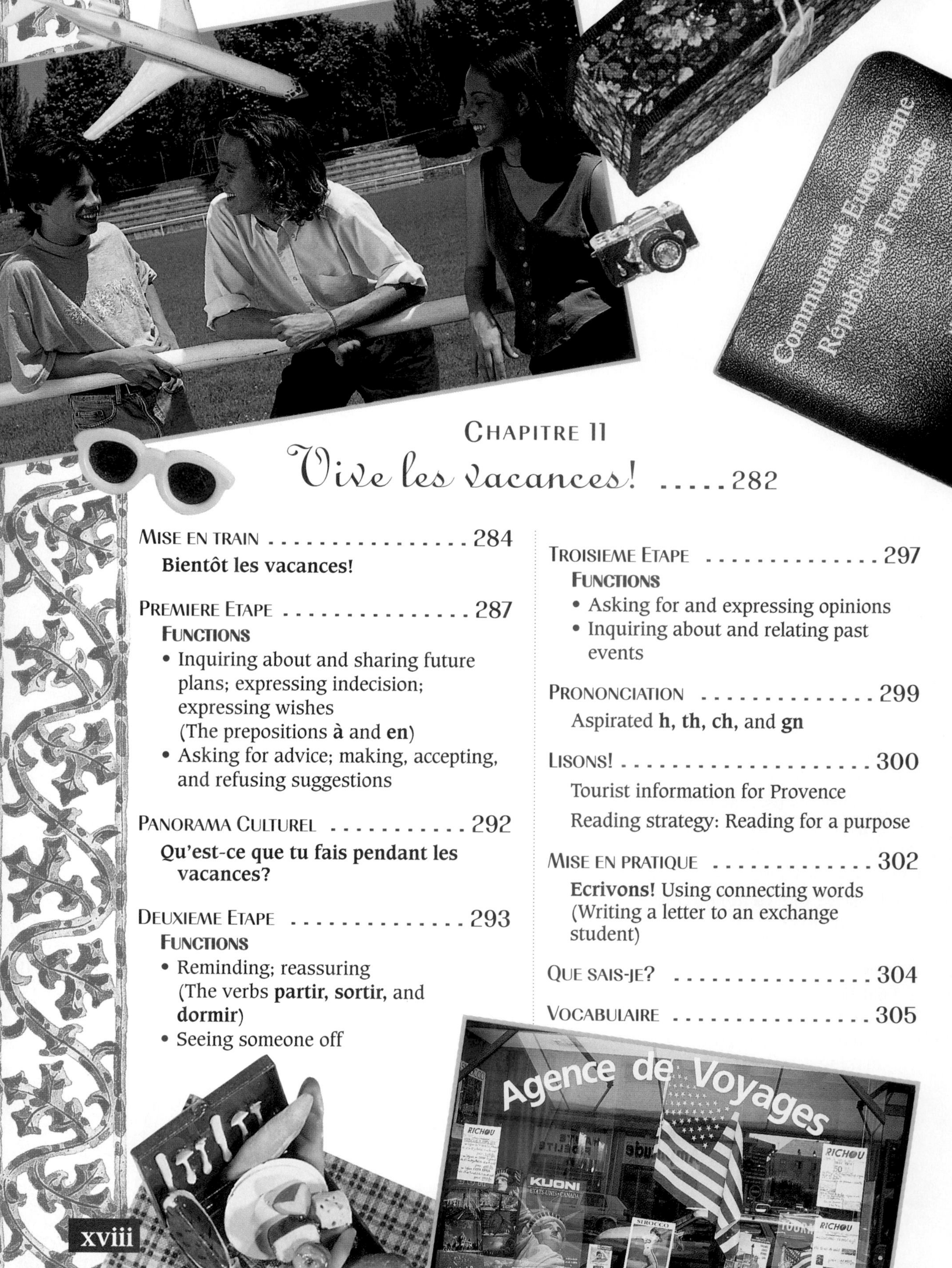

CHAPITRE 11

Vive les vacances! 282

ALLEZ, VIENS

à Fort-de-France!

CHAPITRE 12
En ville 310

REFERENCE SECTION

Cultural References

ADDRESSING PEOPLE

ART

CASTLES AND PALACES

CHURCHES

CINEMA

CITIES

CLOTHING

ENTERTAINMENT

FOLKLORE

FOOD

HOME AND FAMILY LIFE

LEISURE ACTIVITIES

MAPS

MONEY

MONUMENTS AND ATTRACTIONS

NUMBERS

PARKS

PEOPLE

RESTAURANTS AND CAFES

SCHOOL LIFE

SHOPPING

SPORTS

TELEPHONE

TIME AND TEMPERATURE

TRANSPORTATION

La France

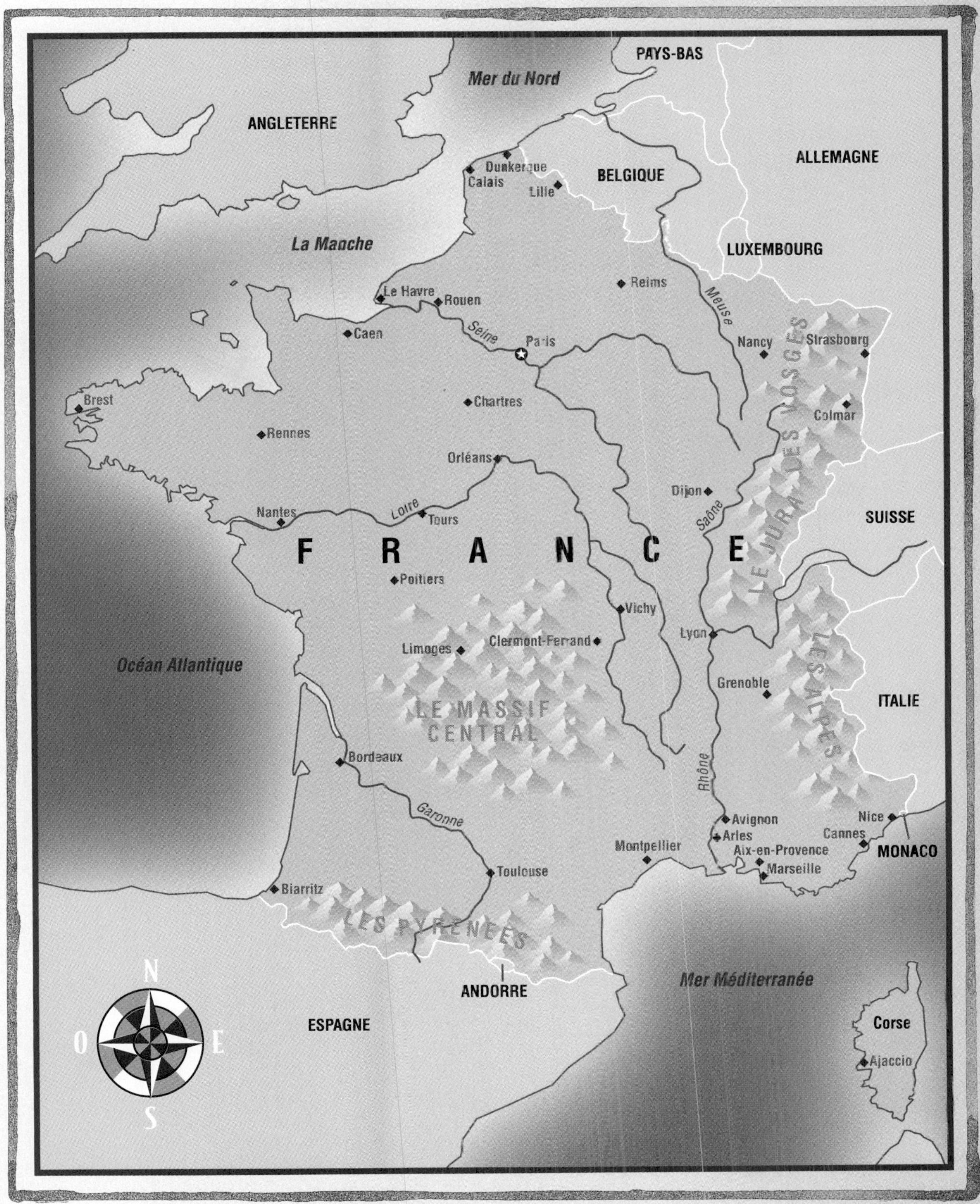

PAYS-BAS
Mer du Nord
ANGLETERRE
ALLEMAGNE
Dunkerque
Calais
BELGIQUE
Lille
La Manche
LUXEMBOURG
Reims
Meuse
Le Havre
Rouen
Caen
Seine
Paris
Nancy
Strasbourg
LES VOSGES
Brest
Chartres
Colmar
Rennes
Orléans
Dijon
Nantes
Loire
Tours
Saône
SUISSE
F R A N C E
LE JURA
Poitiers
Vichy
Lyon
Limoges
Clermont-Ferrand
Océan Atlantique
LES ALPES
Grenoble
ITALIE
LE MASSIF CENTRAL
Bordeaux
Rhône
Garonne
Avignon
Nice
Arles
Cannes
Montpellier
Aix-en-Provence
MONACO
Marseille
Toulouse
Biarritz
LES PYRÉNÉES
N
ANDORRE
Mer Méditerranée
O
E
ESPAGNE
Corse
Ajaccio
S

L'Afrique francophone

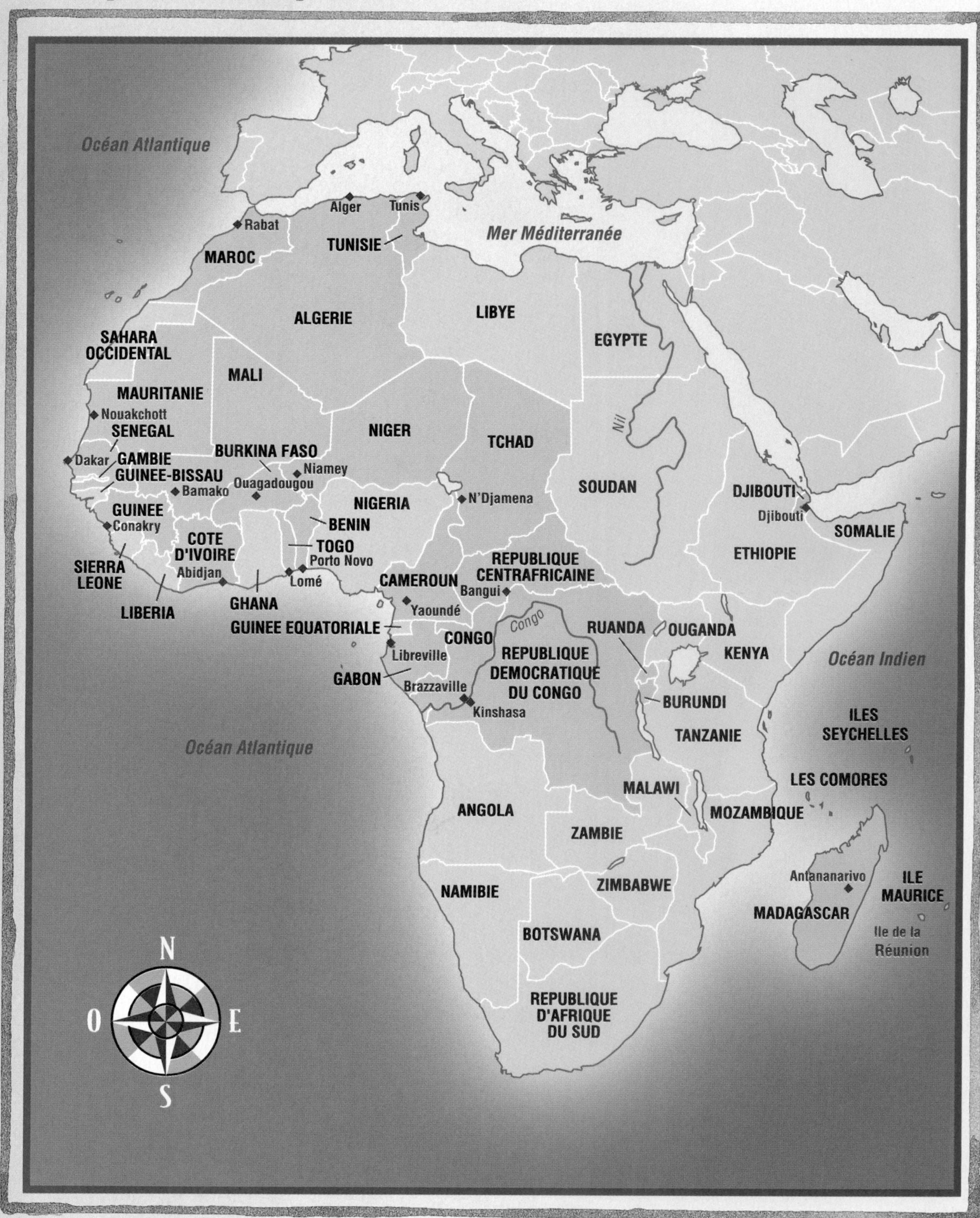

L'Amérique francophone

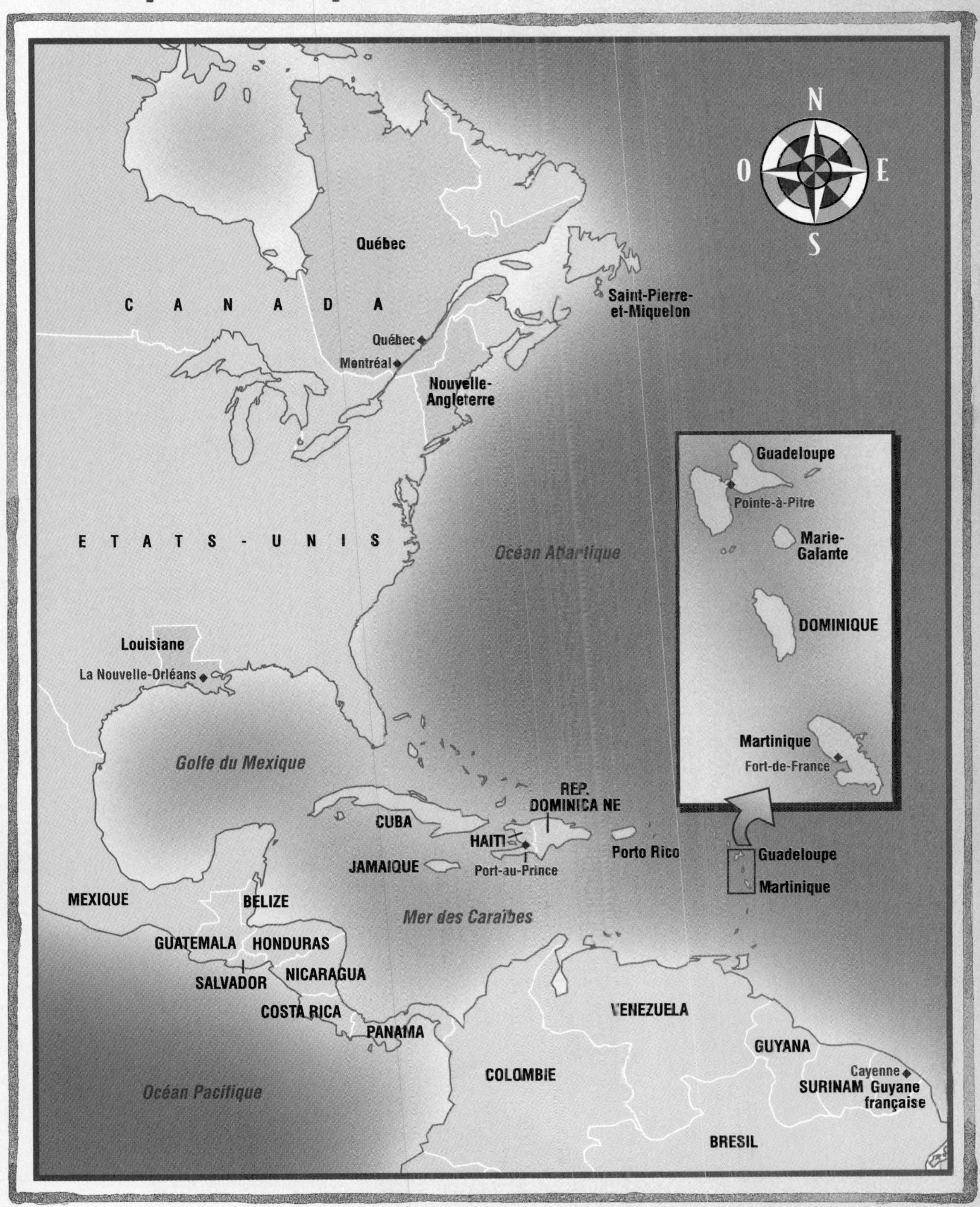

N
O
E
S
Québec
C A N A D A
Québec
Montréal
Saint-Pierre-
et-Miquelon
Nouvelle-
Angleterre
E T A T S - U N I S
Océan Atlantique
Louisiane
La Nouvelle-Orléans
Golfe du Mexique
CUBA
REP.
DOMINICAINE
HAITI
Port-au-Prince
JAMAIQUE
Porto Rico
Guadeloupe
Martinique
MEXIQUE
BELIZE
Mer des Caraïbes
GUATEMALA
HONDURAS
SALVADOR
NICARAGUA
COSTA RICA
PANAMA
VENEZUELA
GUYANA
COLOMBIE
Cayenne
SURINAM
Guyane
française
BRESIL
Océan Pacifique
Guadeloupe
Pointe-à-Pitre
Marie-
Galante
DOMINIQUE
Martinique
Fort-de-France

CHAPITRE PRELIMINAIRE

Allez, viens!

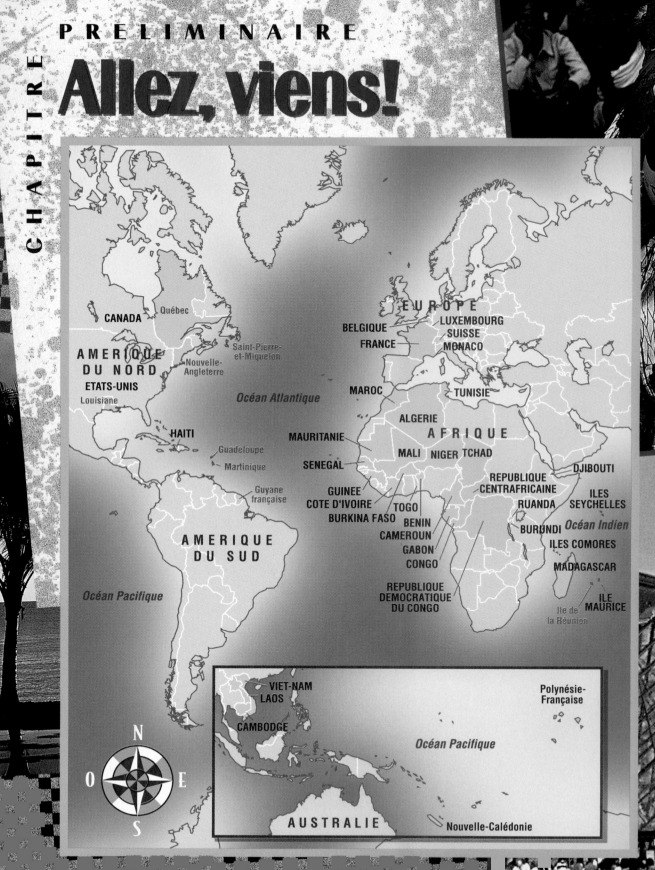

CANADA
Québec
AMERIQUE DU NORD
ETATS-UNIS
Louisiane
Saint-Pierre-et-Miquelon
Nouvelle-Angleterre
HAITI
Guadeloupe
Martinique
Guyane française
AMERIQUE DU SUD
Océan Pacifique
Océan Atlantique
EUROPE
BELGIQUE
LUXEMBOURG
SUISSE
FRANCE
MONACO
MAROC
TUNISIE
ALGERIE
AFRIQUE
MAURITANIE
MALI
NIGER
TCHAD
SENEGAL
DJIBOUTI
REPUBLIQUE CENTRAFRICAINE
GUINEE
COTE D'IVOIRE
TOGO
BURKINA FASO
BENIN
CAMEROUN
GABON
CONGO
REPUBLIQUE DEMOCRATIQUE DU CONGO
ILES SEYCHELLES
RUANDA
BURUNDI
Océan Indien
ILES COMORES
MADAGASCAR
ILE MAURICE
Ile de la Réunion
VIET-NAM
LAOS
CAMBODGE
Polynésie-Française
Océan Pacifique
AUSTRALIE
Nouvelle-Calédonie
N
O
E
S

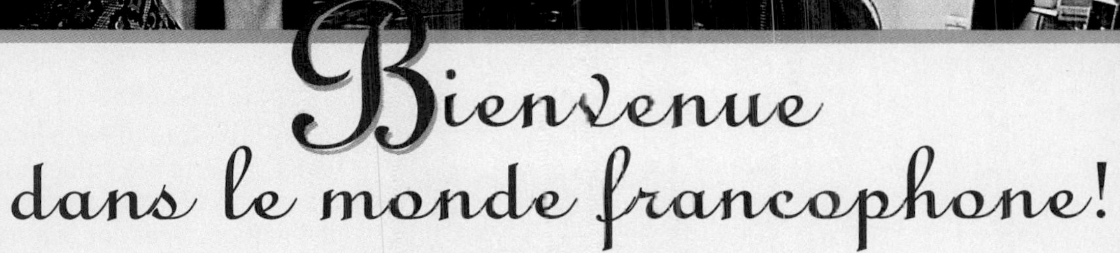

Bienvenue dans le monde francophone!

Welcome to the French-speaking world!

You know, of course, that French is spoken in France, but did you know that French is spoken by many people in North America? About one-third of Canadians speak French, mostly in Quebec province **(le Québec)**. In the United States, about 375,000 people in New England **(la Nouvelle-Angleterre)**, whose ancestors immigrated from Canada, speak or understand French. French is also an official language in the state of Louisiana **(la Louisiane)**.

French is the official language of France's overseas possessions. These include the islands of Martinique **(la Martinique)** and Guadeloupe **(la Guadeloupe)** in the Caribbean Sea, French Guiana **(la Guyane française)** in South America, the island of Réunion **(la Réunion)** in the Indian Ocean, and several islands in the Pacific Ocean. French is also spoken in Haiti **(Haïti)**.

Did you know that French is also widely used in Africa? Over twenty African countries have retained French as an official language. Many people in West and Central African countries, such as Senegal **(le Sénégal)**, the Republic of Côte d'Ivoire **(la République de Côte d'Ivoire)**, Mali **(le Mali)**, Niger **(le Niger)**, and Chad **(le Tchad)**, speak French. In North Africa, French has played an important role in Algeria **(l'Algérie)**, Tunisia **(la Tunisie)**, and Morocco **(le Maroc)**. Although Arabic is the official language of these North African countries, French is used in many schools across North Africa and in parts of the Middle East.

Take a minute to find France on the map. Several of the countries bordering France use French as an official language. It's the first or second language of many people in Belgium **(la Belgique)**, Switzerland **(la Suisse)**, Luxembourg **(le Luxembourg)**, and Andorra **(l'Andorre)**, as well as in the principality of Monaco **(Monaco)**.

As you look at the map, what other places can you find where French is spoken? Can you imagine how French came to be spoken in these places?

TU LES CONNAIS? *Do you know them?*

In science, politics, technology, and the arts, French-speaking people have made important contributions. How many of these people can you match with their descriptions?

a.

b.

c.

d.

1. Léopold Senghor (b. 1906)
A key advocate of **Négritude,** which asserts the values and the spirit of black African civilization, Senghor is a man of many talents. He was the first black African high school teacher in France. He was President of Senegal from 1960 to 1980. He was also the first black member of the **Académie Française.**

2. Isabelle Adjani (b. 1955)
A talented actress and producer, Isabelle Yasmine Adjani is well known for her award-winning roles in French films. In the 1980s, Adjani publicly acknowledged her Algerian heritage and began a personal campaign to raise consciousness about racism in France.

3. Victor Hugo (1802-1885)
Novelist, poet, and political activist, Hugo led the Romantic Movement in French literature. In his most famous works, *Notre-Dame de Paris (The Hunchback of Notre Dame)* and *Les Misérables,* he sympathizes with the victims of poverty and condemns a corrupt political system.

4. Marie-José Pérec (b. 1968)
At the 1996 Olympic Games®, Pérec became only the second woman in history to win the 200 m. and 400 m. titles in the same Olympics. Her numerous victories have made her one of the premier female track athletes of our time.

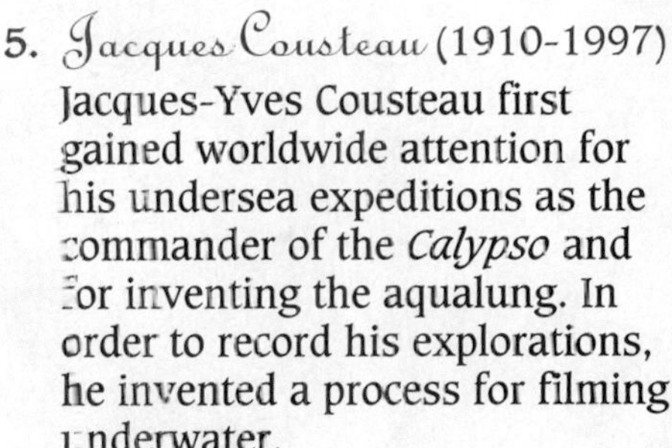

5. Jacques Cousteau (1910-1997)
Jacques-Yves Cousteau first gained worldwide attention for his undersea expeditions as the commander of the *Calypso* and for inventing the aqualung. In order to record his explorations, he invented a process for filming underwater.

6. Céline Dion (b. 1968)
A native of Quebec, Dion is an award-winning singer whose work includes hit songs in both English and French. In 1996, her album *Falling Into You* was awarded the Grammy® for Album of the Year and Best Pop Album. Dion also performed in the opening ceremonies of the 1996 Olympic Games in Atlanta, Georgia.

7. Gérard Depardieu (b. 1948)
Gérard Depardieu is a popular actor, director, and producer, who has appeared in over 70 films. His performance in the 1990 movie *Green Card,* which won him a Golden Globe award, marked his American film debut.

8. Marie Curie (1867-1934)
Along with her husband Pierre, Marie Curie won a Nobel prize in physics for her study of radioactivity. Several years later, she also won an individual Nobel prize for chemistry. Marie Curie was the first woman to teach at the Sorbonne in Paris.

1e 2a 3h 4b 5g 6f 7d 8c

POURQUOI APPRENDRE LE FRANÇAIS? *Why learn French?*

When you study a language, you learn much more than vocabulary and grammar. You learn about the people who speak the language and the influence they've had on our lives. Francophone (French-speaking) cultures continue to make notable contributions to many fields, including art, literature, movies, fashion, cuisine, science, and technology.

Someday you may live, travel, or be an exchange student in one of the more than 30 countries all over the world where French is spoken. You can imagine how much more meaningful your experience will be if you can talk to people in their own language.

Being able to communicate in another language can be an advantage when you're looking for employment in almost any field. As a journalist, sportscaster, hotel receptionist, tour guide, travel agent, buyer for a large company, lawyer, engineer, economist, financial expert, flight attendant, diplomat, translator, teacher, writer, interpreter, publisher, or librarian, you may have the opportunity to use French in your work. Did you know that nearly 4,000 American companies have offices in France?

Perhaps the best reason for studying French is for the fun of it. Studying another language is a challenge to your mind, and you'll get a great feeling of accomplishment the first time you have a conversation in French.

QUI SUIS-JE? *Who am I?*

Here's how you introduce yourself to young people who speak French.

To ask someone's name:
Tu t'appelles comment?

To give your name:
Je m'appelle...

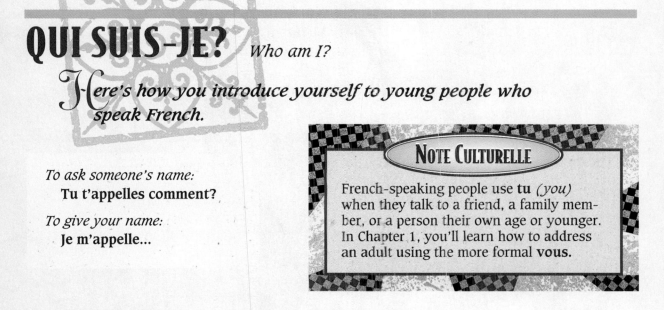

French-speaking people use **tu** *(you)* when they talk to a friend, a family member, or a person their own age or younger. In Chapter 1, you'll learn how to address an adult using the more formal **vous.**

Here's a list of some popular French names for girls and boys. Can you find your name, or a name similar to yours?

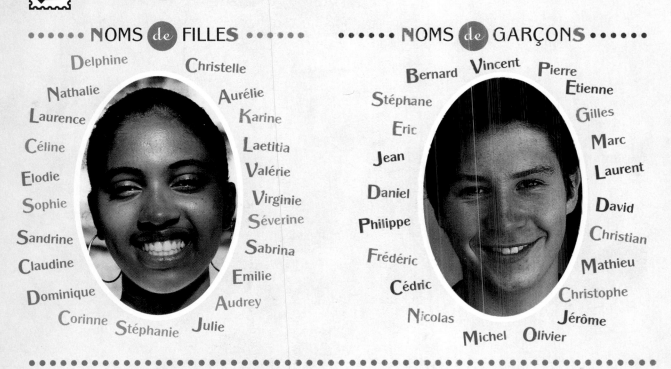

NOMS de FILLES

Delphine, Christelle, Nathalie, Aurélie, Laurence, Karine, Céline, Laetitia, Elodie, Valérie, Sophie, Virginie, Séverine, Sandrine, Sabrina, Claudine, Emilie, Dominique, Audrey, Corinne, Stéphanie, Julie

NOMS de GARÇONS

1 Présente-toi! *Introduce yourself!*

If you like, choose a French name for yourself. Introduce yourself to two or three students in the class, using your own name or your new French name. Ask them their names, too.

L'ALPHABET

The French alphabet looks the same as the English alphabet. The difference is in pronunciation. Look at the letters and words below as your teacher pronounces them or as you listen to the audio recording. Which letters sound similar in English and French? Which ones have a different sound?

Have you noticed that many French words look like English words? Words in different languages that look alike are called *cognates*. Although they're pronounced differently, cognates have the same meaning in French and English. You may not realize it, but you already know hundreds of French words.

Can you figure out what these words mean?

2 Le dictionnaire

Scan the French-English vocabulary list in the back of your book to see if you can find ten cognates.

3 Ecoute! *Listen!*

Write down the words as you hear them spelled. Then, match the words you've written with the pictures. Be careful! One of the words isn't a cognate.

a.

b.

c.

d.

e.

f.

4 Tu t'appelles comment?

Can you spell your name, pronouncing the letters in French?

LES ACCENTS *Accent marks*

Have you noticed the marks over some of the letters in French words? These marks are called accents. They're very important to the spelling, the pronunciation, and even the meaning of French words.

- The **accent aigu** (´) tells you to pronounce an *e* similar to the *a* in the English word *date:*

éléphant **Sénégal**

- The **accent grave** (`) tells you to pronounce an *e* like the *e* in the English word *jet:*

zèbre **chèque**

However, an **accent grave** over an *a* or *u* doesn't change the sound of these letters:

à **où**

- The **accent circonflexe** (ˆ) can appear over any vowel, and it doesn't change the sound of the letter:

pâté **forêt** **île** **hôtel** **flûte**

- The **cédille** (¸) under a *c* tells you to pronounce the *c* like an *s*:

français **ça**

- When two vowels appear next to each other, a **tréma** (¨) over the second one tells you to pronounce each vowel separately:

Noël **Haïti**

- You usually will not see accents on capital letters.

île **Ile** **état** **Etats-Unis**

- When you spell a word aloud, be sure to say the accents, as well as the letters.

5 Ecoute!

Write down the words as you hear them spelled.

LES CHIFFRES DE 0 A 20 *Numbers from 0 to 20*

How many times a day do you use numbers? Giving someone a phone number, checking grades, and getting change at the store all involve numbers. Here are the French numbers from 0 to 20.

0	1	2	3
zéro	un	deux	trois
4	5	6	7
quatre	cinq	six	sept
8	9	10	11
huit	neuf	dix	onze
12	13	14	15
douze	treize	quatorze	quinze
16	17	18	19
seize	dix-sept	dix-huit	dix-neuf

20

vingt

NOTE CULTURELLE

When you count on your fingers, which finger do you start with? The French way is to start counting with your thumb as number *one,* your index finger as *two,* and so on. How would you show *four* the French way? And *eight?*

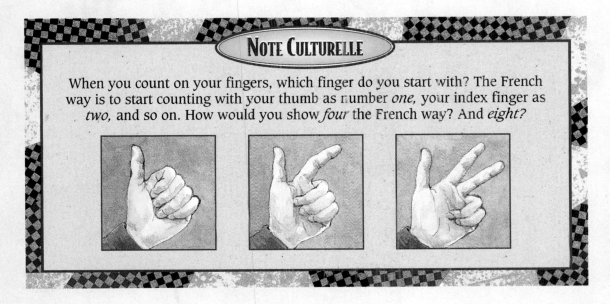

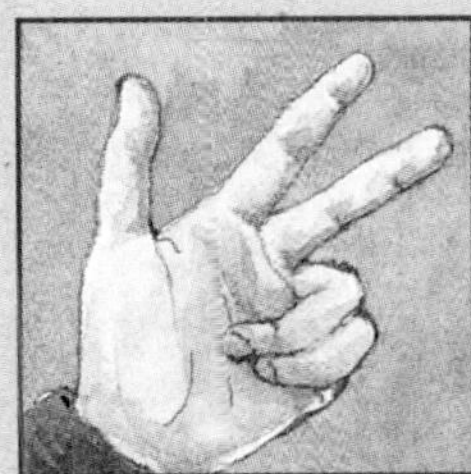

6 Ecoute!

Listen as Nicole, Paul, Vincent, and Corinne tell you their phone numbers. Then, match the numbers with their names.

1. Paul
2. Nicole
3. Vincent
4. Corinne

a. 03. 20. 16. 05. 17
b. 03. 20. 18. 11. 19
c. 03. 20. 17. 07. 18
d. 03. 20. 15. 04. 13
e. 03. 20. 14. 08. 12

7 Devine! *Guess!*

Think of a number between one and twenty. Your partner will try to guess your number. Help out by saying **plus** *(higher)* or **moins** *(lower)* as your partner guesses. Take turns.

8 Plaques d'immatriculation *License plates*

Look at the license plates pictured below. Take turns with a partner reading aloud the numbers and letters you see.

90 ZD 972

1.

2.

1872 LD 94

3.

Québec
WFW 547
Je me souviens

4.

2463 RP 13

5.

1869
AR01
CI

6.

A L'ECOLE *At school*

You should familiarize yourself with these common French instructions. You'll hear your teacher using them in class.

Ecoutez! *Listen!*
Répétez! *Repeat!*
Levez-vous! *Stand up!*
Levez la main! *Raise your hand!*
Asseyez-vous! *Sit down!*
Ouvrez vos livres à la page... !
Open your books to page . . . !

Fermez la porte! *Close the door!*
Sortez une feuille de papier!
Take out a sheet of paper!
Allez au tableau!
Go to the blackboard!
Regardez la carte! *Look at the map!*

9 Ecoute!

Listen to the teacher in this French class tell his students what to do. Then, decide which student is following each instruction.

CHAPITRES 1, 2, 3
Allez, viens à Poitiers!
Poitiers — ville d'art et d'histoire

Poitiers
ANGLETERRE
BELGIQUE
ALLEMAGNE
Lille
LUXEMBOURG
Paris
Strasbourg
Chartres
Tours
SUISSE
Poitiers
Océan Atlantique
FRANCE
Lyon
ITALIE
Bordeaux
Nice
Arles
Aix-en-Provence
N
CORSE
ESPAGNE
Mer Méditerranée
Capital of Poitou-Charentes
Population: more than 120,000
Points of interest: the Futuroscope theme park, the Saint-Pierre Cathedral, the Palais de Justice
Museums: Sainte-Croix, Hypogée des Dunes
Industries: agriculture, fishing, electrical and mechanical manufacturing, forestry, furniture production
Famous people: Saint-Hilaire, Diane de Poitiers, Aliénor d'Aquitaine
Regional specialties: goat cheese, nougat, snails, cream-cheese pastries, chocolates
HRW
go.hrw.com
WA0 POITIERS

Poitiers

Poitiers is famous for its art and history. It was here in 732 A.D. that Charles Martel defeated the Saracens in the Battle of Poitiers. Home to an important university and attractions such as a futuristic park devoted to cinematic technology, Poitiers is also a very modern city.

① People of all ages enjoy the **Futuroscope**, a popular futuristic theme park filled with cinematic exhibits. Of particular interest are the 360-degree theater and the **Kinémax** with its 600-square-meter screen.

② The heart of French cities and towns is called **le centre-ville**. In Poitiers, it is the bustling center of town where people gather in cafés and frequent the many shops.

③ At least once a week, French towns usually have an outdoor market such as this **marché aux fleurs**.

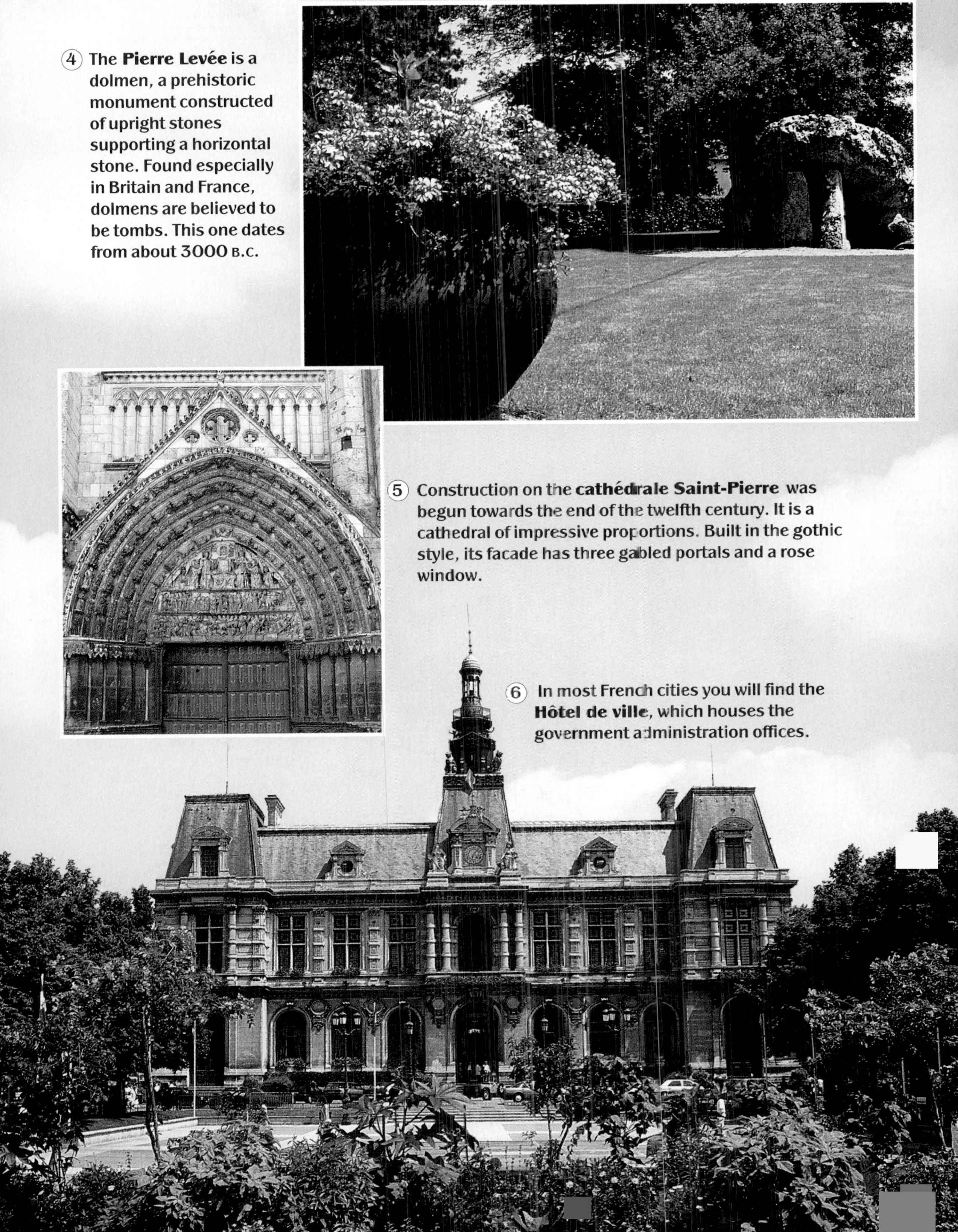

(4) The **Pierre Levée** is a dolmen, a prehistoric monument constructed of upright stones supporting a horizontal stone. Found especially in Britain and France, dolmens are believed to be tombs. This one dates from about 3000 B.C.

(5) Construction on the **cathédrale Saint-Pierre** was begun towards the end of the twelfth century. It is a cathedral of impressive proportions. Built in the gothic style, its facade has three gabled portals and a rose window.

(6) In most French cities you will find the **Hôtel de ville**, which houses the government administration offices.

CHAPITRE

1 Faisons connaissance!

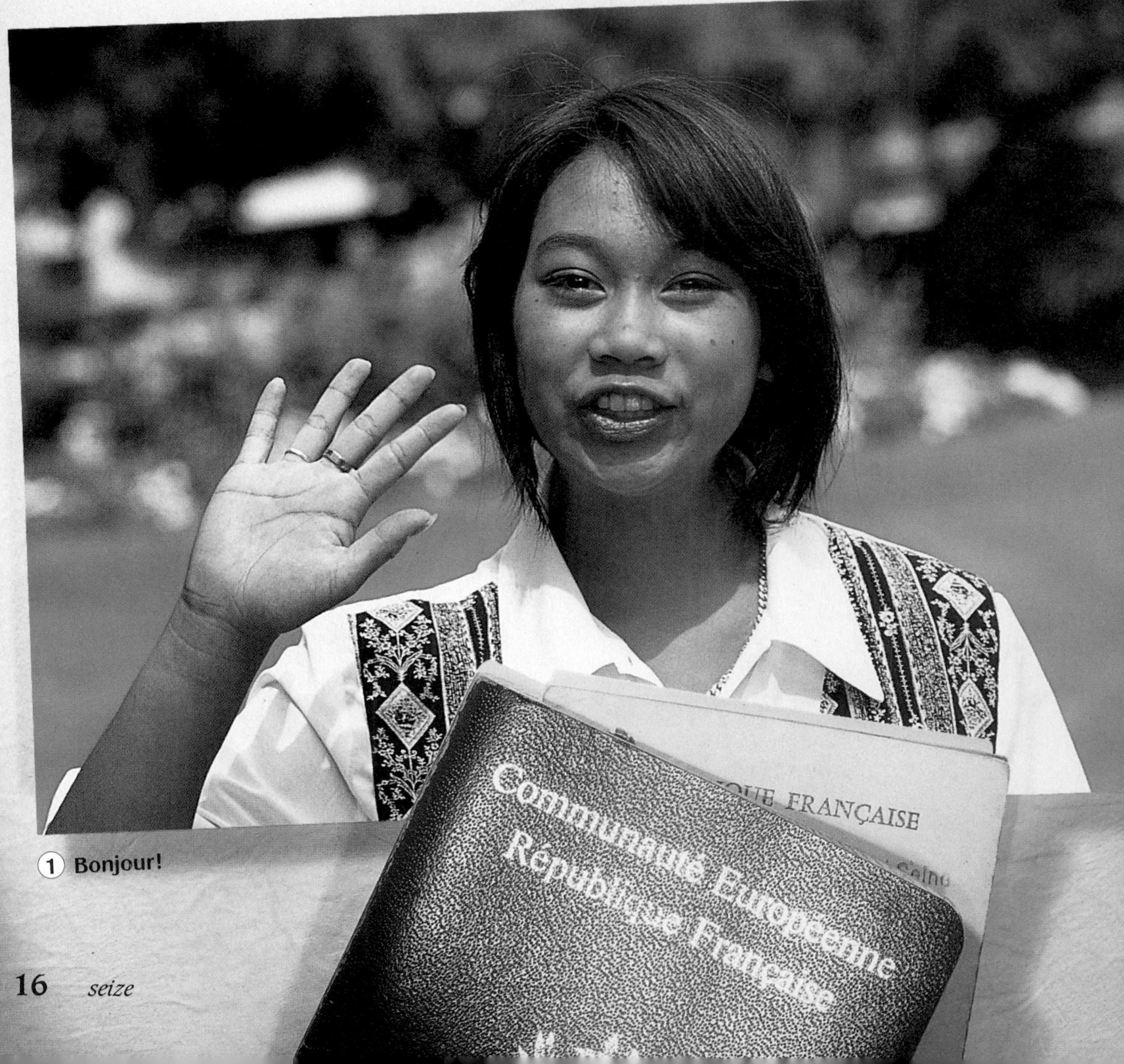

1 Bonjour!

When you meet new people, it's fun to find out what you have in common with them—and even what you don't!

In this chapter you will learn

- to greet people and say goodbye; to ask how people are and tell how you are; to ask someone's name and age and give yours
- to express likes, dislikes, and preferences about things
- to express likes, dislikes, and preferences about activities

And you will

- listen to French-speaking students tell what they like to do
- read about French-speaking teenagers who are looking for pen pals
- write a letter of introduction to a pen pal
- find out how French-speaking people greet one another

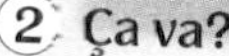

2 Ça va?

3 J'aime les desserts!

Mise en train

Salut, les copains!

What can you tell about these teenagers just by looking at their photos?

Claire

Bonjour! Ça va? Je m'appelle Claire. J'ai 15 ans. Je suis française, de Poitiers. J'adore le cinéma. Mais j'aime aussi danser, lire, voyager et écouter de la musique.

Djeneba

Salut! Je m'appelle Djeneba. J'ai 16 ans. Je suis ivoirienne. J'aime étudier, mais j'aime mieux faire du sport. C'est super cool!

Ahmed

Salut! Je m'appelle Ahmed. Je suis marocain. J'aime tous les sports, surtout le football. J'aime aussi faire du vélo.

Thuy

Salut! Ça va? Je m'appelle Thuy. J'ai 14 ans. Je suis vietnamienne. J'aime faire les magasins. En général, je n'aime pas la télévision. J'aime mieux aller au cinéma.

Didier

Salut! Je m'appelle Didier. J'ai 13 ans. Je suis belge. J'aime écouter de la musique. J'aime aussi les vacances. J'aime surtout voyager!

Stéphane

Bonjour! Je m'appelle Stéphane. J'ai 15 ans et je suis martiniquais. J'aime la plage, la mer, le soleil, la musique et j'aime aussi nager. J'aime surtout danser.

André

Tiens, bonjour! Comment ça va? Je m'appelle André. J'ai 17 ans et je suis suisse. Je parle français et allemand. J'aime beaucoup la télévision. J'aime aussi parler au téléphone avec mes copains.

Emilie

Bonjour! Je m'appelle Emilie. J'ai 16 ans. Je suis québécoise. J'adore faire du sport, surtout du ski et du patin. J'aime bien aussi faire de l'équitation.

1 Tu as compris? *Did you understand?*

Answer the following questions about the teenagers you've just met. Look back at **Salut, les copains!** if you have to. Don't be afraid to guess.

1. What are these teenagers talking about?
2. What information do they give you in the first few lines of their introductions?
3. What are some of the things they like?
4. Which of them have interests in common?

2 Vrai ou faux? *True or false?*

According to **Salut, les copains!**, are the following statements true **(vrai)** or false **(faux)**?

1. André aime parler au téléphone.
2. Ahmed n'aime pas le sport.
3. Stéphane aime écouter de la musique.
4. Claire aime voyager et danser.
5. Didier n'aime pas voyager.
6. Emilie aime faire de l'équitation.
7. Thuy aime la télévision.
8. Djeneba n'aime pas faire du sport.

3 Cherche les expressions *Look for the expressions*

Look back at **Salut, les copains!** How do the teenagers . . .

1. say hello?
2. give their name?
3. give their age?
4. say they like something?

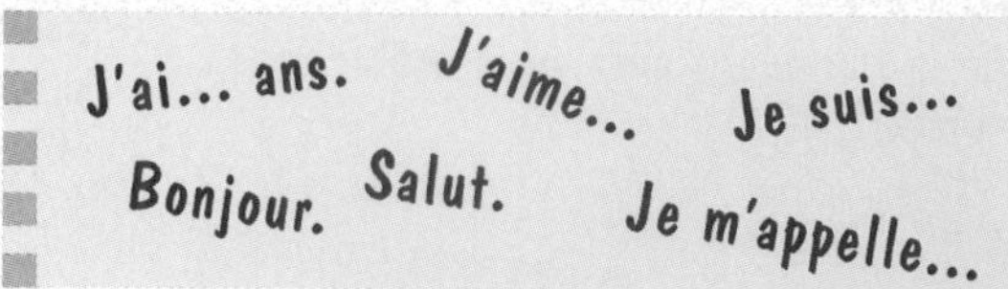

J'ai... ans.
J'aime...
Je suis...
Bonjour.
Salut.
Je m'appelle...

4 Qui est-ce? *Who is it?*

Can you identify the teenagers in **Salut, les copains!** from these descriptions?

1. Elle est québécoise.
2. Il parle allemand.
3. Il a quinze ans.
4. Il aime voyager.
5. Elle adore le ski.
6. Elle n'aime pas la télévision.
7. Il adore le football.
8. Elle aime étudier.

5 Et maintenant, à toi *And now, it's your turn*

Which of the students in **Salut, les copains!** would you most like to meet? Why? Jot down your thoughts and share them with a classmate.

RENCONTRE CULTURELLE

Look at what the people in these photos are doing.

—Salut, Mireille!
—Salut, Lucien!

—Bonjour, maman!
—Bonjour, mon chou!

—Salut, Lucien!
—Salut, Jean-Philippe!

—Salut, Agnès!
—Tchao, Mireille!

—Bonjour, Monsieur Balland.
—Bonjour, Marc.

—Au revoir, Monsieur Legrand.
—Au revoir, Isabelle.

Qu'en penses-tu? *What do you think?*

1. How do the teenagers greet adults? Other teenagers? What gestures do they use?
2. How do they say goodbye? What gestures do they use?
3. Is this similar to the way you greet people and say goodbye in the United States?

Savais-tu que...? *Did you know . . . ?*

In France, girls kiss both girls and boys on the cheek when they meet or say goodbye. The number of kisses varies from two to four depending on the region. Boys shake hands with one another. Teenagers may kiss adults who are family members or friends of the family, but they shake hands when they greet other adults.

To address adults who aren't family members, teenagers generally use the titles **madame, mademoiselle,** or **monsieur. Mme, Mlle,** and **M.** are the written abbreviations of these titles.

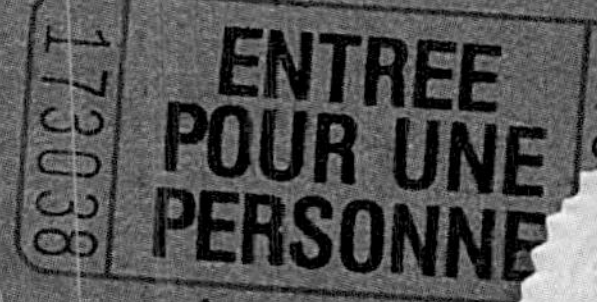

PREMIERE ETAPE

Greeting people and saying goodbye; asking how people are and telling how you are; asking someone's name and age and giving yours

COMMENT DIT-ON... ?

Greeting people and saying goodbye

To anyone:	**Bonjour.** *Hello.*	**Au revoir.** *Goodbye.* **A tout à l'heure.** *See you later.* **A bientôt.** *See you soon.* **A demain.** *See you tomorrow.*
To someone your own age or younger:	**Salut.** *Hi.*	**Salut.** *Bye.* **Tchao.** *Bye.*

6 Ecoute!

Imagine you overhear the following short conversations on the street in Poitiers. Listen carefully and decide whether the speakers are saying hello or goodbye.

7 Comment le dire? *How should you say it?*

How would you say hello to these people in French?

Mme Leblanc

M. Diab

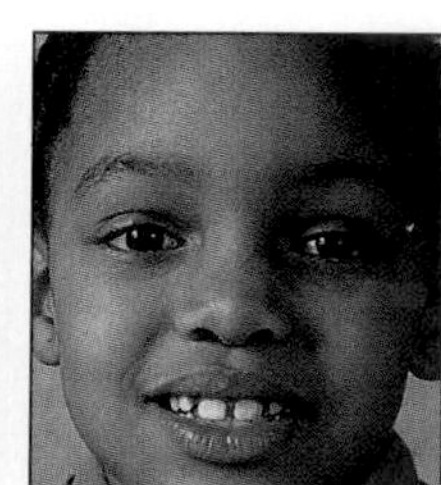

Nadia

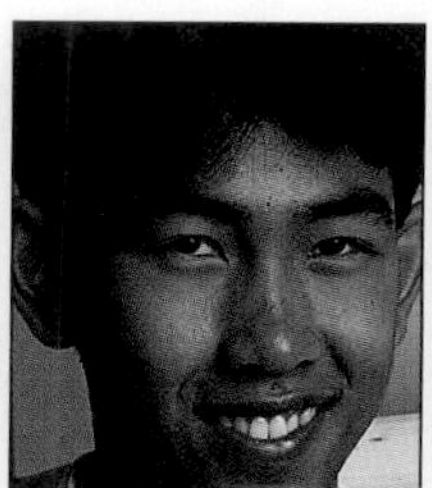

Eric

Mme Desrochers

8 Comment répondre? *How should you answer?*

How would you respond to the greeting from each of the following people?

1.

2.

3.

4.

COMMENT DIT-ON... ?

Asking how people are and telling how you are

To ask how your friend is: **Comment ça va?** *or* **Ça va?**

To tell how you are:

Super! *Great!*
Très bien. *Very well.*

Ça va. *Fine.*
Comme ci, comme ça. *So-so.*
Pas mal. *Not bad.*
Bof! *(expression of indifference)*

Pas terrible. *Not so great.*

To keep a conversation going: **Et toi?** *And you?*

A la française

To ask an adult how he or she is, you can say:
Comment allez-vous?

To keep a conversation with an adult going, you can say:
Et vous?

You'll learn more about using **vous** later in this chapter.

9 Ecoute!

You're going to hear a student ask Valérie, Jean-Michel, Anne, Marie, and Karim how they're feeling. Are they feeling good, fair, or bad?

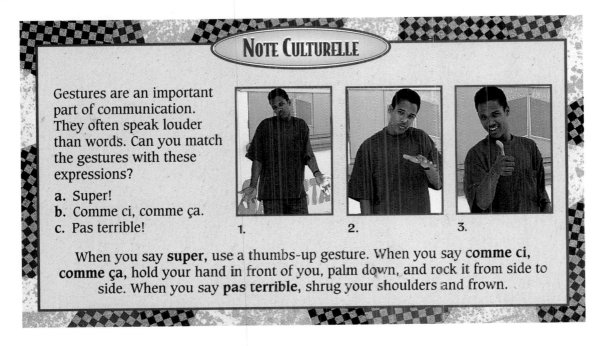

Note Culturelle

Gestures are an important part of communication. They often speak louder than words. Can you match the gestures with these expressions?

a. Super!
b. Comme ci, comme ça.
c. Pas terrible!

1.

2.

3.

When you say **super,** use a thumbs-up gesture. When you say **comme ci, comme ça,** hold your hand in front of you, palm down, and rock it from side to side. When you say **pas terrible,** shrug your shoulders and frown.

10 Méli-mélo! *Mishmash!*

Work with a classmate to rewrite this conversation in the correct order, using your own names. Then, act it out with your partner. Remember to use the appropriate gestures.

Très bien. Super! Et toi? Tchao. Salut,... ! Ça va? Bonjour,... ! Bon. Alors, à tout à l'heure!

11 Et ton voisin (ta voisine)? *And your neighbor?*

Create a conversation with a partner. Be sure to greet your partner, ask how he or she is feeling, respond to any questions your partner asks you, and say goodbye. Don't forget to include the gestures you learned in the **Note Culturelle** on page 23.

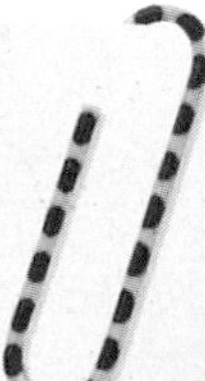

COMMENT DIT-ON... ?

Asking someone's name and giving yours

—Tu t'appelles comment?
—Je m'appelle Magali.

To ask someone his or her name:
Tu t'appelles comment?

To ask someone else's name:
Il/Elle s'appelle comment? *What is his/her name?*

To give your name:
Je m'appelle...

To give someone else's name:
Il/Elle s'appelle... *His/Her name is . . .*

12 Ecoute!

Listen as some French teenagers tell you about their friends. Are they talking about a boy **(un garçon)** or a girl **(une fille)**?

13 Ecoute!

You're going to hear a song called **S'appeler rap.** Which of the following names are mentioned in the song?

Emilie — Jean — Thomas — Laurence — Pierre — Linda — Robert — Laurent — Julie

14 Je te présente... *Let me introduce . . .*

Select a French name for yourself from the list of names on page 5, or ask your teacher to suggest others. Then, say hello to a classmate, introduce yourself, and ask his or her name. Now, introduce your partner to the rest of the class, using **il s'appelle** or **elle s'appelle.**

COMMENT DIT-ON... ?

Asking someone's age and giving yours

To find out someone's age:
Tu as quel âge?

To give your age:
J'ai douze **ans.**
treize
quatorze
quinze
seize
dix-sept
dix-huit

15 Ecoute!

Listen as Bruno, Véronique, Laurent, and Céline introduce themselves to you. Write down each student's age.

16 Faisons connaissance! *Let's get to know one another!*

Create a conversation with two other classmates. Introduce yourself, ask your partners' names and ages, and ask how they are.

17 Mon journal *My journal*

A good way to learn French is to use it to express your own thoughts and feelings. From time to time, you'll be asked to write about yourself in French in a journal. As your first journal entry, identify yourself—give your name, your age, and anything else important to you that you've learned how to say in French.

DEUXIEME ETAPE

Expressing likes, dislikes, and preferences about things

COMMENT DIT-ON... ?

Expressing likes, dislikes, and preferences about things

To ask if someone likes something:
Tu aimes les hamburgers?
Tu aimes le vélo **ou** le ski? *Do you like . . . , or . . . ?*

To say that you like something:
J'adore le chocolat.
J'aime bien le sport.
J'aime les hamburgers.

To say that you dislike something:
Je n'aime pas les hamburgers.

To say that you prefer something:
J'aime les frites, **mais j'aime mieux** le chocolat. *I like . . ., but I prefer . . .*
Je préfère le français.

J'aime la pizza.

Je n'aime pas la pizza.

NOTE DE GRAMMAIRE

Look at the sentences in the illustrations to the left. Can you figure out when to use **ne (n')... pas**?

You put **ne (n')... pas** around the verb **aime** to make the sentence negative. Notice the contraction **n'** before the vowel.

J'aime le sport.
Je **n'**aime **pas** le sport.

18 Ecoute!

a. Listen to Paul and Sophie Dubois discuss names for their baby girl. Which of the names does Paul prefer? And Sophie?

Claude Sandrine Claudette
Laetitia Claudine

b. Do you agree with Paul and Sophie's choices? With a partner, discuss whether you like or dislike the names Paul and Sophie mention. What's your favorite French girl's name? And your favorite French boy's name? You might refer to the list of names on page 5.

— Tu aimes... ?
— Oui, mais je n'aime pas...

19 Quel film? *Which movie?*

With two of your classmates, decide on a movie you all like.

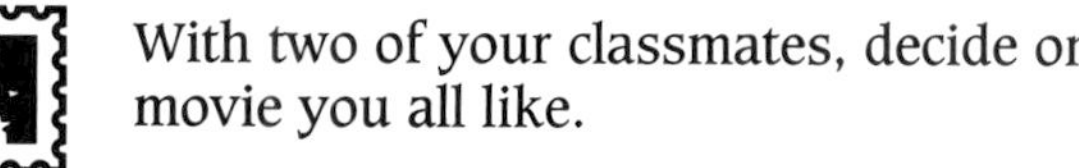

CASABLANCA RE
1942. 1h40. Film d'aventures américain en noir et blanc de Michael Curtiz avec Humphrey Bogart, Ingrid Bergman, Paul Henreid, Conrad Veidt, Claude Rains.
Casablanca à l'heure de Vichy. Un réfugié américain retrouve une femme follement aimée et fuit la persécution nazie. Une distribution étincelante et une mise en scène efficace.
• V.O. Saint Lambert 96

— J'aime *Twister*®*!* Et toi?
— Moi, je n'aime pas *Twister*. Tu aimes *Independence Day*®*?*
— Oui, j'aime *Independence Day,* mais j'aime mieux *Casablanca!*

VOCABULAIRE

les amis (m.)

le cinéma

le ski

le football

le magasin

la plage

le vélo

la glace

l'école (f.)

le français

les frites (f.)

le chocolat

l'anglais (m.)

les examens (f.)

les vacances (f.)

les escargots (m.)

You can probably guess what these words mean:

les concerts (m.) **les hamburgers** (m.) **les maths** (f.) **la pizza** **le sport**

20 Ecoute!

Listen as several French teenagers call in to a radio talk-show poll of their likes and dislikes. Match their names with the pictures that illustrate the activities they like or dislike.

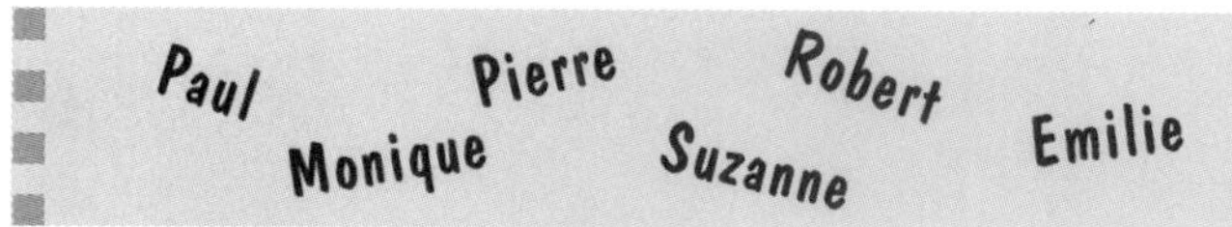

a.

b.

c.

d.

e.

f.

GRAMMAIRE The definite articles **le, la, l'**, and **les**

There are four ways to say *the* in French: **le, la, l'**, and **les.** These words are called *definite articles.* Look at the articles and nouns below. Can you tell when to use **les**? When to use **l'**?

le français	la glace	l'école	les escargots
le football	la pizza	l'anglais	les magasins

- As you may have guessed, you always use **les** before plural nouns.
- Before a singular noun, you use **l'** if the noun begins with a vowel sound, **le** if the noun is masculine, or **la** if the noun is feminine. How do you know which nouns are masculine and which are feminine? While it is usually true that nouns that refer to males are masculine (**le garçon** *the boy*) and those that refer to females are feminine (**la fille** *the girl*), there are no hard-and-fast rules for other nouns. You'll just have to learn the definite article that goes with each one.

21 Et toi, qu'est-ce que tu aimes?

Lucie and Gilbert are talking about the things they like. With a partner, complete their conversation according to the pictures.

LUCIE Moi, j'aime bien  . Et toi?

GILBERT Moi, j'aime mieux 

. J'aime bien aussi sortir avec  .

J'adore le sport aussi. Et toi, tu aimes le sport?

LUCIE Oui, j'adore  et j'aime bien  aussi.

How can you remember if a noun is masculine or feminine? Here are a few hints. Choose the one that works best for you.

- Practice saying each noun aloud with **le** or **la** in front of it. (NOTE: This won't help with nouns that begin with vowels!)
- Write the feminine nouns in one column and the masculine nouns in another. You might even write the feminine nouns in one color and the masculine nouns in a second color.
- Make flash cards of the nouns, writing the feminine and masculine nouns in different colors.

22 Tu aimes...? *Do you like . . . ?*

Choose six things from the vocabulary on page 27. Next, write down which of those things you like and which you dislike. Then, with a partner, try to guess each other's likes and dislikes by asking **Tu aimes... ?**

A la française

Two common words you can use to connect your ideas are **et** *(and)* and **mais** *(but)*. Here's how you can use them to combine sentences.

J'aime les hamburgers. J'aime le chocolat.
J'aime les hamburgers **et** le chocolat.

J'aime le français. Je n'aime pas les maths.
J'aime le français, **mais** je n'aime pas les maths.

23 Mon journal

In your journal, write down some of your likes and dislikes. Use **et** and **mais** to connect your sentences. You might want to illustrate your journal entry.

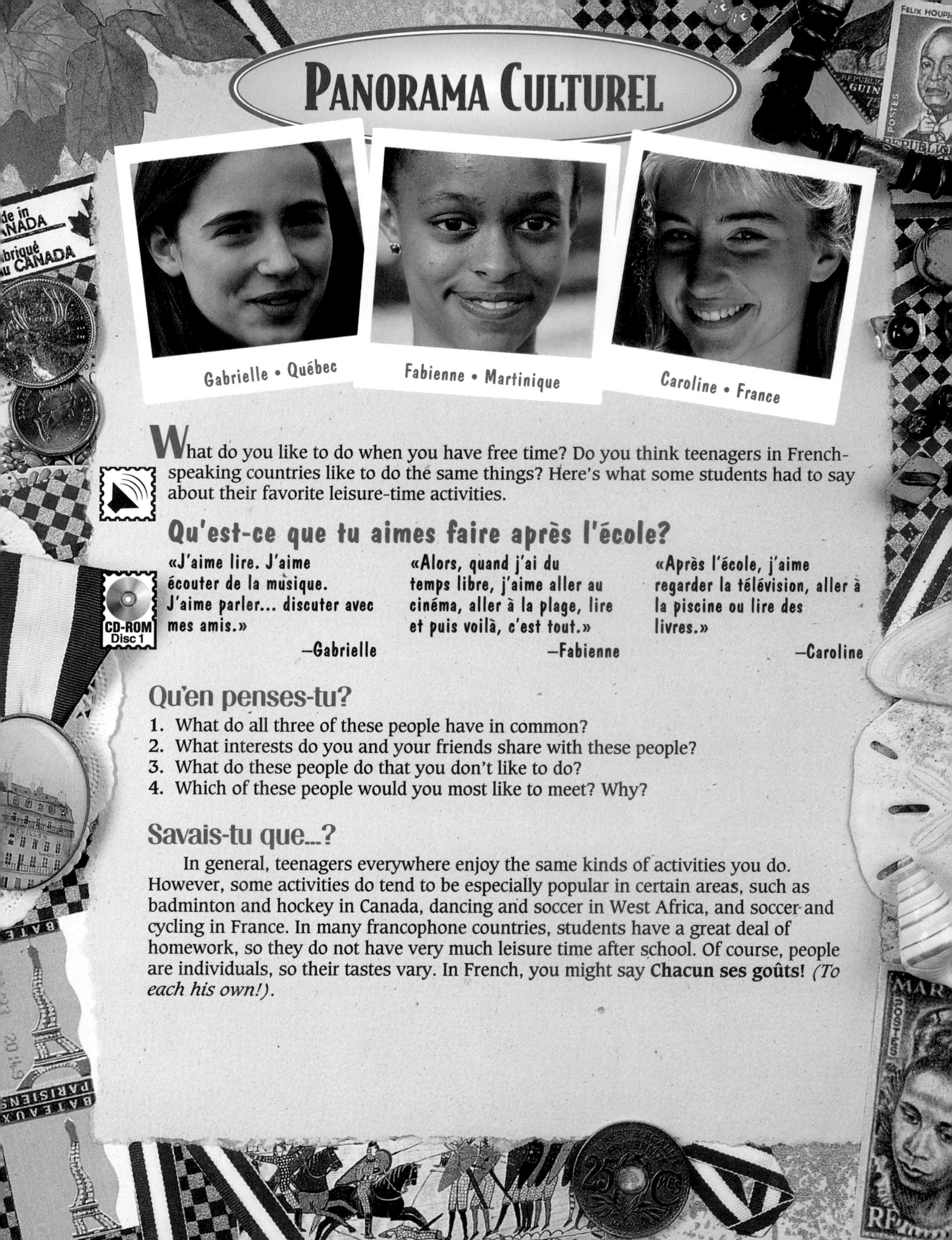

Panorama Culturel

Gabrielle • Québec

Fabienne • Martinique

Caroline • France

What do you like to do when you have free time? Do you think teenagers in French-speaking countries like to do the same things? Here's what some students had to say about their favorite leisure-time activities.

CD-ROM Disc 1

Qu'est-ce que tu aimes faire après l'école?

«J'aime lire. J'aime écouter de la musique. J'aime parler... discuter avec mes amis.»

—Gabrielle

«Alors, quand j'ai du temps libre, j'aime aller au cinéma, aller à la plage, lire et puis voilà, c'est tout.»

—Fabienne

«Après l'école, j'aime regarder la télévision, aller à la piscine ou lire des livres.»

—Caroline

Qu'en penses-tu?

1. What do all three of these people have in common?
2. What interests do you and your friends share with these people?
3. What do these people do that you don't like to do?
4. Which of these people would you most like to meet? Why?

Savais-tu que...?

In general, teenagers everywhere enjoy the same kinds of activities you do. However, some activities do tend to be especially popular in certain areas, such as badminton and hockey in Canada, dancing and soccer in West Africa, and soccer and cycling in France. In many francophone countries, students have a great deal of homework, so they do not have very much leisure time after school. Of course, people are individuals, so their tastes vary. In French, you might say **Chacun ses goûts!** *(To each his own!)*.

TROISIEME ETAPE

Expressing likes, dislikes, and preferences about activities

VOCABULAIRE

CD-ROM Disc 1

Stéphanie adore **regarder la télé.**

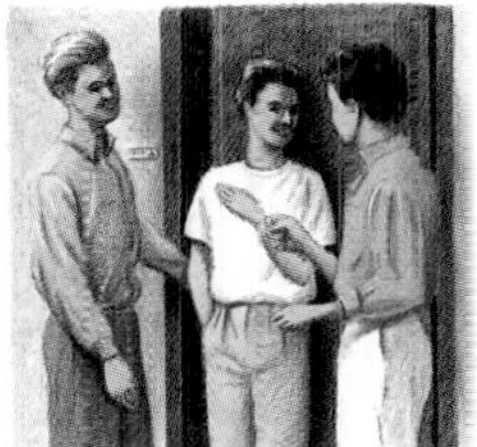

Etienne aime **sortir avec les copains.**

Nicolas aime **parler au téléphone.**

Olivier aime **dormir.**

Danielle aime **étudier.**

Sylvie aime bien **faire du sport.**

Michèle aime **faire les magasins.**

Hervé aime **faire le ménage.**

Raymond aime **faire de l'équitation.**

Serge aime **voyager.**

Eric aime **écouter de la musique.**

Laurence aime bien **nager.**

Solange adore **danser.**

Annie aime **lire.**

24 Ecoute!

You're going to hear six students tell you what they like to do. For each statement you hear, decide which of the students pictured on page 31 is speaking.

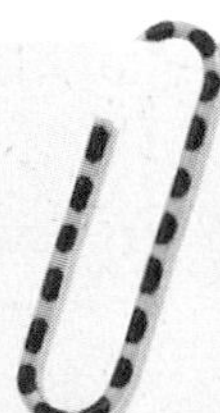

COMMENT DIT-ON... ?
Expressing likes, dislikes, and preferences about activities

CD-ROM Disc 1

To ask if someone likes an activity:
Tu aimes voyager?

To tell what you like to do:
J'aime voyager.
J'adore danser.
J'aime bien dormir.

To tell what you don't like to do:
Je n'aime pas aller aux concerts.

To tell what you prefer to do:
J'aime mieux regarder la télévision.
Je préfère lire.

25 Sondage *Poll*

a. Complete the following poll.

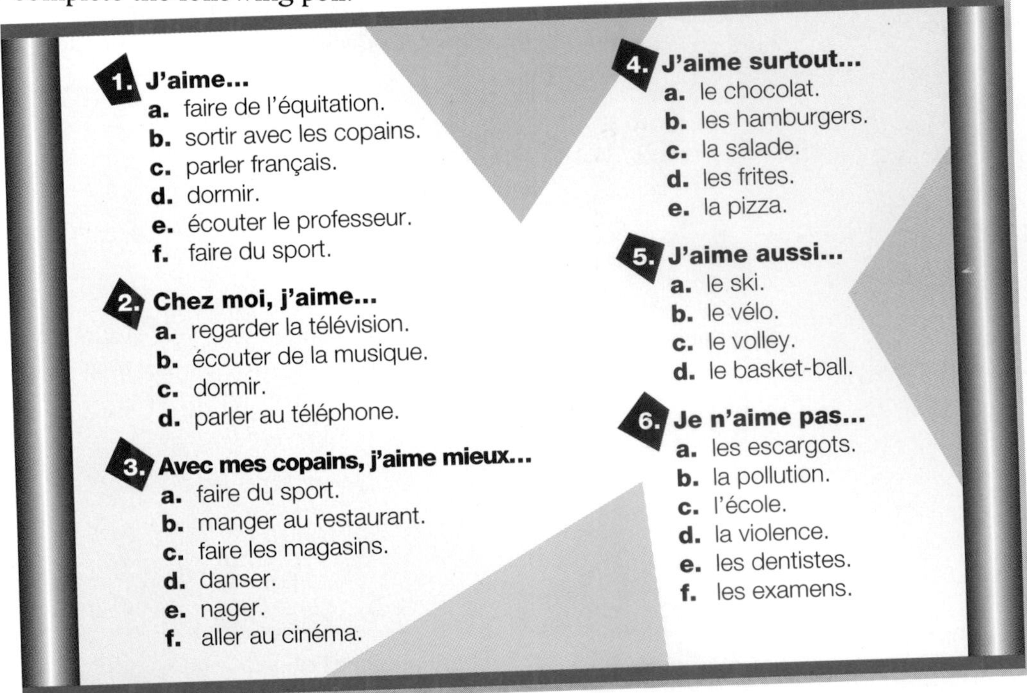

1. J'aime...
- a. faire de l'équitation.
- b. sortir avec les copains.
- c. parler français.
- d. dormir.
- e. écouter le professeur.
- f. faire du sport.

2. Chez moi, j'aime...
- a. regarder la télévision.
- b. écouter de la musique.
- c. dormir.
- d. parler au téléphone.

3. Avec mes copains, j'aime mieux...
- a. faire du sport.
- b. manger au restaurant.
- c. faire les magasins.
- d. danser.
- e. nager.
- f. aller au cinéma.

4. J'aime surtout...
- a. le chocolat.
- b. les hamburgers.
- c. la salade.
- d. les frites.
- e. la pizza.

5. J'aime aussi...
- a. le ski.
- b. le vélo.
- c. le volley.
- d. le basket-ball.

6. Je n'aime pas...
- a. les escargots.
- b. la pollution.
- c. l'école.
- d. la violence.
- e. les dentistes.
- f. les examens.

b. Compare your responses to the poll with those of a classmate. Which interests do you have in common?

GRAMMAIRE Subject pronouns and -er verbs

The verb **aimer** has different forms. In French, the verb forms change according to the subjects just as they do in English: *I like, you like,* but *he* or *she likes.*

Look at the chart below. Most **-er** verbs, that is, verbs whose infinitive ends in **-er**, follow this pattern.

aimer *(to like)*

J'aime Tu aimes Il/Elle aime	les vacances.	Nous aimons Vous aimez Ils/Elles aiment	les vacances.

- The forms **aime, aimes,** and **aiment** sound the same.
- The subject pronouns in French are **je/j'** *(I)*, **tu** *(you)*, **il** *(he* or *it)*, **elle** *(she or it)*, **nous** *(we)*, **vous** *(you)*, **ils** *(they)*, and **elles** *(they)*.
- Notice that there are two pronouns for *they*. Use **elles** to refer to a group of females. Use **ils** to refer to a group of males or a group of males and females.
- **Tu** and **vous** both mean *you.* Use **vous** when you talk to more than one person or to an adult who is not a family member. Use **tu** when you talk to a friend, family member, or someone your own age.
- Noun subjects take the same verb forms as their pronouns.

Philippe aime la salade   **Sophie et Julie aiment** faire du sport.
Il aime la salade   **Elles aiment** faire du sport.

26 «Tu» ou «vous»?

a. Would you use **tu** or **vous** to greet the following people? How would you ask them if they like a certain thing or activity?

M. et Mme Roland

Mlle Normand

Flore et Loïc

Lucie

b. Now complete the following phrases to tell what these people like, according to the illustrations above.

1. M. et Mme Roland...
2. Mlle Normand...
3. Flore et moi, nous...
4. Moi, je m'appelle Lucie. J'...

27 Qu'est-ce qu'ils aiment faire?

Your French pen pal wants to know what your friends like to do. Use the following photographs as cues.

Julio

Robert

Mark, David et Thomas

Pam

Marie

Eric

Karen

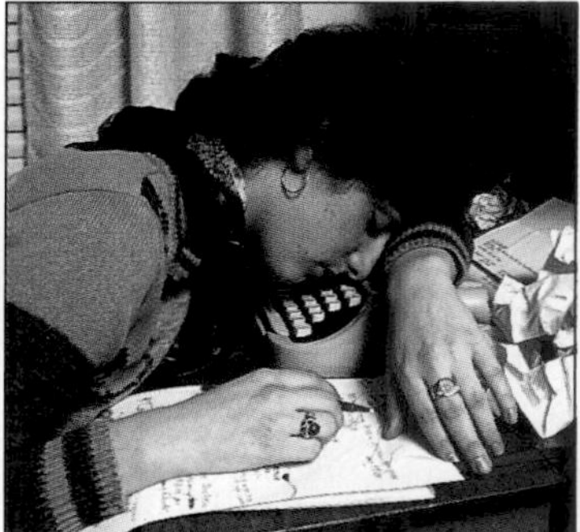

Blair

Emily et Raymond

28 Les vedettes! *Celebrities!*

a. Make a list of three public figures you admire (movie stars, musicians, athletes, and so on). Write down one or two things you think each person might like to do.

Shaquille O'Neal aime faire du sport, surtout *(especially)* du basket-ball!

b. Now, get together with a classmate. Tell your partner what one of the celebrities you've chosen likes to do. Use **il** or **elle** instead of the person's name. Your partner will try to identify the celebrity. Take turns.

29 Enquête *Survey*

Get together with three classmates. Ask questions to find out who shares your likes and dislikes. After you've discovered what you have in common, report your findings to the rest of the class.

Paul et moi, nous aimons le français et l'anglais, mais nous n'aimons pas le sport.

30 Mon journal

Expand your previous journal entry by adding the activities you like and dislike. Tell which activities you and your friends like to do together. Find or draw pictures to illustrate the activities.

PRONONCIATION

Intonation

As you speak, your voice rises and falls. This is called *intonation*.

A. A prononcer

In French, your voice rises at the end of each group of words within a statement and falls at the end of a statement. Repeat each of the following phrases:

J'aime les frites, les hamburgers et la pizza.

Il aime le football, mais il n'aime pas le vélo.

If you want to change a statement into a question, raise your voice at the end of the sentence. Repeat these questions.

Tu aimes l'anglais?

Tu t'appelles Julie?

B. A écouter

Decide whether each of the following is a statement or a question.

C. A écrire

You're going to hear two short dialogues. Write down what the people say.

LISONS!

When you look through French magazines, you'll often find a section where people place personal or business ads.

DE BONS CONSEILS You can often figure out what a reading selection is about simply by looking at the titles, subtitles, illustrations, and captions.

A. Look at the pictures and titles of this article from a French magazine. What do you think the article is about?

B. Do you remember what you've learned about cognates? Can you find at least five cognates in this article?

C. What do you think **Petites annonces** means?

D. Which of the pen pals would you choose if you were searching for the following?

Quelqu'un qui *(someone who)...*

aime faire les boutiques

aime les animaux

parle français et espagnol

aime la musique et le cinéma

aime le rap et la techno

COPAINS ★ COPINES ★ COPAIN

PETITES

Christiane Saulnier
Marseille

Si vous aimez la télévision, les animaux et les vacances, qu'est-ce que vous attendez pour m'écrire et m'envoyer votre photo! Je voudrais correspondre avec des filles ou des garçons de 13 à 16 ans. J'attends votre réponse avec impatience!

Karim Marzouk
Tunis, Tunisie

J'adorerais recevoir des lettres de personnes habitant le monde entier; j'adore voyager, écouter de la musique, aller au concert et lire sur la plage. J'aime bien les langues et je parle aussi l'arabe et l'espagnol. A bientôt.

Mireille Lacombe
Nantes

J'ai 15 ans et je voudrais bien correspondre avec des filles et des garçons de 13 à 17 ans. J'aime le rap et surtout la techno. Je fais aussi de l'équitation. Ecrivez-moi vite et je promets de vous répondre (photos S.V.P.)!

Didier Kouassi
Abidjan, Côte d'Ivoire

La techno me fait délirer et je suis aussi très sportif. Je cherche des correspondants filles ou garçons entre 15 et 17 ans. N'hésitez pas à m'écrire!

ion Air Mail Par avion

INES ★ COPAINS ★ COPINES

ANNONCES

Laurence Simon
Le Marin, Martinique

J'ai 16 ans, je suis dingue de sport, j'aime les soirs de fête entre copains. Le week-end, j'aime faire les magasins. Alors, si vous me ressemblez, dépêchez-vous de m'écrire. Réponse assurée à 100%!

Etienne Hubert
Poitiers

Je suis blond aux yeux bleus, assez grand, timide mais très sympa. J'aime sortir et j'aime lire la science-fiction. Je cherche des amis entre 14 et 16 ans. Répondez vite!

Hugues Vallet
La Rochelle

Je voudrais correspondre avec des filles et des garçons de 16 à 18 ans. J'aime sortir, délirer et faire les boutiques. Je suis fan de Vanessa Paradis et de Julia Roberts. Alors, j'attends vos lettres!

Amélie Perrin
Périgord

Je voudrais correspondre avec des jeunes de 14 à 17 ans qui aiment faire la fête, écouter de la musique et aller au cinéma. Moi, j'étudie la danse et la photographie. Ecrivez-moi et je me ferai une joie de vous répondre.

Vous voulez correspondre avec des gens sympa? Écrivez votre petite annonce en précisant vos nom, prénom, âge et adresse, et en y joignant une photo d'identité.

Rachel M
3904-1

E. Several of your friends are looking for pen pals. Based on their wishes, find a good match for each of them in **Petites annonces.**

1. My pen pal should like sports.
2. I'd like to hear from someone who likes going out.
3. I'm looking for a pen pal who likes to go to the movies.
4. It would be great to have a pen pal who enjoys shopping.
5. I'd like to hear from someone from Africa.
6. I'd like a pen pal who likes to travel.

F. If you want to place an ad for a pen pal, what should you do?

G. One of your classmates is looking for a pen pal. Make a short list of questions that will help you identify which pen pal has the most in common with your classmate. Then, interview your classmate, compare his or her answers with the ads included in **Petites annonces,** and decide which pen pal would be the best match. Find out if your classmate agrees with your decision.

H. Jot down a few things you might like to include in your own letter requesting a pen pal. Using your notes, write your own request for a pen pal like the ones you read in **Petites annonces.**

MISE EN PRATIQUE

1 Do the following photos represent French culture, American culture, or both?

1.

2.

3.

4.

5.

2 **L'Organisation internationale de correspondants (l'O.I.C.),** a pen pal organization you wrote to, has left a phone message on your answering machine. Listen carefully to the message and write down your pen pal's name, age, phone number, likes, and dislikes.

Nom :
Age :
Numéro :
Aime :
N'aime pas :

3 Tell a classmate in French about your new pen pal.

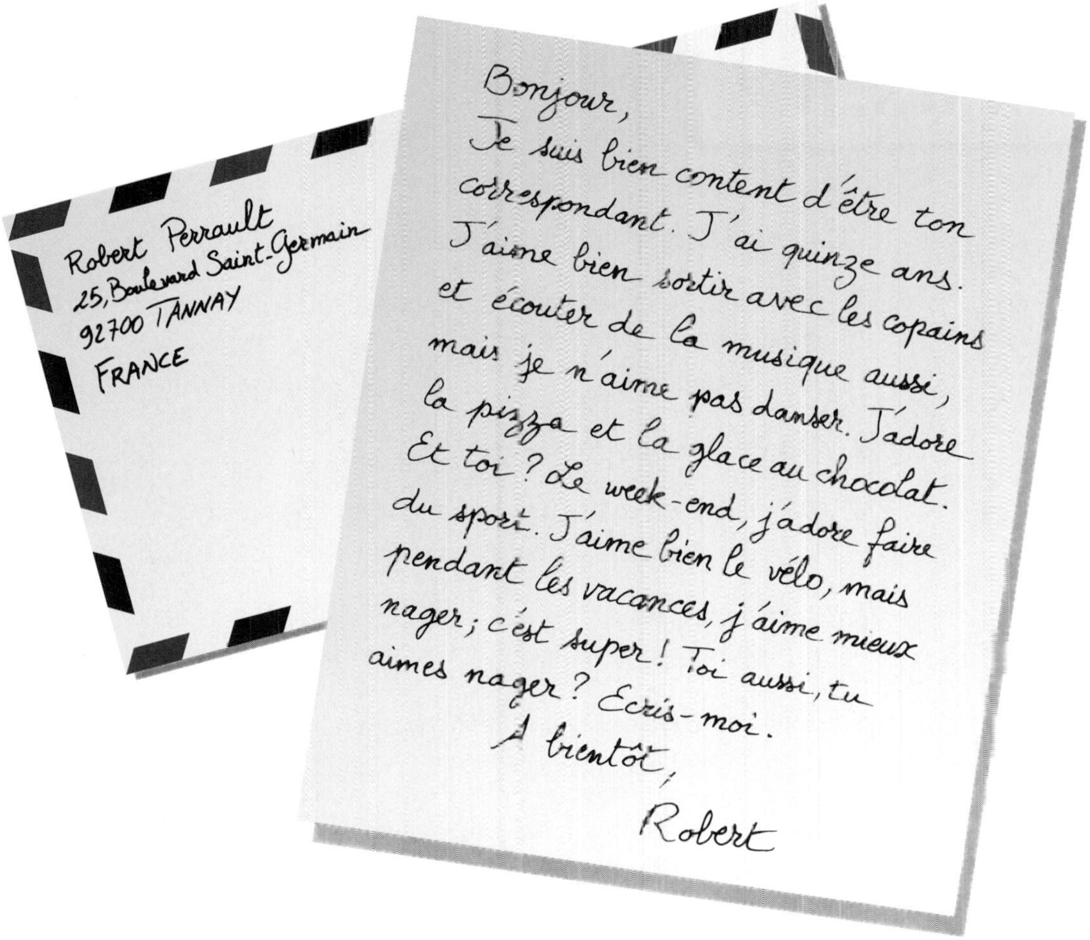

Robert Perrault
25, Boulevard Saint-Germain
92700 TANNAY
FRANCE

Bonjour,

Je suis bien content d'être ton correspondant. J'ai quinze ans. J'aime bien sortir avec les copains et écouter de la musique aussi, mais je n'aime pas danser. J'adore la pizza et la glace au chocolat. Et toi? Le week-end, j'adore faire du sport. J'aime bien le vélo, mais pendant les vacances, j'aime mieux nager; c'est super! Toi aussi, tu aimes nager? Ecris-moi.

A bientôt,

Robert

4 You've received your first letter from Robert Perrault. Read it twice— the first time for general understanding, the second time for details. Then, answer the questions below in English.

1. How old is Robert?
2. What sports does he like?
3. What foods does he like?
4. What doesn't he like to do?

5 Now, answer Robert's letter. Begin your reply with **Cher Robert.** Be sure to . . .

- introduce yourself.
- ask how he's doing.
- tell about your likes and dislikes.
- ask him about other likes and dislikes he might have.
- answer his questions to you.
- say goodbye.

6

JEU DE ROLE

A French exchange student has just arrived at your school. How would you find out his or her name? Age? Likes and dislikes? Act out the scene with a partner. Take turns playing the role of the French student.

QUE SAIS-JE?

Can you use what you've learned in this chapter?

Can you greet people and say goodbye? p. 22

1 How would you say hello and goodbye to the following people? What gestures would you use?

1. a classmate
2. your French teacher

Can you ask how people are and tell how you are? p. 23

2 Can you ask how someone is?

3 If someone asks you how you are, what do you say if . . .

1. you feel great?
2. you feel OK?
3. you don't feel well?

Can you ask someone's name and age and give yours? pp. 24–25

4 How would you . . .

1. ask someone's name?
2. tell someone your name?

5 How would you . . .

1. find out someone's age?
2. tell someone how old you are?

Can you express likes, dislikes, and preferences? pp. 26, 32

6 Can you tell what you like and dislike, using the verb **aimer**?

1. horseback riding
2. soccer
3. going out with friends
4. shopping
5. the movies

7 Can you ask a friend in French if he or she likes . . .

a.

b.

c.

d.

e.

8 Can you tell in French what these people like, dislike, or prefer?

1. Robert never studies.
2. Emilie thinks reading is the greatest.
3. Hervé prefers pizza.
4. Nathalie never goes to the beach.
5. Nicole is always biking or playing soccer.

VOCABULAIRE

PREMIERE ETAPE

Greeting people and saying goodbye

Bonjour! *Hello!*
Salut! *Hi!* or *Goodbye!*
Au revoir! *Goodbye!*
A tout à l'heure! *See you later!*
A bientôt. *See you soon.*
A demain. *See you tomorrow.*
Tchao! *Bye!*
madame (Mme) *ma'am; Mrs.*
mademoiselle (Mlle) *miss; Miss*
monsieur (M.) *sir; Mr.*

Asking how people are and telling how you are

(Comment) ça va? *How's it going?*
Ça va. *Fine.*
Super! *Great!*
Très bien. *Very well.*
Comme ci, comme ça. *So-so*
Bof! *(expression of indifference)*
Pas mal. *Not bad.*
Pas terrible. *Not so great.*
Et toi? *And you?*

Asking someone's name and giving yours

Tu t'appelles comment? *What's your name?*
Je m'appelle... *My name is . . .*
Il/Elle s'appelle comment? *What's his/her name?*
Il/Elle s'appelle... *His/Her name is . . .*

Asking someone's age and giving yours

Tu as quel âge? *How old are you?*
J'ai... ans. *I am . . . years old.*
douze *twelve*
treize *thirteen*
quatorze *fourteen*
quinze *fifteen*
seize *sixteen*
dix-sept *seventeen*
dix-huit *eighteen*

DEUXIEME ETAPE

Expressing likes, dislikes, and preferences about things

Moi, j'aime (bien)... *I (really) like . . .*
Je n'aime pas... *I don't like . . .*
J'aime mieux... *I prefer . . .*
Je préfère... *I prefer . . .*
J'adore... *I adore . . .*
Tu aimes... ? *Do you like . . . ?*
les amis (m.) *friends*
l'anglais (m.) *English*
le chocolat *chocolate*
le cinéma *the movies*
les concerts (m.) *concerts*
l'école (f.) *school*
les escargots (m.) *snails*
les examens (m.) *tests*
le football *soccer*
le français *French*
les frites (f.) *French fries*
la glace *ice cream*
les hamburgers (m.) *hamburgers*
les magasins (m.) *stores*
les maths (f.) *math*
la pizza *pizza*
la plage *beach*
le ski *skiing*
le sport *sports*
les vacances (f.) *vacation*
le vélo *biking*

Other useful expressions

et *and*
mais *but*
non *no*
oui *yes*
ou *or*

TROISIEME ETAPE

Expressing likes, dislikes, and preferences about activities

aimer *to like*
danser *to dance*
dormir *to sleep*
écouter de la musique *to listen to music*
étudier *to study*
faire de l'équitation *to go horseback riding*
faire les magasins *to go shopping*
faire le ménage *to do housework*
faire du sport *to play sports*
lire *to read*
nager *to swim*
parler au téléphone *to talk on the phone*
regarder la télé *to watch TV*
sortir avec les copains *to go out with friends*
voyager *to travel*

Other useful expressions

aussi *also*
surtout *especially*

For subject pronouns see page 33.

CHAPITRE

2 Vive l'école!

1 — J'adore le sport!
— Moi aussi!

When school starts, new schedules are the main topic of conversation, at least for a while. What classes do you have? How do you feel about them?

In this chapter you will learn

- to agree and disagree
- to ask for and give information
- to ask for and express opinions

And you will

- listen to French-speaking students talk about their classes
- read a French student's class schedule
- write about your own classes
- compare schools in francophone countries with schools in the United States

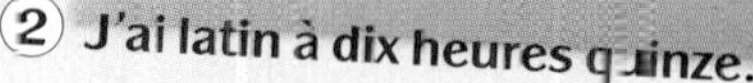
(2) J'ai latin à dix heures quinze.

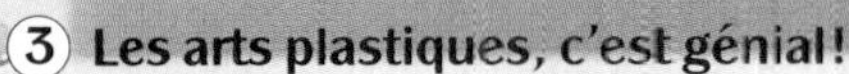
(3) Les arts plastiques, c'est génial!

Mise en train

La rentrée

Where do you think these teenagers are? What do you think they're talking about? How do you know?

Les jeunes de Poitiers :

Claire

Delphine

Marc

Jérôme

et du Texas :

Ann

C'est la première semaine de cours...

1
Tu as quel cours maintenant?
Allemand. J'adore. Et toi, tu as quoi?
Sciences nat.
2
Pourquoi?
C'est difficile, les sciences nat.
Mais non, c'est passionnant. Et le prof est sympa.
Ecoutez. Je ne veux pas être en retard. Bon courage!

3
Alors, les garçons, ça boume?
Super.
Bof. Pas terrible.

4
Qu'est-ce qu'il y a?
Oh rien. J'ai maths.
Tu n'aimes pas les maths?
Non, c'est nul.

Moi, j'adore. C'est super intéressant.
J'aime mieux le sport. C'est plus cool.
Et après, tu as quoi?
Après les maths, j'ai géographie.
Et toi, Jérôme, tu as quoi maintenant?
Euh, je ne sais pas très bien.
Tu n'as pas allemand?
Si, tu as raison.
Tu aimes l'allemand, toi?
Oui, mais j'aime encore mieux l'espagnol. C'est plus facile pour moi.
Tu étudies aussi l'espagnol?
Oui. Et l'anglais aussi.
Dis, tu as sport cet aprèm?
Oui, à quatorze heures.
Génial! Nous aussi!
Alors, on a tous sport cet aprèm.
Il est quelle heure?
Huit heures! Vite. Allons-y! On est en retard!
Eh bien, Jérôme? Qu'est-ce qu'il y a?
Je n'ai pas mes baskets.

1 Tu as compris?

Answer the following questions about **La rentrée.**

1. What are the students discussing?
2. What do you think **La rentrée** means?
3. What class do they all have together?
4. Why are they in a hurry at the end of the conversation?
5. What is Jérôme worried about?

2 Vrai ou faux?

1. Ann est américaine.
2. Jérôme n'aime pas l'espagnol.
3. Ann et Marc n'aiment pas les maths.
4. Jérôme a allemand.
5. Marc n'a pas sport cet aprèm.

3 Cherche les expressions

In **La rentrée**, what do the students say to . . .

1. ask what class someone has?
2. tell why they like a class?
3. tell why they don't like a class?
4. tell which class they prefer?
5. ask what time it is?

C'est difficile. C'est nul. Il est quelle heure?
C'est super intéressant. J'aime encore mieux...
C'est plus cool.
Tu as quel cours? Tu as quoi?
J'aime mieux...
Le prof est sympa. C'est passionnant.

4 Ils aiment ou pas?

Do these students like or dislike the subjects or teachers they're talking about?

1. «Les sciences nat, c'est passionnant.»
2. «Les maths, c'est nul.»
3. «C'est super intéressant, les maths.»
4. «Le prof est sympa.»

5 Qu'est-ce qui manque? *What's missing?*

Choose the correct words from the box to complete these sentences based on **La rentrée.**

1. Après maths, Marc a _____.
2. Jérôme a _____.
3. Jérôme aime mieux _____ que l'allemand.
4. On a tous sport à _____ heures.
5. On est en retard! Il est _____ heures.

géographie allemand quatorze
huit l'espagnol

6 Et maintenant, à toi

Which students in **La rentrée** share your own likes or dislikes about school subjects?

PREMIERE ETAPE

Agreeing and disagreeing

VOCABULAIRE

LYCEE VOLTAIRE

LES SCIENCES NATURELLES

L'INFORMATIQUE

LES TRAVAUX PRATIQUES DE CHIMIE

L'HISTOIRE

LA GEOGRAPHIE

L'ALLEMAND

L'EDUCATION PHYSIQUE ET SPORTIVE

L'ESPAGNOL

LES ARTS PLASTIQUES

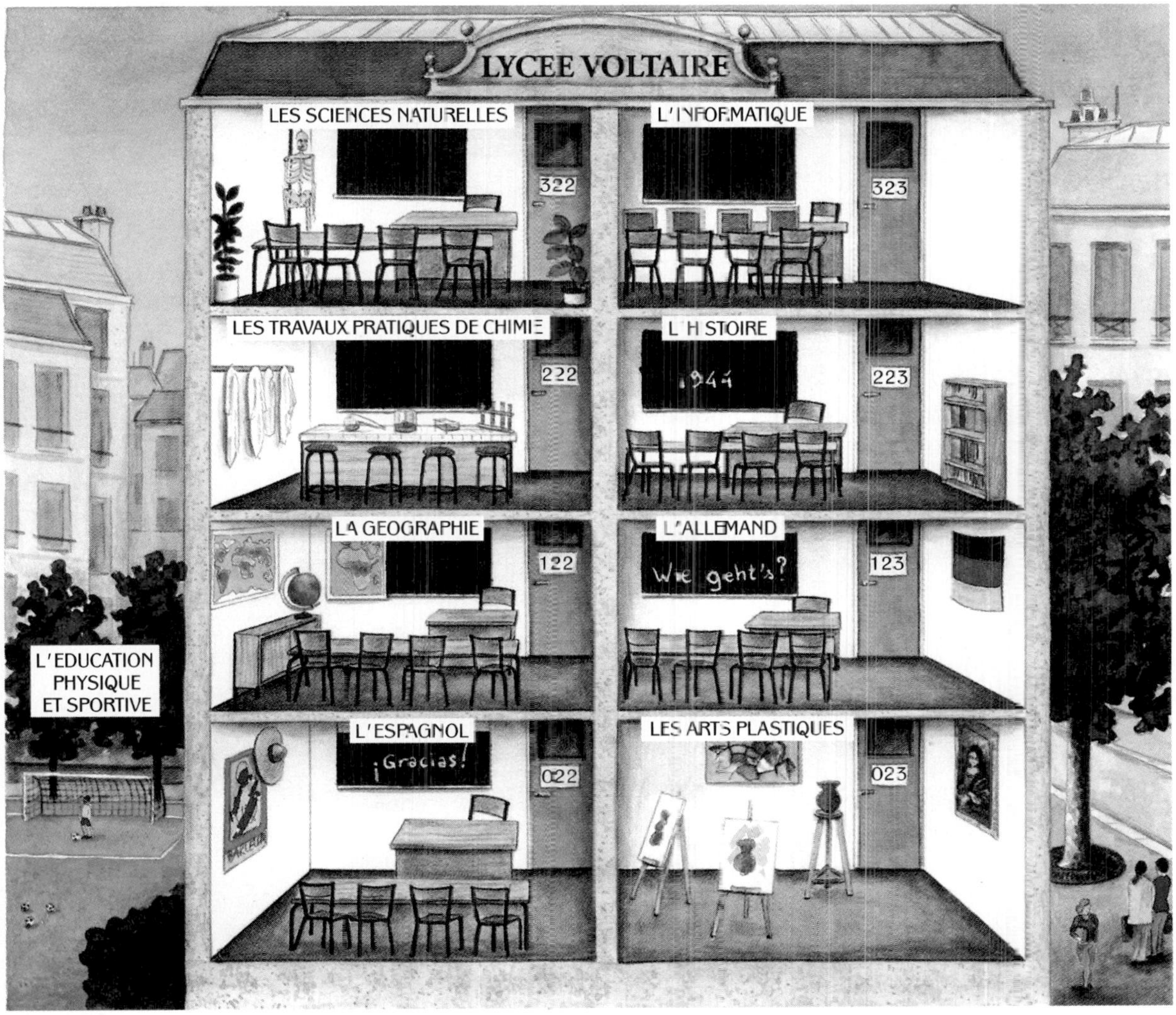

l'algèbre (f.)	*algebra*	**la chorale**	*choir*	**la musique**	*music*
la biologie	*biology*	**le cours de développement personnel et social (DPS)**	*health*	**le cours**	*course, school subject*
la chimie	*chemistry*	**la danse**	*dance*	**les devoirs** (m.)	*homework*
la géométrie	*geometry*	**le latin**	*Latin*	**l'élève** (m./f.)	*student*
la physique	*physics*			**le professeur**	*teacher*

*You can abbreviate **Education Physique et Sportive** as **EPS.** In conversation, students often say **le sport** instead of **EPS.**

7 Ecoute!

On the first day of school, Céline and Aurélie are looking for their French class. As you listen to their conversation, look at the drawing of the school on page 47 and write the numbers of the classrooms they're looking into.

8 Ils aiment quels cours? *What subjects do they like?*

Name three subjects Nicole and Gérard probably like, according to their interests.

Nicole

Gérard

9 C'est qui? *Who is it?*

Tell your partner what subject one of these students likes, without naming the person. Your partner will try to guess the person's name. Take turns until you've identified all of the students.

Michel

— Il aime le français.
— C'est Michel.

Julien

Nathalie

Virginie

Guillaume

Franck

Karine

Study at regular intervals. It's best to learn language in small chunks and to review frequently. Cramming will not usually work for French. Study at least a little bit every day, whether you have an assignment or not. The more often you review words and structures, the easier it will be for you to understand and participate in class.

NOTE CULTURELLE

In France and other countries that follow the French educational system, the grade levels are numbered in descending order. When students begin junior high **(le collège)** at about 10 or 11 years of age, the grade they are in is called **sixième.** Then they go into **cinquième, quatrième,** and **troisième.** The grade levels at the high school **(le lycée)** are called **seconde, première,** and **terminale.**

Le baccalauréat, or **le bac,** is a national exam taken at the end of study at a **lycée** Not all students take the **bac,** but those who plan to go on to a university must pass it. It's an extremely difficult oral and written test that covers all major subjects. Students spend the final year of the **lycée, la terminale,** preparing for this exam. There are three major categories of **baccalauréat** exams: **le bac général, le bac technologique,** and **le bac professionnel.** Each category is divided into a more specialized series of exams, depending upon a student's chosen field of study. For example, a student specializing in literature would take the **bac général littéraire,** or simply **le bac L.**

Baccalauréat 1996: Les hauts et les bas

Taux de réussite par série (en %).

Examen et série	Total	En 1995	Changement
Bac Général			
Littéraire (L)	71,9	71,7	+0,2
Economique et social (ES)	71,1	73,2	- 2,1
Sciences (S)	77,8	78,4	- 0,6
Bac Technologique			
Sciences et technologies industrielles (STI)	73,4	67,5	+5,9
Sciences et technologies de laboratoire (STL)	79,7	75,2	+4,5
Sciences médico-sociales (SMS)	81	73,5	+7,5
Sciences et technologies tertiaires (STT)	80,6	80,6	0
Bac Professionnel			
Industriel	74,3	70,2	+4,1
Tertiaire	81	74,8	+6,2
Total France métropolitaine	76	75,2	+0,8

10 Mon journal

Make a list of your favorite school subjects in your journal. If you were taking these subjects in France, which **bac** do you think you would take?

Je passerais le bac... *(I would take* **bac** *. . .)*

COMMENT DIT-ON... ?
Agreeing and disagreeing

To agree:
Oui, beaucoup. *Yes, very much.*
Moi aussi. *Me too.*
Moi non plus. *Neither do I.*

To disagree:
Moi, non. *I don't.*
Non, pas trop. *No, not too much.*
Moi, si. *I do.*
Pas moi. *Not me.*

11 Ecoute!

Listen as Hélène and Gérard talk about the subjects they like and dislike. Which one do they agree on? Which one do they disagree on?

12 Parlons! *Let's talk!*

Ask your partner's opinion about several subjects and then agree or disagree. Take turns.

— Tu aimes les arts plastiques?
— Non, pas trop.
— Moi, si.

NOTE DE GRAMMAIRE

Use **si** instead of **oui** to contradict a negative statement or question.

— Tu **n'**aimes **pas** la biologie?
— Mais **si**! J'adore la bio!

13 Ça te plaît? *Do you like it?*

Get together with two classmates. Find at least two things or activities that you all like. Then, tell the rest of the class what you agree on.

ELEVE 1 — J'aime les hamburgers. Et toi?
ELEVE 2 — Oui, beaucoup.
ELEVE 3 — Moi aussi.
ELEVE 1 — Nous aimons tous *(all)* les hamburgers.

le cinéma — le foot — les concerts — la pizza — faire du sport — écouter de la musique — faire les magasins — la glace — le ski

DEUXIEME ETAPE

Asking for and giving information

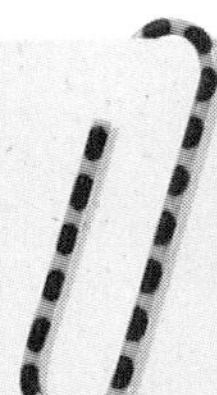

COMMENT DIT-ON... ?
Asking for and giving information

To ask about someone's classes:
Tu as quels cours aujourd'hui?
What classes do you have . . . ?
Tu as quoi le matin?
What do you have . . . ?
Vous avez espagnol l'après-midi?
Do you have . . . ?

To tell what classes you have:
J'ai arts plastiques et physique.
I have . . .
J'ai algèbre, DPS et sport.

Oui, et **nous avons** aussi géo.
. . . we have . . .

14 On a quoi? *What do we have?*

a. Find out what subjects your partner has in the morning and in the afternoon.

— Tu as quoi le matin (l'après-midi)?
— Bio, algèbre et chorale. Et toi?
— Moi, j'ai algèbre, chimie, chorale et DPS.

b. Now, tell the rest of the class which subjects you and your partner have in common.

Marc et moi, nous avons algèbre et chorale.

VOCABULAIRE

le matin	*in the morning*
l'après-midi	*in the afternoon*
aujourd'hui	*today*
demain	*tomorrow*
maintenant	*now*

GRAMMAIRE The verb avoir

Avoir is an irregular verb. That means it doesn't follow the pattern of the **-er** verbs you learned in Chapter 1.

avoir *(to have)*

J' **ai** / Tu **as** / Il/Elle/On **a**	chimie maintenant.	Nous **avons** / Vous **avez** / Ils/Elles **ont**	chimie maintenant.

As you saw in Chapter 1, you often use an article **(le, la, l'**, or **les)** before a noun. When you're telling which school subjects you have, however, you don't use an article.

15 Ils ont quels cours?

Some students are day-dreaming about the future. What classes are they taking to prepare for these careers?

Ils ont géométrie, physique et géographie.

1.

2.

3.

4.

VOCABULAIRE

Voilà l'emploi du temps de Stéphanie Lambert.

EMPLOI DU TEMPS — **NOM:** Stéphanie Lambert — **CLASSE:** 3e

		LUNDI	MARDI	MERCREDI	JEUDI	VENDREDI	SAMEDI	DIMANCHE
MATIN	**8h00**	Allemand	Arts plastiques	Mathématiques	Mathématiques	Français		
	9h00	Français	Arts plastiques	Anglais	Sciences nat	Français	Anglais	
	10h00	**Récréation**	**Récréation**	**Récréation**	**Récréation**	**Récréation**	TP physique	**L**
	10h15	EPS	Allemand	Français	EPS	Sciences nat	TP physique	**I**
	11h15	Sciences nat	**Etude**	Histoire/Géo	**Etude**	Arts plastiques	**[Sortie]**	
	12h15	**Déjeuner**	**Déjeuner**	**[Sortie]**	**Déjeuner**	**Déjeuner**	**APRES-MIDI**	**B**
APRES-MIDI	**14h00**	Histoire/Géo	Mathématiques	**APRES-MIDI**	Histoire/Géo	Allemand	**LIBRE**	
	15h00	Anglais	Physique/Chimie	**LIBRE**	Physique/Chimie	Mathématiques		**R**
	16h00	**Récréation**	**[Sortie]**		**Récréation**	**[Sortie]**		
	16h15	Mathématiques			Arts plastiques			**E**
	17h15	**[Sortie]**			**[Sortie]**			

16 Tu comprends?

Answer the following questions about Stéphanie Lambert's schedule on page 52.

1. Can you find and copy the words in the schedule that refer to days of the week?
2. **Déjeuner** and **Récréation** don't refer to school subjects. What do you think they mean?
3. What do you think **14h00** means?
4. If **étudier** means *to study,* what do you think **Etude** means?
5. You know that **sortir** means *to go out.* What do you think **Sortie** means?
6. Can you list two differences between Stéphanie's schedule and yours?

17 L'Emploi du temps de Stéphanie

Stéphanie is telling a friend about her schedule. Complete her statements according to her schedule on page 52.

Le __1__ matin, j'ai allemand, français, EPS et sciences nat. Je n'aime pas trop les sciences. J'ai histoire-géo le __2__, le __3__ et le __4__. J'adore l'histoire! Et le mercredi __5__, je n'ai pas cours. Normalement, j'ai __6__ à 10h00, mais le __7__, j'ai travaux pratiques de physique à 10h00. Je n'ai pas cours le __8__.

18 Ecoute!

Look at Stéphanie's schedule as you listen to three of her friends call her on the phone. They're going to tell her what subjects they have on a certain day of the week. Do they have the same subjects as Stéphanie on that day?

VOCABULAIRE

You've already learned the numbers 0–20. Here are the numbers 21–59 in French.

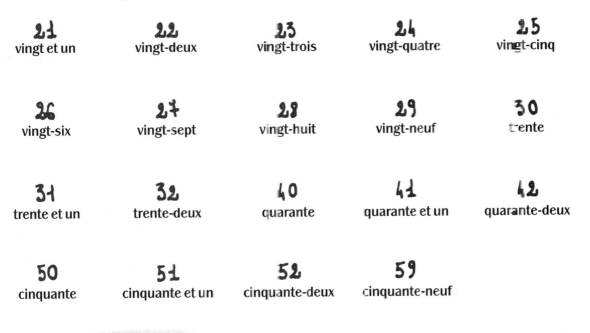

21 vingt et un	22 vingt-deux	23 vingt-trois	24 vingt-quatre	25 vingt-cinq
26 vingt-six	27 vingt-sept	28 vingt-huit	29 vingt-neuf	30 trente
31 trente et un	32 trente-deux	40 quarante	41 quarante et un	42 quarante-deux
50 cinquante	51 cinquante et un	52 cinquante-deux	59 cinquante-neuf	

19 Quels sont les nombres?

1. Say these numbers in French.

   a. 25 **b.** 37 **c.** 46 **d.** 53

2. Write the numerals for these numbers.

   a. vingt-huit **b.** trente-quatre **c.** quarante et un **d.** cinquante-cinq

COMMENT DIT-ON... ?

Telling when you have class

To find out at what time someone has a certain class:

Tu as maths **à quelle heure**?

To tell at what time you have a certain class:

J'ai maths **à neuf heures.**

huit heures

dix heures quinze

sept heures vingt

quinze heures trente

seize heures quarante-cinq

20 Ecoute!

Listen as Jérôme answers Ann's questions about his schedule. At what time does he have these classes: **anglais, espagnol, histoire,** and **maths**?

A la française

In casual conversation, you might try using the abbreviated forms of words just as French teenagers do. For example, **la récréation** can be abbreviated to **la récré.** Do you recall the abbreviated forms of the words listed below? If not, look for them in **La rentrée** or in Stéphanie's schedule.

les sciences naturelles
la géographie
l'éducation physique et sportive
l'après-midi
les mathématiques
le professeur

NOTE CULTURELLE

Although in familiar conversation people may use the 12-hour system to give the time, they use the 24-hour system **(l'heure officielle)** to give schedules for transportation, schools, stores, and movies. For example, the school day generally begins at 8h00 **(huit heures)** and continues until 17h00 **(dix-sept heures)** or 18h00 **(dix-huit heures)** with a break from 12h00 **(douze heures)** to 14h00 **(quatorze heures)**. You will learn about the 12-hour system in Chapter 6.

21 Une journée chargée

A busy day

Claudine is busy today. What does she have at each of the times listed?

A huit heures, elle a géographie.

1. 8h00

2. 9h35

3. 11h50

4. 14h05

5. 16h20

22 Nos emplois du temps *Our schedules*

a. You and your partner prepare schedules showing only the times classes meet at your school. Take turns asking at what time you each have the classes listed here. Fill in each other's schedule, writing the subjects next to the appropriate times.

— Tu as histoire à quelle heure?
— A onze heures trente.

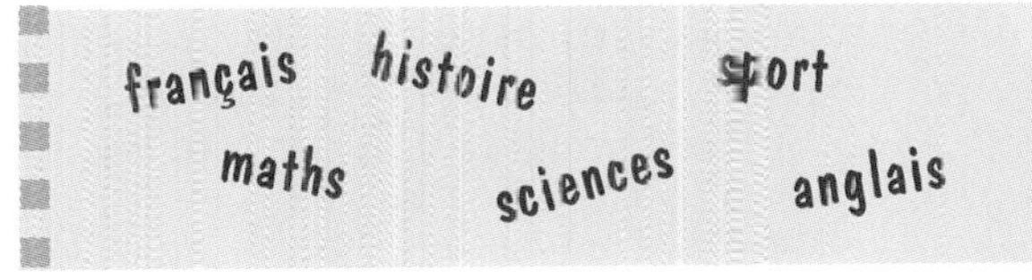

b. Now complete the schedules by asking what subjects you each have at the remaining times.

— Tu as quoi à treize heures?

23 Mon journal

In your journal, make a list of your classes. Include the days and times you have them and the names of your teachers.

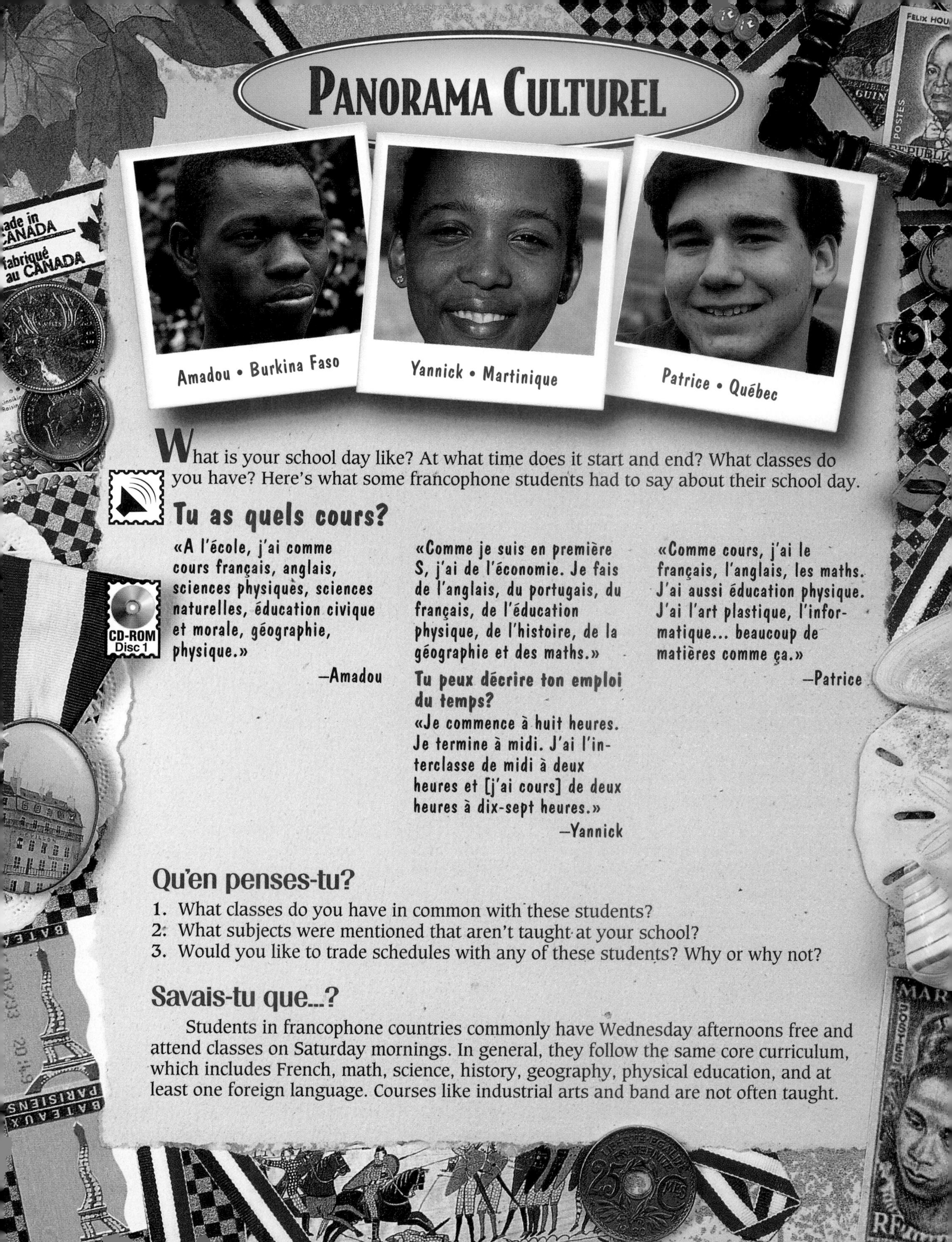

Panorama Culturel

Amadou • Burkina Faso

Yannick • Martinique

Patrice • Québec

What is your school day like? At what time does it start and end? What classes do you have? Here's what some francophone students had to say about their school day.

Tu as quels cours?

CD-ROM Disc 1

«A l'école, j'ai comme cours français, anglais, sciences physiques, sciences naturelles, éducation civique et morale, géographie, physique.»

—Amadou

«Comme je suis en première S, j'ai de l'économie. Je fais de l'anglais, du portugais, du français, de l'éducation physique, de l'histoire, de la géographie et des maths.»

Tu peux décrire ton emploi du temps?

«Je commence à huit heures. Je termine à midi. J'ai l'interclasse de midi à deux heures et [j'ai cours] de deux heures à dix-sept heures.»

—Yannick

«Comme cours, j'ai le français, l'anglais, les maths. J'ai aussi éducation physique. J'ai l'art plastique, l'informatique... beaucoup de matières comme ça.»

—Patrice

Qu'en penses-tu?

1. What classes do you have in common with these students?
2. What subjects were mentioned that aren't taught at your school?
3. Would you like to trade schedules with any of these students? Why or why not?

Savais-tu que...?

Students in francophone countries commonly have Wednesday afternoons free and attend classes on Saturday mornings. In general, they follow the same core curriculum, which includes French, math, science, history, geography, physical education, and at least one foreign language. Courses like industrial arts and band are not often taught.

TROISIEME ETAPE

Asking for and expressing opinions

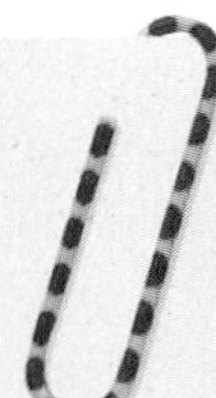

COMMENT DIT-ON... ?

Asking for and expressing opinions

To ask someone's opinion:

Comment tu trouves ça?
Comment tu trouves le cours de biologie?

To express a favorable opinion:

C'est... *It's . . .*
- **facile.** *easy.*
- **génial.** *great.*
- **super.** *super.*
- **cool.** *cool.*
- **intéressant.** *interesting.*
- **passionnant.** *fascinating.*

To express indifference:

C'est pas mal. *It's not bad.*
Ça va. *It's OK.*

To express an unfavorable opinion:

C'est... *It's . . .*
- **difficile.** *hard.*
- **pas terrible.** *not so great.*
- **pas super.** *not so hot.*
- **zéro.** *a waste of time.*
- **nul.** *useless.*
- **barbant.** *boring.*

A la française

In informal conversation, French speakers will often leave out the **ne** in a negative sentence.

J'aime pas les hamburgers, moi.
C'est pas super, la géo.

In writing, you should include the **ne** in negative sentences.

24 Ecoute!

Listen as Aurélie and Eric talk about their subjects. Which ones does Eric like? Which doesn't he like? And Aurélie?

les sciences nat
la géo
l'anglais
l'allemand
l'espagnol
l'histoire
les maths

The French system of grading is based on a scale of 0–20. A score of less than 8 isn't a passing grade. Students are usually pleased with a score of 10 or higher. They must work very hard to receive a 17 or an 18, and it's very rare to earn a 19 or a 20.

25 Qu'est-ce qu'on dit? *What are they saying?*

What do you think these students are saying?

1. L'histoire, c'est...

2. La géométrie, c'est...

3. L'algèbre, c'est...

4. La biologie, c'est...

5. L'espagnol, c'est...

6. Les arts plastiques, c'est...

26 La vie scolaire *School life*

Read this letter that your new pen pal Laurent wrote to you after his first day of class. Then, write your reply.

Salut!
Ça va au lycée? Tu aimes tes cours? Moi, mes cours sont pas mal. J'adore les maths, c'est facile. Mais la physique, c'est barbant. Et la bio, c'est difficile. Et toi? Tu aimes les sciences? Pas moi. J'aime mieux les langues. C'est génial, et c'est plus intéressant. J'ai sport l'après-midi. J'aime bien; c'est cool. Et toi? Tu as sport aussi? Ça te plaît?

A bientôt,
Laurent

27 Comment tu trouves?

With your partner, discuss how you feel about your classes.

— Tu as maths?
— Oui, à neuf heures.
— Comment tu trouves ça?
— C'est super!

28 Un sondage

What is your favorite in each of the following categories? Ask at least three of your classmates how they like your favorites.

— Comment tu trouves *Star Wars*®?
— C'est pas terrible.

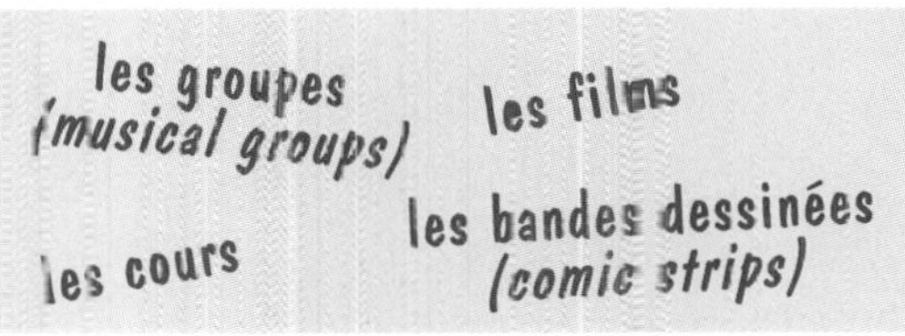

les groupes (musical groups)
les films
les cours
les bandes dessinées (comic strips)

PRONONCIATION

Liaison

In French you don't usually pronounce consonants at the end of a word, such as the **s** in **les** and the **t** in **c'est.** But you do pronounce some final consonants if the following word begins with a vowel sound. This linking of the final consonant of one word with the beginning vowel of the next word is called **liaison.**

les examens	**C'est intéressant.**	**vous avez**	**deux élèves**
z	t	z	z

A. A prononcer

Repeat the following phrases and sentences.

les maths / les escargots
nous n'aimons pas / nous aimons
C'est super. / C'est intéressant.
les profs / les élèves

B. A lire

Take turns with a partner reading the following sentences aloud. Make all necessary liaisons.

1. Ils ont maths.
2. Elles ont histoire.
3. Elles aiment l'espagnol.
4. Elle a deux examens lundi.
5. Vous avez cours le samedi?
6. Nous aimons les arts plastiques.

C. A écrire

You're going to hear two short dialogues. Write down what you hear.

LISONS!

How do most American students feel about their classes and their teachers? Do you think French students feel the same way?

DE BONS CONSEILS
You'll find photos, drawings, charts, and other visual clues when you read newspapers, magazines, and even your textbooks! These illustrations will usually give you an idea of what you're going to read before you begin.

A. First, look at the illustrations. Based on what you see, do you think you're going to read . . .

1. price lists?
2. math exercises?
3. results from a survey?
4. ads from a sales catalogue?

B. Now, scan the titles and texts. Based on the titles and the drawings, do you think these articles are about . . .

1. teenagers' favorite pastimes?
2. grades given to students on exams?
3. students' attitudes toward school?
4. prices at several stores?

C. Here are some cognates from the graph entitled **Profs.** What do you think these words mean in English?

distants respectueux compétents absents

SONDAGE
Les lycéens ont-ils le moral?

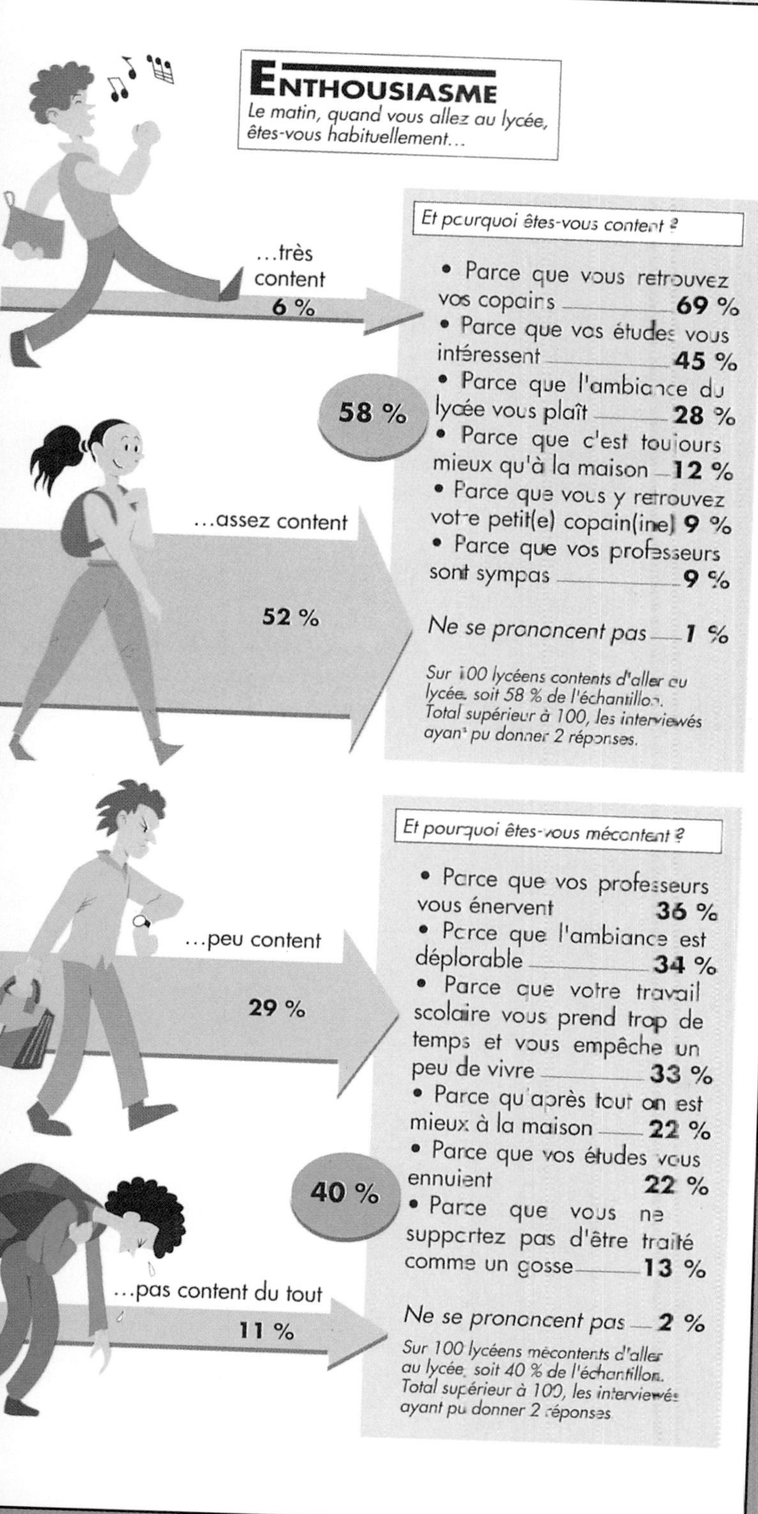

ENTHOUSIASME
Le matin, quand vous allez au lycée, êtes-vous habituellement...
...très content
6 %
Et pourquoi êtes-vous content ?
• Parce que vous retrouvez vos copains 69 %
• Parce que vos études vous intéressent 45 %
• Parce que l'ambiance du lycée vous plaît 28 %
• Parce que c'est toujours mieux qu'à la maison 12 %
• Parce que vous y retrouvez votre petit(e) copain(ine) 9 %
• Parce que vos professeurs sont sympas 9 %
Ne se prononcent pas 1 %
Sur 100 lycéens contents d'aller au lycée, soit 58 % de l'échantillon.
Total supérieur à 100, les interviewés ayant pu donner 2 réponses.
58 %
...assez content
52 %
Et pourquoi êtes-vous mécontent ?
• Parce que vos professeurs vous énervent 36 %
• Parce que l'ambiance est déplorable 34 %
• Parce que votre travail scolaire vous prend trop de temps et vous empêche un peu de vivre 33 %
• Parce qu'après tout on est mieux à la maison 22 %
• Parce que vos études vous ennuient 22 %
• Parce que vous ne supportez pas d'être traité comme un gosse 13 %
Ne se prononcent pas 2 %
Sur 100 lycéens mécontents d'aller au lycée, soit 40 % de l'échantillon.
Total supérieur à 100, les interviewés ayant pu donner 2 réponses.
...peu content
29 %
40 %
...pas content du tout
11 %

D. Knowing that the words at each end of the bar on the graph are opposites, what do you think the following words mean?

1. **assidus**
2. **incompétents**
3. **pas intéressants**
4. **méprisants**
5. **amicaux**

E. According to the graph . . .

1. do French students generally have a positive or negative image of their teachers?
2. how do most of the students feel about their teachers?
3. what do the students criticize the most?

F. Look at the drawings for **Enthousiasme.** What do you think the following categories mean in English? Which category is the best? Which is the worst?

peu content   très content
pas content du tout
assez content

G. According to the percentages, do most of the students have a positive or a negative attitude when they go to the **lycée?**

H. Conduct the same surveys in your class and compile the results. How do the attitudes of your classmates compare with those of the French **lycéens?**

MISE EN PRATIQUE

1 Listen as André, a French exchange student, tells you how he feels about his American schedule. What is his reaction to his schedule in general? At what times does he have the following subjects: **chimie, sport, latin, informatique**?

2 Answer these questions according to Eliane's schedule.

1. Eliane a quoi le lundi matin?
2. Elle a quels cours le jeudi après-midi?
3. Quels jours et à quelle heure est-ce qu'elle a histoire? Anglais? Maths?

EMPLOI DU TEMPS **NOM:** Eliane Soulard **CLASSE:** 3e

		LUNDI	MARDI	MERCREDI	JEUDI	VENDREDI	SAMEDI	DIMANCHE
MATIN	8h00	Anglais	Arts plastiques	Histoire/Géo	Mathématiques	Musique		
	9h00	Français	Musique	Anglais	Sciences nat	Arts plastiques	Anglais	L
	10h00	Récréation	Récréation	Récréation	Récréation	Récréation	TP physique	
	10h15	EPS	Mathématiques	Sciences nat	EPS	Sciences nat	TP physique	I
	11h15	Sciences nat	Etude	Arts plastiques	Etude	Français	[Sortie]	
	2h15	**Déjeuner**	**Déjeuner**	**[Sortie]**	**Déjeuner**	**Déjeuner**	**APRES-MIDI**	B
APRES-MIDI	14h00	Arts plastiques	Mathématiques	**APRES-MIDI**	Histoire/Géo	Physique	**LIBRE**	
	15h00	Musique	Physique	**LIBRE**	Physique	Anglais		R
	16h00	Récréation	[Sortie]		Récréation	[Sortie]		
	16h15	Mathématiques			Français			E
	17h15	[Sortie]			[Sortie]			

3 Tell three classmates whether or not you like Eliane's schedule and why. Then, ask them if they like it.

> J'aime l'emploi du temps d'Eliane. Elle a étude et arts plastiques. C'est cool! Et vous?

4 How does an American class schedule compare with Eliane's? With a partner, make a list of similarities and differences.

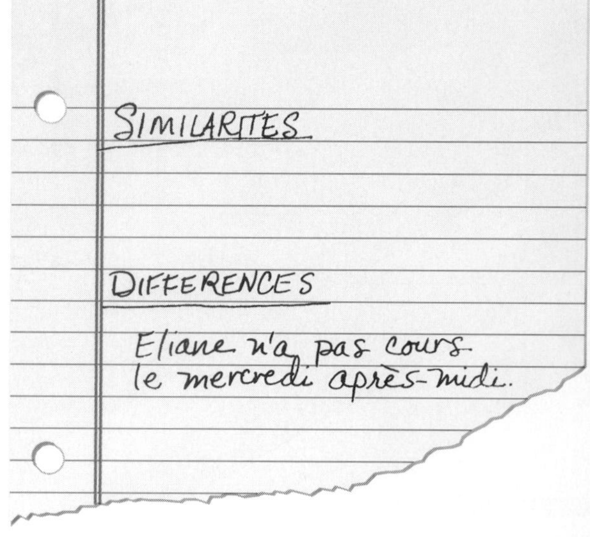

SIMILARITES
DIFFERENCES
Eliane n'a pas cours
le mercredi après-midi.

5 Answer these questions according to Eliane's report card.

1. What are Eliane's best subjects?
2. What would she probably say about French class? Music class? Science class?

BULLETIN TRIMESTRIEL

Année scolaire : 1998 - 1999

NOM et Prénom: Soulard Eliane   Classe de: 3e

MATIERES D'ENSEIGNEMENT	Moyenne de l'élève	OBSERVATIONS
Français	5	Montre peu d'enthousiasme
Anglais	8	Assez mauvais travail!
Mathématiques	18	Très bonne élève!
Histoire-Géographie	11	Travail moyen
Sciences naturelles	17	Elève sérieuse
Education physique	12	Un peu paresseuse
Physique-Chimie	18	Très douée pour la physique
Arts plastiques	14	Bon travail.
Musique	13	Fait des efforts.

Ce bulletin doit être conservé précieusement par les parents.
Il n'en sera pas délivré de duplicata.

6 Create your ideal schedule showing subjects, days, and times. Write it down in the form of a French **emploi du temps**.

7 **JEU DE ROLE**

Create a conversation with two classmates. Talk about . . .

a. the subjects you like best and your opinion of them.
b. the subjects you don't like and your opinion of them.
c. whether or not you agree with your classmates' likes and dislikes.

QUE SAIS-JE?

Can you use what you've learned in this chapter?

Can you agree and disagree? p. 50

1 How would you agree if your friend said the following? How would you disagree with your friend?

1. J'adore l'histoire!
2. J'aime les sciences nat. Et toi?
3. Je n'aime pas le français.

Can you ask for and give information? pp. 51, 54

2 How would you ask . . .

1. what subjects your friend has in the morning?
2. what subjects your friend has in the afternoon?
3. what subjects your friend has on Tuesdays?
4. if your friend has music class?
5. if your friend has English today?

3 How would you say in French that the following students have these classes, using the verb **avoir?**

1. you / French and choir
2. Paul / physics
3. we / gym
4. Francine and Séverine / Spanish

Can you tell when you have class? p. 54

4 How would you ask your friend at what time he or she has these classes?

1.

2.

3.

5 How would you tell your friend that you have the following classes at the times given?

1. 9h15

2. 11h45

3. 15h50

Can you ask for and express opinions? p. 57

6 How would you tell your friend that your geography class is . . .

1. fascinating?
2. not so great?
3. boring?

VOCABULAIRE

PREMIERE ETAPE

School subjects

l'algèbre (f.) *algebra*
l'allemand (m.) *German*
les arts (m.) **plastiques** *art class*
la biologie *biology*
la chimie *chemistry*
la chorale *choir*
le cours de développement personnel et social (DPS) *health*
la danse *dance*
l'éducation (f.) **physique et sportive (EPS)** *physical education*
l'espagnol (m.) *Spanish*
la géographie *geography*
la géométrie *geometry*
l'histoire (f.) *history*
l'informatique (f.) *computer science*
le latin *Latin*
la musique *music*
la physique *physics*
les sciences (f.) **naturelles** *natural science*
le sport *gym*
les travaux (m.) **pratiques** *lab*

School-related words

le cours *course*
les devoirs (m.) *homework*
l'élève (m./f.) *student*
le professeur (le prof) *teacher*

Agreeing and disagreeing

Oui, beaucoup. *Yes, very much.*
Moi aussi. *Me too.*
Moi, non. *I don't.*
Non, pas trop. *No, not too much.*
Moi non plus. *Neither do I.*
Moi, si. *I do.*
Pas moi. *Not me.*

DEUXIEME ETAPE

Asking for and giving information

Tu as quels cours... ? *What classes do you have . . . ?*
Tu as quoi... ? *What do you have . . . ?*
J'ai... *I have . . .*
Vous avez... ? *Do you have . . . ?*
Nous avons... *We have . . .*
avoir *to have*

Telling when you have class

Tu as... à quelle heure? *At what time do you have . . . ?*
à... heures *at . . . o'clock*
à... heures quinze *at . . . fifteen*
à... heures trente *at . . . thirty*
à... heures quarante-cinq *at . . . forty-five*
aujourd'hui *today*
demain *tomorrow*
maintenant *now*
le matin *in the morning*
l'après-midi (m.) *in the afternoon*
le lundi *on Mondays*
le mardi *on Tuesdays*
le mercredi *on Wednesdays*
le jeudi *on Thursdays*
le vendredi *on Fridays*
le samedi *on Saturdays*
le dimanche *on Sundays*

Parts of the school day

la récréation *break*
l'étude (f.) *study hall*
le déjeuner *lunch*
la sortie *dismissal*
l'après-midi libre *afternoon off*

Numbers

See page 53 for the numbers 21 through 59.

TROISIEME ETAPE

Asking for and expressing opinions

Comment tu trouves... ? *What do you think of . . . ?*
Comment tu trouves ça? *What do you think of that/it?*
Ça va. *It's OK.*
C'est... *It's . . .*
super. *super.*
cool. *cool.*
facile. *easy.*
génial. *great.*
intéressant. *interesting.*
passionnant. *fascinating.*
pas mal. *not bad.*
barbant. *boring.*
difficile. *difficult.*
nul. *useless.*
pas super. *not so hot.*
pas terrible. *not so great.*
zéro. *a waste of time.*

CHAPITRE

3

Tout pour la rentrée

① C'est combien, cette calculatrice?

At the start of a new school year, French students have to buy supplies, including their textbooks, at the store. They may also buy things that are less essential for school, like compact discs and clothes.

In this chapter you will learn

- to make and respond to requests; to ask others what they need and tell what you need
- to tell what you'd like and what you'd like to do
- to get someone's attention; to ask for information; to express thanks

And you will

- listen to teenagers talk about what they need for school
- read a page from a French catalogue
- write a list of supplies you need for your classes
- find out about the school supplies French teenagers buy

(2) Il me faut un sac.

(3) Je voudrais ce tee-shirt.

Mise en train

Claire

Mme Millet

La vendeuse

Pas question!

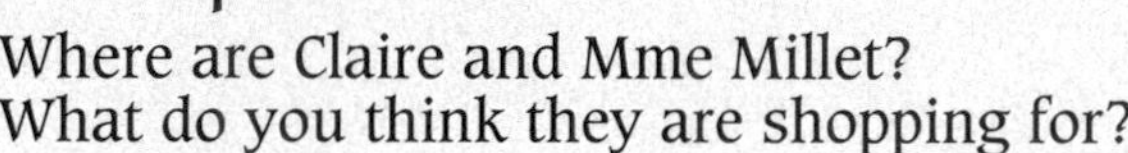
Where are Claire and Mme Millet?
What do you think they are shopping for?

1
Alors, qu'est-ce qu'il te faut?
Eh bien, des crayons, des stylos, une gomme, une calculatrice, un pot de colle...

2
Pardon, mademoiselle, vous avez des trousses, s'il vous plaît?
Bien sûr. Là, à côté des cahiers.
Merci.

3
C'est combien, ces cahiers-ci?
12 F.

4
Ah, regarde, maman, une calculatrice-traductrice.
C'est pour les maths ou pour l'anglais?
Euh, il me faut une calculatrice pour les maths... Mais une calculatrice-traductrice, c'est pratique pour l'anglais.
C'EST LA RENTRÉE

5
C'est combien, s'il vous plaît?
590 F.
C'EST LA RENTRÉE

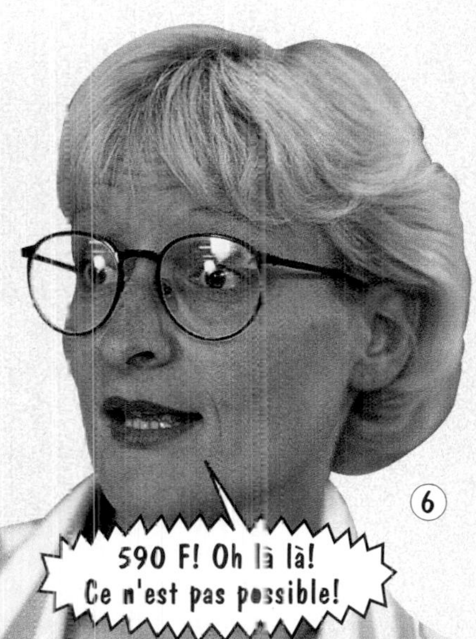
6
590 F! Oh là là!
Ce n'est pas possible!

Et cette calculatrice-là?

7
120 F.
Bien. Alors, la calculatrice.
Mais, maman...
Non, c'est trop cher.
C'EST LA RENTRÉE

8
Eh, maman, regarde ce sac vert. Il est super!
Oui. Pas mal. Mais cher. Moi, j'aime mieux ce sac-là, à 70 F.

9
Oh non! Il est horrible!
Ecoute, Claire, un sac, c'est un sac.

10
Non. Je voudrais ce sac-ci.
Et moi, je n'achète pas un sac à 215 F.
Alors, j'aime mieux aller à l'école sans sac!

1 Tu as compris?

Answer the following questions based on **Pas question!**

1. What is the relationship between Claire and Mme Millet? How do you know?
2. Where are they?
3. What are they doing there?
4. Why does Claire need a calculator?
5. What is Mme Millet's main concern?
6. What do you think of Claire's decision at the end of **Pas question!**?

2 Claire ou sa mère?

Does **elle** in each of the following sentences refer to Claire or Mme Millet?

1. Elle aime la calculatrice à 590 F.
2. Elle voudrait une calculatrice-traductrice.
3. Elle aime mieux le sac à 70 F.
4. Elle aime mieux le sac vert.
5. Elle va aller à l'école sans sac.
6. Elle n'achète pas un sac à 215 F.

3 Cherche les expressions

Can you find an expression in **Pas question!** to . . .

1. ask what someone needs?
2. tell what you need?
3. get a salesperson's attention?
4. ask the price of something?
5. say you like or prefer something?
6. say you don't like something?

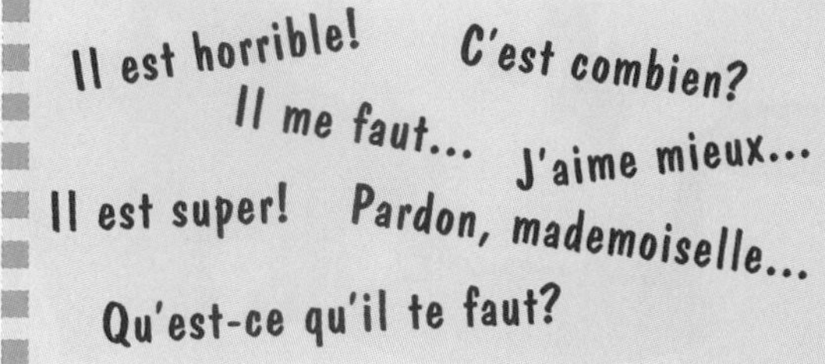

Il est horrible!
C'est combien?
Il me faut...
J'aime mieux...
Il est super!
Pardon, mademoiselle...
Qu'est-ce qu'il te faut?

4 Mets en ordre

Put these sentences about **Pas question!** in chronological order.

1. Mme Millet asks the price of a calculator.
2. Mme Millet asks a salesperson if she has any pencil cases.
3. Claire says she will go to school without a bag.
4. Mme Millet asks Claire what she needs for school.
5. Mme Millet asks the price of the notebooks.
6. Claire points out a bag she likes.

5 Et maintenant, à toi

What do you think will happen next in the story? Discuss your ideas with a partner.

PREMIERE ETAPE

Making and responding to requests; asking others what they need and telling what you need

VOCABULAIRE

De bons conseils

Make flashcards to learn new words. On one side of a card, write the French word you want to learn. (If the word is a noun, include an article to help you remember the gender.) On the other side, paste or draw a picture to illustrate the meaning of the word. Then, ask a classmate to show you the picture while you try to name the object, or use the cards to test yourself.

6 Ecoute!

Listen as Hafaïdh and Karine check the contents of their bookbags. Then, look at the pictures and decide which bag belongs to each of them.

a.

b.

c.

7 Objets trouvés

Lost and found

When Paulette gets home from the store, she realizes that she forgot to put some of her school supplies into her bag. Look at the receipt showing what she bought and make a list, in French, of the missing items.

Elle n'a pas le...

VEN 13-05-99 3004
047CA BELLIOT Stephanie

GOMME CAOUTCH	3.30
CRAYONS GRAH.	5.15
REGLE GRADUEE	5.20
CAH. BROUILLON	1.90
COPIES DBLES PF GC	4.25
CLASSEUR 17X22	16.15
TROUSSE	28.10
SOUS/TOTAL	64.05
TOTAL	64.05
REÇU	100.00
RENDU	35.95

00617 7 ARTC 16:36TM

Note Culturelle

In large stores in France, customers are expected to place their items on the conveyer belt and then remove and bag them as well. Most stores provide small plastic sacks, but many shoppers bring their own basket **(un panier)** or net bag **(un filet)**. Since space is limited in small stores and boutiques, browsing inside stores is not common. Instead, items and their prices are placed in window displays. Most people window-shop until they are ready to make a purchase. A store that reads **Entrée libre** welcomes browsers.

8 Devine!

Write down the name of one of the objects from the **Vocabulaire** on page 71. Don't let the other members of your group know what you've chosen. They will then take turns guessing which object you chose.

—C'est un taille-crayon?
—Oui, c'est ça. *or* Non, ce n'est pas ça.

—Tu as une calculatrice, Paul?
—J'ai un stylo, un crayon, une règle et des feuilles de papier, mais je n'ai pas de calculatrice!

COMMENT DIT-ON... ?
Making and responding to requests

To ask someone for something:
Tu as un stylo?
Vous avez un crayon?

To respond:
Oui. **Voilà.** *Here.*
Non. **Je regrette. Je n'ai pas de** crayons. *Sorry. I don't have . . .*

GRAMMAIRE The indefinite articles un, une, and des

The articles **un** and **une** both mean *a* or *an*. Use **un** with masculine nouns and **une** with feminine nouns. Use **des** *(some)* with plural nouns. Notice that **un, une,** and **des** change to **de** after **ne... pas.**

J'ai **un** crayon, mais je n'ai pas **de** papier.

9 Ecoute!

Listen as Nadine asks her friends for some school supplies. Match her friends' responses to the appropriate pictures.

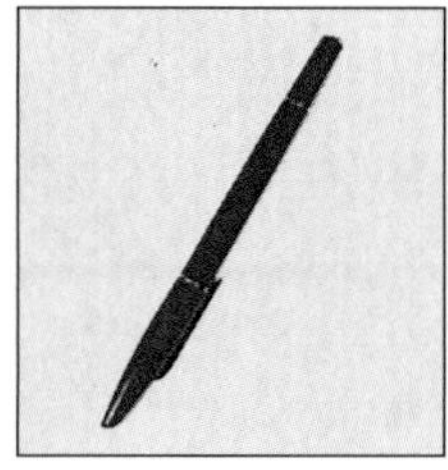
a.

b.

c.

d.

e.

10 Tu as ça, toi?

With a partner, take turns pointing out the differences you notice between Christophe's desk and Annick's.

Regarde! Christophe a une gomme, mais Annick n'a pas de gomme.

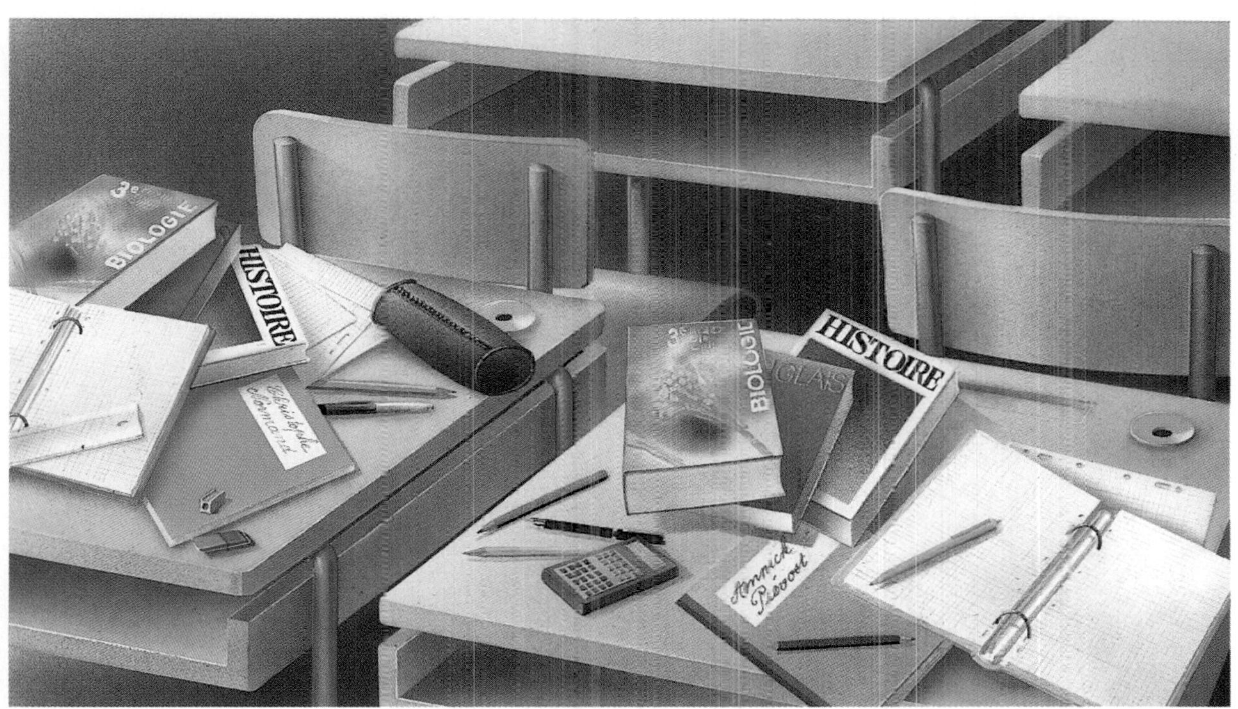

COMMENT DIT-ON... ?

Asking others what they need and telling what you need

To ask what someone needs:

Qu'est-ce qu'il te faut pour la bio?
What do you need for . . . ? (informal)

Qu'est-ce qu'il vous faut pour la géo?
What do you need for . . . ? (formal)

To tell what you need:

Il me faut un stylo et un classeur.

11 Qu'est-ce qu'il te faut?

Make a list of your school subjects. Exchange lists with a partner. Then take turns asking each other what you need for various classes.

— Qu'est-ce qu'il te faut pour les maths?
— Il me faut une calculatrice et un crayon.

Vocabulaire à la carte

Here are some additional words you can use to talk about your school supplies.

un compas	*a compass*
des crayons (m.) **de couleur**	*some colored pencils*
un feutre	*a marker*
du liquide correcteur	*some correction fluid*
du ruban adhésif (m.)	*some transparent tape*
une tenue de gymnastique	*a gym suit*

12 Aide-mémoire

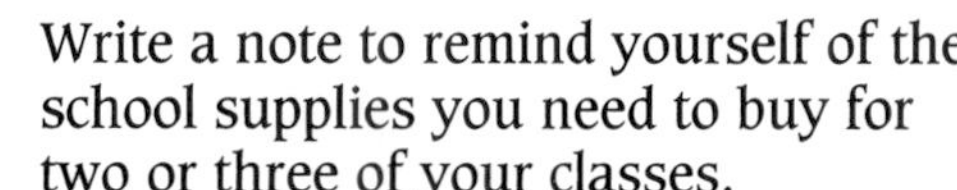

Write a note to remind yourself of the school supplies you need to buy for two or three of your classes.

13 Un petit service

You're late for class, and you've forgotten your supplies. Ask a friend if he or she has what you need. Your friend should respond appropriately. Then, change roles.

— Oh là là! J'ai histoire! Il me faut un stylo et un cahier. Tu as un stylo?
— Non, je regrette.
— Zut! *(Darn!)*

Panorama Culturel

Séverine • Martinique

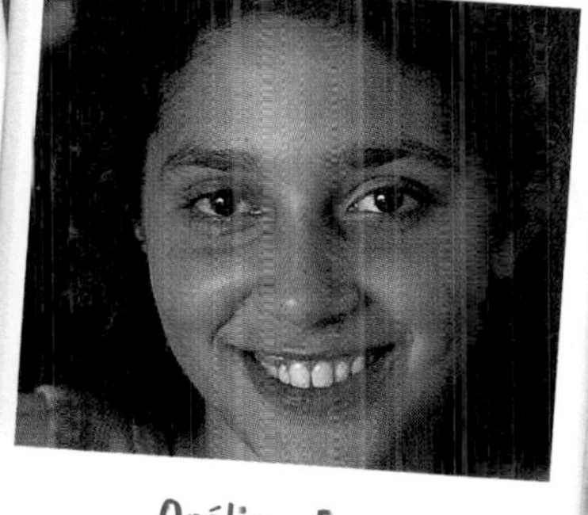

Onélia • France

Marius • Côte d'Ivoire

We asked some francophone students what supplies they bought for the opening of school, **la rentrée.** Here's what they had to say.

CD-ROM Disc 1

Qu'est-ce qu'il te faut comme fournitures scolaires?

«Alors, donc pour l'école j'ai acheté un nouveau sac à dos, des livres pour étudier, des vêtements, entre autres des jeans, des chaussures, bien sûr et puis bon, des tee-shirts, des jupes, des robes.»

—Séverine

«Il faut des classeurs, des cahiers, des crayons, des règles, des instruments de géométrie, [une] calculatrice pour les mathématiques, des feuilles... C'est tout.»

—Onélia

«Pour l'école, il faut des règles, des bics, des stylos, des cahiers, des livres et la tenue.»

—Marius

Qu'en penses-tu?

1. What school supplies did you have to purchase for the school year?
2. What did these students buy that is usually provided by schools in the United States?
3. What are the advantages and disadvantages of each system?
4. What other items do you usually buy at the beginning of a school year?

Savais-tu que...?

In French-speaking countries, students usually buy their own textbooks and even maintain their own grade book, **un livret scolaire.** Some schools require students to purchase school uniforms. A store that specializes in school supplies, textbooks, and paper products is called **une librairie-papeterie.**

DEUXIEME ETAPE

Telling what you'd like and what you'd like to do

Vocabulaire

Qu'est-ce qu'on va acheter?

Hervé regarde **un short.**

Odile regarde **des baskets.**

Denis regarde **un roman.**

Stéphane regarde **un disque compact/un CD.**

Dorothée regarde **un jean.**

Mme Roussel regarde **un ordinateur.**

M. Beauvois regarde **une montre.**

M. Prévost regarde **un portefeuille.**

You can probably figure out what these words mean:

un bracelet	**un magazine**	**une radio**	**une télévision**
une cassette	**un poster**	**un sweat-shirt**	**une vidéocassette**
un dictionnaire	**un pull-over**	**un tee-shirt**	

14 Ecoute!

Several shoppers in the **Vocabulaire** are going to tell you what they would like to buy. As you listen to each speaker, look at the illustrations above and identify the person. Write down his or her name.

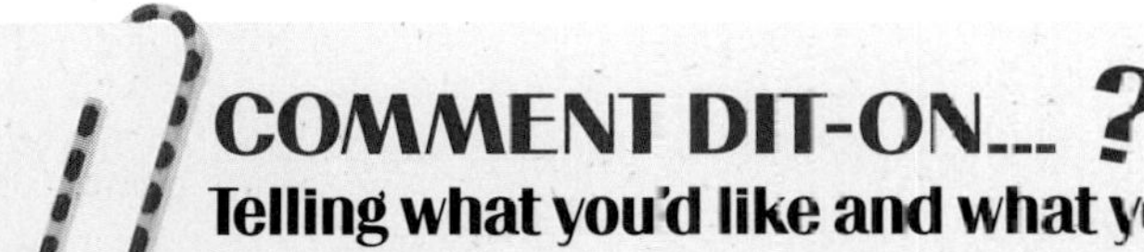

COMMENT DIT-ON... ?

Telling what you'd like and what you'd like to do

Je voudrais un sac. *I'd like . . .*
Je voudrais acheter un tee-shirt. *I'd like to buy . . .*

15 Ecoute!

Georges has just won a gift certificate from his favorite department store. Listen as he tells you what he would like to buy and make a list of his choices.

16 Vive le week-end!

What would you like to do this weekend? Find three classmates who want to do the same thing.

—Je voudrais sortir avec des copains. Et toi?
—Moi aussi. *or* Moi, je voudrais faire du sport.

faire les magasins
dormir
danser
écouter de la musique
parler au téléphone
étudier
regarder la télévision
nager
sortir avec des copains
faire le ménage
faire du sport

17 Un cadeau *A gift*

Make a list of what you would like to buy for . . .

1. a friend who likes horror movies and books.
2. a friend who loves sports.
3. someone who's always late for class.
4. a friend who loves music.
5. someone who loves French.
6. your best friend.

18 Mon journal

You earned 100 dollars this summer. Write down three or four items you'd like to buy for yourself.

GRAMMAIRE The demonstrative adjectives **ce**, **cet**, **cette**, and **ces**

Ce, **cet**, and **cette** mean *this* or *that*. **Ces** means *these* or *those*.

	Singular	*Plural*
Masculine before a consonant sound	**ce** stylo	**ces** stylos
Masculine before a vowel sound	**cet** examen	**ces** examens
Feminine	**cette** école	**ces** écoles

When you want to specify *that* as opposed to *this*, add **-là** *(there)* to the end of the noun.

—J'aime **ce** sac.
—Moi, j'aime mieux **ce** sac-**là**.

19 Le cadeau parfait *The perfect gift*

Claire is shopping for a gift for her mother. The salesperson is making suggestions. Choose the correct articles to complete their conversation.

LE VENDEUR Vous aimez **(ce/cette)** montre, mademoiselle?
CLAIRE Oui, mais ma mère a déjà **(un/une)** montre.
LE VENDEUR Et **(ces/ce)** roman?
CLAIRE Non, elle n'aime pas lire.
LE VENDEUR Elle aime **(la /l')** musique?
CLAIRE Oui. Elle adore le jazz.
LE VENDEUR **(Cet/Cette)** cassette de Wynton Marsalis, peut-être?
CLAIRE C'est une bonne idée.

20 Qu'est-ce que tu aimes mieux?

Take turns with a partner asking and answering questions about the items below.

— Tu aimes ce sac?
— Non. J'aime mieux ce sac-là!

Moi aussi. Non, je n'aime pas ça.
Non. Oui, j'adore!
Oui, mais j'aime mieux...
J'aime bien. Moi non plus.

1.

2.

3.

4.

VOCABULAIRE

De quelle couleur est...

le sac?	la trousse?
ROUGE	ROUGE
ORANGE	ORANGE
JAUNE	JAUNE
VERT	VERTE
BLEU	BLEUE
VIOLET	VIOLETTE

le sac?	la trousse?
ROSE	ROSE
BLANC	BLANCHE
GRIS	GRISE
NOIR	NOIRE
MARRON	MARRON

21 Vrai ou faux?

Tell whether the statements below are true **(vrai)** or false **(faux)** according to the picture.

1. Claire a un sac jaune.
2. Claire et Thierry ont des tee-shirts bleus.
3. Claire a un short marron.
4. Thierry a des baskets bleues.
5. Thierry a un classeur rouge.
6. Claire et Thierry ont des shorts noirs.

GRAMMAIRE Adjective agreement and placement

Did you notice in the **Vocabulaire** on page 78 that the spelling of some colors changes according to the nouns they describe?

	Singular	*Plural*
Masculine	le classeur vert	les classeurs vert**s**
Feminine	la gomme vert**e**	les gommes vert**es**

- Usually, you add an **e** to make an adjective feminine; however, when an adjective ends in an unaccented **e**, you don't have to add another **e: le classeur rouge, la gomme rouge.**
- Some adjectives don't follow this pattern: **blanc, blanche; violet, violette.**
- Usually, you add an **s** to make an adjective plural; however, when an adjective ends in an **s**, you don't have to add another **s: les crayons gris.**
- Some adjectives don't change form. Two examples are **orange** and **marron.**
- What do you notice about where the adjectives are placed in relation to the nouns they describe?*

22 Chasse au trésor *Scavenger hunt*

Create a list of six objects. Ask your classmates if they have the items on your list. When you find someone who does, find out what color each item is and write the person's name next to the appropriate item.

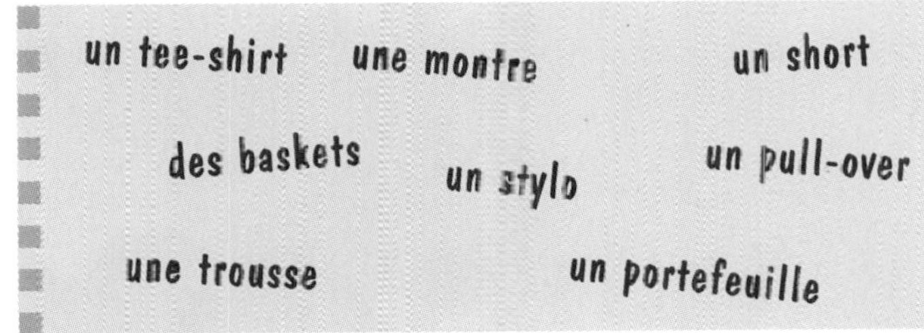

un tee-shirt
une montre
un short
des baskets
un stylo
un pull-over
une trousse
un portefeuille

* Colors and many other adjectives are placed **after** the nouns they describe.

TROISIEME ETAPE

Getting someone's attention; asking for information; expressing thanks

VOCABULAIRE

60	70	71	72	80	81
soixante	soixante-dix	soixante et onze	soixante-douze	quatre-vingts	quatre-vingt-un
90	**91**	**100**	**101**	**200**	**201**
quatre-vingt-dix	quatre-vingt-onze	cent	cent un	deux cents	deux cent un

CD-ROM Disc 1

23 Ecoute!

Listen to four French disc jockeys announce the dial frequencies of their radio stations. Then, match the frequency to the station logo.

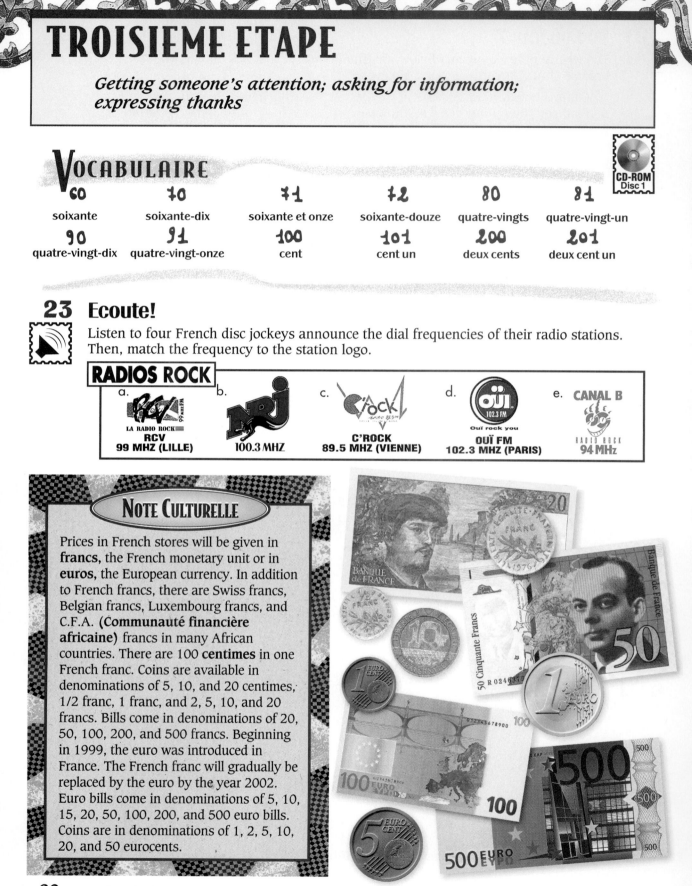

RADIOS ROCK

a. 

RCV
99 MHZ (LILLE)

b. 

100.3 MHZ

c. 

C'ROCK
89.5 MHZ (VIENNE)

d. 

OUÏ FM
102.3 MHZ (PARIS)

e. 

94 MHz

NOTE CULTURELLE

Prices in French stores will be given in **francs,** the French monetary unit or in **euros,** the European currency. In addition to French francs, there are Swiss francs, Belgian francs, Luxembourg francs, and C.F.A. **(Communauté financière africaine)** francs in many African countries. There are 100 **centimes** in one French franc. Coins are available in denominations of 5, 10, and 20 centimes, 1/2 franc, 1 franc, and 2, 5, 10, and 20 francs. Bills come in denominations of 20, 50, 100, 200, and 500 francs. Beginning in 1999, the euro was introduced in France. The French franc will gradually be replaced by the euro by the year 2002. Euro bills come in denominations of 5, 10, 15, 20, 50, 100, 200, and 500 euro bills. Coins are in denominations of 1, 2, 5, 10, 20, and 50 eurocents.

24 Ça fait combien? *How much is it?*

How much money is shown in each illustration? Give the totals in French.

1.

2.

25 C'est combien?

Look at the drawing of the store display below. How much money does each of these customers spend in **Papier Plume?**

1. Alain achète deux stylos et une trousse.
2. Geneviève achète un classeur, un dictionnaire et un cahier.
3. Paul achète six crayons et un taille-crayon.
4. Marcel achète une règle, une gomme et un stylo.
5. Sarah achète deux cahiers et un dictionnaire.
6. Cécile achète une règle et une calculatrice.

26 Mon journal

Do you budget your money? Make a list of the items you've bought in the last month and the approximate price of each in francs. To convert American prices to francs, look up the current exchange rate in the newspaper.

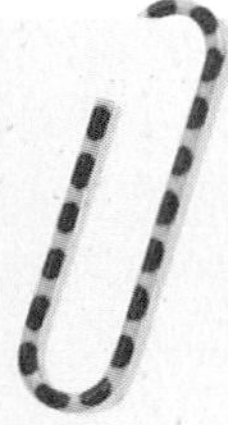

COMMENT DIT-ON... ?

Getting someone's attention; asking for information; expressing thanks

To get someone's attention:
Pardon, monsieur/madame/ mademoiselle.
Excusez-moi, monsieur/madame/ mademoiselle.

To ask how much something costs:
C'est combien?

To express thanks:
Merci.

27 Ecoute!

In a department store in France, you overhear shoppers asking salespeople for the prices of various items. As you listen to the conversations, write down the items mentioned and their prices.

28 Jeu de rôle

You're buying school supplies in a French **librairie-papeterie.** For each item you want, get the salesperson's attention and ask how much the item costs. The salesperson will give you the price. Act out this scene with a partner. Then, change roles.

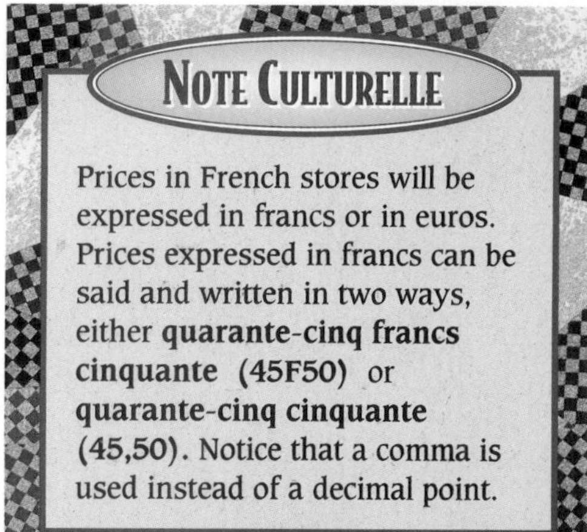

Note Culturelle

Prices in French stores will be expressed in francs or in euros. Prices expressed in francs can be said and written in two ways, either **quarante-cinq francs cinquante (45F50)** or **quarante-cinq cinquante (45,50)**. Notice that a comma is used instead of a decimal point.

29 Les magazines

You've decided to subscribe to a French magazine. Take turns with a partner playing the roles of a customer and a salesperson. Use the advertisement to discuss the prices of several magazines.

Abonnez-vous à :

FEMME A LA MODE	(12 numéros) France 210 FF
DECOUVERTE SCIENTIFIQUE	(22 numéros) France 499 FF
L'AFRIQUE DE NOS JOURS	(12 numéros) France 250 FF, Europe 250 FF, Dom-Tom 250 FF, Afrique 265 FF
TELE-TUBE	(52 numéros) France et Dom-Tom 580 FF, USA $140, Canada $180, Autres pays 855 FF
LA VOIX DU MONDE	(52 numéros) France 728 FF
LES GRANDS MOUVEMENTS DE L'ECONOMIE	(12 numéros) France 170 FF
LA VIE SPORTIVE	(12 numéros) France 215 FF

PRONONCIATION

The r sound

The French **r** is quite different from the American *r*. To pronounce the French **r**, keep the tip of your tongue pressed against your lower front teeth. Arch the back of your tongue upward, almost totally blocking the passage of air in the back of your throat.

A. A prononcer

Repeat the following words.

1. Raoul	rouge	roman	règle
2. crayon	trente	calculatrice	barbe
3. terrible	intéressant	Europe	quarante
4. poster	rare	vert	montre

B. A lire

Take turns with a partner reading the following sentences aloud.

1. Fermez la porte.
2. Regardez le livre de français.
3. Prenez un crayon.
4. Ouvrez la fenêtre.
5. Je voudrais une montre.
6. Je regrette. Je n'ai pas de règle.

C. A écrire

You're going to hear a short dialogue. Write down what you hear.

LISONS!

Look at the information presented on this page. Where would you expect to find a text like this? Would you normally use information like this for a specific purpose? What would it be?

DE BONS CONSEILS

When you read material like this, you are generally looking for specific information—prices, colors, or sizes, for example. When that is your purpose, you don't have to read or understand every word. You can simply scan the material until you find what you are looking for.

A. At what time of year would you expect to see an advertisement like this?

B. When you buy school supplies, what is most important to you? Color? Price? Brand name?

C. Working with a partner, scan the ad for information about price, size, and quantity. Make a list of the words you find in the text that fit each of these categories.

D. What do you think **les 3** means?

E. The word **écolier** is used to describe the notebook. Do you recognize a word you've learned before in this word? What do you think **écolier** means?

F. What is the most expensive item? The least expensive?

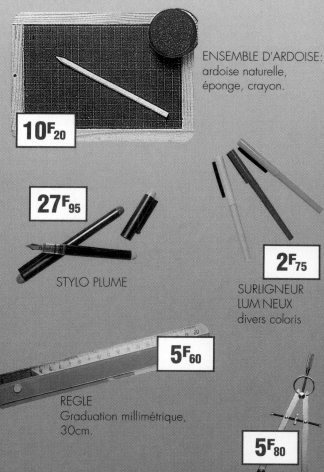

UNIVERS
TOUT POUR LA RENTREE

VENEZ VOIR NOS PRIX REMARQUABLES!

10F20

ENSEMBLE D'ARDOISE: ardoise naturelle, éponge, crayon.

27F95

STYLO PLUME

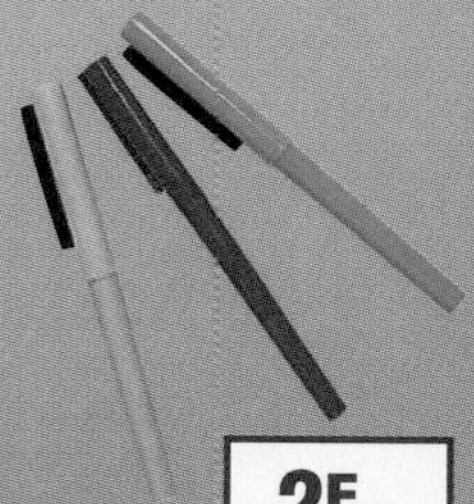

2F75

SURLIGNEUR LUM NEUX divers coloris

5F60

REGLE Graduation millimétrique, 30cm.

5F80

COMPAS POINTE FIXE

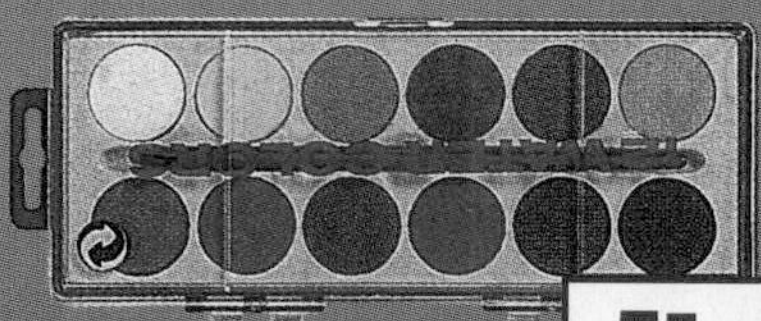

5F95

BOITE DE GOUACHE 12 pastilles de 30 mm et un pinceau.

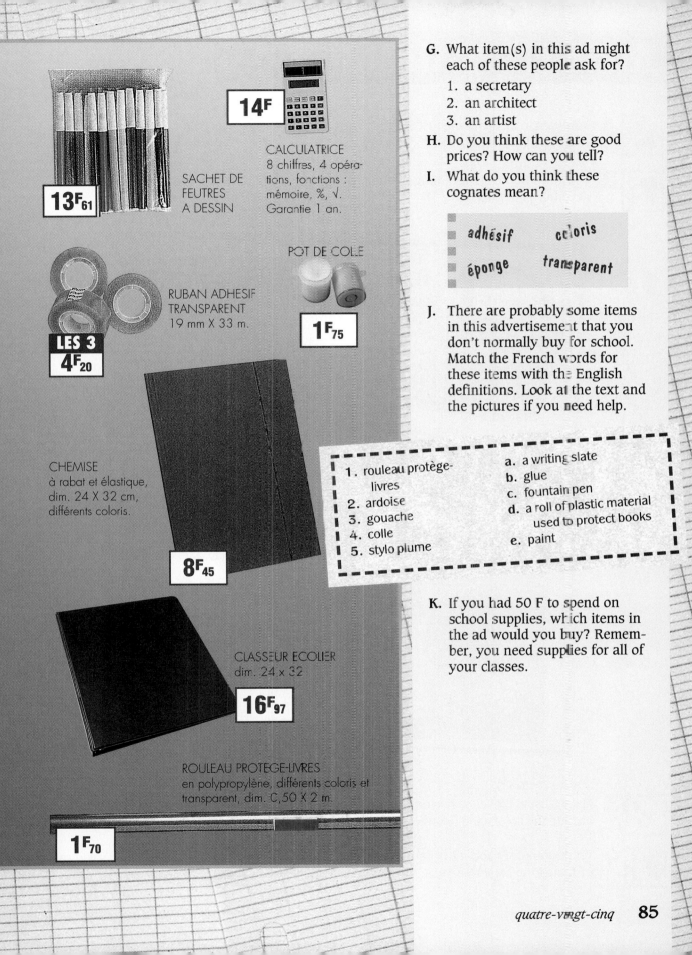

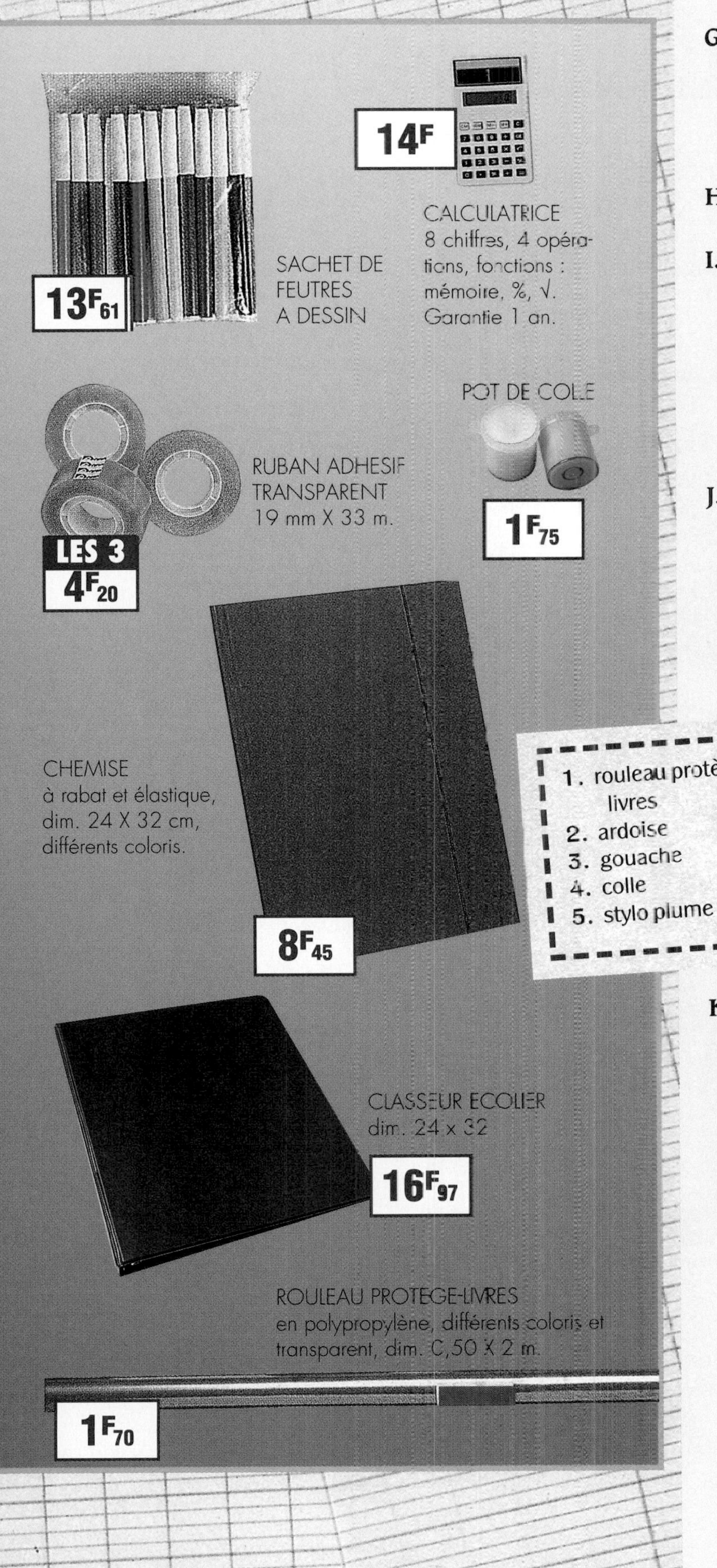

G. What item(s) in this ad might each of these people ask for?

1. a secretary
2. an architect
3. an artist

H. Do you think these are good prices? How can you tell?

I. What do you think these cognates mean?

adhésif	*coloris*
éponge	*transparent*

J. There are probably some items in this advertisement that you don't normally buy for school. Match the French words for these items with the English definitions. Look at the text and the pictures if you need help.

1. rouleau protège-livres	a. a writing slate
2. ardoise	b. glue
3. gouache	c. fountain pen
4. colle	d. a roll of plastic material used to protect books
5. stylo plume	e. paint

K. If you had 50 F to spend on school supplies, which items in the ad would you buy? Remember, you need supplies for all of your classes.

MISE EN PRATIQUE

CD-ROM Disc 1

1 You want to buy your friend a birthday gift. Listen as she gives you some ideas and then make a list of the things she would like.

2 You and a friend are browsing through a magazine. Point out several items you like and several you dislike.

165F.
Sac shopping, 35X10X30 cm, 65 % polyester et 35 % coton.

35F.
Classeur, 21X29,7 cm.

45F.
Stylo plume.

22,50F.
Chemise 3 rabats élastique, 24X32 cm.

195F.
Sac à dos, 65 % polyester et 35 % coton.

59,50F.
Portefeuille, 65 % polyester et 35 % coton.

3 Make a list in French of two or three of the items pictured above that you'd like to buy. Include the colors and prices of the items you choose.

4 Tell your partner about the items you've chosen in Activity 3. Give as much detail as you can, including the color and price.

5 Your friend has been passing notes to you during study hall. Write a response to each one.

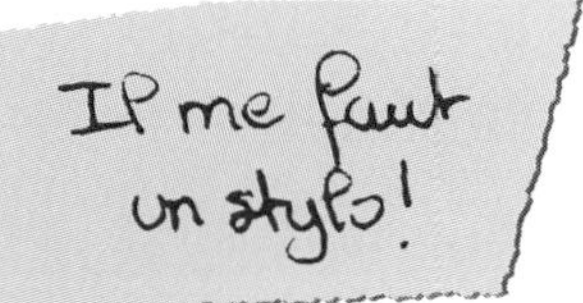
Il me faut
un stylo!

Qu'est-ce qu'il faut pour l'algèbre?

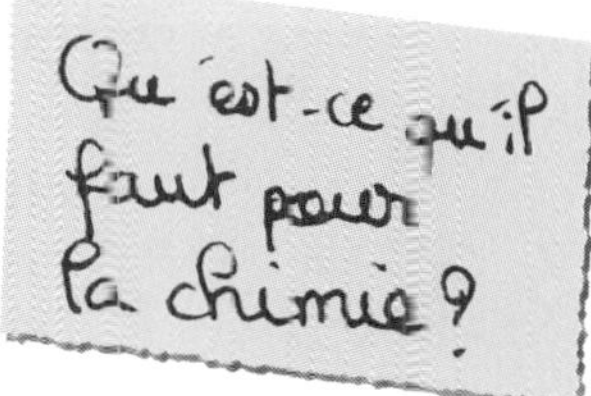
Qu'est-ce qu'il
faut pour
la chimie?

6 If you were in France, what differences would you notice in these areas?

1. money
2. school supplies
3. stores

7

Ecrivons!

You're creating your own department store. First, make a list of possible names for your store. Then, create a list of items you would like to sell in your store, and begin thinking about how these items might be grouped together. Before you start, organize your ideas in a cluster diagram.

STRATEGIE

Cluster diagrams are a helpful way to organize the ideas you develop in your brainstorming. Start by drawing a circle and label it with the name you chose for your store. Then draw two or three other circles, each connected to the first circle. In each of the new circles you draw, write the name of an item you plan to sell. Add more circles as you need them. Connect your circles with lines to group similar items together as they might be organized in a department store.

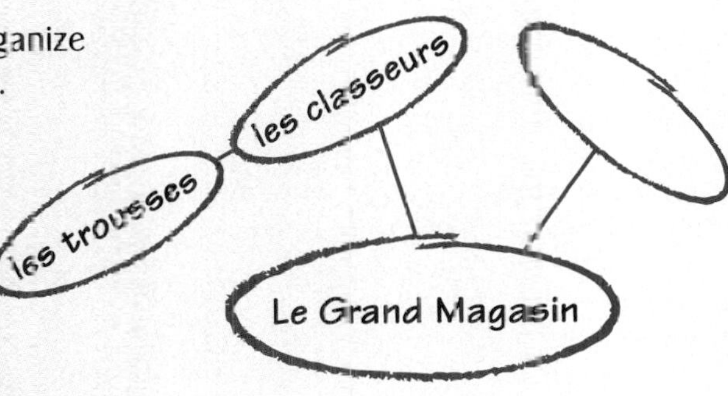
les classeurs
les trousses
Le Grand Magasin

8

JEU DE ROLE

Visit the "store" your partner created and decide on something you'd like to buy. Your partner will play the role of the salesperson. Get the salesperson's attention, tell what you want, ask the price(s), pay for your purchase(s), thank the salesperson, and say goodbye. Your partner should respond appropriately. Then, change roles, using the store you created. Remember to use **madame, monsieur,** or **mademoiselle,** and **vous.**

QUE SAIS-JE?

Can you use what you've learned in this chapter?

Can you make and respond to requests? p. 72

1 How would you ask for the following items using the verb **avoir?** How would you respond to someone's request for one of these items?

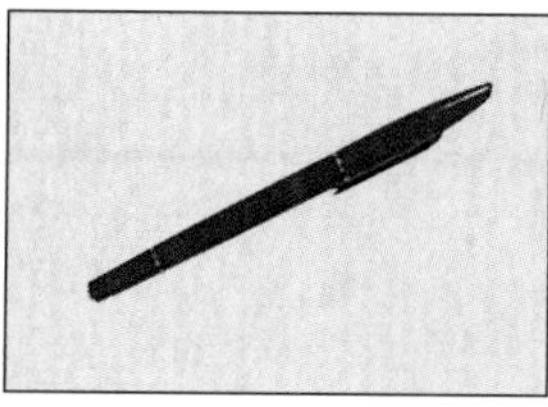
1.

2.

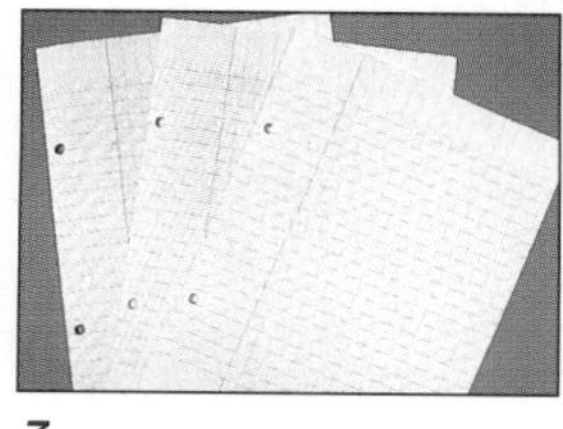
3.

Can you ask others what they need? p. 74

2 How would you ask your friend what he or she needs for each of these school subjects?

1.

2.

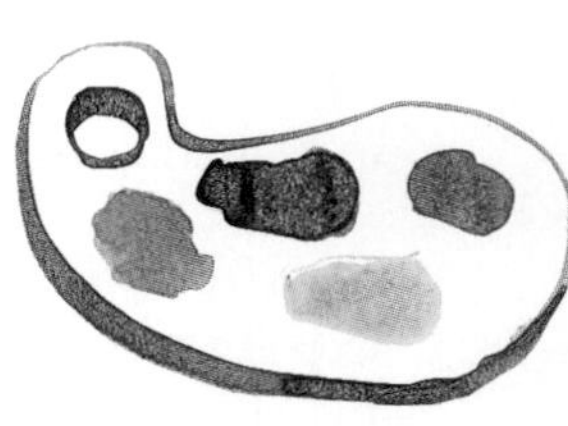
3.

Can you tell what you need? p. 74

3 How would you tell a friend that you need . . .

1 a calculator and an eraser for math?
2. a binder and some sheets of paper for Spanish class?
3. some pens and a notebook for English?
4. a pencil and a ruler for geometry?
5. a backpack and a book for history?

Can you tell what you'd like and what you'd like to do? p. 77

4 How would you tell your friend that you'd like . . .

1. those white sneakers?
2. this blue bag?
3. that purple and black pencil case?
4. to listen to music and talk on the phone?
5. to go shopping?

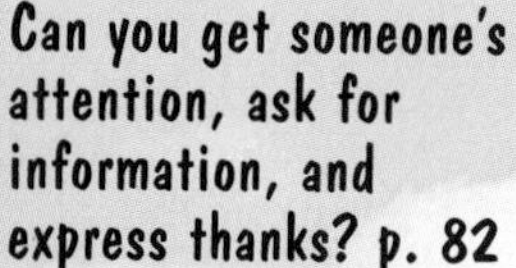

Can you get someone's attention, ask for information, and express thanks? p. 82

5 What would you say in a store to . . .

1. get a salesperson's attention?
2. politely ask the price of something?
3. thank a clerk for helping you?

VOCABULAIRE

PREMIERE ETAPE

Making and responding to requests

Tu as... ? *Do you have . . . ?*
Vous avez... ? *Do you have . . . ?*
Voilà. *Here.*
Je regrette. *Sorry.*
Je n'ai pas de... *I don't have . . .*

Asking others what they need and telling what you need

Qu'est-ce qu'il vous faut pour... ? *What do you need for . . . ?* (formal)
Qu'est-ce qu'il te faut pour... ? *What do you need for . . . ?* (informal)
Il me faut... *I need . . .*
un *a; an*
une *a; an*
des *some*

School supplies

un cahier *notebook*
une calculatrice *calculator*
un classeur *loose-leaf binder*
un crayon *pencil*
des feuilles (f.) de papier *sheets of paper*
une gomme *eraser*
un livre *book*
une règle *ruler*
un sac (à dos) *bag; backpack*
un stylo *pen*
un taille-crayon *pencil sharpener*
une trousse *pencil case*

Other useful expressions

Zut! *Darn!*

DEUXIEME ETAPE

Telling what you'd like and what you'd like to do

Je voudrais... *I'd like . . .*
Je voudrais acheter... *I'd like to buy . . .*

For school and fun

des baskets (f.) *sneakers*
un bracelet *bracelet*
une cassette *cassette tape*
un dictionnaire *dictionary*
un disque compact/un CD *compact disc/CD*
un jean *(a pair of) jeans*
un magazine *magazine*
une montre *watch*
un ordinateur *computer*
un portefeuille *wallet*
un poster *poster*
un pull-over *pullover*
une radio *radio*
un roman *novel*
un short *(a pair of) shorts*
un sweat-shirt *sweatshirt*
un tee-shirt *T-shirt*
une télévision *television*
une vidéocassette *videotape*
ce, cet, cette *this; that*
ces *these; those*
-là *there (noun suffix)*

Colors

De quelle couleur est... ? *What color is . . . ?*
blanc(he) *white*
bleu(e) *blue*
gris(e) *grey*
jaune *yellow*
marron *brown*
noir(e) *black*
orange *orange*
rose *pink*
rouge *red*
vert(e) *green*
violet(te) *purple*

TROISIEME ETAPE

Getting someone's attention; asking for information; expressing thanks

Pardon. *Pardon me.*
Excusez-moi. *Excuse me.*
C'est combien? *How much is it?*
Merci. *Thank you.*
A votre service. *At your service; You're welcome.*
s'il vous/te plaît *please*
franc *(the French monetary unit)*
soixante *sixty*
soixante-dix *seventy*
quatre-vingts *eighty*
quatre-vingt-dix *ninety*
cent *one hundred*
deux cents *two hundred*

Other useful expressions

Bien sûr. *Of course.*

CHAPITRE 4

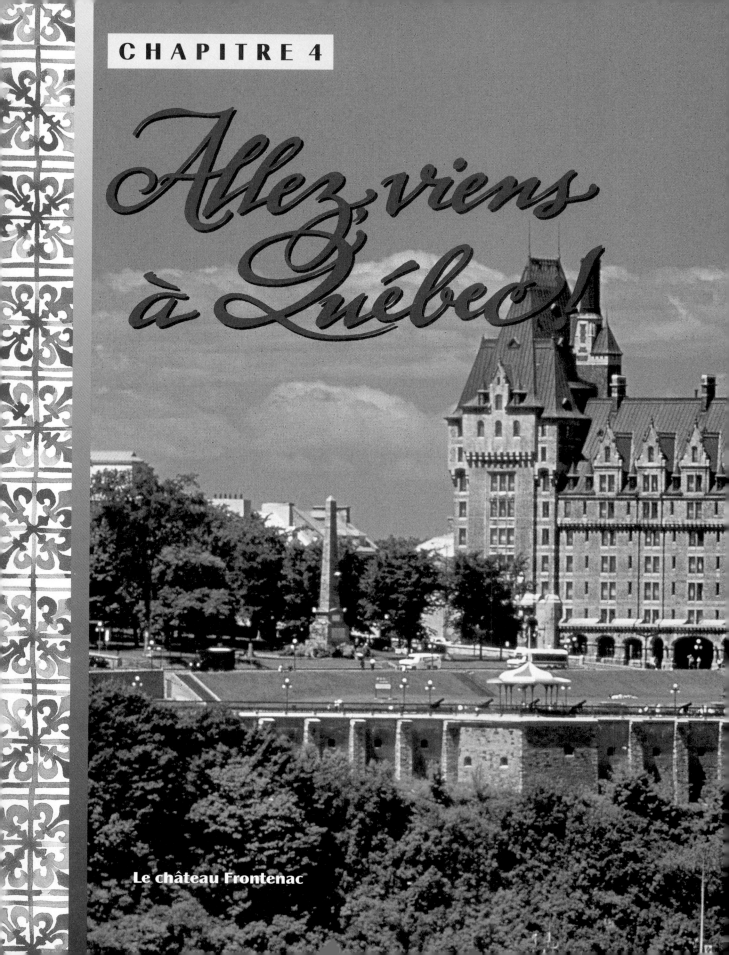

Allez, viens à Québec!

Le château Frontenac

Québec

Capitale de la province du Québec

Population : plus de 600.000

Points d'intérêt : le château Frontenac, l'université Laval, la terrasse Dufferin, le musée du Québec, les fortifications de Québec, les chutes Montmorency, le mont Sainte-Anne, Québec Expérience

Québécois célèbres : Samuel de Champlain, François de Montmorency-Laval, le marquis de Montcalm

Ressources et industries : dérivés du bois, du cuir et de l'érable; tourisme

Spécialités : ragoût de boulettes, tourtière, cretons, soupe aux pois, tarte au sucre, tarte à la ferlouche

Québec

Quebec City, one of the oldest cities in North America, is the capital of ***La Nouvelle-France****, as the French-speaking province of Quebec used to be called. The* ***Québécois*** *people are fiercely proud of their heritage and traditions, and they work hard to maintain their language and culture. The narrow streets and quaint cafés of* ***Vieux-Québec*** *have an old-world feeling, but Quebec is also a dynamic, modern city — as exciting as any you'll find in North America!*

(1) Typical houses in **Vieux-Québec.**

(2) The spectacular **chutes Montmorency** are just outside of the city.

(3) Musicians, jugglers, and other entertainers perform frequently in the streets of **Vieux-Québec.**

(4) **Le quartier Petit-Champlain** is a picturesque shopping district filled with boutiques and cafés.

(5) **La rue du Trésor** is where local artists sell their work. This street in the heart of the old section of town is very popular among tourists.

(6) **Les plaines d'Abraham,** now a 250-acre park, was the site of the battle in which the English defeated the French on September 13, 1759.

(7) **La Grande Allée,** a boulevard lined with businesses and cafés, is the longest road in Quebec.

(8) **La terrasse Dufferin** is a bustling six-kilometer boardwalk that overlooks the St. Lawrence River.

CHAPITRE

4
Sports et passe-temps

1 On aime faire du théâtre!

Teenagers in French-speaking countries find plenty of time for hobbies. They play sports, watch television, listen to music, take photos, and go out with friends. Many of their spare-time activities are similar to yours.

In this chapter you will learn

- to tell how much you like or dislike something
- to exchange information
- to make, accept, and turn down suggestions

And you will

- listen to French-speaking students talk about what they do for fun
- read about a sports resort in Canada
- write about your hobbies and what you do to have fun
- find out about sports and hobbies in francophone countries

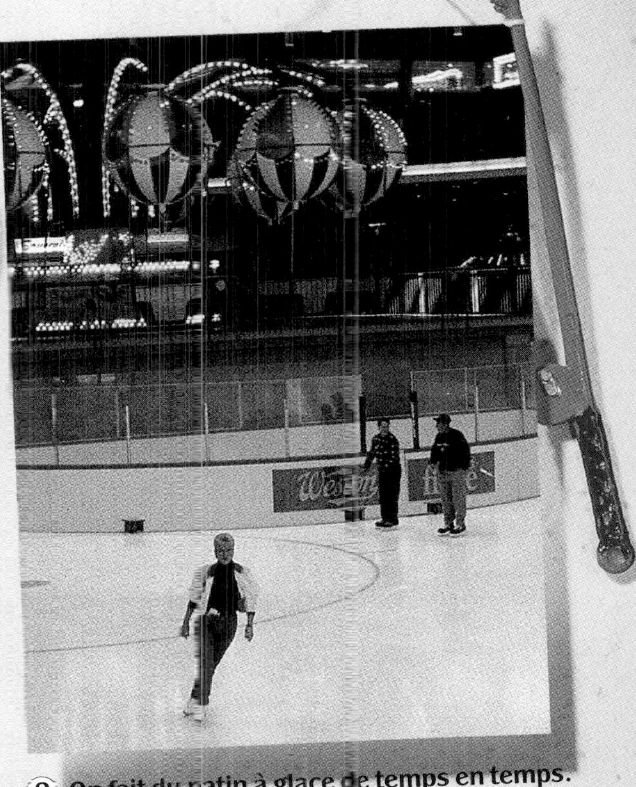

(2) On fait du patin à glace de temps en temps.

(3) En automne, on fait du vélo.

Mise en train

Nouvelles de Québec

Emilie is eager to get to know her American pen pal Leticia. What kind of information do you think Emilie might include in a letter to her new pen pal?

Emilie Tremblay
185, rue des Grisons
Québec, Québec
G1R 4M9
Canada

Leticia Garza
10286 Balboa Ave
San Diego, CA 92
U.S.A.

Salut, Leticia!

Comment ça va? Juste une petite lettre pour accompagner ces photos, une brochure sur le mont Sainte-Anne, une montagne près de Québec et aussi une cassette vidéo sur Québec... et sur moi! Comme ça, tu as une idée des activités ici... C'est l'automne à Québec et il fait déjà froid! Heureusement, il y a du soleil, mais il y a du vent. Quel temps est-ce qu'il fait à San Diego? Est-ce qu'il fait froid aussi? J'aime beaucoup Québec. C'est très sympa. Il y a beaucoup de choses à faire. En automne, je fais du patin et de la natation. J'adore le sport. En été, je fais du deltaplane et de la voile. Au printemps, je fais de l'équitation et je joue au tennis. Et en hiver, bien sûr, je fais du ski. C'est super ici pour le ski. Il neige de novembre à avril! Tu imagines? Est-ce qu'il neige à San Diego? Qu'est-ce qu'on fait comme sport? Du ski? Du base-ball? Quand il fait trop froid, je regarde la télévision et j'écoute de la musique. J'adore le rock et la musique québécoise. Et toi? Qu'est-ce que tu écoutes comme musique? Qu'est-ce qu'on fait à San Diego les fins de semaine? J'ai aussi une autre passion : de temps en temps, je fais des films avec un caméscope. C'est le fun! Tu sais, c'est super, Québec. Et la Californie, c'est comment? C'est le fun ou pas?

A très bientôt

Emilie

① *Ça, c'est notre café préféré.*

② *La musique, c'est super! Tu fais de la musique, toi?*

③ *Au printemps, on joue au tennis. J'adore!*

④ *C'est mon copain Michel. En été, on fait du vélo.*

⑤ *En automne, on fait de l'équitation.*

⑥ *C'est moi! En hiver, on fait du patin.*

1 Tu as compris?

Answer the following questions about Emilie's letter to Leticia. Don't be afraid to guess.

1. What is Emilie sending to Leticia along with her letter?
2. What are some of Emilie's hobbies and pastimes?
3. What would she like to know about Leticia and San Diego?
4. What does Emilie tell Leticia about the city of Quebec?
5. What else have you learned about Emilie from her letter?

2 C'est Emilie?

Tell whether Emilie would be likely or unlikely to say each of the statements below.

1. «J'adore faire du sport.»
2. «Le ski? Ici on n'aime pas beaucoup ça.»
3. «Pour moi, Québec, c'est barbant en hiver.»
4. «Faire des films avec un caméscope, pour moi, c'est passionnant.»
5. «Je regarde la télé en hiver quand il fait trop froid.»
6. «La musique? Bof! Je n'aime pas beaucoup ça.»

3 Cherche les expressions

In **Nouvelles de Québec**, what does Emilie say to . . .

1. greet Leticia?
2. ask how Leticia is?
3. ask about the weather?
4. tell what she likes?
5. express her opinion about something?
6. inquire about California?
7. say goodbye?

C'est super.
Comment ça va?
J'adore...
J'aime...
A très bientôt.
C'est très sympa.
Quel temps est-ce qu'il fait?
Salut!
C'est le fun.
Et la Californie, c'est comment?

4 Les saisons et les sports

D'après la lettre d'Emilie, quels sports est-ce qu'elle fait? En quelle saison? Choisis des sports pour compléter ces phrases.

1. Au printemps, Emilie fait...
2. En hiver, elle fait...
3. En automne, elle fait...
4. En été, elle fait...

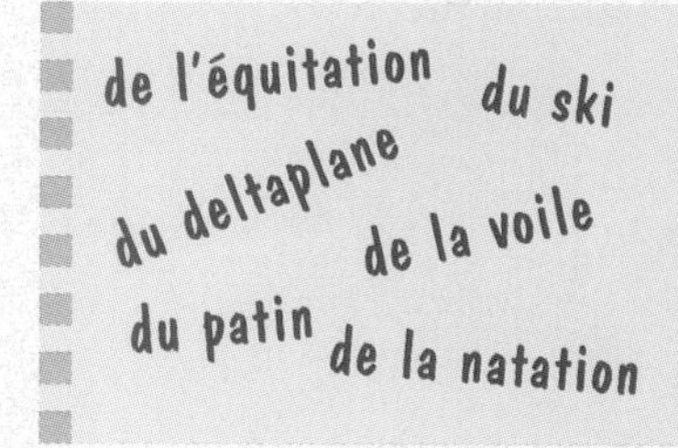

de l'équitation
du ski
du deltaplane
de la voile
du patin
de la natation

5 Et maintenant, à toi

Emilie fait beaucoup de choses! Tu fais les mêmes choses? Pour chaque activité, réponds **Moi aussi** ou **Moi, non.**

1. Emilie fait du ski.
2. Elle écoute de la musique.
3. Emilie fait des films avec un caméscope.
4. Elle fait de l'équitation.
5. Quand il fait trop froid pour sortir, Emilie regarde la télé.
6. Emilie joue au tennis.

What do you know about Quebec? What impressions do you get of Quebec when you look at these photos?

Qu'en penses-tu?

1. What things do you see that are typically American?
2. What do you see in these photos that you might not see in the United States?

Savais-tu que... ?

One of the first things you'll notice about Quebec City is its fascinating blend of styles—old and new, European and North American. Old Quebec (**le Vieux-Québec**) is filled with quaint neighborhood cafés and shops that maintain the old-world flavor of Europe. And yet, it is surrounded by a vibrant, modern city with high-rise hotels, office buildings, and a complex network of freeways. All of these elements together give the city its unique character.

PREMIERE ETAPE

Telling how much you like or dislike something

VOCABULAIRE

Qu'est-ce que tu aimes faire après l'école?

jouer au foot(ball)

jouer au football américain

faire de la vidéo

faire du roller en ligne

faire du patin à glace

faire du théâtre

faire de l'athlétisme

faire du vélo

faire de la natation *

You can probably guess what these activities are:

faire de l'aérobic	faire du ski (nautique)	jouer au basket(-ball)	jouer à des jeux vidéo
faire du jogging	jouer aux cartes	jouer au golf	jouer au tennis
faire de la/des photo(s)	jouer au base-ball	jouer au hockey	jouer au volley(-ball)

6 Ecoute!

Listen to this conversation between Philippe and Pascal. List at least two activities Pascal likes and two he doesn't like.

* Remember that **nager** also means *to swim.*

GRAMMAIRE Expressions with **faire** and **jouer**

You use **faire** *(to make, to do)* followed by the preposition **de** with activities, including sports.

- When the sport is a masculine noun, **de** becomes **du.**
  faire **du** ski faire **du** patin
- If the activity is plural, **de** becomes **des.**
  faire **des** photos
- The preposition **de** doesn't change before **la** or **l'**.
  faire **de la** natation faire **de l'**aérobic

You use **jouer** *(to play)* with games or sports that you play. It is followed by the preposition **à.**

- When the game or sport is a masculine noun, **à** becomes **au.**
  jouer **au** football
- When the game or sport is plural, **à** becomes **aux.**
  jouer **aux** cartes
- The preposition **à** doesn't change before **la, l'** or **des.**

7 Qu'est-ce que tu aimes faire?

Ariane and Serge are telling each other about the activities they like to do after school. Complete their conversation by substituting the activities suggested by the pictures.

ARIANE Qu'est-ce que tu aimes faire après l'école?

SERGE Moi, j'aime  avec mes copains. Et toi?

ARIANE Moi, j'aime  et j'adore  .

SERGE Tu aimes  ? On va jouer à la plage demain. Tu viens?

ARIANE Non, merci. J'aime mieux  avec des copains.

8 Après l'école

You and a Canadian student are discussing what you like to do after school on different days of the week. Create the conversation with one of your classmates.

— Qu'est-ce que tu aimes faire le lundi après l'école?
— J'aime jouer au basket le lundi. Et toi?
— Moi, j'aime faire du vélo.

COMMENT DIT-ON... ?
Telling how much you like or dislike something

To tell how much you like something:
J'aime **beaucoup** le sport. *I like . . . a lot!*
J'aime **surtout** faire du ski. *I especially like . . .*

To tell how much you dislike something:
Je n'aime **pas tellement** le football. *I don't like . . . too much.*
Je n'aime **pas beaucoup** le volley-ball. *I don't like . . . very much.*
Je n'aime **pas du tout** la natation. *I don't like . . . at all.*

You can use the expressions in bold type alone as short answers:
— Tu aimes faire du sport?
— Oui, **beaucoup!** *or*
Non, **pas tellement.**

9 Ecoute!

On a school trip to Quebec, you listen to your classmate talk to a Canadian student. Write down at least one sport or game each speaker likes and one each speaker dislikes.

10 Pas d'accord!

You and a Canadian exchange student want to watch sports on TV, but you can't agree on what to watch. Each time one of you finds something you like, the other doesn't like it and changes the channel. Act this out with a partner.

— Oh! J'aime bien le football. Et toi, tu aimes?
— Pas beaucoup. Regarde, un match de tennis. Tu aimes le tennis?

le patin à glace
le hockey
le football américain
oui, beaucoup
le basket-ball
pas tellement
pas du tout
pas beaucoup
le ski
moi, si
la natation

11 Qu'est-ce qu'ils aiment faire?

The Canadian exchange student is visiting your school. He'd like to get to know your friends better, so he asks you about their interests. Tell him how much each of your friends likes or dislikes the activity pictured, using the cue provided.

—Est-ce que Marc aime... ? —Non, il n'aime pas trop...

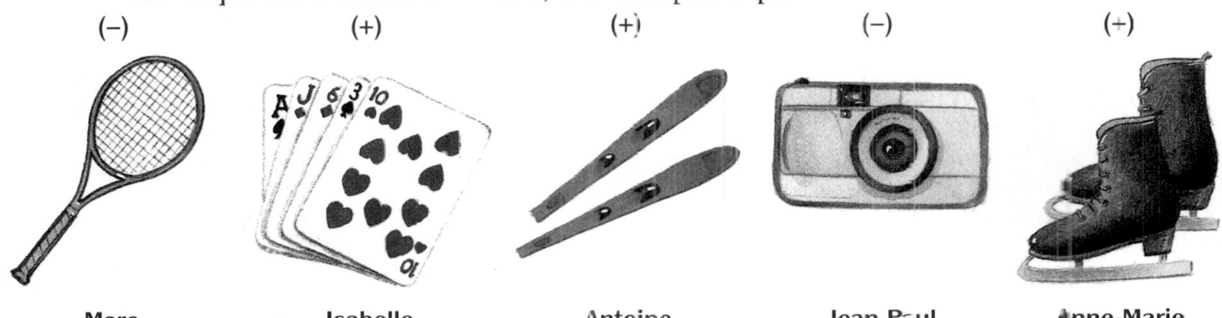

1. Est-ce que Marc aime... ?
2. Est-ce qu'Isabelle aime... ?
3. Et Antoine, est-ce qu'il aime... ?
4. Et Jean-Paul, est-ce qu'il aime... ?
5. Est-ce qu'Anne-Marie aime... ?

GRAMMAIRE Question formation

You've already learned to make a yes-or-no question by raising the pitch of your voice at the end of a sentence. Another way to ask a yes-or-no question is to say **est-ce que** before a statement and raise your voice at the very end.

Est-ce que tu aimes faire du vélo?

12 Et toi?

With a partner, discuss the sports and hobbies you both like to do. Take turns asking and answering questions. Be sure to vary the kinds of questions you ask.

— Est-ce que tu aimes jouer au football américain?
— Non! J'aime mieux faire de l'aérobic, du théâtre et du roller en ligne.

Vocabulaire à la carte

faire un pique-nique	*to have a picnic*
faire de la randonnée	*to go hiking*
faire des haltères	*to lift weights*
faire de la gymnastique	*to do gymnastics*
faire du surf	*to surf*
faire de la voile	*to go sailing*

13 Enquête

Poll five of your classmates about the sports and hobbies they like to do. Which activity is the most popular? Which is the least popular?

DEUXIEME ETAPE

Exchanging information

Exchanging information

To find out a friend's interests:

Qu'est-ce que tu fais comme sport? *What sports do you play?*
Qu'est-ce que tu fais pour t'amuser? *What do you do to have fun?*

To tell about your interests:

Je fais de l'athlétisme. *I do . . .*
Je joue au volley-ball. *I play . . .*
Je ne fais pas de ski. *I don't . . .*
Je ne joue pas au foot. *I don't play . . .*

NOTE DE GRAMMAIRE

Du, de la, and **de l'** usually become **de** (or **d'**) in a negative sentence.

Je ne fais pas **de** jogging.
Je ne fais pas **d'**athlétisme.

14 Qu'est-ce que tu fais pour t'amuser?

With a partner, take turns asking each other about your sports and hobbies.

— Qu'est-ce que tu fais pour t'amuser?
— Je fais du jogging et du ski. Et toi?
— Moi, je...

GRAMMAIRE The verb **faire**

The irregular verb **faire** is used in many different expressions.

faire (*to do, to play,* or *to make)*

Je **fais**	du sport.	Nous **faisons**	du sport.
Tu **fais**		Vous **faites**	
Il/Elle/On **fait**		Ils/Elles **font**	

15 Quels sports?

Complete the following conversation with the correct forms of the verb **faire.**

— Tu __1__ quels sports?
— Moi, je __2__ surtout du ski et du patin.
— Et tes copains, qu'est-ce qu'ils __3__ comme sport?
— Michel __4__ de la natation et Hélène __5__ du roller en ligne.
— Hélène et toi, est-ce que vous __6__ du sport ensemble?
— Oui, nous __7__ souvent du vélo.

16 Jean et Luc

Jean and Luc are identical twins. They even enjoy the same activities. Tell what activities they do, based on what you see in their room.

GRAMMAIRE The pronoun on

- The subject pronoun **on** is used with the **il/elle** form of the verb. In conversational French, **on** usually means *we.*
  Le samedi, **on** fait du sport. *On Saturdays, we play sports.*
- **On** can mean *they* or *you* when it refers to people in general.
  En France, **on** parle français.
- You will have to use context, the surrounding words and phrases, to tell how a speaker is using **on.**

17 Au Cercle français *At the French Club*

Based on the activities shown in the photos, talk about some of the activities you do or don't do with your friends.

Mes copains et moi, on fait...

1.

2.

3.

4.

5.

Vocabulaire

Quel temps fait-il?

Il fait beau.

Il fait chaud.

Il fait froid.

Il fait frais.

Il pleut.

Il neige.

18 C'est agréable ou désagréable?

Is each of these activities pleasant (**agréable**) or unpleasant (**désagréable**)?

1. faire du vélo quand *(when)* il fait froid
2. faire de la natation quand il fait chaud
3. regarder la télé quand il neige
4. faire du jogging quand il fait frais
5. jouer au football américain quand il pleut

19 Et toi?

Qu'est-ce que tu aimes faire quand...

1. il fait froid?
2. il pleut?
3. il fait beau?
4. il neige?

Vocabulaire

Les mois de l'année

janvier
février
mars
avril
mai
juin
juillet
août
septembre
octobre
novembre
décembre

Francophone countries, like most other countries of the world, use the metric system, so temperature is measured in degrees centigrade or Celsius rather than Fahrenheit. This means that the freezing point of water is 0°C, and its boiling point is 100°C. A comfortable temperature would be 25°C (77°F). If the temperature were more than 35°C, it would be very hot. If the temperature were 18°C (64.4°F), you would probably need a jacket. If the temperature were 15°C, what month might it be?

20 Il fait quel temps?

In these months, what is the weather usually like where you live?

1. en mai
2. en février
3. en juillet
4. en octobre
5. en avril
6. en décembre

Il fait froid. Il pleut. Il neige. Il fait frais. Il fait beau. Il fait chaud.

Do you remember the endings that you learned to use with the verb **aimer** in Chapter 1? Those endings are exactly the same for all regular **-er** verbs, which include many French verbs. Here's how the verb **jouer** fits the pattern.

jouer *(to play)*

Je **joue** / Tu **joues** / Il/Elle/On **joue** } au tennis.

Nous **jouons** / Vous **jouez** / Ils/Elles **jouent** } au tennis.

21 Ecoute!

Listen as a newspaper reporter asks three Canadian teenagers, Paul, Anne, and Julie, about their hobbies and pastimes. Then, answer the questions below.

1. Which teenagers don't watch TV?
2. Which ones like to listen to music?
3. Which ones play hockey?
4. Which ones like to dance?
5. Which teenagers like to go to the movies?

22 Prisonnier des neiges

Imagine that you've been snowed in during a winter storm. Write a note to a friend telling him or her about the weather, what you're doing to pass the time, and how you feel about the situation.

Vocabulaire

Qu'est-ce que tu fais...

en vacances?

le soir?

le week-end?

en automne?

en hiver?

au printemps?

en été?

23 Un questionnaire

To help pair up campers for activities, a camp counselor has sent out the survey you see on the right. Give one answer in each category.

1. En automne, je...
a. fais du patin à glace.
b. joue au hockey.
c. écoute de la musique.
d. fais du ski.
e. fais autre chose.

2. En hiver, je...
a. joue au football américain.
b. joue au foot.
c. fais du théâtre.
d. joue au volley.
e. fais autre chose.

3. Au printemps, je...
a. joue au base-ball.
b. fais de l'athlétisme.
c. fais du vélo.
d. fais de la vidéo.
e. fais autre chose.

4. En été, je...
a. fais de la natation.
b. fais du roller en ligne.
c. regarde la télé.
d. fais du ski nautique.
e. fais autre chose.

24 Et toi?

Tell other students in your class what activities you do in each season and ask what they do. Try to find someone who does at least two of the same things that you do.

— En hiver, je fais du patin à glace. Et toi?
— Moi, non! Quand il fait froid, j'écoute de la musique.

25 Une lettre

In preparation for a visit to Canada, you've decided to write to your French-Canadian pen pal. Write a brief paragraph, asking about your pen pal's sports and hobbies and telling which ones you do and don't do.

Marius • Côte d'Ivoire

Aljosa • France

Mélanie • Québec

What sports do you play? Where do you go to practice them? We asked some young people about their favorite sports. Here's what they had to say.

Qu'est-ce que tu fais comme sport?

«Je fais beaucoup de sport, mais surtout le football. Je fais le football et le skate, le patin à roulettes et puis j'aime aussi le tennis.»

—Marius

«Comme sport, j'aime bien faire le tennis. J'aime bien aller à la piscine, voilà. J'aime bien [le] bowling.»

—Aljosa

«Avec mes amies, moi je fais beaucoup de sport. Je fais partie de l'équipe interscolaire de volley-ball et de badminton de l'école. Je fais de la natation. Je fais du patinage. Je fais de la course. Je fais du tennis aussi souvent l'été. L'hiver, je patine.»

—Mélanie

Qu'en penses-tu?

1. Which of these students enjoy the same sports that you do?
2. Which sports that they mention are not played in your area?
3. Can you guess which sports are associated with the following events and places?*
   - a. La Coupe du monde
   - b. Le Grand Prix de Monaco
   - c. Le Tour de France
   - d. Le stade Roland-Garros

Savais-tu que... ?

While schools in francophone countries do offer extracurricular sports, serious athletes often participate through clubs outside of school. Activities such as swimming, tennis, or volleyball are often organized by parent volunteers or communities. In France, recreation centers **(Maisons des jeunes et de la culture** or **MJC)** sponsor all kinds of social, cultural, and educational activities for young people.

* a. soccer b. auto racing c. cycling d. tennis (the French Open)

TROISIEME ETAPE

Making, accepting, and turning down suggestions

COMMENT DIT-ON... ?

Making, accepting, and turning down suggestions

To make a suggestion:

On fait du patin?
How about . . . ?
On joue au foot?
How about . . . ?

To accept a suggestion:

D'accord. *OK.*
Bonne idée. *Good idea.*
Oui, c'est génial!
Allons-y! *Let's go!*

To turn down a suggestion:

Désolé(e), mais je ne peux pas.
Sorry, but I can't.
Ça ne me dit rien.
That doesn't interest me.
Non, c'est barbant!

26 Ecoute!

Listen as Germain calls his friends Lise, Renaud, Philippe, and Monique to suggest activities for the weekend. Do his friends accept or turn down his suggestions?

27 Qu'est-ce qu'on fait?

Write down one or two things that you'd like to do this weekend. Then, find three classmates who'd like to join you.

— On fait du jogging ce week-end?
— Le jogging, c'est barbant! *or* D'accord. C'est génial, le jogging.

GRAMMAIRE Adverbs of frequency

- To tell how often you do something, use **quelquefois** (*sometimes*), **de temps en temps** (*from time to time*), une **fois par semaine** (*. . . time(s) a week*), **souvent** (*often*), **d'habitude** (*usually*), **rarement** (*rarely*), and **ne... jamais** (*never*).
- Short adverbs usually come after the verb. Longer adverbs can be placed at the beginning or the end of a sentence. Put **d'habitude** at the beginning of a sentence and **une fois par semaine** at the end. Put **ne... jamais** around the verb, as you do with **ne... pas.**

Je fais **souvent** du ski.
D'habitude, je fais du ski au printemps.
Je fais du ski **une fois par semaine.**
Je **ne** fais **jamais** de ski.

28 Ecoute!

Listen as Emile, a reporter for the school newspaper in Quebec City, interviews his classmates about sports. How often does each person practice sports?

29 L'agenda de Pauline *Pauline's planner*

Pauline is an active, French-Canadian teenager. Based on her calendar, take turns with a partner asking about her activities and how often she does them.

— Est-ce qu'elle fait de l'aérobic?
— Oui, de temps en temps.

NOVEMBRE

DIMANCHE	LUNDI	MARDI	MERCREDI	JEUDI	VENDREDI	SAMEDI
		1 jogging	2 photo	3 jogging	4 théâtre	5 patin à glace
6 aérobic	7 jogging	8 photo	9	10 jogging	11	12 jogging
13 photo	14 jogging	15	16 aérobic	17 jogging	18 théâtre	19
20 patin à glace	21 jogging	22 jogging	23 photo	24 ski	25	26 aérobic
27 jogging	28	29 jogging	30 photo			

30 Moi, je fais souvent...

With a partner, discuss your favorite pastimes and how often you do them. Ask questions to keep the conversation going.

— Qu'est-ce que tu fais pour t'amuser?
— En été, je fais souvent du ski nautique. Et toi?
— Je fais du vélo. Et toi? Tu fais du vélo... ?

le week-end? en vacances?
quand il fait froid? en été?
quand il fait beau?

31 Sondage

a. Make a chart like the one shown here. In the left-hand column, list the activities you enjoy. In the middle column, tell when you do them, and in the right-hand column, tell how often.

ACTIVITE	SAISON	FREQUENCE
Je fais du ski. Je fais...	en hiver	de temps en temps

b. Now, share this information with three other classmates. Ask questions to find out what you have in common and what you don't.

— Je fais du ski de temps en temps.
— Pas moi! Je ne fais jamais de ski.

32 Le sportif

Your French pen pal Lucien is coming to visit soon. Read his letter and tell whether he would answer **D'accord** or **Ça ne me dit rien** if you were to suggest the following activities.

1. On fait de la vidéo ce week-end?
2. On fait du ski nautique?
3. On joue au foot?
4. On fait de la natation ce soir?
5. On joue au football américain ce week-end?

Salut!
J'espère que ça va. Moi, ça va bien. Je fais beaucoup de sport maintenant. Et toi, tu aimes faire du sport? Moi, j'aime jouer au foot, mais je n'aime pas trop le football américain; c'est barbant. D'habitude, le week-end, je joue au tennis ou je fais de la natation. La natation, c'est génial. Mais je n'aime pas faire du ski nautique; c'est nul. Quand il fait froid, je fais de l'aérobic. A part le sport, quelquefois, je fais de la vidéo. Et toi? Qu'est-ce que tu fais le week-end? Ecris-moi vite!
A bientôt,

Lucien

33 Cher Lucien, ...

Now, answer Lucien's letter. Be sure to . . .

- tell him what activities you like and why you like them.
- tell him when and how often you do each activity.
- tell him what you don't like to do and why not.
- suggest one or two things you might do together and when.

34 Une interview

a. You are a guest at a French-Canadian school and you'll soon be interviewed on local television. You've received a list of questions you'll be asked. Write down your answers.

1. Tu fais souvent du sport?
2. Qu'est-ce que tu fais comme sport en hiver?
3. Tu regardes souvent la télé?
4. Qu'est-ce que tu fais le week-end?
5. Qu'est-ce que tu fais en vacances?
6. Tu fais quoi le soir?
7. Tu écoutes souvent de la musique? (Du rock? Du jazz? De la musique classique?)
8. Qu'est-ce que tu fais quand il fait froid?

b. With a partner, take turns asking and answering the questions.

35 Mon journal

Using the information in the chart you made for Activity 31, tell about your favorite weekend and after-school activities and how often you do them. Give your opinions of the activities, too.

PRONONCIATION

The sounds [u] and [y]

The sound [u] occurs in such English words as *Sue, shoe,* and *too.* The French [u] is shorter, tenser, and more rounded than the vowel sound in English. Listen to these French words: **tout, nous, vous.** The sound [u] is usually represented by the letter combination **ou.**

The sound [y] is represented in the words **salut, super,** and **musique.** This sound does not exist in English. To pronounce [y], start by saying [i], as in the English word *me.* Then, round your lips as if you were going to say the English word *moon,* keeping your tongue pressed behind your lower front teeth.

A. A prononcer

Now, practice first the sound [u] and then [y]. Repeat these words.

1. vous
2. nous
3. douze
4. rouge
5. cours
6. joue
7. tu
8. musique
9. nul
10. étude
11. une
12. du

B. A lire

Take turns with a partner reading the following sentences aloud.

1. Salut! Tu t'appelles Louis?
2. J'ai cours aujourd'hui.
3. Tu aimes la trousse rouge?
4. Elle n'aime pas du tout faire du ski.
5. Nous aimons écouter de la musique.
6. Vous jouez souvent au foot?

C. A écrire

You're going to hear a short dialogue. Write down what you hear.

LISONS!

What are your favorite free-time activities? In this article, you will get some additional information about the activities enjoyed by francophone students.

DE BONS CONSEILS
When you first glance at a reading selection, you might try to predict what information the article will give you. This will give you a better idea of what you're going to read. Remember to use headings, subheadings, and the organization of the text to help you understand what you're reading.

A. The title of this selection is **Allez, c'est à vous de choisir!** What do you think this title means? What do you think the article will be about?

B. Look at the organization of the article and the two major headings. What type of information do you think will be included under **Pour les artistes?** What about **Pour les sportifs?** What do you know about the activities in each category?

C. What type of information do you find in each section? Do all the sections have the same type of information? If not, how do they differ?

Pour les artistes

D. Scan the sections titled **La musique, Le théâtre,** and **La danse.** Make a list of the cognates you find. You should find at least ten.

Allez, c'est à vous de choisir!

Cette année, c'est décidé, vous vous lancez dans une activité! Nous vous en proposons ici quelques exemples, à vous de choisir...

POUR LES ARTISTES

LA MUSIQUE

- Il n'y a pas d'âge pour commencer. L'important, c'est d'être motivé. Et de bien choisir son instrument.
- Vous devez avoir votre instrument. Au début, il est possible de le louer.
- Rythme : en général 1 heure de solfège par semaine et 1/2 h de cours d'instrument. Pour progresser, il faut prévoir 1/4 h de travail chaque jour.

LE THEATRE

- C'est souvent à l'adolescence qu'on commence. On découvre à la fois les joies (et les doutes) de l'improvisation et les grands auteurs.
- Rythme : entre 2 et 3 heures par semaine, plus des textes à apprendre.
- Renseignez-vous auprès de votre mairie ou à l'École de Musique, 4, rue Beaubourg, 75004 Paris. Tel : 01 42 71 25 07.

LA DANSE

- Peu de garçons s'inscrivent au cours de danse et c'est bien dommage car la danse apprend à aimer et maîtriser son corps... et à s'éclater aussi!
- Débutant à tout âge!
- Pour commencer, un caleçon chaud (pour les muscles) et un tee-shirt près du corps (pour que le prof voie vos mouvements) peuvent suffire. Et des chaussures ballerines ou rythmiques.
- Rythme : 1 heure et demie par semaine.
- Fédération française de danse : 12, rue Saint-Germain-d'Auxerrois, 75013 Paris. Tel : 01 42 36 12 61.

POUR LES SPORTIFS

LE TENNIS

•Des matchs sont organisés par les clubs. Ils permettent de se préparer à la compétition.

•Le coût varie selon les clubs et votre niveau. Choisissez un forfait qui comprend les cours et l'accès aux courts.

•Comptez au moins 250 francs pour une raquette de bonne qualité et choisissez des chaussures adaptées, pas les tennis mode que vous portez tous les jours!

•Rythme : 1 heure par semaine, plus les tournois. Si vous jouez beaucoup, faites un autre sport en complément, pour éviter les problèmes de dos.

•Fédération française de tennis : Stade Roland Garros, 2 avenue Gordon Bennett, 75016 Paris. Tel : 01 47 43 48 00.

LE FOOTBALL

•Avec quelques copains et un ballon, on peut s'amuser presque partout. Mais pour jouer dans les règles de l'art, mieux vaut s'inscrire dans un club.

•Souvent, le short et le maillot sont fournis par le club, mais les chaussures à crampons vissés coûtent entre 150 et 900 francs.

•Rythme : en général 2 heures par semaine. Rencontres entre clubs le samedi ou le dimanche.

•Fédération française de football : 60 bis, avenue d'Iéna, 75763 Paris cédex 16. Tel : 01 44 31 73 00.

LE KARTING

•Il existe une formule de location de kart avec cours adaptés dès 12 ans.

•Coût : environ 3.000 francs par an, comprenant les cours et le matériel.

•Rythme : 1 heure par semaine, plus quelques courses (souvent le samedi ou le dimanche).

•Groupement national de karting : 203, rue Lafayette, 75010 Paris. Tel : 01 42 05 09 44.

E. What do you think the word **débutant** means? Can you think of any words in English that are related to this word?

F. At what age do people usually . . .

1. learn how to play an instrument
2. begin drama?
3. learn how to dance?

G. According to the article, how often do you need to practice playing an instrument to improve quickly?

Pour les sportifs

H. What do you think **Rythme** means? How do you know?

I. What do you think Le Karting means? Is this an activity that is popular in your area?

J. According to the article, how much does a tennis racket cost?

K. Which of these activities . . .

1. require(s) special shoes?
2. require(s) two or more hours a week?

L. For which activities is it recommended that you join a club?

M. Which activity costs the most to participate in? Why?

N. Conduct a survey among your classmates to see which of these activities are the most and least popular and why. You might also find out in how many of these activities your classmates have participated, which ones are the most interesting, and why. Make a list of questions you need to include in your survey.

MISE EN PRATIQUE

1 Listen to this radio commercial for the **Village des Sports**, a resort in Quebec. List at least one activity offered in each season.

2 You've decided to spend part of your vacation at the **Village des Sports.** Read the information you've received about the resort. Then, answer the questions that follow.

Village des Sports

c'est l'fun fun fun!

en hiver comme en été

Le plus grand centre du sport au Canada offre du plaisir pour toute la famille. Services d'accueil, de restauration et de location sur place.

EN ETE
- le tennis
- le volley
- l'athlétisme
- le base-ball
- le roller en ligne
- le ski nautique
- la natation
- l'équitation
- la voile

EN AUTOMNE
- le football
- l'équitation
- la randonnée
- le volley

EN HIVER
- le hockey
- le ski
- le patin à glace
- la luge

AU PRINTEMPS
- le base-ball
- la randonnée
- le roller en ligne
- le tennis

Village des Sports
1860, boul. Vlaicartier
(418) 844-3725
à 24 km du centre-ville de Québec via la route 371 Nord

1. Would the **Village des Sports** be good for a family vacation? Why or why not?
2. According to the brochure, in what season(s) can you go . . .
   a. in-line skating?
   b. water skiing?
   c. hiking?
   d. horseback riding?
3. You have a friend who doesn't like cold weather. What three activities could your friend do at the **Village des Sports?**

3 a. You've arrived at the **Village des Sports**. You meet your three roommates, get to know them, and ask them about the activities they enjoy.
b. You and your roommates decide to participate in an activity together. Each of you suggests an activity until you all agree on one.

4 What differences are there between the way students in your area and students in Quebec spend their free time?

5

Ecrivons!

You're going to write a letter to your French class back home describing your activities at the **Village des Sports.** Organizing your ideas using the strategy below will help you create your letter.

STRATEGIE

Arranging ideas logically is a helpful way to organize your ideas before you begin writing.

J'aime	Je n'aime pas	Le temps
faire du ski		Il fait froid.

1. Divide a sheet of paper into three separate columns.
2. Label the first column on your paper **J'aime...** , the next column **Je n'aime pas...** , and the third column **Le temps.**
3. In the first column, list the activities that you like to participate in at the **Village des Sports.** In the next column, list the activities you dislike, and in the third column, tell what the weather is like there.
4. Now you are ready to write your letter.

6

JEU DE ROLE

You're a famous Canadian athlete. Your partner, a reporter for the local television station, will interview you about your busy training routine. Tell the interviewer what you do at different times of the year, in various weather conditions, and how often. Then, take the role of the reporter and interview your partner, who will assume the identity of a different Canadian athlete.

QUE SAIS-JE?

Can you use what you've learned in this chapter?

Can you tell how much you like or dislike something? p. 102

1 Can you tell someone how much you like or dislike these activities?

1.

2.

3.

4.

5.

2 Can you tell someone which sports and activities you enjoy a lot? Which ones you don't enjoy at all?

Can you exchange information? p. 104

3 How would you tell someone about a few of your sports and hobbies, using the verbs **jouer** and **faire**?

4 How would you find out if someone plays these games?

1.

2.

3.

5 How would you tell someone in French . . .

1. what you do in a certain season?
2. what you like to do in a certain month?
3. what you do in certain weather?
4. what you like to do at a certain time of day?

Can you make, accept, and turn down suggestions? p. 110

6 How would you suggest that . . .

1. you and a friend go waterskiing?
2. you and your friends play baseball?

7 If a friend asked you to go jogging, how would you accept the suggestion? How would you turn it down?

VOCABULAIRE

PREMIERE ETAPE

Telling how much you like or dislike something

Beaucoup. *A lot.*
surtout *especially*
Pas tellement. *Not too much.*
Pas beaucoup. *Not very much.*
Pas du tout. *Not at all.*

Sports and hobbies

faire de l'aérobic *to do aerobics*
de l'athlétisme *to do track and field*
du jogging *to jog*
de la natation *to swim*
du patin à glace *to ice-skate*
de la photo *to do photography*
des photos *to take pictures*
du roller en ligne *to in-line skate*
du ski *to ski*
du ski nautique *to water-ski*
du théâtre *to do drama*
du vélo *to bike*
de la vidéo *to make videos*
jouer au base-ball *to play baseball*
au basket(-ball) *to play basketball*
au foot(ball) *to play soccer*
au football américain *to play football*
au golf *to play golf*
au hockey *to play hockey*
à des jeux vidéo *to play video games*
au tennis *to play tennis*
au volley(-ball) *to play volleyball*
aux cartes *to play cards*

Other useful expressions

Est-ce que *(introduces a yes-or-no question)*

DEUXIEME ETAPE

Exchanging information

Qu'est-ce que tu fais comme sport? *What sports do you play?*
Qu'est-ce que tu fais pour t'amuser? *What do you do to have fun?*
Je fais... *I play/do . . .*
Je joue... *I play . . .*
Je ne fais pas de... *I don't play/do . . .*
Je ne joue pas... *I don't play . . .*
faire *to do, to play, to make*
jouer *to play*

Weather

Quel temps fait-il? *What's the weather like?*
Il fait beau. *It's nice weather.*
Il fait chaud. *It's hot.*
Il fait frais. *It's cool.*
Il fait froid. *It's cold.*
Il pleut. *It's raining.*
Il neige. *It's snowing.*

Seasons, months, and times

Qu'est-ce que tu fais... *What do you do . . .*
le week-end? *on weekends?*
le soir? *in the evening?*
en vacances? *on vacation?*
au printemps? *in the spring?*
en été? *in the summer?*
en automne? *in the fall?*
en hiver? *in the winter?*
en janvier?
en février?
en mars?
en avril?
en mai?
en juin?
en juillet?
en août?
en septembre?
en octobre?
en novembre?
en décembre?

Other useful expressions

on *we, they, you*

TROISIEME ETAPE

Making, accepting, and turning down suggestions

On... ? *How about . . . ?*
D'accord. *OK.*
Bonne idée. *Good idea.*
Allons-y! *Let's go!*
Oui, c'est... *Yes, it's . . .*
Désolé(e), mais je ne peux pas. *Sorry, but I can't.*
Ça ne me dit rien. *That doesn't interest me.*
Non, c'est... *No, it's (that's) . . .*

Expressions of frequency

quelquefois *sometimes*
...fois par semaine *. . . time(s) a week*
de temps en temps *from time to time*
souvent *often*
rarement *rarely*
ne... jamais *never*
d'habitude *usually*

CHAPITRES 5, 6, 7

Allez, viens à Paris!

L'avenue des Champs-Elysées et l'Arc de triomphe

Paris

Capitale de la France

Population : plus de 2.150.000; région parisienne : plus de 10.000.000

Points d'intérêt : la tour Eiffel, l'Arc de triomphe, la cathédrale Notre-Dame, le centre Georges Pompidou, la basilique du Sacré-Cœur

Musées : l'Orangerie, le musée du Louvre, le musée d'Orsay, le musée de l'Homme, le musée Rodin

Parcs et jardins : le jardin du Luxembourg, le Champ-de-Mars, les Tuileries

Parisiens célèbres : Charles Baudelaire, Colette, Victor Hugo, Edith Piaf, Auguste Rodin, Jean-Paul Sartre

Industries : haute couture, finance, technologie, transport, tourisme

go.hrw.com
WAO PARIS

Paris

Paris is a city that has no equal. It is the intellectual and cultural capital of the French-speaking world and also the largest city in Europe, if you include the greater Parisian area. Whether you like to visit museums, go to the theater, sit in cafés, or stroll along tree-lined boulevards, there's something for everyone here. Paris is one of the world's most beautiful and exciting cities!

① **Le centre Georges Pompidou** houses a major library and the National Museum of Modern Art. Outside, you can see jugglers, magicians, and all kinds of entertainers. It is one of Paris's most popular tourist attractions.

② Many of the streets in the **Montmartre** district are lined with artists who sell their work and will even paint your portrait.

③ In the shadow of **la cathédrale Notre-Dame,** booksellers, called **bouquinistes,** sell rare books and posters along the banks of the river Seine.

(4) In Paris, the terrace of a café is a wonderful place to sit and watch the world go by.

(5) **La tour Eiffel** was erected as a temporary exhibit for the Centennial Exposition in 1889 and has been the object of controversy ever since. It is 320.75 meters tall, including the television antenna added in 1957. To reach the top platform, ride one of the hydraulic elevators or climb the 1,792 stairs!

(6) The Paris subway, **le métro,** is one of the world's most efficient mass-transit systems.

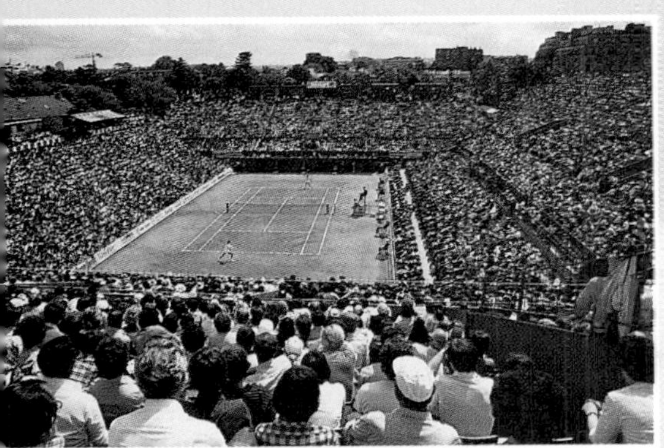

(7) **Le stade Roland-Garros** is the site of the French Open, one of the Grand-Slam tennis tournaments.

CHAPITRE

5 On va au café?

1 On va au café?

Where are your favorite places to meet and relax with your friends? In France, people of all ages meet at cafés to talk, have a snack, or just watch the people go by!

② Miam, miam! Je vais prendre un croque-monsieur.

In this chapter you will learn

- to make suggestions; to make excuses; to make a recommendation
- to get someone's attention; to order food and beverages
- to inquire about and express likes and dislikes; to pay the check

And you will

- listen to people ordering in a café
- read a café menu
- write about your food and drink preferences
- find out about French cafés

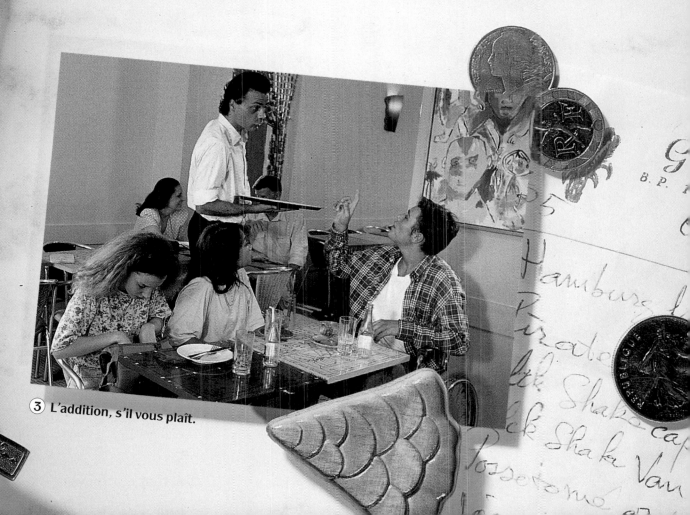

③ L'addition, s'il vous plaît.

Mise en train

Qu'est-ce qu'on prend?

Where does this story take place? What are the people doing? Why do you think they look upset at the end?

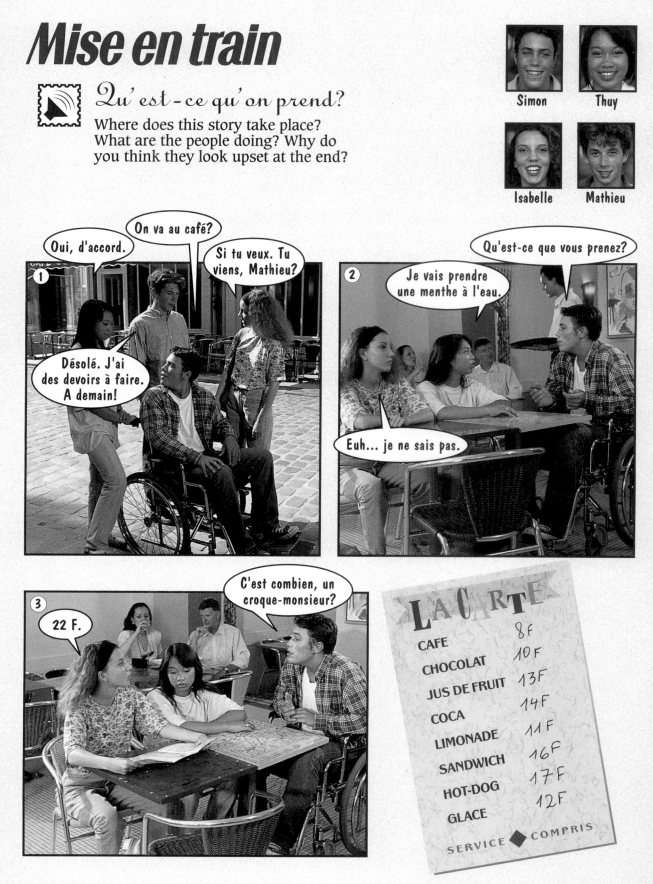

Simon

Thuy

Isabelle

Mathieu

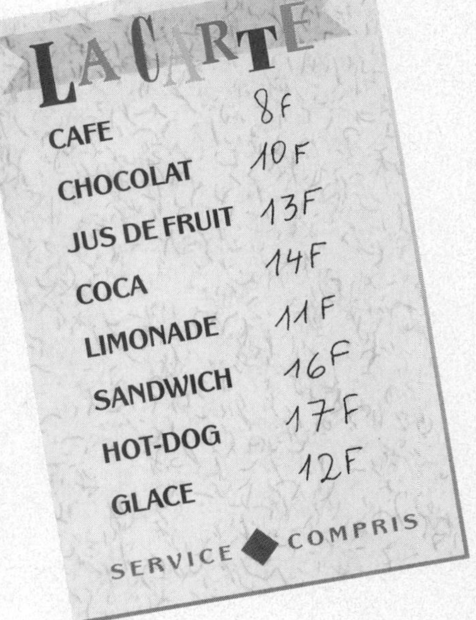

4
Vous avez choisi?
Apportez-moi une menthe à l'eau, s'il vous plaît.
Euh, je ne sais toujours pas.
Moi, je vais prendre une coupe melba et une bouteille d'eau minérale, s'il vous plaît. Et toi, Isabelle?
5
Vous avez des pizzas?
Non, je regrette. Nous n'avons pas de pizzas.
Tu aimes les sandwiches? Eh bien, prends un croque-monsieur.
D'accord. Un croque-monsieur pour moi.

Et comme boisson, qu'est-ce que vous prenez?
Qu'est-ce que vous avez comme jus de fruit?
6
Nous avons du jus d'orange, du jus de pomme...
Un jus d'orange, s'il vous plaît.
Parfait. C'est tout?
7
Non... Une coupe melba aussi pour moi, s'il vous plaît.
8

Plus tard...
9
Monsieur! L'addition, s'il vous plaît.
Tout de suite.
Eh, je ne trouve pas mon porte-monnaie! Je n'ai pas d'argent!

10
Ce n'est pas vrai!
Voilà, ça fait 129 F.

1 Tu as compris?

Answer the following questions about **Qu'est-ce qu'on prend?**

1. What is the relationship between the teenagers in **Qu'est-ce qu'on prend?**
2. Where are they at the beginning of the story?
3. Where do they decide to go?
4. What does each person order?
5. Who has trouble deciding what to order?
6. What is the problem at the end of the story?

2 Mets en ordre

Mets les phrases suivantes en ordre d'après **Qu'est-ce qu'on prend?**

1. Thuy commande une menthe à l'eau.
2. Simon demande l'addition.
3. Simon propose à Isabelle, Thuy et Mathieu d'aller au café.
4. Isabelle ne retrouve pas son argent.
5. Le serveur apporte l'addition.
6. Isabelle commande un jus d'orange.

3 Les deux font la paire

Choisis la bonne réponse d'après **Qu'est-ce qu'on prend?**

1. On va au café?
2. Qu'est-ce que vous prenez?
3. C'est combien, un croque-monsieur?
4. Vous avez des pizzas?
5. Qu'est-ce que vous avez comme jus de fruit?

a. Nous avons du jus d'orange, du jus de pomme...
b. Je vais prendre une menthe à l'eau.
c. Désolé. J'ai des devoirs à faire.
d. Vingt-deux francs.
e. Non, je regrette.

4 Cherche les expressions

Look back at **Qu'est-ce qu'on prend?** What do the students say to . . .

1. suggest that everyone go to the café?
2. give an excuse?
3. ask what someone's going to order?
4. order food?
5. ask what kind of fruit juice the restaurant serves?
6. ask how much something costs?
7. ask for the check?

On va au café? Qu'est-ce que vous prenez?
Apportez-moi... L'addition, s'il vous plaît.
Désolé. J'ai des devoirs à faire.
Je vais prendre...
C'est combien,... ? Qu'est-ce que vous avez comme jus de fruit?

5 Et maintenant, à toi

Isabelle is in an embarrassing situation. What do you think she is going to do? Take turns with a partner suggesting ways Isabelle and her friends might resolve their problem.

PREMIERE ETAPE

Making suggestions; making excuses; making a recommendation

COMMENT DIT-ON... ?

Making suggestions; making excuses

To make suggestions:

On va au café? *How about going to the café?*
On fait du ski?
On joue au base-ball?

To make excuses:

Désolé(e). J'ai des devoirs à faire. *Sorry. I have homework to do.*
J'ai des courses à faire. *I have errands to do.*
J'ai des trucs à faire. *I have some things to do.*
J'ai des tas de choses à faire. *I have lots of things to do.*
Je ne peux pas parce que... *I can't because . . .*

6 Ecoute!

Listen to the following dialogues. Do the speakers accept or turn down the suggestions?

Tu te rappelles?

Do you remember the following ways to accept a suggestion?

D'accord.
Bonne idée.

Do you remember the following ways to turn down a suggestion?

Ça ne me dit rien. J'aime mieux...
Désolé(e), mais je ne peux pas.

7 Qu'est-ce qu'on fait?

Suggest to your friends that you all do these activities after class. They will either accept your suggestions or turn them down and make excuses. Take turns making suggestions.

—On... ?
—D'accord,... *or* Désolé(e),...

1.

2.

3.

4.

5.

8 Un petit mot

You and your friend have agreed to go to the café on Saturday. You can't make it. Write your friend a note saying that you can't go, make an excuse, and suggest another activity at another time.

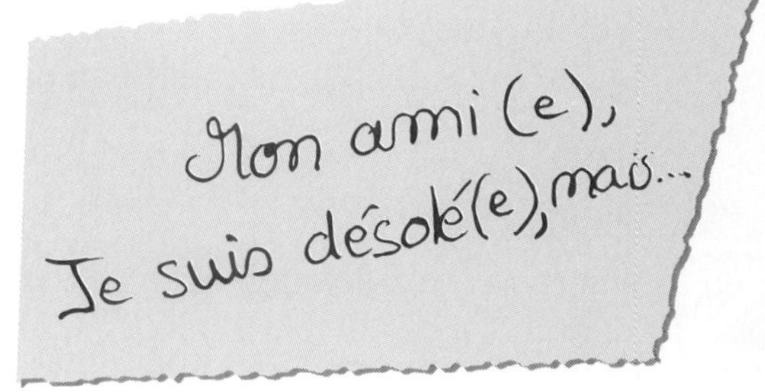
Mon ami(e),
Je suis désolé(e), mais...

Vocabulaire

CD-ROM Disc 2

Au café...

9 Ecoute!

Look at the picture. As the boys tell the waiter what they would like, decide which boy is ordering.

Didier Minh Paul Mamadou Nabil

10 Vous désirez?

Now, take the role of the server in Activity 9. Write down each boy's order.

11 La fête internationale

Your French class is going to participate in an international food fair at school. You've been assigned to poll your classmates about the types of food and drink they would like to have at the party. Make a list of five questions you might ask.

COMMENT DIT-ON... ?

Making a recommendation

To recommend something to eat or drink:

Prends une limonade. (informal) *Have . . .*
Prenez un sandwich. (formal) *Have . . .*

GRAMMAIRE The verb **prendre**

Prendre is an irregular verb.

prendre *(to take; to have food or drink)*

Je **prends**	des frites.	Nous **prenons**	un croque-monsieur.
Tu **prends**		Vous **prenez**	
Il/Elle/On **prend**		Ils/Elles **prennent**	

12 Qu'est-ce que je vais prendre?

You and your friends are deciding what to have in a café. Complete the conversation with the appropriate forms of the verb **prendre.**

—Alors, qu'est-ce que vous __1__ ?
—Moi, j'ai très faim, je __2__ un steak-frites.
—Et toi, Anne, qu'est-ce que tu __3__ ?
—Michel et moi, nous __4__ une pizza.
—Et Isabelle, qu'est-ce qu'elle __5__ ?
—Isabelle et Sylvie n'ont pas faim mais elles ont très soif, alors elles __6__ un coca.

De bons conseils

Resist the temptation to match English with French word-for-word. In many cases, it doesn't work. For example, in English you say *I am hungry*, while in French you say **J'ai faim** (literally, *I have hunger*).

13 Qu'est-ce qu'ils prennent?

Panorama Culturel

Déjan • France

Clémentine • France

Armande • Côte d'Ivoire

Where do you go to meet with your friends? Here's what some francophone students had to say about where they go and what they do.

Où retrouves-tu tes amis?

CD-ROM Disc 2

«J'aime bien aller au café après l'école. On va jouer un peu au baby, au flipper et après, je rentre chez moi faire les devoirs. On a un parc à côté de chez nous et on rencontre tous nos amis.»

—Déjan

«Nous allons dans des cafés ou chez d'autres amis. Quand il fait beau, [on va] à la piscine. Ça dépend du temps qu'il fait.»

—Clémentine

«Je vais à la maison, soit chez moi, ou bien chez eux [mes amis]. Puis on va à l'Alocodrome, enfin pour prendre un peu d'aloco, puis on revient à la maison.»

—Armande

Qu'en penses-tu?

1. Where do these students go to meet their friends?
2. Do you and your friends like to go to the same places and do the same things as these teenagers? Where do you go? What do you do?

Savais-tu que... ?

Many cultures have a particular kind of place where people gather. In many francophone countries, a café is more than just a place to eat; it's a social institution! Cafés primarily serve beverages. They may also serve bread **(pain)** or flaky crescent rolls **(croissants)** in the morning, and some cafés serve lunch. If you order something, you may stay in most cafés as long as you like. In some African countries, people like to go to open-air restaurants called **maquis.** They usually open only in the evening and serve traditional snack foods such as fried plantains **(aloco)**, as well as full meals.

DEUXIEME ETAPE

Getting someone's attention; ordering food and beverages

COMMENT DIT-ON... ?

Getting someone's attention; ordering food and beverages

To get the server's attention:
Excusez-moi.
Monsieur! Madame! Mademoiselle!
La carte, s'il vous plaît. *The menu, please.*

The server may ask:
Vous avez choisi? *Have you decided/chosen?*
Vous prenez? *What are you having?*

You might want to ask:
Vous avez des jus de fruit?
Qu'est-ce que vous avez comme boissons? *What kind of drinks do you have?*
Qu'est-ce qu'il y a à boire? *What is there to drink?*

To order:
Je voudrais un hamburger.
Je vais prendre un coca, **s'il vous plaît.** *I'll have . . . , please.*
Un sandwich, **s'il vous plaît.** *. . . , please.*
Donnez-moi un hot-dog, **s'il vous plaît.** *Please give me . . .*
Apportez-moi une limonade, **s'il vous plaît.** *Please bring me . . .*

14 Ecoute!

Listen to these remarks and decide whether the server **(le serveur/la serveuse)** or the customer **(le client/la cliente)** is speaking.

15 Méli-mélo!

Unscramble the following conversation between a server and a customer. Then, act it out with a partner.

—Qu'est-ce qu'il y a comme sandwiches?
—Bien sûr.
—Eh bien, donnez-moi un sandwich au fromage, s'il vous plaît.
—Vous avez choisi?
—Il y a des sandwiches au jambon, au saucisson, au fromage...

A la française

If you need time to think during a conversation, you can say **Eh bien**... and pause for a moment before you continue speaking.

—Vous prenez, mademoiselle?
—Eh bien... un steak-frites, s'il vous plaît.

At first you'll have to make a conscious effort to do this. The more you practice, the more natural it will become.

16 On prend un sandwich?

You've stopped at a café for lunch. Get the server's attention, look at the menu, and order. Take turns playing the role of the server.

LA MAISON DU SANDWICH

NOS SANDWICHES

au jambon de Paris	19 F	au gruyère	19 F
au jambon de pays	25 F	au camembert	19 F
au saucisson	19 F	au saumon	34 F
au pâté	21 F	au crabe	32 F
mixte (jambon et gruyère)	26 F	végétarien	28 F

GRAMMAIRE The imperative

Did you notice the subject **vous** isn't used in **Donnez-moi...** and **Apportez-moi...** ? When you give a command in French, you leave off the subject pronoun **tu** or **vous,** just as we leave off the subject pronoun *you* in English commands.

- When you write the **tu** form of an **-er** verb as a command, drop the final **s** of the usual verb ending.

  Tu écoutes... ⟶ **Ecoute!**
  Tu regardes... ⟶ **Regarde!**

- If the verb isn't a regular **-er** verb, the spelling of the command form doesn't change.

  Tu fais... ⟶ **Fais** les devoirs!
  Tu prends... ⟶ **Prends** un hot-dog, Paul!

- Remember to use the **tu** form when you talk with family members and people your own age or younger. Use the **vous** form when you talk with people older than you or with more than one person.

  Prenez un coca, Marc et Eve.

17 Que faire?

Your friends can't decide how they want to spend their Saturday afternoon. You're the one they always turn to for advice. Respond to each of their statements below by telling them what they should do.

—Nous avons faim.
—Prenez un sandwich.

1. Nous avons soif.
2. J'aime beaucoup la musique.
3. Il fait beau aujourd'hui.
4. Nous avons un examen demain.
5. Il fait frais.
6. Je voudrais faire du sport.

18 Que prendre?

You don't know what to order at the café. The server makes some suggestions for you, but you don't like the suggestions. Take turns playing the server.

—Prenez un sandwich au fromage.
—Non, je n'aime pas le fromage.
—Alors, prenez un sandwich au jambon.
—Non, apportez-moi un hot-dog, s'il vous plaît.

19 A la crêperie

You and some friends get together at a **crêperie.** Look at the menu and order. Take turns playing the server.

NOTE CULTURELLE

In France, waiters and waitresses are considered professionals. In better restaurants, waiters and waitresses must not only be good servers but they must also be knowledgeable about food and wine. Even in simple restaurants or cafés, servers take great pride in their work. Contrary to what you may have seen in American movies, it is impolite to address a waiter as **Garçon.** It is more polite to say **Monsieur** to a waiter, and **Madame** or **Mademoiselle** to a waitress. It is expected that diners will take time to enjoy their food, so service in French restaurants may seem slow to Americans. It is not uncommon for a meal to last several hours.

La Crêperie Normande

Crêpes salées :

Jambon - fromage	35
Epinards - crème fraîche	35
Champignons	38

Crêpes sucrées :

Sucre	28
Banane - Chantilly	35
Chocolat	32
Glace vanille - sauce noisette	38

20 Mon journal

Make a list of the foods and drinks you like to have when you go out with your friends. Then, mention several items you'd try if you were at a café in France.

TROISIEME ETAPE

Inquiring about and expressing likes and dislikes; paying the check

COMMENT DIT-ON... ?

Inquiring about and expressing likes and dislikes

To ask how someone likes the food or drink:
Comment tu trouves ça? *How do you like it?*

To say you like your food/drink:
C'est... *It's . . .*
bon! *good!*
excellent! *excellent!*
délicieux! *delicious!*
pas mauvais. *pretty good.*

To say you don't like your food/drink:
C'est... *It's . . .*
pas bon. *not good.*
pas terrible. *not so great.*
dégoûtant. *gross.*
mauvais. *bad.*

21 Ecoute!

Listen to the following remarks. Do the speakers like or dislike the food they've been served?

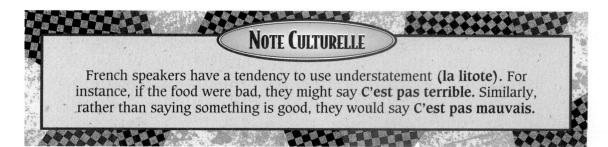

NOTE CULTURELLE

French speakers have a tendency to use understatement **(la litote)**. For instance, if the food were bad, they might say **C'est pas terrible.** Similarly, rather than saying something is good, they would say **C'est pas mauvais.**

22 A mon avis...

The school cafeteria is thinking of adding some items to the menu. A poll is being taken among the students. Discuss each of the items below with a partner.

1.

2.

3.

4.

23 Ça, c'est bon.

You and your partner are in a café. Ask if your partner has decided what to order and tell what you think of his or her choice.

— Tu as choisi? Qu'est-ce que tu vas prendre?
— Euh... je vais prendre un hot-dog.
— Un hot-dog? C'est dégoûtant! *or* Bonne idée. C'est délicieux.

24 Chère correspondante

Your French pen pal Cécile asked you what teenagers in America eat or drink when they get together. Write a brief note in French telling her what you and your friends have when you go out and what you think of each item.

COMMENT DIT-ON... ?

Paying the check

To ask for the check:
L'addition, s'il vous plaît. *The check, please.*

The server might answer:
Oui, tout de suite. *Yes, right away.*
Un moment, s'il vous plaît.

To ask how much something is:
C'est combien, un sandwich?
Ça fait combien, s'il vous plaît?
How much is it, . . . ? (total)

C'est huit **francs.**
Ça fait cinquante **francs.** *It's . . . francs.* (total)

25 Ecoute!

Listen to the following remarks. Are the speakers ordering or getting ready to pay the check?

Tu te rappelles?

Do you remember the numbers from 20–100?

20	vingt	50	cinquante	80	quatre-vingts
30	trente	60	soixante	90	quatre-vingt-dix
40	quarante	70	soixante-dix	100	cent

NOTE CULTURELLE

In cafés and restaurants, a 15% tip is included in the check if the words **service compris** are posted or written on the menu. If you're not sure, it's acceptable to ask **Le service est compris?** It's customary, however, to leave a little extra if the service is particularly good.

LA GIRAFE
Port de Cavalaire
Tél : 04 94 64 40 31

28-09-99

CROQUE-MONSIEUR 23,00
STEAK-FRITES 29,00
EAU MINERALE 9,00
COCA 14,00

TOTAL 75,00 F

La Direction souhaite
que cet instant de
détente vous ait été
AGREABLE

26 Ça fait combien?

You and your friend have just finished eating at a café. Look at the check, tell what you had **(Moi, j'ai pris...)**, and figure out how much each of you owes.

—Moi, j'ai pris...
—Ça fait... francs.

27 Qu'est-ce qu'on dit?

Write what you think the people in this scene are saying. Then, with a partner, compare what you both have written.

CAFE SPORT

Sandwiches		BOISSONS	
Fromage	15 F	Jus de fruit	13 F
Jambon	19 F	orange, pomme, pamplemousse	
Saucisson	18 F		
Hamburger	22 F	Limonade	11 F
Hot-dog	17 F	Café	8 F
Steak-frites	33 F	Cola	14 F
Croque-monsieur	22 F	Eau minérale	10 F
Pizza	20 F	Chocolat	10 F
Frites	10 F		
Glace	12 F		

28 Jeu de rôle

Act out a scene in a café. One student is the server and the others are customers. The customers should get the server's attention, order, comment on the food, and then pay the check.

PRONONCIATION

The nasal sound [ã]

Listen carefully to the vowel sounds in the following words: **ans, en**. These words contain the nasal sound [ã]. It's called a nasal sound because part of the air goes through the back of your mouth and nose when you make the sound. Listen to the English word *sandwich,* and the French **sandwich**. Is the first syllable pronounced the same in the two words? The sound in French is a pure nasal sound, with no trace of the *n* sound in it. In English you say *envy,* but in French you say **envie**. The nasal sound [ã] has four possible spellings: **an, am, en,** and **em**.

These letter combinations don't always represent a nasal sound. If another vowel follows the **n** or the **m,** or if the **n** or **m** is doubled, there may not be a nasal sound. You'll have to learn the pronunciation when you learn the word.

Listen to the following pairs of words and compare the sounds.

Fr*ance*/*ani*mal   pr*end*/pr*enez*   j*amb*on/*ami*   *env*ie/*enne*mi

A. A prononcer

Repeat the following words.

en France	attendez	comment	soixante
anglais	dimanche	jambon	temps
orange	tellement	vent	souvent

B. A lire

Take turns with a partner reading the following sentences aloud.

1. Il a cent francs.
2. J'ai un excellent roman allemand.
3. Elle a danse et sciences nat vendredi.
4. Moi, je vais prendre un sandwich au jambon.

C. A écrire

You're going to hear a short dialogue. Write down what you hear.

LISONS!

Do you like to go out to eat with your friends? Where do you like to go?

DE BONS CONSEILS

When you're faced with something new to read, look for anything that is familiar, anything that will help you identify the type of reading selection that you're dealing with. For example, a quick glance at these reading selections tells you that they're menus. Since you're familiar with menus, you should have a general idea of the kind of information these will contain, even if you don't know what all the words mean.

A. When you look at menus, what information are you usually looking for? Can you find this type of information on these menus?

B. French cuisine is enjoyed the world over. However, you can often find dishes from other cultures at French cafés and restaurants.

1. Which items on the menus are typical American dishes?
2. What French words might you find on American menus?
3. What other French words do you know that are related to food and restaurants?

C. In the Café des Lauriers, what ingredients do the **salade niçoise**, the **salade mexicaine**, and the **salade sicilienne** have in common?

SALADE VERTE 20

SALADE NIÇOISE 38
(salade verte, tomates, œufs, haricots verts, thon, olives)

SALADE MEXICAINE 40
(salade verte, tomates, maïs, poivrons, thon, olives)

SALADE SICILIENNE 40
(salade verte, tomates, basilic, mozzarella, huile d'olive)

ASSIETTE ANGLAISE 45
(jambon blanc, saucisson, rôti de porc, beurre)

SANDWICHES
jambon blanc 28
saucisson 28
pâté 30
fromage 26

CROQUE-MONSIEUR 27

PORTION FROMAGE 18

PIZZA 30

QUICHE 30

HAMBURGER 30

FONTAINE ELYSÉE

SANDWICHES

Jambon cru	30
Jambon de Paris	24
Pâté	24
Mixte	36
Roquefort aux noix	28

OMELETTES

Jambon	35
Fromage	35
Mixte	41

PLATS DIVERS

Croque-monsieur	30
Escargots (les 6)	52
Hot-Dog 1 Saucisse	32
Hot-Dog 2 Saucisses	57

BOISSONS CHAUDES

Café express	15
Décaféiné	15
Café ou chocolat viennois	32
Café crème	27
Cappuccino	33

BOISSONS FRAICHES

Eau minérale, limonade	26
Cola	28
Jus de fruit raisin, poire, abricot, pamplemousse, ananas	28

SPECIALITES

COUPE CHAMPS-ELYSEES : Chocolat - Pistache - Caramel - Sauce Chocolat - Mandarine Impériale - Chantilly	53
BANANA SPLIT : Glace -Vanille - Chocolat - Banane Fruit - Sauce Chocolat - Chantilly	44
COUPE MELBA : Vanille - Pêche Fruit - Chantilly - Sauce Fraise	44

D. Which café lists the beverages served? Do you recognize any of them? What is the difference between **BOISSONS FRAICHES** and **BOISSONS CHAUDES?**

E. How many different cognates can you find on the menus? (You should be able to find at least ten!)

F. Read the following statements about your friends' likes and dislikes. Which café would you recommend to each one?

1. Chantal a soif, mais elle n'a pas faim. Elle aime les jus de fruit.
2. Michel adore la glace.
3. Jean-Paul est végétarien.
4. Mai voudrait une omelette.
5. Alain aime les quiches.

G. Judging from the menus, what are the differences between the two cafés? What are the specialties of each one?

H. If your parents invited you to go out, which café would you choose? Why? Which would you choose if you had to pay?

I. If you had 100 F to spend, what would you order?

J. Now, make your own menu. Plan what you want to serve and how you want the menu to look. Will you have any illustrations? Don't forget to include prices.

MISE EN PRATIQUE

1 In which café would you most likely hear these conversations?

Café de Paris

15, Place du Palais - 75004 Paris
Téléphone 01-43-54-20-21

Nos glaces

Coupe Melba	50
Coupe Nougat	46
Banana Split	42

Nos boissons

Eau minérale	14
Jus de fruit	16
Café	10
Thé	8

SERVICE COMPRIS 15%

87, Avenue Victor Hugo - 75017 Paris
Tél. 01-45-62-52-53

Sandwiches

Croque-monsieur	30
Sandwich au jambon	25
Sandwich au fromage	20
Sandwich au rosbif	25

Boissons

Orangina, Coca	10
Eau minérale	12
Café	8
Jus de fruit	14

Café Américain

135, Boulevard d'Argençon • 75008 Paris
• Téléphone 01-44-15-30-33

★ Pizzas ★

Trois fromages	50
Suprême	65

★ Plats ★

Couscous	50
Steak-frites	45

★ Boissons ★

Coca	12
Limonade	15
Eau minérale	13

SERVICE COMPRIS 15 %

2 You and your partner are hungry. Suggest that you go to a café, decide what you both want to eat, and choose one of the cafés above.

3 From what you know about French cafés, are these statements true or false?

1. If you don't see **service compris** on the menu, you should leave a tip.
2. To call the waiter, you should say **Garçon!**
3. It is usually acceptable to stay in a French café for a long time, as long as you've ordered something to eat or drink.
4. If a French person says **C'est pas mauvais,** he or she doesn't like the food.

4 *Ecrivons!*

The French Club at your school is going to have a picnic to raise money. Plan the picnic with two classmates and then create your own poster announcing it.

STRATEGIE

Arranging ideas spatially is a useful way to organize information before you write. It's a way of creating a type of blueprint to show how your finished product will look.

First, create a name and catchy slogan to attract attention to your event. Determine the time and place of the picnic, the food, and the activities. Include a brief description of the purpose of the event. You should also decide how much each item will cost. Jot down all of your decisions.

Now, you're ready to create your blueprint. On a sheet of paper, draw a box for each item that will be included on your poster (title, slogan, date, time, place, food, and so on) indicating where you want the information to appear. Label each box with the type of information that will go in that space.

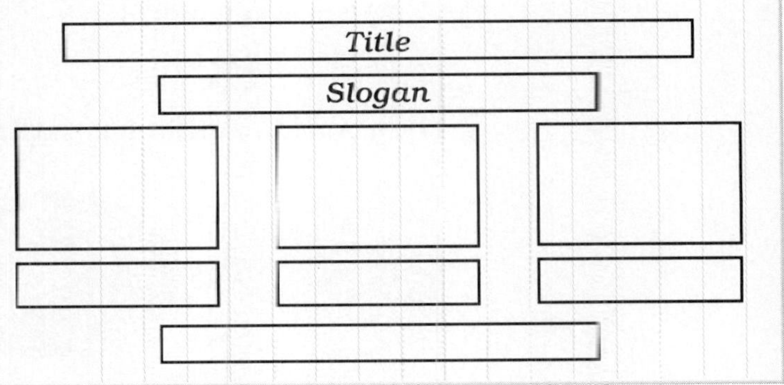

Next, using the blueprint you've developed, create your poster promoting the French Club picnic. Use the material you've learned in this chapter, such as commands. You might add drawings or magazine cutouts to illustrate your poster.

5

JEU DE ROLE

The day of the French Club picnic has arrived. One person in your group will act as host, the others will be the guests. The host will ask people what they want. Guests will tell what they want and talk about how they like the food and drink. After eating, suggest activities and decide which one you'll participate in.

QUE SAIS-JE?

Can you use what you've learned in this chapter?

Can you make suggestions, excuses, and recommendations? pp. 129, 132

1 How would you suggest to a friend that you . . .

1. go to the café?
2. play tennis?

2 How would you turn down a suggestion and make an excuse?

3 How would you recommend to a friend something . . .

1. to eat?
2. to drink?

Can you get someone's attention and order food and beverages? p. 135

4 In a café, how would you . . .

1. get the server's attention?
2. ask what kinds of sandwiches they serve?
3. ask what there is to drink?

5 How would you say that you're . . .

1. hungry?
2. thirsty?

6 How would you order . . .

1. something to eat?
2. something to drink?

7 How would you tell what people are having, using the verb **prendre**?

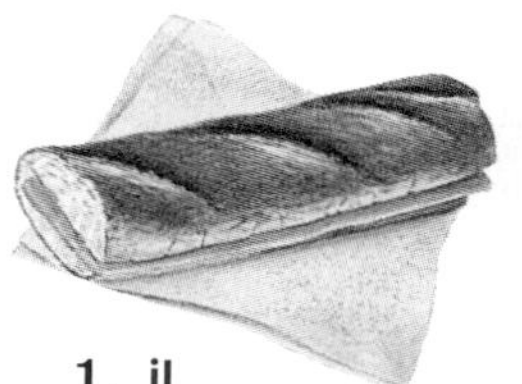
1. il

2. tu

3. nous

4. ils

Can you inquire about and express likes and dislikes? p. 138

8 How would you ask a friend how he or she likes a certain food?

9 How would you tell someone what you think of these items?

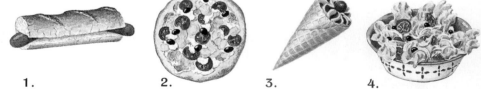

1.

2.

3.

4.

Can you pay the check? p. 139

10 How would you ask how much each item in number 9 costs?

11 How would you ask for the check?

12 How would you ask what the total is?

VOCABULAIRE

PREMIERE ETAPE

Making suggestions; making excuses

On va au café? *How about going to the café?*
On... ? *How about . . . ?*
Désolé(e). J'ai des devoirs à faire. *Sorry. I have homework to do.*
J'ai des courses à faire. *I have errands to do.*
J'ai des trucs à faire. *I have some things to do.*
J'ai des tas de choses à faire. *I have lots of things to do.*
Je ne peux pas parce que... *I can't because . . .*

Foods and beverages

un sandwich au jambon *ham sandwich*
au saucisson *salami sandwich*
au fromage *cheese sandwich*
un hot-dog *hot dog*
un croque-monsieur *toasted cheese and ham sandwich*
un steak-frites *steak and French fries*
une quiche *quiche*
une omelette *omelet*
une crêpe *very thin pancake*
une eau minérale *mineral water*
une limonade *lemon soda*
un citron pressé *lemonade*
un sirop de fraise (à l'eau) *water with strawberry syrup*
un coca *cola*
un jus d'orange *orange juice*
un jus de pomme *apple juice*
un café *coffee*
un chocolat *hot chocolate*

Making a recommendation

Prends/Prenez... *Have . . .*
prendre *to take; to have food or drink*

Other useful expressions

avoir soif *to be thirsty*
avoir faim *to be hungry*

DEUXIEME ETAPE

Getting someone's attention

Excusez-moi. *Excuse me.*
Monsieur! *Waiter!*
Madame! *Waitress!*
Mademoiselle! *Waitress!*
La carte, s'il vous plaît. *The menu, please.*

Ordering food and beverages

Vous avez choisi? *Have you decided/chosen?*
Vous prenez? *What are you having?*
Vous avez... ? *Do you have . . . ?*
Qu'est-ce que vous avez comme boissons? *What do you have to drink?*
Qu'est-ce qu'il y a à boire? *What is there to drink?*
Je voudrais... *I'd like . . .*
Je vais prendre..., s'il vous plaît. *I'll have . . . , please.*
..., s'il vous plaît. *. . . , please.*
Donnez-moi..., s'il vous plaît. *Please give me . . .*
Apportez-moi..., s'il vous plaît. *Please bring me . . .*

TROISIEME ETAPE

Inquiring about and expressing likes and dislikes

Comment tu trouves ça? *How do you like it?*
C'est... *It's . . .*
bon! *good!*
excellent! *excellent!*
délicieux! *delicious!*
pas mauvais! *pretty good!*
pas bon. *not good.*
pas terrible. *not so great.*
dégoûtant. *gross.*
mauvais. *bad.*

Paying the check

L'addition, s'il vous plaît. *The check, please.*
Oui, tout de suite. *Yes, right away.*
Un moment, s'il vous plaît. *One moment, please.*
C'est combien,... ? *How much is . . . ?*
Ça fait combien, s'il vous plaît? *How much is it, please?*
C'est... francs. *It's . . . francs.*
Ça fait... francs. *It's . . . francs.*

CHAPITRE

6 Amusons-nous!

1 On va au centre Georges Pompidou?

Teenagers everywhere love to go out with their friends. In Paris there are so many events and activities that it is almost impossible to choose. If you were in Paris, what would you want to do?

In this chapter you will learn

- to make plans
- to extend and respond to invitations
- to arrange to meet someone

And you will

- listen to French teenagers talk about where they go to have fun
- read brochures and advertisements
- write about your plans for the weekend
- find out what French-speaking young people do and where they go to have fun

② On se retrouve au métro Palais-Royal?

③ Je voudrais bien aller au cinéma.

LOUV

MUSEE

036585A
Ministère de la Culture
C.N.M.H.S.
DROIT D'ENTRÉE
26 F

RATP
CARNET 2 CL
SECTION URBAINE
M BUS RER T
19115

Mise en train

Projets de week-end

What do you think Mathieu and Isabelle are talking about? Why do you think so?

Vendredi après-midi...

1
Salut, Isabelle. Dis, qu'est-ce que tu vas faire demain?
Oh, pas grand-chose. Le matin, je vais aller à mon cours de danse. L'après-midi, je vais faire les magasins. Mais le soir, je suis libre.

2
Il y a un concert super à Bercy : Patrick Bruel. J'aimerais bien y aller. Tu veux venir avec moi?
Oh non, je n'ai pas envie d'aller à un concert.
Ah, dommage...

3
Et dimanche après-midi, tu es libre?
Dimanche? Oui, je n'ai rien de prévu.
Tu veux aller au zoo?
Ah, non, je déteste les zoos.

4
Alors, allons au Louvre!
Non, je n'aime pas trop les musées.

Qu'est-ce que tu veux faire, alors?

S'il fait beau, on peut faire une promenade au palais de Chaillot. On peut même monter au sommet de la tour Eiffel.
Bof.

J'ai une idée! Tu ne veux pas aller faire un tour dans un bateau-mouche?
BATEAUX MOUCHES
Ça, non. C'est pas terrible.

On va au Sacré-Cœur?
Non, j'ai pas envie.

On peut tout simplement aller au cinéma. Tu veux?
D'accord. Je veux bien. Qu'est-ce que tu veux voir comme film?
Moi, je propose *Dracula*. Ça passe à 16h40 et à 18h55.

Oh non, je n'aime pas les films d'horreur. Je préfère aller voir un film comique.
Oh non! Encore un film comique?! Tu sais, c'est bizarre. On n'est jamais d'accord!

1 Tu as compris?

Answer the following questions according to **Projets de week-end.** Don't be afraid to guess.

1. What are Isabelle's plans for tomorrow?
2. What day and time of day is it?
3. Can you name three places where Mathieu suggests they go?
4. Can you name three things that Isabelle prefers to do?
5. What do they finally agree to do? What problem remains?

2 Vrai ou faux?

1. Isabelle aime aller au zoo.
2. Isabelle a un cours de danse.
3. Mathieu aime la musique de Patrick Bruel.
4. Isabelle aime bien les musées.
5. Isabelle veut voir un film d'horreur dimanche après-midi.

3 Mets en ordre

Mets les phrases en ordre d'après **Projets de week-end.**

1. Isabelle propose d'aller au palais de Chaillot.
2. Mathieu propose d'aller au zoo.
3. Isabelle propose d'aller au Sacré-Cœur.
4. Mathieu ne veut pas faire de promenade.
5. Isabelle refuse d'aller au concert.
6. Isabelle accepte d'aller au cinéma.

4 Où est-ce qu'on veut aller?

Choisis les activités qu'Isabelle veut faire et les activités que Mathieu préfère.

aller voir un film comique
faire une promenade au palais de Chaillot
aller à un concert
aller voir un film d'horreur
aller au musée
aller au zoo
faire un tour en bateau
aller au Sacré-Cœur

5 Invitations et refus

Match Mathieu's suggestions for weekend activities with Isabelle's refusals.

Tu veux...

1. aller au concert de Patrick Bruel?
2. aller au Louvre?
3. aller au zoo?
4. aller voir *Dracula*?

Désolée, mais...

a. je déteste les zoos.
b. je préfère aller voir un film comique.
c. je n'aime pas trop les musées.
d. je n'ai pas envie.

6 Et maintenant, à toi

How would you react to Mathieu and Isabelle's suggestions for the weekend? Which would you choose to do? Why? Compare your answers with a partner's.

PREMIERE ETAPE

Making plans

COMMENT DIT-ON... ?

Making plans

To ask what a friend's planning to do:

Qu'est-ce que tu vas faire demain? *What are you going to do . . . ?*
Tu vas faire quoi ce week-end? *What are you going to do . . . ?*

To tell what you're going to do:

Vendredi, **je vais** faire du vélo.
Samedi après-midi, **je vais** aller au café. } *I'm going to . . .*
Dimanche, **je vais** regarder la télé.
Pas grand-chose. *Not much.*
Rien de spécial. *Nothing special.*

7 Ecoute!

Listen as Sophie asks Thérèse about her plans for the weekend. Write down at least three things Thérèse plans to do.

8 Qu'est-ce que tu vas faire?

a. Write down three activities you have planned for the weekend.

b. Now, tell your partner what you plan to do and ask about his or her plans.

Je vais voir un film. Et toi, qu'est-ce que tu vas faire?

VOCABULAIRE

regarder un match	*to watch a game (on TV)*
manger quelque chose	*to eat something*
voir un film	*to see a movie*
aller voir un match	*to go see a game*
voir une pièce	*to see a play*
faire une promenade	*to go for a walk*
faire les vitrines	*to window-shop*
faire un pique-nique	*to have a picnic*
aller à une boum	*to go to a party*

NOTE DE GRAMMAIRE

If you want to say that you do an activity regularly on a certain day of the week, use the article **le** before the day of the week.

Je fais du patin à glace **le mercredi** *(on Wednesdays)*.

To say that you are doing something only on one particular day, use the day of the week without an article before it.

Je vais faire du patin à glace **mercredi** *(on Wednesday)*.

GRAMMAIRE The verb **aller**

Aller is an irregular verb.

aller *(to go)*

Je **vais** au café.	Nous **allons** au café.
Tu **vas** au café.	Vous **allez** au café.
Il/Elle/On **va** au café.	Ils/Elles **vont** au café.

- You can use a form of the verb **aller** with the infinitive of another verb to say that you're *going to do something* in the future.

  Je vais jouer au base-ball demain.

- To say that you're *not going to do something* in the near future, put **ne... pas** around the conjugated form of the verb **aller.**

  Je *ne* vais *pas* jouer au base-ball demain.

9 Ecoute!

Listen to the following sentences and decide whether the people are talking about what they're doing or what they're going to do.

10 Qu'est-ce que tu vas faire?

You have a busy weekend planned! Tell what you're going to do and on what day you plan to do it.

1.

2.

3.

4.

5.

6.

11 Qu'est-ce qu'ils vont faire?

What are these people going to do?

1. Elles

2. Ils

3. Je

4. Nous

5. Vous

6. Elle

A la française

The French often use the present tense of a verb to say that something will happen in the near future, just as we do in English.

Samedi matin, je vais jouer au tennis. *Saturday morning, I'm going to play tennis.*

Samedi matin, je joue au tennis. *Saturday morning, I'm playing tennis.*

12 Enquête

Ask the members of your group what they're going to do this weekend and tell them what you're planning. Then, tell the class what you're all planning to do.

—Qu'est-ce que tu fais ce week-end, Nicole?
—Samedi après-midi, je fais du ski nautique. Et toi?
—Moi, je vais à une boum.
(to the class)
—Je vais à une boum et Nicole fait du ski nautique samedi après-midi.

VOCABULAIRE

Where do you and your friends like to go in your spare time?

au restaurant

au cinéma

au parc

au stade

au zoo

au centre commercial

à la plage

à la piscine

au musée

à la Maison des jeunes

au théâtre

à la bibliothèque

13 Où vas-tu?

Où est-ce que tu vas pour faire ces activités?

1. Je vais faire de la natation...
2. Je vais faire les vitrines...
3. Je vais voir un film...
4. Je vais manger quelque chose...
5. Je vais voir un match...
6. Je vais voir une pièce...

a. au cinéma.
b. au théâtre.
c. au centre commercial.
d. à la piscine.
e. au café.
f. au stade.

GRAMMAIRE Contractions with à

The preposition **à** usually means *to* or *at.*
When you use **à** before **le** or **les**, make the following contractions:

à + le = au Je vais **au** stade.
à + les = aux Martine va aller **aux** Tuileries.

The preposition **à** doesn't contract with **l'** or **la**:

Cet après-midi, on ne va pas **à la** Maison des jeunes. On va **à l'**école.

14 Projets de week-end

Christine and Alain are talking about where they like to go on weekends. Complete their conversation according to the pictures.

CHRISTINE Moi, j'adore aller 

avec mes copains. Après, on va souvent  . Et toi?

ALAIN Moi, j'aime mieux aller  . J'adore le sport. J'aime bien aller  aussi. On y joue souvent au foot.

CHRISTINE Qu'est-ce que tu vas faire ce week-end? On va  ?

ALAIN Ah, non, je n'aime pas trop nager. Tu veux aller  ?

15 Qu'est-ce qu'on fait?

You're trying to decide what to do after school. With a partner, take turns suggesting places to go. Then, accept or reject each other's suggestions.

le café le musée la piscine le parc
la piscine la Maison des jeunes le zoo
la bibliothèque le centre commercial

16 Mon journal

Tu as des projets pour le week-end? Qu'est-ce que tu vas faire? Où vas-tu? Quand?

Vendredi après-midi, je vais faire mes devoirs. Samedi, je...

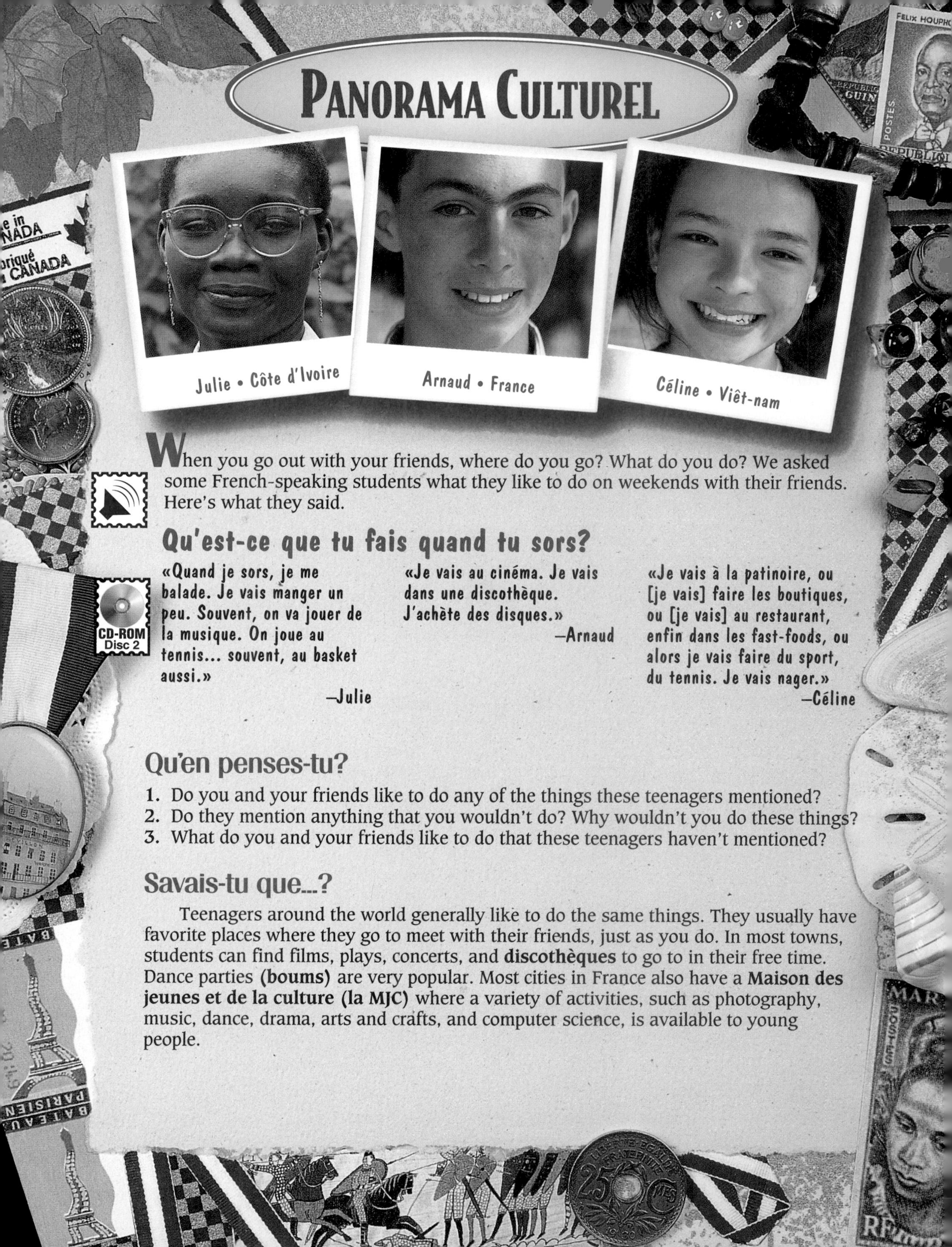

PANORAMA CULTUREL

Julie • Côte d'Ivoire

Arnaud • France

Céline • Viêt-nam

When you go out with your friends, where do you go? What do you do? We asked some French-speaking students what they like to do on weekends with their friends. Here's what they said.

Qu'est-ce que tu fais quand tu sors?

CD-ROM Disc 2

«Quand je sors, je me balade. Je vais manger un peu. Souvent, on va jouer de la musique. On joue au tennis... souvent, au basket aussi.»

—Julie

«Je vais au cinéma. Je vais dans une discothèque. J'achète des disques.»

—Arnaud

«Je vais à la patinoire, ou [je vais] faire les boutiques, ou [je vais] au restaurant, enfin dans les fast-foods, ou alors je vais faire du sport, du tennis. Je vais nager.»

—Céline

Qu'en penses-tu?

1. Do you and your friends like to do any of the things these teenagers mentioned?
2. Do they mention anything that you wouldn't do? Why wouldn't you do these things?
3. What do you and your friends like to do that these teenagers haven't mentioned?

Savais-tu que...?

Teenagers around the world generally like to do the same things. They usually have favorite places where they go to meet with their friends, just as you do. In most towns, students can find films, plays, concerts, and **discothèques** to go to in their free time. Dance parties **(boums)** are very popular. Most cities in France also have a **Maison des jeunes et de la culture (la MJC)** where a variety of activities, such as photography, music, dance, drama, arts and crafts, and computer science, is available to young people.

DEUXIEME ETAPE

Extending and responding to invitations

COMMENT DIT-ON... ?
Extending and responding to invitations

CD-ROM Disc 2

To extend an invitation:

Allons au parc! *Let's go . . . !*
Tu veux aller au café **avec moi?** *Do you want to . . . with me?*
Je voudrais aller faire du vélo. **Tu viens?** *Will you come?*
On peut faire du ski. *We can . . .*

To accept an invitation:

D'accord.
Bonne idée.
Je veux bien. *I'd really like to.*
Pourquoi pas? *Why not?*

To refuse an invitation:

Ça ne me dit rien.
J'ai des trucs à faire.
Désolé(e), je ne peux pas.
Désolé(e), je suis occupé(e).
Sorry, I'm busy.

17 Ecoute!

Ecoute ces dialogues. Est-ce qu'on accepte ou refuse l'invitation?

Les loisirs préférés	15-25 ans
Cinéma	90
Discothèque	69
Fête foraine	58
Concert de rock	42
Parc d'attractions	37
Match (payant)	36
Monument historique	31
Bal public	30
Musée	27
Théâtre	17
Concert de jazz	11
Cirque	10
Concert classique	6
Spectacle de danse	5
Opéra	3

18 Et toi? Tu veux?

Choisis la bonne réponse.

1. J'ai faim.
2. Je voudrais faire un pique-nique.
3. Tu ne viens pas?
4. Je voudrais voir un match de foot.
5. Tu veux voir une pièce?

a. Allons au parc!
b. J'ai des trucs à faire.
c. Pourquoi pas? Allons au théâtre!
d. Tu veux aller au café?
e. Allons au stade!

19 Tu acceptes?

Your partner will invite you to participate in some of the following activities. Accept or refuse, telling where you're going or what you're going to do instead. Exchange roles.

1.

2.

3.

4.

5.

6.

GRAMMAIRE The verb **vouloir**

Vouloir is an irregular verb.

vouloir *(to want)*

Je **veux** / Tu **veux** / Il/Elle/On **veut**	aller au café.	Nous **voulons** / Vous **voulez** / Ils/Elles **veulent**	aller au café.

Je voudrais *(I would like)* is a more polite form of **je veux.**

20 Qu'est-ce qu'on veut faire ce soir?

1. Pierre et Marc

2. Alain

3. Moi, je...

4. Elodie et Guy

5. Mes copains et moi, nous...

6. David et Monique

21 Invitations pour le week-end

You're making plans for the upcoming weekend. Take turns with a partner suggesting activities and accepting or politely refusing the suggestions.

22 Vous voulez faire quoi?

You and your friends can't decide what to do this weekend. Each of you makes a suggestion, and the others react to it. See if you can find three things you'd all like to do.

—Vous voulez faire du vélo?
—Oui, je veux bien.
—Moi, je ne veux pas. Je n'aime pas faire du vélo.

23 A la boum!

The French Club is having a party. Invite three students. Before they accept or refuse your invitation, they want to know what you're planning to do. Tell them about the activities you're planning. Your friends will either accept or refuse.

écouter de la musique québécoise
danser
voir un film français
parler français avec des copains
manger des escargots

L'ambiance sera extra!

Le Cercle Français
t'invite
à une fête
le 10 mai
de 7h à 10h

Si tu viens, ce sera plus sympa!

Rencontre Culturelle

Qu'en penses-tu?

1. Judging from these photos, how would you describe a typical date in France?
2. Do American teenagers usually go out on dates in groups or in couples? Which do you think is preferable? Why?
3. What do you think is the best age to begin dating? Why?

Savais-tu que... ?

French teenagers tend to go out in groups. They usually do not "date" in the same way American teenagers do. They do not generally pair off into couples until they are older. Those who do have a boyfriend or girlfriend still go out with a group — but they almost always pay their own way.

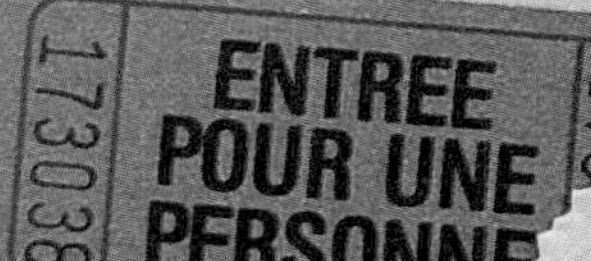

TROISIEME ETAPE

Arranging to meet someone

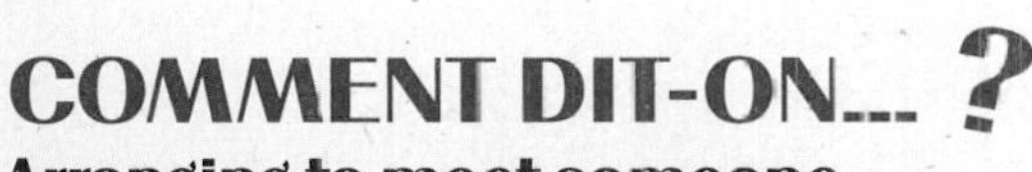

Arranging to meet someone

To ask when: **Quand?** **Quand ça?**	*To tell when:* **Lundi./Demain matin./Ce week-end.** **Tout de suite.** *Right away.*
To ask where: **Où?** **Où ça?**	*To tell where:* **Au** café. *At the . . .* **Devant** le cinéma. *In front of . . .* **Dans** le café. *In . . .* **Au métro** Saint-Michel. *At the . . . subway stop.* **Chez** moi. *At . . . house.*
To ask with whom: **Avec qui?**	*To tell with whom:* **Avec** Ahmed et Nathalie.
To ask at what time: **A quelle heure?**	*To tell at what time:* **A dix heures du matin.** *At ten in the morning.* **A cinq heures de l'après-midi.** *At five in the afternoon.* **A cinq heures et quart.** *At quarter past five.* **A cinq heures et demie.** *At half past five.* **Vers six heures.** *About six o'clock.*
To ask the time: **Quelle heure est-il?** *What time is it?*	*To give the time:* **Il est six heures.** *It's six o'clock.* **Il est six heures moins le quart.** *It's a quarter to six.* **Il est six heures dix.** *It's ten after six.* **Il est midi.** *It's noon.*/**Il est minuit.** *It's midnight.*

To confirm:

Bon, on se retrouve à trois heures. *OK, we'll meet . . .*
Rendez-vous mardi au café. *We'll meet . . .*
Entendu. *OK.*

24 Ecoute!

While you're waiting to use a public phone in Paris, you overhear a young woman inviting a friend to go out. Listen to the conversation and then choose the correct answers to these questions.

1. Sylvie parle **avec qui**?
   a. Marc b. Anna c. Paul
2. Elle va **où?**
   a. au musée b. au parc c. au stade
3. **A quelle heure?**
   a. 1h30 b. 10h15 c. 12h00
4. **Où** est-ce qu'ils se retrouvent?
   a. au métro Solférino b. dans un café c. devant le musée

Note Culturelle

You've already learned that train, airline, school, and other official schedules use a 24-hour system called **l'heure officielle.** When you look in an entertainment guide such as *Pariscope,* you may see that a movie starts at 20h00, which is 8:00 P.M. In everyday conversation, however, people use a 12-hour system. For example, for 1:30 P.M., you may hear, **une heure et demie de l'après-midi,** rather than **treize heures trente.** Expressions such as **et demie, et quart,** and **moins le quart** are used only in conversational time, never in official time.

25 A quelle heure?

Où est-ce que Christian et Noëlle vont aujourd'hui? Qu'est-ce qu'ils vont faire? A quelle heure?

1. 9h00

2. 12h00

3. 5h45

4. 8h30

26 Ecoute!

Listen to these three messages on your answering machine and write down who they're from and where you're being invited to go. Listen a second time and write down the meeting time and place.

27 Qu'est-ce que tu vas faire ce soir?

a. Make a list of at least three things that you're going to do tonight. Be sure to include the time and place.

b. Now, ask what your partner is going to do tonight. Then, continue to ask questions about his or her plans.

GRAMMAIRE Information questions

There are several ways to ask information questions in French.

- People often ask information questions using only a question word or phrase. They will sometimes add **ça** after the question word to make it sound less abrupt.

  Où ça?
  Quand ça?

- Another way to ask an information question is to attach the question word or phrase at the end of a statement.

  Tu vas **où?**
  Tu veux faire **quoi?**
  Tu vas au cinéma **à quelle heure?**
  Tu vas au parc **avec qui?**

- Still another way is to begin an information question with the question word or phrase, followed by **est-ce que (qu')**.

  Où est-ce que tu vas?
  Qu'est-ce que tu veux faire ce soir?
  Avec qui est-ce que tu vas au cinéma?
  A quelle heure est-ce qu'on se retrouve?

28 On va où?

Some friends are inviting you to join them. Ask questions to get more information about their plans. Complete the conversation with the appropriate words or phrases.

— Tu veux aller au cinéma?
— ______
— Demain soir.
— ______
— Vers six heures.
— ______
— Au cinéma Gaumont.
— ______
— Avec Catherine et Michel.
— D'accord!
— Bon, on se retrouve...

29 Qu'est-ce qu'on fait chez toi?

You'd like to find out more about what teenagers in France normally do. Write down at least six questions to ask your pen pal about his or her classes, activities, and hobbies.

30 Allons au cinéma!

Look at the movie schedule below. Choose a movie you want to see and invite your partner to go with you. When you've agreed on a movie to see, decide at which time you want to go and arrange a time and place to meet.

Le Beaumont **15, Bd des Italiens • 75002 PARIS**

- **Astérix chez les Bretons,** *v.f. Séances : 12h, 14h15, 16h30, 18h45, 21h00*
- **Les Randonneurs,** *v.f. Séances : 11h55, 13h55, 15h55*
- **Roméo et Juliette,** *v.f. Séances : 13h40, 16h15, 18h55, 21h30*
- **La Guerre des étoiles,** *v.o. Séances : 11h30, 14h, 16h30, 19h, 21h30*
- **Le Cinquième Elément,** *v.f. Séances : 13h30, 15h, 16h30*
- **Les 101 Dalmatiens,** *v.o. Séances : 11h05, 13h45, 16h20, 19h, 21h35*
- **Hercules,** *v.f. Séances : 21h*
- **Les Visiteurs,** *v.f. Séances : 13h30, 16h30*
- **Volcan,** *v.f. Séances : 12h30, 14h, 16h*
- **Casablanca,** *v.o. Séances : 16h30, 19h*

31 Ça te dit?

A friend has written you this note suggesting some things to do this weekend. Write an answer, accepting the invitations or making suggestions of your own.

Salut! Ça va? Tu veux faire quoi ce week-end? Moi, je voudrais faire les magasins vendredi soir et jouer au tennis samedi après-midi. On va au ciné samedi soir vers huit heures et demie. Tu viens? Et dimanche matin, tu veux aller au café? Qu'est-ce que tu en penses? Fabienne

32 Mon journal

What are you and your friends going to do during the next school vacation? Write about your plans. Tell what you're going to do, with whom, when, where, and so on

PRONONCIATION

The vowel sounds [ø] and [œ]

The vowel sound [ø] in **veux** is represented by the letter combination **eu.** It is pronounced with the lips rounded and the tongue pressed against the back of the lower front teeth. To produce this sound, first make the sound **è**, as in **algèbre,** and hold it. Then round the lips slightly to the position for closed **o**, as in **photo.** Repeat these words.

jeudi veux peu deux

The vowel sound [œ] in the word **heure** is similar to the sound in **veux** and is also represented by the letters **eu.** This sound is more open, however, and occurs when these letters are followed by a consonant sound in the same syllable. To produce this sound, first make the sound **è**, as in **algèbre**, and hold it. Then round the lips slightly to the position for open **o**, as in **short.** Repeat these words.

classeur feuille heure

A. A prononcer

Repeat the following words.

1. jeudi	déjeuner	peux
2. deux	veut	mieux
3. ordinateur	jeunes	heure
4. feuille	classeur	veulent

B. A lire

Take turns with a partner reading each of the following sentences aloud.

1. Tu as deux ordinateurs? On peut étudier chez toi jeudi?
2. Tu veux manger des escargots? C'est délicieux!
3. On va à la Maison des jeunes? A quelle heure?
4. Tu as une feuille de papier? Je n'ai pas mon classeur.

C. A écrire

You're going to hear a short dialogue. Write down what you hear.

LISONS!

Where do you like to go on the weekend? Look at these brochures to see where Parisians go for fun.

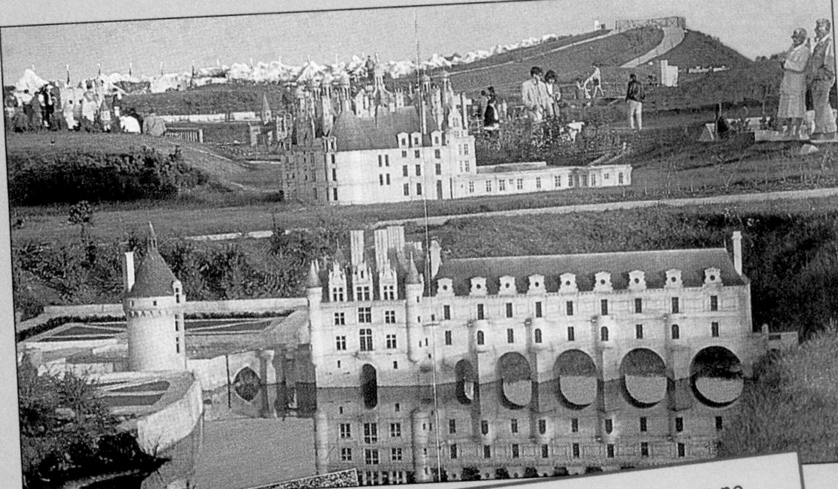

Le Pays FRANCE MINIATURE, c'est la France comme vous ne l'avez jamais vue! Sur une immense carte en relief, sont regroupées les plus belles richesses de notre patrimoine : 166 monuments historiques, 15 villages typiques de nos régions, les paysages et les scènes de la vie quotidienne à l'échelle 1/30ème... au cœur d'un environnement naturel extraordinaire.

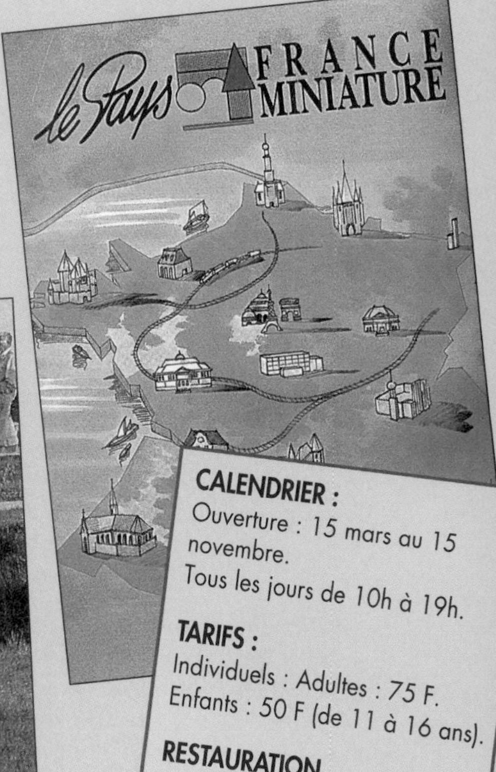

CALENDRIER :
Ouverture : 15 mars au 15 novembre.
Tous les jours de 10h à 19h.

TARIFS :
Individuels : Adultes : 75 F.
Enfants : 50 F (de 11 à 16 ans).

RESTAURATION
Deux restaurants de 300 places chacun et 2 kiosques proposent des menus de différentes régions de France (un restaurant ouvert le samedi soir). Aire de pique-nique aménagée.

DE BONS CONSEILS

When you run across a word you don't know, use context to guess the meaning of the word. You automatically use this strategy in your own language. For example, you may not know the English word *dingo,* but when you see it in a sentence, you can make an intelligent guess about what it means. Read this sentence: *He thought that the kangaroos and the koala bears were cute, but that the dingos were mean-looking.* You can guess that a *dingo* is a possibly vicious animal found in Australia. It is, in fact, a wild dog.

A. What kinds of places do these brochures describe?

B. One of your friends visited **France Miniature** and told you about it. Check the brochure to see if what he said was accurate or not.

1. "I saw more than 150 monuments!"
2. "There were twenty villages represented."
3. "The size of everything was on a scale of 1/25."
4. "It was more expensive than **Parc Astérix.**"
5. "We stayed until midnight."
6. "We went on my birthday, June 15th."

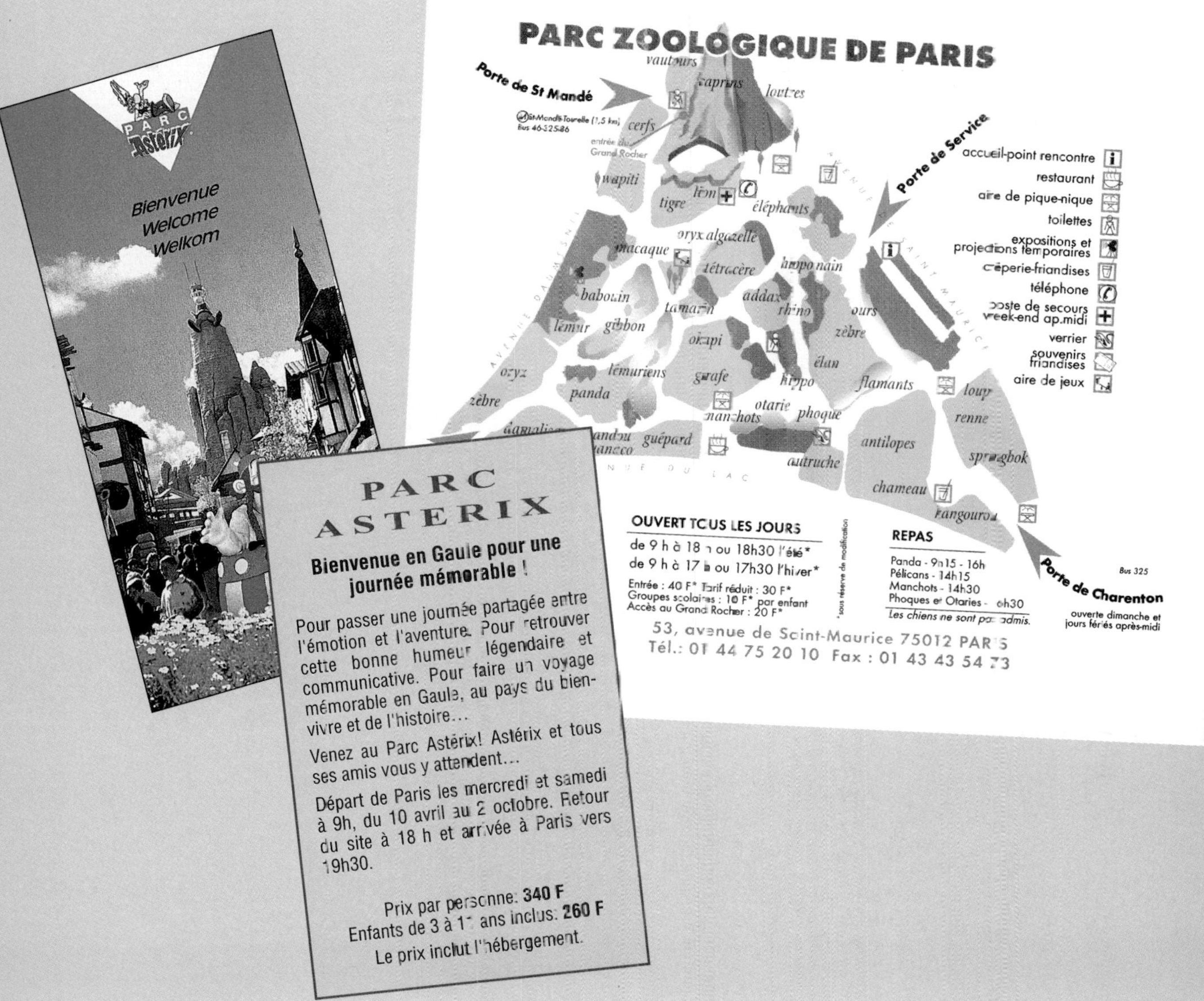

PARC ASTÉRIX
Bienvenue
Welcome
Welkom
PARC ZOOLOGIQUE DE PARIS
Porte de St Mandé
Porte de Service
accueil-point rencontre
restaurant
aire de pique-nique
toilettes
expositions et projections temporaires
crêperie-friandises
téléphone
poste de secours week-end ap.midi
verrier
souvenirs friandises
aire de jeux
wapiti
tigre
éléphants
macaque
tétracère
babouin
lémur
gibbon
okapi
girafe
zèbre
élan
flamants
panda
lémuriens
otarie
phoque
guépard
antilopes
renne
autruche
chameau
OUVERT TOUS LES JOURS
de 9 h à 18 h ou 18h30 l'été*
de 9 h à 17 h ou 17h30 l'hiver*
Entrée : 40 F* Tarif réduit : 30 F*
Groupes scolaires : 10 F* par enfant
Accès au Grand Rocher : 20 F*
* sous réserve de modification
REPAS
Panda - 9h15 - 16h
Pélicans - 14h15
Manchots - 14h30
Phoques et Otaries - 16h30
Les chiens ne sont pas admis.
Porte de Charenton
Bus 325
ouverte dimanche et jours fériés après-midi
53, avenue de Saint-Maurice 75012 PARIS
Tél.: 01 44 75 20 10 Fax : 01 43 43 54 73
PARC ASTERIX
Bienvenue en Gaule pour une journée mémorable !
Pour passer une journée partagée entre l'émotion et l'aventure. Pour retrouver cette bonne humeur légendaire et communicative. Pour faire un voyage mémorable en Gaule, au pays du bien-vivre et de l'histoire…
Venez au Parc Astérix! Astérix et tous ses amis vous y attendent…
Départ de Paris les mercredi et samedi à 9h, du 10 avril au 2 octobre. Retour du site à 18 h et arrivée à Paris vers 19h30.
Prix par personne: 340 F
Enfants de 3 à 11 ans inclus: 260 F
Le prix inclut l'hébergement.

C. Look at the brochure for **Parc Astérix** and answer the following questions.

1. During which months would you not be able to go on this trip?
2. On which days of the week can you take this trip to **Parc Astérix**?
3. If you took the trip in the advertisement, at what time would you leave Paris?
4. At what time would you leave the park for the trip back?
5. If you go with three friends and one of you brings your ten-year-old sister, how much will it cost?

D. Imagine you and a friend want to go to the **Parc zoologique de Paris.**

1. Is the park open on Sundays? Is there a restaurant?
2. How much is it going to cost? Will it make a difference if you're students?
3. How late can you stay in the summer? In the winter?
4. What are some of the animals you'll get to see?
5. At what time do the pelicans eat? The pandas?
6. How many picnic areas are there? What is near the first-aid station? Where can you buy a gift?

E. Which of these places would you like to go to most? Why?

MISE EN PRATIQUE

La tour Eiffel est le monument parisien le plus connu au monde. Elle a été construite pour l'Exposition universelle de 1889. Jusqu'à la construction de l'Empire State Building de New York en 1931, la tour Eiffel était la plus haute tour du monde avec ses 320 mètres, antenne comprise. La Tour a trois étages. Il y a un restaurant au premier et au deuxième étages. Le troisième étage offre un superbe point de vue sur la ville. Horaires : 9h30 à 23 h. Tarifs : 20 F à 56 F.

Le musée d'Orsay a été installé dans l'ancienne gare d'Orsay, construite par Victor Laloux et inaugurée en 1900 au moment de l'Exposition universelle. C'est en 1977 qu'un Conseil des ministres a décidé de transformer la gare et son hôtel en un musée consacré à la création artistique du XIXe siècle (1848-1914). Collections : Arts Décoratifs, Histoire, Littérature, Mobilier, Peinture, Photographie, Sculpture. L'intérieur a été réalisé par l'architecte italienne Gae Aulenti. 1, rue de Bellechasse, 7e. Tél. : 01 40 49 48 14. Métro : Solférino. Horaires : tous les jours sauf le lundi de 10h-18h, le jeudi jusqu'à 21h45. Tarifs : 35 F.

Notre-Dame de Paris est un chef-d'œuvre de l'art gothique français, construite entre 1163 et 1330. La façade principale est composée de trois gigantesques portails. Visite guidée et gratuite de la cathédrale tous les jours : à 12 h du lundi au vendredi, à 14h30 le samedi, à 14 h le dimanche. Visite payante des tours tous les jours de 10 h à 17h30. Concerts gratuits tous les dimanches à 17h45. Visites et ascension fermées les jours fériés. Tél : 01 42 34 56 10. Tarifs : Visite des tours : 31 F.

1 Look over the advertisements and answer the questions below.

1. Which place(s) offer(s) a view of Paris?
2. Where can you go to a free concert? On what day?
3. Are any of these places open in the evening? If so, which ones?
4. Where can you see nineteenth-century French art?
5. Which attraction is closed on holidays?
6. Which places list their prices?
7. Which attraction is closed on Mondays?
8. Which attraction costs the most to visit?
9. At which place can you buy something to eat?

2 Your French friends are discussing which Paris attraction to visit. Listen to their conversation and write down the attraction they decide on. Listen again and tell when and where they agree to meet.

3 Using what you've learned about French culture, answer the following questions.

1. Where do French teenagers like to go to have fun?
2. Would a French teenager be surprised at American dating customs? Why?

4 *Ecrivons!*

You have one day in Paris to do whatever you like. Write a note to your French class back home telling everyone what you plan to do during your day in Paris.

STRATEGIE

Arranging your ideas chronologically is helpful when planning activities for the day. To do this, take a sheet of paper, turn it sideways, and divide it into five columns. Label the first column **de 8h à 10h,** the second column **de 10h à midi,** and so on, in two-hour increments up to 6:00 in the evening. Next, decide what you would like to do at these times and write the information in the appropriate columns.

de 8h à 10h	de 10h à midi	de midi à 2h
visiter la tour Eiffel	aller au zoo	

Now, using the information from the chart you've prepared, write the note to your French class. Tell everyone what you plan to see and do throughout the day. Here are some connecting words that may help your writing flow more smoothly: **d'abord** *(first),* **ensuite** *(next),* and **après ça** *(after that).*

5 **JEU DE ROLE**

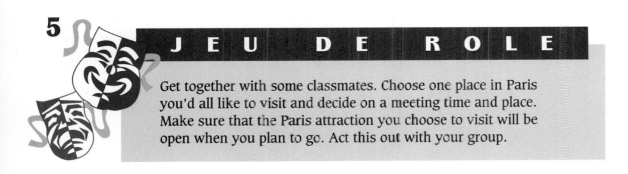

Get together with some classmates. Choose one place in Paris you'd all like to visit and decide on a meeting time and place. Make sure that the Paris attraction you choose to visit will be open when you plan to go. Act this out with your group.

QUE SAIS-JE?

Can you use what you've learned in this chapter?

Can you make plans? p. 153

1 How would you say that these people are going to these places?

1. Je

2. Nous

3. Anne et Etienne

2 How would you tell what you're planning to do this weekend?

Can you extend and respond to invitations? p. 159

3 How would you invite a friend to . . .

1. go window shopping?
2. go for a walk?
3. go see a basketball game?
4. go to the café?

4 How would you accept the following invitations? How would you refuse them?

1. Je voudrais aller faire du ski. Tu viens?
2. Allons à la Maison des jeunes!
3. On va au restaurant. Tu viens?
4. Tu veux aller au cinéma?

5 How would you say that the following people want to go to these places?

1. Ahmed

2. Isabelle et Ferdinand

3. Mon amie et moi

Can you arrange to meet someone? p. 163

6 If someone invited you to go to the movies, what are three questions you might ask to find out more information?

7 What are some possible answers to the following questions?

1. Où ça?
2. Avec qui?
3. A quelle heure?
4. Quand ça?

VOCABULAIRE

PREMIERE ETAPE

Making plans

Qu'est-ce que tu vas faire... ? *What are you going to do . . . ?*
Tu vas faire quoi...? *What are you going to do . . . ?*
Je vais... *I'm going . . .*
Pas grand-chose. *Not much.*
Rien de spécial. *Nothing special.*

Things to do

aller à une boum *to go to a party*
faire une promenade *to go for a walk*
faire un pique-nique *to have a picnic*
faire les vitrines *to window-shop*
manger quelque chose *to eat something*
regarder un match *to watch a game (on TV)*
voir un film *to see a movie*
aller voir un match *to go see a game*
voir une pièce *to see a play*

Places to go

la bibliothèque *the library*
le centre commercial *the mall*
le cinéma *the movie theater*
la Maison des jeunes et de la culture (MJC) *the recreation center*
le musée *the museum*
le parc *the park*
la piscine *the swimming pool*
la plage *the beach*
le restaurant *the restaurant*
le stade *the stadium*
le théâtre *the theater*
le zoo *the zoo*

Other useful expressions

aller *to go*
au/à la/à l'/aux *to, at*

DEUXIEME ETAPE

Extending invitations

Allons... ! *Let's go . . . !*
Tu veux... avec moi? *Do you want . . . with me?*
Tu viens? *Will you come?*
On peut... *We can . . .*

Accepting invitations

D'accord. *OK.*
Bonne idée. *Good idea.*
Je veux bien. *I'd really like to.*
Pourquoi pas? *Why not?*

Refusing invitations

Ça ne me dit rien. *I don't feel like it.*
J'ai des trucs à faire. *I've got things to do.*
Désolé(e), je ne peux pas. *Sorry, I can't.*
Désolé(e), je suis occupé(e). *Sorry, I'm busy.*

Other useful expressions

je voudrais... *I'd like . . .*
vouloir *to want*

TROISIEME ETAPE

Arranging to meet someone

Quand (ça)? *When?*
tout de suite *right away*
Où (ça)? *Where?*
dans *in*
devant *in front of*
au (métro)... *at the . . . (metro stop)*
chez... *at . . . ('s) house*
Avec qui? *With whom?*
avec... *with . . .*
A quelle heure? *At what time?*
A cinq heures. *At five o'clock.*
et demie *half past*
et quart *quarter past*
moins le quart *quarter to*
moins cinq *five to*
Quelle heure est-il? *What time is it?*
Il est midi. *It's noon.*
Il est minuit. *It's midnight.*
Il est midi (minuit) et demi. *It's half past noon (midnight).*
vers *about*
Bon, on se retrouve... *OK, we'll meet . . .*
Rendez-vous... *We'll meet . . .*
Entendu. *OK.*

Other useful expressions

ce week-end *this weekend*
demain *tomorrow*
est-ce que *(introduces a yes-no question)*

CHAPITRE

7 La famille

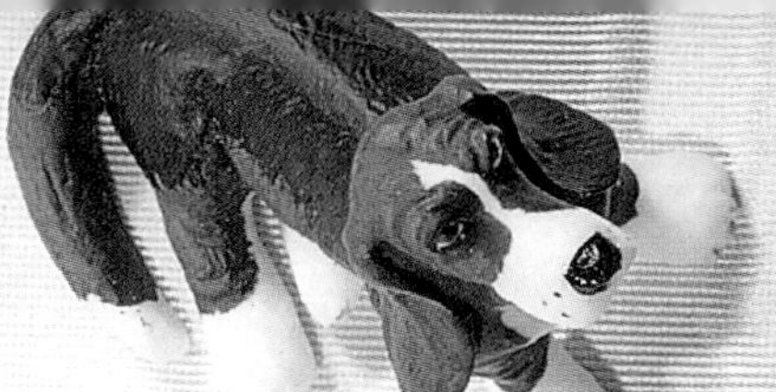

1 Je te présente mon frère Alexandre.

Families provide support and nurturing for their members. Being part of a family also involves duties and responsibilities. Do you think families in francophone cultures are different from families here in the United States?

In this chapter you will learn

- to identify and introduce people
- to describe and characterize people
- to ask for, give, and refuse permission

And you will

- listen to French-speaking teenagers talk about their families
- read magazine articles about pets
- write a description of someone you know
- find out about pets in France

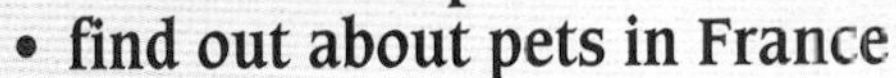

2 Ma cousine? Comment est-elle? Elle est très gentille!

3 Je peux aller au cinéma ce soir, s'il te plaît?

Mise en train

Sympa, la famille!

Look at the people pictured in the photo album. Can you guess how they're related to Isabelle?

1
Tiens, j'adore regarder les photos. Je peux les voir?
Bien sûr!

Ce sont mes grands-parents. Ils sont heureux sur cette photo. Ils fêtent leur quarantième anniversaire de mariage.

C'est une photo de papa et maman.

Là, c'est mon oncle et ma tante, le frère de ma mère et sa femme. Et au milieu, ce sont leurs enfants, mes cousins. Ils habitent tous en Bretagne. Ça, c'est Loïc. Il a 18 ans.

C'est Julie. Elle a 8 ans. Elle est adorable.

Et elle, c'est ma cousine Patricia. Elle est très intelligente. En maths, elle a toujours 18 sur 20!

Là, c'est moi. Quel amour de bébé, n'est-ce pas? Je suis toute petite... peut-être un an et demi.
5
6
C'est mon frère Alexandre. Il a 11 ans. Il est parfois pénible.
7
C'est ma tante du côté de mon père. Elle s'appelle Véronique. Ça, c'est son chat Musica. Elle adore les animaux. Elle a aussi deux chiens!
Et toi, tu n'as pas de frères ou de sœurs?
Non. Je suis fille unique.
Tu as de la chance.

1 Tu as compris?

Answer these questions about **Sympa, la famille!**

1. What are Isabelle and Thuy talking about?
2. Does Isabelle have brothers or sisters? If so, what are their names?
3. How many cousins does she have?
4. Who are some of the other family members she mentions?
5. How does Isabelle feel about her family? How can you tell?

2 Vrai ou faux?

1. Julie a huit ans.
2. Julie est blonde.
3. Les cousins d'Isabelle habitent à Paris.
4. Tante Véronique n'a pas d'animaux.
5. Thuy a un frère.

3 Quelle photo?

De quelle photo est-ce qu'Isabelle parle?

1. Il a onze ans.
2. En maths, elle a toujours 18 sur 20.
3. J'ai un an et demi, je crois...
4. Elle a huit ans.

a.

b.

c.

d.

4 Cherche les expressions

In **Sympa, la famille!**, what does Isabelle or Thuy say to . . .

1. ask permission?
2. identify family members?
3. describe someone?
4. pay a compliment?
5. tell someone's age?
6. complain about someone?

Je peux... ?
C'est...
Elle est très intelligente.
Elle est adorable.
Ce sont...
Il/Elle a... ans.
Il est parfois pénible.
Ils sont heureux.

5 Et maintenant, à toi

How does Isabelle's family resemble or differ from families you know?

PREMIERE ETAPE

Identifying and introducing people

To identify people:

C'est ma tante Véronique.
Ce sont mes cousins Loïc et Julie. *These/Those are . . .*
Voici mon frère Alexandre. *Here's . . .*
Voilà Patricia. *There's . . .*

6 C'est qui?

With a partner, take turns creating identities for the people in this picture.

Vocabulaire

Les membres de la famille d'Isabelle

Ma grand-mère et mon grand-père, Eugénie et Jean-Marie Ménard

Other family relationships:
la femme *wife*
le mari *husband*
la fille *daughter*
le fils *son*
l'enfant *child*
le parent *parent, relative*

Ma tante Véronique, la sœur de mon père

Mon père et ma mère, Raymond et Josette Guérin

Mon oncle et ma tante, Guillaume et Micheline Ménard

Mon frère Alexandre

C'est moi!

Mes cousines Patricia et Julie, et mon cousin Loïc

Mon chien

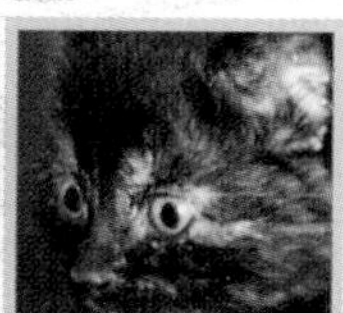

Mon chat

Mon canari

Mon poisson

7 Qui est-ce?

Which member of Isabelle's family does each of these statements refer to?

Le frère de Véronique, c'est Raymond.

1. C'est le père d'Alexandre.
2. C'est la femme de Guillaume.
3. C'est le grand-père de Julie.
4. C'est la mère de Patricia.
5. Ce sont les sœurs de Loïc.
6. C'est le cousin de Patricia.

NOTE DE GRAMMAIRE

Use **de (d')** to indicate relationship or ownership.

C'est la mère **de** Paul.
That's Paul's mother.
Voici le chien **d'**Agnès.
Here's Agnès' dog.
C'est le copain **du** prof.
That's the teacher's friend.

8 Ecoute!

Alain montre des photos de sa famille à Jay. De quelle photo est-ce qu'il parle?

a. b. c. d. e.

GRAMMAIRE Possessive adjectives

	Before a masculine singular noun		*Before a feminine singular noun*		*Before a plural noun*	
my	**mon**	frère	**ma**	sœur	**mes**	frères
your	**ton**		**ta**		**tes**	
his/her/its	**son**		**sa**		**ses**	
our	**notre**		**notre**		**nos**	
your	**votre**		**votre**		**vos**	
their	**leur**		**leur**		**leurs**	

- **Son, sa,** and **ses** may mean either *her* or *his.*
  C'est **son** père. That's *her* father. *or* That's *his* father.
  C'est **sa** mère. That's *her* mother. *or* That's *his* mother.
  Ce sont **ses** parents. Those are *her* parents. *or* Those are *his* parents.
- **Mon, ton,** and **son** are used before all singular nouns that begin with a vowel sound, whether the noun is masculine or feminine.
  C'est **ton amie** Marianne?
  C'est **mon oncle** Xavier.
- Liaison is always made with **mon, ton,** and **son,** and with all the plural forms.
  mon‿école **nos‿amis**
- Can you figure out when to use **ton, ta, tes,** and when to use **votre** and **vos?***

9 Ecoute!

Listen to Roland and Odile. Are they talking about their own pets or someone else's? Then, listen again to find out what kind of pets they're talking about.

*Use **ton, ta,** and **tes** with people you would normally address with **tu.** Use **votre** and **vos** with people you would normally address with **vous.**

Note Culturelle

Family life plays an important role in French society. Although modern times have brought changes to the family's daily life (more working mothers, less time for family activities, more divorces, and so on), France is working hard to maintain the family unit. To do this, the French government provides subsidies **(allocations familiales)** to all families with two or more children. Other social benefits also encourage larger families in a country with an ever-decreasing birth rate. These benefits include a paid maternity leave of at least 14 weeks, a renewable maternity or paternity leave of one year, free day-care, and a birth allowance **(allocation de naissance)** for every child after the second. Families also receive subsidies for each child attending school or college.

10 Ma famille française

You're showing a classmate a photo of the family you stayed with in France. Take turns with a partner identifying the people and asking questions about them.

—C'est qui, ça?
—C'est ma sœur.
—Elle joue souvent au tennis?
—Oui. Une fois par semaine.

11 Devine! *Guess!*

Identify the teenagers in the photos below and tell how you think the other people in the photos are related to them. Take turns with a partner.

C'est Nadine et son grand-père.

Nadine

Hassan

Thierry

Liliane

Monique et Annie

COMMENT DIT-ON... ?

Introducing people

To introduce someone to a friend:

C'est Jean-Michel.

Je te présente mon ami Jean-Michel.
I'd like you to meet . . .

To introduce someone to an adult:

Je vous présente Jean-Michel.

To respond to an introduction:

Salut, Jean-Michel. **Ça va?**

Bonjour.

Très heureux (heureuse). *Pleased to meet you.* (FORMAL)

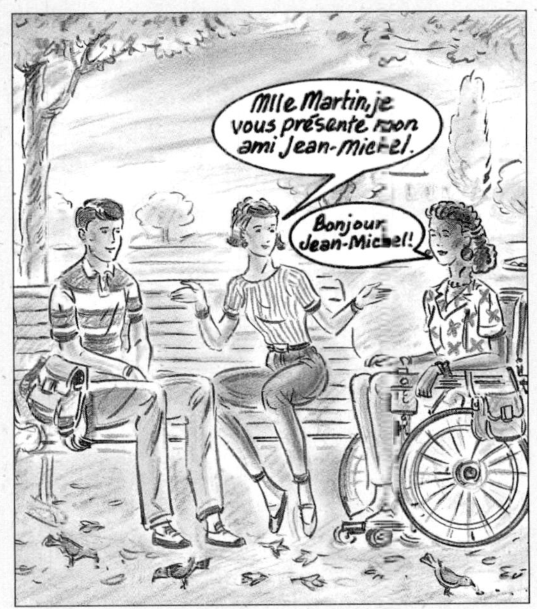

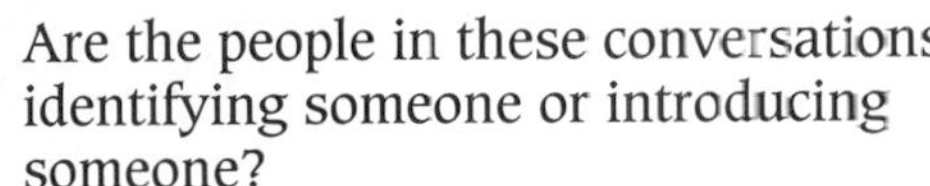

12 Ecoute!

Are the people in these conversations identifying someone or introducing someone?

13 Je te présente...

A new student from France has just arrived at your school and asks you the names and ages of some students in your class. Introduce him or her to those classmates. Act this out in your group, changing roles.

14 Mon journal

Write about your family, giving the names and ages of each person. Tell what each of them likes to do. You may choose to create an imaginary family or you may want to write about a famous family in real life or on TV.

Tu te rappelles?

Do you remember how to ask for and give people's names and ages?

—Elle s'appelle comment?
—Magali.
—Elle a quel âge?
—Seize ans.

Vocabulaire à la carte

Here are some other words you might need to talk about your family.

des petits-enfants	*grandchildren*
un demi-frère	*stepbrother; half brother*
une demi-sœur	*stepsister; half sister*
un(e) enfant unique	*an only child*
une belle-mère	*stepmother/mother-in-law*
un beau-père	*stepfather/father-in-law*
un petit-fils	*grandson*
une petite-fille	*granddaughter*
une nièce	*niece*
un neveu	*nephew*

DEUXIEME ETAPE

Describing and characterizing people

VOCABULAIRE

Ils sont comment?

You can also use these descriptive words:

mignon(mignonne)(s) *cute* **ne... ni grand(e)(s) ni petit(e)(s)** *. . . neither tall nor short*

You can use these words to characterize people:

amusant(e)(s)	*funny*	**sympathique(s)/sympa**	*nice*	**embêtant(e)(s)**	*annoying*
timide(s)	*shy*	**intelligent(e)(s)**	*smart*	**pénible(s)**	*a pain in the neck*
gentil(le)(s)	*nice*	**content(e)(s)**	*happy*	**mechant(e)(s)**	*mean*
		fort(e)(s)	*strong*		

De bons conseils

Organizing vocabulary in various ways can help you remember words. Group words by categories, like foods, sports, numbers, colors, and so forth. Try to associate words with a certain context, such as school (school subjects, classroom objects) or a store (items for sale, salesperson). Try to use associations like opposites, such as **petit—grand** or **gros—mince.**

15 Ecoute!

Match the descriptions you hear with the students' names.

Roger Denise Julie Martin Carmen

COMMENT DIT-ON... ?

Describing and characterizing people

To ask what someone is like:

Il est comment? *What is he like?*
Elle est comment? *What is she like?*
Ils/Elles sont comment? *What are they like?*

To describe someone:

Il n'est ni grand **ni** petit.
Elle est brune.
Ils/Elles sont âgé(e)s.

To characterize someone:

Il est pénible.
Elle est timide.
Ils/Elles sont amusant(e)s.

16 Ecoute!

Ariane is telling a friend about her cousins. Does she have a favorable or unfavorable opinion of them?

17 Des familles bizarres

Comment sont les membres de ces familles?

GRAMMAIRE Adjective agreement

As you may remember from Chapter 3, you often change the pronunciation and spelling of adjectives according to the nouns they describe.

- If the adjective describes a feminine noun, you usually add an **e** to the masculine form of the adjective.
- If the adjective describes a plural noun, you usually add an **s** to the singular form, masculine or feminine.
- If an adjective describes both males and females, you always use the masculine plural form.
- Some adjectives have special (irregular) feminine or plural forms. Here are some irregular adjectives that you've seen in this chapter.

Masculine	Feminine
Il est **roux.**	Elle est **rousse.**
Ils sont **roux.**	Elles sont **rousses.**
Il est **mignon.**	Elle est **mignonne.**
Ils sont **mignons.**	Elles sont **mignonnes.**
Il est **gentil.**	Elle est **gentille.**
Ils sont **gentils.**	Elles sont **gentilles.**
Il est **gros.**	Elle est **grosse.**
Ils sont **gros.**	Elles sont **grosses.**

- In the masculine forms, the final consonant sound is silent. In the feminine forms, the final consonant sound is pronounced.
- A few adjectives don't ever change. Here are some that you've already seen.

marron **orange** **cool** **super** **sympa**

18 On est différents!

Frédéric and Denise are brother and sister. Look at the picture and tell how they're alike and how they're different.

Frédéric est grand, mais Denise est petite.

19 Les meilleurs amis

Take turns with a partner describing your best friends. Tell about your friends' appearance, personality, and interests.

GRAMMAIRE The verb être

Etre is an irregular verb.

être *(to be)*

Je **suis** intelligent(e).	Nous **sommes** intelligent(e)s.
Tu **es** intelligent(e).	Vous **êtes** intelligent(e)(s).
Il/Elle/On **est** intelligent(e).	Ils/Elles **sont** intelligent(e)s.

20 On est très différents

Albain is describing everyone, including himself. Complete his descriptions with the appropriate forms of **être.**

Je __1__ blond, mais Rénato et Jacob, ils __2__ bruns. Francette et Babette, vous __3__ rousses. Et toi, Francette, tu __4__ grande aussi. Rénato aussi __5__ grand, et pénible. Babette __6__ très gentille et mignonne. Mais les différences ne __7__ pas importantes. Nous __8__ tous intelligents.

21 Devine!

Describe a member of the Louvain family to your partner, without naming the family member. He or she will try to figure out who it is. Take turns.

22 Mon journal

Write a paragraph describing a family member whom you admire. Tell what he or she likes to do and where he or she likes to go. If you prefer, choose a member of your favorite TV family and describe and characterize that person.

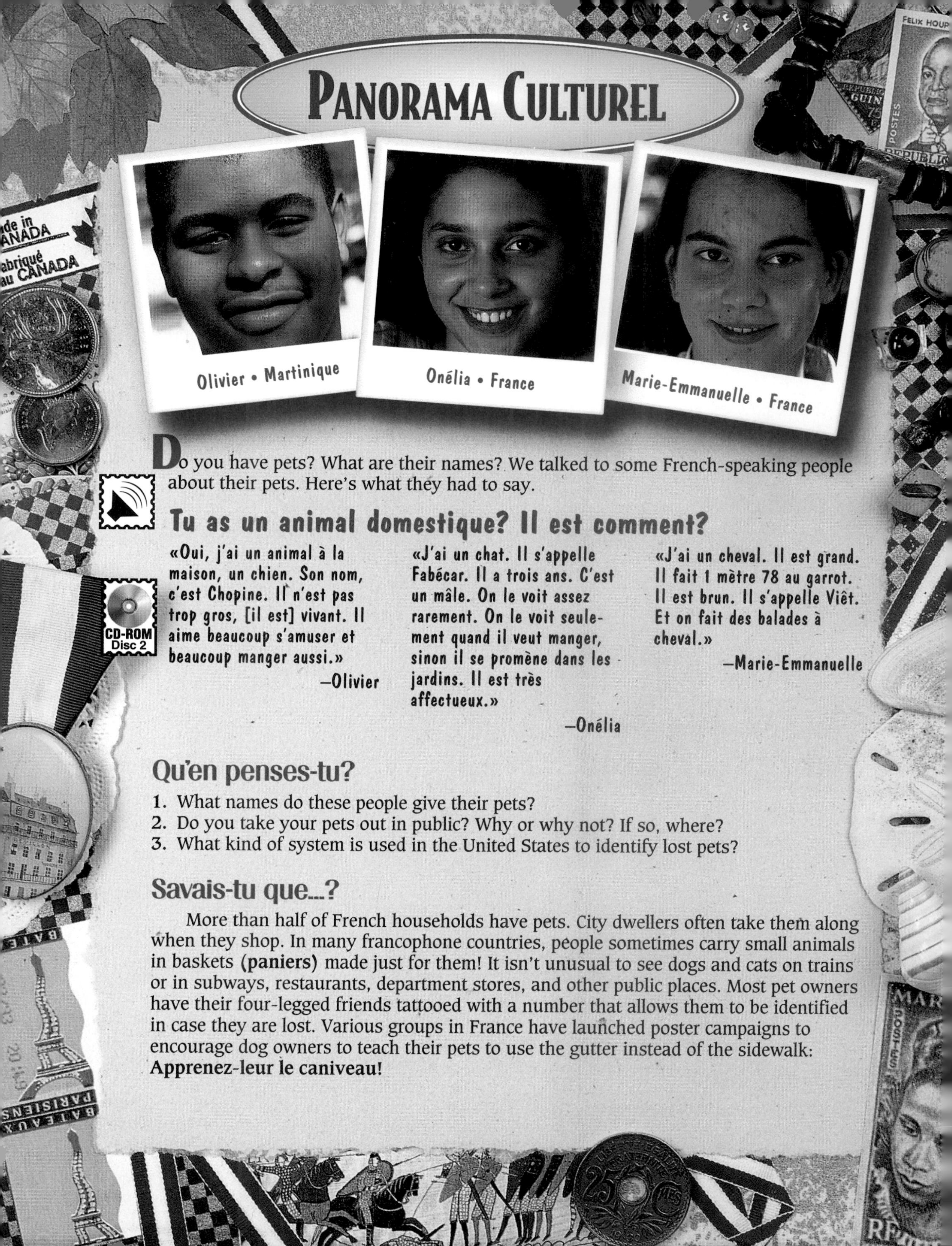

Panorama Culturel

Olivier • Martinique

Onélia • France

Marie-Emmanuelle • France

Do you have pets? What are their names? We talked to some French-speaking people about their pets. Here's what they had to say.

CD-ROM Disc 2

Tu as un animal domestique? Il est comment?

«Oui, j'ai un animal à la maison, un chien. Son nom, c'est Chopine. Il n'est pas trop gros, [il est] vivant. Il aime beaucoup s'amuser et beaucoup manger aussi.»

—Olivier

«J'ai un chat. Il s'appelle Fabécar. Il a trois ans. C'est un mâle. On le voit assez rarement. On le voit seulement quand il veut manger, sinon il se promène dans les jardins. Il est très affectueux.»

—Onélia

«J'ai un cheval. Il est grand. Il fait 1 mètre 78 au garrot. Il est brun. Il s'appelle Viêt. Et on fait des balades à cheval.»

—Marie-Emmanuelle

Qu'en penses-tu?

1. What names do these people give their pets?
2. Do you take your pets out in public? Why or why not? If so, where?
3. What kind of system is used in the United States to identify lost pets?

Savais-tu que...?

More than half of French households have pets. City dwellers often take them along when they shop. In many francophone countries, people sometimes carry small animals in baskets **(paniers)** made just for them! It isn't unusual to see dogs and cats on trains or in subways, restaurants, department stores, and other public places. Most pet owners have their four-legged friends tattooed with a number that allows them to be identified in case they are lost. Various groups in France have launched poster campaigns to encourage dog owners to teach their pets to use the gutter instead of the sidewalk: **Apprenez-leur le caniveau!**

TROISIEME ETAPE

Asking for, giving, and refusing permission

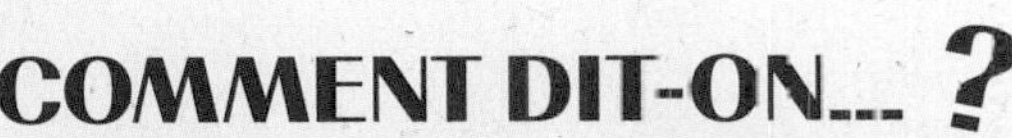

COMMENT DIT-ON... ?

Asking for, giving, and refusing permission

To ask for permission:

Je voudrais aller au cinéma. **Tu es d'accord?**
Is that OK with you?

(Est-ce que) je peux sortir? *May I . . .*

To give permission:

Oui, si tu veux. *Yes, if you want to.*

Pourquoi pas?

Oui, bien sûr.

D'accord, si tu fais **d'abord** la vaisselle.
OK, if you . . . first.

To refuse permission:

Pas question! *Out of the question!*

Non, c'est impossible. *No, that's impossible.*

Non, tu dois faire tes devoirs.
No, you've got to . . .

Pas ce soir. *Not . . .*

23 Ecoute!

Listen to these people ask for permission. Are they given or refused permission?

VOCABULAIRE

débarrasser la table	*to clear the table*
faire les courses	*to do the shopping*
faire le ménage	*to clean house*
faire la vaisselle	*to do the dishes*
garder ta petite sœur	*to look after . . .*
laver la voiture	*to wash the car*
passer l'aspirateur	*to vacuum*
promener le chien	*to walk the dog*
ranger ta chambre	*to pick up your room*
sortir la poubelle	*to take out the trash*
tondre le gazon	*to mow the lawn*

24 Ecoute!

Listen to some French teenagers ask permission to go out with their friends. Which picture represents the outcome of each dialogue?

a.

b.

c.

d.

e.

f.

25 Qui doit le faire?

Ask your partner who does various chores at his or her house. Then, change roles.

—Qui promène le chien?
—Mon frère. Et moi aussi quelquefois.

26 Qu'est-ce qu'ils disent? *What are they saying?*

1.

2.

3.

4.

27 Et toi?

Give or refuse permission in these situations.

1. Your little sister or brother asks to listen to your cassette.
2. Your friend wants to read your novel.
3. Your little sister or brother wants to go to the movies with you and your friend.

28 Jeu de rôle

Pretend you're a parent. Your partner asks permission to do several activities this weekend. Refuse permission for some, give permission for others, and give reasons. Change roles.

PRONONCIATION

The nasal sounds [ɔ̃], [ɛ̃], and [œ̃]

In Chapter 5 you learned about the nasal sound [ɑ̃]. Now listen to the other French nasal sounds [ɔ̃], [ɛ̃], and [œ̃]. As you repeat the following words, try not to put a trace of the consonant **n** in your nasal sounds.

on hein un

How are these nasal sounds represented in writing? The nasal sound [ɔ̃] is represented by a combination of **on** or **om.** Several letter combinations can represent the sound [ɛ̃], for example, **in, im, ain, aim, (i)en.** The nasal sound [œ̃] is spelled **un** or **um.** A vowel after these groups of letters or, in some cases, a doubling of the consonants **n** or **m** will result in a non-nasal sound, as in **limonade** and **ennemi**.

A. A prononcer

Repeat the following words.

1. ton	blond	pardon	nombre
2. cousin	impossible	copain	faim
3. un	lundi	brun	humble

B. A lire

Take turns with a partner reading the following sentences aloud.

1. Ils ont très faim. Ils vont prendre des sandwiches au jambon. C'est bon!
2. Allons faire du patin ou bien, allons au concert!
3. Ce garçon est blond et ce garçon-là est brun. Ils sont minces et mignons!
4. Pardon. C'est combien, cette montre? Cent soixante-quinze francs?

C. A écrire

You're going to hear a short dialogue. Write down what you hear.

LISONS!

Have you ever read an article about animals in an American magazine or newspaper? Here are some articles that appeared in the French magazine *Femme Actuelle.*

DE BONS CONSEILS When you read something, it's important to separate the main idea from the supporting details. Sometimes the main idea is clearly stated at the beginning, other times it's just implied.

A. Which completion best expresses the main idea of these articles?

These articles are about . . .

1. animals that are missing.
2. animals that have performed heroic rescues.
3. animals that are up for adoption.
4. animals that have won prizes at cat and dog shows.

B. Now that you've decided what the main idea of the reading is, make a list of the kinds of details you expect to find in each of the articles.

C. How is Mayo different from the other animals? What is the main idea of the article about him? What other details are given?

D. Each of the articles includes a description of the animal. Look at the articles again and answer these questions.

1. Which animal is the oldest? The youngest?
2. Which animals get along well with children?

EN DIRECT DES REFUGES

Cet animal vous attend au refuge de la Société normande de protection aux animaux, 7 bis, avenue Jacques-Chastellain, Ile Lacroix 76000 Rouen. Tél.: (02) 35.70.20.36. Si Camel a été adopté, pensez à ses voisins de cage.

IL VOUS ATTEND, ADOPTEZ-LE

CAMEL, 5 ANS

Ce sympathique bobtail blanc et gris est arrivé au refuge à la suite du décès accidentel de son maître. Il est vif, joyeux, a bon caractère et s'entend très bien avec les enfants. En échange de son dévouement et de sa fidélité, ce sportif robuste demande un grand espace afin de pouvoir courir et s'ébattre à son aise.

Continuez à nous écrire, et envoyez-nous votre photo avec votre protégé, une surprise vous attend!

Cet animal vous attend au refuge de l'Eden, Rod A'char, 29430 Lanhouarneau. Tél.: (02) 98.61.64.55. Colette Di Faostino tient seule, sans aucune subvention, ce havre exemplaire mais pauvre. Si Dady avait été adoptée, pensez à ses compagnons de malchance !

ELLE VOUS ATTEND, ADOPTEZ-LA

DADY, 2 ANS

Toute blanche, à l'exception de quelques petites taches et des oreilles noires bien dressées, Dady a un petit air de spitz, opulente fourrure en moins. Gentille, enjouée, très attachante, elle a été abandonnée après la séparation de ses maîtres et attend une famille qui accepterait de s'occuper d'elle un peu, beaucoup, passionnément.

Mayo a trouvé une famille

Mayo a été adopté à la SPA de Valenciennes par Françoise Robeaux qui rêvait d'un chat gris ! Il a ainsi rejoint l'autre «fils» de la famille, un superbe siamois âgé de 13 ans.

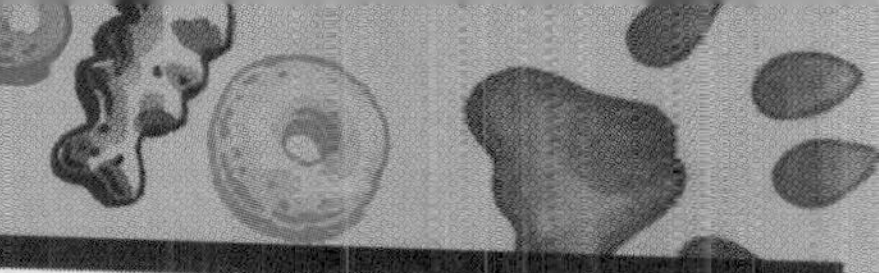

ELLE VOUS ATTEND, ADOPTEZ-LA

POUPETTE, 3 ANS

Cette jolie chatte stérilisée au regard tendre et étonné a été recueillie à l'âge de quelques semaines par une vieille dame, dont elle a été la dernière compagne. Sa maîtresse est malheureusement décédée après un long séjour à l'hôpital. Poupette, l'orpheline, ne comprend pas ce qui lui arrive et commence à trouver le temps long ! Elle a hâte de retrouver un foyer «sympa», des bras caressants et une paire de genoux pour ronronner.

Cet animal vous attend avec espoir au refuge Grammont de la SPA 30, av. du Général-de-Gaulle 92230 Gennevilliers. Tél.: (01) 47.98.57.40. Rens. sur Minitel: 36.15 SPA. Si Poupette est déjà partie, pensez aux autres!

IL VOUS ATTEND, ADOPTEZ-LE

JUPITER, 7 MOIS

Cet adorable chaton tigré et blanc vient tout juste d'être castré et est dûment tatoué. Très joueur et affectueux, il a été recueilli au refuge parce que, malheureusement, sa maîtresse a dû être hospitalisée pour un séjour de longue durée. Sociable, il s'entend très bien avec les jeunes enfants et accepterait volontiers un chien pour compagnon.

Cet animal vous attend au refuge de la fondation Assistance aux animaux, 8, rue des Plantes 77410 Villevaudé. Tél.: (01) 60.26.20.48 (l'après-midi seulement).

ELLE VOUS ATTEND, ADOPTEZ-LA

FLORA, 3 ANS

C'est une pure braque Saint Germain roux et blanc. Elle ne pense qu'à jouer, s'entend bien avec les enfants et témoigne d'une gentillesse infatigable. Flora a été abandonnée car elle ne s'intéressait pas à la chasse. Son sport passion : la course derrière la «baballe».

Elle vous attend au refuge de l'Eden, Rod A'char, 29430 Lanhouarneau. Tél.: (02) 98.61.64.55. Colette Di Faostino tient seule, sans aucune subvention, ce havre exemplaire mais pauvre. Si Flora est adoptée, pensez à ses compagnons !

Vous avez recueilli un animal par notre intermédiaire ? Envoyez-nous votre photo avec votre protégé, une surprise vous attend!

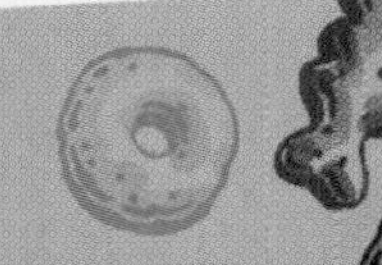

3. Which animal needs a lot of space?
4. Which animals love to play?

E. Make a list of all the adjectives of physical description that you can find in the articles. Now, list the adjectives that describe the animals' characteristics.

F. Each article also explains why these animals were sent to the animal shelter.

1. Which animal wasn't interested in hunting?
2. Whose owner was involved in an accident?
3. Whose owner had to go to the hospital for a long time?
4. Whose family got separated?

G. A third kind of detail tells where you can go to adopt these animals. Can you find the French word for *animal shelter*?

H. Now, write your own classified ad to try to find a home for a lost pet. Remember to give the animal's name and age, tell what the animal looks like, and describe his or her character.

or

Write a letter to the animal shelter telling them what kind of pet you would like to adopt.

1. First, make a list of all of the characteristics you're looking for in a pet. Will you choose to adopt a cat or a dog? What will he or she look like? Act like? Like to do?
2. Write a short letter, including all the important information about your desired pet.
3. Don't forget to give your address and telephone number!

ouah - ouah

MISE EN PRATIQUE

1 Ecoute Nathalie qui va te parler de sa famille. Puis, réponds aux questions.

1. Comment s'appelle le frère de Nathalie?
2. Il a quel âge?
3. Est-ce qu'elle a un chien ou un chat?
4. Comment est son animal?

2 Skim these documents. Then, read them more thoroughly and answer the questions below.

1. What kind of document is this? How do you know?
2. Who is Michel Louis Raymond?
3. Who are Denise Morel-Tissot and Raymond Tissot?
4. What happened on May 20, 1999?

Nous avons la joie
de vous annoncer la naissance
de notre fils

Michel Louis Raymond
20 mai 1999

Denise Morel-Tissot
Raymond Tissot

Christelle et Nicolas

ont le plaisir de vous faire part de leur mariage

qui aura lieu le treize février 1999 à 15 heures, en la Mairie de Saint-Cyr-sur-Loire

M. et Mme Lionel Desombre
305 Rue des Marronniers
37540 Saint-Cyr-sur-Loire

5. What kind of document is this? How do you know?
6. Who are Christelle and Nicolas?
7. What happened on February 13, 1999, at three o'clock?
8. Who do you think M. and Mme Lionel Desombre are?

3 Are the following sentences representative of French culture, American culture, or both?

1. Dogs are not allowed in restaurants or department stores.
2. The government gives money to all families with two or more children.
3. Pets are tattooed with an identification number.
4. Women have a paid maternity leave of 14 weeks.

4 *Ecrivons!*

Write a paragraph describing the family in the picture. Give French names to all the family members, tell their ages, give brief physical descriptions, say something about their personalities, and mention one or two things they each like to do.

A cluster diagram, like the one you created in Chapter 3, will help you organize your thoughts. Make a large circle for each family member, then attach smaller circles for age, physical description, and so on.

STRATEGIE

Using details to describe people will enable you to help your reader develop a clearer mental picture of what you're writing about. The more detailed the writing, the sharper the mental image the reader gets of the subject.

Using the information you organized in your cluster diagram, write a paragraph describing the family in the picture. Imagine that your readers have never seen this picture before. After reading your paragraph, they should feel as if they know the members of the family personally. Be sure to use descriptive words you learned in this chapter, but remember those you've learned in previous chapters as well!

5

JEU DE ROLE

Your friends arrive at your door and suggest that you go out with them. Your parent tells them that you can go out if you finish your chores, so your friends offer to help. As you work around the house, you discuss where to go and what to do. Create a conversation with your classmates. Be prepared to act out the scene, using props.

QUE SAIS-JE?

Can you use what you've learned in this chapter?

Can you identify people? p. 179

1 How would you point out and identify Isabelle's relatives? How would you give their names and approximate ages? See page 180.

1. her grandparents
2. her uncle
3. her cousin Loïc
4. her brother

Can you introduce people? p. 183

2 How would you introduce your friend to . . .

1. an adult relative?
2. a classmate?

Can you describe and characterize people? p. 185

3 How would you describe these people?

1.

2.

4 How would you . . .

1. tell a friend that he or she is nice?
2. tell several friends that they're annoying?
3. say that you and your friend are intelligent?

Can you ask for, give, and refuse permission? p. 189

5 How would you ask permission to . . .

1. go to the movies?
2. go out with your friends?
3. go shopping?
4. go ice-skating?

6 How would you give someone permission to do something? How would you refuse?

7 What are three things your parents might ask you to do before allowing you to go out with your friends?

VOCABULAIRE

PREMIERE ETAPE

Identifying people

C'est... *This/That is . . .*
Ce sont... *These/those are . . .*
Voici... *Here's . . .*
Voilà... *There's . . .*

Family members

la famille *family*
le grand-père *grandfather*
la grand-mère *grandmother*
la mère *mother*
le père *father*
le parent *parent, relative*
la femme *wife*
le mari *husband*
la sœur *sister*
le frère *brother*
la fille *daughter*
le fils *son*
l'enfant (m./f.) *child*
l'oncle (m.) *uncle*
la tante *aunt*
la cousine *girl cousin*
le cousin *boy cousin*
le chat *cat*
le chien *dog*
le canari *canary*
le poisson *fish*

Possessive adjectives

mon/ma/mes *my*
ton/ta/tes *your*
son/sa/ses *his, her*
notre/nos *our*
votre/vos *your*
leur/leurs *their*

Introducing people

C'est... *This is . . .*
Je te/vous présente... *I'd like you to meet . . .*
Très heureux (heureuse). *Pleased to meet you.* (FORMAL)

Other useful expressions

de *of (indicates relationship or ownership)*

DEUXIEME ETAPE

Describing and characterizing people

Il est comment? *What is he like?*
Elle est comment? *What is she like?*
Ils/Elles sont comment? *What are they like?*
Il est... *He is . . .*
Elle est... *She is . . .*
Ils/Elles sont... *They're . . .*
amusant(e) *funny*
content(e) *happy*
embêtant(e) *annoying*
fort(e) *strong*
gentil (gentille) *nice*
intelligent(e) *smart*
méchant(e) *mean*
pénible *annoying; a pain in the neck*
sympa(thique) *nice*
timide *shy*
âgé(e) *older*
blond(e) *blond*
brun(e) *brunette*
grand(e) *tall*
gros (grosse) *fat*
jeune *young*
mince *slender*
mignon (mignonne) *cute*
ne... ni grand(e) ni petit(e) *neither tall nor short*
petit(e) *short*
roux (rousse) *redheaded*
être *to be*

TROISIEME ETAPE

Asking for, giving, and refusing permission

Tu es d'accord? *Is that OK with you?*
(Est-ce que) je peux... ? *May I . . . ?*
Oui, si tu veux. *Yes, if you want to.*
Pourquoi pas? *Why not?*
Oui, bien sûr. *Yes, of course.*
D'accord, si tu... d'abord... *OK, if you . . . first.*
Pas question! *Out of the question!*
Non, c'est impossible. *No, that's impossible.*
Non, tu dois... *No, you've got to . . .*
Pas ce soir. *Not tonight.*

Chores

débarrasser la table *to clear the table*
faire la vaisselle *to do the dishes*
faire le ménage *to do housework*
faire les courses *to do the shopping*
garder... *to look after . . .*
laver la voiture *to wash the car*
passer l'aspirateur *to vacuum*
promener le chien *to walk the dog*
ranger ta chambre *to pick up your room*
sortir la poubelle *to take out the trash*
tondre le gazon *to mow the lawn*

CHAPITRE 8

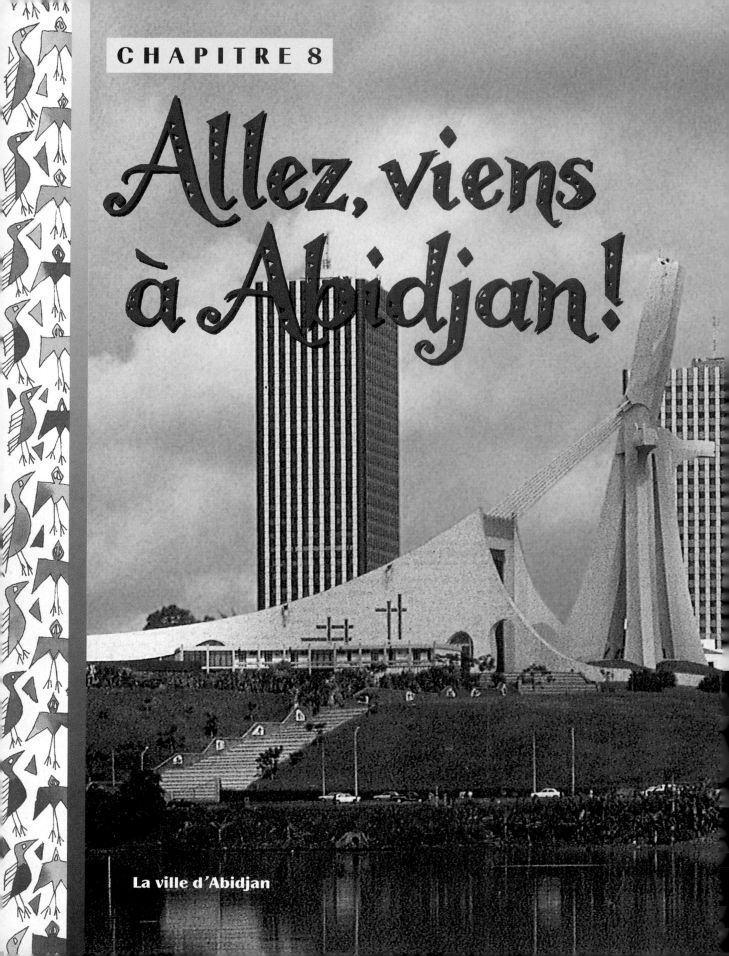

Allez, viens à Abidjan!

La ville d'Abidjan

Abidjan

Ville principale de la République de Côte d'Ivoire

Population : plus de 2.100.000

Points d'intérêt : l'Assemblée nationale, le palais du Président, le parc national du Banco, le Musée national

Abidjanais célèbres : Bernard Dadié, Goffi Jadeau, Amon d'Aby, Abdoulaye Traoré

Ressources et industries : café, cacao, bananes, textiles, bois

Spécialités : foutou, aloco, kedjenou, attiéké, sauce arachide, sauce graine, sauce claire

Abidjan

*Abidjan is a modern city that lies on the **baie de Cocody** in Côte d'Ivoire. It is a bustling metropolitan area sometimes called the "melting pot of Africa." The office buildings and hotels of **Le Plateau** contrast sharply with the lively and colorful district of **Treichville,** the cultural heart of Abidjan.*

(1) Côte d'Ivoire is famous for its brightly colored fabrics and weavings.

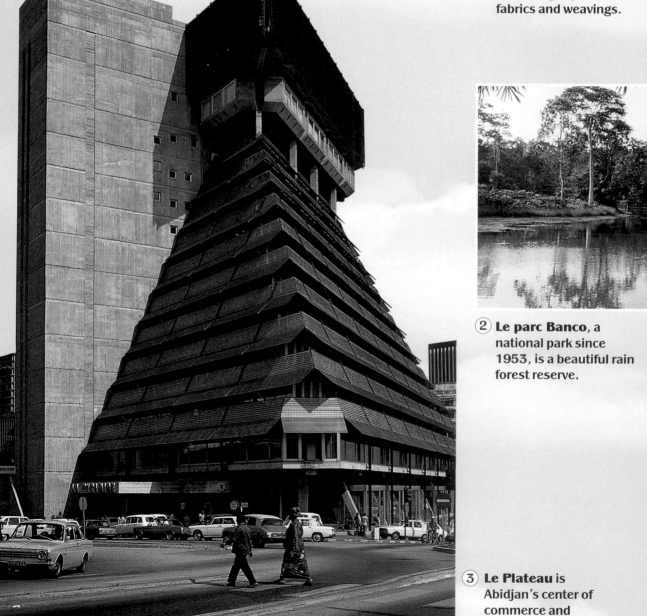

(2) **Le parc Banco**, a national park since 1953, is a beautiful rain forest reserve.

(3) **Le Plateau** is Abidjan's center of commerce and government.

④ The port of **Adjamé** is one of the busiest in West Africa.

⑤ Many different kinds of traditional masks are displayed in the National Museum in Abidjan.

⑥ **Treichville** is the main shopping district of Abidjan. The combination of colors, sounds, and aromas of this lively quarter of town will awaken all the senses.

CHAPITRE

8 Au marché

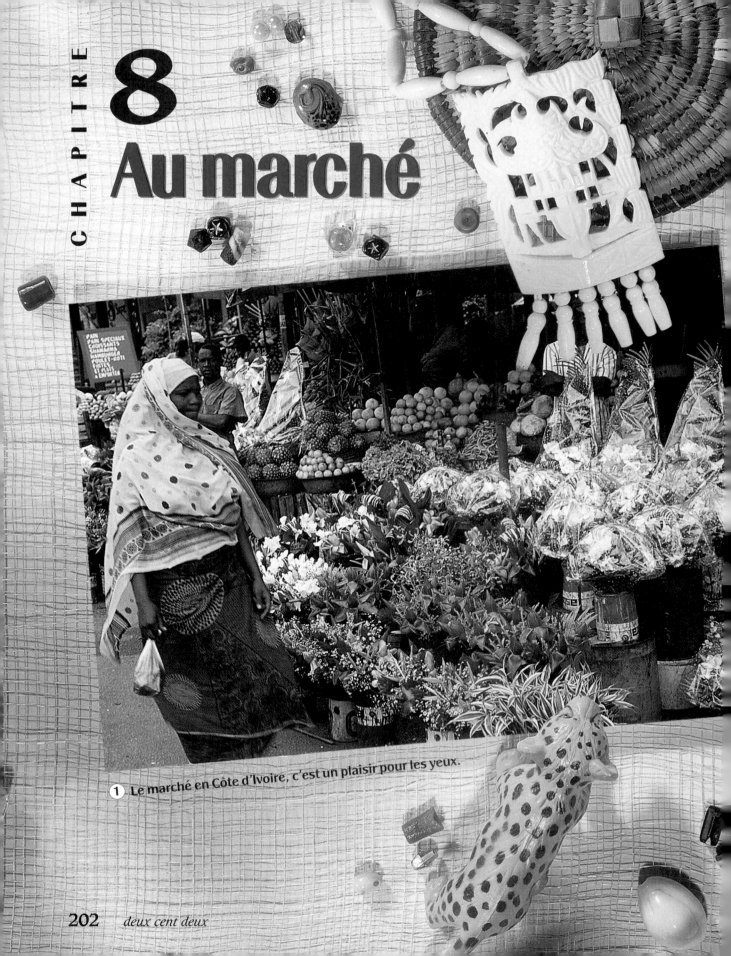

1 Le marché en Côte d'Ivoire, c'est un plaisir pour les yeux.

Imagine shopping for food in the Republic of Côte d'Ivoire—the tropical fruits, lively marketplace, and Ivorian merchants would make it an adventure. You'd also gain experience with the metric system and the currency of francophone Africa, *le franc de la Communauté financière africaine (CFA)*.

In this chapter you will learn

- to express need
- to make, accept, and decline requests; to tell someone what to do
- to offer, accept, or refuse food

And you will

- listen to French-speaking people talk about the foods they like
- read recipes for African dishes
- write about your favorite and least favorite foods
- find out about the metric system of weights and measures

2 Tu me rapportes des fruits?

3 Tiens, Djeneba, tu peux m'aider?

Mise en train

Une invitée pour le déjeuner

Djeneba

Mme Diomandé

Aminata

Where does Djeneba go to do the grocery shopping?
Do you recognize any of the food items she buys?

Le matin chez les Diomandé, à Abidjan. C'est l'heure du petit déjeuner.

1 kilo de riz
250 grammes de pâte d'arachide
1 poisson
7 oignons
1 douzaine de tomates
3 citrons
un paquet de beurre
du pain

Plus tard...

...puis, elle rentre chez elle.

Mme Diomandé fait la cuisine.

Toc toc toc!

9

Ah, j'ai oublié... Devine qui j'ai vu au marché.

Aucune idée... Va voir qui est à la porte.

1 Tu as compris?

1. What time of day is it?
2. What does Mme Diomandé want Djeneba to do? Why?
3. What are some of the things Djeneba buys?
4. What happens at the end of the story?
5. Judging from the story title, what do you think Djeneba forgot to tell Mme Diomandé?

2 Vrai ou faux?

1. Aminata va au marché.
2. Mme Diomandé va faire du foutou avec de la sauce arachide.
3. Djeneba ne veut pas aller au marché.
4. Djeneba achète des bananes au marché.
5. Djeneba oublie *(forgets)* le pain.

3 Choisis la photo

Match the foods that Djeneba bought with their pictures.

1. du poisson 2. des tomates 3. des oignons 4. des citrons 5. du pain

a.

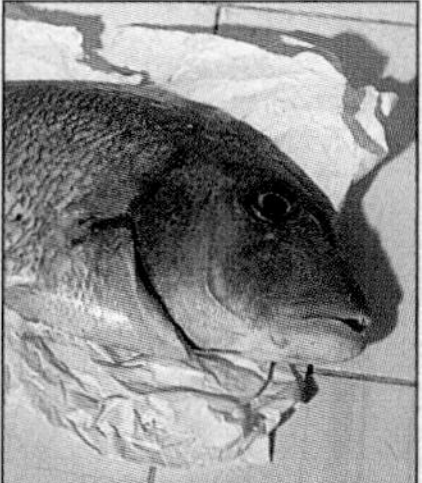
b.

c.

d.

e.

4 C'est qui?

1. «Non, merci. Je n'ai plus faim.»
2. «Tu me fais le marché?»
3. «J'ai aussi acheté un paquet de beurre, de la pâte de tomates, du pain et du riz.»
4. «Ah, j'ai oublié... »
5. «Va voir qui est à la porte.»

5 Cherche les expressions

In **Une invitée pour le déjeuner**, how does . . .

1. Mme Diomandé offer more food to Aminata?
2. Aminata refuse the offer?
3. Mme Diomandé ask Djeneba to do the shopping?
4. Mme Diomandé tell Djeneba what she needs?
5. Djeneba agree to do what Mme Diomandé asks?

Volontiers! Tu me fais le marché?
Non, merci. Je n'ai plus faim.
Bon, d'accord. Il me faut...
Encore du pain?

6 Et maintenant, à toi

Who does the grocery shopping in your family? Where do they do the shopping?

PREMIERE ETAPE

Expressing need

VOCABULAIRE

Qu'est-ce qu'on trouve **au marché? Au supermarché?**

Légumes

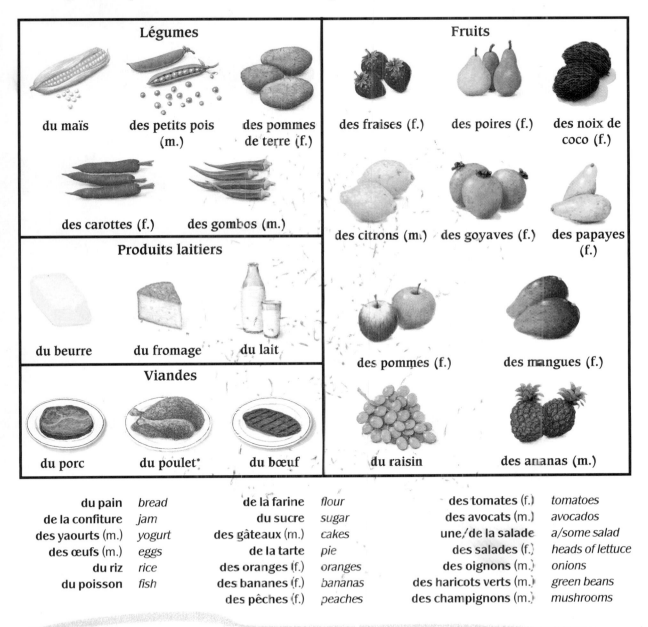

du maïs — **des petits pois (m.)** — **des pommes de terre (f.)** — **des carottes (f.)** — **des gombos (m.)**

Produits laitiers

du beurre — **du fromage** — **du lait**

Viandes

du porc — **du poulet*** — **du bœuf**

Fruits

des fraises (f.) — **des poires (f.)** — **des noix de coco (f.)** — **des citrons (m.)** — **des goyaves (f.)** — **des papayes (f.)** — **des pommes (f.)** — **des mangues (f.)** — **du raisin** — **des ananas (m.)**

du pain	*bread*	**de la farine**	*flour*	**des tomates** (f.)	*tomatoes*
de la confiture	*jam*	**du sucre**	*sugar*	**des avocats** (m.)	*avocados*
des yaourts (m.)	*yogurt*	**des gâteaux** (m.)	*cakes*	**une/de la salade**	*a/some salad*
des œufs (m.)	*eggs*	**de la tarte**	*pie*	**des salades** (f.)	*heads of lettuce*
du riz	*rice*	**des oranges** (f.)	*oranges*	**des oignons** (m.)	*onions*
du poisson	*fish*	**des bananes** (f.)	*bananas*	**des haricots verts** (m.)	*green beans*
		des pêches (f.)	*peaches*	**des champignons** (m.)	*mushrooms*

* **Poule** usually refers to live chickens, while **poulet** usually refers to chicken as a food item.

7 Ecoute!

Listen to the dialogues and decide if the people are talking about fruit, vegetables, fish, or poultry.

GRAMMAIRE The partitive and indefinite articles

You already know how to use **un** and **une** with singular nouns and **des** with plural nouns. Use **du, de la, de l'**, or **des** to indicate *some of* or *part of* something.

Je voudrais **du** gâteau.
Tu veux **de la** salade?
Elle va prendre **de** l'eau minérale.
Il me faut **des** oranges.

- If you want to talk about a whole item, use the indefinite articles **un** and **une.**

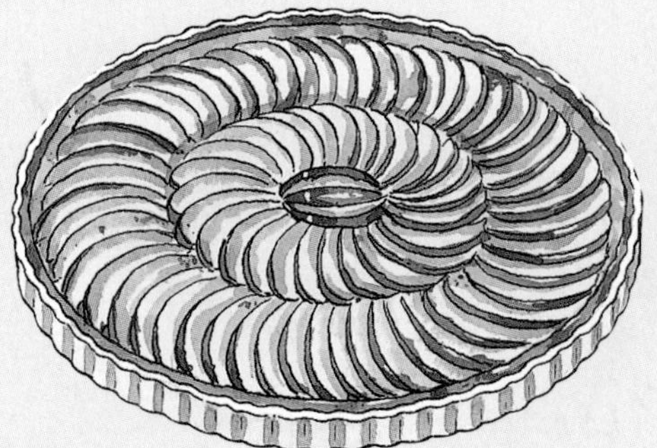

Il achète **une** tarte.

Il prend **de la** tarte.

- In a negative sentence, **du, de la, de l'**, and **des** change to **de/d'** *(none* or *any).*

—Tu as **du** pain?
—Désolée, je n'ai pas **de** pain.

—Tu prends **de la** viande?
—Merci, je ne prends jamais **de** viande.

- You can't leave out the article in French as you do in English.
  Elle mange **du** fromage. *She's eating cheese.*

8 Qu'est-ce qu'on mange?

Complète ce dialogue avec du, de la, de l', de, d', ou des.

ASSIKA Dis, maman, qu'est-ce qu'on mange à midi? J'ai très faim!
MAMAN __1__ poisson, __2__ riz et __3__ haricots verts.
ASSIKA Est-ce qu'on a encore __4__ pain?
MAMAN Non. Et on n'a pas __5__ bananes non plus. Est-ce que tu peux aller en acheter?
ASSIKA Bon, d'accord. C'est tout?
MAMAN Non. Prends aussi __6__ yaourts, __7__ farine et __8__ sucre. Je vais faire un gâteau pour ce soir.
ASSIKA Super!
MAMAN Merci, ma chérie.

9 Qu'est-ce qu'elles achètent?

What are Prisca, Clémentine, and Adjoua buying at the market?

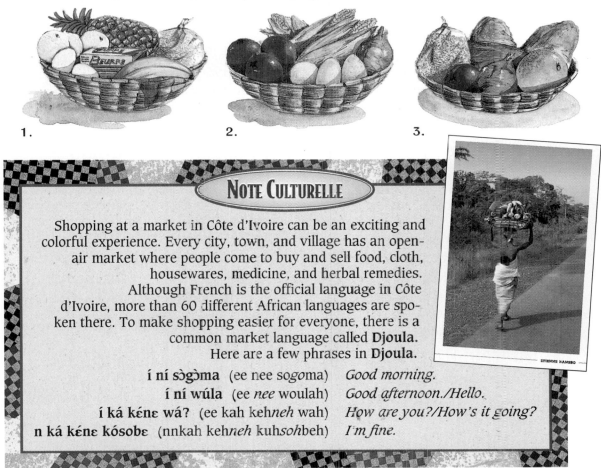

1.

2.

3.

NOTE CULTURELLE

Shopping at a market in Côte d'Ivoire can be an exciting and colorful experience. Every city, town, and village has an open-air market where people come to buy and sell food, cloth, housewares, medicine, and herbal remedies.

Although French is the official language in Côte d'Ivoire, more than 60 different African languages are spoken there. To make shopping easier for everyone, there is a common market language called **Djoula.** Here are a few phrases in **Djoula.**

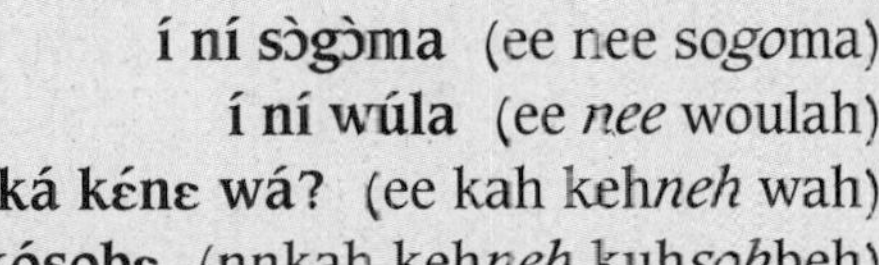

í ní sɔ̀gɔ̀ma	(ee nee sogoma)	*Good morning.*
í ní wúla	(ee *nee* woulah)	*Good afternoon./Hello.*
í ká kɛ́nɛ wá?	(ee kah keh*neh* wah)	*How are you?/How's it going?*
n ká kɛ́nɛ kósobɛ	(nnkah keh*neh* kuh*soh*beh)	*I'm fine.*

ETIENNE NANGBO

10 Qu'est-ce qu'il y a dans le chariot?

Your partner has mixed his or her shopping cart with five others whose contents are listed below. Ask about the contents until you have enough information to guess which cart belongs to your partner. Then, change roles.

— Tu as acheté des tomates? — Non.
— Tu as acheté du poisson? — Oui.
— Ton chariot, c'est le numéro... ? — Oui.

1. du poisson
   des tomates
   des bananes
   du fromage
   du lait
2. du pain
   des œufs
   des oignons
   du poisson
   des haricots verts
3. du sucre
   des ananas
   du lait
   du maïs
   des tomates
4. des tomates
   des haricots verts
   des œufs
   du sucre
   du maïs
5. des ananas
   des bananes
   du fromage
   des oignons
   des haricots verts
6. des bananes
   des œufs
   du poisson
   du pain
   des tomates

COMMENT DIT-ON... ?
Expressing need

— **Qu'est-ce qu'il te faut?**
— **Il me faut** des bananes, du riz et de l'eau minérale.

— **De quoi est-ce que tu as besoin?** *What do you need?*
— **J'ai besoin de** riz pour faire du foutou. *I need . . .*

NOTE DE GRAMMAIRE

The expression **avoir besoin de** can be followed by a noun or a verb. The partitive article is not used with this expression.

Tu **as besoin de** tomates?
Nous **avons besoin d'**œufs pour l'omelette.
J'**ai besoin d'**aller au marché.

A la française

Many French expressions involve foods: **On est dans la purée** *(We're in trouble)*; **C'est pas de la tarte** *(It's not easy)*. Can you guess what **C'est du gâteau** means? *

Vocabulaire à la carte

Here are some additional words you may want to know:

du concombre	*cucumber*
des cornichons (m.)	*pickles*
de la mayonnaise	*mayonnaise*
de la moutarde	*mustard*
des noix (f.)	*nuts*
du poivre	*pepper*
du sel	*salt*

11 Que faut-il?

Tu as besoin de quoi pour faire...

1. un bon sandwich?
2. une quiche?
3. une salade?
4. une salade de fruits?
5. un banana split?

12 Un repas entre amis

Sandrine is having a party, but she's keeping the menu a secret. Based on what she needs, try to guess what she's preparing.

1. J'ai besoin de salade, de tomates, de carottes, d'oignons...
2. J'ai besoin de fromage, de pain, de jambon...
3. J'ai besoin d'œufs, de champignons, de fromage, de lait...
4. J'ai besoin de bananes, de pommes, d'oranges...

une tarte aux pommes
un banana split
une salade de fruits
un sandwich
une salade
une omelette

13 De quoi est-ce que tu as besoin?

You're going to cook a special meal for your host family. Decide what you want to make. Then, go to the market and buy what you need. Take turns with a partner playing the role of the merchant.

* It means *It's easy; it's a piece of cake.*

PANORAMA CULTUREL

Louise • France

Angèle • Côte d'Ivoire

Micheline • Belgique

Where does your family go to shop for groceries? People in francophone countries have several options. We asked these people where they shop. Here's what they had to say.

CD-ROM Disc 2

Où est-ce que tu aimes faire des provisions?

«Je vais le plus souvent au supermarché, mais je préfère le marché, parce que le marché, c'est dehors et puis, l'ambiance est meilleure.»

—Louise

«Je préfère aller au supermarché pour aller faire des achats parce que là-bas, c'est plus sûr et bien conservé.»

—Angèle

«Je préfère aller au marché, chez les petits commerçants, parce qu'il y a le contact personnel, il y a le choix, il y a les odeurs, les couleurs, le plaisir de la promenade aussi dans le marché.»

—Micheline

Qu'en penses-tu?

1. Where do these people shop for groceries?
2. What are the advantages and disadvantages of shopping in these different places?
3. Are there outdoor farmers' markets in your community? What can you buy there?
4. Does your family sometimes shop in small specialty stores? If so, what do they buy there?

Savais-tu que... ?

Many people in francophone countries grocery shop in supermarkets (**supermarchés**) or hypermarkets (**hypermarchés**) because it's convenient. Others prefer to shop in small grocery stores (**épiceries**) or outdoor markets (**marchés en plein air**). **Supermarchés** are similar to their American counterparts. **Hypermarchés** are very large stores that carry just about anything you can imagine—all under one roof! Americans may be surprised to learn, however, that stores are not open 24 hours a day or even late in the evening. **Epiceries** are usually closed between 12:30 P.M. and 4 P.M. and all day on either Sunday or Monday.

DEUXIEME ETAPE

Making, accepting, and declining requests; telling someone what to do

COMMENT DIT-ON... ?

Making, accepting, and declining requests; telling someone what to do

To make requests:

Tu peux aller faire les courses?
Can you . . . ?

Tu me rapportes des œufs?
Will you bring me . . . ?

To tell someone what to do:

Rapporte(-moi) du beurre.
Bring (me) back . . .

Prends du lait. *Get . . .*

Achète(-moi) du riz. *Buy (me) . . .*

N'oublie pas d'acheter le lait.
Don't forget to . . .

To accept:

Pourquoi pas?

Bon, d'accord.

Je veux bien. *Gladly.*

J'y vais tout de suite.
I'll go right away.

To decline:

Je ne peux pas maintenant.

Je regrette, mais je n'ai pas le temps. *I'm sorry, but I don't have time.*

J'ai des trucs à faire.

J'ai des tas de choses à faire.

14 Ecoute!

a. Listen to these dialogues. Is the first speaker making a request or telling someone what to do?

b. Now, listen again. Does the second speaker accept or decline the request or command?

A la française

You already know that the verb **faire** means *to do*. What do you think the verb **refaire** might mean? The prefix **re-** in front of a verb means *to redo* something; to do something again. Use **r-** in front of a verb that begins with a vowel

Tu dois **re**lire ce livre. *You need to reread this book.*
On va **re**cheter du lait. *We'll buy milk again.*
Rapporte-moi du beurre! *Bring me back some butter!*

Does this same rule apply in English?

GRAMMAIRE The verb pouvoir

Pouvoir is an irregular verb. Notice how similar it is to the verb **vouloir**, which you learned in Chapter 6.

pouvoir *(to be able to, can, may)*

Je **peux**	faire les courses?	Nous **pouvons**	promener le chien?
Tu **peux**		Vous **pouvez**	
Il/Elle/On **peut**		Ils/Elles **peuvent**	

15 Qui va faire les courses?

Complete this conversation with the appropriate forms of **pouvoir**.

M. BONFILS Sim, tu __1__ aller au marché pour moi?
SIM Non, je ne __2__ pas. J'ai des trucs à faire!
ARMANDE Papa, Julie et moi, nous __3__ y aller si tu veux.
M. BONFILS Merci, les filles. Vous __4__ me prendre un ananas et des mangues? Ah, et du pain aussi.
JULIE On __5__ acheter les fruits, mais Sim et Marius ne font jamais rien. Ils __6__ bien acheter le pain pour une fois!

16 On peut?

Find out if your classmates can do these things with or for you.

—Vous pouvez écouter de la musique après l'école?
—Non, nous ne pouvons pas.

regarder la télé après l'école
aller nager
faire des courses avec moi
me rapporter un sandwich
jouer au foot demain
sortir ce soir

VOCABULAIRE

Vous en voulez combien?

un kilo(gramme) de pommes de terre et **une livre d'**oignons

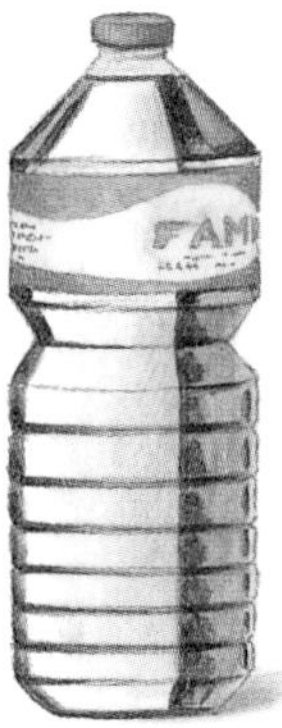

une bouteille d'eau minérale

une douzaine d'œufs

une boîte de tomates

un paquet de sucre

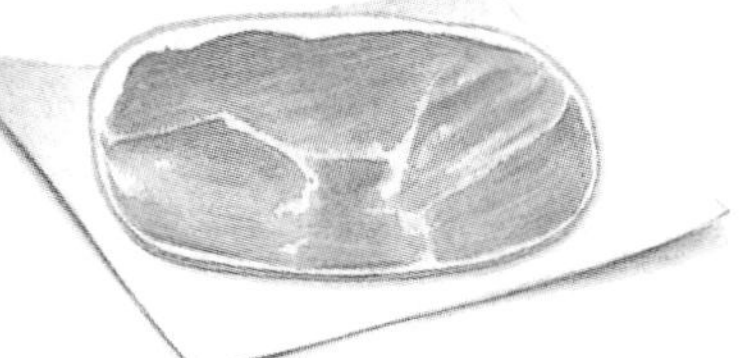

une tranche de jambon

un morceau de fromage

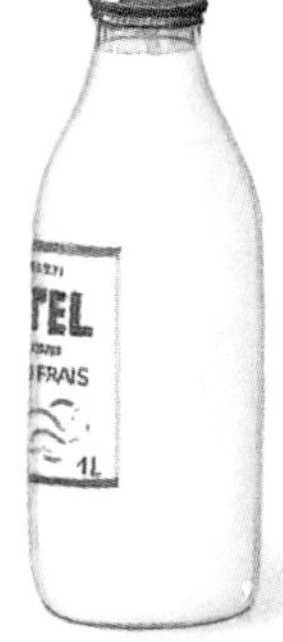

un litre de lait

NOTE DE GRAMMAIRE

Notice that you use **de** or **d'** after these expressions of quantity.

Une tranche **de** jambon, s'il vous plaît.

Je voudrais un kilo **d'**oranges.

NOTE CULTURELLE

The metric system was created shortly after the French Revolution and has since been adopted by nearly all countries in the world. Although the United States is officially trying to convert to the metric system, many people aren't yet used to it. In the metric system, lengths are measured in centimeters and meters, rather than inches and yards. Distances are measured in kilometers. Grams and kilograms are the standard measures of weight. **Une livre** is half a kilogram. Liquids, including gasoline, are measured in liters. To convert metric measurements, use the following table:

1 centimeter	= .39 inches	1 gram	= .035 ounces
1 meter	= 39.37 inches	1 kilogram	= 2.2 pounds
1 kilometer	= .62 miles	1 liter	= 1.06 quarts

17 Ecoute!

Listen to Sophie as she does her shopping. Write down the items and the quantities she asks for.

18 Qu'est-ce que tu veux?

Your mother and grandmother are planning a dinner party. They have asked you to go to the market for them. Complete the conversation below with an appropriate quantity from the expressions given.

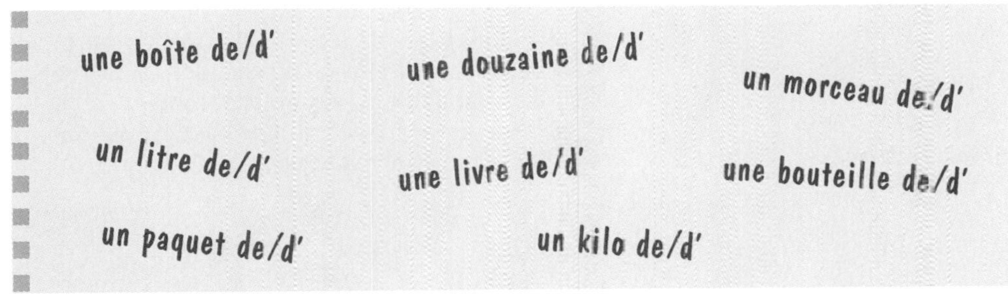

une boîte de/d'
une douzaine de/d'
un morceau de/d'
un litre de/d'
une livre de/d'
une bouteille de/d'
un paquet de/d'
un kilo de/d'

—Alors, Maman, qu'est-ce qu'il te faut?
—Il me faut __1__ bœuf, __2__ fromage et __3__ eau minérale.
—Et pour le dessert?
—Achète-moi __4__ farine, __5__ pêches et __6__ œufs.
—Et toi, Mémé, de quoi est-ce que tu as besoin?
—Rapporte-moi __7__ oignons et __8__ lait, s'il te plaît.
—D'accord. A tout à l'heure.

19 Allons au marché!

You're shopping for groceries. Make sure that you place your orders in appropriate quantities. Your partner will be the merchant. Then, change roles.

Vous avez choisi?
Voilà.
Et avec ça?
C'est tout?
Vous désirez?
Je voudrais...
Il me faut...
Je prends...

avocats
tomates
vinaigre
oignons
oeufs
pain
huile d'olive
fromage
riz
haricots verts
raisin
sucre

20 Jeu de rôle

You're working as a volunteer to pick up groceries for senior citizens. Make a list of what you need to get and the quantity of each item. Take turns with your partner playing the role of the senior citizen.

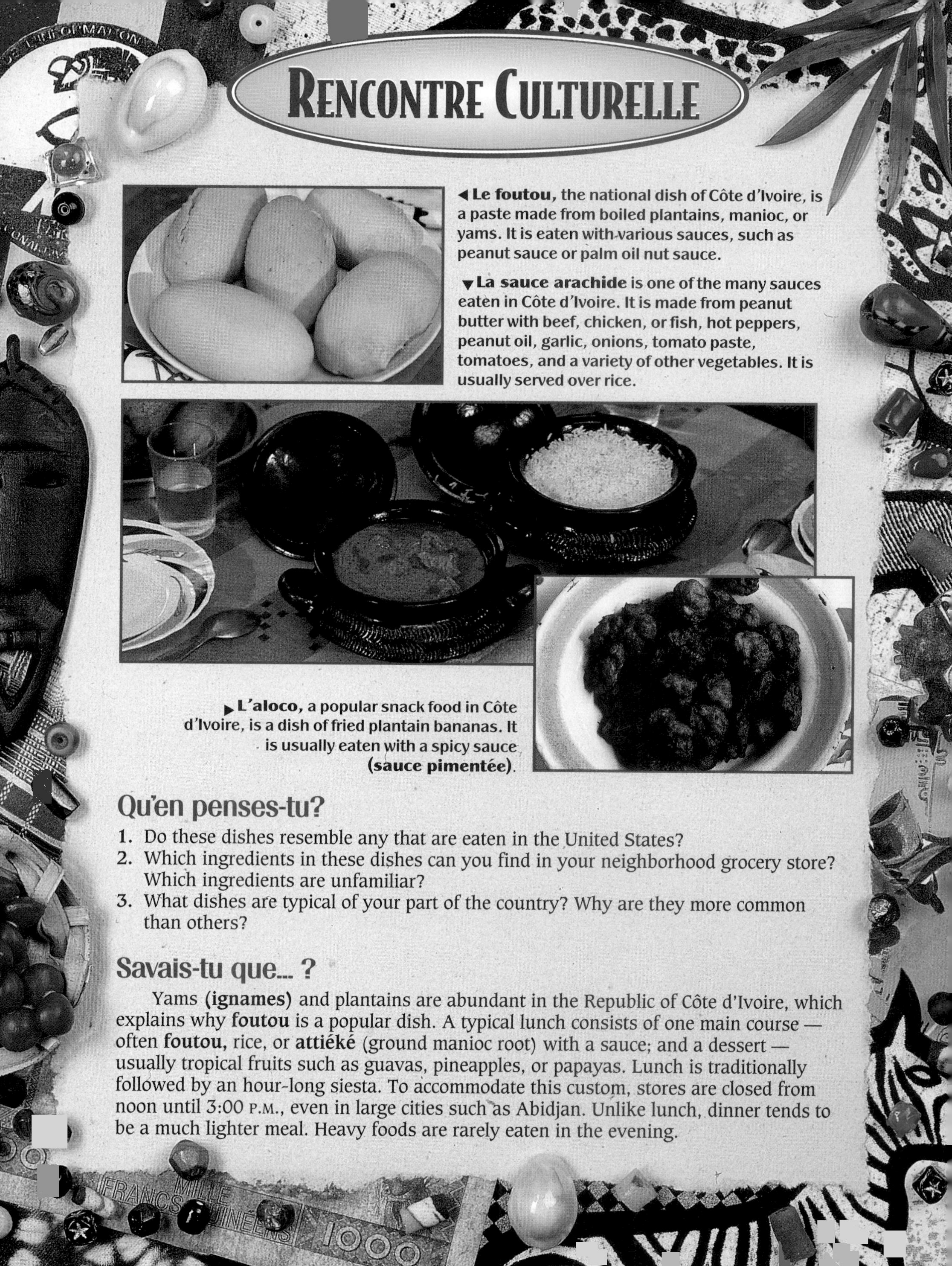

Rencontre Culturelle

◀ **Le foutou,** the national dish of Côte d'Ivoire, is a paste made from boiled plantains, manioc, or yams. It is eaten with various sauces, such as peanut sauce or palm oil nut sauce.

▼ **La sauce arachide** is one of the many sauces eaten in Côte d'Ivoire. It is made from peanut butter with beef, chicken, or fish, hot peppers, peanut oil, garlic, onions, tomato paste, tomatoes, and a variety of other vegetables. It is usually served over rice.

▶ **L'aloco,** a popular snack food in Côte d'Ivoire, is a dish of fried plantain bananas. It is usually eaten with a spicy sauce **(sauce pimentée)**.

Qu'en penses-tu?

1. Do these dishes resemble any that are eaten in the United States?
2. Which ingredients in these dishes can you find in your neighborhood grocery store? Which ingredients are unfamiliar?
3. What dishes are typical of your part of the country? Why are they more common than others?

Savais-tu que... ?

Yams **(ignames)** and plantains are abundant in the Republic of Côte d'Ivoire, which explains why **foutou** is a popular dish. A typical lunch consists of one main course — often **foutou,** rice, or **attiéké** (ground manioc root) with a sauce; and a dessert — usually tropical fruits such as guavas, pineapples, or papayas. Lunch is traditionally followed by an hour-long siesta. To accommodate this custom, stores are closed from noon until 3:00 P.M., even in large cities such as Abidjan. Unlike lunch, dinner tends to be a much lighter meal. Heavy foods are rarely eaten in the evening.

TROISIEME ETAPE

Offering, accepting, or refusing food

VOCABULAIRE

Qu'est-ce qu'on mange au...

petit déjeuner?

déjeuner?

goûter?

dîner?

21 Ecoute!

Listen to these people tell what they have for breakfast. Match each speaker with his or her breakfast.

a.

b.

c.

NOTE CULTURELLE

In the morning, most people in francophone countries have a very light breakfast. Coffee with hot milk **(café au lait)** and hot chocolate are the drinks of choice. They are usually served with bread or croissants, butter, and jam. Children may eat cereal for breakfast as well, sometimes with warm milk. The largest meal of the day, **le déjeuner,** has traditionally been between noon and 1:00 P.M. Dinner **(le dîner)** is eaten after 7:00 P.M.

22 Un repas typique

Look at each illustration below and tell at which meal(s) you might eat the items. Then, decide whether each set of items would typically be served in the United States, in a francophone country, or in both.

1.

2.

3.

4.

5.

6.

23 Quel repas?

Describe one of these meals to your partner. He or she will try to guess which meal you're talking about. Take turns.

Il y a du poulet,...

1.

2.

3.

24 Devine!

Write down what you think you'll have for your meals tomorrow, using the **Vocabulaire** on page 207. Your partner will do the same. Take turns guessing what each of you will have.

—Au petit déjeuner, tu vas manger... ?
—Oui, c'est ça. *or* Non, pas de...

COMMENT DIT-ON... ?

Offering, accepting, or refusing food

To offer food to someone:
Tu veux du riz?
Vous voulez de l'eau minérale?
Vous prenez du fromage?
Tu prends du fromage?
Encore du pain? *More . . . ?*

To accept:
Oui, s'il vous/te plaît.
Oui, j'en veux bien. *Yes, I'd like some.*
Oui, avec plaisir. *Yes, with pleasure.*

To refuse:
Non, merci.
Je n'en veux plus. *I don't want any more.*
Non, merci. Je n'ai plus faim. *No thanks. I'm not hungry anymore.*

25 Ecoute!

Is the speaker offering, accepting, or refusing food?

26 Encore du pain?

An Ivorian exchange student is having dinner at your house. Encourage him or her to try some of the foods on the table. Your friend will accept or politely refuse.

De bons conseils

Look for opportunities to practice your French wherever you go. Try to meet French-speaking people and talk with them. Ask your teacher to help you find a pen pal in a French-speaking country. Rent videocassettes of French films. See how many French products you can find at the grocery store and the cosmetic counter, and how many French dishes you can find on restaurant menus.

GRAMMAIRE The pronoun en

En takes the place of a phrase beginning with **du, de la, de l', des,** or **de** to avoid repetition. **En** usually means *some (of it/them)* or simply *it/them.*

— Tu veux **des mangues**?
— Oui, j'**en** veux bien.
— Tu manges **des légumes**?
— Oui, j'**en** mange souvent.

In a negative sentence, **en** means *any* or *none.*

— Tu veux **du beurre**?
— Merci, je n'**en** veux pas.

27 Elle en a combien?

What quantity of each of these items does Aïssata have in her basket?

Des haricots? Elle en a un kilo.

1. Du lait?
2. Du beurre?
3. Des tomates?
4. Du riz?
5. Des œufs?
6. De l'eau minérale?
7. Des ananas?

28 Tu en veux?

Take turns with a partner asking each other if you eat the foods shown in Activity 26. Use the pronoun **en** in your answers.

— Tu manges du poulet?
— Oui, j'en mange souvent.

29 Bienvenue chez nous!

Write a conversation between an Ivorian family and an American family who are having dinner together. During the meal, the hosts offer various foods to their guests, who respond politely and comment favorably on what they're eating.

PRONONCIATION

The sounds [o] and [ɔ]

The sound [o] is similar to the vowel sound in the English word *boat.* To make the sound [o], hold your mouth in a whistling position. Keep the lips and tongue steady to avoid the glide heard in *boat.* Repeat each of these words: **trop, kilo, mot.** The spellings **au, eau, ô,** and sometimes **o** represent the sound [o]. Now, repeat these words: **jaune, chaud, beau, rôle.**

The sound [ɔ] is between the vowel sounds in the English words *boat* and *bought.* Usually, this sound is followed by a consonant sound in the same syllable. The sound [ɔ] is more open, so hold your mouth in a semi-whistling position to produce it. This sound is usually spelled with the letter **o.** Now repeat these words: **bof, donne, fort, carotte.**

A. A prononcer

Repeat the following words and phrases.

1. au revoir	un stylo jaune	au restaurant
2. un gâteau	moi aussi	des haricots verts
3. des pommes	d'abord	une promenade
4. encore	dormir	l'école

B. A lire

Take turns with a partner reading each of the following sentences aloud.

1. Elle a une gomme violette et un stylo jaune.
2. Tu aimes les carottes? Moi, j'adore. J'aime bien aussi les escargots et le porc.
3. Elle est occupée aujourd'hui. Elle a informatique et biologie.
4. Il me faut un short parce qu'il fait trop chaud.
5. Tu peux sortir si tu promènes d'abord le chien.

C. A écrire

You're going to hear a short dialogue. Write down what you hear.

LISONS!

Skim the titles and photographs. What will you be reading?

DE BONS CONSEILS Remember to look for cognates to help you figure out what you're reading. Occasionally, you will encounter false cognates, words that look alike in two languages but have different meanings.

Context clues can sometimes help you recognize false cognates. An example of a false cognate is the French phrase **fruits de mer. Fruits de mer** may make you think of the English word *fruit,* but it means *seafood.*

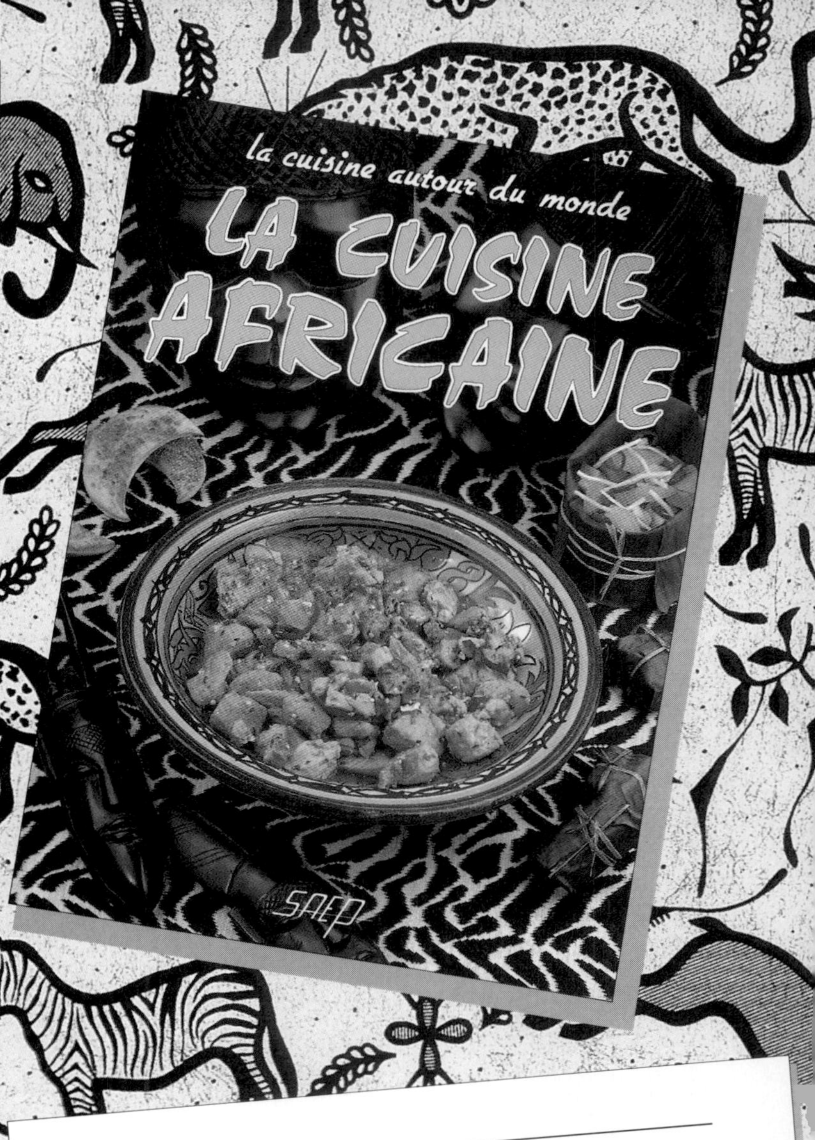

A. You already know a few false cognates. Try to figure out the meaning of the false cognates in the sentences below.

1. Je vais à San Francisco à 11h00. Maintenant, il est 10h40, et **j'attends** le train.
   a. I'm attending
   b. I'm late for
   c. I'm waiting for
2. J'adore les sciences. Ce soir, je vais **assister** à une conférence sur l'ozone.
   a. to attend
   b. to assist
   c. to teach

Les desserts

Croissants au coco et au sésame
(Afrique occidentale)

Prép. : 30 mn. - Cuiss. : 10 mn.
Repos : 1 h. - 8 pers.

2 œufs
140 g de sucre
190 g de noix de coco râpée
170 g de farine
Vanille en poudre
Graines de sésame.

Mélanger la noix de coco râpée, le sucre, la vanille et les œufs entiers. Incorporer la farine. Travailler la pâte. Former une boule. Laisser reposer 1 heure au frais.

Etaler la pâte sur 1/2 cm. Découper en croissants. Les rouler dans le sésame. Cuire au four à 200 °C, (th. 6-7), 10 minutes.

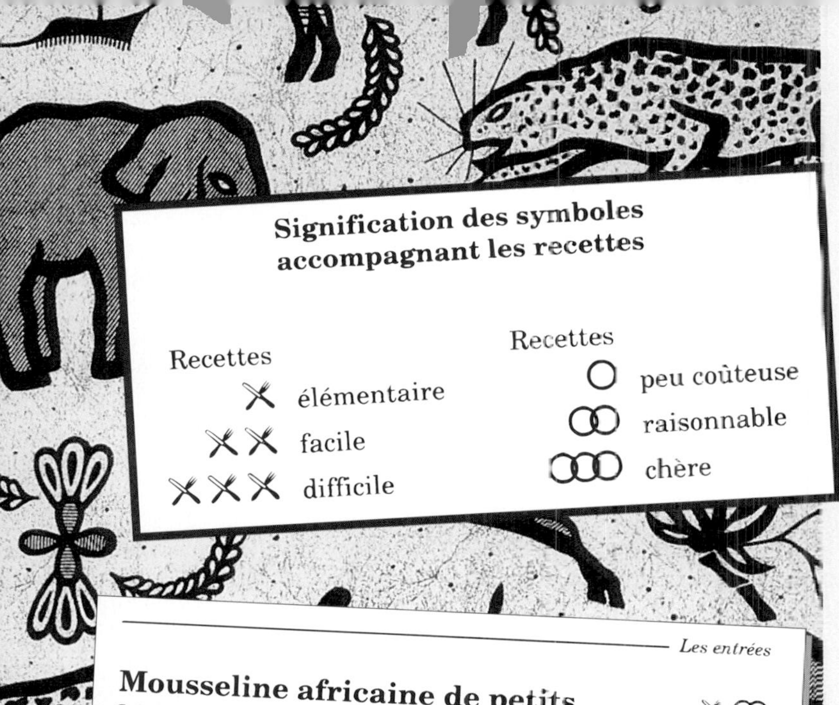

Signification des symboles accompagnant les recettes

Recettes		Recettes	
✕	élémentaire	○	peu coûteuse
✕✕	facile	○○	raisonnable
✕✕✕	difficile	○○○	chère

Les entrées

Mousseline africaine de petits légumes

(Afrique occidentale - Bénin - Togo)

✕ ○○

Prép. : 40 mn - Cuiss. : 15 mn.
4 pers.

2 petits concombres	*1 avocat*
Ail	*1 épi de maïs*
1 lime	*Graines de carvi*
1 radis noir	*4 petites brioches*
1/2 papaye	*Sel.*

Eplucher les concombres. Les détailler en dés. Faire la même chose avec l'avocat.

Débarrasser l'épis de maïs des feuilles et des barbes. Le faire cuire durant 15 minutes à l'eau bouillante. Saler en fin de cuisson.

Egréner le maïs. Débarrasser la papaye de ses graines La découper en petits dés. Emincer le radis noir. Parfumer de graines de carvi et d'ail haché. Arroser la salade de jus de lime.

Retirer le chapeau des brioches. Les évider. Les garnir de la salade parfumée.

Les brioches ne doivent pas être sucrées. Si on les fabrique, il convient d'ôter le sucre.

Ne pas saler l'épi de maïs au début de la cuisson mais à la fin afin d'éviter qu'il durcisse.

B. With a partner, scan the reading and write down all of the cognates you can find in these selections.

C. Did you find any false cognates? Were you able to figure out what they mean? If so, how?

D. Where would you expect to find these reading selections? Where are these dishes from?

E. Which of the dishes would make a good dessert?

F. Are these dishes easy or difficult to make? How do you know? Are they expensive or inexpensive to make? How do you know?

G. To make **croissants**, how long do you need to chill the dough? At what temperature do you bake them? What temperature is that on the Fahrenheit scale? (To convert from Celsius to Fahrenheit, multiply by $\frac{9}{5}$ and add 32.)

H. To make **mousseline**, how long do you have to cook the corn? Do you think this dish would taste sweet or salty? How many people does this dish serve?

I. Now, with a partner, write the instructions for an easy recipe that you know how to make. Include the ingredients, the steps required to prepare the dish, and the cooking and preparation time required.

The background design on the two **Lisons!** pages is from a piece of cloth purchased in Côte d'Ivoire.

MISE EN PRATIQUE

1 Listen to this supermarket advertisement. List four of the foods that are on sale. Then, listen again for the prices of the four items you listed.

2

LES GROUPES D'ALIMENTS

Les aliments sont regroupés en 6 catégories selon leurs caractéristiques nutritionnelles :

- **Le lait et les produits laitiers** sont nos principaux fournisseurs de calcium.
- **Viandes, poissons et œufs** sont nos sources essentielles de protéines de bonne qualité.
- **Le groupe du pain, des féculents et des légumes secs** apporte les «glucides lents» libérant progressivement l'énergie nécessaire à notre organisme.
- **Légumes et fruits** sont nos sources de fibres, vitamines et minéraux.
- **Les matières grasses** sont les sources énergétiques les plus importantes pour notre corps.
- **Le sucre et ses dérivés** apportent les «glucides rapides» nécessaires au bon fonctionnement cérébral et musculaire.

Groupe	Lait Produits Laitiers	Viandes Poissons Œufs	Pains Féculents	Fruits Légumes	Matières Grasses	Sucre Dérivés
Intérêt Principal	Calcium	Protéines	Glucides	Fibres Vitamines A et B	Lipides	Glucides
Intérêt Secon-daire	Protéines Vitamines A, B, D	Fer Vitamine B	Fibres	Glucides	Vitamines (A, E, selon mat. grasses)	

L'ensemble de ces catégories permet, au sein d'une alimentation diversifiée, de couvrir tous nos besoins.

1. What kind of chart is this?
2. What do the six categories listed mean?
3. According to the chart, what are some of the nutrients found in . . .
   a. produits laitiers?
   b. viandes?
   c. pain?
   d. fruits et légumes?
   e. matières grasses?
   f. sucre et ses dérivés?
4. Give some examples of foods you know in French that fall into each category.
5. Name three foods that are high in protein and three that are high in calcium.

3 What are some differences between meals in Africa, France, and the United States?

4 ## Ecrivons!

Imagine that you're the producer of a certain food item that you're trying to market. Write an ad that encourages people to buy the item, telling when they might eat it and why it's good. Consider who would be likely to buy your product. Include logos and pictures in your ad as well.

STRATEGIE

Arranging your ideas spatially is a good way to organize ideas for your advertisement. First, brainstorm some catchy phrases and convincing arguments you might write in your ad to persuade people to buy your product. Also, decide what types of illustrations you might use (photos, logos, and so on) and where to place them in your ad. Then, create a sketch of how you want your ad to look.

Persuasive writing encourages people to do a certain thing or to think a certain way. Advertisements are a type of persuasive writing because advertisers try to convince people that their products are better than any others.

Using the sketch you prepared, create the ad for your product. Structure is very important in persuasive writing. You should choose what you feel is the greatest benefit or most appealing characteristic of the product and draw attention to it. You can do this by writing it in larger print or in an eye-catching color. Less attention should be drawn to what you feel are your product's weaker points. However, try to avoid relying too heavily on illustrations and layout; your ad should be informative as well as eye-catching. Be sure to use descriptive terms that illustrate the qualities of your product.

5

JEU DE ROLE

a. Make a list in French of what you've eaten for the last two days. Use the food vocabulary that you've learned in this chapter.

b. Now, you go to a nutrition counselor. The counselor will evaluate your diet, telling you what you need to eat more of and what you shouldn't eat anymore. Act out this scene with a partner. Then, change roles.

QUE SAIS-JE?

Can you use what you've learned in this chapter?

Can you express need? p. 210

1 How would you tell someone that you need these things?

Can you make, accept, and decline requests or tell someone what to do? p. 212

2 How would you . . .

1. ask someone to go grocery shopping for you?
2. tell someone to bring back some groceries for you?

3 How would you accept the requests in Activity 2? How would you refuse?

4 How would you ask for a specific quantity of these foods?

1. œufs
2. lait
3. oranges
4. beurre
5. jambon
6. eau minérale

Can you offer, accept, or refuse food? p. 219

5 How would you offer someone these foods?

1. some rice
2. some oranges
3. some milk

6 How would you accept the foods listed in number 5 if they were offered? How would you refuse them?

7 How would you tell someone what you have for . . .

1. breakfast?
2. lunch?
3. an afternoon snack?
4. dinner?

VOCABULAIRE

PREMIERE ETAPE

Expressing need

Qu'est-ce qu'il te faut? *What do you need?*
Il me faut... *I need . . .*
De quoi est-ce que tu as besoin? *What do you need?*
J'ai besoin de... *I need . . .*
du, de la, de l' *some*

Foods; Shopping

des ananas (m.) *pineapples*
des avocats (m.) *avocados*
des bananes (f.) *bananas*
du beurre *butter*
du bœuf *beef*
des carottes (f.) *carrots*
des champignons (m.) *mushrooms*
des citrons (m.) *lemons*
de la confiture *jam*
de la farine *flour*
des fraises (f.) *strawberries*
du fromage *cheese*
des fruits (m.) *fruit*
des gâteaux (m.) *cakes*
des gombos (m.) *okra*
des goyaves (f.) *guavas*
des haricots verts (m.) *green beans*
du lait *milk*
des légumes (m.) *vegetables*
du maïs *corn*
des mangues (f.) *mangoes*
des noix de coco (f.) *coconuts*
des œufs (m.) *eggs*
des oignons (m.) *onions*
des oranges (f.) *oranges*
du pain *bread*
des papayes (f.) *papayas*
des pêches (f.) *peaches*
des petits pois (m.) *peas*
des poires (f.) *pears*
du poisson *fish*
des pommes (f.) *apples*
des pommes de terre (f.) *potatoes*
du porc *pork*
des poules (f.) *live chickens*
du poulet *chicken*
des produits (m.) **laitiers** *dairy products*
du raisin *grapes*
du riz *rice*
une/de la salade *a/some salad*
des salades *heads of lettuce*
du sucre *sugar*
de la tarte (f.) *pie*
des tomates (f.) *tomatoes*
de la viande *meat*
des yaourts (m.) *yogurt*
le marché *market*
le supermarché *supermarket*

DEUXIEME ETAPE

Making, accepting, and declining requests

Tu peux... ? *Can you . . . ?*
Tu me rapportes... ? *Will you bring me . . . ?*
Bon, d'accord. *Well, OK.*
Je veux bien. *Gladly.*
J'y vais tout de suite. *I'll go right away.*
Je regrette, mais je n'ai pas le temps. *I'm sorry, but I don't have time.*
Je ne peux pas maintenant. *I can't right now.*

Telling someone what to do

Rapporte(-moi)... *Bring (me) back . . .*
Prends... *Get . . .*
Achète(-moi)... *Buy (me) . . .*
N'oublie pas de... *Don't forget . . .*
pouvoir *to be able to, can, may*

Quantities

une boîte de *a can of*
une bouteille de *a bottle of*
une douzaine de *a dozen*
un kilo(gramme) de *a kilogram of*
un litre de *a liter of*
une livre de *a pound of*
un morceau de *a piece of*
un paquet de *a package/box of*
une tranche de *a slice of*

TROISIEME ETAPE

Offering, accepting, or refusing food

Tu veux... ? *Do you want . . . ?*
Vous voulez... ? *Do you want . . . ?*
Vous prenez... ? *Will you have . . . ?*
Tu prends... ? *Will you have . . . ?*
Encore de... ? *More . . . ?*
Oui, s'il vous/te plaît. *Yes, please.*
Oui, j'en veux bien. *Yes, I'd like some.*
Oui, avec plaisir. *Yes, with pleasure.*
Non, merci. *No, thank you.*
Je n'en veux plus. *I don't want any more.*
Non, merci. Je n'ai plus faim. *No thanks. I'm not hungry anymore.*
en *some, of it, of them, any*

Meals

le petit déjeuner *breakfast*
le déjeuner *lunch*
le goûter *afternoon snack*
le dîner *dinner*

La ville d'Arles

Arles

Population : plus de 50.000

Points d'intérêt : la place Richelme, la place du Forum, les arènes romaines, les thermes de Constantin, les Alyscamps, le théâtre antique

Aux environs d'Arles : les Baux-de-Provence, les Antiques à St-Rémy-de-Provence, le moulin d'Alphonse Daudet

Personnages célèbres : Alphonse Daudet, Vincent Van Gogh, Frédéric Mistral

Musées : le musée Réattu, le musée de l'Arles Antique, le Museon Arlaten

Industries : riz, papier, industries chimiques et métalliques

Arles 

Founded by the Greeks in the fifth century B.C., Arles later prospered for hundreds of years under Roman rule. It was the largest city in Provence and the capital of ancient Gaul. In the Middle Ages, Arles was an important religious center. It did not become a part of France until 1481. In 1888, Vincent Van Gogh moved to Arles and painted some of his most famous works. Today, Arles still attracts artists, as well as historians and archeologists. Festivals, the many museums, and the beautiful countryside draw thousands of other visitors every year to this very special place known to some as "the soul of Provence."

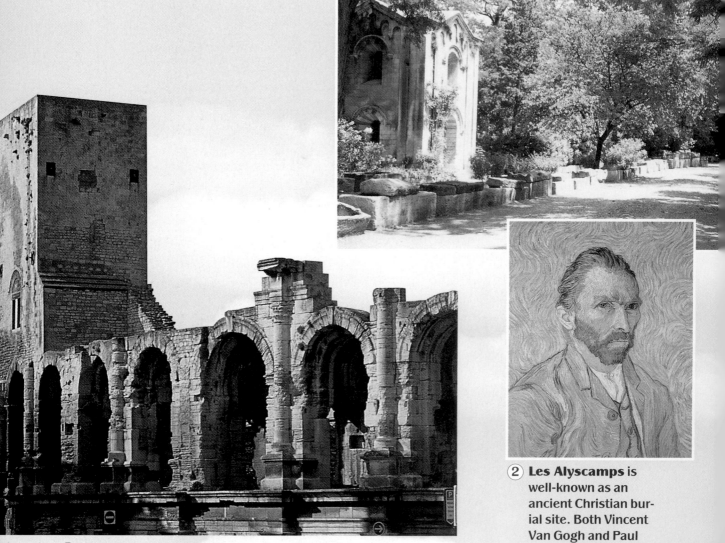

① **Les arènes romaines** is one of the most ancient Roman amphitheaters in the world. Measuring 136 meters long and 107 meters wide, it is also one of the largest arenas, holding 12,000 spectators.

② **Les Alyscamps** is well-known as an ancient Christian burial site. Both Vincent Van Gogh and Paul Gauguin immortalized it in their paintings.

③ The marshland known as **la Camargue** is a stunningly beautiful nature reserve. It is particularly known for its pink flamingos and wild horses.

④ Arles is home to several festivals that feature dancers from all over Provence dressed in their traditional costumes.

⑤ **Le théâtre antique**, constructed in the first century B.C., is still in use. It is here that the Festival d'Arles, the Rencontres internationales de la photographie, and numerous shows are staged.

CHAPITRE

9 Au téléphone

① Allô? C'est Hélène à l'appareil.

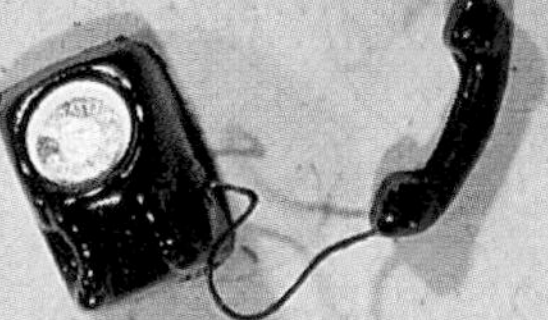

Teenagers in francophone countries like to talk to their friends about the good things that are happening to them, as well as their problems, just as teenagers do in the United States.

In this chapter you will learn

- to ask for and express opinions; to inquire about and relate past events
- to make and answer a telephone call
- to share confidences and console others; to ask for and give advice

And you will

- listen to French-speaking students talk about what they did during the weekend
- read about French teenagers' telephone habits
- write about what you did over the weekend
- learn about the French telephone system

② Tu as passé un bon week-end?

③ J'ai un petit problème.

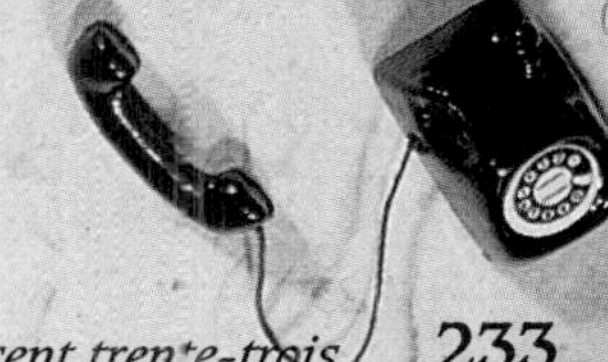

cile Clém...
04.67.64.12.98
CD
EF
r. et Mme Colin
GH
, rue Victor Hugo
IJ
4000 Montpellier
KL
MN

Mise en train

Un week-end spécial

What is the subject of Hélène and Magali's telephone conversation? How do you know?

Hélène

Magali

Florent

Ahmed

Hélène et Magali sont au téléphone et racontent ce qu'elles ont fait pendant le week-end. Magali a fait beaucoup de choses. La conversation dure...

Allô?
Hélène? C'est Magali à l'appareil. Tu as passé un bon week-end?
Bof, ça a été. Je n'ai rien fait de spécial.

1

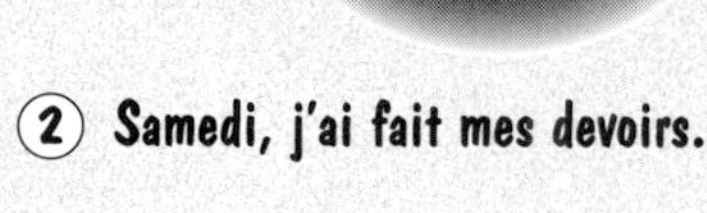

2 Samedi, j'ai fait mes devoirs.

3 Dimanche, j'ai regardé la télévision...

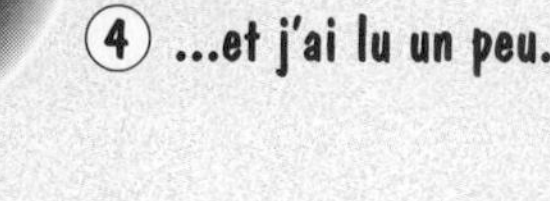

4 ...et j'ai lu un peu.

5
Et toi? Tu as passé un bon week-end?
Excellent! J'ai passé un week-end super!
Ah oui? Qu'est-ce que tu as fait?
Je suis allée au théâtre antique avec Florent.
6 Il m'a présenté un garçon très sympa. Il s'appelle Ahmed. Il est super gentil.
7 Nous avons beaucoup parlé. Tu sais, il adore le sport. Il aime le tennis, comme moi.
8 Dimanche, nous sommes tous allés aux Baux-de-Provence.
Qu'est-ce que vous avez fait là-bas?
Je vais te raconter une histoire incroyable!
Je t'écoute.
Attends une seconde... Ecoute, Hélène, mon père veut téléphoner. Je te rappelle plus tard.
9
10
Mais, qu'est-ce qui s'est passé aux Baux-de-Provence?

1 Tu as compris?

1. How was Hélène's weekend?
2. Did Magali have a good weekend? Why? Why not?
3. Do you think Magali likes Ahmed? How can you tell?
4. Why does Magali have to hang up?

2 Magali ou Hélène?

Qui a fait ça, Magali ou Hélène?

1. aller aux Baux
2. faire ses devoirs
3. lire
4. aller au théâtre antique
5. regarder la télévision
6. ne rien faire de spécial

3 Mets en ordre

Put Magali's activities in order according to **Un week-end spécial.**

1. Elle est allée au théâtre antique.
2. Elle est allée aux Baux-de-Provence.
3. Elle a parlé avec Hélène au téléphone.
4. Elle a rencontré un garçon sympa.

4 C'est qui?

Match the photos of these people with the sentences that refer to them.

Magali

Hélène

Ahmed

le père de Magali

1. Cette personne veut téléphoner.
2. Cette personne a passé un bon week-end.
3. Cette personne est super gentille.
4. Pendant le week-end, cette personne n'a rien fait de spécial.
5. Cette personne va téléphoner plus tard.

5 Cherche les expressions

According to **Un week-end spécial,** what do you say in French . . .

1. to answer the phone?
2. to identify yourself on the phone?
3. to ask if someone had a good weekend?
4. to ask what someone did?
5. to tell someone to hold?
6. to ask what happened?

C'est... à l'appareil. Qu'est-ce qui s'est passé?
Attends une seconde.
Allô? Qu'est-ce que tu as fait?
Tu as passé un bon week-end?

6 Et maintenant, à toi

What do you think happened to Magali at les Baux?

PREMIERE ETAPE

Asking for and expressing opinions; inquiring about and relating past events

COMMENT DIT-ON... ?

Asking for and expressing opinions

To ask for someone's opinion:
Tu as passé un bon week-end?
Did you have a good weekend?

To express indifference:
Oui, ça a été. *Yes, it was OK.*
Oh, pas mauvais.

To express satisfaction:
Oui, très chouette. *Yes, super.*
Oui, excellent.
Oui, très bon.

To express dissatisfaction:
Très mauvais.
C'était épouvantable.
It was horrible.

7 Ecoute!

Listen to these people talk about their weekend. Tell if they had a really good time, a mildly good time, or no fun at all.

8 Tu as passé un bon week-end?

Find out if some of your classmates had a good or bad weekend. Then, tell them how your weekend was.

COMMENT DIT-ON... ?

Inquiring about and relating past events

To inquire about past events:

Qu'est-ce qui s'est passé (hier)?
What happened (yesterday)?

Qu'est-ce que tu as fait vendredi?
What did you do . . . ?

Et après? *And then?*

Tu es allé(e) où? *Where did you go?*

To relate past events:

Nous avons parlé. *We talked.*

D'abord, j'ai fait mes devoirs.
First, . . .

Ensuite, j'ai téléphoné à un copain.
Then, . . .

Après, je suis sorti(e).
Afterwards, I went out.

Et après ça, j'ai téléphoné à Luc.
And after that, . . .

Finalement/Enfin, je suis allé(e) chez Paul.
Finally, I went . . .

9 Méli-mélo!

Remets la conversation entre Albert et Marcel dans le bon ordre.

—Salut, Marcel! Ça va?

—Vendredi et samedi, rien de spécial.

—Et après ça?

—Pas mal. Dis, qu'est-ce que tu as fait ce week-end?

—Vous êtes allés où?

—Après, nous sommes allés au café et nous avons parlé jusqu'à minuit.

—Dimanche, j'ai téléphoné à Gisèle et nous avons décidé de sortir.

—Et dimanche?

—D'abord, nous avons fait un pique-nique. Ensuite, nous sommes allés au cinéma.

—Oui, ça va bien. Et toi?

GRAMMAIRE The passé composé with avoir

To tell what happened in the past, use the **passé composé** of the verb. The **passé composé** is composed of two parts: *(a)* a present-tense form of the helping verb **avoir** or **être**—which you've already learned—and *(b)* the past participle of the verb you want to use. You use **avoir** as the helping verb with most verbs. Only with a small number of French verbs, like **aller**, do you use **être** as the helping verb. You'll learn more about these verbs later.

Helping Verb +		*Past Participle*
J'	**ai**	
Tu	**as**	
Il/Elle/On	**a**	**parlé** au téléphone.
Nous	**avons**	
Vous	**avez**	
Ils/Elles	**ont**	

- To form the past participle of a verb that ends in **-er**, drop the **-er** and add **-é**.
- To make a verb in the **passé composé** negative, put **ne (n')... pas** around the helping verb.

  Je **n'**ai **pas** étudié.

- Some French verbs have irregular past participles, that is, they don't follow a regular pattern. You'll have to memorize them when you learn the verb. Here are the past participles of some irregular verbs that you've already seen.

faire	**fait**	J'ai **fait** mes devoirs.
prendre	**pris**	Ils ont **pris** un taxi.
voir	**vu**	Il a **vu** sa grand-mère.
lire	**lu**	Elle a **lu** un roman français.

10 Ecoute!

Listen to these conversations and decide whether the speakers are talking about what they did last weekend or what they're going to do next weekend.

11 Une journée à la plage

Qu'est-ce que Claire et ses amis ont fait à la plage?

1.

2.

3.

12 Qu'est-ce qu'on a fait?

Take turns with a partner asking and telling what you did and didn't do over the weekend. Then, tell another classmate about your partner's weekend activities.

faire mes devoirs
laver la voiture
acheter une montre
sortir la poubelle
faire le ménage
ranger ma chambre
promener le chien
prendre un café avec mes amis
faire un pique-nique
lire un roman
voir un film français

NOTE DE GRAMMAIRE

When you use the **passé composé** with adverbs such as **trop, beaucoup, pas encore** *(not yet),* **bien** *(well),* **mal** *(badly),* and **déjà** *(already),* place the adverb before the past participle of the verb.

J'ai **déjà** mangé.

Nadine n'a **pas encore** vu ce film.

13 Mais pourquoi?

Using the words in the box, give a logical explanation for each of the statements below. Be sure to put the verbs in the **passé composé.**

Céline a gagné le match de tennis.
Elle a bien joué.

1. Marie-Louise a eu 18 à son interro de maths!
2. Jérôme n'a pas d'énergie.
3. Sabine veut aller voir *Les Misérables.*
4. Luc n'a plus faim.
5. Etienne ne veut pas lire *Le Petit Prince.*

bien
étudier
travailler
déjà
voir
pas encore
manger
beaucoup
trop
lire

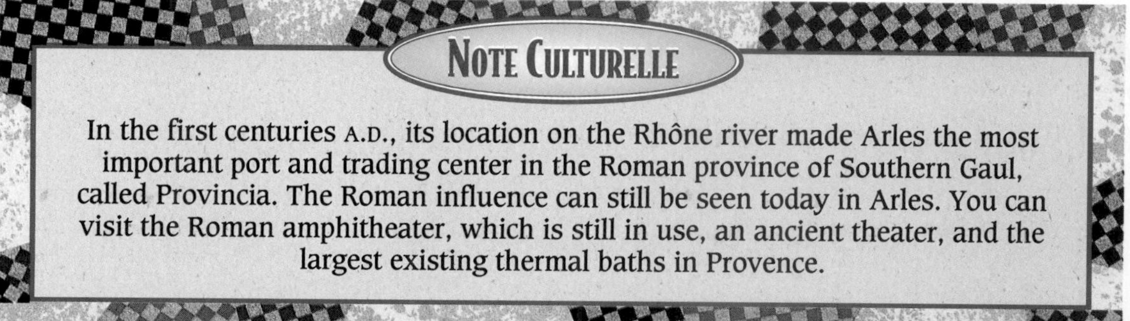

NOTE CULTURELLE

In the first centuries A.D., its location on the Rhône river made Arles the most important port and trading center in the Roman province of Southern Gaul, called Provincia. The Roman influence can still be seen today in Arles. You can visit the Roman amphitheater, which is still in use, an ancient theater, and the largest existing thermal baths in Provence.

Vocabulaire

J'ai raté le bus.

J'ai trouvé cinquante francs.

J'ai oublié mes devoirs.

J'ai déjeuné à la cantine.

J'ai rencontré une fille (un garçon) sympa.

J'ai chanté dans la chorale.

J'ai acheté un CD.

J'ai travaillé au fast-food.

Here are some other verbs and expressions you may want to use to talk about what you've done during your day.

apporter	*to bring*	**gagner**	*to win, to earn*	**répéter**	*to rehearse, to practice music*
chercher	*to look for*	**montrer**	*to show*		
commencer	*to begin, to start*	**passer un examen**	*to take an exam*	**retrouver**	*to meet with*
dîner	*to have dinner*	**rater une interro**	*to fail a quiz*	**visiter**	*to visit (a place)*

14 Qu'est-ce qu'ils ont fait le week-end dernier?

1. 

2. 

3. 

4. 

5. 

6. 

15 Pierre a fait quoi?

Pierre spent a week at a sports camp. Which of the activities below do you think he did and which do you think he didn't do?

chanter avec des copains
rater le bus
gagner un match
faire du ski nautique
rater un examen
nager
acheter un CD
manger des escargots

De bons conseils

French words that look similar are often related in meaning, so you can use words you already know to guess the meanings of new words. If you already know what **chanter** means, you can probably guess the meaning of **une chanteuse.** You know what **commencer** means, so what do you think **le commencement** means? Likewise, you should be able to figure out **le visiteur** from the verb **visiter.**

16 Tu as déjà fait ça?

Make a list of ten activities that you or a classmate might have done last week. Then, try to find a classmate who did each activity. When you find someone who did one of the activities, write his or her name on your list next to the activity. Try to find a different person for each activity.

Activités	Nom
1. J'ai gagné cent dollars.	Jeff
2. J'ai chanté dans la chorale.	Lisa

17 Mon journal

Write down five things you did last weekend. Be sure to tell when you did each activity, with whom, and add as many other details as you can think of.

DEUXIEME ETAPE

Making and answering a telephone call

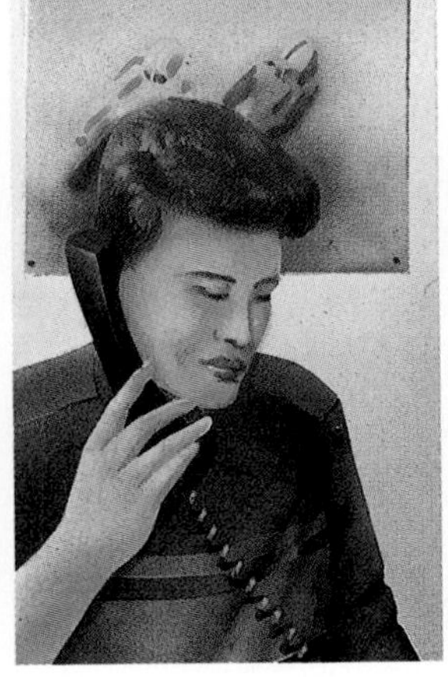

—Allô, Anita?
—Oui. C'est moi.
—Salut. C'est François.

—Allô? C'est Michel. Véronique est là, s'il vous plaît?
—Une seconde.
—Merci.

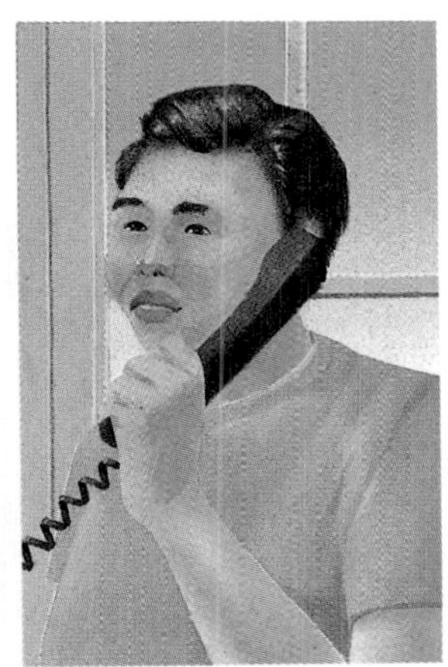

—Allô? Est-ce que Xuan est là, s'il vous plaît?
—Non, il est chez Robert.
—Est-ce que je peux laisser un message?
—Bien sûr.
—Vous pouvez lui dire qu'Emmanuel a téléphoné?
—D'accord.
—Merci.

18 Au téléphone

Answer these questions about the conversations.

1. What do the people say to begin the conversation?
2. Who has to wait a few seconds to speak to his or her friend?
3. Who gets to talk right away to the person he or she is calling?
4. Who isn't home?

COMMENT DIT-ON... ?

Making and answering a telephone call

CD-ROM Disc 3

To make a phone call:

Bonjour.

Je suis bien chez Véronique?
Is this . . . 's house?

C'est Michel.

(Est-ce que) Véronique **est là, s'il vous plaît?**

Je peux parler à Véronique?

Je peux laisser un message?
May I leave a message?

Vous pouvez lui dire que j'ai téléphoné?
Can you tell her/him that I called?

To answer a phone call:

Allô?

Qui est à l'appareil?
Who's calling?

Vous pouvez rappeler plus tard?
Can you call back later?

Une seconde, s'il vous plaît.

D'accord.

Bien sûr.

Here are some additional phrases you may need:

Ne quittez pas. *Hold on.*

Ça ne répond pas.
There's no answer.

C'est occupé.
It's busy.

19 Ecoute!

Ecoute ces conversations téléphoniques. Qui téléphone? A qui voudrait-il/-elle parler?

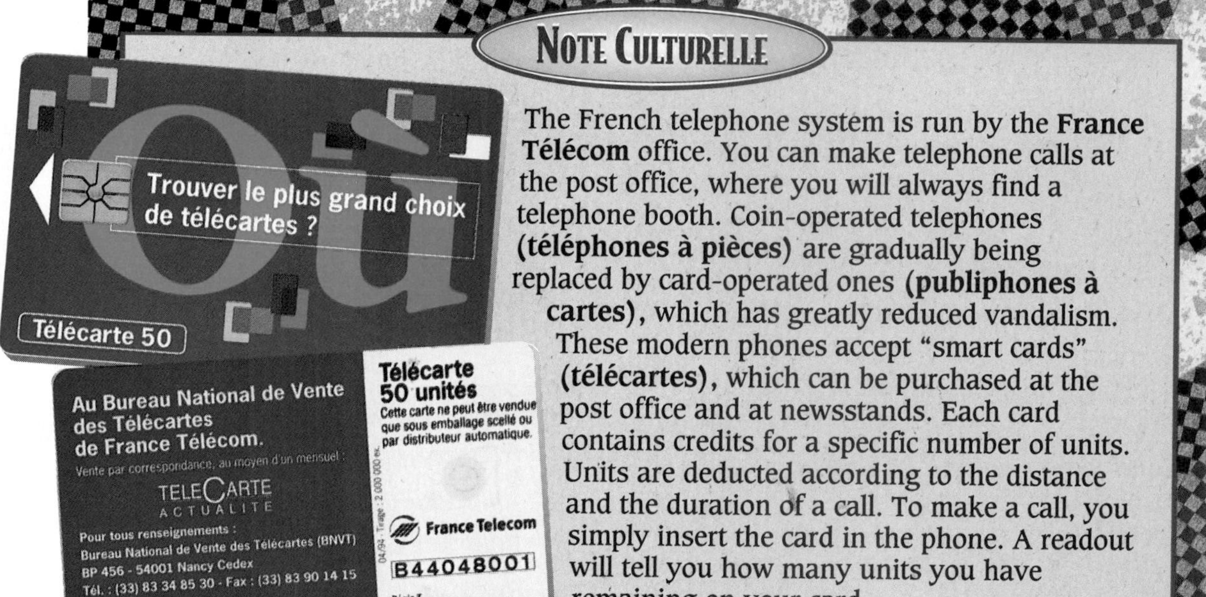

NOTE CULTURELLE

The French telephone system is run by the **France Télécom** office. You can make telephone calls at the post office, where you will always find a telephone booth. Coin-operated telephones **(téléphones à pièces)** are gradually being replaced by card-operated ones **(publiphones à cartes)**, which has greatly reduced vandalism. These modern phones accept "smart cards" **(télécartes)**, which can be purchased at the post office and at newsstands. Each card contains credits for a specific number of units. Units are deducted according to the distance and the duration of a call. To make a call, you simply insert the card in the phone. A readout will tell you how many units you have remaining on your card.

20 Méli-mélo!

Mets cette conversation dans le bon ordre.

D'accord.

Allô?

C'est Aurélie.

Tu peux lui dire que j'ai téléphoné?

Salut, Aurélie. Désolée, elle n'est pas là.

Allô, bonjour. Je peux parler à Nicole?

Qui est à l'appareil?

Bien sûr.

Est-ce que je peux laisser un message?

21 Ecoute!

During your exchange visit to France, you stay with a French family, **les Tissot**. You're the only one at home today. Several of their friends call and leave messages. Write down the messages and compare your notes with a classmate's.

22 Jeu de rôle

The friend you're phoning isn't home, so you leave a message. Take turns playing the role of the friend's parent.

GRAMMAIRE -re verbs

Like -**er** verbs, most verbs that end in -**re** follow a regular pattern. Drop the -**re** from the infinitive and add the endings below. Notice that you don't add an ending to the **il/elle/on** form of the verb.

répondre *(to answer)*

je répond**s**	nous répond**ons**
tu répond**s**	vous répond**ez**
il/elle/on répond	ils/elles répond**ent**

- **Répondre** is followed by a form of the preposition **à**.
  Nathalie répond **à** Lucas. Je réponds **au** professeur.
- Some other -**re** verbs you might want to use are **vendre** *(to sell)*, **attendre** *(to wait for)*, and **perdre** *(to lose)*.
- To form the past participle of an -**re** verb, drop the -**re** and add -**u**.
  Il a **répondu** à sa lettre. Nous avons **perdu** nos cahiers.

23 A l'école

Sébastien overhears the following comments before class. Complete the comments with the appropriate forms of the verbs **répondre, vendre, attendre**, and **perdre**.

1. «Nous ____ le professeur. Il est en retard.»
2. «Attention, Luc! Tu _____ ton argent. Tu dois fermer *(to close)* ton sac à dos.»
3. «Ils ____ toujours bien aux questions du professeur!»
4. «Est-ce qu'on ____ des calculatrices à la Papeterie Simonet? Il me faut une calculatrice.»
5. «Je ____ à la lettre de Marianne. Elle est à Nice avec sa famille.»
6. «On va _____ des tee-shirts pour gagner de l'argent pour le Cercle français.»

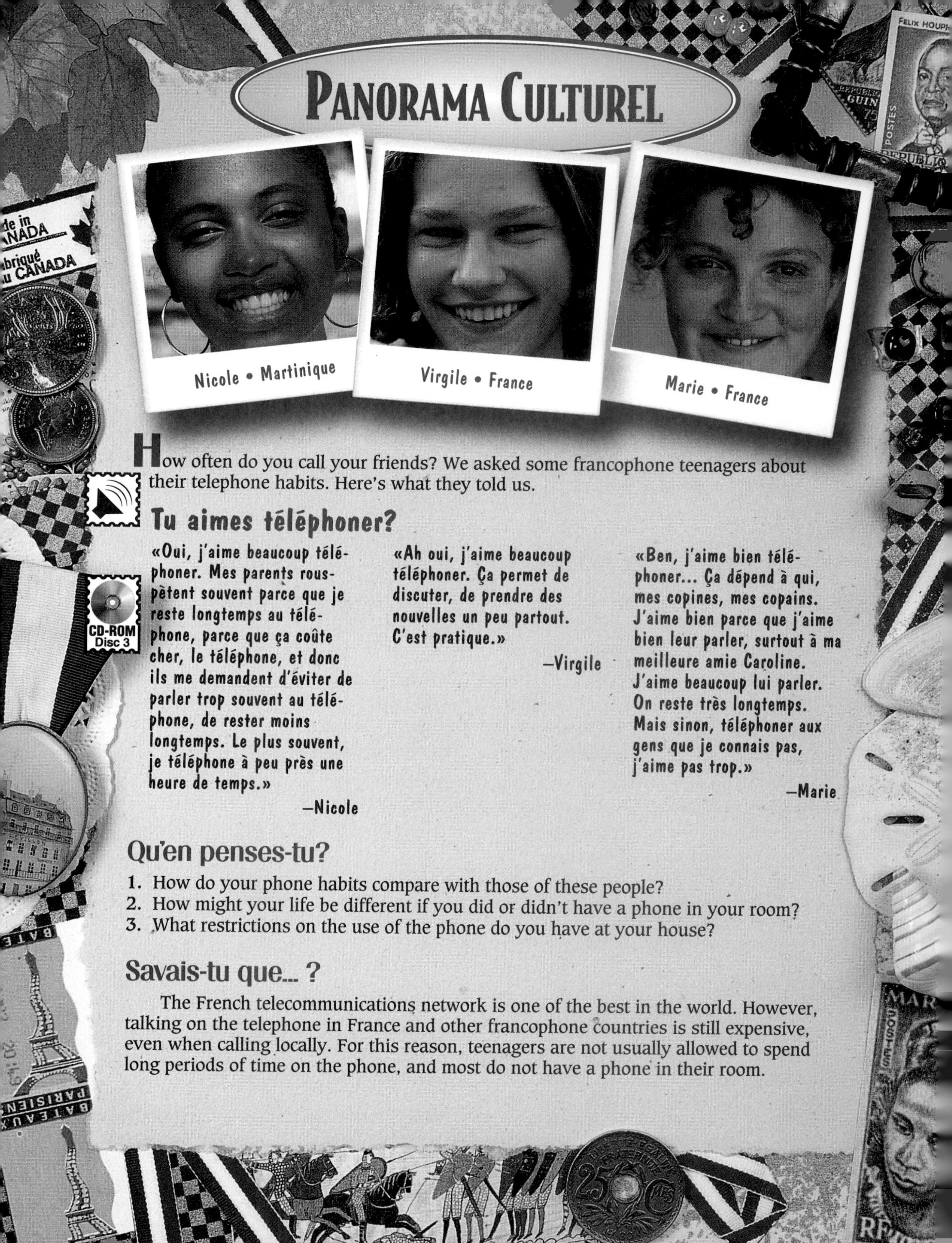

PANORAMA CULTUREL

Nicole • Martinique

Virgile • France

Marie • France

How often do you call your friends? We asked some francophone teenagers about their telephone habits. Here's what they told us.

Tu aimes téléphoner?

«Oui, j'aime beaucoup téléphoner. Mes parents rouspètent souvent parce que je reste longtemps au téléphone, parce que ça coûte cher, le téléphone, et donc ils me demandent d'éviter de parler trop souvent au téléphone, de rester moins longtemps. Le plus souvent, je téléphone à peu près une heure de temps.»

—Nicole

«Ah oui, j'aime beaucoup téléphoner. Ça permet de discuter, de prendre des nouvelles un peu partout. C'est pratique.»

—Virgile

«Ben, j'aime bien téléphoner... Ça dépend à qui, mes copines, mes copains. J'aime bien parce que j'aime bien leur parler, surtout à ma meilleure amie Caroline. J'aime beaucoup lui parler. On reste très longtemps. Mais sinon, téléphoner aux gens que je connais pas, j'aime pas trop.»

—Marie

Qu'en penses-tu?

1. How do your phone habits compare with those of these people?
2. How might your life be different if you did or didn't have a phone in your room?
3. What restrictions on the use of the phone do you have at your house?

Savais-tu que... ?

The French telecommunications network is one of the best in the world. However, talking on the telephone in France and other francophone countries is still expensive, even when calling locally. For this reason, teenagers are not usually allowed to spend long periods of time on the phone, and most do not have a phone in their room.

TROISIEME ETAPE

Sharing confidences and consoling others; asking for and giving advice

COMMENT DIT-ON... ?

Sharing confidences and consoling others; asking for and giving advice

To share a confidence:

J'ai un petit problème.
I've got a little problem.

Je peux te parler?
Can I talk to you?

Tu as une minute?
Do you have a minute?

To ask for advice:

A ton avis, qu'est-ce que je fais?
In your opinion, what do I do?

Qu'est-ce que tu me conseilles?
What do you advise me to do?

To console someone:

Je t'écoute. *I'm listening.*

Qu'est-ce que je peux faire?
What can I do?

Ne t'en fais pas! *Don't worry!*

Ça va aller mieux!
It's going to get better!

To give advice:

Oublie-le/-la/-les!
Forget him/her/it/them!

Téléphone-lui/-leur!
Call him/her/them!

Tu devrais lui/leur parler.
You should talk to him/her/them.

Pourquoi tu ne téléphones pas?
Why don't you . . . ?

NOTE DE GRAMMAIRE

In the expressions above, **le, la,** and **les** *(him, her, it, them)* are object pronouns that refer to people or things. The pronouns **lui** and **leur** *(to him, to her, to them)* refer only to people. You will learn more about these pronouns later.

De bons conseils

Study at regular intervals. It's best to learn language in small chunks and to review frequently. Cramming will not usually work for French. Study at least a little bit every day, whether you have an assignment or not. The more often you review words and structures, the easier it will be for you to understand and speak in class. And don't forget to talk to yourself or to a classmate in French!

24 Ecoute!

Are these people giving advice or asking for advice?

25 Ecoute!

Ecoute cette conversation entre Mireille et Simone. Simone a un problème. Quel est son problème?

26 J'ai un petit problème

Match each of the following problems with a logical solution.

1. Mon frère ne me parle plus depuis *(for)* cinq jours.
2. Je veux acheter un vélo, mais je n'ai pas d'argent.
3. J'ai oublié mes devoirs.
4. Je vais rater l'interro d'anglais.

a. Tu devrais étudier plus souvent.
b. Pourquoi tu ne travailles pas?
c. Refais-les!
d. Parle-lui!

27 Pauvre Hervé!

Console Hervé.

1.

2.

3.

28 Et à ton avis?

Your friend phones and asks to speak to you. He or she has some problems and wants to ask your advice about them. Console your friend and offer some advice. Then, change roles.

veut rencontrer de nouveaux copains.

n'a pas acheté de cadeau pour l'anniversaire de sa sœur.

veut faire une boum, mais ses parents ne sont pas d'accord.

n'a pas d'argent pour acheter des baskets.

a raté un examen.

ne peut pas trouver de travail pour l'été.

n'aime pas le prof de biologie.

n'a pas parlé avec son petit ami (sa petite amie) depuis *(for)* 3 jours.

n'a pas gagné son match de tennis.

a oublié ses devoirs.

29 Ne t'en fais pas!

Your friend asks you to listen to his or her account of a very bad day. Console your friend. Act this out with a partner. Then, change roles.

PRONONCIATION

The vowel sounds [e] and [ɛ]

Listen to the vowels in the word **préfère.** How are they different? The first one is pronounced [e], and the second one [ɛ]. To make the vowel sound [e], hold your mouth in a closed smiling position. Keep your lips and tongue steady to avoid the glide as in the English word *day*. Repeat these words.

été désolé occupé répondre

Now, take a smiling position once again, but this time open your mouth wider. This will produce the vowel sound [ɛ]. Repeat these words.

règle algèbre achète frère

In the examples, you can see that **é** represents the sound [e], while **è** represents the sound [ɛ] in writing. You've probably noticed that **e** with no accent and some other letter combinations can represent these sounds as well. Repeat these words.

apportez trouver

You see that the spellings **ez** and **er** normally represent the sound [e]. This is true of all infinitives ending in **-er.** Now repeat these words.

fait	français	neige	bête
elle	cassette	examen	cherche

Some spellings of the vowel sound [ɛ] are **ait, ais, ei,** and **ê**. An unaccented **e** is pronounced as open [ɛ] when it is followed by a double consonant, such as **ll** or **tt,** when followed by **x,** and, in most cases, when followed by **r,** or by any pronounced consonant.

A. A prononcer

Repeat the following words.

1. délicieux	méchant	théâtre	vélo
2. après-midi	père	mère	très
3. février	chanter	chez	prenez
4. cette	française	treize	pêches

B. A lire

Take turns with a partner reading each of the following sentences aloud.

1. Ne quittez pas! Je vais chercher mon frère.
2. Marcel a visité Arles en mai. Il est allé au musée, à la cathédrale et aux arènes.
3. Elle n'aime pas trop l'algèbre et la géométrie, mais elle aime bien l'espagnol.
4. Tu ne peux pas aller au cinéma. Tu n'as pas fait la vaisselle.

C. A écrire

You're going to hear a short dialogue. Write down what you hear.

LISONS!

Do you talk on the telephone much? Whom do you call? What do you talk about? What advantages are there to talking on the phone? Are there disadvantages? Based on the title of this article, what do you think it will be about?

DE BONS CONSEILS

As you read, you use many different reading strategies at the same time. You may start by looking at illustrations, then move on to the titles and subtitles. You may need to skim the passage to get the general idea, then scan for specific details, and finally read the passage for more complete comprehension.

A. Skim the article. What kind of information do you expect to find?

B. What is the purpose of each section? How does the second section differ from the others?

Emmanuelle

C. How old was Emmanuelle when she started using the telephone? How did her parents feel about her using the telephone?

D. Read Emmanuelle's statement and list all the cognates you find. Then, match these terms with their English equivalents.

1. carte téléphonique	a. stationery
2. cervelle	b. phone card
3. remboursement	c. brain
4. cabine téléphonique	d. reimbursement
5. papier à lettres	e. telephone booth

Et moi, et moi... et eux !

Je passe ma vie au téléphone

Il y en a qui chantent : «Qui a eu cette idée folle, un jour, d'inventer l'école?» Moi, si j'en avais le talent, je chanterais : «Qui a eu cette idée folle, un jour, d'inventer le phone?»

Je ne pouvais plus me passer du téléphone. Et pourtant, j'ai tout essayé : punitions des parents, remboursement des communications, cures de quinze jours et plus en colonie... J'en ai découvert l'usage à dix ou onze ans, l'utilisation quasi quotidienne à treize ans. Et cela pour n'importe quel motif : discuter du travail scolaire, appeler les copains de colo qui habitent parfois à plus de 100 km de chez moi...

C'est à ce moment-là que mes parents sont intervenus. Au début, mes coups de fil ne se voyaient pas sur la note car mes parents restent assez longtemps, eux aussi, au téléphone. Mais du coup, j'ai pris l'habitude des longues conversations et des cris se sont fait entendre. Jusqu'au jour où, las de me réprimander, ils ont décidé de m'acheter une carte téléphonique et des timbres. J'ai vite eu la flemme d'aller à la cabine téléphonique et j'ai donc jeté mon dévolu sur le papier à lettres. En écrivant, j'utilise ma petite cervelle et quel plaisir de recevoir

Emmanuelle : «Qui a eu l'idée, un jour, d'inventer le phone?»

en retour une lettre que je peux lire et relire où et quand je veux! Il ne se passe pas une journée sans que je reçoive ma lecture préférée, celle qui vient du fond du cœur, celle des copains. D'accord, le téléphone est rapide et chaleureux, mais la lettre l'est peut-être encore plus. Bref, le téléphone est une gâterie à consommer avec modération.

Emmanuelle, 15 ans

LE bon usage du téléphone passe par une certaine maîtrise de l'appareil. Il faut savoir se présenter, être clair, précis, articuler... Après quelques années de pratique s'installe une véritable relation avec le combiné magique, merveilleux messager des peines et des espoirs. On attend une soirée entière une hypothétique sonnerie, on sursaute à chaque «Dring!», redoutant que Sylvain annule le rendez-vous pour lequel il a fallu passer trois heures dans la salle de bains. Combien de fois ai-je tourné, hésitante, autour de cet objet mystérieux au clavier soudain terrifiant? Combien de fois a-t-il, avec patience et sans jamais rien dire, recueilli mes rires et mes larmes? C'est pourquoi, aujourd'hui, je tiens à confesser publiquement et solennellement que j'aime mon téléphone!

Géraldine, 17 ans

Géraldine : «Je le confesse : mon téléphone, je l'aime!»

Pour dire bonjour, pour un rien...

Un quart d'heure, une demi-heure, une heure pendus au bout du fil... L'opération se répète quotidiennement. «Mes enfants téléphonent à leurs amis pour un rien, pour se dire bonjour et parfois pour faire leurs devoirs. Ça commence dès qu'ils rentrent du lycée et ça peut durer très longtemps... C'est à croire qu'ils sont nés avec un téléphone à l'oreille!», confie Véronique. Comme le dit Aurélie : «De retour chez soi, la seule façon de conserver un lien avec ceux qu'on vient de quitter, c'est le téléphone.»

Au sens propre comme au sens figuré, l'appareil est un fil qui vous relie au monde, qui vous rassure sur l'amitié des copains. C'est-à-dire sur ce qui est le plus important. Parce que dans l'amitié, on trouve la confiance, le respect, la tolérance et la sécurité dont on a tant besoin, à tout moment. Faute de lien, le risque est de se retrouver seul face à ses angoisses.

Le téléphone, c'est un fil qui vous relie au monde, qui rassure sur l'amitié des copains. Et c'est ce qui est le plus important.

D'ailleurs, peu importe parfois qui vous appelez; quand l'interlocuteur décroche, vous finissez toujours par trouver quelque chose à raconter ou une confidence à partager.

E. How did Emmanuelle break her telephone addiction? How does she communicate with her friends now? Why does she prefer this means of communication?

Pour dire bonjour, pour un rien...

F. In this section, Véronique and Aurélie each make a statement. Which person is a parent? How do you know?

G. Read the selection again and find three reasons why people enjoy talking on the phone. Which reason do you think is most important?

Géraldine

H. What advice does Géraldine give at the beginning of her statement? How does she describe her relationship with the telephone?

I. Who might have made each of the following statements?

"My telephone is my best friend."

"Finally, Arlette answered the letter I wrote her last week!"

"You may not make any more long-distance calls!"

J. Which people give the following reasons for talking on the phone?

1. to say hello to friends
2. to do homework

K. In English, write a statement similar to Emmanuelle's and Geraldine's in which you tell how you feel about the telephone. Give examples to show why you feel the way you do.

MISE EN PRATIQUE

1 A friend has left a message on your answering machine telling you what he did over the weekend. Listen, then decide if these sentences are true or false.

1. Martin a passé un mauvais week-end.
2. Il est allé à la plage.
3. Il a fait beau pendant le week-end.
4. Il a joué au football samedi.
5. Il n'a pas joué au tennis.
6. Dimanche, il a fait de l'aérobic.

2 Scan these letters first and then read them more carefully. What are they about? Who is Agnès? Then, answer the questions that follow.

Chère Agnès

Agnès vous comprend. Vous pouvez lui confier tous vos problèmes. Elle trouve toujours une solution!

Il me dit qu'il veut sortir avec moi. Est-ce vrai?

Chère Agnès,

J'aime beaucoup un garçon, Pierre, qui me dit, dans une lettre très tendre, qu'il veut sortir avec moi. Mais il ne m'appelle jamais. Se moque-t-il de moi? Aide-moi car je suis dingue de lui!

--Monique...

Ne te décourage pas! Tu aimes ce garçon et il t'aime également. Tu t'imagines qu'il se moque de toi, mais lui aussi doit se demander s'il a ses chances. A toi d'aller vers lui. Bonne chance!

Toute ma famille me déteste.

Chère Agnès,

J'ai 14 ans et j'ai un problème : tout le monde dans ma famille me déteste, sauf ma mémé. Mes parents et ma sœur se moquent toujours de moi et me disent que je suis laide. Je suis très déprimée. Au secours!

--S

Ah S...! N'écoute pas ce que ta famille te dit. Et puis, il y a toujours ta mémé qui t'aime. Tu as 14 ans et tes parents ont sûrement peur de perdre leur petite fille. Parle-leur de tes sentiments et tu verras, tout ira mieux.

1. What is Monique's problem?
2. How does Agnès respond?
3. Who is S having difficulties with?
4. What does Agnès advise her to do?

3 Based on what you know about the French telephone system, tell whether the statements below are true or false.

1. The only way to make a call from a public phone in France is to use coins.
2. You can generally find a public phone at the post office.
3. You can't buy phone cards at the post office.
4. Card-operated phones are being replaced by coin-operated ones.
5. If you make a call using a phone card, you will be charged based on the distance and duration of the call.

4 Ecrivons!

Think of a problem that many teenagers face. Describe the problem in a letter to Agnès and ask her to give you some advice. Then, exchange letters with a classmate and write a response offering advice about his or her problem.

STRATEGIE

Answering the five "W" questions (Who? What? Where? When? and Why?) can help you clarify your ideas. It can also help you make sure you don't leave out important information for your audience.

Prewriting
On a sheet of paper, brainstorm ways to explain the problem by asking yourself the "W" questions. Who is involved in the problem? What exactly is the problem? Where do you see the problem? At home? At school? When is the problem most evident? Why do you think this problem occurs?

Writing
Using the answers to your "W" questions, write a letter to Agnès describing the problem. Be as specific as you can in your description. However, don't try to use vocabulary and expressions you don't know or aren't familiar with. Use what you know as effectively as you can; other words and expressions will come later.

Now, exchange letters with a classmate. Each of you should write a response to the other's letter, offering advice on the problem. In writing your response, try to use some of the expressions you've learned for giving advice. After your classmate has read your response, have him or her return it to you, along with the letter you wrote. You're now ready for the final step of the writing process.

Revising
Evaluating your work is another important part of writing. This process involves several steps:

1. Self-evaluation: Reread both your letter and the response you wrote. Are they both arranged well? Are they easy to understand? Are they too wordy or are they lacking information?
2. Proofreading: Now, go over your writing again. This time, look just for misspelled words, punctuation errors, and grammatical mistakes.
3. Revising: Make any changes you feel are necessary.

After these steps are completed, you can submit, or publish, the final copy of your work.

5 JEU DE ROLE

You haven't seen your friend in a while. You want to find out what he or she has been doing. Phone and ask to speak to your friend. Talk about what you both did last weekend. Find out also what your friend is planning to do next summer. Act this out with a partner.

QUE SAIS-JE?

Can you use what you've learned in this chapter?

Can you ask for and express opinions? p. 237

1 How would you ask a friend how his or her weekend went?

2 How would you tell someone that your weekend was . . .

1. great?
2. OK?
3. horrible?

Can you inquire about and relate past events using the *passé composé*? p. 238

3 If you were inquiring about your friend's weekend, how would you ask . . .

1. what your friend did?
2. where your friend went?
3. what happened?

4 How would you tell someone that you did these things?

1.

2.

3.

Can you make and answer a telephone call? p. 244

5 If you were making a telephone call, how would you . . .

1. tell who you are?
2. ask if it's the right house?
3. ask to speak to someone?
4. ask to leave a message?
5. ask someone to say you called?
6. tell someone the line's busy?

6 If you were answering a telephone call, how would you . . .

1. ask who's calling?
2. ask someone to hold?
3. ask someone to call back later?

Can you share confidences, console others, and ask for and give advice? p. 247

7 How would you approach a friend about a problem you have?

8 What would you say to console a friend?

9 How would you ask a friend for advice?

10 How would you tell a friend what you think he or she should do?

VOCABULAIRE

PREMIERE ETAPE

Asking for and expressing opinions

Tu as passé un bon week-end? *Did you have a good weekend?*
Oui, très chouette. *Yes, super.*
Oui, excellent. *Yes, excellent.*
Oui, très bon. *Yes, very good.*
Oui, ça a été. *Yes, it was OK.*
Oh, pas mauvais. *Oh, not bad.*
Très mauvais. *Very bad.*
C'était épouvantable. *It was horrible.*

Inquiring about and relating past events

Qu'est-ce qui s'est passé (hier)? *What happened (yesterday)?*
Nous avons parlé. *We talked.*
Qu'est-ce que tu as fait... ? *What did you do . . . ?*
D'abord,... *First, . . .*
Ensuite,... *Then, . . .*
Après, je suis sorti(e). *Afterwards, I went out.*
Et après (ça)... *And after (that) . . .*
Finalement/Enfin,... *Finally, . . .*
Tu es allé(e) où? *Where did you go?*
Je suis allé(e)... *I went . . .*
j'ai fait *I did, I made*
j'ai pris *I took*
j'ai vu *I saw*
j'ai lu *I read*
déjà *already*
bien *well*
mal *badly*
ne... pas encore *not yet*
acheter *to buy*
apporter *to bring*
chanter *to sing*
chercher *to look for*
commencer *to begin, to start*
déjeuner à la cantine *to have lunch at the cafeteria*
dîner *to have dinner*
gagner *to win, to earn*
montrer *to show*
oublier *to forget*
passer un examen *to take an exam*
rater le bus *to miss the bus*
rater une interro *to fail a quiz*
rencontrer *to meet for the first time*
répéter *to rehearse, to practice music*
retrouver *to meet with*
travailler au fast-food *to work at a fast-food restaurant*
trouver *to find*
visiter *to visit (a place)*
une fille *girl*
un garçon *boy*

DEUXIEME ETAPE

Making and answering a telephone call

Allô? *Hello?*
Je suis bien chez... ? *Is this . . . 's house?*
Qui est à l'appareil? *Who's calling?*
(Est-ce que)... est là, s'il vous plaît? *Is . . . there, please?*
Une seconde, s'il vous plaît. *One second, please.*
(Est-ce que) je peux parler à... ? *May I speak to . . . ?*
Bien sûr. *Certainly.*
Vous pouvez rappeler plus tard? *Can you call back later?*
Je peux laisser un message? *May I leave a message?*
Vous pouvez lui dire que j'ai téléphoné? *Can you tell her/him that I called?*
Ne quittez pas. *Hold on.*
Ça ne répond pas. *There's no answer.*
C'est occupé. *It's busy.*
attendre *to wait for*
perdre *to lose*
répondre (à) *to answer*
vendre *to sell*

TROISIEME ETAPE

Sharing confidences and consoling others

J'ai un petit problème. *I've got a little problem.*
Je peux te parler? *Can we talk?*
Tu as une minute? *Do you have a minute?*
Je t'écoute. *I'm listening.*
Qu'est-ce que je peux faire? *What can I do?*
Ne t'en fais pas! *Don't worry!*
Ça va aller mieux! *It's going to get better!*

Asking for and giving advice

A ton avis, qu'est-ce que je fais? *In your opinion, what do I do?*
Qu'est-ce que tu me conseilles? *What do you advise me to do?*
Oublie-le/-la/-les! *Forget him/her/it/them!*
Téléphone-lui/-leur! *Call him/her/them!*
Tu devrais lui/leur parler. *You should talk to him/her/them.*
Pourquoi tu ne... pas? *Why don't you . . . ?*
le *him, it*
la *her, it*
les *them*
lui *to him, to her*
leur *to them*

CHAPITRE

10 Dans un magasin de vêtements

1 Je ne sais pas quoi mettre pour aller à la boum.

It's not easy to decide what to wear on a special occasion. It's often a welcome excuse to buy something new. But what? It depends on the statement you want to make. Chic? Casual? How do you create just the right look?

In this chapter you will learn

- to ask for and give advice
- to express need; to inquire
- to ask for an opinion; to pay a compliment; to criticize; to hesitate; to make a decision

And you will

- listen to French-speaking students talk about what they like to wear on different occasions
- read about the clothing styles French-speaking teenagers like
- write about what you wear on different occasions
- find out how francophone teenagers feel about fashion

② J'aimerais un foulard pour aller avec cette jupe.

③ C'est tout à fait ton style!

Mise en train

Chacun ses goûts

What event are Hélène and Magali discussing at the beginning of the story? Where does Magali go? Why do you think Hélène doesn't go with her?

1
Oh là là! Je ne sais pas quoi mettre demain. C'est l'anniversaire de Sophie. J'ai envie d'acheter quelque chose de joli. Et toi, qu'est-ce que tu vas mettre?
Oh, je ne sais pas. Sans doute un jean et un tee-shirt.
ARTISANS DU MONDE
IZZERIA

2
Pourquoi est-ce que tu ne trouves pas quelque chose d'original? De mignon?
Ecoute, Magali. Moi, j'aime bien être en jean et en tee-shirt. C'est simple et agréable à porter. Chacun ses goûts.
ARTISANS DU MONDE

Au magasin...

3
Bonjour. Je peux vous aider?
Je cherche quelque chose pour aller à une fête. J'aimerais quelque chose d'original et pas trop cher.

4
Qu'est-ce que vous faites comme taille?
Je fais du 38.

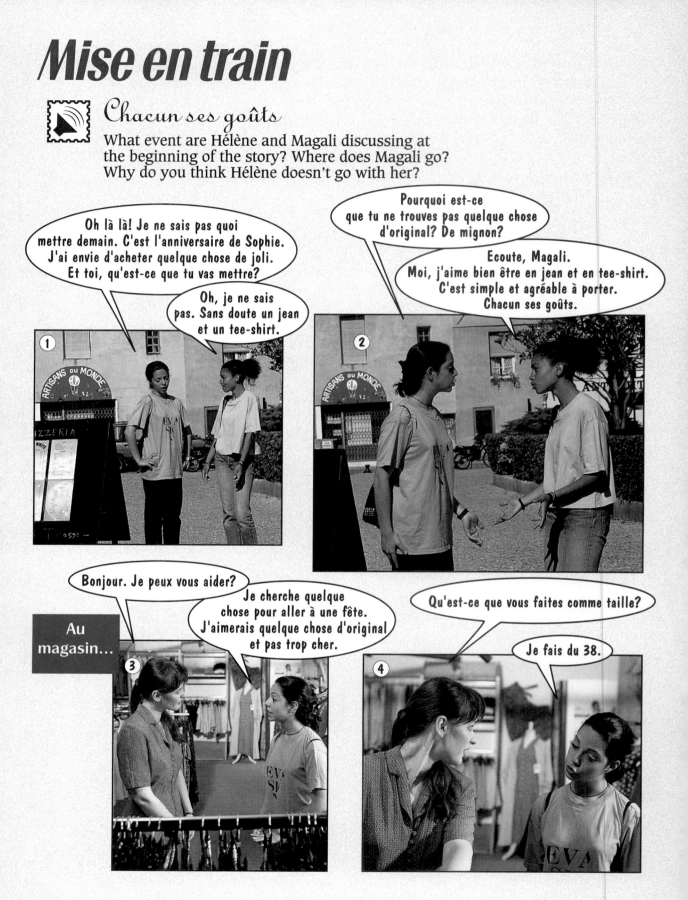

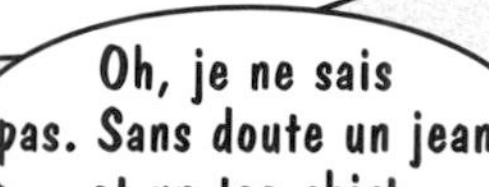

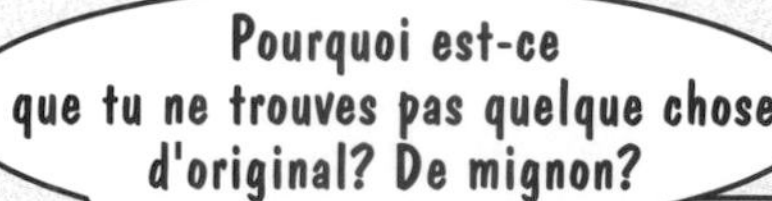

Quelques minutes plus tard...

8

Ah, très chic! C'est tout à fait votre style.

Vous trouvez? Mais, je ne sais pas quoi mettre avec.

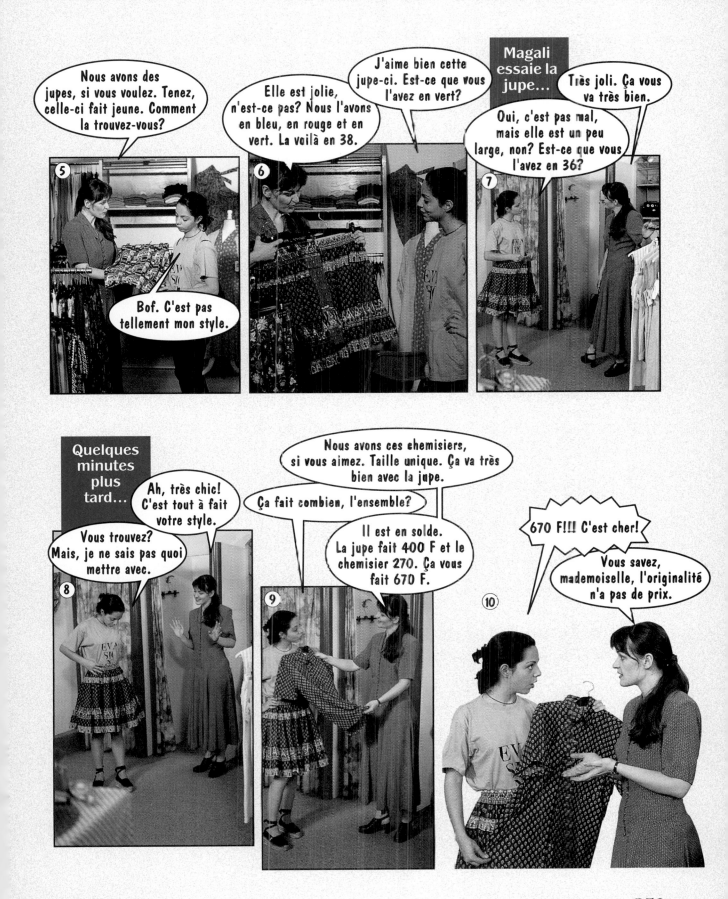

1 Tu as compris?

1. Why does Magali want to buy something new?
2. What is Hélène going to wear? Why?
3. What type of clothing is Magali looking for?
4. What outfit does Magali like?
5. What does she think of the price?

2 C'est qui?

Qui parle? C'est Magali, Hélène ou la vendeuse?

1. «J'aimerais quelque chose d'original et pas trop cher.»
2. «Je peux vous aider?»
3. «Moi, j'aime bien être en jean et en tee-shirt. C'est simple et agréable à porter.»
4. «Qu'est-ce que vous faites comme taille?»
5. «Chacun ses goûts.»
6. «Est-ce que vous l'avez en vert?»
7. «C'est tout à fait votre style.»
8. «Ce n'est pas tellement mon style.»

3 Chacun ses goûts

What does Magali say about these things?

1. le jean et le tee-shirt d'Hélène
2. la jupe verte en 38
3. le prix de l'ensemble

4 Qu'est-ce qu'elle répond?

Qu'est-ce que Magali répond à la vendeuse?

1. Qu'est-ce que vous faites comme taille?
2. Comment la trouvez-vous?
3. Je peux vous aider?
4. Ça vous fait 670 francs.

a. C'est cher!
b. Je fais du 38.
c. Je cherche quelque chose pour aller à une fête.
d. Bof. Ce n'est pas tellement mon style.

5 Cherche les expressions

According to **Chacun ses goûts,** how would you . . .

1. express indecision?
2. express satisfaction with your clothes?
3. tell a salesperson what you want?
4. tell what size you wear?
5. express dissatisfaction with clothes?
6. ask for a certain color or size?
7. ask what all of your purchases cost?

Je fais du...
Ça fait combien, ... ?
C'est simple et agréable à porter.
J'aimerais quelque chose de...
Je ne sais pas quoi mettre.
Est-ce que vous l'avez en... ?
C'est pas tellement mon style.

6 Et maintenant, à toi

Do you prefer Magali's style or Hélène's? What sort of clothes do you like to wear?

PREMIERE ETAPE

Asking for and giving advice

VOCABULAIRE

VETEMENTS

maillot de bain bleu et rouge 119F

chemise blanche ou bleue 129F

veste bleue 720F

chemisier blanc 149F

robe verte à fleurs 439F

blouson bleu ou noir 925F

blouson marron ou noir 1160F

jupe grise 199F

chaussures marron 309F

bottes noires 499F

Accessoires

chaussettes noires, blanches, bleues, pêche 10,20F la paire

lunettes de soleil 61,50F

cravate bleue à rayures 83F

montre noire 449F

écharpe rose et blanche 101,50F

ceinture noire ou marron 99,90F

chapeau gris 255F

boucles d'oreilles 249F

casquette rouge 161F

Here are some other words you may want to use to talk about what you're wearing.

un bracelet	**un manteau**	**des sandales** (f.)
un cardigan	**un pantalon**	**un short**
un jean	**un pull (-over)**	**un sweat-shirt**

7 Ecoute!

Listen as Armelle tells her friend about her big shopping trip. Then, choose the illustration that represents her purchases.

a. b. c.

8 Des cadeaux

Look at the picture and tell what Lise bought for her family.

Elle a acheté... pour...

9 Pas de chance!

On your way to France, the airline lost your luggage. Fortunately, the airline is paying you $500 for new clothes. Make a list of the clothes you'll buy.

D'abord, je vais acheter...

10 La fête

Imagine that you've been invited to a party. Of the clothes you listed in Activity 9, which would you choose to wear? What clothes would you need that aren't on your list?

GRAMMAIRE The verbs **mettre** and **porter**

mettre *(to put, to put on, to wear)*

Je **mets**	un pull.	Nous **mettons**	un pull.
Tu **mets**		Vous **mettez**	
Il/Elle/On **met**		Ils/Elles **mettent**	

- **Mets** and **met** are pronounced alike. You don't pronounce the final consonant(s) **ts** and **t**.
- The past participle of **mettre** is **mis**: Elle **a mis** une jupe.
- You can also use the regular **-er** verb **porter** to tell what someone is wearing:
  Elle **porte** une robe.

11 Qu'est-ce qu'on met pour sortir?

1. **Pour aller à l'école, Sophie...**

2. **Pour aller à une boum, elles...**

3. **Pour aller au café, toi, tu...**

4. **Pour aller au stade, nous...**

12 Qu'est-ce que tu as mis hier?

Ask your partner what he or she wore yesterday and tell what you wore.

Although it's common to feel a little uncomfortable when speaking a new language, the best way to overcome it is to talk and talk and talk. Whenever you answer a question or have a conversation with a partner, try to keep the conversation going as long as possible. Don't worry about making a mistake. The more you think about making mistakes, the less likely you will be to talk.

COMMENT DIT-ON... ?

Asking for and giving advice

To ask for advice:

Je ne sais pas quoi mettre pour aller à la boum. *I don't know what to wear for (to) . . .*

Qu'est-ce que je mets? *What shall I wear?*

To give advice:

Pourquoi est-ce que tu ne mets pas ta robe? *Why don't you wear . . . ?*

Mets ton jean. *Wear . . .*

JE NE SAIS PAS QUOI METTRE POUR ALLER VOIR NICOLE!
POURQUOI EST-CE QUE TU NE METS PAS MA CRAVATE AVEC CETTE CHEMISE?

13 Ecoute!

Are these people asking for or giving advice?

14 Harmonie de couleurs

Ask your partner's advice on what you should wear with the following items. Take turns.

—Qu'est-ce que je mets avec ma jupe noire?
—Pourquoi tu ne mets pas ton pull gris?

1. Avec mon pantalon bleu?
2. Avec ma chemise rouge?
3. Avec mes baskets violettes?
4. Avec mon pull gris?
5. Avec mon short orange?
6. Avec ma veste verte?

15 Qu'est-ce que je mets?

Tell your partner where you'll go and what you'll do during your stay as an exchange student in France. Ask for advice about what you should wear. Then, change roles.

—Pour aller au café, qu'est-ce que je mets?
—Mets un jean et un sweat-shirt.

pour aller à la plage
pour aller au café
pour aller à une boum
pour jouer au football
pour dîner dans un restaurant élégant
pour aller au parc
pour faire du patin à glace
pour aller au théâtre
pour aller au musée
pour faire du ski

16 Mon journal

Write about what you normally wear to school, to parties, to go out with friends, or what you wear to dress up for a special occasion.

DEUXIEME ETAPE

Expressing need; inquiring

COMMENT DIT-ON... ?

Expressing need; inquiring

The salesperson might ask you:

Vous désirez?
(Est-ce que) je peux vous aider?
May I help you?

To express need, you might answer:

Oui, il me faut un chemisier vert.
Oui, vous avez des chapeaux?
Je cherche quelque chose pour aller à une boum.
I'm looking for something to . . .
J'aimerais un chemisier **pour aller avec** ma jupe.
I'd like . . . to go with . . .
Non, merci, je regarde.
No, thanks, I'm just looking.
Je peux l'/les essayer?
Can I try it/them on?
Je peux essayer le/la/l'/les bleu(e)(s)?
Can I try on the . . . ?

To inquire about prices:

C'est combien,... ?
Ça fait combien?

To ask about sizes, colors, and fabrics:

Vous avez ça en (taille) 36?
Do you have that in (size) . . . ?
en bleu?
en coton? *cotton?*
en jean? *denim?*
en cuir? *leather?*

NOTE DE GRAMMAIRE

You can use colors and other adjectives as nouns by putting **le, la,** or **les** before them. Change their spelling according to the things they refer to: **le bleu, la bleue** = *the blue one;* **les verts, les vertes** = *the green ones.*

17 Ecoute!

Listen and decide whether a customer or salesperson is speaking.

18 Ecoute!

Listen and decide whether these people are talking about the color, price, or size of the items they're looking at.

19 Méli-mélo!

Mets cette conversation dans le bon ordre.

—C'est combien?

—Oui. Nous les avons en bleu, en rouge et en orange.

—Voilà, ces maillots de bain sont très chic.

—Oh là là! C'est trop cher, ça!

—Je peux vous aider?

—C'est 450 F.

—Euh, je n'aime pas trop la couleur. Vous les avez en bleu?

—Oui, je cherche un maillot de bain.

20 Quelle couleur?

Blondine and Claire are getting ready for a party. Complete their conversation with **le, la, l'**, or **les** and a color.

—Et avec ma jupe bleue, est-ce que je mets mon chemisier orange ou mon chemisier blanc?
—Pas l'orange! Mets plutôt __1__.
—Et pour les chaussures? __2__ vont mieux avec ma jupe, non?
—Mais non. Mets __3__.
—Et mon sac rose ou le noir? Le rose, non?
—Mmm... je n'aime pas __4__. Tu as une ceinture noire?
—Oui, mais j'ai aussi une ceinture jaune.
—Ah non! Pas la jaune! Mets __5__.

21 Préférences

You and a partner are looking at some clothes in a catalogue. Tell each other which items you like and in which colors.

—J'aime bien ce polo en bleu. Et toi?
—Moi, j'aime mieux le noir.

COLLECTION D'ETE
LES POLOS à 155F
LES JEANS à 245F
blanc
orange
noir
rouge
jaune
bleu
noir
blanc
bleu

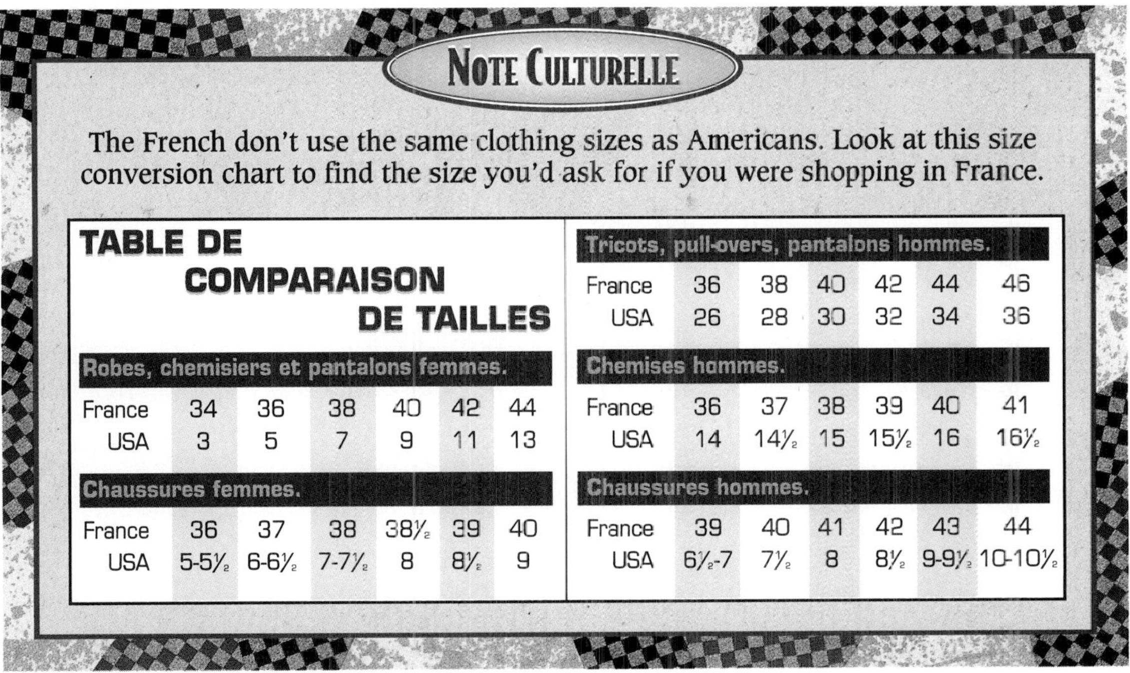

NOTE CULTURELLE

The French don't use the same clothing sizes as Americans. Look at this size conversion chart to find the size you'd ask for if you were shopping in France.

TABLE DE COMPARAISON DE TAILLES

Robes, chemisiers et pantalons femmes.

France	34	36	38	40	42	44
USA	3	5	7	9	11	13

Chaussures femmes.

France	36	37	38	38½	39	40
USA	5-5½	6-6½	7-7½	8	8½	9

Tricots, pull-overs, pantalons hommes.

France	36	38	40	42	44	46
USA	26	28	30	32	34	36

Chemises hommes.

France	36	37	38	39	40	41
USA	14	14½	15	15½	16	16½

Chaussures hommes.

France	39	40	41	42	43	44
USA	6½-7	7½	8	8½	9-9½	10-10½

22 Jeu de rôle

You need something to go with some of the items below. Tell the salesperson what you need and ask about prices and sizes. Act out this scene with a partner. Then, change roles.

un jean
un blouson en jean
une veste en cuir noir
un pull jaune
un short noir
une chemise en coton

Vocabulaire à la carte

à rayures	*striped*	**en laine**	*wool*
à carreaux	*checked*	**en rayonne**	*rayon*
à pois	*polka dot*	**en lin**	*linen*
à fleurs	*flowered*	**en soie**	*silk*
bleu clair	*light blue*	**bleu foncé**	*dark blue*

GRAMMAIRE -ir verbs

You've already learned the forms of regular **-er** and **-re** verbs. There is one more regular verb pattern for you to learn. Here are the forms of regular **-ir** verbs.

choisir *(to choose, to pick)*

Je **choisis**	un manteau noir.	Nous **choisissons**	ce jean-là.
Tu **choisis**		Vous **choisissez**	
Il/Elle/On **choisit**		Ils/Elles **choisissent**	

- The past participle of regular **-ir** verbs ends in **-i**: Elle a choisi une belle robe.
- Other regular **-ir** verbs you might want to use when talking about clothes are: **grandir** *(to grow)*, **maigrir** *(to lose weight)*, and **grossir** *(to gain weight)*.

23 Qu'est-ce qu'ils choisissent?

Qu'est-ce qu'ils choisissent pour aller avec leurs vêtements?

1. Elle...

2. Nous...

3. Il...

4. Vous...

24 Ça ne me va plus!

Why don't these clothes fit anymore? Remember to use the **passé composé** in your answer.

1.

2.

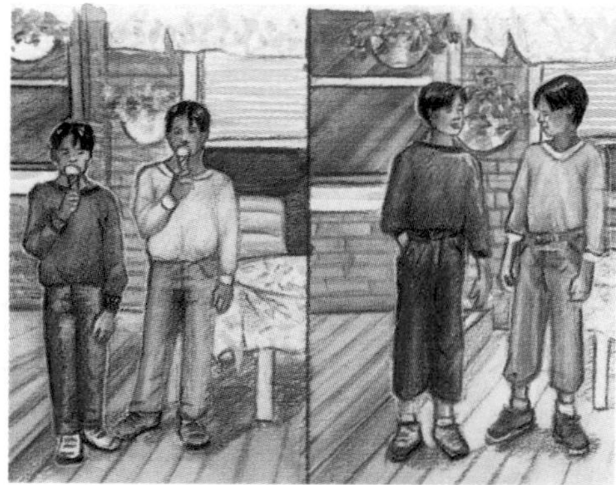

3.

4.

25 Dans un grand magasin

With a partner, act out a scene in a department store between a customer and salesperson. The customer, who's going on a winter vacation, should tell what he or she is looking for, ask about size, colors, styles, fabrics, and prices, and ask to try things on. The salesperson should respond appropriately. Change roles.

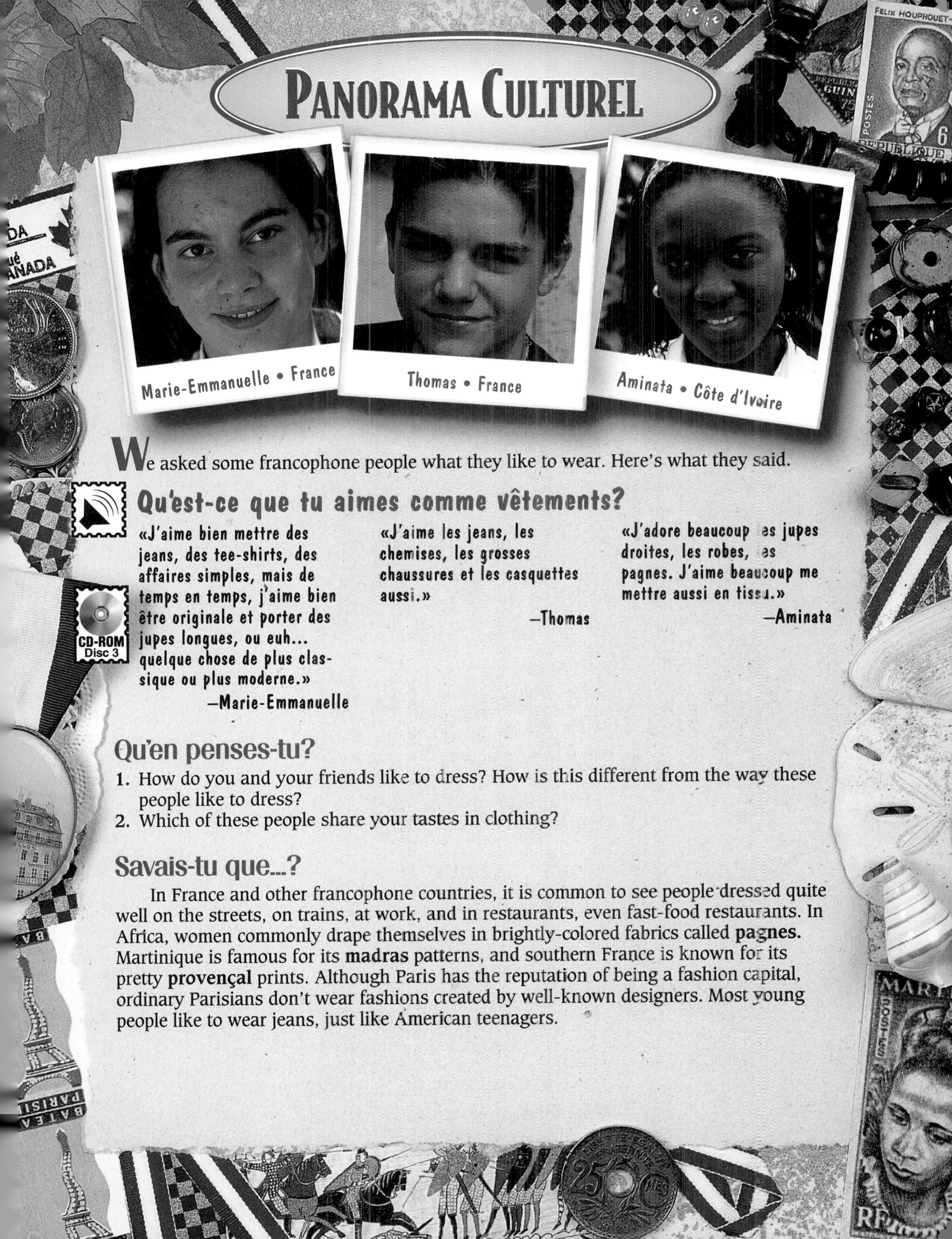

PANORAMA CULTUREL

Marie-Emmanuelle • France

Thomas • France

Aminata • Côte d'Ivoire

We asked some francophone people what they like to wear. Here's what they said.

CD-ROM Disc 3

Qu'est-ce que tu aimes comme vêtements?

«J'aime bien mettre des jeans, des tee-shirts, des affaires simples, mais de temps en temps, j'aime bien être originale et porter des jupes longues, ou euh... quelque chose de plus classique ou plus moderne.»

—Marie-Emmanuelle

«J'aime les jeans, les chemises, les grosses chaussures et les casquettes aussi.»

—Thomas

«J'adore beaucoup les jupes droites, les robes, les pagnes. J'aime beaucoup me mettre aussi en tissu.»

—Aminata

Qu'en penses-tu?

1. How do you and your friends like to dress? How is this different from the way these people like to dress?
2. Which of these people share your tastes in clothing?

Savais-tu que...?

In France and other francophone countries, it is common to see people dressed quite well on the streets, on trains, at work, and in restaurants, even fast-food restaurants. In Africa, women commonly drape themselves in brightly-colored fabrics called **pagnes.** Martinique is famous for its **madras** patterns, and southern France is known for its pretty **provençal** prints. Although Paris has the reputation of being a fashion capital, ordinary Parisians don't wear fashions created by well-known designers. Most young people like to wear jeans, just like American teenagers.

TROISIEME ETAPE

Asking for an opinion; paying a compliment; criticizing; hesitating; making a decision

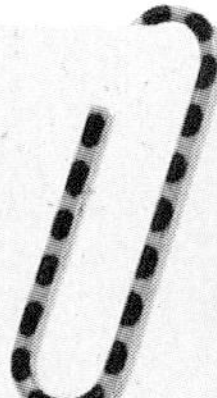

COMMENT DIT-ON... ?

Asking for an opinion, paying a compliment, and criticizing

To ask for an opinion:

Comment tu trouves... ?
Elle me va, cette robe?
Does . . . suit me?
Il te/vous plaît, ce jean?
Do you like . . . ?
Tu aimes mieux le bleu **ou** le noir?

To pay a compliment:

C'est parfait. *It's perfect.*
C'est tout à fait ton/votre style. *It looks great on you!*
Elle te/vous va très bien, cette jupe.
. . . suits you really well.
Il/Elle va très bien avec ta chemise. *It goes very well with . . .*
Je le/la/les trouve... *I think it's/they're . . .*
très à la mode. *in style.*
chic.
mignon(mignonne)(s). *cute.*
sensationnel(le)/sensas. *fantastic.*
rétro.

To criticize:

Il/Elle ne te/vous va pas du tout. *That doesn't look good on you at all.*
Il/Elle est (Ils/Elles sont) trop serré(e)(s). *It's/They're too tight.*
large(s). *baggy.*
petit(e)(s). *small.*
grand(e)(s). *big.*
court(e)(s). *short.*
long(longue)(s). *long.*
Il/Elle ne va pas du tout avec tes chaussures. *That doesn't go at all with . . .*
Je le/la/les trouve moche(s). *I think it's/they're tacky.*
démodé(e)(s). *out of style.*
horrible(s). *terrible.*

26 Ecoute!

Listen to the following conversations and decide if the speakers are complimenting or criticizing each other's clothing.

27 Un après-midi au grand magasin

You and a friend are spending the afternoon shopping at **Le Printemps.** If these people asked you for advice, what would you say?

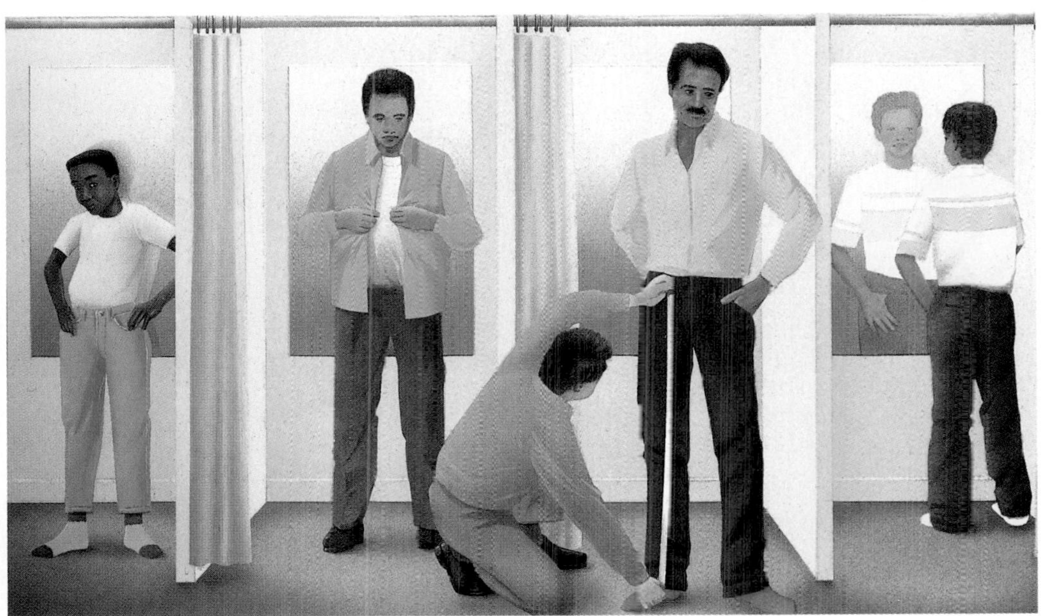

28 Sondage

Complete this survey from a French fashion magazine. How many points did you get? Which category do you fall into? Compare your answers with your partner's.

ENQUETE: LA MODE

Es-tu à la mode?

Fais notre petit test pour savoir si tu es vraiment à la dernière mode.

1 En général, quelle sorte de vêtements est-ce que tu portes?

a. Des vêtements super chic. (3 points)
b. Ça dépend de l'occasion. (2 points)
c. Des jeans, des tee-shirts et des baskets. (1 point)

2 Tu achètes de nouveaux vêtements...

a. très souvent. (3 points)
b. quelquefois. (2 points)
c. presque jamais. (1 point)

3 Quand tu achètes des vêtements, en général, tu...

a. achètes ce qui est à la dernière mode. (3 points)
b. achètes quelque chose que tu aimes. (2 points)
c. achètes ce qui est en solde. (1 point)

4 Dans un magazine de mode, tu vois que les chemises en plastique fluorescentes sont très populaires. Tu...

a. achètes 4 chemises de 4 couleurs différentes. (3 points)
b. attends patiemment pour voir si les autres en portent. (2 points)
c. refuses d'en acheter! Tu ne veux pas être ridicule! (1 point)

Réponses :

10 -12 points : Tu es vraiment à la mode! Attention! Tu risques de perdre ton originalité.
5 - 9 points : Parfaitement raisonnable! Tu es à la mode tout en gardant ton propre style.
0 - 4 points : Tu ne t'intéresses pas à la mode! Tu sais, il y a quelquefois des styles uniques. Essaie de les trouver.

NE PRENDS PAS CE TEST TROP AU SERIEUX!

Read the following dialogues to find out how French people compliment one another.

—J'aime bien ta chemise.
—Ah oui?
—Oui, elle est pas mal.
—Tu trouves? Tu sais, c'est une vieille chemise.

—Il est super, ce chapeau!
—Tu crois?
—Oui, il te va très bien.
—C'est gentil.

—Tu es ravissante aujourd'hui!
—Vraiment? Je n'ai rien fait de spécial.

Qu'en penses-tu?

1. How do these people react to a compliment?
2. How do you usually react to a compliment? How is that different from the French reactions you've just read?

Savais-tu que...?

The French do not compliment freely and generally do so only in exceptional cases. It is common to respond to compliments with **Merci**. However, French people will often respond with a modest expression of disbelief, such as **Vraiment? Tu crois? Tu trouves? Ah oui?** or a comment downplaying the importance of the item complimented, such as **Oh, c'est vieux.**

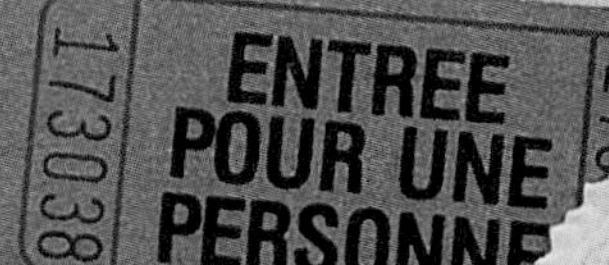

29 Fais des compliments!

Compliment two things that your partner is wearing. He or she should respond in the French way.

—Elles sont sensas, tes baskets!
—Vraiment?
—Oui, elles sont très à la mode!

GRAMMAIRE The direct object pronouns le, la, and les

The pronouns **le**, *him* or *it,* **la,** *her* or *it,* and **les,** *them,* refer to people or things. In the sentences below, what do the pronouns **le, la,** and **les** refer to?*

— Ce pull, il te plaît?	— Oui, je **le** trouve assez chic.
— Comment tu trouves cette robe?	— Je **la** trouve démodée.
— Vous aimez ces chaussures?	— Oui, je vais **les** prendre.

- You normally place the direct object pronouns before the conjugated verb.

Je **le** prends.	Je **l'**ai pris.
Je ne **la** prends pas.	Ne **les** prends pas!

- There are two exceptions to this rule. You place the direct object pronoun after the conjugated verb in a positive command and before an infinitive.

  Prends-**le!**
  Je vais **la** prendre.

- When **le** or **la** comes before a verb that starts with a vowel sound, it changes to **l'**.

  Je vais essayer **le pull.** Je vais l'essayer.

30 Qu'en penses-tu?

Elise and Karim are shopping for clothes. Complete their conversation, using **le, la, l',** and **les.**

ELISE	Dis, Karim, tu aimes ce pantalon, toi?
KARIM	Bof... Je __1__ trouve un peu démodé, mais enfin...
ELISE	Et cette chemise-là?
KARIM	Oui, je __2__ aime bien. Eh! Tu as vu ces chaussures? Elles sont super, non?
ELISE	Oui! Tu vas __3__ prendre?
KARIM	Oh, je sais pas...
ELISE	Si, allez! Prends- __4__ !
KARIM	Bon. Je vais __5__ essayer. Et toi, essaie la chemise. Je __6__ trouve vraiment chouette.
ELISE	D'accord. Mmm... et ce pull violet, il est beau, non?
KARIM	Oui, mais je __7__ préfère en bleu.

* the pullover, the dress, the shoes

COMMENT DIT-ON... ?

Hesitating; making a decision

When the salesperson asks you:

Vous avez choisi?
Vous avez décidé de prendre ce pantalon? *Have you decided to take . . . ?*
Vous le/la/les prenez? *Are you going to take it/them?*

To hesitate, say:

Je ne sais pas.
Euh... J'hésite.
Oh, I'm not sure.
Il/Elle me plaît, mais il/elle est cher/chère.
I like it, but it's expensive.

To make a decision, say:

Je le/la/les prends.
I'll take it/them.
C'est trop cher.
It's too expensive.

NOTE DE GRAMMAIRE

- Use **il/elle/ils/elles** when you are referring to a specific item.
  Comment tu trouves cette robe? **Elle** est chouette, non?
- Use **c'est** when you are speaking in general about an action or something that happened.
  J'aime porter des pantalons parce que **c'est** pratique.
  J'ai réussi à mon examen de maths! **C'est** super!

In the sentences above, **c'est** refers to the general ideas of wearing pants and passing a test.

31 Ecoute!

Listen to these exchanges between a customer and a salesperson. Tell whether the customer takes the item, doesn't take it, or can't decide.

32 Qu'est-ce qu'ils disent?

Write down what you think these people are saying. Then, get together with a partner and compare what you both have written.

1.

2.

3.

4.

33 J'hésite

You're shopping for something new to wear to a party. The salesperson helps you find something. You're unsure, but your friend offers you advice. Take turns.

PRONONCIATION

The glides [j], [w], and [ɥ]

As you listen to people speak French, you may notice a sound that reminds you of the first sound in the English word *yes*. This sound is called a *glide*, because one sound glides into another. Now, try making the sound [j] in these common French words: **mieux, chemisier, bien.** Did you notice that this gliding sound often occurs when the letter **i** is followed by **e**? The sound is also represented by the letters **ill** in words such as **maillot** and **gentille.**

There are two more glides in French. [w] sounds similar to the *w* sound you hear in *west wind.* Listen to these French words: **moi, Louis, jouer.**

The last glide sound is the one you hear in the French word **lui.** It sounds like the French vowel sounds [y] and [i] together. This sound is often written as **ui.** Listen to the glide [ɥ] in these words: **cuir, huit, juillet.**

A. A prononcer

Repeat the following words.

1. travailler	monsieur	combien	conseiller
2. pouvoir	soif	poires	moins
3. suis	minuit	suite	juillet

B. A lire

Take turns with a partner reading each of the following sentences aloud.

1. J'aime bien tes boucles d'oreilles. Elles sont géniales!
2. Il me faut des feuilles de papier, un taille-crayon et un cahier.
3. Elle a choisi un blouson en cuir et une écharpe en soie. C'est chouette!
4. Tu as quoi aujourd'hui? Moi, j'ai histoire et ensuite, je vais faire mes devoirs.
5. —Tu veux promener le chien avec moi?
   —Pourquoi pas?

C. A écrire

You're going to hear a short dialogue. Write down what you hear.

LISONS!

How important is fashion to you? Do you generally favor one style or do you like to vary the look of what you wear?

DE BONS CONSEILS

When you read, be careful to separate facts from opinions. A fact is something that can be proven by observation or specific information. **Le jean est rouge** is a fact that you could prove by looking at the jeans to see if they're red or not. An opinion is someone's personal view of something. **La mode, c'est important** is an opinion. While some people may believe that to be true, it cannot be proven.

A. Think for a moment about the role fashion plays in your life.

1. Do you follow trends you see in magazines or at school?
2. How much influence do your parents have on your wardrobe?
3. Do you think clothing is a reflection of a person's personality or lifestyle?

B. How would you categorize styles that are popular at your school or in your town? What words would you use to describe them?

C. What can you tell about the people who wrote these essays?

D. Which of the students consider fashion important? Which consider it unimportant?

LA MODE AU LYCÉE

Mélanie

• 15 ans. En seconde au lycée Théodore Aubanel, Avignon.

Ce que je trouve dommage aujourd'hui, c'est que les filles ressemblent de plus en plus à des garçons. Au lycée, presque toutes mes copines portent des jeans ou des pantalons avec des sweat-shirts. Moi aussi, j'aime bien les jeans, mais de temps en temps, je préfère m'habiller «en fille» avec des robes ou des jupes. Je porte aussi beaucoup de bijoux, surtout des boucles d'oreilles; j'adore ça. Et puis en même temps, ça fait plaisir à mes parents quand je suis habillée comme ça; ils préfèrent ça au look garçon manqué.

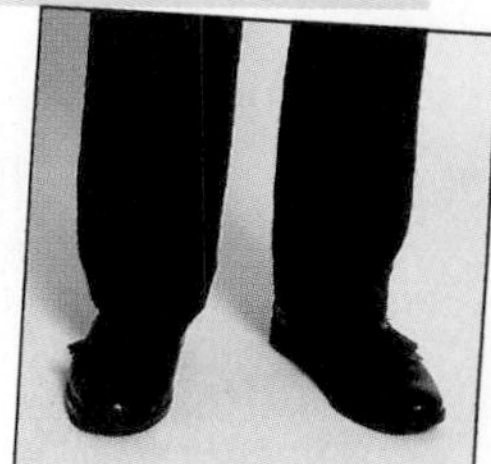

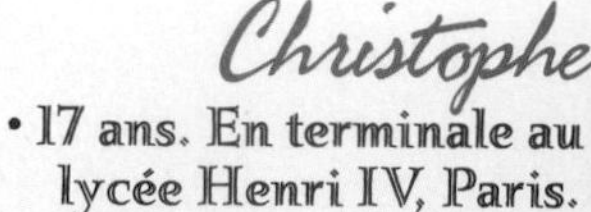

Christophe

• 17 ans. En terminale au lycée Henri IV, Paris.

Moi, ce qui m'énerve avec la mode, c'est que si tu ne la suis pas, tout le monde te regarde d'un air bizarre au lycée. Moi, par exemple, le retour de la mode des années 70, les pattes d'eph et le look grunge, c'est vraiment pas mon truc. Je trouve ça horrible. Alors, je ne vois pas pourquoi je devrais m'habiller comme ça, simplement parce que c'est la mode. Je préfère porter des pantalons à pinces, des blazers et des chemises avec des cravates. Mes copains trouvent que ça fait trop sérieux, trop fils-à-papa, mais ça m'est égal. Je suis sûr que dans quelques années, quand ils travailleront, ils seront tous habillés comme moi et quand ils regarderont des photos de terminale, ils rigoleront bien en voyant les habits qu'ils portaient à 18 ans!

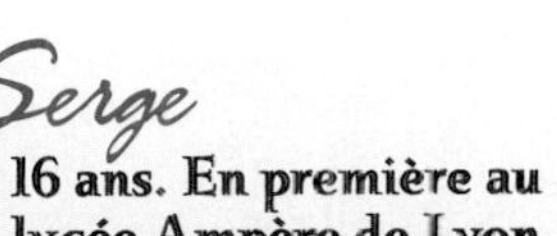

• 16 ans. En première au lycée Ampère de Lyon.

Pour moi, ce qui est vraiment important, c'est d'avoir des vêtements confortables. Je suis très sportif et j'aime pouvoir bouger dans mes habits. Mais, je veux aussi des trucs cool. Pas question de porter des vêtements très serrés ou très chers, par exemple. Je ne vois pas l'intérêt d'avoir un blouson qui coûte 4 000 F. Je préfère un blouson bon marché dans lequel je peux jouer au foot avec les copains. Comme ça, si je tombe ou si je l'abîme, c'est pas tragique. En général, je mets des jeans parce que c'est pratique et sympa. En été, je porte des tee-shirts très simples et en hiver, des sweat-shirts. Et comme chaussures, je préfère les baskets.

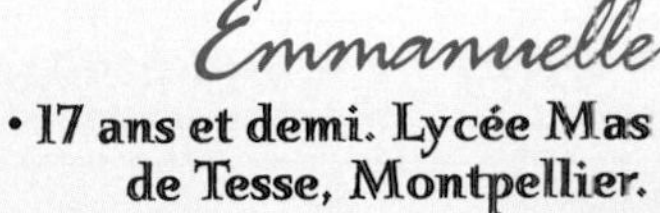

• 17 ans et demi. Lycée Mas de Tesse, Montpellier.

Pour moi, la façon dont quelqu'un s'habille est un reflet de sa personnalité. Au lycée, j'étudie les arts plastiques, et comme on le dit souvent, les artistes sont des gens originaux et créatifs. Je n'aime pas dépenser beaucoup pour mes vêtements. Je n'achète jamais de choses très chères, mais j'utilise mon imagination pour les rendre plus originales. Par exemple, j'ajoute toujours des accessoires sympa : bijoux fantaisie que je fabrique souvent moi-même, foulards, ceintures, sacs... Parfois, je fais même certains de mes vêtements, surtout les jupes car c'est facile. Et comme ça, je suis sûre que personne ne portera la même chose que moi!

E. Although many people consider France a fashion capital, the U.S. also influences fashion. What English words can you find in the essays?

F. Look for the words in the box below in the essays. Then, try to match them with their English equivalents.

1. bijoux	a. fashion
2. la mode	b. things
3. pattes d'eph	c. ruin
4. bouger	d. jewelry
5. abîme	e. to move
6. les trucs	f. bell-bottoms

G. Which student . . .

1. likes clothes that are practical and comfortable?
2. makes some of his or her clothing and jewelry?
3. doesn't buy expensive clothes?
4. thinks girls should wear feminine clothes sometimes?

H. Which of the following sentences are facts and which are opinions?

1. En été, je porte des tee-shirts.
2. Les artistes sont des gens originaux et créatifs.
3. Les filles ressemblent de plus en plus à des garçons.
4. Je n'achète jamais de choses très chères.
5. La façon dont on s'habille est un reflet de sa personnalité.

I. Write a short paragraph in French telling what you like to wear. Mention colors and any other details you feel are important.

MISE EN PRATIQUE

CD-ROM Disc 3

1 Listen to this conversation between Philippe and a saleswoman at a French department store. Then, answer these questions.

1. What does Philippe want to buy?
2. What colors does he prefer?
3. What does the salesperson say about the first item Philippe tries on?
4. How does Philippe feel about the way the item fits?
5. Does he end up buying it?

2 Look over the advertisement below. Then, answer the questions that follow.

NOUVELLE COLLECTION ARIELLE DE LA BRETTINIERE
FEMME : Pantalon à pinces uni, 100 % soie. Du 36 au 44, **399 F**. Existe en vert, bleu, rouge, blanc et noir. **Cardigan** en coton, taille unique, **299 F**. Existe en noir et blanc cassé. **Tee-shirt** cache-cœur noir, manches courtes, **129 F**. **Boucles d'oreilles** et **bracelet** fantaisie, **45 F** et **65 F**.
ENFANT : Robe bleu clair à fleurs multicolores, 100 % coton. Du 2 au 8 ans, **79 F**. **Tee-shirt** uni rose, 100 % coton, **29 F**. Du 2 au 8 ans. Existe en 17 coloris. **Sandales** en cuir blanc, **119 F**. Du 24 au 34.
HOMME : Pantalon à pinces, 100 % lin. Du 38 au 52, **439 F**. Existe en noir, bleu marine, beige et marron. **Chemise** en jean, manches longues. Du 2 au 6, **259 F**. **Pull** rouge, 100 % coton. Du 2 au 6, **299 F**.
VENDUE DANS LES GRANDS MAGASINS

1. Who does **Arielle de la Brettinière** make clothes for?
2. How many colors does the child's T-shirt come in?
3. The women's pants are available in what sizes?
4. What material is the men's shirt made of?
5. What's the most expensive men's item on the page? The most expensive women's item?

3 From what you know about French culture, are these statements true or false?

1. The French are famous for giving lots of compliments.
2. The French tend to downplay the compliments they receive.
3. **Merci** is the only appropriate way to respond to a compliment.
4. A common French way to respond to a compliment on something you're wearing is to say **Tu trouves?**

 4

Ecrivons!

You've been hired by a French magazine to write about fashion trends among American teenagers today. Interview two or three classmates about their tastes in clothing. Then, write a short article in French based on your interviews.

STRATEGIE

Paraphrasing is a useful tool for organizing and simplifying information for your readers. To paraphrase a quote or other piece of information you collect, you state the main points in your own words. At the same time, be sure you don't change the meaning of what was said.

Prewriting

First, brainstorm a list of interview questions that you might ask your classmates about their fashion preferences. You might ask what they like to wear, what they wear to parties **(les boums)**, what colors they like, and what their favorite article of clothing is. Arrange your questions in a logical order. You may want to arrange them so that you begin with more general questions and progress to more specific ones.

Next, conduct your interview with two or three classmates. Be sure to take notes on their responses to each of your questions.

Before you begin your article, rearrange the information you've collected into a logical order. For example, you might group different answers to each question together.

Writing

Expository writing is a process of converting information you've collected into a readable or easily understandable form. Newspaper and magazine articles are good examples of expository writing. Reporters collect information on newsworthy events, fashion trends, etc., and then take that information and turn it into articles that readers can easily understand.

Now, referring to the information you've collected and organized, write a short article that reveals what you found out. It's not necessary to include every detail of the information you collect. For example, if a quote from your interview is too long, you may paraphrase the main points of the quote in your own words.

Revising

Peer evaluation is another helpful step in the evaluation process. Give your article to a classmate and have him or her give you suggestions on how to improve it. After your classmate evaluates your article, make any revisions you feel are necessary, including those you find in proofreading. Now you're ready to submit your finished article.

5

JEU DE ROLE

Choose one of the items from the advertisement on page 278 and ask the salesperson about it. Do they have it in your size? Can you try it on? The salesperson should compliment the way it looks, and you should decide whether to buy it or not. Take turns playing the role of the salesperson.

QUE SAIS-JE?

Can you use what you've learned in this chapter?

Can you ask for and give advice? p. 264

1 How would you ask a friend what you should wear to a party?

2 How would you advise a friend to wear these clothes, using the verb **mettre?**

1.

2.

Can you express need and inquire? p. 265

3 How would you tell a salesperson . . .

1. that you're just looking?
2. what you would like?

4 How would you ask a salesperson . . .

1. if you can try something on?
2. if they have what you want in a different size?
3. if they have what you want in a particular color?
4. how much something costs?

5 How would you tell what these people are choosing?

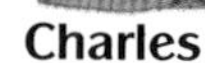

Charles

Jean-Marc et Farid

Astrid

Delphine et Camille

Can you ask for an opinion, pay a compliment, and criticize? p. 270

6 If you were shopping with a friend, how would you ask . . .

1. if your friend likes what you have on?
2. if something looks good on you?
3. if it's too short?

7 How would you compliment a friend's clothing? How would you criticize it?

Can you hesitate and make a decision? p. 274

8 How can you express your hesitation?

9 How would you tell a salesperson what you've decided to do?

VOCABULAIRE

PREMIERE ETAPE

Clothes

un blouson *jacket*
des bottes (f.) *boots*
des boucles d'oreilles (f.) *earrings*
un bracelet *bracelet*
un cardigan *cardigan*
une casquette *cap*
une ceinture *belt*
un chapeau *hat*
des chaussettes (f.) *socks*
des chaussures (f.) *shoes*
une chemise *shirt (men's)*
un chemisier *shirt (women's)*
une cravate *tie*
une écharpe *scarf*
une jupe *skirt*
des lunettes de soleil (f.) *sunglasses*
un maillot de bain *bathing suit*
un manteau *coat*
un pantalon *(a pair of) pants*
une robe *dress*
des sandales (f.) *sandals*
une veste *suit jacket, blazer*
des vêtements *clothes*

Asking for and giving advice

Je ne sais pas quoi mettre pour... *I don't know what to wear for (to) . . .*
Qu'est-ce que je mets? *What shall I wear?*
Pourquoi est-ce que tu ne mets pas... ? *Why don't you wear . . . ?*
Mets... *Wear . . .*
mettre *to put, to put on, to wear*
porter *to wear*

DEUXIEME ETAPE

Expressing need; inquiring

Vous désirez? *What would you like?*
(Est-ce que) je peux vous aider? *May I help you?*
Je cherche quelque chose pour... *I'm looking for something to . . .*
J'aimerais... pour aller avec... *I'd like . . . to go with . . .*
Non, merci, je regarde. *No, thanks, I'm just looking.*
Je peux l'/les essayer? *Can I try it/them on?*
Je peux essayer le/la/les... ? *Can I try on the . . . ?*
Vous avez ça... ? *Do you have that . . . ? (size, fabric, color)*
en taille... ? *in size . . . ?*
en bleu *in blue*
en coton *cotton*
en jean *denim*
en cuir *leather*

Other useful expressions

choisir *to choose, to pick*
grandir *to grow*
maigrir *to lose weight*
grossir *to gain weight*

TROISIEME ETAPE

Asking for an opinion; paying a compliment; criticizing

Comment tu trouves... ? *How do you like . . . ?*
Il/Elle me va? *Does . . . suit me?*
Il/Elle te/vous plaît? *Do you like it?*
C'est parfait. *It's perfect.*
C'est tout à fait ton style. *It looks great on you!*
Il/Elle te/vous va très bien. *It suits you really well.*
Il/Elle va très bien avec... *It goes very well with . . .*
Il/Elle est (Ils/Elles sont) trop... *It's/They're too . . .*
Je le/la/les trouve... *I think it's/they're . . .*
très à la mode *in style*
chic *chic*
mignon (mignonne)(s) *cute*
sensationnel (le)(s)/sensas *fantastic*
rétro *retro*
serré(e)(s) *tight*
large(s) *baggy*
petit(e)(s) *small*
grand(e)(s) *big*
court(e)(s) *short*
long(longue)(s) *long*
moche(s) *tacky*
démodé(e)(s) *out of style*
horrible(s) *terrible*
Il/Elle ne te/vous va pas du tout. *It doesn't look good on you at all.*
Il/Elle ne va pas du tout avec... *It doesn't go at all with . . .*

Hesitating; making a decision

Vous avez choisi? *Have you decided?*
Vous avez décidé de prendre... ? *Have you decided to take . . . ?*
Vous le/la/les prenez? *Are you taking it/them?*
Je ne sais pas. *I don't know.*
Euh... J'hésite. *Well, I'm not sure.*
Il/Elle me plaît, mais il/elle est cher/chère. *I like it, but it's expensive.*
Je le/la/les prends. *I'll take it/them.*
C'est trop cher. *It's too expensive.*

CHAPITRE

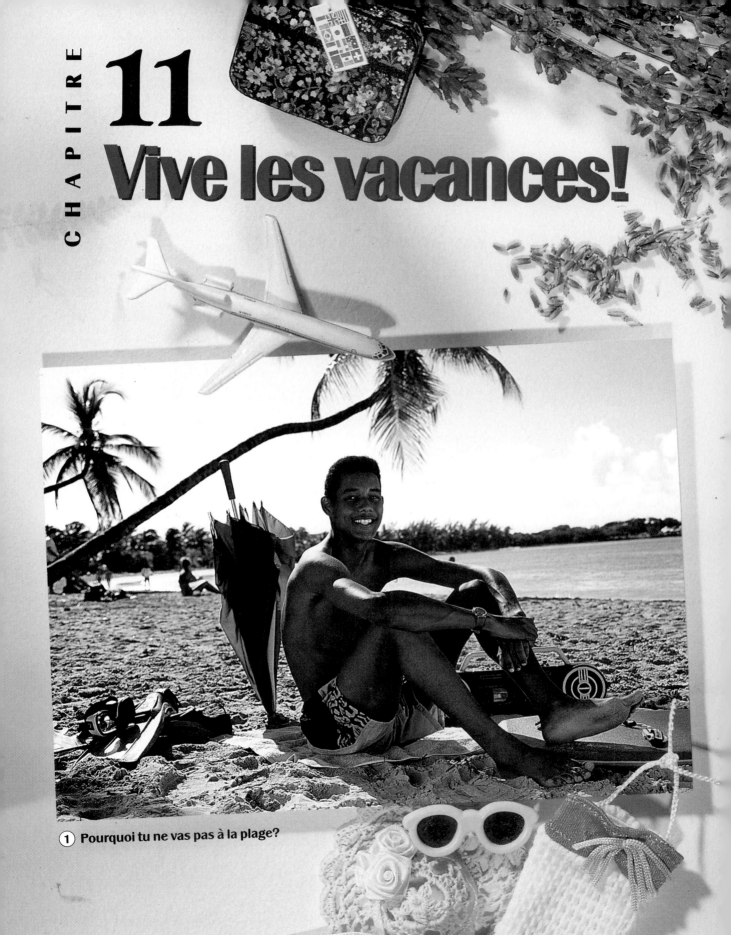

11
Vive les vacances!

1 Pourquoi tu ne vas pas à la plage?

How do you spend your vacation? Do you work? Do you do things in your hometown with your friends? Do you travel to other places and meet new people?

(2) Tu n'as pas oublié ton dictionnaire?

In this chapter you will learn

- to inquire about and share future plans; to express indecision; to express wishes; to ask for advice; to make, accept, and refuse suggestions
- to remind; to reassure; to see someone off
- to ask for and express opinions; to inquire about and relate past events

And you will

- listen to francophone students talk about their vacation plans
- read about tourist attractions in Provence
- write about your ideal vacation
- find out where French-speaking people go and what they do during their vacations

(3) C'était formidable, les vacances en Provence!

Mise en train

Bientôt les vacances!

What are these teenagers discussing? What clues do you have? What is Florent's dilemma?

1

Alors, les copains, qu'est-ce que vous allez faire pendant les vacances?

Moi, je pars en colonie de vacances.

C'est sympa!

2

Et en août, je vais voir mes cousins à la montagne. Ils habitent à Sisteron, dans les Alpes de Haute-Provence. C'est super joli là-bas.

3

Et toi, Ahmed, tu vas à l'étranger?

Non. En juillet, je vais faire du camping dans les Gorges du Verdon.

4

En août, je travaille dans une station-service. J'aimerais bien acheter une mobylette.

C'est génial!

5
Je vais peut-être rester en Arles. J'ai envie d'être ici pour le Festival de la photographie. A part ça, je n'ai rien de prévu. Je n'ai pas encore décidé.
Et toi, Florent?
Pourquoi est-ce que tu ne travailles pas comme pompiste avec moi?
J'aimerais bien, mais je préfère partir en vacances.
6
Tu peux aller en colonie de vacances aussi.
C'est possible.
7
Bon, je dois m'en aller.
Moi aussi. Au revoir à tous!
Salut!
Tchao!
8
Qu'est-ce que je vais faire, moi?

1 Tu as compris?

1. What time of year is it? How do you know?
2. Who is planning to travel during the vacation? Where?
3. Who is going to work during the vacation? Why?
4. What is Florent going to do?

2 C'est qui?

D'après **Bientôt les vacances!** qui a l'intention de (d')...

Florent

Ahmed

Magali

aller dans les Alpes?
travailler en Arles?
rester en Arles?
partir en colonie de vacances?
aller voir ses cousins?
aller à la montagne?
faire du camping?

3 Vrai ou faux?

1. Tous les jeunes restent en France pendant les vacances.
2. Les cousins de Magali habitent à la montagne.
3. Ahmed va faire du camping dans les Alpes.
4. Ahmed va travailler dans un café.
5. Ahmed veut aller au Festival de la photographie.
6. Florent part en colonie de vacances.

4 Cherche les expressions

According to **Bientôt les vacances!**, what can you say in French. . .

1. to ask what someone is going to do?
2. to tell what a place looks like?
3. to express an opinion?
4. to express indecision?
5. to make a suggestion?
6. to express a preference?

C'est génial! C'est super joli...
Je préfère...
Pourquoi est-ce que tu ne... pas?
Qu'est-ce que vous allez faire... ?
Je n'ai pas encore décidé.

5 Et maintenant, à toi

Whose vacation plans are the most interesting to you? Why?

PREMIERE ETAPE

Inquiring about and sharing future plans; expressing indecision; expressing wishes; asking for advice; making, accepting, and refusing suggestions

VOCABULAIRE

Où est-ce que tu vas aller pendant tes vacances?

à la montagne

à la campagne

au bord de la mer

en forêt

en colonie de vacances

chez mes grands-parents

Qu'est-ce qu'on peut y faire? On peut y...

faire du camping.

faire de la randonnée.

faire du bateau.

faire de la plongée.

faire de la planche à voile.

faire de la voile.

6 Ecoute!

Listen as Nathalie, Bruno, Pauline, and Emile tell about their vacation plans. What is each teenager going to do?

De bons conseils

Although there are few hard-and-fast rules to help you remember if a noun is masculine or feminine, you can often predict the gender of a word by its ending. Some of the endings that usually indicate a feminine word are **-tion, -sion, -ie, -ette, -elle, -ine, -ude,** and **-ure.** Endings that often signal a masculine word are **-ment, -age, -oir, -ier, -et,** and **-eau.** But be careful! There are exceptions.

Tu te rappelles?

Do you remember how to tell what is going to happen? Use a form of the verb **aller** *(to go)* plus the infinitive of another verb.

Demain, je **vais faire** du bateau.

Si tu as oublié
the verb aller
va à la page 154.

7 Dans une colonie de vacances

Qu'est-ce que Vincent et Roland vont faire en colonie de vacances?

1.

2.

3.

4.

5.

6.

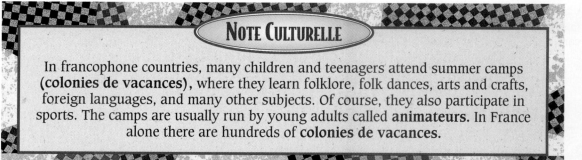

Note Culturelle

In francophone countries, many children and teenagers attend summer camps **(colonies de vacances),** where they learn folklore, folk dances, arts and crafts, foreign languages, and many other subjects. Of course, they also participate in sports. The camps are usually run by young adults called **animateurs.** In France alone there are hundreds of **colonies de vacances.**

COMMENT DIT-ON... ?

Inquiring about and sharing future plans; expressing indecision; expressing wishes

To inquire about someone's plans:
Qu'est-ce que tu vas faire cet été?
Où est-ce que tu vas aller pendant les vacances?

To express indecision:
J'hésite.
Je ne sais pas.
Je n'en sais rien. *I have no idea.*
Je n'ai rien de prévu. *I don't have any plans.*

To share your plans:
En juillet, **je vais** travailler.
En août, **j'ai l'intention d'**aller en Italie. *. . . I intend to . . .*

To express wishes:
Je voudrais bien aller chez mes cousins.
J'ai envie de travailler. *I feel like . . .*

8 Ecoute!

Listen to these speakers talk about their vacations. Do they have definite plans or are they undecided?

9 Les vacances en France

Imagine you're going to France on vacation next summer. Your partner will ask about your vacation plans. Tell what you feel like doing or plan to do there. Then, change roles.

visiter le Louvre
faire des photos
faire du ski
rencontrer de jeunes Français
voir la tour Eiffel
parler français
aller à un concert de rock français
aller au café

NOTE DE GRAMMAIRE

- To say *to* or *in* before the names of most cities, use **à**.

  Tu vas **à** Paris pendant les vacances?

- Names of countries are either masculine or feminine. Feminine countries end in **-e**, but there are exceptions, such as **le Mexique.** Use **au** *(to, in)* before masculine names and **en** *(to, in)* before feminine names and before names of countries that begin with a vowel. Before plural names, use **aux.**

  Vous allez **au** Canada?

  Hélène va **en** Allemagne.

  Nous allons **aux** Etats-Unis.

- States and provinces follow slightly different rules.

Vocabulaire à la carte

en Angleterre	en France
en Allemagne	en Floride
en Australie	en Italie
en Belgique	au Maroc
au Brésil	au Mexique
en Californie	en Russie
en Chine	au Sénégal
en Egypte	en Suisse
en Espagne	au Texas
aux Etats-Unis	au Viêt-Nam

10 Où vont-ils?

Dans quel pays *(country)* vont-ils passer leurs vacances?

1. Murielle va prendre des photos de la tour Eiffel.
2. Monique va visiter le château Frontenac.
3. Joseph va visiter la tour de Londres.
4. Mathieu va voir les pyramides.
5. Than et Laure vont visiter le Texas.
6. Dominique va voir le Kremlin.
7. Paul et Gilles vont aller à Casablanca.

au Canada au Maroc
aux Etats-Unis
en Russie en Angleterre
en Egypte en France

11 On y fait quoi?

Select two of the countries from Activity 10 and decide with your group on at least three activities you would all like to do on vacation in each country.

12 Un voyage gratuit

You've won a trip to go anywhere you want. Where will you go? Why? What will you do there? Discuss this with a partner. Take turns.

Tu te rappelles?

Do you remember how to ask for advice? Make, accept, and refuse suggestions?

To ask for advice:
Je ne sais pas quoi faire (où aller).
Tu as une idée?
Qu'est-ce que tu me conseilles?

To make suggestions:
Je te conseille de...
Tu devrais...

To accept suggestions:
C'est une bonne idée!
Pourquoi pas?
D'accord!
Allons-y!

To refuse suggestions:
Non, ce n'est pas possible.
Non, je ne peux pas.
Ça ne me dit rien.
C'est trop cher.

13 Ecoute!

Ecoute Alain et Valérie qui parlent de leurs vacances. Est-ce que ces phrases sont vraies ou fausses?

1. Alain ne sait pas quoi faire.
2. Valérie n'a pas d'idées.
3. Valérie est déjà allée à la Martinique.
4. Alain ne veut pas aller à la Martinique.

A la française

Use the words **alors** *(so, then, well, in that case)* and **donc** *(so, then, therefore)* to connect your sentences.

J'adore faire de la plongée, **donc** je vais en Australie.
Tu aimes faire du bateau? **Alors,** tu devrais aller à Marseille.

14 Des conseils

Ces élèves rêvent *(are dreaming)* de ce qu'ils aiment. Ils ne savent pas où aller pendant les vacances. Tu as une idée?

Malika

Marion

Hai

Christian

Adrienne

Ali

15 Où aller?

Tell your partner what you like to do on vacation. Your partner will then make some suggestions about where you might want to go. Accept your partner's suggestions, or refuse them and give an excuse. Then, change roles.

16 Mon journal

Décris un voyage que tu vas faire ou que tu voudrais faire. Où veux-tu aller? Quand? Avec qui? Qu'est-ce que tu vas y faire?

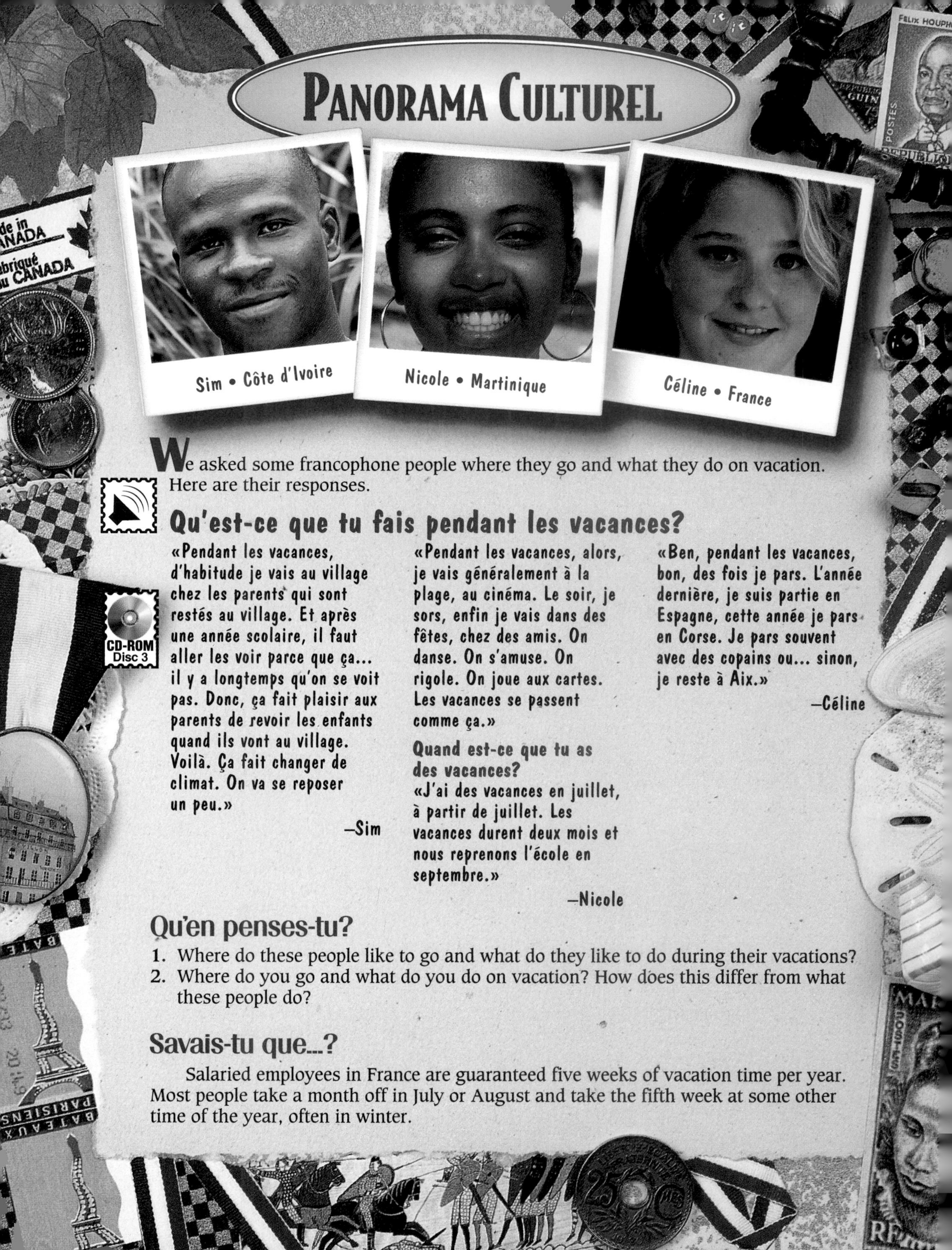

Panorama Culturel

Sim • Côte d'Ivoire

Nicole • Martinique

Céline • France

We asked some francophone people where they go and what they do on vacation. Here are their responses.

CD-ROM Disc 3

Qu'est-ce que tu fais pendant les vacances?

«Pendant les vacances, d'habitude je vais au village chez les parents qui sont restés au village. Et après une année scolaire, il faut aller les voir parce que ça... il y a longtemps qu'on se voit pas. Donc, ça fait plaisir aux parents de revoir les enfants quand ils vont au village. Voilà. Ça fait changer de climat. On va se reposer un peu.»

–Sim

«Pendant les vacances, alors, je vais généralement à la plage, au cinéma. Le soir, je sors, enfin je vais dans des fêtes, chez des amis. On danse. On s'amuse. On rigole. On joue aux cartes. Les vacances se passent comme ça.»

Quand est-ce que tu as des vacances?

«J'ai des vacances en juillet, à partir de juillet. Les vacances durent deux mois et nous reprenons l'école en septembre.»

–Nicole

«Ben, pendant les vacances, bon, des fois je pars. L'année dernière, je suis partie en Espagne, cette année je pars en Corse. Je pars souvent avec des copains ou... sinon, je reste à Aix.»

–Céline

Qu'en penses-tu?

1. Where do these people like to go and what do they like to do during their vacations?
2. Where do you go and what do you do on vacation? How does this differ from what these people do?

Savais-tu que...?

Salaried employees in France are guaranteed five weeks of vacation time per year. Most people take a month off in July or August and take the fifth week at some other time of the year, often in winter.

DEUXIEME ETAPE

Reminding; reassuring; seeing someone off

VOCABULAIRE

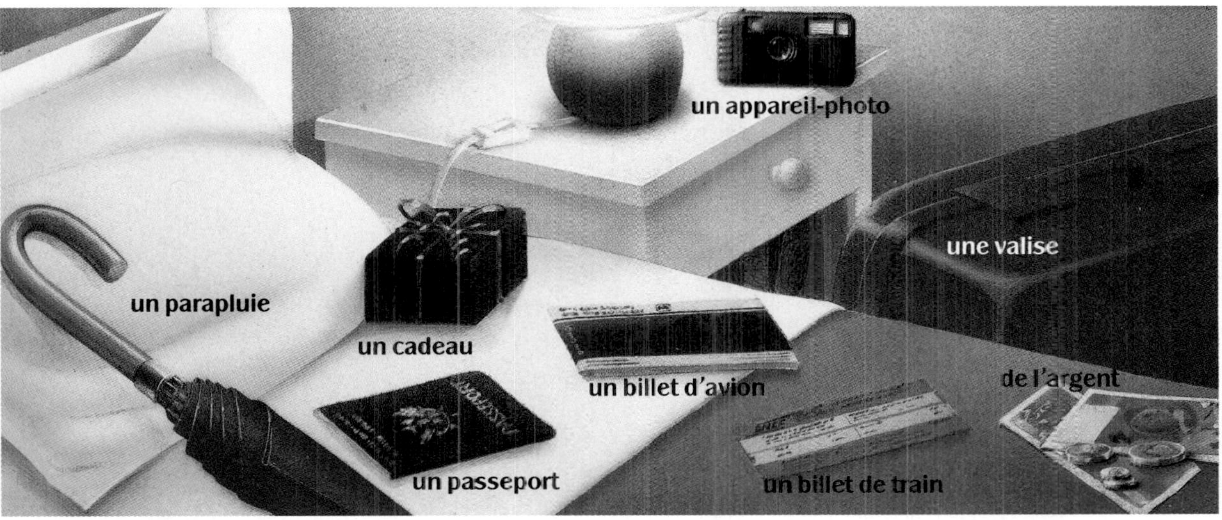

17 Qu'est-ce qu'il te faut?

1. Qu'est-ce qu'il faut quand il pleut?
2. Qu'est-ce qu'il faut pour prendre le train? L'avion?
3. Qu'est-ce qu'il faut pour acheter des souvenirs?
4. Qu'est-ce qu'il faut pour prendre des photos?

COMMENT DIT-ON... ?

Reminding; reassuring

To remind someone of something:

N'oublie pas ton passeport!
Tu n'as pas oublié ton billet d'avion? *You didn't forget . . . ?*
Tu ne peux pas partir sans ton écharpe! *You can't leave without . . . !*
Tu prends ton manteau? *Are you taking . . . ?*

To reassure someone:

Ne t'en fais pas.
J'ai pensé à tout. *I've thought of everything.*
Je n'ai rien oublié. *I didn't forget anything.*

18 Ecoute!

Listen to these speakers. Are they reminding or reassuring someone?

19 Qu'est-ce qu'il a oublié?

Read the list of things Jean-Paul needs for his trip. Make a list of what he's forgotten to pack. Next, play the role of Jean-Paul's parent and remind him what to take. Then, change roles.

appareil-photo
billet d'avion
billet de train
passeport
dictionnaire
magazines
casquette
baskets
shorts
chaussures
chaussettes
cadeaux

20 Jeu de rôle

You're going on a trip to France this summer with the French Club. Ask your friend, who went last year, what you should take. He or she will remind you of some things you'll need. Act this out with a partner and then change roles.

GRAMMAIRE The verb partir

A small group of verbs whose infinitives end in **-ir** follow a pattern different than the one you learned in Chapter 10.

partir *(to leave)*

Je **pars**	à dix heures.	Nous **partons**	à dix heures.
Tu **pars**		Vous **partez**	
Il/Elle/On **part**		Ils/Elles **partent**	

- Don't pronounce the **s** or **t** in **pars** or **part.**
- **Sortir** *(to go out)* and **dormir** *(to sleep)* also follow this pattern.

A la française

French speakers often use the present tense to talk about the future.

Je **pars** à neuf heures. *I'm leaving/I'm going to leave/I will leave . . .*
Je **sors** avec Aline ce soir. *I'm going out/I'm going to go out/I will go out . . .*

21 D'habitude, qu'est-ce que tu fais?

You're exchanging information with your host family about your daily routines. Complete each sentence with the correct form of **partir**, **sortir**, or **dormir.**

1. Je __________ pour l'école à huit heures du matin.
2. Ma sœur et moi, nous __________ jusqu'à dix heures le samedi matin.
3. Mon père et ma mère __________ toujours avant moi le matin.
4. Quand est-ce que vous __________ en vacances?
5. Est-ce que tu __________ beaucoup le week-end?
6. Mon frère Emile __________ le vendredi soir avec son amie Agnès.

22 Vacances en Provence

Regarde l'itinéraire de Marianne. Ensuite, réponds aux questions.

1. D'où part Marianne samedi?
2. Où est-ce qu'elle va?
3. Son voyage va durer *(last)* combien de temps?
4. Qu'est-ce qu'elle a l'intention de faire?

SAMEDI :

départ d'Arles, bus de 9h35;
arrivée aux Baux-de-Provence à 10h10;
* visite de la Cathédrale d'Images;
dîner : Auberge de la Benvengudo

DIMANCHE :

départ pour Saint-Rémy-de-Provence, bus de 9h15;
arrivée à 9h45;
* visite du musée Van Gogh; déjeuner : pique-nique à Fontvieille;
* visite du moulin de Daudet;
retour aux Baux-de-Provence;
départ pour Avignon, bus de 18h16;
arrivée à 19h10 Hôtel le Midi;
dîner

LUNDI :

* visite de la Cité des Papes, le Pont St-Bénezet, promenade du Rocher des Doms, le musée du Petit-Palais;
* spectacle folklorique;
départ pour Grasse 20h15;
arrivée à 22h10 Hôtel les Arômes

MARDI :

* visite de la Parfumerie Fragonard;
* Musée d'Art et d'Histoire de Provence; retour en Arles 17h42;
arrivée à 19h20

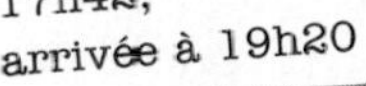

23 Jeu de rôle

You're going to take the same trip as Marianne. Your partner will ask you questions about the trip and remind you what to take.

24 Bonjour de Provence!

Pendant ton voyage en Provence, écris une carte postale à ton ami(e), à tes camarades de classe ou à ton professeur.

Bienvenue en Provence!

COMMENT DIT-ON... ?
Seeing someone off

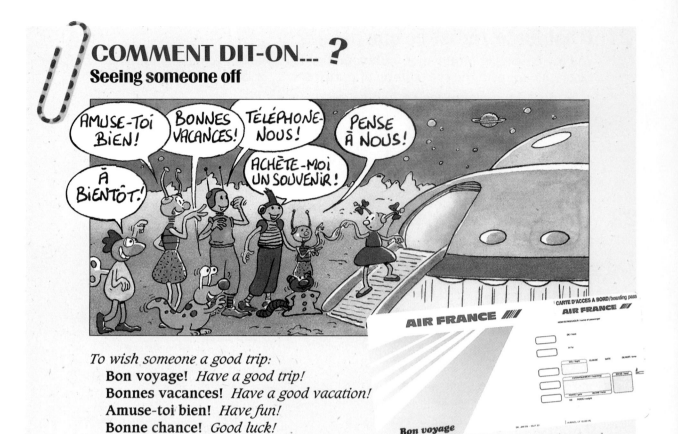

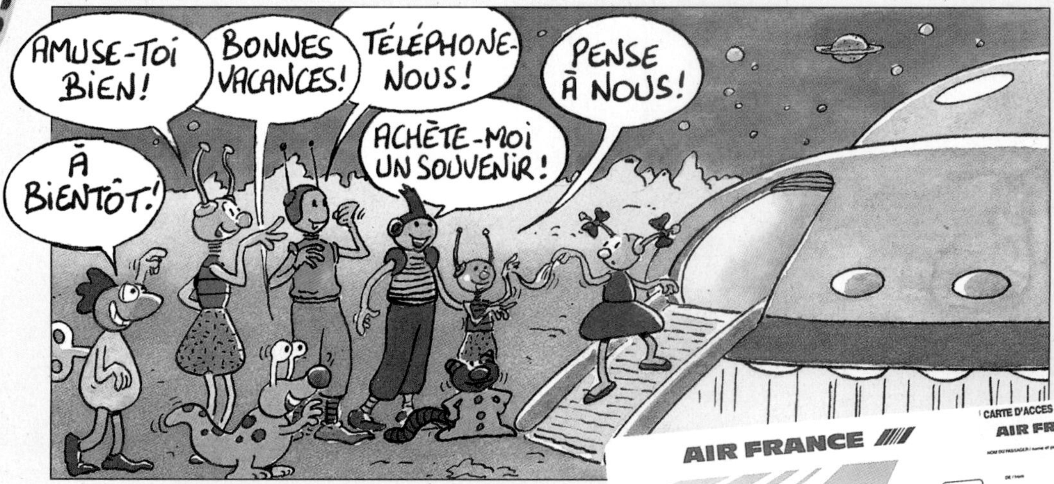

AMUSE-TOI BIEN!
BONNES VACANCES!
TÉLÉPHONE-NOUS!
PENSE À NOUS!
À BIENTÔT!
ACHÈTE-MOI UN SOUVENIR!

AIR FRANCE
CARTE D'ACCES A BORD/boarding pass
Bon voyage

To wish someone a good trip:
Bon voyage! *Have a good trip!*
Bonnes vacances! *Have a good vacation!*
Amuse-toi bien! *Have fun!*
Bonne chance! *Good luck!*

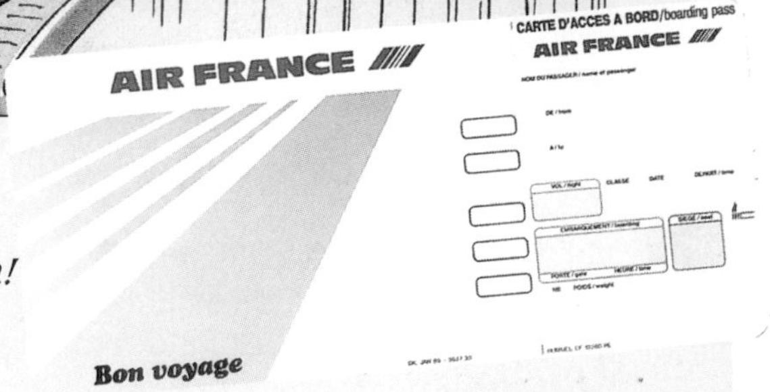

25 Ecoute!

Ecoute ces conversations. On arrive ou on part?

26 Au revoir!

It's time for your French exchange student to return home. See him or her off at the airport. Act this out with your partner.

Tu te rappelles?

Do you remember how to give commands? Use the **tu** or **vous** form of the verb without a subject.

Attends! Allez!

When you use an **-er** verb, remember to drop the final **s** of the **tu** form.

Ecoute!

When you use an object pronoun with a positive command, place it after the verb, separated by a hyphen in writing.

Donnez-moi votre billet, s'il vous plaît.

27 Un grand voyage

You and a friend have decided to take a trip together to a foreign country. Decide where you will go and what you will do there. Talk about the weather conditions and when you will go. Discuss what clothes and other items you each plan to pack and what you will wear on the plane.

Si tu as oublié
weather
va à la page 106.

28 Un petit mot

Your friend is leaving on a trip tomorrow. Write a note wishing him or her well and suggesting things he or she might like to see and do while on vacation.

TROISIEME ETAPE

Asking for and expressing opinions; inquiring about and relating past events

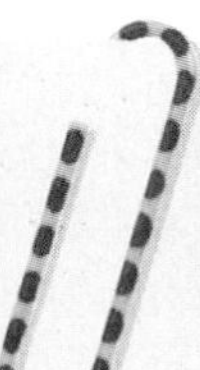

COMMENT DIT-ON... ?

Asking for and expressing opinions

To ask someone's opinion:

Tu as passé un bon été?

Ça s'est bien passé?
Did it go well?

Tu t'es bien amusé(e)?
Did you have fun?

To express an opinion:

Oui, très chouette.
Oui, c'était formidable!
Yes, it was great!
Oui, ça a été.
Oh, pas mauvais.
C'était épouvantable.
Non, pas vraiment. *No, not really.*
C'était un véritable cauchemar!
It was a real nightmare!
C'était ennuyeux. *It was boring.*
C'était barbant.

29 Ecoute!

Listen to these conversations and then tell whether these people had a good, fair, or bad vacation.

30 Méli-mélo!

Remets la conversation entre Thierry et Hervé dans le bon ordre.

Tu te rappelles?

Do you remember how to inquire about and relate events that happened in the past?

Tu es allé(e) où?
Qu'est-ce que tu as fait?
D'abord,... Ensuite,... Après,... Finalement,...

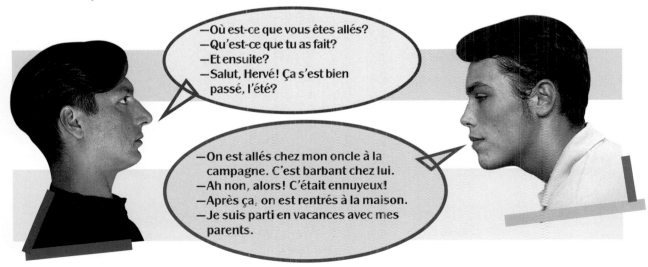

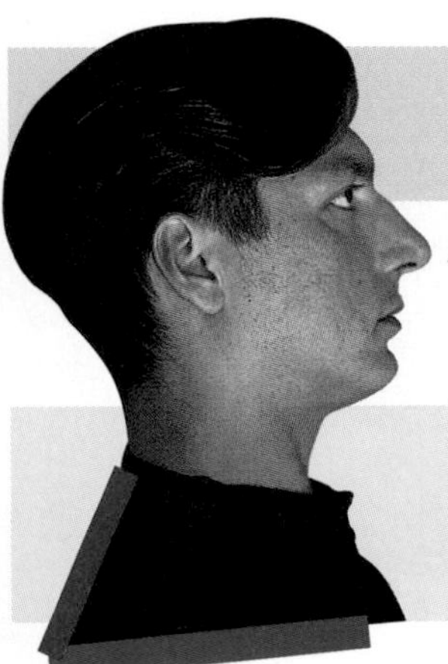

—Où est-ce que vous êtes allés?
—Qu'est-ce que tu as fait?
—Et ensuite?
—Salut, Hervé! Ça s'est bien passé, l'été?

—On est allés chez mon oncle à la campagne. C'est barbant chez lui.
—Ah non, alors! C'était ennuyeux!
—Après ça, on est rentrés à la maison.
—Je suis parti en vacances avec mes parents.

Si tu as oublié
le passé composé
va à la page 239.

Tu te rappelles?

CD-ROM Disc 3

Do you remember how to form the **passé composé?** Use a form of **avoir** as a helping verb with the past participle of the main verb. The past participles of regular **-er**, **-re**, and **-ir** verbs end in **é**, **u**, and **i**.

Nous **avons** beaucoup **mangé**. J'**ai répondu** à leur lettre. Ils **ont fini.**

You have to memorize the past participles of irregular verbs.

J'**ai fait** du camping. Ils **ont vu** un film.

To make a verb in the **passé composé** negative, you place **ne... pas** around the helping verb.

Il **n'**a **pas** fait ses devoirs.

With **aller**, **partir**, and **sortir**, you use **être** as the helping verb instead of **avoir.**

31 Qu'est-ce qu'elle a fait?

Mets ces activités dans le bon ordre d'après l'itinéraire de Marianne à la page 295.

D'abord, elle...

visiter le musée Van Gogh
voir un spectacle folklorique
visiter la parfumerie Fragonard
visiter la Cité des Papes
voir le moulin de Daudet
faire la promenade du Rocher des Doms
faire un pique-nique

32 On fait la même chose?

You and your partner took these photographs on a trip to France last year. Take turns telling where you went, what you did, and what you thought of each place or activity.

Un café sur le Cours Mirabeau

Le palais des Papes, c'est formidable.

La mer Méditerranée

Les arènes en Arles

La Côte d'Azur

33 On est de retour

Tu reviens d'un voyage. Ton ami(e) te demande où tu es allé(e), avec qui, ce que tu as fait et comment ça s'est passé.

PRONONCIATION

Aspirated h, th, ch, and gn

You've learned that you don't pronounce the letter **h** in French. Some words begin with an aspirated **h (h aspiré)**. This means that you don't make elision and liaison with the word that comes before. Repeat these phrases: **le haut-parleur; le houx; les halls; les haricots.**

Haut and **houx** begin with an aspirated **h**, so you can't drop the **e** from the article **le. Halls** and **haricots** also begin with an aspirated **h**, so you don't pronounce the **s** in the article **les.** How will you know which words begin with an aspirated **h**? If you look the words up in the dictionary, you may find an asterisk (*) before an aspirated **h.**

How do you pronounce the combination **th**? Just ignore the letter **h** and pronounce the **t.** Repeat these words: **mathématiques, théâtre, athlète.**

What about the combination **ch**? In French, **ch** is pronounced like the English *sh,* as in the word *show.* Compare these English and French words: *change/***change**, *chocolate/***chocolat**, *chance/***chance.** In some words, **ch** is pronounced like *k.* Listen to these words and repeat them: **chorale, Christine, archéologie.**

Finally, how do you pronounce the combination **gn**? The English sound /ny/, as in the word *onion* is similar. Pronounce these words: **oignon, montagne, magnifique.**

A. A prononcer

Repeat the following words.

1. le héros	la harpe	le hippie	le hockey
2. thème	maths	mythe	bibliothèque
3. Chine	choisir	tranche	pêches
4. espagnol	champignon	montagne	magnifique

B. A lire

Take turns with a partner reading each of the following sentences aloud.

1. J'aime la Hollande, mais je veux aller à la montagne en Allemagne.
2. Je cherche une chemise, des chaussures et un chapeau.
3. Il n'a pas fait ses devoirs de maths et de chimie à la bibliothèque dimanche.
4. Charles a gagné trois hamsters. Ils sont dans ma chambre! Quel cauchemar!

C. A écrire

You're going to hear a short dialogue. Write down what you hear.

LISONS!

What would you like to do if you were visiting Provence?

DE BONS CONSEILS

When you read for a purpose, it's a good idea to decide beforehand what kind of information you want. If you're looking for an overview, a quick, general reading may be all that is required. If you're looking for specific details, you'll have to read more carefully.

A. The information at the top of both pages is from a book entitled *Le Guide du Routard.* Do you think this is
1. a history book?
2. a travel guide?
3. a geography book?

B. You usually read a book like this to gather general information about what is going on, or to find details about a certain place or event. What general categories of information can you find? Under what titles?

C. Where should you stay if . . .
1. you plan to visit Provence in November?
2. you want a balcony?
3. you want the least expensive room you can get?
4. you have a tent and a sleeping bag?

D. Do you think the descriptions of the hotels were written by the hotel management? How do you know?

ARLES (13200)

Où dormir?

Très bon marché

Auberge de jeunesse : 20, av. Foch. ☎ 04-90-96-18-25. Fax : 04-90-96-31-26. Fermée pendant les vacances de Noël. 100 lits. 75 F la première nuit, 65 F les suivantes, draps et petit déjeuner compris. Fait aussi restaurant. Repas à 47 F.

Prix modérés

Hôtel Gauguin : 5, place Voltaire. ☎ 04-90-96-14-35. Fax : 04-90-18-98-87. Fermé du 10 janvier au 15 février et du 15 novembre au 20 décembre. De 170 F à 210 F la double. Sur trois étages. Chambres simples, bien aménagées. Celles qui donnent sur la place ont un balcon. Peu de charme cependant dans ce quartier de l'après-guerre. Le petit plus : tous les matins la météo locale est affichée à la réception!

Plus chic

Hôtel du Musée : 11, rue du Grand-Prieuré. ☎ 04-90-93-88-88. Fax : 04-90-49-98-15. Fermé en janvier. Dans une belle demeure du XVIIe siècle, face au musée Réattu et à deux pas du Rhône, une excellente adresse. De 270 F à 300 F la chambre double. Joli patio pour le petit déjeuner. Très bien situé et très bon accueil.

Camping

Camping City : 67, route de Crau. ☎ 04-90-93-08-86. Fax : 04-90-93-91-07. Fermé du 30 octobre au 1er mars. En allant vers Raphèle-lès-Arles. Assez ombragé, mais plutôt bruyant. Attention aux moustiques, car situé près d'un marécage. Piscine, épicerie, plats à emporter, restaurant-pizzeria, animations en été.

BATEAU « MIREIO »

BATEAU «MIREIO»

Bateau restaurant de 250 places, chauffé, climatisé. Croisières déjeuner sans escale vers Châteauneuf-du-Pape ou avec escale en Arles – visite de la capitale de la Camargue –, à Roquemaure avec dégustation des vins de Côtes du Rhône, à Villeneuve avec visite du village et de ses monuments. Croisières dîner et soirées spectacle devant Avignon et Villeneuve. Animation dansante et commentaires sur toutes les croisières.

84000 AVIGNON -
Tél. : 04 90 85 62 25
Fax : 04 90 85 61 14

CATHEDRALE D'IMAGES

Aux Baux-de-Provence, dans les anciennes carrières du Val-d'Enfer, CATHEDRALE D'IMAGES propose un spectacle permanent en IMAGE TOTALE. 4.000m² d'écrans naturels, 40 sources de projection, 2 500 diapos créent une féerie visuelle et sonore où déambule le spectateur.
–Couvrez-vous car les carrières sont fraîches!–

13520 LES BAUX-DE-PROVENCE -
Tél. : 04 90 54 38 65
Fax : 04 90 54 42 65

CATHEDRALE D'IMAGES

ARLES (13200)

Où manger?

Bon marché

Vitamine : 04-90-93-77-36. 16, rue du Docteur-Fanton derrière la place du Forum. Fermé le samedi soir et le dimanche sauf pendant l'été. Une carte de 50 salades différentes, de 20 à 48 F, et 15 spécialités de pâtes de 32 à 80 F, le tout dans une salle agréablement décorée (expos photos) et avec un accueil décontracté.

Le Grillon : rond-point des Arènes. 04-90-96-70-97. Fermé le mercredi. Ce restaurant-brasserie-crêperie-glacier ne paie pas de mine, mais il y a une agréable terrasse avec une très belle vue sur les arènes. On y découvre de bons petits plats sympathiques. Menu à 81 F (très honnête) le midi, le soir et le week-end, avec soupe de poisson, fricassée de canard à la graine de moutarde, fromage ou dessert. A la carte, compter 70 F pour un plat. Salades copieuses à 49 F.

Le Poisson Banane : 6, rue du Forum. 04-90-96-02-58. Ouvert uniquement le soir. Fermé le dimanche seulement hors saison. Avec sa grande terrasse et sa tonnelle, ce petit resto caché derrière la place du Forum passe facilement inaperçu et c'est dommage. Il est agréable d'aller y goûter une cuisine sucrée-salée inventive avec un menu à 125 F, et une spécialité antillaise : le «poisson-banane», bien sûr. Autre menu à 79 F servi tous les jours jusqu'à 21h.

CHATEAU MUSEE DE L'EMPERI

CHATEAU MUSEE DE L'EMPERI

Le CHATEAU DE L'EMPERI, la plus importante forteresse médiévale en Provence, abrite une des plus somptueuses collections d'art et d'histoire militaire qui soit en Europe. Cette collection unique illustre l'évolution des uniformes et de l'art militaire de Louis XIV à 1918. La période napoléonienne est la plus présente. Le Château de l'Empéri est situé en plein cœur de la ville ancienne.

13300 SALON DE PROVENCE -
Tél : 04 90 56 22 36

GROTTES DE THOUZON

Les décors de stalactites qui parent « le ciel » de ce réseau naturel forment des paysages souterrains merveilleux.
(Photo : M. CROTET)
Grotte réputée pour la finesse de ses stalactites (fistuleuses). Parcours aisé pour les personnes âgées et les enfants. Seule grotte naturelle aménagée pour le tourisme en Provence. Ouvert du 1/04 au 31/10. Groupe toute l'année sur rendez-vous.

84250 LE THOR
Tél. : 04 90 33 93 65
Fax : 04 90 33 74 90

GROTTES DE THOUZON

E. Which restaurant should you try if . . .

1. you want the most expensive meal available?
2. you love salad?
3. you want to go out on Saturday night?

F. At the bottom of both pages, you will find descriptions of several tourist attractions in Provence. After you've read them, match attractions listed below with the sites where you would find them.

1. a dinner cruise
2. stalactites
3. thousands of projection screens
4. a collection of military art and uniforms

a. Cathédrale d'Images
b. Bateau «Mireio»
c. Grottes de Thouzon
d. Château Musée de l'Empéri

G. If you were working at a tourist information office, what would you recommend to someone who . . .

1. wants a comfortable cruise package?
2. would like to visit a medieval castle?
3. likes to explore caves?
4. is interested in military art?

H. Are there similar tourist attractions in your area? What are they?

I. You and your friend have three days to spend in Arles. You're on a very tight budget, but you still want to enjoy your trip. Where will you stay? Where will you eat your lunches and dinners? How much will you spend for these three days?

MISE EN PRATIQUE

1 Listen to this radio advertisement and then answer these questions.

1. What is being advertised?
2. Can you name two places that are mentioned in the advertisement?
3. What activities are mentioned in the advertisement?
4. For whom do they offer discounts?

2 Read the brochure and then answer the questions that follow.

Le rêve américain devient réalité, en séjour Immersion avec EF

Vivre à l'américaine

Qui n'a rêvé un jour de vivre une autre vie ? Ce rêve devient réalité, grâce à la formule EF Immersion : pendant quelques semaines, vous devenez totalement américain. Parce que les familles d'accueil sont soigneusement séléctionnées par EF, votre intégration est immédiate, et vos progrès linguistiques sont aussi spectaculaires que durables. C'est, sans nul doute, la formule qui vous assure la connaissance la plus directe et la plus profonde du mode de vie américain.

Vacances de Printemps

N° de séjour	Date de départ	Date de retour	Durée du séjour	Région	Frais de séjour*
550	11 avril	25 avril	2 sem.	Côte Est	7.730
551	18 avril	2 mai	2 sem.	Côte Est	7.730
552	18 avril	2 mai	2 sem.	Sud-Est	8.170

*Voyage inclus (départ Paris)

1. Where do students go if they sign up for this trip?
2. Where do they stay?
3. What do they learn?
4. In what months can students make this trip?
5. How long does it last?
6. To what regions of the country can students go?
7. How much does this trip cost?

3 Decide whether the statements below are true or false.

1. Only a few French children attend summer camp.
2. French children can study foreign languages at summer camp.
3. Most French people take a one-week summer vacation.

4 *Ecrivons!*

Write a letter to a French-speaking exchange student who is coming to your school. Tell him or her what there is to see and do where you live, what the weather is like there, and what to bring.

STRATEGIE

Using connecting words such as **donc** and **alors** to link your ideas can help your writing flow more naturally.

Prewriting

Before you begin your letter, arrange your ideas logically to make your letter flow more smoothly. You might want to divide a sheet of paper into columns and label each column with a subject you'll address in your letter (**le temps, il te faut...** , and so on). Write each of your ideas in the appropriate column.

Writing

Using the ideas you organized, write a letter to describe the place where you live. Include a lot of detail in your description to help form an image of the places to visit. Try to use connecting words to tie sentences together in the letter. Remember to use expressions you've learned for making suggestions and reminding someone to do something.

Revising

Proofreading is one of the most important steps in the evaluation process. It gives you a chance to correct any mistakes you might have made while you were writing. While writing your first draft, concentrate on being creative. You can make corrections to the grammar, punctuation, and spelling when you proofread.

It's a good idea to proofread in several passes. First, read through your letter to check only for grammar and punctuation mistakes. On your second pass, check for spelling errors. This way, there will be fewer errors in your final draft.

5 JEU DE ROLE

a. You want to take a trip for your vacation, but you're not sure where. Tell your travel agent what you like to do and what you'd like to see. The travel agent will make some suggestions about where you might go and what there is to do there. He or she will also describe the weather conditions and tell you what clothes to take, where you can stay, and when and from where you can leave. The travel agent will also remind you of things you shouldn't forget to take. Act this out with your partner. Then, change roles.

b. You've returned from your trip and your friend wants to know how it went. Tell your friend about your trip and answer any questions he or she has about what you did. Act this out with your partner and then change roles.

QUE SAIS-JE?

Can you use what you've learned in this chapter?

Can you inquire about and share future plans? Express indecision and wishes? p. 289

1 How would you ask where a friend is going on vacation and what he or she is going to do? How would you answer these questions?

2 How would you tell someone . . .

1. you're not sure what to do?
2. where you'd really like to go?

Can you ask for advice? Make, accept, and refuse suggestions? p. 290

3 How would you ask a friend for advice about your vacation?

4 How would you suggest to a friend that he or she . . .

1. go to the country?
2. go camping?
3. work?
4. go to Canada?

5 How would you accept and refuse the suggestions in number 4?

Can you remind and reassure someone? p. 293

6 How would you remind a friend to take these things on a trip?

1.

2.

3.

7 How would you reassure someone you haven't forgotten these things?

1.

2.

3.

Can you see someone off? p. 296

8 How would you tell when these people are leaving, using the verb **partir?**

1. Didier / 14h28
2. Désirée et Annie / 20h46
3. Nous / 11h15
4. Tu / 23h59

9 How would you wish someone a good trip?

Can you ask for and express opinions? p. 297

10 How would you ask a friend how his or her vacation went?

11 How would you tell how your vacation went?

Can you inquire about and relate past events? p. 297

12 How would you find out what a friend did on vacation?

13 How would you tell what you did on vacation?

VOCABULAIRE

PREMIERE ETAPE

Inquiring about and sharing future plans

Qu'est-ce que tu vas faire...? *What are you going to do . . . ?*
Où est-ce que tu vas aller... ? *Where are you going to go . . . ?*
Je vais... *I'm going to . . .*
J'ai l'intention de... *I intend to . . .*

Expressing indecision

J'hésite. *I'm not sure.*
Je ne sais pas. *I don't know.*
Je n'en sais rien. *I have no idea.*
Je n'ai rien de prévu. *I don't have any plans.*

Expressing wishes

Je voudrais bien... *I'd really like to . . .*
J'ai envie de... *I feel like . . .*

Vacation places and activities

à la montagne *to/in the mountains*
en forêt *to/in the forest*
à la campagne *to/in the countryside*
en colonie de vacances *to/at a summer camp*
au bord de la mer *to/on the coast*
chez... *to/at . . . 's house*
faire du camping *to go camping*
faire de la randonnée *to go hiking*
faire du bateau *to go boating*
faire de la plongée *to go scuba diving*
faire de la planche à voile *to go windsurfing*
faire de la voile *to go sailing*
à *to, in (a city or place)*
en *to, in (before a feminine noun)*
au *to, in (before a masculine noun)*
aux *to, in (before a plural noun)*

Asking for advice; making, accepting, and refusing suggestions

See **Tu te rappelles?** on page 290.

DEUXIEME ETAPE

Travel items

un passeport *passport*
un billet de train *train ticket*
un billet d'avion *plane ticket*
une valise *suitcase*
de l'argent *money*
un appareil-photo *camera*
un cadeau *gift*
un parapluie *umbrella*

Reminding, reassuring

N'oublie pas... *Don't forget . . .*
Tu n'as pas oublié... ? *You didn't forget . . . ?*
Tu ne peux pas partir sans... *You can't leave without . . .*
Tu prends... ? *Are you taking . . . ?*
Ne t'en fais pas. *Don't worry.*
Je n'ai rien oublié. *I didn't forget anything.*
J'ai pensé à tout. *I've thought of everything.*
partir *to leave*

Seeing someone off

Bon voyage! *Have a good trip!*
Bonnes vacances! *Have a good vacation!*
Amuse-toi bien! *Have fun!*
Bonne chance! *Good luck!*

TROISIEME ETAPE

Asking for and expressing opinions

Tu as passé un bon... ? *Did you have a good . . . ?*
Ça s'est bien passé? *Did it go well?*
Tu t'es bien amusé(e)? *Did you have fun?*
Oui, très chouette. *Yes, very cool.*
C'était formidable! *It was great!*
Oui, ça a été. *Yes, it was OK*
Oh, pas mauvais. *Oh, not bad.*
C'était épouvantable. *It was horrible.*
Non, pas vraiment. *No, not really.*
C'était un véritable cauchemar! *It was a real nightmare!*
C'était ennuyeux. *It was boring.*
C'était barbant. *It was boring.*

Inquiring about and relating past events

See **Tu te rappelles?** on page 297.

CHAPITRE 12

Allez, viens à Fort-de-France!

La ville de Fort-de-France

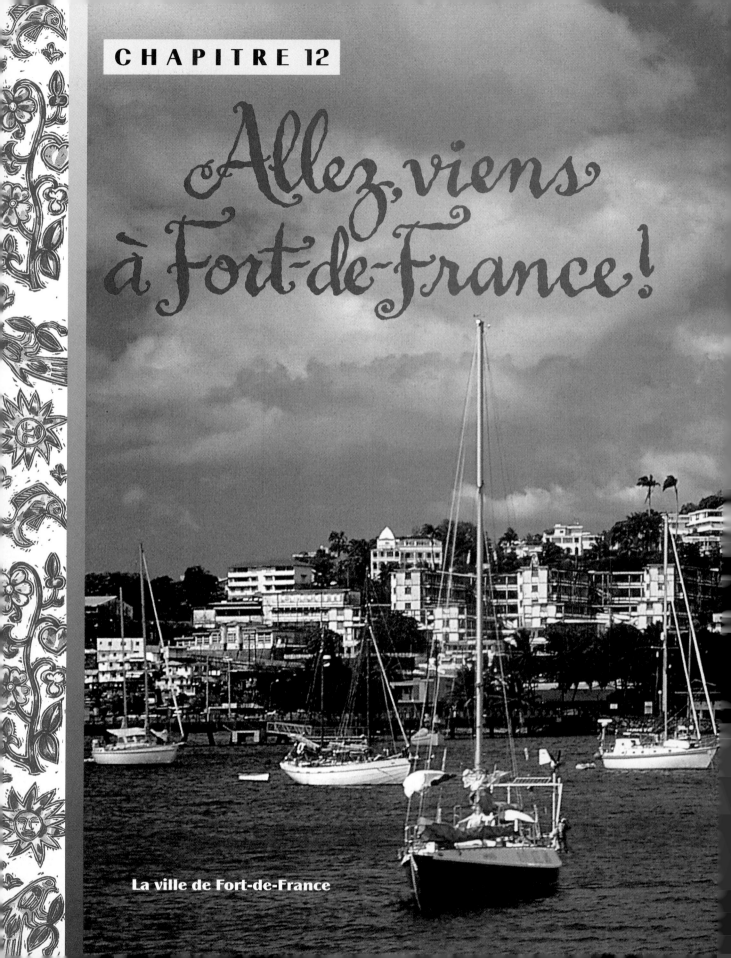

Fort-de-France

Ville principale de la Martinique

Population : plus de 100.000

Langues : français, créole

Points d'intérêt : la bibliothèque Schœlcher, le musée départemental, le fort Saint-Louis, la cathédrale Saint-Louis

Parcs et jardins : la Savane, le Parc floral

Spécialités : crabes farcis, blanc-manger, boudin créole, acras de morue

Evénements : Carnaval, le Festival de Fort-de-France, les Tours des yoles rondes de la Martinique

Fort-de-France

Clinging to the mountains overlooking the Caribbean coast of Martinique, the city of Fort-de-France lies on the ***baie des Flamands****. Nearly one-third of the population of Martinique lives in or near the city. Here you will see a blending of cultures. Although Martinique is 4,261 miles from Paris, it is a* ***département*** *of France. While its character is decidedly French, the pastel-colored buildings and wrought-iron balconies may remind you of New Orleans, and the sounds of the* ***créole*** *language and* ***zouk*** *music are purely West Indian.*

① **La bibliothèque Schœlcher** is a very elaborate building constructed in a blend of byzantine, Egyptian, and romanesque styles. Like the Eiffel Tower, it was built in 1889 for the Paris Exposition. It was later dismantled and rebuilt among the palm trees in Fort-de-France.

② **La Savane** is a 12½-acre landscaped park filled with tropical trees, fountains, benches, and gardens. This is the place to go to meet with friends, take a walk, or play a casual game of soccer.

③ Built on a rocky peninsula, **le fort Saint-Louis** overlooks the port of Fort-de-France.

4 Martinique is known for its colorfully printed fabrics, called **madras.**

5 Fresh fruits and vegetables are sold daily in the colorful **marché.**

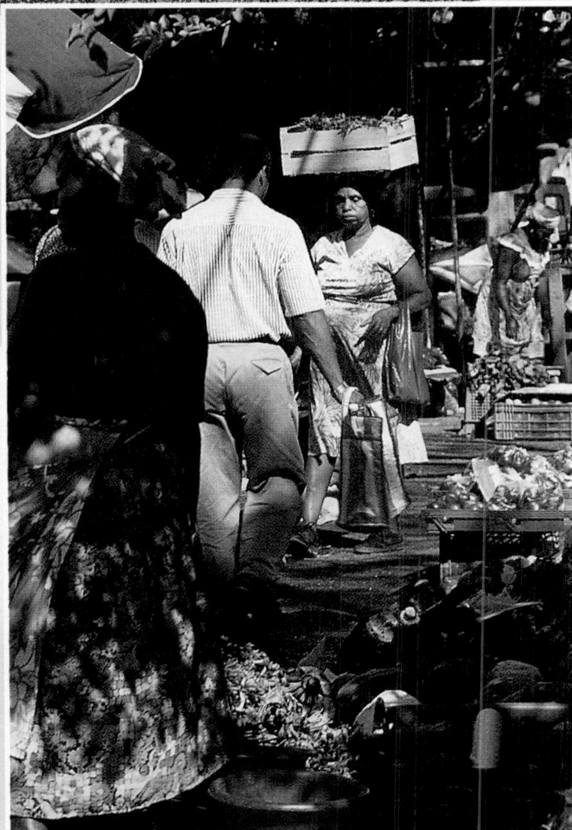

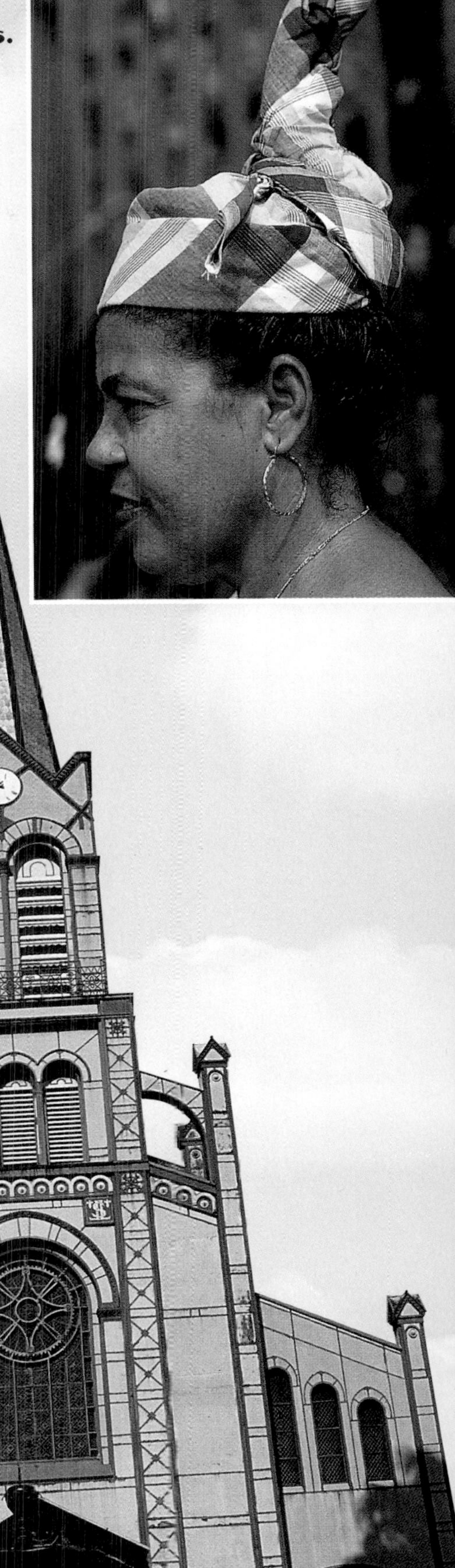

6 The steeple of **la cathédrale Saint-Louis** towers over downtown Fort-de-France.

CHAPITRE

12 En ville

① Regarde, c'est la cathédrale Saint-Louis!

Getting around in a new place can be difficult. Knowing where things are and how to get there makes it much easier.

In this chapter you will review and practice

- pointing out places and things
- making and responding to requests; asking for advice and making suggestions
- asking for and giving directions

And you will

- listen to people give directions
- read a story from Martinique
- write about your hometown
- find out about getting a driver's license in francophone countries

(2) Tu pourrais passer chez le disquaire?

(3) Pardon, monsieur. Nous cherchons le Hit Parade, s'il vous plaît.

Mise en train

Un petit service

Do you ever run errands for your family? What kinds of things do you have to do? Look at the pictures below and see if you can figure out what Lucien's mother, father, and sister are asking him to do.

Lucien

Lisette

La mère

Le père

Une voisine

1
Maman, je vais en ville. J'ai rendez-vous avec Mireille. On va passer la journée à Fort-de-France. Je vais lui faire visiter le fort Saint-Louis.
2
Avant de rentrer, passe au marché et prends de l'ananas, des oranges et des caramboles.

3
Ah, tu peux rendre ces livres à la bibliothèque aussi, s'il te plaît? Et en échange, tu me prends trois autres livres. Voilà ma carte.

4
Est-ce que tu peux aller à la poste et envoyer ce paquet?
Je ne sais pas si je vais avoir le temps.

5
Je vais d'abord au fort Saint-Louis, puis je dois aller au marché et ensuite...
C'est important...
Bon.

6
Tu peux passer chez le disquaire? J'ai commandé un disque-compact.
Bien. C'est tout?

7
Au retour, tu peux aller à la boulangerie? Prends deux baguettes.

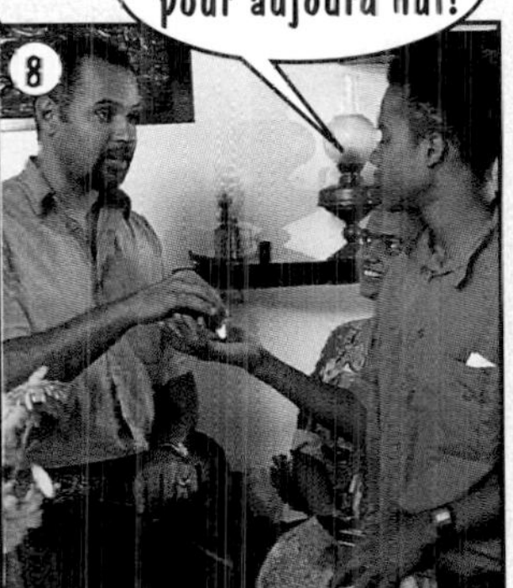
8
Tiens, voilà 5 francs. Prends-moi aussi le journal.
Bon, ça suffit pour aujourd'hui!

9
Tu vas voir, c'est très intéressant, le fort Saint-Louis.
Merci, Lucien. C'est sympa.

10
Bonjour. Est-ce que par hasard vous allez en ville aujourd'hui?
Au secours!

1 Tu as compris?

1. What are Lucien's plans for the day?
2. What are Lucien and his family talking about?
3. Is Lucien happy with the situation? Why or why not?
4. What happens at the end?

2 Qui dit quoi?

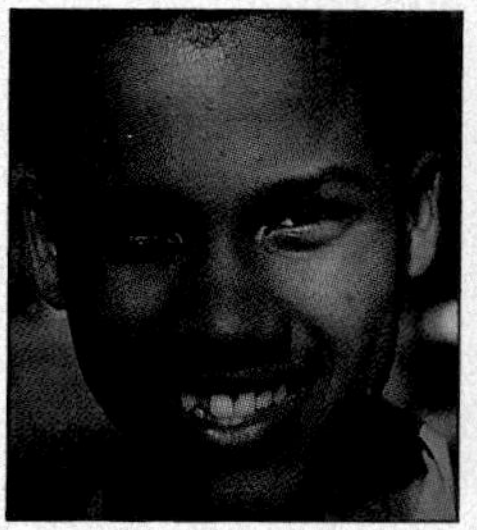
Lucien

Lisette

M. Lapiquonne

Mme Lapiquonne

1. «Tu peux aller à la boulangerie?»
2. «Tu peux rendre ces livres à la bibliothèque aussi, s'il te plaît?»
3. «Est-ce que tu peux aller à la poste et envoyer ce paquet?»
4. «Tu peux passer chez le disquaire?»
5. «Passe au marché et prends de l'ananas, des oranges et des caramboles.»
6. «Prends-moi aussi le journal.»

3 Où va-t-il?

Où est-ce que Lucien va aller pour...

1. acheter des caramboles?
2. envoyer le paquet?
3. rendre les livres?
4. acheter le disque compact?
5. acheter des baguettes?

à la boulangerie
à la poste
chez le disquaire
au marché
à la bibliothèque

4 Vrai ou faux?

1. Lucien va acheter des caramboles, des pêches et des pommes.
2. Il va rendre des livres à la bibliothèque.
3. Lucien va à la boulangerie.
4. Lisette lui donne de l'argent pour acheter un livre.
5. Lucien va chez le disquaire pour son père.
6. Il va acheter le journal pour la voisine.

5 Cherche les expressions

According to **Un petit service**, how do you . . .

1. say you're meeting someone?
2. say you don't know if you'll have time?
3. ask someone to do something for you?
4. express your annoyance?
5. call for help?

Est-ce que tu peux... ? Au secours!
Ça suffit! J'ai rendez-vous avec...
Je ne sais pas si je vais avoir le temps.

6 Et maintenant, à toi

What errands do you do for your family and friends? Do you go to the same places as Lucien?

PREMIERE ETAPE

Storytelling Book
pp. 45, 48

Pointing out places and things

CD-ROM Disc 3

VOCABULAIRE

Où est-ce qu'on va pour faire les courses? On peut aller à ces **endroits** :

à **la boulangerie** pour acheter **des baguettes**

à **la pâtisserie** pour acheter **des pâtisseries**

à **l'épicerie** pour acheter de la confiture

à **la poste** pour acheter **des timbres** et **envoyer des lettres**

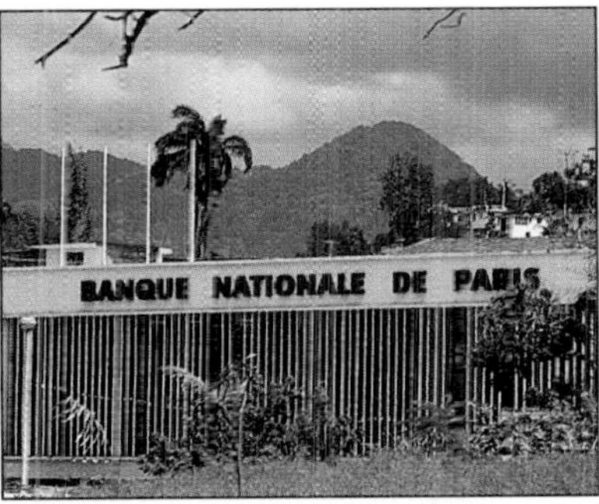

à **la banque** pour **retirer** ou **déposer** de l'argent

à **la librairie-papeterie** pour acheter des livres ou **des enveloppes**

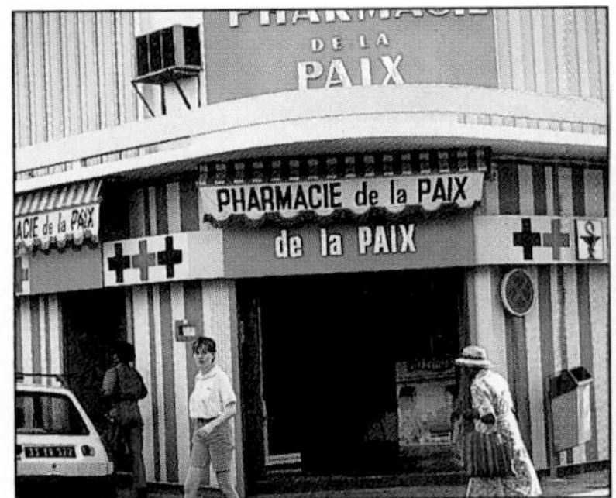

à **la pharmacie** pour acheter **des médicaments**

chez le disquaire pour acheter des disques compacts ou des cassettes

à la bibliothèque pour **emprunter** ou **rendre** des livres

7 Ecoute!

Listen to these conversations and tell where the people are.

8 Un petit mot

Read this note that Frédéric wrote to his friend. Then, list three places he went to and tell what he did there.

Tu te rappelles?

Remember, **au**, **à la**, **à l'**, and **aux** mean *to the* or *at the*. Use **au** before a masculine singular noun, **à la** before a feminine singular noun, **à l'** before any singular noun beginning with a vowel sound, and **aux** before any plural noun.

Je vais { **au** musée. / **à la** boulangerie. / **à l'**épicerie.

Je vais { **à l'**hôtel. / **aux** Etats-Unis.

Cher Pierre,

Ici, rien de bien nouveau. Hier, mes parents sont allés passer la journée chez leurs amis, alors j'étais tout seul. J'en ai profité pour faire des courses. D'abord, je suis allé à la boulangerie acheter du pain. Ensuite, je suis allé à la poste parce que je n'avais plus de timbres, et j'en ai profité pour envoyer une lettre à Jules, mon correspondant québécois. Puis, je suis allé à la bibliothèque emprunter quelques livres parce que j'ai fini de lire toute ma collection. Je n'ai pas trouvé le dernier livre de Stephen King à la bibliothèque (il paraît qu'il est super!), alors je suis allé à la librairie pour l'acheter. Finalement, je suis passé à l'épicerie acheter des légumes et du fromage pour mon déjeuner. Voilà, c'est tout. Ecris-moi vite pour me dire comment tu trouves ton nouveau lycée. Salut.

Frédéric

9 Des courses en ville

Yvette fait des courses en ville. Où est-elle?

1. «Je voudrais ce gâteau au chocolat, s'il vous plaît.»
2. «Je voudrais emprunter ces trois livres, s'il vous plaît.»
3. «Eh bien, je voudrais des médicaments pour ma mère.»
4. «C'est combien pour envoyer cette lettre aux Etats-Unis?»
5. «Zut, alors! Elle est fermée. Je ne peux pas déposer de l'argent!»

Note Culturelle

Stores in France and Martinique don't stay open 24 hours a day. Between 12:30 P.M. and 3:30 P.M., very few small businesses are open; however, they usually remain open until 7:00 P.M. By law, businesses must close one day a week, usually Sunday. Only grocery stores, restaurants, and certain places related to culture and entertainment, such as museums and movie theaters, may stay open on Sunday.

10 Il va où?

a. Regarde la liste d'Armand. Où va-t-il?
b. Qu'est-ce qu'il peut acheter d'autre là où il va?

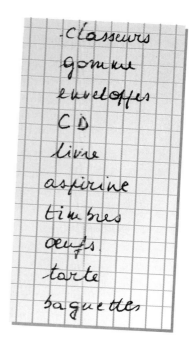

classeurs
gomme
enveloppes
CD
livre
aspirine
timbres
oeufs
tarte
baguettes

De bons conseils

You've already learned that an ending can often help you guess the gender of a word. An ending can also help you guess the meaning of a word. For example, the ending **-erie** often indicates a place where something is sold or made. Look at these words: **poissonnerie, fromagerie, chocolaterie, croissanterie.** What do you think they mean? Another common ending that carries a particular meaning is **-eur (-euse).** It indicates a person who performs a certain activity. In French, **chasser** means *to hunt.* A person who hunts is a **chasseur.** Since **chanter** means *to sing,* how do you think you would say *singer* in French? If **danser** means *to dance,* how would you say *dancer?**

11 Devine!

Think of something that you bought. Then, tell your partner where you went to buy it. Your partner will try to guess what you bought there. Take turns.

— Je suis allé(e) à la boulangerie.
— Tu as acheté des croissants?
— Non.

Si tu as oublié
le passé composé
va à la page 239.

COMMENT DIT-ON... ?

Pointing out places and things

Voici tes timbres.
Regarde, voilà ma maison.
Look, here/there is/are . . .
Ça, c'est la banque.
This/That is . . .
Là, c'est mon disquaire préféré.
There, that is . . .
Là, tu vois, c'est la maison de mes grands-parents.
There, you see, this/that is . . .

VOILÀ LA MAISON DE MES GRANDS-PARENTS.

*chanteur, danseur

12 A la Martinique

During your trip to Martinique you took the photos below. Take turns with your partner pointing out and identifying the places and objects in the photos.

le disquaire
la statue de Joséphine de Beauharnais
la pharmacie
la boulangerie
la bibliothèque Schœlcher
le marché

1.

2.

3.

4.

5.

6.

A la française

When you try to communicate in a foreign language, there will always be times when you can't remember or don't know the exact word you need. One way to get around this problem is to use *circumlocution.* Circumlocution means substituting words and expressions you do know to explain what you mean. For example, if you can't think of the French word for *pharmacy,* you might say **l'endroit où on peut acheter des médicaments** *(the place where you can buy medicine).* Other expressions you can use are **la personne qui/que** *(the person who/whom),* and **le truc qui/que** *(the thing that).*

13 Mon quartier

An exchange student is coming to stay with your family for a semester. Draw a map of your neighborhood and label the school, post office, grocery store, and so on.

14 Jeu de rôle

As your exchange student asks where various places are, point them out on the map you made for Activity 13. Tell what you buy or do there. Take turns playing the role of the exchange student.

Rencontre Culturelle

Look at the illustrations below. Where are these people? What are they talking about?

— Bonjour, Madame Perrot. Vous avez passé de bonnes vacances?
— Très bonnes. On est allés à la Guadeloupe. Vous savez, ma sœur habite là-bas, et...

— Et votre père, il va bien?
— Oui, merci. Il va beaucoup mieux depuis...

— Qu'est-ce que vous allez faire avec ça?
— Ma voisine m'a donné une très bonne recette. C'est très simple. Tout ce qu'il faut faire, c'est...

Qu'en penses-tu?

1. What are the topics of these conversations? What does this tell you about the culture of Martinique?
2. What kind of relationships do you or your family have with the people who work in your town? Do you know them? Do you often make "small talk" with them?

Savais-tu que... ?

In Martinique, as in many parts of France, people like to take the time to say hello, ask how others are doing, and find out what's going on in one another's lives. Of course, the smaller the town, the more likely this is to occur. While it may be frustrating to Americans in a hurry, especially when they are conducting business, in West Indian culture it is considered rude not to take a few minutes to engage in some polite conversation before talking business.

DEUXIEME ETAPE

Making and responding to requests; asking for advice and making suggestions

COMMENT DIT-ON... ?

Making and responding to requests

TU PEUX ALLER A L'EPICERIE POUR ACHETER DU JAMBON?
DIS, EST-CE QUE TU PEUX ALLER A LA POSTE POUR MOI?

To make a request:

(Est-ce que) tu peux aller au marché?

Tu me rapportes des timbres?

Tu pourrais passer à la poste acheter des timbres?
Could you go by . . . ?

To accept requests:

D'accord.

Je veux bien.

J'y vais tout de suite.

Si tu veux. *If you want.*

To decline requests:

Je ne peux pas maintenant.

Je suis désolé(e), mais je n'ai pas le temps.

15 Ecoute!

Listen to the following conversations and decide if the person agrees to or refuses the request.

Tu te rappelles?

Use the partitive articles **du**, **de la**, and **de l'** when you mean *some* of an item. If you mean a whole item instead of a part of it, use the indefinite articles **un**, **une**, and **des. Du, de la, de l', des, un**, and **une** usually become **de/d'** in negative sentences.

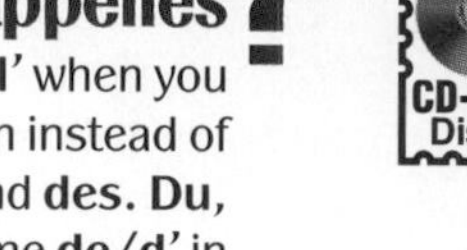

16 Un petit service

What would these people say to ask you a favor?

1.

2.

3.

4.

Si tu as oublié
expressing need
va à la page 210.

17 Il me faut...

Decide which of these items you need and ask your partner to go to the appropriate store. Your partner will accept or decline your request. Take turns.

1.

2.

3.

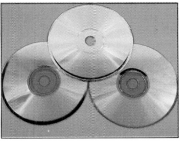

4.

5.

6.

18 Tu pourrais me rendre un service?

Ask your classmates to do these favors for you. They will either accept or decline and make an excuse.

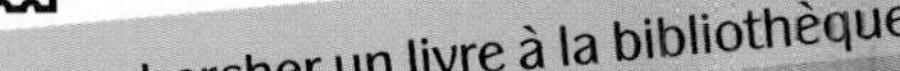

aller chercher un livre à la bibliothèque

acheter un dictionnaire de français à la librairie

acheter un CD chez le disquaire

acheter un sandwich au fast-food

acheter une règle à la papeterie

acheter des timbres à la poste

Si tu as oublié
making an excuse
va à la page 129.

COMMENT DIT-ON... ?

Asking for advice and making suggestions

To ask for advice on how to get somewhere:

Comment est-ce qu'on y va? *How can we get there?*

To suggest how to get somewhere:

On peut y aller en train. *We can go . . .*

On peut prendre le bus. *We can take . . .*

VOCABULAIRE

Comment est-ce qu'on y va?

en bus (m.)

à pied (m.)

à vélo (m.)

en voiture (f.)

en taxi (m.)

en bateau (m.)

en avion (m.)

en train (m.)

en métro (m.)

19 Ecoute!

Listen to these conversations. Where are these people going and how are they going to get there?

20 Comment vont-ils voyager?

1.

2.

3.

4.

CD-ROM
Disc 3

GRAMMAIRE The pronoun y

You've already seen the pronoun **y** *(there)* several times. Can you figure out how to use it?

—Je vais **à la bibliothèque**. Tu **y** vas aussi?
—Non, je n'y vais pas.

—Je vais **chez le disquaire**. Tu veux **y** aller?
—Non, j'y suis allé hier.

It can replace an entire phrase meaning *to, at,* or *in* any place that has already been mentioned. Place it before the conjugated verb, or, if there is an infinitive, place **y** before the infinitive: Je vais **y** aller demain.

21 On va en ville

How do you and your friends get to these places?

Au cinéma? Nous y allons en bus.

au cinéma · au supermarché · à la poste · à la bibliothèque · à la piscine · au centre commercial · au stade · au parc · à la librairie · au lycée · au concert

Si tu as oublié
inviting
va à la page 159.

22 Qu'est-ce qu'on fait vendredi soir?

You call your friend and invite him or her to do something Friday night. When you've decided where you want to go, talk about how to get there.

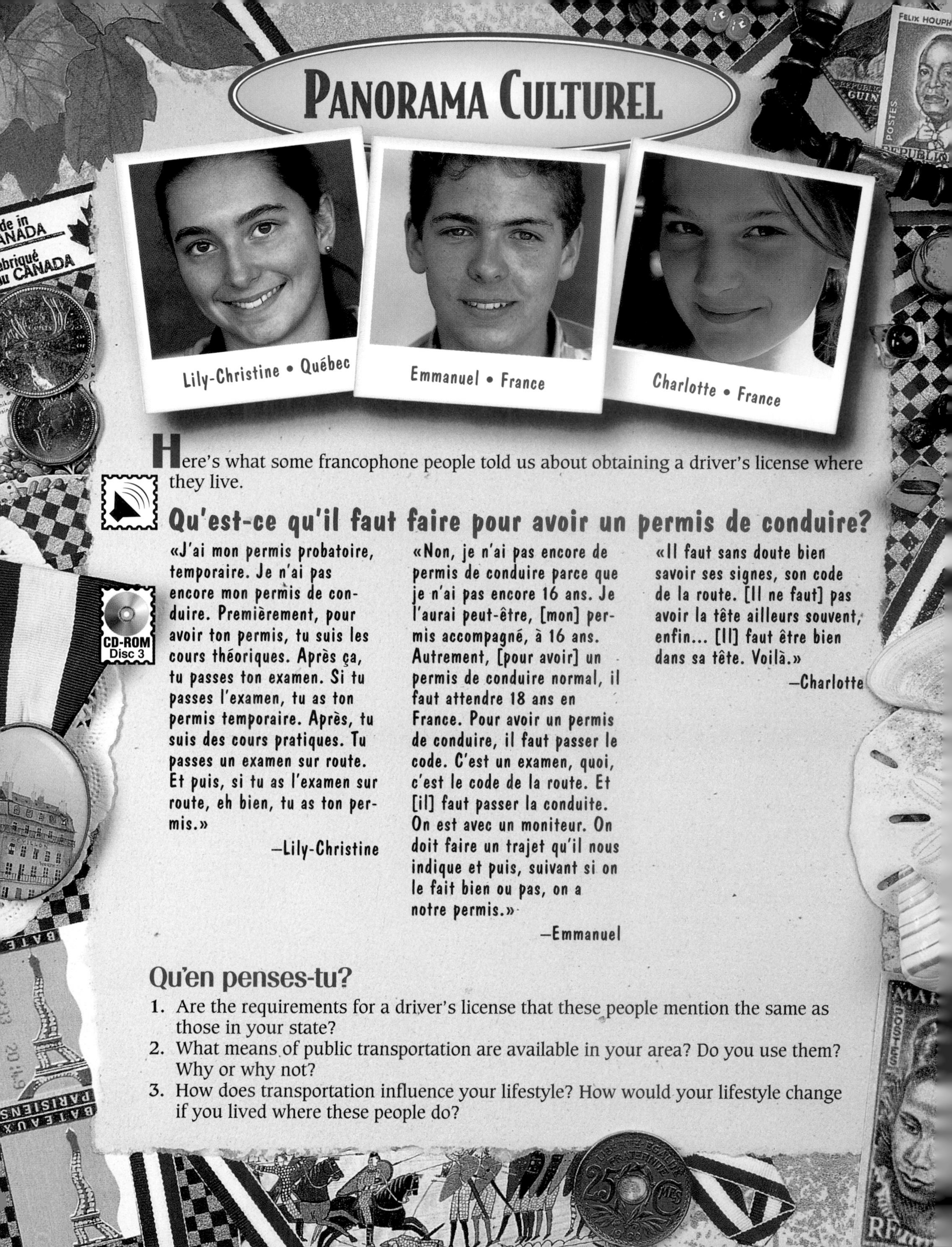

Panorama Culturel

Lily-Christine • Québec

Emmanuel • France

Charlotte • France

Here's what some francophone people told us about obtaining a driver's license where they live.

CD-ROM Disc 3

Qu'est-ce qu'il faut faire pour avoir un permis de conduire?

«J'ai mon permis probatoire, temporaire. Je n'ai pas encore mon permis de conduire. Premièrement, pour avoir ton permis, tu suis les cours théoriques. Après ça, tu passes ton examen. Si tu passes l'examen, tu as ton permis temporaire. Après, tu suis des cours pratiques. Tu passes un examen sur route. Et puis, si tu as l'examen sur route, eh bien, tu as ton permis.»

—Lily-Christine

«Non, je n'ai pas encore de permis de conduire parce que je n'ai pas encore 16 ans. Je l'aurai peut-être, [mon] permis accompagné, à 16 ans. Autrement, [pour avoir] un permis de conduire normal, il faut attendre 18 ans en France. Pour avoir un permis de conduire, il faut passer le code. C'est un examen, quoi, c'est le code de la route. Et [il] faut passer la conduite. On est avec un moniteur. On doit faire un trajet qu'il nous indique et puis, suivant si on le fait bien ou pas, on a notre permis.»

—Emmanuel

«Il faut sans doute bien savoir ses signes, son code de la route. [Il ne faut] pas avoir la tête ailleurs souvent, enfin... [Il] faut être bien dans sa tête. Voilà.»

—Charlotte

Qu'en penses-tu?

1. Are the requirements for a driver's license that these people mention the same as those in your state?
2. What means of public transportation are available in your area? Do you use them? Why or why not?
3. How does transportation influence your lifestyle? How would your lifestyle change if you lived where these people do?

TROISIEME ETAPE

Asking for and giving directions

Vocabulaire

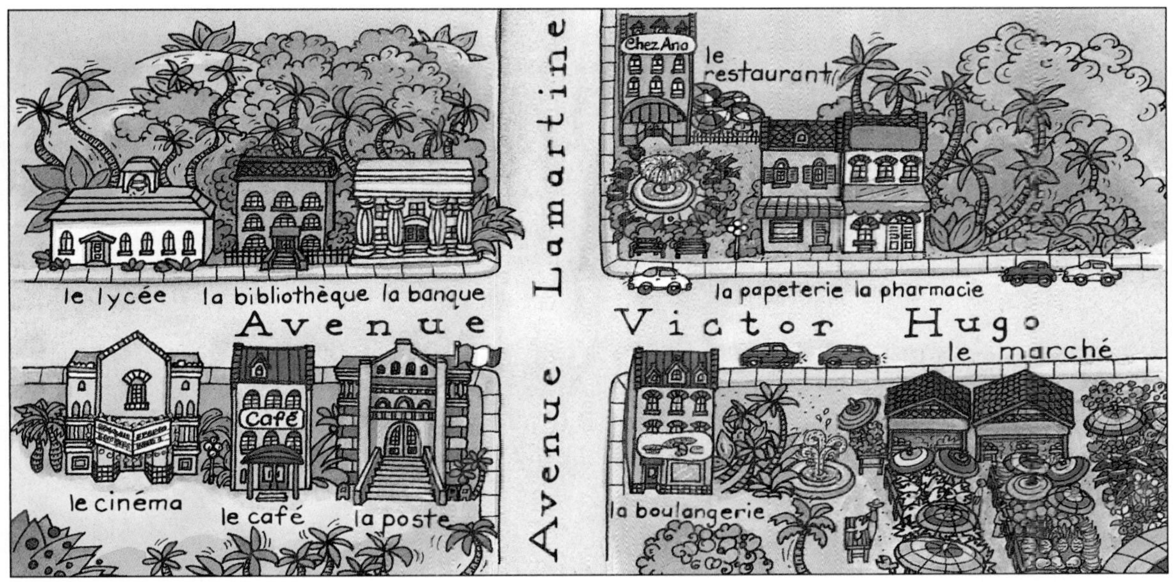

La bibliothèque est **entre** le lycée et la banque.
La poste est **à droite du** café.
Le cinéma est **à gauche du** café.

La boulangerie est **au coin de** la rue.
Le café est **en face de** la bibliothèque.

Here are some other prepositions you may want to use to give directions:

à côté de	*next to*	**loin de**	*far from*
devant	*in front of*	**près de**	*near*
derrière	*behind*		

23 Ecoute!

Listen to the following statements and tell whether they are true or false, according to the **Vocabulaire.**

24 Qui est-ce?

Tell where a classmate is seated in your classroom. The others in your group will try to guess who it is.

Cette personne est derrière David et à côté d'Isabelle.

NOTE DE GRAMMAIRE

The preposition **de** usually means *of* or *from.*

- When you use **de** before **le** or **les,** make the following contractions:

de + le = du	C'est près **du** musée.
de + les = des	Le café est près **des** Alpes.

- **De** doesn't change before **l'** or **la:** C'est au coin **de la** rue.

25 Il est perdu!

Your friend, Hervé, has a poor sense of direction. Everything is in just the opposite direction or location from what he thinks. Help him out by answering his questions.

—La poste est loin de la bibliothèque?
—Mais non, elle est près de la bibliothèque.

1. Est-ce que la papeterie est près de la pharmacie?
2. Le cinéma est devant le centre commercial?
3. La bibliothèque est à droite?
4. Est-ce que le café est derrière le stade?

Note Culturelle

Martinique is an overseas possession of France known as a **département d'outre-mer,** or **DOM.** It has the same administrative status as a department in France, and the people of Martinique, who are citizens of France, have the same rights and responsibilities as other French citizens. Other DOMs include Guadeloupe, French Guiana, and Reunion Island. France also has overseas territories, like New Caledonia and French Polynesia. These territories are called **territoires d'outre-mer,** or **TOMs.**

26 La visite d'Arianne

Arianne a pris des photos pendant sa visite chez son oncle et sa tante. Complète les descriptions des photos avec des prépositions.

1. C'est mon oncle et ma tante dans le jardin _____ leur maison.

2. Là, _____ ma tante, c'est mon cousin Daniel.

3. Et voilà ma cousine Adeline, _____ mon oncle.

4. Il y a une boulangerie _____ leur maison. Les croissants sont délicieux le matin!

5. Leur maison est _____ une autre maison et une épicerie.

6. Il y a un parc au coin de la rue, _____ leur maison.

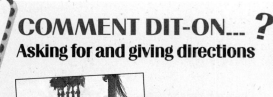

COMMENT DIT-ON... ?

Asking for and giving directions

To ask for directions:

Pardon, madame. La poste, **s'il vous plaît?**

Pardon, mademoiselle. Où est la banque, **s'il vous plaît?**

Pardon, monsieur. Je cherche le musée, **s'il vous plaît.** *Excuse me, sir. I'm looking for . . . please.*

To give directions:

Vous continuez jusqu'au prochain feu rouge. *You keep going until the next light.*

Vous allez tout droit jusqu'au lycée. *You go straight ahead until you get to . . .*

Vous tournez à droite. *You turn . . .*

Prenez la rue Lamartine, **puis traversez la rue** Isambert. *Take . . . Street, then cross . . . Street.*

Vous passez devant la boulangerie. *You'll pass . . .*

C'est tout de suite à gauche. *It's right there on the . . .*

27 Ecoute!

Guy is at the bus station **(la gare routière)** in Fort-de-France. Follow M. Robinet's directions, using the map on page 328. Where does Guy want to go?

Note Culturelle

In many French towns, intersections have a traffic circle **(un rond-point)** at the center, which is often decorated with flowers, fountains, or statues. Vehicles enter and continue around the center island, turning off at the various streets that open into the circle. Most towns have at least one public square, often located in front of a public building or a church. Numerous cities have closed off some of the tiny streets in the **centre-ville** and made pedestrian areas where people can stroll freely, without having to worry about traffic.

28 Où est-ce?

Give directions from school to your favorite restaurant or record store. Your partner will try to guess the name of the place. Take turns.

29 Quel monument est-ce?

Your pen pal from Martinique wrote directions to a site that he thinks you should visit. Follow his directions on the map of Fort-de-France to find out which of these sites it is.

la bibliothèque Schœlcher

la cathédrale Saint-Louis

Quand tu sors de la gare routière, va à droite sur le boulevard du Général de Gaulle. Prends la première à droite – c'est la rue Félix Eboué – et continue tout droit. Tu vas passer devant la préfecture. Traverse l'avenue des Caraïbes et va tout droit dans la rue de la Liberté jusqu'à la poste. Ensuite, tourne à droite rue Blénac et continue tout droit. Ça sera à droite, tout de suite après la rue Schoelcher.

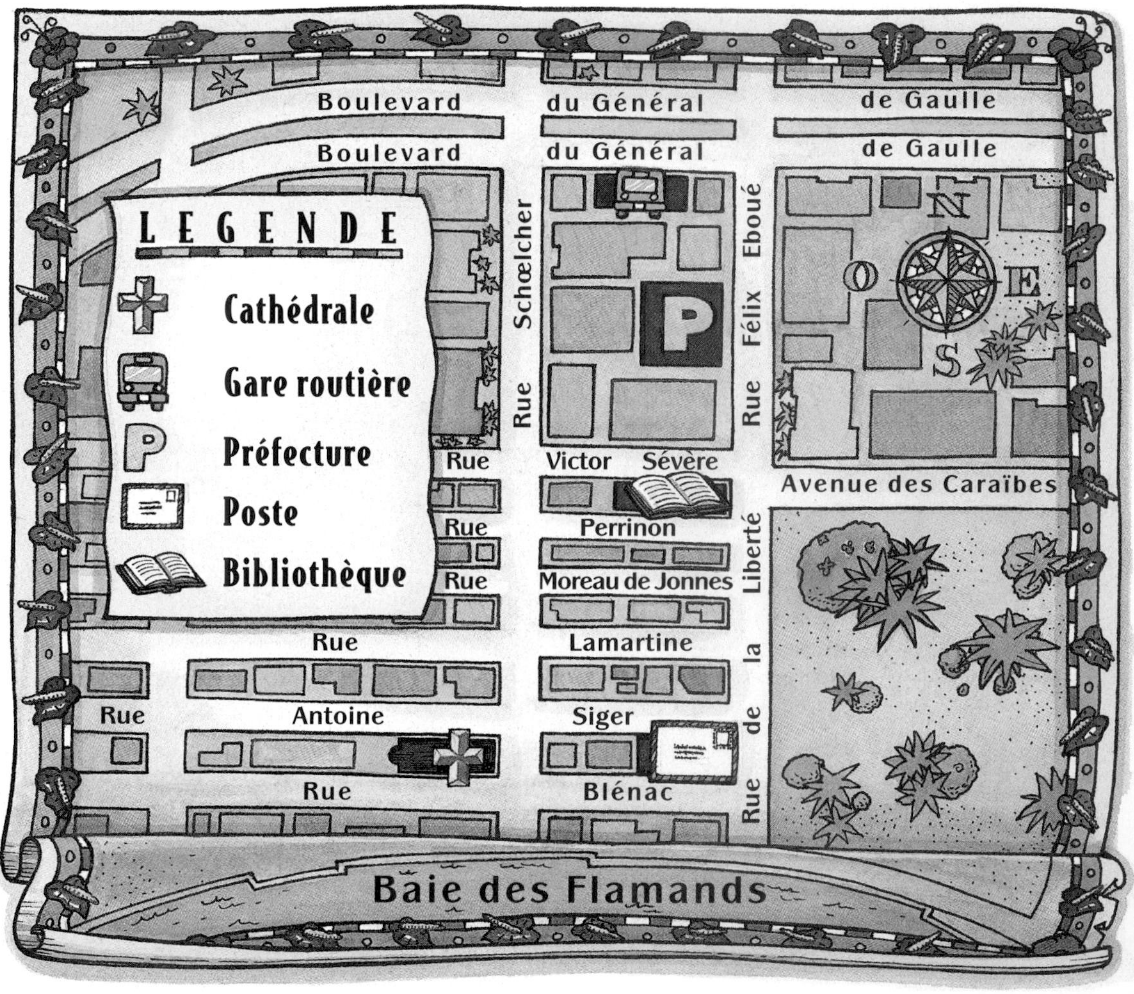

LEGENDE
Cathédrale
Gare routière
Préfecture
Poste
Bibliothèque

Boulevard du Général de Gaulle
Boulevard du Général de Gaulle
Rue Schœlcher
Rue Félix Eboué
Rue Victor Sévère
Avenue des Caraïbes
Rue Perrinon
Rue Moreau de Jonnes
Rue Lamartine
Rue Antoine Siger
Rue Blénac
Rue de la Liberté
N
O
E
S
Baie des Flamands

30 Mon journal

Write a description of your city or neighborhood. What does it look like? Where are things located? Draw a small map to accompany your description.

PRONONCIATION

Prononciation

Do you remember what you've learned about French pronunciation? Here is a quick pronunciation review. If you've forgotten how to produce any of these sounds, check the Pronunciation Index at the back of the book and go back to the chapters where they were introduced. Repeat these words.

[y]	du	étude	[u]	rouge	voudrais
[o]	escargots	gâteau	[ɔ]	pomme	carottes
[ø]	veut	heureux	[œ]	sœur	beurre
[e]	cinéma	trouver	[ɛ]	frère	anglaise
[ɑ̃]	anglais	il prend	[ɔ̃]	allons	poisson
[ɛ̃]	quinze	pain	[œ̃]	lundi	emprunter
[j]	papier	viande	[w]	moi	pouvoir
[ɥ]	lui	ensuite	[t]	maths	théâtre
[r]	très	roux	[ʃ]	chat	chercher
[']	le héros	le hockey	[ɲ]	montagne	Allemagne

A. A prononcer

Repeat the following words.

1. nourriture — boutique — bateau — poste
2. feu — déposer — près — derrière
3. devant — avion — timbre — emprunter
4. pied — voiture — envoyer — tout de suite
5. rue — gauche — prochain — bibliothèque

B. A lire

Take turns with a partner reading each of the following sentences aloud.

1. Quand le chat n'est pas là, les souris dansent.
2. Il est mieux de travailler que de s'amuser.
3. Beaucoup de bruit pour rien.
4. Un poisson n'est jamais trop petit pour être frit.
5. On n'attrape pas les mouches avec du vinaigre.

C. A écrire

You're going to hear a short dialogue. Write down what you hear.

LISONS!

What kinds of stories do you like to read? Stories about the past? About the future? About exotic places?

DE BONS CONSEILS When you read stories, newspaper and magazine articles, or novels that were written for native French speakers, you're bound to come across many unfamiliar words. Just remember to use all the reading tips that you know to try to understand what you're reading.

A. Look at the title and illustrations that accompany the text. What is this story going to be about? Where does the story take place?

B. Scan the story to see if you can find the answers to these questions.

1. Who are the main characters in the story?
2. What is going on when the story starts?
3. Why does Congo come to help the horse?
4. How does Congo help the horse?

C. Read the story carefully and then see if you can put these events in the correct order.

1. Congo burns the blue horse.
2. A child is frightened by the blue horse.
3. Congo first comes to see the blue horse.
4. M. Quinquina and his sons play music.
5. The blue bird is freed.
6. The mayor goes to see Congo.

Cheval de bois

Cette année, la ville de Saint-Pierre accueille le manège de la famille Quinquina pour sa fête patronale. Le manège s'est installé sur la place du marché, face à la mer. Madame Quinquina tient une buvette où elle sert des limonades multicolores.

Monsieur Quinquina et ses deux fils jouent de la flûte de bambou et du "ti-bwa". Au rythme de cette musique, le manège de chevaux de bois, poussé par de robustes jeunes gens, tourne, tourne, tourne.

Cheval bleu, bleu comme l'océan.
Cheval noir, noir comme la nuit.
Cheval blanc, blanc comme les nuages.
Cheval vert, vert comme les bambous.
Cheval rouge, rouge comme le flamboyant.
Cheval jaune, jaune comme l'allamanda.

Les chevaux de bois tournent, tournent et, sur leur dos, tous les enfants sont heureux.

Mais quand la nuit parfumée caresse l'île, les chevaux de bois rêvent. Le cheval bleu, bleu comme l'océan, rêve de partir, partir loin, visiter les îles, visiter le monde. Il a entendu dire que la terre est ronde. Vrai ou faux? Il aimerait bien savoir ! Cela fait si longtemps qu'il porte ce rêve dans sa carcasse de bois que cette nuit-là, son rêve devient oiseau. L'oiseau bat des ailes dans le corps du cheval bleu, bleu comme l'océan.

Au matin, un enfant monte sur le cheval bleu.
Tout à coup, il commence à hurler :
— Maman, maman, il y a une bête dans le cheval. J'ai peur! Je veux descendre.

On arrête la musique, on arrête le manège. C'est un tollé général : les mères rassemblent leurs enfants. En quelques secondes, la place est vide. Le maire et ses conseillers décident d'aller chercher le sage Congo.

...Congo s'approche du manège et caresse les flancs du cheval bleu, bleu comme l'océan :

— Je vais te délivrer ! cheval bleu, bleu comme l'océan, car ton rêve est vivant, il s'est métamorphosé en oiseau.

Congo s'assied près du cheval bleu, bleu comme l'océan. Quand le maire voit Congo tranquillement assis, il sort de la mairie en courant et hurle :

— Que faites-vous?
— J'attends, dit doucement Congo.
— Vous attendez quoi? demande le maire.
— J'attends que la nuit mette son manteau étoilé et ouvre son œil d'or. Je ferai alors un grand feu.

Quand la nuit met son manteau étoilé et ouvre son œil d'or, Congo prend tendrement dans ses bras le cheval bleu, bleu comme l'océan, et le dépose dans les flammes. Le feu crépite, chante, et l'or des flammes devient bleu, bleu comme l'océan. Les habitants de Saint-Pierre voient un immense oiseau bleu, bleu comme l'océan, s'élever dans la nuit étoilée et s'envoler vers l'horizon.
Congo, heureux, murmure :
-Bon vent, oiseau-rêve !

RAPPEL As you read the story, you probably came across some unfamiliar words. Remember, you don't have to understand every word to get a sense of what you're reading. If you decide that the meaning of a particular word is necessary to help you understand the story, there are two techniques you've learned that can help: using the context to figure out the meaning of the word, and trying to see a cognate in the word.

D. Below are some cognates that appear in *Cheval de bois.* See if you can match them with their English equivalents.

1. habitants	a. counselors
2. fête	b. to descend; to get down
3. flammes	c. island
4. conseillers	d. festival
5. île	e. flames
6. descendre	f. inhabitants, people who live in a certain area

E. Make a list of all of the other cognates you can find in *Cheval de bois.* You should be able to find at least six more. Watch out for false cognates!

F. How can you tell this story was written for a young audience?

G. What stories, fairy tales, or myths have you read or heard that are similar to this story? In what ways are they similar? In what ways are they different?

H. Do you think there really was a bird inside the horse? What do you think the bird represents?

I. Compose a fairy tale of your own. Write it out or record it in French. Keep it simple so that your teacher can use it in the future with students who are beginning to learn French! Illustrate your story to make it easier to understand.

MISE EN PRATIQUE

1 You're planning a trip to Martinique and you'll need some transportation. Look at these ads. What kinds of transportation are available?

LOCATION TROIS-ILETS
Anse à l'Ane - 97229 Trois-Ilets

68.40.37
Lundi à Vendredi
8 H - 13 H
et 15 H - 18 H
Week-end :
à la demande

Avec Location TROIS-ILETS, la moto que vous avez louée par téléphone, 48 heures plus tôt, vient à vous. Chez vous. Si vous vous trouvez dans la commune des Trois-Ilets. Location possible pour une semaine au moins.

TAXI FORT-DE-FRANCE
102 Rue de la République -
97200 Fort-de-France

70.44.08 Tous les jours : 5 H - 20 H

Nos taxis répondent sans délais quand vous téléphonez à Taxi Fort-de-France. Déplacement dans toute l'île.

LOCA CENTER
3 Km Route de Schœlcher n. 63 -
97233 Schœlcher

Livraison de voiture (Opel Corsa, Peugeot 106) à domicile (Nord Caraïbe, Schœlcher, Fort-de-France) pour une durée minimum de trois jours. Pas de frais de déplacement. Pendant la haute saison, pour une location de 10 jours au moins, réserver un mois à l'avance. Pour une location d'une durée de 3 à 7 jours, réserver 48 heures à l'avance. Pendant la basse saison, réserver la veille ou le jour même.

61.05.95
61.40.12
Lundi à Vendredi
7 H 30 - 16 H 30
Week-end : à la demande

1. Where can you call if you want a taxi? When is the latest you can call?
2. Where can you call if you want to rent a Renault? What about a motorcycle?
3. What's the minimum length of time you can rent these vehicles?
4. How long in advance do you need to make a reservation?
5. Are these places open on weekends?

2 Listen to Didier tell his family about his trip to Martinique. Put the pictures in order according to Didier's description.

a.

b.

c.

d.

3 *Ecrivons!*

Write a logical conversation to accompany the picture below.

STRATEGIE

Making a writing plan before you begin is important. Study the illustration carefully. Do you know all the vocabulary you'll need? Will you need to use certain verbs or structures frequently? You might want to use your textbook as a reference.

Prewriting

To help form your writing plan, look at the illustration and jot down ideas that immediately come to mind. You might imagine the situation, names for the people, and things they might be saying. Think about the types of vocabulary and structures you will need.

Writing

Now, using the notes you created in your writing plan, create the conversation that goes with the picture. Keep in mind expressions you've learned, such as asking for and giving directions, and vocabulary for telling where something is located.

Revising

When you've completed your writing, set it aside for a while before you do your self-evaluation. This will give you a fresh perspective on how to make it better. Also, when you evaluate what you've written, focus on only one area at a time. For example, don't look for spelling and punctuation mistakes while you're checking to see how well your writing flows. Focus on finding such mistakes when you proofread.

After you've revised your work, let a classmate give you feedback. Then, you can concentrate on making any other necessary revisions.

4 JEU DE ROLE

While visiting Fort-de-France, you stop and mail some postcards at the post office. You ask the employee for directions to two places in town: the library and the cathedral. Using the map on page 328, the employee gives you directions from the post office to each of these places. Be sure to ask questions if something is not clear. Then, ask the employee what means of transportation you should use to get to these places.

QUE SAIS-JE?

Can you use what you've learned in this chapter?

Can you point out places and things? p. 317

1 How would you point out and identify . . .
1. a certain building?
2. a certain store?
3. a certain person?

Can you make and respond to requests? p. 320

2 How would you ask someone to . . .
1. buy some stamps?
2. go to the bookstore?
3. deposit some money?

3 How would you agree to do the favors you asked in number 2? How would you refuse?

Can you ask for advice and make suggestions? p. 322

4 How would you ask a friend which means of transportation you should use to get to a certain store?

5 How would you suggest these means of transportation?

1.

2.

3.

4.

Can you ask for and give directions? p. 327

6 How would you tell someone that you're looking for a certain place?

7 How would you ask someone where a certain place in town is?

8 How would you give someone directions to your house from . . .
1. your school?
2. your favorite restaurant?

VOCABULAIRE

PREMIERE ETAPE

Pointing out places and things

Voici... *Here is/are . . .*
Regarde, voilà... *Look, here/there is/are . . .*
Ça, c'est... *This/That is . . .*
Là, c'est... *There, that is . . .*
Là, tu vois, c'est... *There, you see, this/that is . . .*
un endroit *place*
chez *at (at the place of) . . .*

Buildings

la banque *bank*
la boulangerie *bakery*
le disquaire *record store*
l'épicerie (f.) *small grocery store*
la librairie *bookstore*
la papeterie *stationery store*
la pâtisserie *pastry shop*
la pharmacie *drugstore*
la poste *post office*

Things to do or buy in town

envoyer des lettres *to send letters*
une baguette *long, thin loaf of bread*
un timbre *stamp*
retirer de l'argent (m.) *to withdraw money*
déposer de l'argent *to deposit money*
rendre *to return something*
emprunter *to borrow*
des médicaments (m.) *medicine*
une enveloppe *envelope*
une pâtisserie *pastry*

DEUXIEME ETAPE

Making and responding to requests

Tu peux... ? *Can you . . . ?*
Tu me rapportes... ? *Will you bring me . . . ?*
Tu pourrais passer à... ? *Could you go by . . . ?*
D'accord. *OK.*
Je veux bien. *Gladly.*
J'y vais tout de suite. *I'll go right away.*
Si tu veux. *If you want.*
Je ne peux pas maintenant. *I can't right now.*
Je suis désolé(e), mais je n'ai pas le temps. *I'm sorry, but I don't have time.*

Asking for advice and making suggestions

Comment est-ce qu'on y va? *How can we get there?*
On peut y aller... *We can go . . .*
On peut prendre... *We can take . . .*
y *there*

Means of transportation

en bus (m.) *by bus*
à pied (m.) *on foot*
à vélo (m.) *by bike*
en voiture (f.) *by car*
en taxi (m.) *by taxi*
en bateau (m.) *by boat*
en avion (m.) *by plane*
en train (m.) *by train*
en métro (m.) *by subway*

TROISIEME ETAPE

Asking for and giving directions

Pardon, ..., s'il vous plaît? *Excuse me, . . . please?*
Pardon, ... Où est..., s'il vous plaît? *Excuse me, . . . Where is . . . , please?*
Pardon, ... Je cherche..., s'il vous plaît. *Excuse me, . . . I'm looking for . . . , please.*
Vous continuez jusqu'au prochain feu rouge. *You keep going until the next light.*
Vous allez tout droit jusqu'à... *You go straight ahead until you get to . . .*
Vous tournez... *You turn . . .*
Prenez la rue..., puis traversez la rue... *Take . . . Street, then cross . . . Street.*
Vous passez... *You'll pass . . .*
C'est tout de suite à... *It's right there on the . . .*

Locations

à côté de *next to*
loin de *far from*
près de *close to*
au coin de *on the corner of*
en face de *across from*
derrière *behind*
devant *in front of*
entre *between*
à droite (de) *to the right*
à gauche (de) *to the left*

REFERENCE SECTION

SUMMARY OF FUNCTIONS

Function is another word for the way in which you use language for a specific purpose. When you find yourself in specific situations, such as in a restaurant, in a grocery store, or at school, you'll want to communicate with those around you. In order to communicate in French, you have to "function" in the language.

Each chapter in this book focuses on language functions. You can easily find them in boxes labeled **Comment dit-on... ?** The other features in the chapter—grammar, vocabulary, culture notes—support the functions you're learning.

Here is a list of functions and the French expressions presented in this book. You'll need them in order to communicate in a wide range of situations. Following each function entry, you will find the chapter and page number where each function is presented.

SOCIALIZING

Greeting people **Ch. 1, p. 22**

Bonjour.
Salut.

Saying goodbye **Ch. 1, p. 22**

Salut.
Au revoir.
A tout à l'heure.
A bientôt.
A demain.
Tchao.

Asking how people are and telling how you are
Ch. 1, p. 23

(Comment) ça va?
Ça va.
Super!
Très bien.
Comme ci, comme ça.
Bof.
Pas mal.
Pas terrible.
Et toi?

Expressing and responding to thanks **Ch. 3, p. 82**

Merci.
A votre service.

Extending invitations **Ch. 6, p. 159**

Allons... !
Tu veux... avec moi?
Tu viens?
On peut...

Accepting invitations **Ch. 6, p. 159**

Je veux bien.
Pourquoi pas?
D'accord.
Bonne idée.

Refusing invitations **Ch. 6, p. 159**

Désolé(e), je suis occupé(e).
Ça ne me dit rien.
J'ai des trucs à faire.
Désolé(e), je ne peux pas.

Identifying people **Ch. 7, p. 179**

C'est...
Ce sont...
Voici...
Voilà...

Introducing people **Ch. 7, p. 183**

C'est...
Je te/vous présente...
Très heureux (heureuse). (FORMAL)

Inquiring about past events **Ch. 9, p. 238**

Qu'est-ce que tu as fait... ?
Tu es allé(e) où?
Et après?
Qu'est-ce qui s'est passé?

Relating past events **Ch. 9, p. 238**

D'abord,...
Ensuite,...
Après,...
Je suis allé(e)...
Et après ça,...
Finalement,/Enfin,...

Inquiring about future plans **Ch. 11, p. 289**

Qu'est-ce que tu vas faire... ?
Où est-ce que tu vas aller... ?

Sharing future plans **Ch. 11, p. 289**

J'ai l'intention de...
Je vais...

Seeing someone off **Ch. 11, p. 296**

Bon voyage!
Bonnes vacances!
Amuse-toi bien!
Bonne chance!

EXCHANGING INFORMATION

Asking someone's name and giving yours
Ch. 1, p. 24

Tu t'appelles comment?
Je m'appelle...

Asking and giving someone else's name
Ch. 1, p. 24

Il/Elle s'appelle comment?
Il/Elle s'appelle...

Asking someone's age and giving yours
Ch. 1, p. 25

Tu as quel âge?
J'ai... ans.

Asking for information **Ch. 2, p. 51**

Tu as quels cours... ?
Tu as quoi... ?
Vous avez... ?
Tu as... à quelle heure?

Giving information **Ch. 2, p. 51**

Nous avons...
J'ai...

Telling when you have class **Ch. 2, p. 54**

à... heure(s)
à... heure(s) quinze
à... heure(s) trente
à... heure(s) quarante-cinq

Making requests **Ch. 3, p. 72**

Tu as... ?
Vous avez... ?

Responding to requests **Ch. 3, p. 72**

Voilà.
Je regrette.
Je n'ai pas de...

Asking others what they need and telling what you need **Ch. 3, p. 74**

Qu'est-ce qu'il te faut pour... ?
Qu'est-ce qu'il vous faut pour... ?
Il me faut...

Expressing need **Ch. 8, p. 210; Ch. 10, p. 265**

Qu'est-ce qu'il te faut?
Il me faut...
De quoi est-ce que tu as besoin?
J'ai besoin de...
Oui, il me faut...
Oui, vous avez... ?
Je cherche quelque chose pour...
J'aimerais... pour aller avec...
Non, merci, je regarde.

Asking for information **Ch. 3, p. 82**

C'est combien?

Getting someone's attention
Ch. 3, p. 82; Ch. 5, p. 135

Pardon...
Excusez-moi.
... , s'il vous plaît.
Monsieur!
Madame!
Mademoiselle!

Exchanging information **Ch. 4, p. 104**

Qu'est-ce que tu fais comme sport?
Qu'est-ce que tu fais pour t'amuser?
Je fais...
Je ne fais pas de...
Je (ne) joue (pas)...

Ordering food and beverages **Ch. 5, p. 135**

Vous avez choisi?
Vous prenez?
Je voudrais...
Je vais prendre..., s'il vous plaît.
... , s'il vous plaît.
Donnez-moi... , s'il vous plaît.
Apportez-moi... , s'il vous plaît.
Vous avez... ?
Qu'est-ce que vous avez comme boissons?
Qu'est-ce qu'il y a à boire?

Paying the check **Ch. 5, p. 139**

L'addition, s'il vous plaît.
Oui, tout de suite.
Un moment, s'il vous plaît.
Ça fait combien, s'il vous plaît?
Ça fait... francs.
C'est combien, ... ?
C'est... francs.

Making plans **Ch. 6, p. 153**

Qu'est-ce que tu vas faire... ?
Tu vas faire quoi... ?
Je vais...
Pas grand-chose.
Rien de spécial.

Arranging to meet someone **Ch. 6, p. 163**

Quand (ça)?
tout de suite
Où (ça)?
devant
au métro...
chez...
dans...
Avec qui?
A quelle heure?
A cinq heures...
et demie
et quart
moins le quart
moins cinq
midi (et demi)
minuit (et demi)
vers
Quelle heure est-il?
Il est...
On se retrouve...
Rendez-vous...
Entendu.

Describing and characterizing people
Ch. 7, p. 185

Il est comment?
Elle est comment?
Ils/Elles sont comment?
Il/Elle est...
Ils/Elles sont...
Il/Elle n'est ni... ni...

Making a telephone call **Ch. 9, p. 244**

Bonjour.
Je suis bien chez... ?
C'est...
(Est-ce que)... est là, s'il vous plaît?

(Est-ce que) je peux parler à... ?
Je peux laisser un message?
Vous pouvez lui dire que j'ai téléphoné?
Ça ne répond pas.
C'est occupé.

Answering a telephone call **Ch. 9, p. 244**

Allô?
Qui est à l'appareil?
Une seconde, s'il vous plaît.
D'accord.
Bien sûr.
Vous pouvez rappeler plus tard?
Ne quittez pas.

Inquiring **Ch. 10, p. 265**

(Est-ce que) je peux vous aider?
Vous désirez?
Je peux l'(les) essayer?
Je peux essayer... ?
C'est combien, ... ?
Ça fait combien?
Vous avez ça en... ?

Pointing out places and things **Ch. 12, p. 317**

Là, tu vois, c'est...
Ça, c'est...
Regarde, voilà...
Là, c'est...
Voici...

Asking for advice **Ch. 12, p. 322**

Comment est-ce qu'on y va?

Making suggestions **Ch. 12, p. 322**

On peut y aller...
On peut prendre...

Asking for directions **Ch. 12, p. 327**

Pardon, ..., s'il vous plaît?
Pardon, ... Où est..., s'il vous plaît?
Pardon, ... Je cherche..., s'il vous plaît.

Giving directions **Ch. 12, p. 327**

Vous continuez jusqu'au prochain feu rouge.
Vous tournez...
Vous allez tout droit jusqu'à...
Prenez la rue... puis traversez la rue...
Vous passez...
C'est tout de suite à...

EXPRESSING FEELINGS AND EMOTIONS

Expressing likes, dislikes, and preferences **Ch. 1, pp. 26, 32**

J'aime (bien)...
Je n'aime pas...
Je préfère...
J'aime mieux...
J'adore...

Ch. 5, p. 138

C'est...
bon!
excellent!
délicieux!
pas mauvais!
pas bon!
pas terrible!
dégoûtant!
mauvais!

Telling what you'd like and what you'd like to do **Ch. 3, p. 77**

Je voudrais...
Je voudrais acheter...

Telling how much you like or dislike something **Ch. 4, p. 102**

Beaucoup.
Pas beaucoup.
Pas tellement.
Pas du tout.
surtout

Inquiring about likes and dislikes **Ch. 1, p. 26**

Tu aimes... ?

Ch. 5, p. 138

Comment tu trouves ça?

Sharing confidences **Ch. 9, p. 247**

J'ai un petit problème.
Je peux te parler?
Tu as une minute?

Consoling others **Ch. 9, p. 247**

Je t'écoute.
Ne t'en fais pas!
Ça va aller mieux!
Qu'est-ce que je peux faire?

Making a decision **Ch. 10, p. 274**

Vous avez décidé de prendre... ?
Vous avez choisi?
Vous le/la/les prenez?
Je le/la/les prends.
Non, c'est trop cher.

Hesitating **Ch. 10, p. 274**

Euh... J'hésite.
Je ne sais pas.
Il/Elle me plaît, mais il/elle est...

Expressing indecision **Ch. 11, p. 289**

J'hésite.
Je ne sais pas.
Je n'en sais rien.
Je n'ai rien de prévu.

Expressing wishes **Ch. 11, p. 289**

J'ai envie de...
Je voudrais bien...

EXPRESSING ATTITUDES AND OPINIONS

Agreeing Ch. 2, p. 50

Oui, beaucoup.
Moi aussi.
Moi non plus.

Disagreeing Ch. 2, p. 50

Moi, non.
Non, pas trop.
Moi, si.
Pas moi.

Asking for opinions Ch. 2, p. 57

Comment tu trouves... ?
Comment tu trouves ça?

Ch. 9, p. 237
Tu as passé un bon week-end?

Ch. 10, p. 270
Il/Elle me va?
Il/Elle te/vous plaît?
Tu aimes mieux... ou... ?

Ch. 11, p. 297
Tu as passé un bon... ?
Tu t'es bien amusé(e)?
Ça s'est bien passé?

Expressing opinions Ch. 2, p. 57

C'est...
facile.
génial.
super.
cool.
intéressant.
passionnant.
difficile.
pas terrible.
pas super.
zéro.
barbant.
nul.
pas mal.
Ça va.

Ch. 9, p. 237
Oui, très chouette.
Oui, excellent.
Oui, très bon.
Oui, ça a été.
Oh, pas mauvais.
C'était épouvantable.
Très mauvais.

Ch. 11, p. 297
C'était formidable!
Non, pas vraiment.
C'était ennuyeux.
C'était un véritable cauchemar!

Paying a compliment Ch. 10, p. 270

C'est tout à fait ton style.
Il/Elle te/vous va très bien.
Il/Elle va très bien avec...
Je le/la/les trouve...
C'est parfait.

Criticizing Ch. 10, p. 270

Il/Elle ne te/vous va pas du tout.
Il/Elle ne va pas du tout avec...
Il/Elle est (Ils/Elles sont) trop...
Je le/la/les trouve...

PERSUADING

Making suggestions Ch. 4, p. 110

On... ?
On fait... ?
On joue... ?

Ch. 5, p. 129
On va... ?

Accepting suggestions Ch. 4, p. 110

D'accord.
Bonne idée.
Oui, c'est...
Allons-y!

Turning down suggestions; making excuses
Ch. 4, p. 110

Non, c'est...
Ça ne me dit rien.
Désolé(e), mais je ne peux pas.

Ch. 5, p. 129
Désolé(e). J'ai des devoirs à faire.
J'ai des courses à faire.
J'ai des trucs à faire.
J'ai des tas de choses à faire.
Je ne peux pas parce que...

Making a recommendation Ch. 5, p. 132

Prends...
Prenez...

Asking for permission Ch. 7, p. 189

Tu es d'accord?
(Est-ce que) je peux... ?

Giving permission Ch. 7, p. 189

Oui, si tu veux.
Pourquoi pas?
D'accord, si tu... d'abord...
Oui, bien sûr.

Refusing permission Ch. 7, p. 189

Pas question!
Non, c'est impossible.
Non, tu dois...
Pas ce soir.

Making requests **Ch. 8, p. 212**

Tu peux(aller faire les courses)?
Tu me rapportes... ?

Ch. 12, p. 320
Est-ce que tu peux... ?
Tu pourrais passer à... ?

Accepting requests **Ch. 8, p. 212**

Pourquoi pas?
Bon, d'accord.
Je veux bien.
J'y vais tout de suite.

Ch. 12, p. 320
D'accord.
Si tu veux.

Declining requests **Ch. 8, p. 212**

Je ne peux pas maintenant.
Je regrette, mais je n'ai pas le temps.
J'ai des tas de choses (trucs) à faire.

Ch. 12, p. 320
Je suis désolé(e), mais je n'ai pas le temps.

Telling someone what to do **Ch. 8, p. 212**

Rapporte(-moi)...
Prends...
Achète(-moi)...
N'oublie pas de...

Offering food **Ch. 8, p. 219**

Tu veux... ?
Vous voulez... ?
Vous prenez... ?
Tu prends... ?
Encore... ?

Accepting food **Ch. 8, p. 219**

Oui, s'il vous/te plaît.
Oui, avec plaisir.
Oui, j'en veux bien.

Refusing food **Ch. 8, p. 219**

Non, merci.
Non, merci. Je n'ai plus faim.
Je n'en veux plus.

Asking for advice **Ch. 9, p. 247**

A ton avis, qu'est-ce que je fais?
Qu'est-ce que tu me conseilles?

Ch. 10, p. 264
Je ne sais pas quoi mettre pour...
Qu'est-ce que je mets?

Giving advice **Ch. 9, p. 247**

Oublie-le/-la/-les!
Téléphone-lui/-leur!
Tu devrais...
Pourquoi tu ne... pas?

Ch. 10, p. 264
Pourquoi est-ce que tu ne mets pas... ?
Mets...

Reminding **Ch. 11, p. 293**

N'oublie pas...
Tu n'as pas oublié... ?
Tu ne peux pas partir sans...
Tu prends... ?

Reassuring **Ch. 11, p. 293**

Ne t'en fais pas.
J'ai pensé à tout.
Je n'ai rien oublié.

ADDITIONAL VOCABULARY

This list presents additional vocabulary you may want to use when you're working on the activities in the textbook and workbook. It also includes the optional vocabulary labeled **Vocabulaire à la carte** that appears in several chapters. If you can't find the words you need here, try the French-English and English-French vocabulary lists beginning on page R56.

ADJECTIVES

absurd *absurde*
awesome (impressive) *impressionnant(e)*
boring *ennuyeux/ennuyeuse*
chilly *froid(e), frais* (m.)/*fraîche* (f.)
colorful (thing) *vif/vive*
despicable *ignoble*
eccentric *excentrique*
incredible *incroyable*
tasteful (remark, object) *de bon goût*
tasteless (flavor) *insipide;* (remark, object) *de mauvais goût*
terrifying *terrifiant(e)*
threatening *menaçant(e)*
tremendous (excellent) *formidable*
unforgettable *inoubliable*
unique *unique*

CLOTHING

blazer *un blazer*
button *un bouton*
coat *un manteau*
collar *un col*
eyeglasses *des lunettes* (f.)
gloves *des gants* (m.)
handkerchief *un mouchoir*
high-heeled shoes *des chaussures* (f.) *à talons*
lace *de la dentelle*
linen *du lin*
necklace *un collier*
nylon *du nylon*
pajamas *un pyjama*
polyester *du polyester*
raincoat *un imperméable*
rayon *de la rayonne*
ring *une bague*
sale (discount) *des soldes* (m.)
silk *de la soie*
sleeve *une manche*
slippers *des pantoufles* (f.)
suit (man's) *un costume;* (woman's) *un tailleur*
suspenders *des bretelles* (f.)
velvet *du velours*
vest *un gilet*
wool *de la laine*
zipper *une fermeture éclair®*

COLORS AND PATTERNS

beige *beige*
checked *à carreaux*
colorful *coloré(e), vif/vive*
dark blue *bleu foncé*
dark-colored *foncé(e)*
flowered *à fleurs*
gold (adj.) *d'or, doré(e)*
light blue *bleu clair*
light-colored *clair(e)*
patterned *à motifs*
polka-dotted *à pois*
striped *à rayures*
turquoise *turquoise*

COMPUTERS

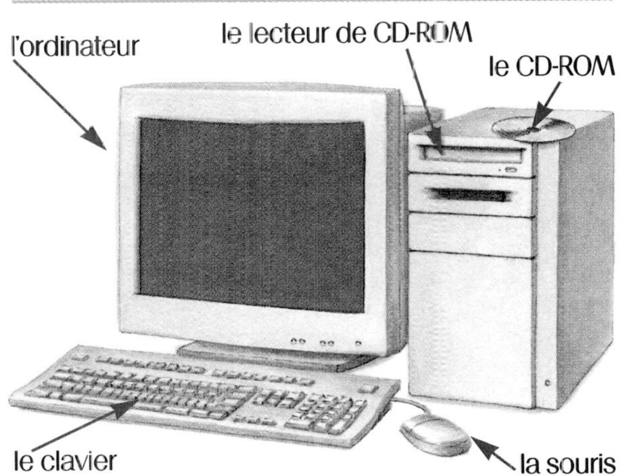

CD-ROM *le CD-ROM, le disque optique compact*
CD-ROM drive *le lecteur de CD-ROM, l'unité* (f.) *de CD-ROM*
to click *cliquer*
computer *l'ordinateur* (m.)
delete key *la touche d'effacement*
disk drive *le lecteur de disquette, l'unité de disquettes* (f.)
diskette, floppy disk *la disquette, la disquette souple*
to drag *glisser, déplacer*
e-mail *le courrier électronique, la messagerie électronique*

file *le dossier*
file (**folder**) *le fichier*
hard drive *le disque dur*
homepage *la page d'accueil*
Internet *Internet* (m.)
keyboard *le clavier*
keyword *le mot clé*
log on *l'ouverture* (f.) *de session*
modem *le modem*
monitor *le moniteur, le logimètre*
mouse *la souris*
password *le mot de passe*
to print *imprimer*
printer *l'imprimante* (f.)
to quit *quitter*
to record *enregistrer*
return key *la touche de retour*
to save *sauvegarder, enregistrer*
screen *l'écran* (m.)
to search *chercher, rechercher*
search engine *le moteur de recherche, l'outil* (m.) *de recherche*
to send *envoyer*
software *le logiciel*
Web site *le site du Web, le site W3*
World Wide Web *le World Wide Web, le Web, le W3*

ENTERTAINMENT

blues *le blues*
CD player *le lecteur de CD*
camera flash *le flash*
folk music *la musique folklorique*
headphones *les écouteurs*
hit (**song**) *le tube*
lens *l'objectif* (m.)
microphone *le micro(phone)*
opera *l'opéra* (m.)
pop music *la musique pop*
reggae *le reggae*
roll of film *la pellicule (photo)*
screen *l'écran* (m.)
speakers *les enceintes* (f.), *les baffles* (m.)
to turn off *éteindre*
to turn on *allumer*
turntable *la platine*
walkman *le balladeur*

FAMILY

adopted *adopté(e), adoptif/adoptive*
brother-in-law *le beau-frère*
child *un(e) enfant*
couple *un couple*
daughter-in-law *la belle-fille*
divorced *divorcé(e)*
engaged *fiancé(e)*
goddaughter *la filleule*
godfather *le parrain*

godmother *la marraine*
godson *le filleul*
grandchildren *les petits-enfants*
granddaughter *la petite-fille*
grandson *le petit-fils*
great-granddaughter *l'arrière-petite-fille* (f.)
great-grandfather *l'arrière-grand-père* (m.)
great-grandmother *l'arrière-grand-mère* (f.)
great-grandson *l'arrière-petit-fils* (m.)
half-brother *le demi-frère*
half-sister *la demi-sœur*
mother-in-law *la belle-mère*
only child *un/une enfant unique*
single *célibataire*
sister-in-law *la belle-sœur*
son-in-law *le gendre; le beau-fils*
stepbrother *le demi-frère*
stepdaughter *la belle-fille*
stepfather *le beau-père*
stepmother *la belle-mère*
stepsister *la demi-sœur*
stepson *le beau-fils*
widow *la veuve*
widower *le veuf*

FOODS AND BEVERAGES

appetizer *une entrée*
apricot *un abricot*
asparagus *des asperges* (f.)
bacon *du bacon*
bowl *un bol*
Brussels sprouts *des choux* (m.) *de Bruxelles*
cabbage *du chou*
cauliflower *du chou-fleur*
cereal *des céréales* (f.)
chestnut *un marron*
cookie *un biscuit*
cucumber *un concombre*
cutlet *une escalope*
fried egg *un œuf au plat;* **hard-boiled egg** *un œuf dur;* **scrambled eggs** *des œufs brouillés;* **soft-boiled egg** *un œuf à la coque*
eggplant *une aubergine*
French bread *une baguette*
garlic *de l'ail* (m.)
grapefruit *un pamplemousse*
honey *du miel*
liver *du foie*
margarine *de la margarine*
marshmallow *une guimauve*
mayonnaise *de la mayonnaise*
melon *un melon*
mustard *de la moutarde*
nuts *des noix* (f.)
peanut butter *du beurre de cacahouètes*
pepper (spice) *du poivre;* (vegetable) *un poivron*
popcorn *du pop-corn*
potato chips *des chips* (f.)
raspberry *une framboise*
salmon *du saumon*

salt *du sel*
shellfish *des fruits* (m.) *de mer*
soup *de la soupe*
spinach *des épinards* (m.)
spoon *une cuillère*
syrup *du sirop*
veal *du veau*
watermelon *une pastèque*
zucchini *une courgette*
bland *doux (douce)*
hot (spicy) *épicé(e)*
juicy (fruit) *juteux/juteuse;* (meat) *tendre*
rare (cooked) *saignant(e)*
medium (cooked) *à point*
spicy *épicé(e)*
well-done (cooked) *bien cuit(e)*
tasty *savoureux/savoureuse*

HOUSEWORK

to clean *nettoyer*
to dry *faire sécher*
to dust *faire la poussière*
to fold *plier*
to hang *pendre*
to iron *repasser*
to put away *ranger*
to rake *ratisser*
to shovel *enlever à la pelle*
to sweep *balayer*

PETS

bird *un oiseau*
cow *une vache*
frog *une grenouille*
goldfish *un poisson rouge*
guinea-pig *un cochon d'Inde*
hamster *un hamster*
horse *un cheval*
kitten *un chaton*
lizard *un lézard*
mouse *une souris*
parrot *un perroquet*
pig *un cochon*
puppy *un chiot*
rabbit *un lapin*
turtle *une tortue*

PLACES AROUND TOWN

airport *l'aéroport* (m.)
beauty shop *le salon de coiffure*
bridge *le pont*
church *l'église* (f.)
consulate *le consulat*
hospital *l'hôpital* (m.)
mosque *la mosquée*
police station *le commissariat de police*
synagogue *la synagogue*
tourist office *l'office du tourisme* (m.)
town hall *l'hôtel* (m.) *de ville*

PROFESSIONS

Note: If only one form is given, that form is used for both men and women. Note that you can also say **une femme banquier, une femme médecin,** and so forth.

archaeologist *un(e) archéologue*
architect *un(e) architecte*
athlete *un(e) athlète*
banker *un banquier*
businessman/businesswoman *un homme d'affaires (une femme d'affaires)*
dancer *un danseur (une danseuse)*
dentist *un(e) dentiste*
doctor *un médecin*
editor *un rédacteur (une rédactrice)*
engineer *un ingénieur*
fashion designer *un(e) styliste de mode*
fashion model *un mannequin*
hairdresser *un coiffeur (une coiffeuse)*
homemaker *un homme au foyer (une femme au foyer)*
lawyer *un(e) avocat(e)*
manager (company) *un directeur (une directrice);* (store, restaurant) *un gérant (une gérante)*
mechanic *un mécanicien (une mécanicienne)*
painter (art) *un peintre;* (buildings) *un peintre en bâtiment*
pilot *un pilote*
plumber *un plombier*
scientist *un(e) scientifique*
secretary *un(e) secrétaire*
social worker *un assistant social (une assistante sociale)*
taxi driver *un chauffeur de taxi*
technician *un technicien (une technicienne)*
truck driver *un routier*
veterinarian *un(e) vétérinaire*
worker *un ouvrier (une ouvrière)*
writer *un écrivain*

SCHOOL SUBJECTS

accounting *la comptabilité*
business *le commerce*
foreign languages *les langues* (f.) *étrangères*
home economics *les arts* (m.) *ménagers*
marching band *la fanfare*
orchestra *l'orchestre* (m.)
social studies *les sciences* (f.) *sociales*
typing *la dactylographie*
woodworking *la menuiserie*
world history *l'histoire* (f.) *mondiale*

SCHOOL SUPPLIES

calendar *un calendrier*
colored pencils *des crayons* (m.) *de couleur*
compass *un compas*
correction fluid *du liquide correcteur*
glue *de la colle*
gym suit *une tenue de gymnastique*
marker *un feutre*
rubber band *un élastique*
scissors *des ciseaux* (m.)
staple *une agrafe*
stapler *une agrafeuse*
transparent tape *du ruban adhésif*

SPORTS AND INTERESTS

badminton *le badminton*
boxing *la boxe*
fishing rod *la canne à pêche*
foot race *la course à pied*
to go for a ride (by bike, car, motorcycle, moped) *faire une promenade, faire un tour (à bicyclette, en voiture, à moto, à vélomoteur)*
to do gymnastics *faire de la gymnastique*
hunting *la chasse*
to lift weights *faire des haltères*
mountain climbing *l'alpinisme* (m.)
to play checkers *jouer aux dames*
to play chess *jouer aux échecs*
to ride a skateboard *faire de la planche à roulettes*
to sew *coudre; faire de la couture*
speed skating *le patinage de vitesse*
to surf *faire du surf*

WEATHER

barometer *le baromètre*
blizzard *la tempête de neige*
cloudy *nuageux*
drizzle *la bruine*
fog *le brouillard*
frost *la gelée*
hail *la grêle*
to hail *grêler*
heat wave *la canicule*
hurricane *l'ouragan* (m.)
ice (on the road) *le verglas*
It's pouring. *Il pleut à verse.*
It's sleeting. *Il tombe de la neige fondue.*
It's sunny. *Il fait du soleil.*
lightning bolt *l'éclair* (m.)
mist *la brume*
shower (rain) *l'averse* (f.)
storm *la tempête*
thermometer *le thermomètre*
thunder *le tonnerre*
thunderstorm *l'orage* (m.)
tornado *la tornade*

CITIES

Algiers *Alger*
Brussels *Bruxelles*
Cairo *Le Caire*
Geneva *Genève*
Lisbon *Lisbonne*
London *Londres*
Montreal *Montréal*
Moscow *Moscou*
New Orleans *La Nouvelle-Orléans*
Quebec City *Québec*
Tangier *Tanger*
Venice *Venise*
Vienna *Vienne*

THE CONTINENTS

Africa *l'Afrique* (f.)
Antarctica *l'Antarctique* (f.)
Asia *l'Asie* (f.)
Australia *l'Océanie* (f.)
Europe *l'Europe* (f.)
North America *l'Amérique* (f.) *du Nord*
South America *l'Amérique* (f.) *du Sud*

COUNTRIES

Algeria *l'Algérie* (f.)
Argentina *l'Argentine* (f.)
Australia *l'Australie* (f.)
Austria *l'Autriche* (f.)
Belgium *la Belgique*
Brazil *le Brésil*
Canada *le Canada*
China *la Chine*
Egypt *l'Egypte* (f.)
England *l'Angleterre* (f.)
France *la France*
Germany *l'Allemagne* (f.)
Greece *la Grèce*
Holland *la Hollande*
India *l'Inde* (f.)
Ireland *l'Irlande* (f.)
Israel *Israël* (m.)
Italy *l'Italie* (f.)
Ivory Coast *la République de Côte d'Ivoire*
Jamaica *la Jamaïque*
Japan *le Japon*
Jordan *la Jordanie*
Lebanon *le Liban*
Libya *la Libye*
Luxembourg *le Luxembourg*
Mexico *le Mexique*
Monaco *Monaco* (f.)
Morocco *le Maroc*
Netherlands *les Pays-Bas* (m.)
North Korea *la Corée du Nord*
Peru *le Pérou*

Philippines *les Philippines* (f.)
Poland *la Pologne*
Portugal *le Portugal*
Russia *la Russie*
Senegal *le Sénégal*
South Korea *la Corée du Sud*
Spain *l'Espagne* (f.)
Switzerland *la Suisse*
Syria *la Syrie*
Tunisia *la Tunisie*
Turkey *la Turquie*
United States *les Etats-Unis* (m.)
Vietnam *le Viêt-nam*

STATES

California *la Californie*
Florida *la Floride*
Georgia *la Géorgie*
Louisiana *la Louisiane*
New Mexico *le Nouveau Mexique*
North Carolina *la Caroline du Nord*
Pennsylvania *la Pennsylvanie*
South Carolina *la Caroline du Sud*
Virginia *la Virginie*

OCEANS AND SEAS

Atlantic Ocean *l'Atlantique* (m.), *l'océan* (m.) *Atlantique*
Caribbean Sea *la mer des Caraïbes*
English Channel *la Manche*
Indian Ocean *l'océan* (m.) *Indien*
Mediterranean Sea *la mer Méditerranée*
Pacific Ocean *le Pacifique, l'océan* (m.) *Pacifique*

OTHER GEOGRAPHICAL TERMS

Alps *les Alpes* (f.)
border *la frontière*
capital *la capitale*
continent *le continent*
country *le pays*
hill *la colline*
lake *le lac*
latitude *la latitude*
longitude *la longitude*
North Africa *l'Afrique* (f.) *du Nord*
ocean *l'océan* (m.)
plain *la plaine*
Pyrenees *les Pyrénées* (f.)
river *la rivière, le fleuve*
sea *la mer*
state *l'état* (m.)
the North Pole *le pôle Nord*
the South Pole *le pôle Sud*
valley *la vallée*

GRAMMAR SUMMARY

ADJECTIVES

REGULAR ADJECTIVES

In French, adjectives agree in gender and number with the nouns that they modify. A regular adjective has four forms: masculine singular, feminine singular, masculine plural, and feminine plural. To make an adjective agree with a feminine noun, add an **-e** to the masculine singular form of the adjective. To make an adjective agree with a plural noun, add an **-s** to the masculine singular form. To make an adjective agree with a feminine plural noun, add **-es** to the masculine singular form. Adjectives ending in **-é,** like **désolé,** also follow these rules.

	SINGULAR	PLURAL
MASCULINE	un jean **vert**	des jeans **verts**
FEMININE	une ceinture **verte**	des ceintures **vertes**

ADJECTIVES THAT END IN AN UNACCENTED -E

When an adjective ends in an unaccented **-e,** the masculine singular and the feminine singular forms are the same. To form the plural of these adjectives, add an **-s** to the singular forms.

	SINGULAR	PLURAL
MASCULINE	un cahier **rouge**	des cahiers **rouges**
FEMININE	une trousse **rouge**	des trousses **rouges**

ADJECTIVES THAT END IN -S

When the masculine singular form of an adjective ends in an **-s,** the masculine plural form does not change. The feminine forms follow the regular adjective rules.

	SINGULAR	PLURAL
MASCULINE	un sac **gris**	des sacs **gris**
FEMININE	une robe **grise**	des robes **grises**

ADJECTIVES THAT END IN -EUX

Adjectives that end in -**eux** do not change in the masculine plural. The feminine singular form of these adjectives is made by replacing the -**x** with -**se.** To form the feminine plural, replace the -**x** with -**ses.**

	SINGULAR	PLURAL
MASCULINE	un garçon **heureux**	des garçons **heureux**
FEMININE	une fille **heureuse**	des filles **heureuses**

ADJECTIVES THAT END IN -IF

To make the feminine singular form of adjectives that end in -**if**, replace -**if** with -**ive**. To make the plural forms of these adjectives, add an -**s** to the singular forms.

	SINGULAR	PLURAL
MASCULINE	un garçon **sportif**	des garçons **sportifs**
FEMININE	une fille **sportive**	des filles **sportives**

ADJECTIVES THAT END IN -IEN

To make the feminine singular and feminine plural forms of masculine singular adjectives that end in -**ien**, add -**ne** and -**nes.** Add an -**s** to form the masculine plural.

	SINGULAR	PLURAL
MASCULINE	un garçon **canadien**	des garçons **canadiens**
FEMININE	une fille **canadienne**	des filles **canadiennes**

ADJECTIVES THAT DOUBLE THE LAST CONSONANT

To make the adjectives **bon, gentil, gros, mignon, nul,** and **violet** agree with a feminine noun, double the last consonant and add an -**e.** To make the plural forms, add an -**s** to the singular forms. Note that with **gros,** the masculine singular and masculine plural forms are the same.

SINGULAR						
MASCULINE	bon	gentil	gros	mignon	nul	violet
FEMININE	bonne	gentille	grosse	mignonne	nulle	violette

PLURAL						
MASCULINE	bons	gentils	gros	mignons	nuls	violets
FEMININE	bonnes	gentilles	grosses	mignonnes	nulles	violettes

INVARIABLE ADJECTIVES

Some adjectives are invariable. They never change form. **Cool, marron, orange, super,** and **sympa** are examples of invariable adjectives. **Sympa,** the shortened form of **sympathique,** is invariable, whereas **sympathique** follows the rules for adjectives that end in an unaccented **-e,** like **rouge.**

Il me faut une montre **marron** et des baskets **orange.**

IRREGULAR ADJECTIVES

The forms of some adjectives must simply be memorized. This is the case for **blanc** and **roux.**

	SINGULAR	PLURAL
MASCULINE	**blanc**	**blancs**
FEMININE	**blanche**	**blanches**

	SINGULAR	PLURAL
MASCULINE	**roux**	**roux**
FEMININE	**rousse**	**rousses**

POSITION OF ADJECTIVES

In French, adjectives are usually placed after the noun that they modify.

C'est une femme **intelligente.**

Certain adjectives precede the noun. Some of these are **bon, jeune, joli, grand,** and **petit.**

C'est un **petit** village.

DEMONSTRATIVE ADJECTIVES

This, that, these, and *those* are demonstrative adjectives. There are two masculine singular forms of these adjectives in French: **ce** and **cet. Cet** is used with masculine singular nouns that begin with a vowel sound. Some examples are **cet ordinateur** and **cet homme.** Demonstrative adjectives always precede the noun that they modify.

	SINGULAR WITH A CONSONANT	SINGULAR WITH A VOWEL SOUND	PLURAL
MASCULINE	**ce** livre	**cet** ordinateur	**ces** posters
FEMININE	**cette** montre	**cette** école	**ces** gommes

GRAMMAR SUMMARY

POSSESSIVE ADJECTIVES

Possessive adjectives come before the noun that they modify and agree in gender and number with the item that they modify. Nouns that begin with a vowel sound use the masculine singular form, for example **mon ami(e), ton ami(e), son ami(e).**

	MASCULINE SINGULAR	FEMININE SINGULAR	MASC./FEM. SINGULAR WITH A VOWEL SOUND	MASC./FEM. PLURAL
my	**mon** père	**ma** mère	**mon** oncle	**mes** cousines
your	**ton** livre	**ta** montre	**ton** écharpe	**tes** cahiers
his, her, its	**son** chien	**sa** sœur	**son** école	**ses** cours

The possessive adjectives for *our, your,* and *their* have only two forms, singular and plural.

	MASC./FEM. SINGULAR	MASC./FEM. PLURAL
our	**notre** frère	**nos** tantes
your	**votre** classeur	**vos** amis
their	**leur** copain	**leurs** trousses

ADJECTIVES AS NOUNS

To use an adjective as a noun, add a definite article before the adjective. The article that you use agrees in gender and number with the noun that the adjective is replacing.

—Tu aimes les chemises rouges ou **les blanches?**
Do you like the red shirts or the white ones?
—J'aime **les blanches.**
I like the white ones.

ADVERBS

POSITION OF ADVERBS

Most adverbs follow the conjugated verb. In the **passé composé,** they usually precede the past participle.

Nathalie fait **souvent** des photos. Je n'ai pas **bien** mangé ce matin.

Adverbs that are made up of more than one word can be placed at the beginning or at the end of a sentence. When you use **ne (n')... jamais,** place it around the conjugated verb.

D'habitude, je fais du tennis le soir.
J'aime faire de l'aérobic **deux fois par semaine.**
Je **n'**ai **jamais** fait de ski.

ARTICLES

DEFINITE ARTICLES

French has four definite articles: **le, la, l'**, and **les.** The form that you use depends on the gender and number of the noun it modifies. Use **le** with masculine singular nouns, **le livre; la** with feminine singular nouns, **la chemise;** and **les** with both masculine and feminine nouns that are plural, **les crayons.** The form **l'** is used with both masculine and feminine nouns that begin with a vowel sound: **l'ami, l'amie, l'homme.** In French, you sometimes use a definite article when no article is required in English.

J'aime **le** chocolat et toi, tu préfères **le** café.

	SINGULAR WITH A CONSONANT	SINGULAR WITH A VOWEL SOUND	PLURAL
MASCULINE	**le** professeur	**l'**ami	**les** livres
FEMININE	**la** pharmacie	**l'**école	**les** pommes

INDEFINITE ARTICLES

In English, there are three indefinite articles: *a, an*, and *some.* In French there are also three: **un, une,** and **des.** The indefinite articles agree in number and gender with the nouns they modify.

	SINGULAR	PLURAL
MASCULINE	**un** poisson	**des** chats
FEMININE	**une** orange	**des** lunettes

PARTITIVE ARTICLES

To say that you want *part* or *some* of an item, use the partitive articles. Use **du** with a masculine noun and **de la** with a feminine noun. Use **de l'** with singular nouns that begin with a vowel sound whether they are masculine or feminine.

Je veux **de la** tarte aux pommes. *I want some apple pie.*

To indicate the whole as opposed to a part of the item, use the indefinite articles **un, une,** and **des.**

Pour la fête, il me faut **des** tartes. *I need (some) pies for the party.*

NEGATION AND THE ARTICLES

When the main verb of a sentence is negated, the indefinite and the partitive articles change to **de/d'.** Definite articles remain the same after a negative verb.

J'ai **le** livre de maths. —> Je n'ai pas **le** livre de maths.
J'ai **des** stylos. —> Je n'ai pas **de** stylos.
J'ai mangé **de la** pizza. —> Je n'ai pas mangé **de** pizza.

INTERROGATIVES

QUESTION FORMATION

There are several ways to ask yes-no questions. One of these is to raise the pitch of your voice at the end of a statement. The other is to place **est-ce que** in front of a statement.

Tu aimes le chocolat. —> **Tu aimes le chocolat?** (intonation) *or*
Est-ce que tu aimes le chocolat?

NEGATIVE QUESTIONS

The answer to a yes-no question depends on the way the question was stated. If the verb in a question is positive, then the answer is **oui** if you agree, and **non** if you don't. If the verb in a question is negative, then **non** is used to agree with the question and **si** to disagree.

QUESTION	AGREEING WITH THE QUESTION	DISAGREEING WITH THE QUESTION
Tu aimes lire?	**Oui,** j'aime lire.	**Non,** je n'aime pas lire.
Tu n'aimes pas lire?	**Non,** je n'aime pas lire.	**Si,** j'aime lire.

INFORMATION QUESTIONS

To ask for specific kinds of information, use the following question words:

A quelle heure? *At what time?* **Où?** *Where?*
Avec qui? *With whom?* **Quand?** *When?*

These words can be used by themselves, at the beginning of a question, at the beginning of the question followed by **est-ce que**, or at the end of a question.

Avec qui?
Avec qui on va au cinéma?
Avec qui est-ce qu'on va au cinéma?
On va au cinéma **avec qui?**

NOUNS

PLURAL FORMS OF NOUNS

In French, you make most nouns plural by adding an -**s** to the end of the word, unless they already end in -**s** or -**x**. Nouns that end in -**eau** are made plural by adding an -**x**, and nouns that end in -**al** are made plural by replacing the -**al** with -**aux**.

	REGULAR NOUNS	-s or -x	-eau	-al
SINGULAR	table	bus	manteau	hôpital
PLURAL	tables	bus	manteaux	hôpitaux

PREPOSITIONS

THE PREPOSITIONS A AND DE

The preposition **à** means *to, at,* or *in,* and **de** means *from* or *of.* When **à** and **de** are used in front of the definite articles **le** and **les**, they form contractions. If they precede any other definite article, there is no contraction.

Il va **à** l'école et **au** musée. *He's going to school and to the museum.*
Nous sommes loin **du** musée. *We are far from the museum.*

	MASCULINE ARTICLE	FEMININE ARTICLE	VOWEL SOUND	PLURAL
à	à + le = **au**	à + la = **à la**	à + l' = **à l'**	à + les = **aux**
de	de + le = **du**	de + la = **de la**	de + l' = **de l'**	de + les = **des**

De can also indicate possession or ownership.

C'est le livre **de** Laurent. *It's Laurent's book.*
C'est le stylo **du** prof. *It's the professor's pen.*

PREPOSITIONS AND PLACES

To say that you are at or going to a place, you need to use a preposition. With cities, use the preposition **à: à Paris.** One notable exception is **en Arles.** When speaking about masculine countries, use **au: au Maroc.** With plural names of countries, use **aux: aux Etats-Unis.** Most countries ending in **-e** are feminine; in these cases, use **en: en France. Le Mexique** is an exception. If a country begins with a vowel, like **Israël,** use **en: en Israël.**

CITIES	MASCULINE COUNTRIES	FEMININE COUNTRIES OR MASCULINE COUNTRIES THAT BEGIN WITH A VOWEL	PLURAL COUNTRIES
à Nantes **à** Paris **en** Arles	**au** Canada **au** Maroc **au** Mexique	**en** Italie **en** Espagne **en** Israël	**aux** Etats-Unis **aux** Philippines **aux** Pays-Bas

PRONOUNS

In French, as in English, a pronoun can refer to a person, place, or thing. Pronouns are used to avoid repetition. In French, pronouns agree in gender and number with the noun that they replace.

SUBJECT PRONOUNS

Subject pronouns replace the subject in a sentence.

je (j')	*I*	**nous**	*we*
tu	*you* (familiar)	**vous**	*you* (plural or formal)
il	*he / it*	**ils**	*they*
elle	*she / it*	**elles**	*they*
on	*we / one / they*		

THE IMPERSONAL PRONOUN IL

Many statements in French begin with the personal pronoun **il.** In these statements, **il** does not refer to any particular person or thing. For this reason, these statements are called impersonal statements.

Il fait beau. *It's nice out.*

Il est huit heures. *It's eight o'clock.*

Il me/te faut... *I/You need . . .*

Il y a... *There is/are . . .*

DIRECT OBJECT PRONOUNS: LE, LA, LES

A direct object is a noun that receives the action of the verb. It answers the questions *What?* or *Whom?* To say *him, her, it,* or *them,* use the pronouns **le, la,** and **les.** In French, you place the direct object pronoun in front of the conjugated verb.

Il regarde **la télé.** —> Il **la** regarde.

If there is an infinitive in the sentence, the direct object pronoun comes before the infinitive.

Je vais attendre **Pierre.** —> Je vais **l'**attendre.

In an affirmative command, the direct object pronoun follows the verb and is connected to it with a hyphen.

Regarde **la télévision.** —> Regarde-**la**!

	SINGULAR	PLURAL
MASCULINE	**le / l'**	**les**
FEMININE	**la / l'**	**les**

INDIRECT OBJECT PRONOUNS: LUI, LEUR

The indirect object answers the question *To whom?* and refers only to people. In French an indirect object follows the preposition **à: Il parle à Marie.** The indirect object pronoun replaces the prepositional phrase **à + a person,** and precedes the conjugated verb.

Nous téléphonons **à Mireille.** —> Nous **lui** téléphonons.

If there is an infinitive in the sentence, the indirect object pronoun comes before the infinitive.

Il n'aime pas parler **à ses parents.** —> Il n'aime pas **leur** parler.

In an affirmative command, the indirect object pronoun follows the verb and is connected to it with a hyphen.

Téléphone **à ta sœur.** —> Téléphone-**lui**!

THE PRONOUN Y

To replace a phrase meaning *to, on, at,* or *in* any place that has already been mentioned, you can use the pronoun **y**. It can replace phrases beginning with prepositions of location such as **à, sur, chez, dans,** and **en + a place or thing.** Place **y** before the conjugated verb.

Elle va **à la pharmacie.** —> Elle **y** va.

If there is an infinitive, place **y** before the infinitive.

Elle va aller **à la poste** demain. —> Elle va **y** aller demain.

THE PRONOUN EN

The pronoun **en** replaces a phrase beginning with **de, du, de la, de l',** or **des.** It usually means *about it, some (of it/of them),* or simply *it/them*, and is placed before the conjugated verb.

Tu achètes **des haricots verts?** —> Oui, j'**en** achète pour le dîner.

En in a negative sentence means *not any* or *none.*

Tu ne bois pas **de café.** —> Tu n'**en** bois pas.

En is placed before the conjugated verb.

Je parle **de mes vacances.** —> J'**en** parle.

If there is an infinitive, place **en** before the infinitive.

Vous aimez manger **des fruits.** —> Vous aimez **en** manger.

Notice that with the **passé composé, en** precedes the helping verb.

Il a mangé **du pain.** —> Il **en** a mangé.

VERBS

THE PRESENT TENSE OF REGULAR VERBS

To conjugate a verb in French, use the following formulas. Which formula you choose depends on the ending of the infinitive. There are three major verb categories: **-er**, **-ir**, and **-re**. Each one has a different conjugation. Within these categories, there are regular and irregular verbs. To conjugate regular verbs, you drop the infinitive endings and add these endings.

	aimer (*to love, to like*)		choisir (*to choose*)		vendre (*to sell*)	
SUBJECT	**STEM**	**ENDING**	**STEM**	**ENDING**	**STEM**	**ENDING**
je/j'	aim	**-e**	chois	**-is**	vend	**-s**
tu		**-es**		**-is**		**-s**
il/elle/on		**-e**		**-it**		—
nous		**-ons**		**-issons**		**-ons**
vous		**-ez**		**-issez**		**-ez**
ils/elles		**-ent**		**-issent**		**-ent**

VERBS WITH STEM AND SPELLING CHANGES

Verbs listed in this section are not irregular, but they do have some stem and spelling changes.

With **acheter** and **promener**, add an **accent grave** over the second-to-last **e** for all forms except **nous** and **vous.** Notice that the accent on the second **e** in **préférer** changes from **é** to **è** in all forms except the **nous** and **vous** forms.

	acheter (*to buy*)	**préférer** (*to prefer*)	**promener** (*to walk (an animal)*)
je/j'	**achète**	**préfère**	**promène**
tu	**achètes**	**préfères**	**promènes**
il/elle/on	**achète**	**préfère**	**promène**
nous	**achetons**	**préférons**	**promenons**
vous	**achetez**	**préférez**	**promenez**
ils/elles	**achètent**	**préfèrent**	**promènent**
PAST PARTICIPLE	**acheté**	**préféré**	**promené**

The following verbs have different stems for **nous** and **vous**.

	appeler *(to call)*	**essayer** *(to try)*
je/j' tu il/elle/on	**appelle** **appelles** **appelle**	**essaie** **essaies** **essaie**
nous vous ils/elles	**appelons** **appelez** **appellent**	**essayons** **essayez** **essaient**
PAST PARTICIPLE	**appelé**	**essayé**

The following verbs show a difference only in the **nous** form.

	commencer *(to start)*	**manger** *(to eat)*
je/j' tu il/elle/on	**commence** **commences** **commence**	**mange** **manges** **mange**
nous vous ils/elles	**commençons** **commencez** **commencent**	**mangeons** **mangez** **mangent**
PAST PARTICIPLE	**commencé**	**mangé**

	nager *(to swim)*	**voyager** *(to travel)*
je/j' tu il/elle/on	**nage** **nages** **nage**	**voyage** **voyages** **voyage**
nous vous ils/elles	**nageons** **nagez** **nagent**	**voyageons** **voyagez** **voyagent**
PAST PARTICIPLE	**nagé**	**voyagé**

VERBS LIKE DORMIR

These verbs follow a different pattern from the one you learned for regular **-ir** verbs. These verbs have two stems: one for the singular subjects, and one for the plural ones.

	dormir *(to sleep)*	**partir** *(to leave)*	**sortir** *(to go out, to take out)*
je/j'	dor**s**	par**s**	sor**s**
tu	dor**s**	par**s**	sor**s**
il/elle/on	dor**t**	par**t**	sor**t**
nous	dorm**ons**	part**ons**	sort**ons**
vous	dorm**ez**	part**ez**	sort**ez**
ils/elles	dorm**ent**	part**ent**	sort**ent**

VERBS WITH IRREGULAR FORMS

Verbs listed in this section do not follow the pattern of verbs like **aimer**, **choisir**, or **vendre.** Therefore, they are called *irregular verbs.* The following four irregular verbs are used frequently.

	aller *(to go)*	**avoir** *(to have)*
je/j'	**vais**	**ai**
tu	**vas**	**as**
il/elle/on	**va**	**a**
nous	**allons**	**avons**
vous	**allez**	**avez**
ils/elles	**vont**	**ont**

	être *(to be)*	**faire** *(to do, to make, to play)*
je/j'	**suis**	**fais**
tu	**es**	**fais**
il/elle/on	**est**	**fait**
nous	**sommes**	**faisons**
vous	**êtes**	**faites**
ils/elles	**sont**	**font**

Devoir, pouvoir, and **vouloir** are also irregular. They are usually followed by an infinitive.

Je peux chanter. *I can sing.*

	devoir *(must, to have to)*	**pouvoir** *(to be able to, can)*	**vouloir** *(to want)*
je/j' tu il/elle/on	**dois** **dois** **doit**	**peux** **peux** **peut**	**veux** **veux** **veut**
nous vous ils/elles	**devons** **devez** **doivent**	**pouvons** **pouvez** **peuvent**	**voulons** **voulez** **veulent**

These verbs also have irregular forms.

	dire *(to say)*	**écrire** *(to write)*	**lire** *(to read)*
je/j' tu il/elle/on	**dis** **dis** **dit**	**écris** **écris** **écrit**	**lis** **lis** **lit**
nous vous ils/elles	**disons** **dites** **disent**	**écrivons** **écrivez** **écrivent**	**lisons** **lisez** **lisent**
PAST PARTICIPLE	**dit**	**écrit**	**lu**

	mettre *(to put, to put on, to wear)*	**prendre** *(to take, to have food or drink)*	**voir** *(to see)*
je/j' tu il/elle/on	**mets** **mets** **met**	**prends** **prends** **prend**	**vois** **vois** **voit**
nous vous ils/elles	**mettons** **mettez** **mettent**	**prenons** **prenez** **prennent**	**voyons** **voyez** **voient**
PAST PARTICIPLE	**mis**	**pris**	**vu**

THE NEAR FUTURE (FUTUR PROCHE)

Like the past tense, the near future is made of two parts. The future tense of a verb consists of the present tense of **aller** plus the infinitive:

Vous **allez sortir** avec vos copains demain. *You're going to go out with your friends tomorrow.*

THE PAST TENSE (PASSE COMPOSE)

The past tense of most verbs is formed with two parts: the present tense form of the helping verb **avoir** and the past participle of the main verb. To form the past participle, use the formulas below. To make a sentence negative in the past, place the **ne... pas** around the helping verb **avoir**.

INFINITIVE	aimer *(to love, to like)*		choisir *(to choose)*		vendre *(to sell)*	
	STEM	ENDING	STEM	ENDING	STEM	ENDING
PAST PARTICIPLE	aim	-é	chois	-i	vend	-u
	aimé		choisi		vendu	
PASSE COMPOSE	**j'ai aimé**		**j'ai choisi**		**j'ai vendu**	

J'**ai mangé** de la pizza.
Elle n'**a** pas **vendu** sa voiture.
Nous **avons choisi** le livre.
Nous n'**avons** pas **mangé** de pizza.

Some verbs have irregular past participles.

faire —> fait
lire —> lu
prendre —> pris
voir —> vu

With some verbs, you use the helping verb **être** instead of **avoir**, for example the verb **aller.** The past participle of these verbs agrees in gender and number with the subject of the sentence.

Je **suis allé(e)** à l'école. Ils **sont allés** à la poste. Elle **est allée** au café.

THE IMPERATIVE (COMMANDS)

To make a request or a command of most verbs, use the **tu**, **nous**, or **vous** form of the present tense of the verb without the subject. Remember to drop the final **-s** in the **tu** form of an **-er** verb.

Mange!
Ecoute le professeur!
Faites vos devoirs!
Prenons un sandwich!

aimer *(to love, to like)*		choisir *(to choose)*		vendre *(to sell)*	
STEM	ENDING	STEM	ENDING	STEM	ENDING
aim	**-e** **-ons** **-ez**	chois	**-is** **-issons** **-issez**	vend	**-s** **-ons** **-ez**

GRAMMAR SUMMARY

ADDITIONAL GRAMMAR PRACTICE

CHAPITRE 1 - FAISONS CONNAISSANCE!

PREMIERE ETAPE

Greeting people and saying goodbye; asking how people are and telling how you are; asking someone's name and age and giving yours

1 Can you find the pattern in these phone numbers? Figure out which number completes each pattern. Then write out the number in French. (See pp. 9, 25.)

EXAMPLE 02. _____ . 20. 29. 38; _____
02. 11. 20. 29. 38; onze

1. 05. 12. _____ . 26. 33; _____
2. 03. 10. _____ . 24. 31; _____
3. 01. _____ . 25. 37. 49;_____
4. 05. _____ . 35. 50. 65; _____
5. 04. 10. _____ . 22. 28; _____
6. 02. _____ . 22. 32. 42; _____

DEUXIEME ETAPE

Expressing likes, dislikes, and preferences about things

2 Complete the following sentences, using the correct form of **aimer** and **ne (n')... pas** when appropriate. (See p. 26.)

EXAMPLE — Tu adores la plage, mais tu n'aimes pas la piscine.

1. Moi, j'aime bien la musique classique, mais je/j' _____ le rock.
2. Tu n'aimes pas le sport, mais tu _____ le vélo.
3. J'adore la glace, mais je/j' _____ le chocolat.
4. J'aime bien l'école, mais je/j' _____ les examens.
5. Tu aimes les concerts, mais tu _____ le cinéma.
6. Tu n'aimes pas les hamburgers, mais tu _____ les frites.
7. J'aime la télé, mais je/j' _____ le cinéma.
8. Tu n'aimes pas l'anglais, mais tu _____ le français.

3 Complete Gabrielle's journal entry with the appropriate definite articles **le, la, l'**, or **les.** (See p. 28.)

J'aime __1__ école. J'aime bien __2__ anglais et __3__ français, mais je n'aime pas __4__ examens. J'adore __5__ sport et __6__ plage. J'aime __7__ football et __8__ vélo aussi.

4 Use the following fragments to create four questions and four answers. Remember to add the appropriate definite articles: **le**, **la**, **l'**, or **les**. (See p. 28.)

EXAMPLE salade/Eric/tu/aimes? Eric, tu aimes la salade?
aime/j'/hamburgers/aussi (*also*) Oui, et j'aime aussi les hamburgers.

1. tu/aimes/frites/Marianne?

   aime/j'/pizza/aussi
   —Oui, et...
2. tu/ne/pas/maths/aimes/Isabelle?

   français/aussi/aime/j'
   —Si (*yes*), et...
3. aimes/escargots/Nathalie/tu?

   j'/aussi/aime/chocolat
   —Oui, et...
4. tu/aimes/ne/pas/magasins?

   plage/j'/aussi/aime
   —Si, et...

TROISIEME ETAPE

Expressing likes, dislikes, and preferences about activities

5 Séverine is looking for a pen pal. Complete her ad with the appropriate forms of the verbs in parentheses. (See p. 33.)

J'ai 16 ans. Je/J' __1__ (adorer) faire du sport. Je/J' __2__ (aimer) aussi sortir avec les copains. Nous __3__ (aimer) bien aller au cinéma, mais nous __4__ (préférer) aller danser. Parfois, nous __5__ (écouter) de la musique. Nous __6__ (adorer) le rap, surtout MC Solaar; il __7__ (danser) très bien. Nous __8__ (aimer) aussi les fast-food. Si vous __9__ (aimer) le sport, écrivez-moi! A bientôt!

6 Etienne and Solange don't have much in common. Complete their conversation with the appropriate forms of the verbs in parentheses. (See p. 33.)

ETIENNE Dis, Solange, tu __1__ (aimer) faire du vélo?
SOLANGE Non, je n' __2__ (aimer) pas le sport, mais j' __3__ (adorer) danser.
ETIENNE Moi, je ne __4__ (danser) pas, mais j' __5__ (écouter) souvent la radio.
SOLANGE Ah oui? Tu __6__ (écouter) quel type de musique?
ETIENNE Moi, j' __7__ (adorer) le rap. Mes copains __8__ (aimer) aller à des concerts de rap, mais moi, j' __9__ (aimer) mieux regarder des vidéoclips à la télé. Et toi, tu __10__ (regarder) la télé?
SOLANGE Moi, non. J' __11__ (aimer) mieux aller au cinéma.

7 There are many things these students like to do, but what do they prefer to do? Complete these conversations with the appropriate subject pronouns. (See p. 33.)

EXAMPLE —Pierre aime les frites. —Oui, mais il aime mieux les escargots.

1. —Lucie et Marie aiment regarder la télé.
   —Oui, mais _____ préfèrent aller au cinéma.
2. —Hugo et toi, vous aimez parler au téléphone?
   —Oui, mais _____ préférons sortir avec les copains.
3. —Olivier et Lise aiment faire les magasins.
   —Oui, mais _____ aiment mieux faire du sport.
4. —Aurélie aime lire.
   —Oui, mais _____ aime mieux dormir.
5. —Christelle et moi, nous aimons le volley.
   —Oui, mais _____ préférez le basket-ball, non?

8 Given their likes and dislikes, what do the following students probably do on week-ends? Complete each sentence, using a personal pronoun and the correct form of the appropriate verb. (See p. 33.)

EXAMPLE Hervé et moi, nous aimons danser.
Le week-end, nous dansons.

1. Mary aime bien parler français avec sa copine.
   Le week-end, ...
2. Jules et Loïc aiment regarder des matchs de football.
   Le week-end, ...
3. Moi, j'adore écouter de la musique.
   Le week-end, ...
4. Sylvie et Marianne aiment bien nager.
   Le week-end, ...
5. Stéphane et toi, vous aimez parler au téléphone.
   Le week-end, ...
6. Toi, tu adores danser.
   Le week-end, ...

CHAPITRE 2 - VIVE L'ECOLE!

PREMIERE ETAPE

Agreeing and disagreeing

1 Would you answer **si** or **oui** to each of the following questions? (See p. 50.)

1. Hervé n'aime pas faire le ménage?
2. Vous aimez le cours de physique?
3. Tu aimes écouter de la musique?
4. Annick et Ahmed n'aiment pas le prof de français?
5. Jean-Paul aime la chorale?
6. Olivia n'aime pas faire du sport?

2 Complete the following conversations, using **si, oui,** or **non,** as appropriate. (See p. 50.)

1. —Tu aimes les sciences naturelles?
   — _____, j'adore!
2. —Marc n'aime pas parler au téléphone?
   — _____, il aime bien parler avec ses copains.
3. —Ils aiment la physique?
   — _____, ils n'aiment pas les cours de science.
4. —Tu n'aimes pas le ski?
   — _____, j'aime bien le sport en général.
5. —Tu aimes faire de l'équitation?
   — _____, mais je préfère lire et regarder la télévision.
6. —Nicole aime les concerts?
   — _____, elle adore la musique.

DEUXIEME ETAPE

Asking for and giving information

3 Complete the conversation below with the correct forms of the verb **avoir.** (See p. 51.)

—Céline, tu ___1___ quels cours aujourd'hui?
—Le matin, j' ___2___ sciences nat et français. L'après-midi, j' ___3___ histoire et géométrie.
—Et Vincent, il ___4___ quels cours?
—Il ___5___ chimie et espagnol le matin, et l'après-midi, il ___6___ informatique.
—Le mardi et le jeudi matin, nous ___7___ travaux pratiques de chimie.

4 Matthieu and some of his friends are discussing their school schedules. Complete each of the following sentences with the correct form of the verb **avoir.** Then, write out the time given in parentheses. (See pp. 51, 54.)

EXAMPLE Sylvie _____ latin à (9h30). Sylvie a latin à neuf heures trente.

1. J' _____ sciences nat à (8h45).
2. Anne et moi, nous _____ EPS à (13h50).
3. Matthieu et Jeanne, vous _____ latin à (11h20), non?
4. Séverine, tu _____ quoi à (15h30)?
5. Chad et Mireille _____ maths à (16h15).

TROISIEME ETAPE

Asking for and expressing opinions

5 Rewrite these informal remarks and questions in formal French. (See pp. 26, 57.)

1. «C'est pas super, l'algèbre.»
2. «Elle aime pas la chimie?»
3. «Ils aiment pas les devoirs.»
4. «Mais non! L'anglais, c'est pas difficile!»
5. «Tu aimes pas la géographie?»

6 David and Olivia are discussing their schedules and their classes. Complete their conversation with either the correct form of the verb in parentheses or the word or phrase that expresses their opinion. (See pp. 33, 51, 57.)

—Olivia, tu ___1___ (avoir) quels cours le lundi matin?

—J' ___2___ (avoir) histoire, maths et français. Et toi, tu ___3___ (avoir) quels cours?

—Florent et moi, nous ___4___ (avoir) chimie, allemand et anglais.

—Vous ___5___ (aimer) la chimie?

—Florent n' ___6___ (aimer) pas ça. Mais moi, j' ___7___ (adorer) la chimie. C'est ___8___ (passionnant/pas super)!

—Ah bon! Florent ___9___ (avoir) biologie le mardi. Il ___10___ (adorer) ça. Et toi, tu ___11___ (aimer) ça, la biologie?

—Moi, non. C'est ___12___ (pas mal/nul).

CHAPITRE 3 - TOUT POUR LA RENTREE

PREMIERE ETAPE

Making and responding to requests; asking others what they need and telling what you need

1 Fill in the missing letters in the following words to find out what Amadou has on his desk. Then write the correct indefinite article for each word. (See p. 73.)

EXAMPLE C __ __ I __ R -> un cahier

1. L __ __ R __ S
2. T __ O __ __ S __
3. S T __ __ O __
4. C __ A __ __ N
5. C __ __ C __ L __ T __ __ C __
6. F __ __ I L __ __ S

2 Rewrite the following conversations, adding **un, une, des,** or **de (d')**. Remember to use the correct form of **avoir**. (See p. 73.)

EXAMPLE Anne/montre/avoir/tu?—Anne, tu as une montre?
Non/pas/montre/ne/avoir/je—Non, je n'ai pas de montre.

1. —Séverine/tu/sac à dos/avoir?
   —Non/ne/avoir/je/pas/sac à dos
2. —Raphaël et Philippe/feuilles de papier/avoir/vous?
   —Non/pas/nous/avoir/ne/feuilles de papier
3. —tu/avoir/Karine/taille-crayon?
   —je/ne/non/pas/avoir/taille-crayon
4. —Valérie et Mireille/vous/calculatrices/avoir?
   —nous/avoir/ne/pas/calculatrices/non

DEUXIEME ETAPE

Telling what you'd like and what you'd like to do

3 You overheard these conversations at a store having a back-to-school sale. Complete the following conversations using **ce, cet, cette,** or **ces.** (See p. 77.)

1. —Tu aimes ____ montre?
   —Oui, mais je préfère ____ bracelet.
2. —Vous aimez ____ jean?
   —Oui, mais il me faut ____ tee-shirt pour l'EPS.
3. —Je voudrais acheter ____ ordinateur.
   —Moi aussi, mais il te faut ____ calculatrice pour la géométrie.
4. —Comment tu trouves ____ baskets?
   —Super! J'aime ____ short aussi.
5. —Je voudrais acheter ____ cassette.
   —Moi, je préfère acheter ____ disque compact.
6. —Il me faut ____ feuilles de papier.
   —Moi aussi. Il me faut ____ règle aussi.

4 Match a verb from column A with a noun from column B, using each word only once. Then, write six logical sentences telling what you would like to do, using **je voudrais,** and **ce, cet, cette**, or **ces.** (See p. 77.)

EXAMPLE étudier roman Je voudrais étudier ce roman.

A	B
1. sortir avec	**a.** magazines
2. regarder	**b.** amis
3. lire	**c.** cours (m. pl.)
4. avoir	**d.** calculatrice
5. acheter	**e.** disque compact
6. écouter	**f.** vidéocassette

5 Unscramble the colors. Then, use them to describe the items you would like to have. Remember to add the appropriate endings to the colors. (See pp. 73, 79.)

EXAMPLE LEBU/des tee-shirts Je voudrais des tee-shirts bleus.

1. RARONM/des trousses
2. NLCAB/des calculatrices
3. ORUEG/des stylos
4. ETVR/une règle
5. RNIO/un sac
6. RIGS/des cahiers
7. OLEVIT/une gomme

6 You're telling the store clerk what school supplies you need to buy. Rewrite each sentence to include the given adjective and place it correctly. (See p. 79.)

1. Il me faut une calculatrice. (gris)
2. Il me faut des baskets. (noir)
3. Il me faut des feuilles de papier. (blanc)
4. Il me faut deux règles. (jaune)
5. Il me faut une trousse. (marron)

TROISIEME ETAPE

Getting someone's attention; asking for information; expressing thanks

7 Ask how much the following items cost, using **ce, cet, cette,** or **ces,** and the appropriate form of the adjectives. (See pp. 77, 79, 82.)

EXAMPLE trousse/bleu C'est combien, cette trousse bleue?

1. crayons/noir
2. montre/violet
3. télévision/gris
4. classeurs/orange
5. bracelet/rose

8 Complete this conversation with the appropriate form of the words in parentheses. (See pp. 73, 77, 79.)

JULIE Excusez-moi, madame, c'est combien, __1__ (ce/cet/cette) ordinateur __2__ (marron)?
VENDEUSE Neuf cents francs!
JULIE C'est pas cher! Et __3__ (ce/cet/cette) montre __4__ (gris)?
VENDEUSE Quatre-vingts francs, mademoiselle. Elle vous plaît?
JULIE Oui, beaucoup. J'aime aussi __5__ (ce/cet/cette) télévision __6__ (blanc). Et vous avez __7__ (des/de/d') calculatrices __8__ (violet)?
VENDEUSE Non. Je regrette, mademoiselle. Je n'ai pas __9__ (des/de/d') calculatrices.

CHAPITRE 4 - SPORTS ET PASSE-TEMPS

PREMIERE ETAPE

Telling how much you like or dislike something

1 Complete the following conversations with **faire** or **jouer** as appropriate. (See p. 101.)

1. —Corinne, est-ce-que tu aimes _____ au golf?
   —Non. Je préfère _____ du ski.
2. —Frédéric et Arthur, est-ce que vous aimez _____ de la vidéo?
   —Pas tellement. Nous aimons mieux _____ du théâtre.
3. —Et Malika, est-ce qu'elle aime _____ aux cartes?
   —Pas du tout. Mais elle aime _____ de la natation.
4. —Georges, est-ce que tu aimes _____ du jogging?
   —Oui. Mais je préfère _____ au hockey.

2 What do you and your friends do in your spare time? Write six sentences telling what you do, using the verbs **faire** and **jouer** and an expression from the box in each sentence. Use each expression only once. (See p. 101.)

jeux vidéo	vélo	ski nautique
tennis	natation	ski

EXAMPLE Ariane aime la piscine (*swimming pool*).
Elle aime faire de la natation.

1. Claude aime tellement la plage.
2. Suzanne aime les bicyclettes (*bicycles*).
3. Olivier et Victor aiment les ordinateurs.
4. Moi, j'aime la neige (*snow*).
5. Tu aimes le sport.

3 You have made a list of the activities your classmates like to do. Double-check your list by transforming your notes into questions, using **est-ce que**, and **tu** or **vous** as appropriate. (See p. 103.)

EXAMPLE Paul et Aurélie aiment faire du ski.
Est-ce que vous aimez faire du ski?

1. Anne-Marie et Louise aiment jouer au foot.
2. Marc aime jouer à des jeux vidéo.
3. Elodie aime faire de la photo.
4. Jacques et Jules aiment jouer au tennis.
5. Alexandrine aime faire du ski nautique.
6. Véronique et Céline aiment faire de l'athlétisme.
7. Miriam aime faire du vélo.
8. Jean et Françoise aiment jouer aux cartes.

DEUXIEME ETAPE

Exchanging information

4 You're having a friend over who doesn't like to do anything. Answer the following questions as your friend would, based on the example. (See p. 104.)

EXAMPLE Tu joues au volley? Non, je ne joue pas au volley.
Tu fais du ski? Non, je ne fais pas de ski.

1. Tu fais de la natation?
2. Tu joues à des jeux vidéo?
3. Tu fais de l'athlétisme?
4. Tu fais du jogging?
5. Tu joues aux cartes?
6. Tu fais des photos?
7. Tu fais du patin à glace?
8. Tu fais du roller en ligne?

5 Pauline and Louise are making plans for the evening. Complete their conversation with the correct forms of **faire**. (See p. 104.)

LOUISE Dis, Pauline, on __1__ de la natation ce soir?
PAULINE Non. Quand il fait froid, moi, je ne __2__ pas de natation! J'aime mieux __3__ du patin à glace! Tu __4__ du patin à glace, toi?
LOUISE Non, ça ne me dit rien. En hiver, quand il neige, mes copines et moi, nous __5__ du ski. C'est génial, le ski!
PAULINE En été, Gilles et Félix __6__ du ski nautique. J'adore le ski nautique! Mais ce soir, moi, je __7__ du patin à glace. C'est décidé!
LOUISE D'accord. Allons-y!

6 Odile is asking her friends if they play certain sports. Based on their answers, what are her questions? Remember to use the correct forms of **faire**. (See p. 104.)

EXAMPLE	ODILE	Vous faites du vélo?
	JEREMY ET VALENTINE	Oui, on adore faire du vélo.

1.	ODILE	_____
	SYLVIE	Oui, j'aime beaucoup faire du jogging.
2.	ODILE	_____
	PIERRE	Oui, Sophie et Marie adorent faire de l'aérobic.
3.	ODILE	_____
	DAVID	Oui, Arthur aime faire de la natation.
4.	ODILE	_____
	MARION ET FRANCINE	Oui, nous aimons bien faire du ski.
5.	ODILE	_____
	VANESSA	Oui, Elodie et Jerôme aiment beaucoup faire du roller en ligne.
6.	ODILE	_____
	CHRISTINE	Oui, Thérèse aime faire de la randonnée.

7 Rewrite the following sentences, replacing the subject with the pronoun **on.** Be sure to make any necessary changes. (See p. 105.)

1. Nous allons à la pharmacie aujourd'hui.
2. Marcel et moi aimons faire de la natation après l'école.
3. Est-ce que vous faites du ski nautique au Texas?
4. Vous jouez aux cartes?
5. Nous faisons de l'aérobic.
6. Est-ce que nous allons faire du roller en ligne ce week-end?
7. Est-ce que vous faites du théâtre dans votre école?

8 Complete the following sentences with the activity most appropriate for the weather condition or time of year stated. (See p. 107.)

jouer au football américain — regarder la télé — jouer au tennis — jouer au hockey — nager — jouer à des jeux vidéo

1. En automne, mon frère _____.
2. Quand il fait chaud, les enfants _____.
3. Quand il neige, Jacqueline _____.
4. Quand il pleut, je _____.
5. Quand il fait frais, mon frère et moi _____.

TROISIEME ETAPE

Making, accepting, and turning down suggestions

9 François is asking Janine how often she plays certain sports. Rewrite their conversation, using the fragments below. Remember to use the correct form of the verbs and to put the adverb in the correct position. (See p. 110.)

FRANÇOIS	tu/est-ce que/souvent/faire/de la natation
JANINE	faire/de la natation/je/souvent/au printemps/oui
FRANÇOIS	faire/du ski/de temps en temps/tu/est-ce que
JANINE	faire/du ski/oui/je/quand il neige
FRANÇOIS	quelquefois/tu/est-ce que/jouer/au foot
JANINE	ne...jamais/jouer/non/au foot/je

10 Vanessa has taken a survey to find out how often teenagers play certain sports. Rewrite her notes, using the adverbs from the box. The meaning of the sentences should remain the same. Use each adverb only once. (See p. 110.)

ne ... jamais d'habitude quelquefois
souvent une fois par semaine

EXAMPLE Camille fait du vélo trois fois par semaine.
Camille fait souvent du vélo.

1. Koffi joue au tennis de temps en temps.
2. Estelle et Olivia font du patin à glace le samedi matin.
3. Quand il pleut, Fatima ne fait pas de jogging.
4. Sébastien joue au golf tous les jours au printemps.

CHAPITRE 5 - ON VA AU CAFE?

PREMIERE ETAPE

Making suggestions; making excuses; making a recommendation

1 Choose the appropriate completion for each sentence. (See p. 133.)

1. Guillaume et Ludovic...	a. prend un jus de pomme; elle a soif.
2. Paul...	b. prenons des hot-dogs.
3. Anne et Lucie...	c. prenez un chocolat.
4. Marie-Lise et toi...	d. prennent du jus d'orange; elles ont très soif.
5. André et moi...	e. prends un croque-monsieur.
6. Alice...	f. prennent un sandwich.
7. Moi, je...	g. prend un steak-frites; il a faim.

2 You and your friends are deciding what to order in a café. Complete the sentences that follow with the correct forms of **prendre**. (See p. 133.)

1. Tu _____ un jus de pomme?
2. Eric _____ un hot-dog.
3. Vous _____ un café?
4. Moi, je _____ une limonade.
5. Elles _____ des sandwichs.
6. Nous _____ des cocas.
7. Jean et Alphonse _____ un steak-frites.
8. Le professeur _____ un croque-monsieur.

DEUXIEME ETAPE

Getting someone's attention; ordering food and beverages

3 You and your friends are browsing through a basket full of items on sale. Tell your friends what to get **(prendre)** based on what they tell you about their favorite colors. (See p. 136.)

un jean noir — des baskets bleues — un short blanc — un bracelet rose — des sweat-shirts orange — un tee-shirt rouge — des pull-overs verts

EXAMPLE Céline : J'aime le rouge. Prends le tee-shirt rouge!

1. Valentine et Sophie : On adore l'orange.
2. Jérôme : Moi, j'aime bien le noir.
3. Clément : Moi, j'aime le blanc.
4. Anne et Lydie : On aime bien le bleu.
5. Aurélie : Moi, j'aime le rose.
6. Marcel et Pascal : On adore le vert.

4 A physical education teacher is encouraging her students to exercise. Based on their answers, write what she told them to do. (See p. 136.)

EXAMPLE —Faites du sport!
—Mais on n'aime pas faire du sport!

1. —Mais je n'aime pas faire de la natation!
2. —Mais on n'aime pas faire du jogging!
3. —Mais on n'aime pas jouer au basket!
4. —Mais je n'aime pas jouer au tennis!
5. —Mais nous n'aimons pas jouer au football!
6. —Mais je n'aime pas faire du roller en ligne!

5 Rewrite the following requests, using the imperative of the verbs in parentheses followed by **-moi**. (See p. 136.)

EXAMPLE —Monsieur, je voudrais un café, s'il vous plaît! (apporter)
—Apportez-moi un café, s'il vous plaît!

1. —Maman, je voudrais une limonade, s'il te plaît! (apporter)
   —_____, s'il te plaît!
2. —Jérémy, je voudrais un sandwich au fromage, s'il te plaît! (donner)
   —_____, s'il te plaît!
3. —Monsieur, je voudrais une eau minérale, s'il vous plaît! (donner)
   —_____, s'il vous plaît!
4. —Mademoiselle, je voudrais un coca, s'il vous plaît! (apporter)
   —_____, s'il vous plaît!
5. —Bérénice, je voudrais un chocolat, s'il te plaît! (apporter)
   —_____, s'il te plaît!
6. —Papa, je voudrais de l'argent, s'il te plaît! (donner)
   —_____, s'il te plaît!

TROISIEME ETAPE

Inquiring about and expressing likes and dislikes; paying the check

6 Maud would like to know how much the following items cost. Write the waiter's answers to her questions. The prices are given in parentheses. Write out the amounts in French. (See p. 139.)

EXAMPLE C'est combien, la pizza suprême? (65F) Soixante-cinq francs.

1. C'est combien, le steak-frites? (45F)
2. C'est combien, l'omelette au jambon? (36F)
3. C'est combien, la salade niçoise? (28F)
4. C'est combien, trois sandwiches au rosbif? (75F)
5. C'est combien, le couscous? (53F)
6. C'est combien, le croque-monsieur et le café? (61F)

7 Write out in French the number that would come next in each of the series below. (See p. 139.)

1. vingt-deux, quarante-quatre, soixante-six...
2. seize, trente-deux, quarante-huit...
3. onze, trente et un, cinquante et un...
4. quatre-vingt-quinze, quatre-vingt-dix, quatre-vingt-cinq...
5. soixante-dix, quatre-vingts, quatre-vingt-dix...
6. vingt-cinq, trente-cinq, quarante-cinq...

CHAPITRE 6 - AMUSONS-NOUS!

PREMIERE ETAPE

Making plans

1 Malika is leaving a message on Axel's answering machine. Complete her message with **le** when appropriate. Be careful! In some cases, you won't need to add anything. (See p. 153.)

Salut, Axel! C'est moi, Malika! Ça va? Ecoute! On va au Café Américain __1__ lundi soir. Tu viens? On va souvent à la crêperie __2__ lundi, mais cette semaine, on va aller au café. Bonne idée, non? __3__ mercredi après-midi, on va aller voir une pièce. On va quelquefois au théâtre __4__ mercredi. C'est super, le théâtre! Est-ce que tu peux venir? Ah, oui, __5__ samedi, on va à la boum de Nadine. Qu'est-ce que tu fais d'habitude __6__ samedi soir? Tu veux venir avec nous? Eh bien, à bientôt peut-être. Tchao!

2 Fernand and Michèle are discussing what to do this coming Saturday. Complete their conversation with the correct forms of **aller**. (See p. 154.)

FERNAND Dis, Michèle, tu __1__ faire quoi demain?
MICHELE Bof. Rien de spécial. D'habitude, le samedi, je fais les vitrines.
FERNAND Eric et moi, on __2__ faire un pique-nique. Tu viens avec nous?
MICHELE Désolée, mais ça ne me dit rien, les pique-niques.
FERNAND Mais écoute, Michèle! Les pique-niques, c'est génial! Tous les copains __3__ venir! On __4__ jouer au foot! Julien et Juliette __5__ apporter des hot-dogs! Nous __6__ nous amuser!
MICHELE D'accord. Pourquoi pas? On se retrouve où?
FERNAND Devant la MJC. Vers trois heures.
MICHELE Entendu. Je __7__ passer chez toi vers deux heures et demie.

3 Combine these fragments into sentences. Remember to use the correct form of **aller**. (See p. 154.)

EXAMPLE Marc et Li/faire les vitrines Marc et Li vont faire les vitrines.

1. Toi, tu/aller au café
2. Moi, je/aller au théâtre
3. Marc/voir un film
4. Simone et moi, nous/voir un match
5. Pascal et Maurice, vous/faire une promenade

4 Imagine that you and your friends are going on a trip to Paris this summer. Complete your plans using **à, à la, au,** and **aux.** (See p. 157.)

1. Christine va aller ___ Cathédrale (f.) Notre-Dame.
2. Nous allons aller ___ Louvre et _____ cafés.
3. Marc va aller ___ concerts de rock.
4. Moi, je vais ___ Maison des jeunes.
5. Les garçons ne vont pas aller ___ centre commercial.

DEUXIEME ETAPE

Extending and responding to invitations

5 Complete the sentences that follow with the correct form of the verb **vouloir**. (See p. 160.)

1. Mes copines _____ aller au restaurant.
2. Mais moi, je _____ aller au café.
3. Et vous, vous _____ manger quelque chose?
4. Non. Nous _____ voir un film.
5. Et toi, Eric, tu _____ faire quoi?
6. Patricia et moi, on _____ faire les vitrines.

6 Based on their preferences, write what the following students want to do. Be sure to use the appropriate subject pronoun, the correct form of **vouloir**, and an expression from the box. Use each expression only once. (See p. 160.)

voir un film — regarder un match de foot à la télé — voir une pièce — manger quelque chose — aller à une boum — aller à la bibliothèque — aller à la piscine

EXAMPLE Marianne a faim. Elle veut manger quelque chose.

1. Suzanne et Monique adorent nager.
2. J'aime lire.
3. Vous adorez le théâtre.
4. Gilles aime bien le cinéma.
5. Anne et moi, nous aimons danser.
6. Tu aimes le football.

TROISIEME ETAPE

Arranging to meet someone

7 Complete this conversation with the correct answer to each question. (See p. 165.)

Avec Lise. — A sept heures et demie. — Chez moi. — Ce soir.

DIANE Tu viens manger avec nous, Isabelle?
ISABELLE Oui. Je veux bien. Quand ça?
DIANE __1__
ISABELLE Où est-ce qu'on se retrouve?
DIANE __2__
ISABELLE Avec qui on va manger?
DIANE __3__
ISABELLE On se retrouve à quelle heure?
DIANE __4__

8 Match the response from column A with the question asked from column B. (See p. 165.)

A	B
1. Mireille et Matthieu.	a. Où est-ce qu'on se retrouve?
2. On va voir "Les Randonneurs."	b. Qu'est-ce tu vas voir?
3. Demain, à deux heures et demie de l'après-midi.	c. Tu vas avec qui?
4. Je vais voir un film.	d. Quand ça?
5. Au cinéma Beaubourg.	e. Qu'est-ce que tu vas faire ce week-end?

CHAPITRE 7 - LA FAMILLE

PREMIERE ETAPE

Identifying and introducing people

1 Ahmed is new to your neighborhood. He needs you to help him identify some people. Answer his questions, using **c'est** or **ce sont** and the words in parentheses in the order in which they are listed. (See pp. 179, 180.)

EXAMPLE C'est qui, Karim et Mohamed? (les oncles/Samira)
Ce sont les oncles de Samira.

1. C'est qui, Claudette? (la grand-mère/Guy)
2. C'est qui, Arnaud et Martin? (les frères/Marie)
3. C'est qui, Mourad? (le fils/Fatima)
4. C'est qui, Jacqueline et Jeanne? (les tantes/Paul)
5. C'est qui, Ismaïl? (le grand-père/Saïdou)

2 Sabine and Claire are asking their younger brother Luc to bring them some items they forgot in their room. Complete their statements with the appropriate possessive adjectives. (See p. 181.)

EXAMPLE Luc, apporte-nous nos calculatrices, s'il te plaît!

1. Apporte-nous _____ stylos, s'il te plaît!
2. Apporte-moi _____ trousse, s'il te plaît!
3. Apporte-moi _____ cahiers, s'il te plaît!
4. Apporte-nous _____ dictionnaire, s'il te plaît!

3 Luc cannot find the items his sisters want, so he asks them where they are. Complete his questions by adding the appropriate possessive adjectives. (See p. 181.)

1. Ils sont où, _____ stylos?
2. Elle est où, _____ trousse, Claire?
3. Ils sont où, _____ cahiers, Sabrine?
4. Il est où, _____ dictionnaire?

4 Mazarine and Jean-Luc are talking about their pets. Complete their conversation with the appropriate possessive adjectives. (See p. 181.)

MAZARINE Il a quel âge, __1__ chien, Jean-Luc?
JEAN-LUC __2__ chien? Je n'ai pas de chien. Par contre, j'ai des poissons rouges!
MAZARINE Ah, c'est cool, ça! Ils s'appellent comment, __3__ poissons?
JEAN-LUC Elvis et Presley. Tu aimes les poissons rouges, toi?
MAZARINE Oui, beaucoup, mais j'aime mieux les chats et les canaris. __4__ sœur a deux chats et trois canaris.
JEAN-LUC Ils sont comment, les chats de __5__ sœur?
MAZARINE Très mignons!
JEAN-LUC Et __6__ canaris?
MAZARINE Eh bien, ils sont jaunes.
JEAN-LUC Ah! Très drôle! Est-ce que __7__ parents aiment bien les animaux?
MAZARINE Oui. Chez moi, tout le monde *(everybody)* adore les animaux.

DEUXIEME ETAPE

Describing and characterizing people

5 Unscramble the adjectives. Then, write the correct form of each adjective. Remember to make the adjective agree with the subject it describes. (See p. 186.)

1. Daniel est UNBR.
2. Ses amis sont LNBOD.
3. Ses tantes sont NILTEG.
4. Ses frères sont TNSUAMA.
5. Ses sœurs sont OFRT.
6. Son chien est BNTAMEET.
7. Sa grand-mère est ETPIT.
8. Ses chats sont ROGS.
9. Sa mère est XRUO.
10. Son cousin est ENBLEPI.

6 Complete the following sentences by choosing the appropriate endings. (See p. 187.)

1. Je...
2. Elles...
3. Tu...
4. Julien et moi, on...
5. Jeanne...
6. Alice et moi, nous...
7. Mes frères...
8. Marie et toi, vous...

a. est très gentille.
b. suis grand et fort.
c. sont embêtants.
d. sommes très minces.
e. es méchant!
f. êtes un peu pénibles!
g. est roux.
h. sont intelligentes.

TROISIEME ETAPE

Asking for, giving, and refusing permission

7 There are many things Onélia would like to do, but first she has to ask her parents for permission. Complete her questions with the correct forms of **être**. (See pp. 187, 189.)

1. Je voudrais sortir avec mes copains. Tu _____ d'accord, maman?
2. Je voudrais aller au cinéma. Vous _____ d'accord?
3. Je voudrais aller à la MJC. Tu _____ d'accord, papa?
4. Je _____ invitée à la boum de Pierre. Vous _____ d'accord?

8 Mme Ménard is asking her children to do some work around the house. Complete their answers with the correct form of **être.** (See pp. 187, 189.)

1. MME MENARD Fabienne, tu fais les courses, s'il te plaît?
   FABIENNE Désolée, je _____ occupée. J'ai des devoirs à faire.
2. MME MENARD Anne et Eva, vous faites la vaisselle, s'il vous plaît?
   ANNE ET EVA Désolées, nous _____ occupées.
3. MME MENARD Paul et Eric, vous pouvez débarrasser la table?
   PAUL ET ERIC Désolés, on _____ occupés. On a des trucs à faire.
4. MME MENARD Lise, tu peux promener le chien?
   LISE Oui, bien sûr!
   MME MENARD Merci. Tu _____ très gentille!

CHAPITRE 8 - AU MARCHE

PREMIERE ETAPE

Expressing need

1 Eric is planning a party and has made a list of what he needs to do to get ready. Complete his list with **du, de la, de l',** and **des** as needed. (See p. 208.)

Pour ma boum, je vais faire des sandwiches, alors je vais acheter _____ pain, _____ fromage et ___ jambon. Mes amis aiment manger _____ salade. Dans la salade, je vais mettre _____ tomates, _____ maïs et _____ champignons. Pour le dessert, je vais préparer une salade de fruits avec _____ oranges, _____ bananes et _____ pommes.

2 Read the recipes below. Then write a note reminding yourself what you need to buy at the market, using the articles **du, de la, de l'**, and **des**. (See p. 208.)

1.

Les crêpes bretonnes
500 g de farine
3 œufs
20 g de beurre
3 g de sel (m.; *salt*)
5 g de levure (f.; *yeast*)
1 cl de jus de pomme
1/4 litre de lait

Il me faut... de la farine,

2.

La sauce arachide
4 oignons
2 tomates
5 cl d'huile d'arachide
100 g de pâte (f.) d'arachide
100 g de pâte (f.) de tomates
10 g de sel
1/4 botte *(bunch)* de piments rouges

Il me faut...

3 Rewrite the following sentences, using the expressions **avoir besoin de** or **il me/te faut** and the partitive article. (See pp. 208, 210.)

EXAMPLE Il me faut des bananes. J'ai besoin de bananes.
Tu as besoin de lait? Il te faut du lait?

1. Il me faut des noix de coco.
2. Il te faut des papayes?
3. Tu as besoin de confiture?
4. Il me faut du raisin.
5. J'ai besoin d'eau minérale.
6. Il te faut des ananas?

DEUXIEME ETAPE

Making, accepting, and declining requests; telling someone what to do

4 You and your friends are planning a party and you're writing down what people are volunteering to bring. Fill in the correct forms of the verb **pouvoir**. (See p. 213.)

1. Isabelle _________ acheter des avocats et des tomates.
2. Moi, je _________ acheter des tartes.
3. Henri, tu _________ acheter des fraises et des citrons?
4. Carol et Sylvain, vous _________ acheter de la salade et du pain.
5. Barbara, Serge et Françoise _________ acheter une bouteille d'eau.

5 Choose the appropriate completion for each sentence. (See p. 213.)

A	B
1. Est-ce que tu...	**a.** ne peuvent pas aller au cinéma ce soir. Ils sont occupés.
2. Elle...	**b.** ne peux pas sortir la poubelle. Je n'ai pas le temps.
3. Nous...	**c.** peux débarrasser la table, s'il te plaît?
4. Angèle et toi, vous...	**d.** ne pouvons pas faire la vaisselle. Nous avons des trucs à faire.
5. Moi, je...	**e.** ne peut pas sortir avec ses copines. Elle a des devoirs à faire.
6. Mes copains...	**f.** pouvez promener le chien?

6 Unscramble the names of the food items. Then combine the fragments to create sentences telling Djeneba what to get you from the market. (See p. 214.)

EXAMPLE RUERBE / un paquet/s'il te plaît/prends
Prends un paquet de beurre, s'il te plaît!

1. ITESPT OSPI / une boîte/rapporte-moi/s'il te plaît
2. NDVAIE / s'il te plaît/un morceau/achète-moi
3. SECHEP / prends/une douzaine
4. SJU ASANAN D' / une bouteille/acheter/n'oublie pas de
5. AMCHNONPIGS / tu peux/s'il te plaît/une livre/acheter
6. IRNAFE / un kilo/s'il te plaît/rapporte-moi

TROISIEME ETAPE

Offering, accepting, or refusing food

7 You're asking Didier about his family's eating habits. Write down his answers to your questions, using the pronoun **en** and the correct form of **prendre**. (See pp. 133, 220.)

EXAMPLE Tu prends du café au lait au petit déjeuner? Oui, j'en prends.

1. Tu prends du lait au dîner? Non, ...
2. Tes parents prennent du pain avec leur fromage? Oui, ...
3. Ta sœur prend des légumes au déjeuner? Oui, ...
4. Ton petit frère prend des gâteaux au goûter? Non, ...
5. Ta cousine et toi, vous prenez de la viande au déjeuner? Non, on ...
6. Tu prends de la sauce arachide avec ton riz? Oui, ...

8 Read the four sentences in the box below and tell what Armelle's friends like and dislike and how they're feeling. With this information in mind, write down their answers to Armelle's offers of various foods and drinks. Use the correct form of **vouloir** and the pronoun **en** in each answer. (See pp. 160, 220.)

> **Marius n'a plus faim, mais il a très soif.**
> **Irène aime les fruits, mais elle n'aime pas tellement le fromage.**
> **Isabelle n'aime pas la viande, mais elle adore le poisson.**
> **Léopold a très faim, mais il n'a plus soif.**

EXAMPLE Irène, encore du fromage? Non, merci. Je n'en veux plus.

1. Marius, tu veux de l'eau?
2. Irène, tu veux des pêches?
3. Isabelle, encore du rosbif?
4. Léopold, tu veux du gâteau?
5. Isabelle, tu veux du poisson?
6. Marius, encore du riz?

CHAPITRE 9 - AU TELEPHONE

PREMIERE ETAPE

Asking for and expressing opinions; inquiring about and relating past events

1 Françoise and Julie are talking about what they did over the weekend. Complete their conversation with the **passé composé** of the verbs in parentheses. (See p. 239.)

FRANÇOIS Salut Julie. Tu __1__ (passer) un bon week-end?
JULIE Oh, ça __2__ (être). J' __3__ (visiter) ma grand-mère et j' __4__ (lire) mon roman. Et toi? Qu'est-ce que tu __5__ (faire)?
FRANÇOIS J' __6__ (prendre) la voiture de ma mère, et mon sœur et moi, nous __7__ (voir) un film.

2 Complete Pierre's journal entry about his busy weekend by putting each verb into the **passé composé** (See p. 239.)

Hier, j' _____ (retrouver) mes amis Jean et Françoise au café. Nous _____ (déjeuner) ensemble puis nous _____ (parler) de notre week-end. Samedi, Françoise _____ (lire) un livre et Jean _____ (étudier). Le soir, ils _____ (acheter) un billet de loto mais ils _____ (ne pas gagner). Dimanche, j' _____ (voir) un bon film et ensuite j' _____ (faire) mes devoirs.

3 Edouard always wants to do what Milo just did. Read what Edouard says he'll be doing. Then write six sentences saying that Milo did the same thing yesterday. Remember to put the verbs in the **passé composé**, and to make all necessary changes. (See p. 239.)

EXAMPLE Demain, je vais acheter des baskets. Hier, Milo a acheté des baskets.

1. Je vais laver la voiture de mon père demain. Hier,...
2. Je vais déjeuner à la cantine demain. Hier,...
3. Demain, je vais retrouver mes copains. Hier,...
4. Demain, je vais répéter avec la chorale. Hier,...
5. Je vais dîner avec ma grand-mère demain. Hier,...
6. Demain, je vais ranger ma chambre. Hier,...

4 Elissa's mother is asking her if she and her brothers and sisters have done their chores. Write Elissa's answers, using **déjà** or **ne (n')... pas encore**. Remember to make all the necessary changes. (See p. 240.)

EXAMPLE MAMAN Tu as passé l'aspirateur?
ELISSA Non, je n'ai pas encore passé l'aspirateur.

1. MAMAN Claire et toi, vous avez rangé vos chambres?
   ELISSA Non,
2. MAMAN Tu as débarrassé la table?
   ELISSA Oui,
3. MAMAN Et Guillaume, est-ce qu'il a fait les courses?
   ELISSA Oui,
4. MAMAN Est-ce que tu as promené le chien?
   ELISSA Non,
5. MAMAN Est-ce que Claire et Sophie ont fait le ménage?
   ELISSA Non,

DEUXIEME ETAPE

Making and answering a telephone call

5 Pierre, David, and Yves are discussing what their friends are doing today. Complete their conversation with the correct forms of **répondre** and **attendre.** (See p. 245.)

PIERRE Tiens, salut! Vous __1__ le bus?
YVES Non, nous __2__ Paul. Il va au stade avec nous.
PIERRE Où est Lise?
DAVID Elle est chez elle. Elle __3__ sa mère pour aller au musée.
PIERRE Ah oui! C'est vrai. Et Bruno, qu'est-ce qu'il fait ce matin?
YVES Il __4__ à la lettre de son correspondant américain. Et toi, qu'est-ce que tu fais, alors?
PIERRE Rien de spécial.
DAVID Tu __5__ Paul avec nous?
PIERRE Oui, pourquoi pas?

6 Write complete sentences using the fragments below. Watch for clues that tell you when to use the **passé composé.** (See p. 245.)

1. hier/Paul/perdre/son portefeuille/au centre commercial
2. nous/répondre/au téléphone/quand/notre père/travailler
3. ne/pas/perdre/votre argent
4. mes parents/vendre/leur voiture/bleu/la semaine dernière
5. Michel/vendre/des bonbons/pour/gagner de l'argent

TROISIEME ETAPE

Sharing confidences and consoling others; asking for and giving advice

7 Léon is asking Diane for advice. Complete their conversation with **le, la, l',** or **lui.** (See p. 247.)

LEON	Dis, Diane, tu as une minute?
DIANE	Oui. Bien sûr. Je t'écoute.
LEON	Ben, hier, au café, j'ai rencontré une fille. On a parlé pendant *(for)* deux heures. Ce matin, elle m'a téléphoné pour me dire qu'elle veut sortir avec moi. A ton avis, qu'est-ce que je fais?
DIANE	Elle est comment cette fille? Tu __1__ (l', les) aimes bien?
LEON	Oui. Je __2__ (l', la) aime beaucoup. Elle est super sympa.
DIANE	Qu'est-ce que tu __3__ (lui, leur) as répondu alors?
LEON	Je ne __4__ (la, lui) ai pas répondu. A ton avis, qu'est-ce que je fais?
DIANE	Téléphone- __5__ (lui, leur) tout de suite!
LEON	Mais je ne trouve plus son numéro de téléphone!
DIANE	Cherche- __6__ (le, leur)!
LEON	Non, c'est pas possible. Je ne peux pas __7__ (le, lui) téléphoner. Je suis trop timide!
DIANE	Ah, bon! Alors, oublie- __8__ (la, les)!

8 You and your friend Max are giving advice to Odile. Repeat Max's advice using an object pronoun **(le, la, les, lui,** or **leur).** (See p. 247.)

EXAMPLE	MAX	Achète les pommes rouges!
	TOI	Oui. Achète-les!

1. Téléphone à tes copains!
2. Prends la trousse violette!
3. Apporte tes disques compacts!
4. Oublie ce garçon!
5. Attends les vacances!
6. Ecris à Caroline!
7. Parle à tes parents!
8. Achète ces stylos!

CHAPITRE 10 - DANS UN MAGASIN DE VETEMENTS

PREMIERE ETAPE

Asking for and giving advice

1 Fill in the blanks to create the correct present tense form of **mettre** for each of the sentences below. (See p. 263.)

1. Qu'est-ce que je __ E __ __ pour la boum de Charles?
2. Pourquoi tu ne M __ T __ pas ta robe blanche?
3. Odile et Béatrice __ __ T __ E __ __ souvent des robes à fleurs.
4. Boris et moi, nous __ E __ __ __ N __ des lunettes de soleil pour aller à des boums.
5. Vous __ __ T __ E __ des lunettes de soleil quand il pleut comme ça?
6. Oui, on __ E __ toujours des lunettes de soleil et des baskets.

2 Marie-France is asking Patricia for advice on what to wear to a party. Complete their conversation with the appropriate forms of **mettre** and **porter.** Remember to use the past tense when indicated. (See p. 263.)

MARIE-FRANCE	Je ne sais pas quoi __1__ (mettre) pour aller au théâtre.
PATRICIA	__2__ (mettre) ta jupe noire avec ton chemisier blanc.
MARIE-FRANCE	Non, ce n'est pas très chic. Et j' __3__ (déjà mettre) mon chemisier blanc avec ma veste cette semaine.
PATRICIA	Pourquoi tu ne __4__ (mettre) pas ton chemisier bleu avec une écharpe alors?
MARIE-FRANCE	Non, j' __5__ (déjà porter) mon écharpe à la boum de Jean-Marc.
PATRICIA	__6__ (mettre) ta robe noire.
MARIE-FRANCE	Bonne idée. Et je vais __7__ aussi mes chaussures noires. Enfin, c'est décidé.

DEUXIEME ETAPE

Expressing need; inquiring

3 Nadia is asking Clara what to wear for Raphaël's party. Write Clara's advice, using **mets** and the correct forms of the adjectives in parentheses. (See pp. 263, 265.)

EXAMPLE NADIA Je mets ma robe violette? (gris)
CLARA Je la trouve trop serrée. Mets la grise!

1. NADIA Je mets mes sandales jaunes? (blanc)
   CLARA Je les trouve un peu démodées. _____
2. NADIA Je mets mon cardigan orange? (noir)
   CLARA C'est pas ton style. _____
3. NADIA Je mets mon écharpe rouge? (rose)
   CLARA Elle ne te va pas. _____
4. NADIA Je mets ma ceinture verte? (bleu)
   CLARA Elle ne va pas avec ta robe. _____
5. NADIA Je mets mes boucles d'oreilles marron? (vert)
   CLARA Je les trouve trop grosses. _____

4 Given their likes and dislikes, write what these students choose to wear to Mélanie's party, using the correct form of **choisir**. Remember to make all the necessary changes. (See p. 267.)

EXAMPLE Suzanne aime les jupes courtes. Elle choisit une jupe courte.

1. Pierre et Philippe aiment bien les cravates à pois.
2. Armelle adore les robes rétro.
3. Moi, j'aime les boucles d'oreilles noires.
4. Tu préfères les chemisiers à fleurs.
5. Elsa et toi, vous aimez bien les chaussures en cuir.
6. Toi et moi, nous adorons les blousons en jean.

5 Write complete sentences using the words below. Remember to put the verbs in the present tense and to make all necessary changes. (See p. 267.)

1. vous/ne/pas/grossir/parce que/vous/faire du sport
2. on/grandir/si/on/manger/assez
3. tu/maigrir/parce que/tu/jouer au foot/tous les jours
4. nous/grossir/facilement/si/nous/ne/pas/faire du jogging
5. je/grossir/parce que/je/manger/beaucoup de gâteaux
6. mes petites sœurs/grandir/tous les jours
7. il/maigrir/si/il/ne/pas/manger/trois fois par jour
8. vous/grandir/quand/vous/manger vos légumes
9. ma sœur/maigrir/facilement/quand/elle/faire de l'aérobic
10. tu/manger/beaucoup/mais/tu/ne/jamais/grossir

6 Why can't these students wear their clothes anymore? Give the explanation, using the **passé composé** of the verbs in parentheses and the cues provided. (See p. 267.)

EXAMPLE Armelle, ce cardigan ne te va plus. (grandir) J'ai grandi.

1. Sophie, ce pantalon ne te va plus. (maigrir)
2. Pierre et Jean, ces chemises ne vous vont plus. (grandir)
3. Valentine, cette robe ne te va plus. (grossir)
4. Ce pantalon ne me va plus. (grandir)
5. Ahmed et Karim, ces vestes ne vous vont plus. (maigrir)
6. Dis donc, ce blouson ne me va plus. (grossir)

TROISIEME ETAPE

Asking for an opinion; paying a compliment; criticizing; hesitating; making a decision

7 You're shopping with a friend. She is having trouble deciding what to buy and asks for your advice. Respond to each of these statements, replacing the object with **le**, **la**, or **les**. Remember to use commands when necessary. (See p. 273.)

1. Est-ce que tu aimes cette robe?
2. Comment tu trouves ce pantalon?
3. Je veux acheter cette veste, mais j'hésite.
4. J'aime bien cette veste mais elle est chère et un peu grande.
5. Est-ce que tu vas acheter ces chaussures aussi?

8 Anne is shopping for clothes. Complete her conversations with the salesperson according to the pattern shown in the example. Remember to use the direct object pronouns **le, la, l'**, and **les** in your answers. (See p. 273.)

EXAMPLE		
	ANNE	Ces bottes vont très bien avec mon manteau. <u>Je peux les essayer?</u>
	VENDEUR	Elles vous vont très bien, mademoiselle! <u>Vous les prenez?</u>
	ANNE	Oui. <u>Je les prends.</u>

1. ANNE Ce blouson va très bien avec mon pantalon noir.
   _____?
   VENDEUR Il vous va très bien, mademoiselle.
   _____?
   ANNE Oui. _____.
2. ANNE Ces sandales vont très bien avec ma jupe en jean.
   _____?
   VENDEUR Elles vous vont très bien, mademoiselle.
   _____?
   ANNE Euh... J'hésite... Non. _____. Elles sont trop chères.
3. ANNE Cette robe va très bien avec mes chaussures.
   _____?
   VENDEUR Elle vous va très bien, mademoiselle.
   _____?
   ANNE Elle me plaît beaucoup. Oui. _____.
4. ANNE Ces lunettes de soleil vont très bien avec mon maillot de bain. _____?
   VENDEUR Elles vous vont très bien, mademoiselle.
   _____?
   ANNE Elles sont super cool. Oui. _____.

9 Complete Flavien's statements with **il est, elle est,** or **c'est**. (See p. 274.)

1. Comment tu trouves ce chapeau? _____ sensas, non?
2. Moi, j'aime beaucoup porter un chapeau parce que _____ sympa.
3. Cédric porte souvent une casquette. _____ en cuir, sa casquette. Très chic!
4. Tu aimes les choses en cuir, toi? Moi, non. Je préfère le jean. _____ plus pratique!
5. Tu dis? Ah, oui. J'adore le look rétro. _____ chouette, le rétro!

CHAPITRE 11 - VIVE LES VACANCES!

PREMIERE ETAPE

Inquiring about and sharing future plans; expressing indecision; expressing wishes; asking for advice; making, accepting, and refusing suggestions

1 The following sentences state what these people generally do during the summer. Rewrite the sentences in the future using the verb **aller**. (See pp. 154, 288.)

1. Antoine fait du bateau.
2. Sophie et sa sœur font de la voile.
3. Ma famille et moi, nous allons au bord de la mer.
4. Anne et toi, vous faites de la randonnée.

2 The names of these exchange students begin with the same letter as their countries of origin. Match each of the students with a country listed in the box. Then tell where he or she will be going this summer. (See p. 290.)

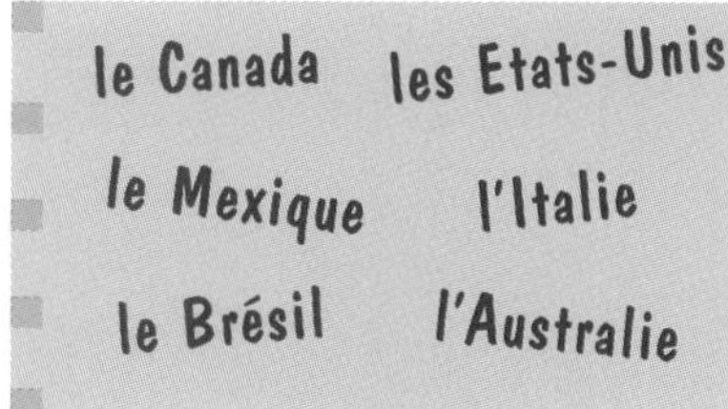

EXAMPLE Bélinda/le Brésil -> Elle va aller au Brésil.

1. Anne/ _____ - _____
2. Erin/_____ - _____
3. Maria/_____ - _____
4. Isabella/_____ - _____
5. Céline/ _____ - _____

3 Jeanne and her friends are asking you for advice. Based on their likes and wishes, write four suggestions, using a location from the box. (See p. 290.)

la Californie | le Mexique | la Suisse | la France | l'Egypte

EXAMPLE J'aime faire de la randonnée! Pourquoi tu ne vas pas en Suisse?

1. J'adore les quiches et les croque-monsieur!
   _____
2. Nous aimons la plage.
   _____
3. Je voudrais visiter les pyramides.
   _____
4. Nous adorons parler espagnol.
   _____

DEUXIEME ETAPE

Reminding; reassuring; seeing someone off

4 Write six sentences telling when you and your friends usually leave home to go to school, using the verb **partir.** (See p. 294.)

EXAMPLE Marianne (8h30) Elle part à huit heures et demie.

1. Antoine et moi (6h15)
2. Et toi, Maryse (7h00)
3. Lise et Marie (7h30)
4. Philippe et toi (8h00)
5. Stéphane (8h45)

5 Omar and Larissa are getting ready to leave for their grandmother's house. Complete their conversation with the correct forms of the verbs in parentheses. (See p. 294.)

OMAR	Dis, Larissa, tu __1__ (dormir) toujours?
LARISSA	Oui. Je __2__ (dormir)!
OMAR	Mais c'est pas possible! On __3__ (partir) dans une heure!
LARISSA	On __4__ (aller) où?
OMAR	Tu ne te rappelles pas? Nous __5__ (partir) en vacances aujourd'hui! Au bord de la mer! Chez mémé!
LARISSA	Ah, mais c'est vrai! J'avais oublié! C'est super! Qu'est-ce que je __6__ (prendre)? Mon maillot de bain?
OMAR	Oui. __7__ (prendre) - le! Il __8__ (aller) faire chaud! Et n' __9__ (oublier) pas une robe! On va __10__ (sortir) avec les copains tous les soirs.
LARISSA	Je __11__ (pouvoir) prendre la valise de maman?
OMAR	Oui. Si tu __12__ (vouloir).
LARISSA	Dis, Omar, tu, n' __13__ (avoir) pas oublié le cadeau pour mémé?
OMAR	Mais non. Je n' __14__ (avoir) rien oublié. J' __15__ (avoir) pensé à tout.

6 There are some things you and your friends cannot leave without, so your parents are telling you to bring them on vacation. Write what they tell you, using the appropriate object pronoun (**le, la,** or **les**). (See pp. 247, 296.)

EXAMPLE Je ne peux pas partir sans mon blouson en jean.
Eh bien, prends-le!

1. Je ne peux pas partir sans ma valise!
2. Je ne peux pas partir sans mon passeport!
3. Nous ne pouvons pas partir sans nos chaussures en cuir!
4. Je ne peux pas partir sans mon appareil-photo!
5. Nous ne pouvons pas partir sans nos lunettes de soleil!
6. Je ne peux pas partir sans ma cravate à fleurs.

TROISIEME ETAPE

Asking for and expressing opinions; inquiring about and relating past events

7 Combine these fragments into eight complete sentences telling what you and your friends did during your vacation. Remember to put the verb in the **passé composé.** (See pp. 239, 298.)

1. Karim et moi/pièce/voir/une/super/nous
2. Tu/de/au bord de/la/faire/mer/voile/la/non?
3. Christelle/jusqu'à midi/dormir
4. Jacques et Simon/la télé/regarder/pendant des heures
5. Jonathan et toi/de/randonnée?/vous/la/faire
6. Larissa et moi/des/sensas/lire/romans/nous
7. Véra et Julie/visiter/le Louvre
8. Moi/à/des/répondre/lettres/je

CHAPITRE 12 - EN VILLE

PREMIERE ETAPE

Pointing out places and things

1 Write five sentences telling where these people are going to go, based on what they need. Use the present tense of **aller** and one word from the box in each sentence. (see pp. 154, 157, 316.)

la boulangerie	la banque	la papeterie	
la poste	l'épicerie	le marché	la pharmacie

EXAMPLE J'ai besoin de pain. Je vais à la boulangerie.

1. Il me faut des feuilles de papier et des gommes.
2. Tu as besoin de retirer de l'argent.
3. Il vous faut des timbres.
4. Mme Bonjean a besoin de farine et de beurre.
5. Pierre et moi, nous avons besoin de médicaments.

2 You're asking your friends what they did during the weekend. Write their answers, using the activities in parenthèses. Remember to put the verbs in the **passé composé**. (See pp. 239, 317.)

EXAMPLE Malika, tu as passé un bon week-end? (visiter le fort Saint-Louis)
Oui. J'ai visité le fort Saint-Louis.

1. Lisette, qu'est-ce que tu as fait pendant le week-end? (lire des magazines)
   J'...
2. Cécile et Julien, vous avez passé un bon week-end? (faire de la plongée)
   Oui, nous...
3. Tu as passé un bon week-end, Martin? (voir un film génial)
   Oui, j'...
4. Romain, tu as passé un bon week-end? (prendre des photos de mes chiens)
   Oui, j'...

DEUXIEME ETAPE

Making and responding to requests; asking for advice and making suggestions

3 Rewrite the following sentences, replacing the words indicating a specific amount with the appropriate partitive or indefinite article (**du, de la, de l'**, or **des**). (See pp. 208, 320.)

EXAMPLE Tu pourrais me rapporter une bouteille de lait?
Tu pourrais me rapporter du lait?

1. Tu me rapportes un kilo de farine, s'il te plaît?
2. Tu me prends un paquet de beurre, s'il te plaît?
3. Tu m'achètes une livre de carottes?
4. Rapporte-moi trois tranches de jambon, s'il te plaît!
5. Tu me rapportes deux bouteilles d'eau minérale?

4 You're asking your friends how they're going to get to their vacation destinations. Write their answers, using the pronoun **y**. (See p. 323.)

EXAMPLE Philippe, comment est-ce que tu vas aux Etats-Unis? (en avion)
J'y vais en avion.

1. Mohamed et Yasmina, comment est-ce que vous allez au bord de la mer? (en train) Nous...
2. Azzedine, comment tu vas à la campagne? (à vélo)
3. Comment est-ce que Fatima va en Angleterre? (en bateau)
4. Hannah et Raphaël, comment vous allez à la montagne? (en bus)
5. Aziz, comment est-ce que tu vas à Paris? (en voiture)

5 Complete the following conversations with **y** and the correct form and tense of the verbs in parentheses. Be careful! Some of the verbs will be in the present tense and some will be in the **passé composé.** (See p. 323.)

—Salut, Michèle, tu vas à la bibliothèque?

—Oui, je/j' __1__ (y/aller) cet aprèm. J'ai des livres à rendre. Tu __2__ (vouloir) venir?

—Oui, je veux bien. On __3__ (y/aller) à quelle heure?

—Dis, Florence, c'est vrai que tu __4__ (trouver) un billet de cent francs devant la banque?

—Pas tout à fait. Je/j' __5__ (y trouver) une pièce de dix francs.

—Tu __6__ (avoir) de la chance, quand même!

—Tu __7__ (pouvoir) me rendre un service, ma chérie!

—Oui, maman.

—Je/j' __8__ (avoir) besoin de bananes et de citrons. Tu __9__ (pouvoir) aller au marché, s'il te plaît?

—Au marché? C'est loin! Comment est-ce que je/j' __10__ (y/aller)? A pied?

—Mais non. Pourquoi tu ne/n' __11__ (y/aller) pas à vélo?

—Bonne idée. Je __12__ (partir) tout de suite.

TROISIEME ETAPE

Asking for and giving directions

6 Unscramble the following location words. Then combine the fragments to create five sentences telling where the places are located. Use the places in the order in which they are given. (See p. 325.)

EXAMPLE EN CEFA ED/l'école/le café   L'école est en face du café.

1. REDEIRER/la poste/le stade
2. ED TOIRDE A/la pharmacie/la boulangerie
3. SERP ED/l'épicerie/le cinéma
4. CHUGEA ED A/la pâtisserie/la bibliothèque
5. ED NOIL/la banque/la papeterie

PRONUNCIATION INDEX

CHAPTER	LETTER COMBINATION	IPA SYMBOL	EXAMPLE
Ch. 1, p. 35 Intonation			
Ch. 2, p. 59 Liaison			vous‿avez des‿amis
Ch. 3, p. 83 The **r** sound	the letter **r**	/ʀ/	rouge vert
Ch. 4, p. 113 The sounds [y] and [u]	the letter **u** the letter combination **ou**	/y/ /u/	une nous
Ch. 5, p. 141 The nasal sound [ɑ̃]	the letter combination **an** the letter combination **am** the letter combination **en** the letter combination **em**	/ɑ̃/	anglais jambon comment temps
Ch. 6, p. 167 The vowel sounds [ø] and [œ]	the letter combination **eu** the letter combination **eu**	/ø/ /œ/	deux heure
Ch. 7, p. 191 The nasal sounds [ɔ̃], [ɛ̃], and [œ̃]	the letter combination **on** the letter combination **om** the letter combination **in** the letter combination **im** the letter combination **ain** the letter combination **aim** the letter combination **(i)en** the letter combination **un** the letter combination **um**	/ɔ̃/ /ɛ̃/ /œ̃/	pardon nombre cousin impossible copain faim bien lundi humble
Ch. 8, p. 221 The sounds [o] and [ɔ]	the letter combination **au** the letter combination **eau** the letter **ô** the letter **o**	/o/ /ɔ/	jaune beau rôle carotte
Ch. 9, p. 249 The vowel sounds [e] and [ɛ]	the letter combination **ez** the letter combination **er** the letter combination **ait** the letter combination **ais** the letter combination **ei** the letter **ê**	/e/ /ɛ/	apportez trouver fait français neige bête
Ch. 10, p. 275 The glides [j], [w], and [ɥ]	the letter **i** the letter combination **ill** the letter combination **oi** the letter combination **oui** the letter combination **ui**	/j/ /w/ /ɥ/	mieux maillot moi Louis huit
Ch. 11, p. 299 **h aspiré**, **th**, **ch**, and **gn**	the letter **h** the letter combination **th** the letter combination **ch** the letter combination **gn**	/'/ /t/ /ʃ/ /ɲ/	les halls théâtre chocolat oignon
Ch. 12, p. 329 Review			

NUMBERS

LES NOMBRES CARDINAUX

0	zéro	20	vingt	80	quatre-vingts
1	un(e)	21	vingt et un(e)	81	quatre-vingt-un(e)
2	deux	22	vingt-deux	82	quatre-vingt-deux
3	trois	23	vingt-trois	90	quatre-vingt-dix
4	quatre	24	vingt-quatre	91	quatre-vingt-onze
5	cinq	25	vingt-cinq	92	quatre-vingt-douze
6	six	26	vingt-six	100	cent
7	sept	27	vingt-sept	101	cent un
8	huit	28	vingt-huit	200	deux cents
9	neuf	29	vingt-neuf	300	trois cents
10	dix	30	trente	800	huit cents
11	onze	31	trente et un(e)	900	neuf cents
12	douze	32	trente-deux	1.000	mille
13	treize	40	quarante	2.000	deux mille
14	quatorze	50	cinquante	3.000	trois mille
15	quinze	60	soixante	10.000	dix mille
16	seize	70	soixante-dix	19.000	dix-neuf mille
17	dix-sept	71	soixante et onze	40.000	quarante mille
18	dix-huit	72	soixante-douze	500.000	cinq cent mille
19	dix-neuf	73	soixante-treize	1.000.000	un million

- The word **et** is used only in 21, 31, 41, 51, 61, and 71.
- **Vingt (trente, quarante,** and so on) **et une** is used when the number refers to a feminine noun: **trente et une cassettes.**
- The **s** is dropped from **quatre-vingts** and is not added to multiples of **cent** when these numbers are followed by another number: **quatre-vingt-cinq; deux cents,** *but* **deux cent six.** The number **mille** never takes an **s: deux mille insectes.**
- **Un million** is followed by **de** + a noun: **un million de francs.**
- In writing numbers, a period is used in French where a comma is used in English.

LES NOMBRES ORDINAUX

1er, 1ère	premier, première	9e	neuvième	17e	dix-septième
2e	deuxième	10e	dixième	18e	dix-huitième
3e	troisième	11e	onzième	19e	dix-neuvième
4e	quatrième	12e	douzième	20e	vingtième
5e	cinquième	13e	treizième	21e	vingt et unième
6e	sixième	14e	quatorzième	22e	vingt-deuxième
7e	septième	15e	quinzième	30e	trentième
8e	huitième	16e	seizième	40e	quarantième

FRENCH-ENGLISH VOCABULARY

This list includes both active and passive vocabulary in this textbook. Active words and phrases are those listed in the **Vocabulaire** section at the end of each chapter. You are expected to know and be able to use active vocabulary. All entries in heavy black type in this list are active. All other words are passive. Passive vocabulary is for recognition only.

The number after each entry refers to the chapter where the word or phrase is introduced. Nouns are always given with an article. If it is not clear whether the noun is masculine or feminine, *m.* (masculine) or *f.* (feminine) follows the noun. Some nouns that are generally seen only in the plural, as well as irregular plurals, are also given with gender indications and the abbreviation *pl.* (plural) following them. An asterisk (*) before a word beginning with *h* indicates an aspirate *h.* Phrases are alphabetized by the key word(s) in the phrase.

The following abbreviations are also used in this vocabulary: *pp.* (past participle), *inv.* (invariable), and *adj.* (adjective).

A

à *to, in (a city or place),* 11; **à côté de** *next to,* 12; **à la** *to, at,* 6; **A bientôt.** *See you soon.* 1; à carreaux *checked,* 10; **A demain.** *See you tomorrow.* 1; à fleurs *flowered,* 10; à la carte *pick and choose,* 3; à la française *French-style,* 1; **à la mode** *in style,* 10; à part ça *aside from that,* 11; à pois *polka dot,* 10; **A quelle heure?** *At what time?* 6; à rayures *striped,* 10; **A tout à l'heure!** *See you later!* 1; **A votre service.** *At your service; You're welcome.* 3; Et maintenant, à toi. *And now, it's your turn,* 1

l' abbaye (f.) *abbey,* 6

abîmer *to ruin,* 10

s' abonner *to subscribe*; abonnez-vous à... *subscribe to . . . ,* 3

l' abricot (m.) *apricot,* 5

abriter *to house,* 11

absent(e) *absent,* 2

accompagner *to accompany,* 4

l' accueil (m.) *reception, welcome,* 4

accueille (accueillir) *to welcome*

acheter *to buy,* 9; **Achète (-moi)...** *Buy (me) . . . ,* 8; Je n'achète pas... *I don't buy / I'm not buying . . . ,* 3

l' acra de morue (m.) *cod fritter*

l' activité (f.) *activity,* 4

l' addition (f.) *check, bill,* 5; **L'addition, s'il vous plaît.** *The check, please.* 5

adorer *to adore,* 1; **J'adore...** *I adore . . .* 1; J'adorerais... *I would adore . . . ,* 1

l' aérobic (f.) *aerobics,* 4; **faire de l'aérobic** *to do aerobics,* 4

affectueux (-euse) *affectionate,* 7

afin de *in order to,* 7

l' âge (m.) *age,* 1; **Tu as quel âge?** *How old are you?* 1

âgé(e) *older,* 7

l' agenda (m.) *planner,* 4

agit : il s'agit de *it's concerned with; it's about,* 6

agréable *pleasant,* 4

ai : J'ai... *I have . . . ,* 2; **J'ai... ans.** *I am . . . years old.* 1; **J'ai besoin de...** *I need . . . ,* 8; **J'ai faim.** *I'm hungry.* 5; **J'ai l'intention de...** *I intend to . . . ,* 11; **J'ai soif.** *I'm thirsty.* 5; **Je n'ai pas de...** *I don't have . . . ,* 3

aider *to help,* 10; **(Est-ce que) je peux vous aider?** *May I help you?* 10

l' ail (m.) *garlic,* 8

les ailes (f.) *wings,* 12

aimé(e) (pp. of aimer) *loved,* 1

aimer *to like,* 1; **J'aime mieux...** *I prefer . . . ,* 1; **J'aimerais... pour aller avec...** *I'd like . . . to go with . . . ,* 10; **Je n'aime pas...** *I don't like . . . ,* 1; **Moi, j'aime (bien)...** *I (really) like . . . ,* 1; **Tu aimes... ?** *Do you like . . . ?* 1

l' aire de pique-nique aménagée (f.) *equipped picnic area,* 6

l' aise (f.) *ease,* 7

ajouter *to add,* 10

l' algèbre (f.) *algebra,* 2

l' Algérie (f.) *Algeria,* 0

l' alimentation (f.) *food,* 12

les aliments (m.) *nutrients,* 8

allé(e) (pp. of aller) *went,* 9; **Je suis allé(e)...** *I went . . . ,* 9; **Tu es allé(e) où?** *Where did you go?* 9

l' allemand (m.) *German (language),* 2

aller *to go,* 6; **Ça va aller mieux!** *It's going to get better!* 9; **On peut y aller...** *We can go there . . . ,* 12

allez : Allez au tableau! *Go to the blackboard!* 0; **Allez, viens!** *Come along!* 0

Allô? *Hello?* 9

l' allocation de naissance (f.) *money provided as a birth allowance by the French government,* 7; l'allocation familiale (f.) *money provided by the French government to large families,* 7

allons : Allons-y! *Let's go!* 4; **Allons...** *Let's go . . . ,* 6

l' aloco (m.) *dish from West Africa made from fried plantain bananas and usually eaten as a snack,* 5

alors *well, then,* 3

l' alphabet (m.) *alphabet,* 0

l' ambiance (f.) *atmosphere,* 2

aménagé(e) *equipped,* 6

américain(e) *American* (adj.), 0

l' ami(e) *friend,* 1

amical(e) (pl. amicaux) *friendly,* 2

amicalement *sincerely (to close a letter),* 1

l' amitié (f.) *friendship,* 1

l' amour (m.) *love,* 1
amusant(e) *funny,* 7
s' amuser *to have fun,* 11; **Amuse-toi bien!** *Have fun!* 11; **Qu'est-ce que tu fais pour t'amuser?** *What do you do to have fun?* 4; **Tu t'es bien amusé(e)?** *Did you have fun?* 11
l' an (m.) *year,* 1; **J'ai... ans.** *I am . . . years old.* 1
l' ananas (m.) *pineapple,* 8
ancien(ne) *old; former,* 6; l'ancienne gare *the former train station,* 6
l' Andorre (article not commonly used) *Andorra,* 0
l' anglais (m.) *English (language),* 1
l' animal (m.) *animal,* 1
l' animateur (m.) *camp counselor,* 11
les animations (f.) *activities,* 11
l' année (f.) *year,* 4
l' année scolaire (f.) *school year,* 2
l' anniversaire (m.) *anniversary; birthday,* 7
les annonces (f.) *ads,* 1; les petites annonces *personal or business ads,* 1
anthracite *charcoal grey,* 10
antique *ancient,* 9
les antiquités (f.) *antiquities, antiques,* 6
août *August,* 4; **en août** *in August,* 4
l' appareil (m.) *phone,* 9; **Qui est à l'appareil?** *Who's calling?* 9
l' appareil-photo (m.) *camera,* 11
appartient (appartenir) à *to belong to,* 9
s' appeler *to call oneself, to be called,* 1; **Il/Elle s'appelle comment?** *What's his/her name?* 1; **Il/Elle s'appelle...** *His/Her name is . . . ,* 1; **Je m'appelle...** *My name is . . . ,* 1; **Tu t'appelles comment?** *What's your name?* 1
apporter *to bring,* 9; **Apportez-moi... , s'il vous plaît.** *Please bring me . . . ,* 5
apprendre *to learn,* 0
l' aprèm (m.) *afternoon,* 2; cet aprèm *this afternoon,* 2
après-guerre *post-war,* 11
l' après-midi (m.) *afternoon; in the afternoon,* 2; **l'après-midi libre** *afternoon off,* 2
après *after, afterward,* 9; **Et après?** *And afterwards?* 9
l' arabe (m.) *Arabic (language),* 1
l' ardoise (f.) *writing slate,* 3
l' arène (f.) *amphitheater,* 9
l' argent (m.) *money,* 11
l' arrivée (f.) *arrival,* 6
arroser *to sprinkle,* 8
l' artiste (m./f.) *artist,* 0
les arts plastiques (m. pl.) *art class,* 2
as : Tu as... ? *Do you have . . . ?* 3; **Tu as quel âge?** *How old are you?* 1; **De quoi est-ce que tu as besoin?** *What do you need?* 8
l' ascenseur (m.) *elevator,* 6
l' ascension (f.) *ascent, climb,* 6; ascension en haut de la tour *ascent/climb to the top of the tower,* 6
l' aspirateur (m.) *vacuum cleaner,* 7; **passer l'aspirateur** *to vacuum,* 7
l' aspirine (f.) *aspirin,* 12
Asseyez : Asseyez-vous! *Sit down!* 0
assez *enough, fairly,* 2
assidu(e) *regular (punctual),* 2
l' assiette (f.) *plate,* 5
assuré(e) (pp. of assurer) *assured,* 1
l' athlétisme (m.) *track and field,* 4; **faire de l'athlétisme** *to do track and field,* 4
attachant(e) *loving,* 7
attendre *to wait for,* 9
l' attiéké (m.) *ground manioc root,* 8
au *to, at,* 6; *to, in (before a masculine noun),* 11; **au métro...** *at the metro stop,* 6; au milieu *in the middle,* 7; **au revoir** *goodbye,* 1; au secours *help,* 9
l' auberge de jeunesse (f.) *youth hostel,* 11
aucun(e) *none,* 7
aujourd'hui *today,* 2
aussi *also,* 1; **Moi aussi.** *Me too.* 2
l' automne (m.) *autumn, fall,* 4; **en automne** *in the fall,* 4
autour de *around,* 8
autre *other,* 4
aux *to, in (before a plural noun),* 6
Av. (abbrev. of avenue) *avenue,* 6
avant *before,* 1
avec *with,* 1; **avec moi** *with me,* 6; **Avec qui?** *With whom?* 6
avez : Qu'est-ce que vous avez comme ... ? *What kind of . . . do you have?* 5; **Vous avez... ?** *Do you have . . . ?* 2
l' avion (m.) *plane,* 12; **en avion** *by plane,* 12, **un billet d'avion** *plane ticket,* 11
l' avis (m.) *opinion,* 9; **A ton avis, qu'est-ce que je fais?** *In your opinion, what do I do?* 9
l' avocat (m.) *avocado,* 8
avoir *to have,* 2; **avoir faim** *to be hungry,* 5; avoir hâte de *to be in a hurry (to do something),* 7; avoir la flemme *to be lazy,* 9; avoir lieu *to take place,* 7; avoir raison *to be right,* 2; **avoir soif** *to be thirsty,* 5
avons : Nous avons... *We have . . . ,* 2
avril April, 4; **en avril** *in April,* 4
ayant : ayant pu donner *having been able to give,* 2

B

le baby (foot) *table soccer game,* 5
le bac(calauréat) *secondary school exam for entering a university,* 2
le bachelier *someone who has passed the* **bac,** 2
la baguette *long, thin loaf of bread,* 12
la baie *bay*
se balader *to stroll,* 6
la balade à cheval *horseback ride,* 7
le ballon *ball,* 4
le bambou *bamboo,* 12
la banane *banana,* 8
les bandes dessinées (f.) *comic strips,* 2
la banque *bank,* 12
barbant(e) *boring,* 2
le base-ball *baseball,* 4; **jouer au base-ball** *to play baseball,* 4
le basilic *basil,* 5
le basket(-ball) *basketball,* 4; **jouer au basket(-ball)** *to play basketball,* 4
les baskets (f.) *sneakers,* 3
le bateau *boat,* 11; **en bateau** *by boat,* 12; **faire du bateau** *to go boating,* 11
le bâteau-mouche *river boat,* 6
Bd (abbrev. of **boulevard**) (m.) *boulevard,* 6
le beau-père *stepfather; father-in-law,* 7
beau *nice, pretty,* 4; **Il fait beau.** *It's nice weather.* 4
Beaucoup. *A lot.* 4; **Oui, beaucoup.** *Yes, very much.* 2; **Pas beaucoup.** *Not very much.* 4

belge *Belgian* (adj.), 1
la Belgique *Belgium,* 0
la belle-mère *stepmother; mother-in-law,* 7
le besoin *need,* 8; **De quoi est-ce que tu as besoin?** *What do you need?* 8; **J'ai besoin de...** *I need . . . ,* 8
la bête *animal,* 12
le beurre *butter,* 8
la bibliothèque *library,* 6
le bic *ballpoint pen,* 3
bien *well,* 1; **Je veux bien.** *Gladly.* 8; **Je veux bien.** *I'd really like to.* 6; **J'en veux bien.** *I'd like some.* 8; **Moi, j'aime (bien)...** *I (really) like . . . ,* 1; **Très bien.** *Very well.* 1
Bien sûr. *Of course.* 3; *certainly,* 9; **Oui, bien sûr.** *Yes, of course.* 7
bientôt *soon,* 1; **A bientôt.** *See you soon.* 1
le bien-vivre *good living, the good life,* 6
Bienvenue! *Welcome!* 0
le bifteck *steak,* 8
les bijoux (m.) *jewelry,* 10
le billet *ticket,* 11; **un billet d'avion** *plane ticket,* 11; **un billet de train** *train ticket,* 11
la biologie *biology,* 2
bizarre *strange,* 7
blanc(he) *white,* 3
le blanc-manger *coconut pudding*
bleu(e) *blue,* 3; le bleu clair *light blue,* 10; le bleu foncé *dark blue,* 10
blond(e) *blond,* 7
le blouson *jacket,* 10
le bœuf *beef,* 8
Bof! *(expression of indifference),* 1
boire *to drink,* 5; **Qu'est-ce qu'il y a à boire?** *What is there to drink?* 5
la boisson *drink, beverage,* 5; **Qu'est-ce que vous avez comme boissons?** *What do you have to drink?* 5
la boîte *box, can,* 8; **une boîte de** *a can of,* 8
le bon *coupon,* 6
bon *good,* 5; **Bon courage!** *Good luck!* 2; **Bon voyage!** *Have a good trip!* 11; **Bon, d'accord.** *Well, OK.* 8; de bons conseils *good advice,* 1; **Oui, très bon.** *Yes, very good.* 9; **pas bon** *not good,* 5
Bonjour *Hello,* 1
bonne (f. of **bon**) *good,* 5; **Bonne chance!** *Good luck!* 11; **Bonne idée.** *Good idea.* 4; **Bonnes vacances!** *Have a good vacation!* 11
le bord *side, edge;* **au bord de la mer** *to/on the coast,* 11
les bottes (f.) *boots,* 10
les boucles d'oreilles (f.) *earrings,* 10
le boudin créole *spicy creole sausage,* 12
bouger *to move,* 10
bouillant(e) *boiling,* 8
la boulangerie *bakery,* 12
la boule *ball,* 8
la boum *party,* 6; **aller à une boum** *to go to a party,* 6
la bouteille *bottle,* 8; **une bouteille de** *a bottle of,* 8
la boutique *store, shop,* 3; une boutique de souvenirs *souvenir shop,* 3
le bracelet *bracelet,* 3
la brioche *brioche, light slightly sweet bread made with a rich yeast dough,* 8
la brochure *brochure,* 4
la broderie *embroidery,* 10
brun(e) *brunette,* 7
le bulletin trimestriel *report card,* 2
le bus *bus,* 12; **en bus** *by bus,* 12, **rater le bus** *to miss the bus,* 9
la buvette *refreshment stand,* 12

C'est... *It's . . . ,* 2; **C'est...** *This is . . . ,* 7; C'est qui? *Who is it?* 2; **C'est combien?** *How much is it?* 3; C'est du gâteau. *It's a piece of cake.* 8; **C'est... francs.** *It's . . . francs.* 5; C'est pas de la tarte. *It's not easy.* 8; C'est tout. *That's all.* 1; **Ça, c'est...** *This/That is . . . ,* 12; **Non, c'est impossible.** *No, that's impossible.* 7
C'était barbant! *It was boring!* **11**
ça *that; it;* Ça boume? *How's it going?* 2; **Ça va.** *Fine.* 1; **Ça va?** *How are things going?* 1; **Ça, c'est...** *This/That is . . . ,* 12; Ça m'est égal *It doesn't matter; I don't care.* 10; **Ça ne me dit rien.** *That doesn't interest me.* 4; *I don't feel like it.* 6; ça suffit *that's enough,* 12; **Et après ça...** *And after that,. . . ,* 9; **Oui, ça a été.** *Yes, it was fine.* 9
ça fait : Ça fait combien, s'il vous plaît? *How much is it, please?* 5; **Ça fait... francs.** *It's . . . francs.* 5
le cabinet de toilette *small room with a sink and counter,* 11
caché(e) (pp. of cacher) *hidden,* 11
le cadeau *gift,* 11
le café *coffee, café,* 5; le café au lait *coffee with hot milk,* 8; le café crème *coffee with cream,* 5
le cahier *notebook,* 0
la calculatrice *calculator,* 3; une calculatrice-traductrice *translating calculator,* 3
le caleçon *leggings,* 4
la Californie *California,* 4
le caméscope *camcorder,* 4
la campagne *countryside,* 11; **à la campagne** *to/in the countryside,* 11
le camping *camping,* 11; **faire du camping** *to go camping,* 11
le canal *channel,* 3
le canari *canary,* 7
le caniveau *sidewalk gutter,* 7
la cantine *cafeteria,* 9; **à la cantine** *at the school cafeteria,* 9
car *because,* 4
la carcasse *body,* 12
le cardigan *sweater,* 10
la carotte *carrot,* 8
la carrière *quarry,* 11
la carte *map,* 0; à la carte *pick and choose,* 3; **La carte, s'il vous plaît.** *The menu, please.* 5
les cartes (f.) *cards,* 4; **jouer aux cartes** *to play cards,* 4
la cartouche *cartridge,* 3; cartouche d'encre *ink cartridge,* 3
le carvi *cumin* (Afrique), 8; graines de carvi *cumin seeds,* 8
la casquette *cap,* 10
la cassette *cassette tape,* 3
la cassette vidéo *videocassette,* 4
la cathédrale *cathedral,* 1
le cauchemar *nightmare,* 11; **C'était un véritable cauchemar!** *It was a real nightmare!* 11
ce *this; that,* 3; **Ce sont...** *These/Those are . . . ,* 7
la ceinture *belt,* 10
cent *one hundred,* 3; **deux cents** *two hundred,* 3
le centre commercial *mall,* 6
le centre-ville *city center,* 12
cependant *however,* 11
le cercle *circle, group,* 6; au cercle

français *at French Club,* 4
ces *these, those,* 3
cet *this, that,* 3
cette *this; that,* 3
chacun *each (person),* 5; Chacun ses goûts! *To each his own!* 1
la chaise *chair,* 0
chaleureux (-euse) *warm,* 9
la chambre *room,* 7; **ranger ta chambre** *to pick up your room,* 7
le champignon *mushroom,* 8
la chance *luck,* 11; **Bonne chance!** *Good luck!* 11
chanter *to sing,* 9
le chanteur *singer (male),* 9
la chanteuse *singer (female),* 9
Chantilly : la crème Chantilly *sweetened whipped cream,* 5
le chapeau *hat,* 10
chaque *each,* 4
chargé(e) *busy,* 2
le chariot *shopping cart,* 8
la chasse *hunting,* 7; une chasse au trésor *treasure hunt,* 3
le chat *cat,* 7
le chaton *kitten,* 7
chaud *hot,* 4; **Il fait chaud.** *It's hot.* 4
chauffé(e) *heated,* 11
les chaussettes (f.) *socks,* 10
les chaussures (f.) *shoes,* 10; les chaussures à crampons *spikes,* 4
le chef-d'œuvre *masterpiece,* 6
la chemise *shirt (man's),* 10
la chemise *folder,* 3
le chemisier *shirt (woman's),* 10
le chèque *check,* 0
cher (chère) *dear,* 1; *expensive,* 3; **C'est trop cher.** *It's too expensive.* 10
chercher *to look for,* 9; **Je cherche quelque chose pour...** *I'm looking for something for . . . ,* 10
le cheval *horse,* 12; le cheval de bois *wooden horse, carousel horse,* 12
chez... *to/at . . . 's house,* 6; **chez le disquaire** *at the record store,* 12; **Je suis bien chez... ?** *Is this . . . 's house?* 9
chic *chic,* 10
le chien *dog,* 7; **promener le chien** *to walk the dog,* 7
le chiffre *number,* 0
la chimie *chemistry,* 2
chimique *chemical,* 9
le chocolat *chocolate,* 1; **un chocolat** *hot chocolate,* 5
la chocolaterie *chocolate shop,* 12
choisi (pp. of choisir) *decided, chosen;* **Vous avez choisi?** *Have you decided/chosen?* 5
choisir *to choose, to pick,* 10
le choix *choice,* 8
la chorale *choir,* 2
la chose *thing,* 5; **J'ai des tas de choses (trucs) à faire.** *I have lots of things to do.* 5
le chou *cabbage,* 1; mon chou *my darling, dear,* 1
chouette *cool,* 9; **Très chouette.** *Very cool.* 9
chrétien(ne) *Christian,* 9
le cinéma *movie theater,* 6; *movies,* 1
le citron *lemon,* 8
le citron pressé *lemonade,* 5
clair(e) *light (color),* 10
le classeur *loose-leaf binder,* 3
classique *classical,* 4
le climat *climate,* 11
climatisé(e) *air-conditioned,* 11
le coca *cola,* 5
le coco *coconut,* 8
le code de la route *rules of the road; rules of the road test,* 12
le coin *corner,* 12; **au coin de** *on the corner of,* 12
le col *collar,* 10; au col montant *with turtleneck,* 10
le collant *hose,* 10
la colle *glue,* 3; un pot de colle *container of glue,* 3
le collège *junior high school,* 2
la colonie de vacances *summer camp,* 11
le coloris *color, shade,* 3
combien *how much, how many,* 3; **C'est combien,... ?** *How much is . . . ?* 5; **C'est combien?** *How much is it?* 3; **Ça fait combien, s'il vous plaît?** *How much is it, please?* 5
le combiné *(telephone) receiver,* 9
comme *like, as,* 4; **Comme ci, comme ça.** *So-so.* 1; Qu'est-ce qu'ils aiment comme cours? *What subjects do they like?* 2; **Qu'est-ce que tu fais comme sport?** *What sports do you play?* 4; **Qu'est-ce que vous avez comme... ?** *What kind of . . . do you have?* 5
le commencement *beginning,* 9
commencer *to begin, to start,* 9
comment *what,* 0; *how,* 1; **(Comment) ça va?** *How's it going?* 1; Comment dit-on? *How do you say it?* 1; Comment le dire? How should you say it? 1; **Comment tu trouves... ?** *What do you think of . . . ?* 2; **Comment tu trouves ça?** *What do you think of that/it?* 2; **Il/Elle est comment?** *What is he/she like?* 7; **Ils/Elles sont comment?** *What are they like?* 7; **Tu t'appelles comment?** *What is your name?* 0
le commerçant *store owner,* 8
le compagnon *companion,* 7
le compas *compass,* 3
compétent(e) *competent,* 2
compléter *to complete,* 4
compris *included,* 5
compris (pp. of comprendre): Tu as compris? *Did you understand?* 1
le concert *concert,* 1
le concombre *cucumber,* 8
conçu(e) (pp. of concevoir) *conceived,* 9
confier *to confide,* 9
la confiture *jam,* 8
connais : Tu les connais? *Do you know them?* 0
la connaissance *acquaintance;* Faisons connaissance! *Let's get acquainted.* 1
connu(e) (pp. of connaître) *knew; known;* le plus connu *the best-known* (adj.), 6
le conseil *advice,* 1; de bons conseils *good advice,* 1
conseiller *to advise, to counsel;* **Qu'est-ce que tu me conseilles?** *What do you advise me to do?* 9
le conseiller *adviser,* 12
la conseillère *adviser,* 12
conservé(e) (pp. of conserver) *kept,* 2; ce bulletin doit être conservé *this report card must be kept,* 2
content(e) *happy, pleased,* 7
continuer *to continue,* 12; **Vous continuez jusqu'au prochain feu rouge.** *You keep going until the next light.* 12
contre *against,* 2
cool *cool,* 2
le copain (la copine) *friend,* 1
le cordon *cord, string;* le cordon de serrage *drawstring,* 10
le cornichon *pickle,* 8
le corps *body,* 8
le correspondant (la correspondante) *pen pal,* 1
correspondre *to write; to correspond,* 1
le côté *side;* **à côté de** *next to,* 12; du côté de mon père *on*

my father's side (of the family), 7
le coton *cotton,* 10; **en coton** *(made of) cotton,* 10
la couleur *color,* 3; **De quelle couleur est... ?** *What color is . . . ?* 3
le coup *hit, blow;* le coup de fil *phone call,* 9
la coupe *dish(ful),* 5
la coupe melba *vanilla ice cream, peaches, whipped cream, and fruit sauce,* 5
courir *to run,* 7
le cours *course,* 2; **le cours de développement personnel et social (DPS)** *health,* 2; **Tu as quels cours... ?** *What classes do you have . . . ?* 2
les courses (f.) *shopping, errands,* 7; **faire les courses** *to do the shopping,*7; **J'ai des courses à faire.** *I have errands to do.* 5
court(e) *short (length),* 10
le cousin *male cousin,* 7
la cousine *female cousin,* 7
coûteux (-euse) *expensive,* 8
les crabes farcis (m.) *deviled land crabs*
la cravate *tie,* 10
le crayon *pencil,* 3; des crayons de couleur *colored pencils,* 3
créer *to create,* 11
la crêpe *very thin pancake,* 5
la crêperie *café or restaurant which specializes in crêpes,* 5
crépiter *to crackle,* 12
croire *to believe;* Tu crois? *Do you think so?* 10
la croisière *cruise,* 11
la croissanterie *croissant shop,* 12
le croque-monsieur *toasted cheese and ham sandwich,* 5
cru(e) *uncooked,* 5
le cuir *leather,* 10; **en cuir** *(made of) leather,* 10
cuire *to cook, to bake,* 8
culturel(le) *cultural,* 0

D

D'abord, ... *First, . . . ,* 9
D'accord. *OK.* 4; **Bon, d'accord.** *Well, OK.* 8; **D'accord, si tu... d'abord...** *OK, if you. . . , first.* 7; **Tu es d'accord?** *Is that OK with you?* 7
d'habitude *usually,* 4
dans *in,* 6
danser *to dance,* 1
la danse *dance,* 2
de *from,* 0; *of,* 0; **de l'** *some,* 8; **de la** *some,* 8; **Je n'ai pas de...** *I don't have . . . ,* 3; **Je ne fais pas de...** *I don't play/do . . . ,* 4
déambuler *to stroll,* 11
débarrasser la table *to clear the table,* 7
décaféiné(e) *decaffeinated,* 5
décédé(e) *deceased,* 7
décembre *December,* 4; **en décembre** *in December,* 4
le décès *death,* 7
décider *to decide,* 5; **Vous avez décidé de prendre... ?** *Have you decided to take . . . ?* 10
décontracté(e) *relaxed,* 11
la découverte *discovery,* 3
décrocher *to take down; to unhook;* quand l'interlocuteur décroche *when the speaker picks up (the phone),* 9
dedans *inside,* 3
dégoûtant(e) *gross,* 5
dehors *outside,* 8
déjà *already,* 9
déjeuner *to have lunch,* 9; **le déjeuner** *lunch,* 2
délicieux (-euse) *delicious,* 5
délirer *to be delirious;* La techno me fait délirer. *I'm wild about technology.* 1
délivré(e) (pp. of delivrer) : il n'en sera pas délivré de duplicata *duplicates will not be issued,* 2
le deltaplane *hang-glider;* faire du deltaplane *to go hang-gliding,* 4
demain *tomorrow,* 2; **A demain.** *See you tomorrow.* 1
le demi-frère *stepbrother,* 7; *half-brother,* 7
la demi-sœur *stepsister,* 7; *half-sister,* 7
demi(e) *half;* **et demi** *half past (after* **midi** *and* **minuit***),* 6; **et demie** *half past,* 6
démodé(e) *out of style,* 10
le dentiste (la dentiste) *dentist,* 1
le départ *departure,* 6
le département d'outre-mer *overseas department,* 12
dépêchez : Dépêchez-vous de... *hurry up and . . . ,* 1
déplorable *deplorable,* 2
déposer *to deposit,* 12
deprimé(e) *depressed,* 9
depuis *for (a certain amount of time),* 9; *since,* 12
le dérivé *derivative, by-product;* le sucre et ses dérivés *sugar and its by-products,* 8
derrière *behind,* 12
des *some,* 3
les dés (m.) *dice;* découper en dés *to dice,* 8
dès que *as soon as,* 9
désagréable *unpleasant,* 4
désirer *to desire, to want;* **Vous désirez?** *What would you like?* 10
désolé(e) : Désolé(e), je suis occupé(e). *Sorry, I'm busy.* 6; **Désolé(e), mais je ne peux pas.** *Sorry, but I can't.* 4
le dessert *dessert,* 0
le dessin *drawing,* 3
détailler *to slice,* 8
devant *in front of,* 6
deviennent : Que deviennent... ? *What happened to . . . ?* 7
Devine! *Guess!* 0
les devoirs (m.) *homework,* 2; **J'ai des devoirs à faire.** *I've got homework to do.* 5
le dévouement *devotion,* 7
devrais : Tu devrais... *You should . . . ,* 9
la diapo (sitive) *photographic slide,* 11
la dictée *dictation,* 0
le dictionnaire *dictionary,* 3
difficile *difficult,* 2
dimanche *Sunday,* 2; **le dimanche** *on Sundays,* 2
dîner *to have dinner,* 9; **le dîner** *dinner,* 8
dingue *crazy,* 1; Je suis dingue de... *I'm crazy about . . . ,* 1
dire *to say;* 1; *to tell,* 9; Comment le dire? *How should you say it?* 1; Dis,... *Say, . . . ,* 2; **Ça ne me dit rien.** *That doesn't interest me.* 4; Comment dit-on... ? *How do you say . . . ?* 1; Jacques a dit... *Simon says . . . ,* 0; Qu'est-ce qu'on se dit? *What are they saying to themselves?* 2; **Vous pouvez lui dire que j'ai téléphoné?** *Can you tell her/him that I called?* 9
direct(e) *direct;* en direct *live,* 7
la discothèque *dance club,* 6
discuter *to discuss,* 7; Ne discute pas! *Don't argue!* 3
disponible *available,* 8
le disquaire *record store,* 12; **chez le disquaire** *at the record store,* 12
le disque compact/CD *compact disc/CD,* 3
distant(e) *distant,* 2
la distribution *cast (of a movie, play, etc.),* 1; une distribution étincelante *a brilliant cast,* 1
divers *various,* 3
dois : Non, tu dois... *No, you've*

got to . . ., 7
le domicile *place of residence,* 4
dommage *too bad,* 10
donc *so, therefore,* 11
donner *to give,* 5; **Donnez-moi... , s'il vous plaît.** *Please give me . . .*, 5
donner sur *to overlook,* 11
dont *of which,* 7
dormir *to sleep,* 1
le dos *back,* 12; **un sac à dos** *backpack,* 3
doucement *gently,* 12
la douche *shower,* 11; avec douche ou bains *with shower or bath,* 11
doué(e) *gifted, talented,* 2
la douzaine *dozen,* 8; **une douzaine de** *a dozen,* 8
les draps (m.) *linens, sheets,* 11
dressé(e) *pointed,* 7
droit(e) *straight,* 10
la droite *right (direction);* **à droite (de)** *to the right,* 12
du *some,* 8
le duplicata (inv.) *duplicate;* il n'en sera pas délivré de duplicata *duplicates will not be issued,* 2
durable *long-lasting,* 11
durcir *to harden,* 8
la durée *duration,* 7
durer *to last,* 11

E

l' **eau** (f.) *water,* 5; **l'eau minérale** *mineral water,* 5; **le sirop de fraise (à l'eau)** *water with strawberry syrup,* 5
s' ébattre *to frolic,* 7
l' échange (m.) *exchange,* 7; en échange de *in exchange for,* 7
l' échantillon (m.) *sample,* 2
l' **écharpe** (f.) *scarf,* 10
l' échelle (f.) *scale,* 6
s' éclater *to have fun, to have a ball,* 4
l' **école** (f.) *school,* 1; A l'école *At school,* 0
l' économie (f.) *economics,* 2
écouter *to listen,* 1; Ecoute! *Listen!* 0; **écouter de la musique** *to listen to music,* 1; **Ecoutez!** *Listen!* 0; **Je t'écoute.** *I'm listening.* 9
l' écran (m.) *screen,* 11
l' écrin (m.) *case,* 6
écrire *to write,* 2; Ecris-moi. *Write me.* 1
l' édifice (m.) *edifice, building,* 6
l' **éducation physique et sportive (EPS)** (f.) *physical education,* 2; l'éducation civique et morale (f.) *civics class,* 2
efficace *efficient,* 9
égrener *to shell,* 8
égyptien(ne) *Egyptian* (adj.), 6
Eh bien... *Umm . . . (expression of hesitation),* 5
élastique *elastic* (adj.), 3
élémentaire *elementary; basic,* 8
l' éléphant (m.) *elephant,* 0
l' **élève** (m./f.) *student,* 2
l' emballage (m.) *packaging,* 9
embêtant(e) *annoying,* 7
émincer *to slice thinly,* 8
l' émission (f.) *TV program,* 4
empêche (empêcher) *to prevent, to keep from doing,* 2
l' emploi *use; job;* un emploi du temps *schedule,* 2
emprunter *to borrow,* 12
en *in,* 1; **en** *some, of it, of them, any, none,* 8; **en** *to, in (before a feminine country),* 11; **en coton** *(made of) cotton,* 10; **en cuir** *(made of) leather,* 10; en français *in French,* 1; **en jean** *(made of) denim,* 10; en retard *late,* 2; en solde *on sale,* 10; **en vacances** *on vacation,* 4; **Je n'en veux plus.** *I don't want anymore,* 8; **Oui, j'en veux bien.** *Yes, I'd like some.* 8; Qu'en penses-tu? *What do you think (about it)?* 1; **Vous avez ça en... ?** *Do you have that in . . . ? (size, fabric, color),* 10
encore *again, more;* **Encore de... ?** *More. . . ?* 8
l' **endroit** (m.) *place,* 12
énerver *to annoy,* 2
l' **enfant** (m./f.) *child,* 7; l'enfant unique *only child,* 7
enfin *finally,* 9
enjoué(e) *playful,* 7
ennuyer *to bore,* 2
ennuyeux (-euse) *boring,* 11; **C'était ennuyeux.** *It was boring,* 11
l' enquête (f.) *survey,* 1
l' enseignement (m.) *teaching,* 2
ensemble *together,* 4
l' ensemble (m.) *collection, ensemble,* 3
ensuite : Ensuite, ... *Next,/Then, . . .*, 9
entendre *to hear;* s'entendre avec *to get along with,* 7
entendu dire que : Il a entendu dire que... *He heard that . . .*, 12
Entendu. *Agreed.* 6
l' enthousiasme (m.) *enthusiasm,* 2
entier (-ière) *whole, entire;* le monde entier *all over the world,* 1
entrant *entering,* 2
entre *between,* 12
l' entrée (f.) *entry, entrance;* Entrée libre *"Browsers welcomed,"* 3
l' **enveloppe** (f.) *envelope,* 12
l' **envie** (f.) *desire; need;* **J'ai envie de...** *I feel like . . .*, 11
les environs (m. pl.) *surroundings,* 9
s' envoler *to fly away,* 12
envoyer *to send,* 12; **envoyer des lettres** *to send letters,* 12
l' épi (m.) *ear (of a plant),* 8; l'épi de maïs *ear of corn,* 8
l' **épicerie** (f.) *grocery store,* 12
éplucher *to clean, to peel,* 8
l' éponge (f.) *sponge,* 3
épouvantable *terrible, horrible,* 9; **C'était épouvantable.** *It was horrible.* 9
l' équipe interscolaire (f.) *school team,* 4
l' **équitation** (f.) *horseback riding,* 1; **faire de l'équitation** *to go horseback riding,* 1
es : Tu es d'accord? *Is that OK with you?* 7
l' escale (f.) *docking (of a boat),* 11
l' escalier (m.) *staircase,* 6
les escargots (m.) *snails,* 1
l' espace (m.) *space, area,* 7
l' **espagnol** (m.) *Spanish (language),* 2
espère : J'espère que oui. *I hope so.* 1
l' espoir (m.) *hope,* 7
essayer *to try; to try on,* 10; **Je peux essayer... ?** *Can I try on . . . ?* 10; **Je peux l'/les essayer?** *Can I try it/them on?* 10
est : Il/Elle est... *He/She is . . .*, 7; **Quelle heure est-il?** *What time is it?* 6; **Qui est à l'appareil?** *Who's calling?* 9
Est-ce que *(Introduces a yes-or-no question),* 4; **(Est-ce que) je peux... ?** *May I . . . ?* 7
et *and,* 1; **Et après ça...** *And after that, . . .*, 9; **Et toi?** *And you?* 1
l' étage (m.) *floor, story (of a building),* 6
était : C'était épouvantable. *It was horrible.* 9
étaler *to spread,* 8
l' étape (f.) *part,* 1; première étape *first part,* 1; deuxième étape

second part, 1; troisième étape *third part,* 1
l' état (m.) *state,* 0
les Etats-Unis (m. pl.) United States, 0
l' été (m.) *summer,* 4; **en été** *in the summer,* 4
été (pp. of être) *was,* 9
étincelant(e) *brilliant,* 1
étoilé(e) *starry,* 12
étonné(e) (pp. of étonner) *surprised,* 7
étranger (-ère) *foreign,* 11
l' étranger (m.) *foreign countries;* à l'étranger *abroad,* 11
être *to be,* 7; **C'est...** *This is . . . ,* 7; **Ce sont...** *These (those) are . . . ,* 7; **Elle est...** *She is . . . ,* 7; **Il est...** *He is . . . ,* 7; **Il est...** *It is . . . (time),* 6; **Ils/Elles sont...** *They're . . . ,* 7; **Oui, ça a été.** *Yes, it was fine.* 9
l' étude (f.) *study hall,* 2
étudier *to study,* 1
l' euro *European Community monetary unit,* 3
l' Europe (f.) *Europe,* 0
évider *to scoop out,* 8
éviter *to avoid,* 9
l' examen (m.) *exam,* 1; **passer un examen** *to take a test,* 9
excellent(e) *excellent,* 5; **Oui, excellent.** *Yes, excellent.* 9
excusez : Excusez-moi. *Excuse me.* 3
exemplaire *exemplary,* 7

la face *face, side;* **en face de** *across from,* 12
facile *easy,* 2
la façon *way, manner,* 10
la faim *hunger;* **avoir faim** *to be hungry,* 5; **Non, merci. Je n'ai plus faim.** *No thanks. I'm not hungry anymore.* 8
faire *to do, to make, to play,* 4; **Désolé(e), j'ai des devoirs à faire.** *Sorry, I have homework to do.* 5; **J'ai des courses à faire.** *I have errands to do.* 5; **Qu'est-ce que tu vas faire... ?** *What are you going to do . . . ?* 6; **Tu vas faire quoi... ?** *What are you going to do . . . ?* 6; **faire de l'équitation** *to go horseback riding,* 1; faire de la course *to race (running),* 4; faire de la gymnastique *to do gymnastics,* 4; faire des haltères *to lift weights,* 4; **faire du bateau** *to go sailing,* **faire du sport** *to play sports,* 1; faire du surf *to surf,* 4; faire la cuisine *to cook, do the cooking,* 8; **faire la vaisselle** *to do the dishes,* 7; **faire le ménage** *to do housework,* 1; faire les boutiques *to go shopping,* 1; **faire les courses** *to do the shopping,* 7; **faire les magasins** *to go shopping,* 1; **faire les vitrines** *to window-shop,* 6; **faire un pique-nique** *to have a picnic,* 6; **faire une promenade** *to go for a walk,* 6
fais : A ton avis, qu'est-ce que je fais? *In your opinion, what do I do?* 9; Fais-moi... *Make me . . . ,* 3; **Je fais...** *I play/do . . . ,* 4; **Ne t'en fais pas!** *Don't worry!* 9; **Qu'est-ce que tu fais comme sport?** *What sports do you play?* 4; **Qu'est-ce que tu fais pour t'amuser?** *What do you do to have fun?* 4; **Qu'est-ce que tu fais... ?** *What do you do . . . ?* 4
faisons : Faisons connaissance! *Let's get acquainted.* 1
fait : Quel temps fait-il? *What's the weather like?* 4; **Il fait beau.** *It's nice weather.* 4; **Il fait chaud.** *It's hot.* 4; **Il fait frais.** *It's cool.* 4; **Il fait froid.** *It's cold.* 4
fait (pp. of faire) *done, made,* 9; **J'ai fait...** *I did/made . . . ,* 9; **Qu'est-ce que tu as fait?** *What did you do?* 9
la famille *family,* 7
la fantaisie *fancy,* 10
le fantôme *ghost,* 0
la farine *flour,* 8
le fast-food *fast-food restaurant,* 6
faut : Il me faut... *I need . . . ,* 3; **Qu'est-ce qu'il te faut pour... ?** *What do you need for . . . ? (informal),* 3; **Qu'est-ce qu'il te faut?** *What do you need?* 8; **Qu'est-ce qu'il vous faut pour... ?** *What do you need for . . . ? (formal),* 3
le fauve *wildcat,* 6
faux (fausse) *false,* 2
les féculents (m.) *starches,* 8
la féerie *extravaganza,* 11
la femme *wife,* 7
la fenêtre *window,* 0
ferai : je me ferai une joie de... *I'll gladly . . . ,* 1
fermez : Fermez la porte. *Close the door.* 0
la fête *party,* 1; faire la fête *to live it up,* 1
le feu *fire,* 12
le feu rouge *traffic light,* 12; **Vous continuez jusqu'au prochain feu rouge.** *You keep going until the next light.* 12
la feuille *sheet; leaf;* **une feuille de papier** *sheet of paper,* 0
le feutre *marker,* 3
février *February,* 4; **en février** *in February,* 4
la fidélité *loyalty,* 7
le filet *a type of net or mesh bag,* 3
la fille *girl,* 0; **la fille** *daughter,* 7
le film *movie,* 6; **voir un film** *to see a movie,* 6; un film d'aventures *adventure film,* 1
le fil *cord, thread;* sans fil *cordless,* 9
le fils *son,* 7
fils-à-papa *daddy's boy,* 10
la fin *end,* 4
finalement *finally,* 9
fistuleux (-euse) *hollow,* 11
la flamme *flame,* 12
le flanc *side; flank,* 12
le flipper *pinball,* 5
la flûte *flute,* 0
la fois *time;* **une fois par semaine** *once a week,* 4
follement *madly,* 1
foncé(e) *dark (color),* 10
le foot *soccer,* 4
le football *soccer,* 1; **le football américain** *football,* 4; **jouer au foot(ball)** *to play soccer,* 4; **jouer au football américain** *to play football,* 4
la forêt *forest,* 0; **en forêt** *to/in the forest,* 11
formidable : C'était formidable! *It was great!* 11
fort(e) *strong,* 7
fou (folle) *crazy,* 9
le foulard *scarf,* 10
le four *oven,* 8
le fournisseur *supplier,* 8
les fournitures (f. pl.) scolaires *school supplies,* 3
la fourrure *fur,* 7
le foutou *a paste made from boiled plantains, manioc, or yams; It is common in Côte d'Ivoire.* 8
le foyer home, 7
fraîche *cool, cold,* 5
le frais *cool place,* 8; au frais *in a cool place,* 8
les frais (m. pl.) *cost, expenses,* 11
frais *cool (temperature),* 4; **Il fait frais.** *It's cool.* 4
la fraise *strawberry,* 8; **un sirop de fraises (à l'eau)** *water with strawberry syrup,* 5

le franc *(the French monetary unit)*, 3; **C'est... francs.** *It's . . . francs.* 5
le franc de la Communauté financière africaine (CFA) *the currency of francophone Africa*, 8
le français *French (language)*, 1; français(e) *French* (adj.), 0; *À la française* French-style, 2
francophone *French-speaking*, 0
le frère *brother*, 7
les friandises (f.) *sweets*, 6
les frites (f. pl.) *French fries*, 1
froid *cold*, 4; **Il fait froid.** *It's cold.* 4
le fromage *cheese*, 5
la fromagerie *cheese shop*, 12
les fruits (m.) *fruit*, 8
fuit (pp. of fuir) *fled*, 1
le fun *fun*, 4; C'est le fun! (in Canada) *It's fun!* 4

G

gagner *to win, to earn*, 9
le garçon *boy*, 9
garder *to look after*, 7
la gare *train station*, 6
le garrot *withers, shoulder height of an animal, such as a horse*, 7
le gâteau *cake*, 8
la gâterie *little treat*, 9
la gauche *left (direction)*; **à gauche** *to the left*, 12
le gazon *lawn*, 7; **tondre le gazon** *to mow the lawn*, 7
généralement *in general, usually*, 11
génial(e) *great*, 2
le génie *genius*, 6
les genoux (m.) *knees*, 7; une paire de genoux *pair of knees, lap*, 7
les gens (m. pl.) *people*, 9
gentil(le) *nice*, 7
la géographie *geography*, 2
la géométrie *geometry*, 2
la glace *ice cream*, 1
la glace *ice*; **faire du patin à glace** *to ice-skate*, 4
le golf golf, 4; **jouer au golf** *to play golf*, 4
les gombos (m.) *okra*, 8
la gomme *eraser*, 3
la gosse *kid*, 2; être traité comme une gosse *to be treated like a kid*, 2
le gouache *paint*, 3
le goûter *afternoon snack*, 8
goûter *to taste*, 8
le goût (m.) *taste*, 4
la goyave *guava*, 8
grâce à *thanks to*, 11
gradué(e) *graduated*, 3; une règle graduée *graduated ruler*, 3
la graine *seed*, 8
la grammaire *grammar*, 1
grand(e) *tall*, 7; *big*, 10
grand-chose : Pas grand-chose. *Not much*. 6
la grand-mère *grandmother*, 7
le grand-père *grandfather*, 7
grandir *to grow*, 10
gratuit(e) *free*, 6
grec *Greek* (adj.), 6
gris(e) *grey*, 3
gros(se) *fat*, 7
grossir *to gain weight*, 10
la grotte *cave*, 11
le groupe *musical group*, 2
la Guadeloupe *Guadeloupe*, 0
le guichet *ticket window*, 6
la Guyane Française *French Guiana*, 0

H

habitant : habitant le monde entier *living all over the world*, 1
habite : J'habite à... *I live in . . .*, 1
l' habitude (f.) *habit*, 4; **d'habitude** *usually*, 4
habituellement *usually*, 2
* haché(e) (pp of hacher) *minced*, 8
Haïti (no article) *Haiti*, 0
***le hamburger** *hamburger*, 1
*les haricots (m.) *beans*, 8; **les haricots verts** (m. pl.) *green beans*, 8
*la harpe *harp*, 11
*la hâte *hurry, haste;* Elle a hâte de... *She can't wait to . . .*, 7
* haut(e) *tall, high*, 6
*le haut-parleur *loudspeaker*, 11
*le havre *haven*, 7
l' hébergement (m.) *lodging*, 6
l' hélicoptère (m.) *helicopter*, 0
*le héros *hero*, 11
hésite : Euh... J'hésite. *Well, I'm not sure*. 10
l' heure (f.) *hour; time*, 1; **à l'heure de** *at the time of*, 1; **A quelle heure?** *At what time?* 6; **A tout à l'heure!** *See you later!* 1; l'heure officielle *official time (24-hour system)*, 2; **Quelle heure est-il?** *What time is it?* 6; **Tu as... à quelle heure?** *At what time do you have . . . ?* 2
heures *o'clock*, 2; **à... heures** *at . . . o'clock*, 2; **à... heures quarante-cinq** *at . . . forty-five*, 2; **à... heures quinze** *at . . . fifteen*, 2; **à... heures trente** *at . . . thirty*, 2
heureusement *luckily, fortunately*, 4
heureux (-euse) *happy;* **Très heureux-(-euse).** *Pleased to meet you.* 7
hier *yesterday*, 9
l' histoire (f.) *history*, 2
l' hiver (m.) *winter*, 4; **en hiver** *in the winter*, 4
***le hockey** *hockey*, 4; **jouer au hockey** *to play hockey*, 4
l' hôpital (pl. -aux) *hospital*, 0
horrible *terrible*, 10
***le hot-dog** *hot dog*, 5
l' hôtel (m.) *hotel* 0
*le houx *holly*, 11
l' huile d'olive (f.) *olive oil*, 5
* hurler *to shriek, to cry out*, 12

I

l' idée (f.) *idea*, 4; **Bonne idée.** *Good idea.* 4
l' identité (f.) *identity;* une photo d'identité *photo ID*, 1
l' igloo (m.) *igloo*, 0
l' igname (f.) *yam*, 8
il y a *there is, there are*, 5; il y a du soleil/du vent *it's sunny/windy*, 4; **Qu'est-ce qu'il y a à boire?** *What is there to drink?* 5
l' île (f.) *island*, 0
imagines : Tu imagines? *Can you imagine?* 4
imprimé(e) *printed*, 10
inaperçu(e) *unnoticed*, 11
inclus(e) *included*, 6
incompétent(e) *incompetent*, 2
incroyable *unbelievable*, 9
l' informatique (f.) *computer science*, 2
intelligent(e) *smart*, 7
l' intention (f.) *intention;* **J'ai l'intention de...** *I intend to . . .*, 11
l' interclasse (m.) *break (between classes)*, 2
intéressant(e) *interesting*, 2
international(e) *international*, 5
l' interphone (m.) *intercom*, 9
l' interro(gation) (f.) *quiz*, 9; **rater une interro** *to fail a quiz*, 9
intervenu(e) (pp. of intervenir) *intervened*, 9

l' interviewé(e) (m./f.) *interviewee,* 2
intime *personal,* 1
l' invité(e) (m./f.) *guest,* 8
ivoirien(ne) *from the Republic of Côte d'Ivoire,* 1

jamais : ne... jamais *never,* 4
le jambon *ham,* 5
janvier *January,* 4; **en janvier** *in January,* 4
le jardin *garden,* 0
jaune *yellow,* 3
le jazz *jazz,* 4
je *I,* 0
le jean *(pair of) jeans,* 3; **en jean** *made of denim,* 10
le jeu *game;* un jeu de rôle *role-playing exercise,* 1; **jouer à des jeux vidéo** *to play video games,* 4
jeudi *Thursday,* 2; **le jeudi** *on Thursdays,* 2
jeune *young,* 7; les jeunes *youths,* 4
le jogging *jogging,* 4; **faire du jogging** *to jog,* 4
la joie *joy,* 1
joignant (joindre) *attached,* 1
joli(e) *pretty,* 4
jouer *to play,* 4; **Je joue...** *I play . . . ,* 4; **Je ne joue pas...** *I don't play . . . ,* 4; **jouer à...** *to play (a game) . . . ,* 4
joueur (-euse) *playful,* 7
le jour *day,* 2; le jour férié (m.) *holiday,* 6
le journal *journal,* 1; *newspaper,* 12
la journée *day,* 2
juillet *July,* 4; **en juillet** *in July,* 4
juin *June,* 4; **en juin** *in June,* 4
la jupe *skirt,* 10
le jus d'orange *orange juice,* 5
le jus de fruit *fruit juice,* 5
le jus de pomme *apple juice,* 5
jusqu'à *up to, until,* 12; **Vous allez tout droit jusqu'à...** *You go straight ahead until you get to . . . ,* 12
juste *just,* 4

K

le kangourou *kangaroo,* 0
le kilo(gramme) *kilogram,* 8; **un kilo de** *a kilogram of,* 8

L

la *the,* 1; *her, it* (f.), 9
là *there,* 12; **-là** *there (noun suffix),* 3; **(Est-ce que)... est là, s'il vous plaît?** *Is . . . , there, please?* 9; là-bas *there; over there,* 8
laid(e) *ugly,* 9
la laine *wool,* 10
laisser *to leave,* 9; **Je peux laisser un message?** *Can I leave a message?* 9
le lait *milk,* 8
laitier (-ière) *dairy,* 8; **les produits laitiers (m.)** *dairy products,* 8
la langue *language,* 1
large *baggy,* 10
le latin *Latin, (language),* 2
laver *to wash,* 7; **laver la voiture** *to wash the car,* 7
le *the,* 1; *him, it,* 9
la légèreté *lightness,* 6
les légumes (m.) *vegetables,* 8
la lettre *letter,* 12; **envoyer des lettres** *to send letters,* 12
les *the,* 1; *them,* 9
leur *to them,* 9
leur/leurs *their,* 7
levez : Levez la main! *Raise your hand!* 0; **Levez-vous!** *Stand up!* 0
la librairie *bookstore,* 12
la librairie-papeterie *bookstore and stationary store,* 3
libre *free,* 2
liégeois : café ou chocolat liégeois *coffee or chocolate ice cream with whipped cream,* 5
le lieu *place;* avoir lieu *to take place,* 7; ... aura lieu... *. . . will take place . . . ,* 7
la limonade *lemon soda,* 5
le lin *linen,* 10
le lion *lion,* 0
le liquide correcteur *correction fluid,* 3
lire *to read,* 1
lisons : Lisons! *Let's read!* 1
la litote *understatement,* 5
le litre *liter,* 8; **un litre de** *a liter of,* 8
la livraison *delivery,* 12
la livre *pound,* 8; **une livre de** *a pound of,* 8
le livre *book,* 0
le livret scolaire *a student's personal gradebook,* 3
la location *rental,* 4
loin *far,* 12; **loin de** *far from,* 12
long(ue) *long,* 10
la longueur *length,* 10
louer *to rent,* 12
la Louisiane *Louisiana,* 0
lu (pp. of lire) *read,* 9
lui *to him, to her,* 9
lundi *Monday,* 2; **le lundi** *on Mondays,* 2
les lunettes de soleil (f. pl.) *sunglasses,* 10
le Luxembourg *Luxembourg,* 0
le lycée *high school,* 2
le lycéen *high school student,* 2

ma *my,* 7
madame (Mme) *ma'am; Mrs.,* 1; **Madame!** *Waitress!* 5
mademoiselle (Mlle) *miss; Miss,* 1; **Mademoiselle!** *Waitress!* 5
le magasin *store,* 1; **faire les magasins** *to go shopping,* 1
le magazine *magazine,* 3
le magnétoscope *videocassette recorder,* VCR, 0
mai *May,* 4; **en mai** *in May,* 4
maigrir *to lose weight,* 10
le maillot de bain *bathing suit,* 10
la main *hand,* 0
maintenant *now,* 2; **Je ne peux pas maintenant.** *I can't right now.* 8
le maire *mayor,* 12
la mairie *city hall,* 4
mais *but,* 1
le maïs *corn,* 8
la Maison des jeunes et de la culture (MJC) *recreation center,* 6
le maître *master, owner,* 7
maîtriser *to master,* 4
la majorité *majority,* 2
mal *bad,* 1; **Pas mal.** *Not bad.* 1
la malchance *misfortune,* 7
le mâle *male (refers to animals),* 7
malheureusement *unfortunately,* 7
le Mali *Mali,* 0
la manche *sleeve,* 10
le manchot *penguin,* 6
le manège *carousel,* 12
manger *to eat,* 6
la mangue *mango,* 8
manqué(e) (pp. of manquer) *missed;* garçon manqué *tomboy,* 10
manque : Qu'est-ce qui manque? *What's missing?* 2
le manteau *coat,* 10
le marché *market,* 8
mardi *Tuesday 2;* **le mardi** *on Tuesdays,* 2
le mari *husband,* 7

le mariage *marriage*, 7
le Maroc *Morocco*, 0
marocain(e) *Moroccan* (adj.), 1
marron (inv.) *brown*, 3
mars *March*, 4; **en mars** *in March*, 4
martiniquais(e) *from Martinique*, 1
la Martinique *Martinique*, 0
le match *game*, 6; **regarder un match** *to watch a game (on TV)*, 6; **aller voir un match** *to go see a game (in person)*, 6
les maths (les mathématiques) (f. pl.) *math*, 1
la matière *school subject*, 2
les matières grasses (f.) *fat*, 8
le matin *morning; in the morning*, 2
mauvais(e) *bad*, 5; **C'est pas mauvais!** *It's pretty good!* 5; **Oh, pas mauvais.** *Oh, not bad.* 9; **Très mauvais.** *Very bad.* 9
méchant(e) *mean*, 7
mécontent(e) *unhappy*, 2
les médicaments (m.) *medicine*, 12
meilleur(e) *best*, 7; les meilleurs amis *best friends*, 7
mélanger *to mix*, 8
méli-mélo *mishmash*, 1
la mémé *granny, grandma*, 9
le ménage *housework*, 1; **faire le ménage** *to do housework*, 1
le mensuel *monthly publication*, 9
méprisant(e) *contemptuous*, 2
la mer *sea;* **au bord de la mer** *to/on the coast*, 11
Merci. *Thank you*, 3; **Non, merci.** *No, thank you.* 8
mercredi *Wednesday*, 2; **le mercredi** *on Wednesdays*, 2
la mère *mother*, 7
mes *my*, 7
le message *message*, 9; **Je peux laisser un message?** *May I leave a message?*, 9
le métro *subway*, 12; **au métro...** *at the . . . metro stop*, 6; **en métro** *by subway*, 12
métropolitain(e) *metropolitan*, 2
mets : mets en ordre *put into order*, 6
mettre *to put, to put on, to wear*, 10; **Je ne sais pas quoi mettre pour...** *I don't know what to wear for (to) . . . ,* 10; **Mets...** *Wear . . . ,* 10; **Qu'est-ce que je mets?** *What shall I wear?* 10
meublé(e) *furnished*, 11
miam, miam *yum-yum*, 5
midi *noon*, 6; **Il est midi.** *It's noon.* 6; **Il est midi et demi.** *It's half past noon.* 6
mieux *better*, 9; **Ça va aller mieux!** *It's going to get better!* 9; **J'aime mieux...** *I prefer . . . ,* 1
mignon(ne) *cute*, 7
mince *slender*, 7
minuit *midnight*, 6; **Il est minuit.** *It's midnight.* 6; **Il est minuit et demi.** *It's half past midnight.* 6
la minute *minute*, 9; **Tu as une minute?** *Do you have a minute?* 9
la mise en scène *production*, 1
la mise *putting, setting;* mise en pratique *putting into practice*, 1; mise en train *getting started*, 1
mixte *mixed*, 5
le mobilier *furniture*, 6
la mobylette *motor scooter*, 11
moche *tacky*, 10
le mode d'emploi *instructions*, 9
la mode *style*, 10; **à la mode** *in style*, 10; à la dernière mode *in the latest fashion*, 10
modéré(e) *moderate*, 11
moi *me*, 2; **Moi aussi.** *Me too.* 2; **Moi, non.** *I don't.* 2; **Moi non plus.** *Neither do I.* 2; **Moi, si.** *I do.* 2; **Pas moi.** *Not me.*
moins *(with numbers) minus, lower*, 0; **moins cinq** *five to*, 6; **moins le quart** *quarter to*, 6
le mois *month*, 4
le moment *moment*, 5; **Un moment, s'il vous plaît.** *One moment, please.* 5
mon *my*, 7
Monaco *Monaco*, 0
le monde *world*, 0
le moniteur *monitor*, 12
monsieur (M.) *sir (Mr.)* 1; **Monsieur!** *Waiter!* 5
le monstre *monster*, 0
la montagne *mountain*, 4; **à la montagne** *to/in the mountains*, 11
la montée *ascent*, 6
la montre *watch*, 3
montrer *to show*, 9
le monument *monument*, 6
se moquer de *to make fun of*, 9
le moral *morale*, 2
le morceau *piece*, 8; **un morceau de** *a piece of*, 8
le motif *reason*, 9
la moto(cyclette) *motorcycle*, 12
le moulin *windmill*, 9
la mousseline *chiffon*, 8
la moutarde *mustard*, 8
moyen(ne) *average*, 2; travail moyen *average work*, 2
la moyenne *average*, 2
le musée *museum*, 6
la musique *music*, 2; **écouter de la musique** *to listen to music*, 1; la musique classique *classical music*, 4
le mystère *mystery*, 5

nager *to swim*, 1
le nain *dwarf*, 6
la naissance *birth*, 7
la natation *swimming*, 4; **faire de la natation** *to swim*, 4
nautique *nautical;* **faire du ski nautique** *to water ski*, 4
ne : ne... pas *not*, 1; **ne... pas encore** *not yet*, 9; **ne... jamais** *never*, 4; **ne... ni grand(e) ni petit(e)** *neither tall nor short*, 7
né(e) (pp. of naître) *born*, 9
la Négritude *movement which asserts the values and spirit of black African civilizations*, 0
neige : Il neige. *It's snowing.* 4
le neveu *nephew*, 7
la nièce *niece*, 7
le Niger *Niger*, 0
le niveau *level*, 6
le nocturne *late-night opening*, 6
le Noël *Christmas*, 0
noir(e) *black*, 3
la noisette *hazelnut*, 5
la noix *nut*, 5
la noix de coco *coconut*, 8
le nom *name*, 1; nom de famille *last name*
le nombre *number*, 2
non *no*, 1; **Moi non plus.** *Neither do I.* 2; **Moi, non.** *I don't.* 2; **Non, c'est...** *No, it's . . . ,* 4; **Non, merci.** *No, thank you.* 8; **Non, pas trop.** *No, not too much.* 2
nos *our*, 7
notre *our*, 7
la Nouvelle-Angleterre *New England*, 0
les nouvelles (f.) *news*, 9
novembre *November*, 4; **en novembre** *in November*, 4
le nuage *cloud*, 12
nul(le) *useless*, 2
le numéro *number*, 0; un numéro de téléphone *telephone number*, 3; les numéros *issues (for magazines, etc.)*, 3

l' objet (m.) *object*, 6; objets trouvés *lost and found*, 3

occupé(e) : C'est occupé. *It's busy.* 9; **Désolé(e), je suis occupé(e).** *Sorry, I'm busy.* 6; s'occuper de *to take care of,* 7
octobre *October,* 4; **en octobre** *in October,* 4
l' odeur (f.) *aroma; smell,* 8
l' œil (m.) *eye,* 12
l' œuf (m.) *egg,* 8
l' oignon (m.) *onion,* 8
l' oiseau (m.) *bird,* 12
ombragé(e) (pp. of ombrager) *shaded,* 11
l' omelette (f.) *omelette,* 5
on *one, we, you, they,* 1; Comment dit-on... ? *How do you say . . . ?* 1; On est dans la purée. *We're in trouble.* 8; **On fait du ski?** *How about skiing?* 5; **On joue au base-ball?** *How about playing baseball?* 5; **On peut...** *We can . . . ,* 6; **On va au café?** *Shall we go to the café?* 5; **On... ?** *How about . . . ?* 4
l' oncle (m.) *uncle,* 7
opulent(e) *rich,* 7
l' or (m.) *gold,* 12
orange (inv.) *orange (color),* 3
l' orange (f.) *orange,* 8; **le jus d'orange** *orange juice*
l' ordinateur (m.) *computer,* 3
l' otarie (f.) *sea lion,* 6
ôter *to cut out,* 8
ou *or,* 1
où *where,* 6; **Où (ça)?** *Where?* 6; **Où est-ce que tu vas aller... ?** *Where are you going to go . . . ?* 11; **Tu es allé(e) où?** *Where did you go?* 9
oublier *to forget,* 9; **Je n'ai rien oublié.** *I didn't forget anything.* 11; **Oublie-le/-la/-les!** *Forget him/her/them!* 9; J'ai oublié. *I forgot.* 3; **N'oublie pas de...** *Don't forget . . . ,* 8; **Tu n'as pas oublié... ?** *You didn't forget . . . ?* 11
oui *yes,* 1; **Oui, c'est...** *Yes it's . . . ,* 4; **Oui, s'il te/vous plaît.** *Yes, please.* 8
ouvert(e) *open,* 6
l' ouverture (f.) *opening,* 6
ouvrez : Ouvrez vos livres à la page... *Open your books to page . . . ,* 0

P

la page *page,* 0
la pagne *a piece of dyed African cloth,* 10
le pain *bread,* 8
le palais *palace,* 1; le palais de justice *court, courthouse,* 1
le pamplemousse *grapefruit,* 5
le panier *basket,* 3
le pantalon *pair of pants,* 10
la papaye *papaya,* 8
la papeterie *stationery store,* 12; librairie-papeterie *bookstore/stationery store,* 3
le papier *paper,* 0; **des feuilles** (f.) **de papier** *sheets of paper,* 3
le paquet *package, box,* 8; **un paquet de** *a package/box of,* 8
par *by,* 12; *per,* 6; par hasard *by chance,* 12; prix par personne *price per person,* 6
le parachute *parachute,* 0
paraître *to appear; seem,* 12
le parapluie *umbrella,* 11
le parc *park,* 6
parce que *because,* 5; **Je ne peux pas parce que...** *I can't because . . . ,* 5
Pardon. *Pardon me.* 3; **Pardon, madame... , s'il vous plaît?** *Excuse me, ma'am . . . , please?* 12; **Pardon, monsieur. Je cherche... , s'il vous plaît.** *Excuse me, sir. I'm looking for. . . , please.* 12
le parent *parent; relative,* 7
paresseux (-euse) *lazy,* 2
parfait(e) *perfect,* 3; **C'est parfait.** *It's perfect.* 10
parfois *sometimes,* 4
parfumer *to flavor,* 8
parlé (pp. of parler) *talked, spoke,* 9; **Nous avons parlé.** *We talked.* 9
parler *to talk,* 1; *to speak,* 9; **(Est-ce que) je peux parler à... ?** *Could I speak to. . . ?* 9; **Je peux te parler?** *Can I talk to you?* 9; **parler au téléphone** *to talk on the phone,* 1; Parlons! *Let's talk!* 2
partagé(e) *split, shared,* 6
partir *to leave,* 11; **Tu ne peux pas partir sans...** *You can't leave without . . . ,* 11
pas *not,* **1: pas bon** *not good,* 5; **Pas ce soir.** *Not tonight.* 7; pas content du tout *not happy at all,* 2; **Il/Elle ne va pas du tout avec...** *It doesn't go at all with . . . ,* 10; **Pas grand-chose.** *Not much.* 6; **Pas mal.** *Not bad.* 1; **pas mauvais** *not bad,* 9; **Pas question!** *Out of the question!* 7; **pas super** *not so hot,* 2; **Pas terrible.** *Not so great.* 1
les passe-temps (m. pl.) *pastimes,* 4
passé : Ça s'est bien passé? *Did it go well?* 11; **Qu'est-ce qui s'est passé?** *What happened?* 9; **Tu as passé un bon week-end?** *Did you have a good weekend?* 9
le passeport *passport,* 11
passé (pp. of passer) : **Qu'est-ce qui s'est passé?** *What happened?* 9; **Tu as passé un bon week-end?** *Did you have a good weekend?* 9
passer *to pass,* 12; *to go by,* 12; **Tu pourrais passer à... ?** *Could you go by . . . ?* 12; **Vous passez...** *You'll pass . . . ,* 12; **passer l'aspirateur** *to vacuum,* 7; **passer un examen** *to take a test,* 9
passerais : je passerais le bac... *I would take bac . . . ,* 2
passionnant(e) *fascinating,* 2
la pastille *tablet,* 3
la pâte *dough,* 8; la pâte d'arachide *peanut butter,* 8; la pâte de tomates *tomato paste,* 8
le pâté *pâté,* 0
les pâtes (f. pl.) *pasta,* 11
le patin *skating,* 1; **faire du patin à glace** *to ice skate,* 4
le patin à roulettes *rollerskating,* 4
le patinage *skating,* 4
patiner *to skate,* 4
la patinoire *skating rink,* 6
la pâtisserie *pastry shop, pastry,* 12
le patrimoine *heritage,* 6
patronal(e) *having to do with saints;* la fête patronale *patron saint's holiday,* 12
les pattes d'eph (f. pl.) *bell-bottoms,* 10
pauvre *poor,* 7
le pays *country,* 6
le paysage *landscape,* 11
la pêche *peach,* 8
la peinture *painting,* 6
pendant *during,* 1
pénible *annoying,* 7
penser *to think;* **J'ai pensé à tout.** *I've thought of everything.* 11; Qu'en penses-tu? *What do you think (about it)?* 1
perdre *to lose,* 9
le père *father,* 7
permettre *to allow,* 9
le permis de conduire *driver's license,* 12; le permis accompagné *learner's permit (driving),* 12; le permis probatoire *learner's permit (driving),* 12
le personnage *individual, character,* 9

personnel(le) *personal,* 4
le petit copain *boyfriend,* 2
le petit déjeuner *breakfast,* 8
petit(e) *short (height),* 7; *small (size),* 10; petites annonces *classified ads,* 1
le petit-fils *grandson,* 7
la petite copine *girlfriend,* 2
la petite-fille *granddaughter,* 7
les petits pois (m.) *peas,* 8
les petits-enfants (m.) *grandchildren,* 7
peu *not very,* 2; à peu près *about, approximately,* 9; peu content *not very happy,* 2; un peu *a little,* 6
peut : On peut... *We can . . . ,* 6
peut-être *maybe; perhaps,* 11
peux : Désolé(e), mais je ne peux pas. *Sorry, but I can't.* 4; **Tu peux... ?** *Can you . . . ?* 8
la pharmacie *drugstore,* 12
la philosophie *philosophy,* 2
le phoque *seal,* 6
la photo *picture, photo,* 4; **faire de la photo** *to do photography,* 4; **faire des photos** *to take pictures,* 4
la photographie *photography,* 1
les photographies (f. pl.) *photographs,* 6
la phrase *sentence,* 4
la physique *physics,* 2
la pièce *play,* 6; **voir une pièce** *to see a play,* 6
le pied *foot,* 12; **à pied** *on foot,* 12
le pinceau *paintbrush,* 3
la pince : des pantalons à pinces *pleated pants,* 10
le pingouin *penguin,* 0
le pique-nique *picnic,* 6; **faire un pique-nique** *to have a picnic,* 6
la piscine *swimming pool,* 6
la pizza *pizza,* 1
la plage *beach,* 1
le plaisir *pleasure, enjoyment,* 4; **Oui, avec plaisir.** *Yes, with pleasure.* 8
plaît : Il/Elle me plaît, mais il/elle est cher/chère. *I like it, but it's expensive.* 10; **Il/Elle te/vous plaît?** *Do you like it?* 10; Ça te plaît? *Do you like it?* 2; **s'il vous/te plaît** *please,* 3
la planche *board;* **faire de la planche à voile** *to go windsurfing,* 11
la plaque *plate (of metal or glass);* la plaque d'immatriculation *license plate,* 0
les plats à emporter (m.) *food to go,* 11
pleut : Il pleut. *It's raining.* 4
la plongée *diving;* **faire de la plongée** *to go scuba diving,* 11
plus *plus (math),* 2; *(with numbers) higher,* 0; **Je n'en veux plus.** *I don't want any more,* 8; **Moi non plus.** *Neither do I.* 2; **Non, merci. Je n'ai plus faim.** *No thanks. I'm not hungry anymore.* 8
la poche *pocket,* 10
le poème *poem,* 0
la poire *pear,* 8
le poisson *fish,* 7
la poissonnerie *fish shop,* 12
la poitrine *chest,* 10
le poivre *pepper,* 8
le poivron *green or red pepper,* 5
la pollution *pollution,* 1
la pomme *apple,* 8; **jus de pomme** *apple juice,* 5
la pomme de terre (f.) *potato,* 8
le pompiste *gas pump attendant,* 11
le porc *pork,* 8
la porte *door,* 0
le porte-monnaie *change purse,* 5
le portefeuille *wallet,* 3
porter *to wear,* 10
le portugais *Portuguese (language),* 2
la poste *post office,* 12
le poster *poster,* 0
le pot de colle *container of glue,* 3
la poubelle *trashcan,* 7; **sortir la poubelle** *to take out the trash,* 7
la poudre *powder,* 8
la poule *(animal) chicken* 8
le poulet *chicken (meat),* 8
pour *for,* 2; **Qu'est-ce qu'il te faut pour...** *What do you need for . . . ? (informal),* 3; **Qu'est-ce que tu fais pour t'amuser?** *What do you do to have fun?* 4
pourquoi *why,* 0; **Pourquoi est-ce que tu ne mets pas... ?** *Why don't you wear . . . ?* 10; **Pourquoi pas?** *Why not?* 6; **Pourquoi tu ne... pas?** *Why don't you . . . ?* 9
pourtant *yet; nevertheless,* 9
pourrais : Tu pourrais passer à ...? *Could you go by . . . ?* 12
pouvoir *to be able to, can,* 8; **(Est-ce que) je peux... ?** *May I . . . ?* 7; **Tu peux... ?** *Can you . . . ?* 8; **Je ne peux pas maintenant.** *I can't right now.* 8; **Je peux te parler?** *Can I talk to you?,* 9; **Non, je ne peux pas.** *No, I can't.* 12; **On peut...** *We can . . . ,* 6; **Qu'est-ce que je peux faire?** *What can I do?* 9; **(Est-ce que) tu pourrais me rendre un petit service?** *Could you do me a favor?* 12; **Tu pourrais passer à... ?** *Could you go by . . . ?,* 12
précieusement *carefully,* 2
précisant : en précisant *specifying,* 1
préféré(e) *favorite,* 4
la préférence *preference,* 3
préférer *to prefer,* 1; **Je préfère...** *I prefer . . . ,* 1
premier (-ière) *first,* 1
prendre *to take or to have (food or drink),* 5; **Je vais prendre... , s'il vous plaît.** *I'm going to have . . . , please.* 5; **On peut prendre...** *We can take . . . ,* 12; **Prends...** *Get . . . ,* 8; *Have . . . ,* 5; **Je le/la/les prends.** *I'll take it/them.* 10; **Tu prends... ?** *Will you have . . . ?,* 8; *Are you taking. . . ?,* 11; **Prenez une feuille de papier.** *Take out a sheet of paper.* 0; **Vous prenez... ?** *What are you having?* 5; *Will you have . . . ?,* 8 **Prenez la rue... puis traversez la rue...** *You take . . . Street, then cross . . . Street,* 12; **Vous avez décidé de prendre... ?** *Have you decided to take . . . ?* 10; **Vous le/la/les prenez?** *Are you going to take it/them?* 10
le prénom *first name,* 1
près *close,* 12 **près de** *close to,* 12
présenter: *to introduce;* **Je te (vous) présente...** *I'd like you to meet . . . ,* 7; Présente-toi! *Introduce yourself!* 0
prévoir *to anticipate,* 4
prévu(e) (pp. of prévoir) *planned;* **Je n'ai rien de prévu.** *I don't have any plans.* 11
principal(e) *main;* la ville principale *main city,* 12
le printemps *spring,* 4; **au printemps** *in the spring,* 4
pris (pp. of prendre) *took, taken,* 9
le prisonnier *prisoner,* 4
le prix *price,* 6
le problème *problem,* 9; **J'ai un petit problème.** *I've got a little problem.* 9

prochain(e) *next,* 12; **Vous continuez jusqu'au prochain feu rouge.** *You keep going until the next light.* 12
les produits laitiers (m.) *dairy products,* 8
le prof(esseur) *teacher,* 0
les progrès (m.) *progress,* 11
la promenade *walk,* 6; **faire une promenade** *to go for a walk,* 6
promener *to walk,* 6; **promener le chien** *to walk the dog,* 7
promets (promettre) *to promise,* 1
prononcer *to pronounce,* 1; prononcent : ne se prononcent pas *no response,* 2
la prononciation *pronunciation,* 2
la protéine *protein,* 8
le publiphone à cartes *card-operated telephone,* 9
puis *then,* 12; **Prenez la rue... puis traversez la rue...** *Take . . . Street, then cross . . . Street,* 12
le pull(-over) *pullover sweater,* 3
la punition *punishment,* 9

qu'est-ce que *what,* 1; **Qu'est-ce qu'il te faut pour... ?** *What do you need for . . . ?* (informal), 3; **Qu'est-ce qu'il vous faut pour... ?** *What do you need for . . . ?* (formal), 3; Qu'est-ce qu'il y a dans...? *What's in the . . . ?* 3; Qu'est-ce qu'il y a? *What's wrong?* 2; Qu'est-ce qu'on fait? *What are we/they doing?* 4; **Qu'est-ce que je peux faire?** *What can I do?* 9; **Qu'est-ce que tu as fait... ?** *What did you do . . . ?* 9; **Qu'est-ce que tu fais... ?** *What do you do . . . ?* 4; **Qu'est-ce que tu vas faire... ?** *What are you going to do . . . ?* 6; **Qu'est-ce que vous avez comme boissons?** *What do you have to drink?* 5; **Qu'est-ce qu'il y a à boire?** *What is there to drink?* 5; Qu'est-ce qui manque? *What's missing?* 2
qu'est-ce qui *what* (subj.), 9; **Qu'est-ce qui s'est passé?** *What happened?* 9
quand *when,* 6; **Quand (ça)?** *When?* 6
le quart *quarter,* 6; **et quart** *quarter past,* 6; **moins le quart** *quarter to,* 6
que *that; what,* 1; Que sais-je? *Self-check (What do I know?),* 1
le Québec *Quebec,* 0
québécois(e) *from Quebec,* 1
quel(le) *what, which,* 1; Ils ont quels cours? *What classes do they have?* 2; **Tu as quel âge?** *How old are you?* 1; **Tu as quels cours... ?** *What classes do you have . . . ?* 2; **Tu as... à quelle heure?** *At what time do you have . . . ?* 2; **Quelle heure est-il?** *What time is it?* 6; **Quel temps fait-il?** *What's the weather like?* 4
quelqu'un *someone,* 1
quelque chose *something,* 6; **Je cherche quelque chose pour...** *I'm looking for something for . . . ,* 10
quelquefois *sometimes,* 4
la question *question,* 0
le questionnaire *questionnaire, survey,* 4
qui *who,* 0; **Avec qui?** *With whom?* 6; C'est qui? *Who is it?* 2; Qui suis-je? *Who am I?* 0
la quiche *quiche: a type of custard pie with a filling, such as ham, bacon, cheese, or spinach,* 5
quittez : Ne quittez pas. *Hold on.* 9
quoi *what,* 10; **De quoi est-ce que tu as besoin?** *What do you need?* 5; **Je ne sais pas quoi mettre pour...** *I don't know what to wear for/to . . . ,* 10; **Tu as quoi... ?** *What do you have. . .?* 2 **Tu vas faire quoi?** *What are you going to do?* 6
quotidien(ne) *everyday,* 6

le rabat *flap,* 3
le raccourci *short cut,* 2
raconter *to tell,* 9
la radio *radio,* 3
le radis *radish,* 8
le raisin *grapes,* 8
la randonnée *hike,* 11; **faire de la randonnée** *to go hiking,* 11
ranger *to arrange, straighten;* **ranger ta chambre** *to pick up your room,* 7
le rap *rap music,* 1
râpé(e) (pp. of râper) *grated,* 8
rappeler *to call back,* 9; **Vous pouvez rappeler plus tard?** *Can you call back later?* 9; Tu te rappelles? *Do you remember?* 3
rapporter *to bring back,* 8; **Rapporte-moi...** *Bring me back . . . ,* 8; **Tu me rapportes... ?** *Will you bring me . . . ?* 8
rarement *rarely,* 4
rater *to fail,* 9; *to miss,* 9; **rater le bus** *to miss the bus,* 9; **rater une interro** *to fail a quiz,* 9
le rayon *department,* 3; au rayon de musique *in the music department,* 3
la rayonne *rayon,* 10
la réalité *reality,* 11
la recette *recipe,* 8
recevoir *to receive,* 1
la récréation *break,* 2
recueilli (pp. of recueillir) *to take in,* 7
refaire *to redo, remake,* 8
réfléchir *to think about,* 2; *to reflect;* Réfléchissez. *Think about it.* 2
le reflet *reflection,* 10
le refuge *animal shelter,* 7
le réfugié *refugee,* 1
le refus *refusal,* 6
le regard *look,* 7
regarder *to look,* 10; *to watch,* 1; **Non, merci, je regarde.** *No, thanks, I'm just looking.* 10; **Regarde, voilà...** *Look, here's/there's/it's . . . ,* 12; **regarder la télé** *to watch TV,* 1; **regarder un match** *to watch a game (on TV),* 6; **Regardez la carte!** *Look at the map!* 0
la règle *ruler,* 3
regrette : Je regrette. *Sorry.* 3; **Je regrette, mais je n'ai pas le temps.** *I'm sorry, but I don't have time.* 8
regroupé(e) *rearranged,* 6
rejoint (pp. of rejoindre) *rejoined,* 7
relier *to connect,* 9
le remboursement *repayment,* 9
la rencontre *encounter,* 1
rencontrer *to meet,* 9
rendre *to return something,* 12; **Rendez-vous...** *We'll meet . . . ,* 6; pour les rendre plus originales *to make them more original,* 10
le renfort *reinforcement;* renforts aux épaules *reinforced shoulder seams,* 10

les renseignements (m.) *information*, 9
la rentrée *back to school*, 2
le repas *meal*, 8
le répertoire *index*, 9
répéter *to rehearse, practice*, 9; **Répétez!** *Repeat!* 0
le répondant *respondent*, 4
le répondeur *answering machine*, 9
répondre *to answer*, 9; **Ça ne répond pas.** *There's no answer.* 9
la réponse *response, answer*, 2
reposer *to rest; to relax;* laisser reposer *to let stand*, 8; se reposer *to relax*, 11
la République de Côte d'Ivoire *the Republic of Côte d'Ivoire*, 0
respectueux (-euse) *respectful*, 2
ressemblez : si vous me ressemblez *if you're like me*, 1
le restaurant *restaurant*, 6
la restauration *dining*, 6
le resto *restaurant*, 11
retard : en retard *late*, 2
retirer *to take out, to remove;* **retirer de l'argent** *to withdraw money*, 12
le retour *return*, 6
rétro (inv.) *retro*, 10
retrouve : Bon, on se retrouve... *OK, we'll meet . . .*, 6
retrouver *to find again*, 6
la Réunion *the island of Réunion*, 0
rêvait (imp. of rêver) *to dream*, 7
le rêve *dream*, 11
revenir *to come back*, 5
ridicule *ridiculous*, 10
rien *nothing*, 6; *anything*, 11; **Ça ne me dit rien.** *I don't feel like it.* 4; **Je n'ai rien oublié.** *I didn't forget anything.* 11; **Rien de spécial.** *Nothing special.* 6
rigoler *to laugh*, 10
le riz *rice*, 8
la robe *dress*, 10
le rock *rock (music)*, 4
le roller *skate;* **faire du roller en ligne** *to in-line skate*, 4
romain(e) *Roman* (adj.), 9
le roman *novel*, 3
rond(e) *round*, 12
ronronner *to purr*, 7
le rosbif *roast beef*, 5
rose *pink*, 3
la rose *rose*, 0
le rôti *roast*, 5
rouge *red*, 3
le rouleau *roll*, 3; un rouleau protège-livres *a roll of plastic material to protect books*, 3
rouspètent (rouspéter) *to complain*, 9
roux (rousse) redheaded, 7
le ruban *ribbon; tape;* ruban adhésif transparent *transparent adhesive tape*, 3
la rue street, 12

S

s'il te plaît (informal) *please*, 3; **Oui, s'il te plaît.** *Yes, please.* (informal), 8
s'il vous plaît *please*, 3 (formal); **Oui, s'il vous plaît.** *Yes, please.* (formal), 8
sa *his, her*, 7
le sac *bag;* **le sac à dos** *backpack*, 3
sage *wise*, 12
sais : Je n'en sais rien. *I have no idea.* 11; **Je ne sais pas.** *I don't know.* 10; Que sais-je? *Self-check (What do I know?)*, 1
la saison *season*, 4; la basse saison *off season*, 12; la haute saison *tourist season*, 12
la salade *salad*, 8
les salades (f.) *heads of lettuce*, 8
saler *to salt*, 8
la salle *room*, 2; la salle de classe *classroom*, 2
Salut *Hi! or Goodbye!* 1
samedi *Saturday*, 2; **le samedi** *on Saturdays*, 2
les sandales (f.) *sandals*, 10
le sandwich *sandwich*, 5; **un sandwich au fromage** *cheese sandwich*, 5; **un sandwich au jambon** *ham sandwich*, 5; **un sandwich au saucisson** *salami sandwich*, 5;
sans *without*, 3; sans doute *probably*, 10
la sauce arachide *sauce made of peanut butter with beef chicken, or fish, hot peppers, peanut oil, garlic, onions, tomato paste, tomatoes, and other vegetables*, 8
la sauce pimentée *spicy sauce*, 8
le saucisson *salami*, 5
savais : Savais-tu que... ? *Did you know . . . ?* 2
savoir *to know*, 1
scellé(e) (pp. of sceller) *sealed*, 9
la science-fiction *science fiction*, 1
les sciences naturelles (f. pl.) *natural science*, 2
scolaire *having to do with school*, 2; la vie scolaire *school life*, 2
la séance *showing (at the movies)*, 6
la seconde *second*, 9; **Une seconde, s'il vous plaît.** *One second, please.* 9
le secours *aid, help;* le poste de secours *first-aid station*, 6
le séjour *stay, residence*, 7
le sel *salt*, 8
selon *according to*, 8
la semaine *week*, 4; **une fois par semaine** *once a week*, 4
le Sénégal *Senegal*, 0
sensas (sensationnel) *fantastic*, 10
septembre *September*, 4; **en septembre** *in September*, 4
sera : ce sera *it will be*, 6
le serpent *snake*, 0
serré(e) *tight*, 10
service compris *tip included*, 5
le service *service*, 3; **A votre service.** *At your service; You're welcome*, 3
ses *his, her*, 7
le sésame *sesame*, 8
sévère *severe, harsh*, 0
le short *(pair of) shorts*, 3
si *yes (to contradict a negative question)*, 2; **Moi, si.** *I do.* 2; **Oui, si tu veux.** *Yes, if you want to.* 7
le siècle *century*, 5
le signe *sign*, 12
sinon *otherwise; other than that*, 9
le sirop de fraise (à l'eau) *water with strawberry syrup*, 5
le ski *skiing*, 1; **faire du ski** *to ski*, 4; **faire du ski nautique** *to water-ski*, 4
la sœur *sister*, 7
la soie *silk*, 10
la soif *thirst;* **avoir soif** *to be thirsty*, 5
soigné(e) *with attention to detail*, 10
soigneusement *carefully*, 11
le soir *evening; in the evening*, 4; **Pas ce soir.** *Not tonight.* 7
sois *(command form of être)* : Ne sois pas découragée! *Don't be discouraged!* 9
soit *either;* soit chez moi, ou bien chez eux *whether at my house or at theirs*, 5
les soldes (m.) *sales*, 6
le soleil *sun, sunshine*, 4
le solfège *music theory*, 4
le sommet *top; summit*, 6
son *his, her*, 7
le sondage *poll*, 1
la sonnerie *ringing (of the telephone)*, 9
sont : Ce sont... *These/Those are . . .*, 7; **Ils/Elles sont...** *They are . . .*, 7; **Ils/Elles sont**

comment? *What are they like?* 7
sorti(e) (pp. of sortir) *went out,* 9; **Après, je suis sorti(e).** *Afterwards, I went out.* 9
la sortie *dismissal (when school gets out),* 2
sortir *to go out,* 1; *to take out,* 7; **sortir avec les copains** *to go out with friends,* 1; **sortir la poubelle** *to take out the trash,* 7
souterrain(e) *underground,* 11
souvent *often,* 4
spécial(e) *special,* 6; **Rien de spécial.** *Nothing special.* 6
le spectacle *show,* 11
le sport *gym,* 2; *sports,* 1; **faire du sport** *to play sports,* 1; **Qu'est-ce que tu fais comme sport?** *What sports do you play?* 4
le sportif (la sportive) *sportsman (sportswoman),* 4
le stade *stadium,* 6
la stalactite *stalactite,* 11
la station-service *service station, gas station,* 11
le steak-frites *steak and French fries,* 5
le style *style;* **C'est tout à fait ton style.** *It looks great on you!* 10
le stylo *pen,* 0; un stylo plume *fountain pen,* 3
la subvention *subsidy,* 7
le sucre *sugar,* 8
sucré(e) *sweet,* 8
suis : Qui suis-je? *Who am I?* 0; **Désolé(e), je suis occupé(e).** *Sorry, I'm busy.* 6; **Je suis bien chez . . . ?** *Is this . . . . 's house?* 9
suisse *Swiss* (adj.), 1; la Suisse *Switzerland,* 0
suivre *to follow,* 9
super *super,* 2; **Super!** *Great!* 1; **pas super** *not so hot,* 2
le supermarché *supermarket,* 8
supportez (supporter) *to put up with,* 2
sur *on;* sur place *on-site,* 4; sur un total de *out of a total of,* 4
le surligneur *highlighting marker,* 3
surtout *especially,* 1
le sweat-shirt *sweatshirt,* 3
sympa (inv.; abbrev. of **sympathique**) *nice,* 7

ta *your,* 7
le tableau *blackboard,* 0
la tache *spot,* 7
la taille *size,* 10; taille unique *one size fits all,* 10; **en taille...** *in size. . . ,* 10
la taille élastiquée *elastic waist,* 10
le taille-crayon *pencil sharpener,* 3
tant : tant privée que professionelle *private as well as professional,* 9
la tante *aunt,* 7
le tarif : tarif réduit *reduced fee,* 6
la tarte *pie,* 8
le tas *pile, heap;* **J'ai des tas de choses à faire.** *I have lots of things to do.* 5
le taux de réussite *rate of success,* 2
le taxi *taxi,* 12; **en taxi** *by taxi,* 12
le Tchad *Chad,* 0
Tchao! *Bye!* 1
la techno *techno music,* 1
le tee-shirt *T-shirt,* 3
la télécarte *phone card,* 9
le télécopieur *fax machine,* 9
le téléphone *telephone,* 0; **parler au téléphone** *to talk on the phone,* 1; le téléphone à pièces *coin-operated telephone,* 9; le téléphone sans fil *cordless telephone,* 9
téléphoné (pp. of téléphoner) *called, phoned,* 9; **Vous pouvez lui dire que j'ai téléphoné?** *Can you tell him/her that I called?* 9
téléphoner *to call, to phone,* 9; **Téléphone-lui/-leur!** *Call him/her/them!* 9
la télévision *television,* 0; **regarder la télé(vision)** *to watch TV,* 1
tellement *so; so much;* **Pas tellement.** *Not too much.* 4
le temps *time,* 4; *weather,* 4; **de temps en temps** *from time to time,* 4; **Je regrette, mais je n'ai pas le temps.** *I'm sorry, but I don't have time.* 8; Quel temps est-ce qu'il fait à... ? *How's the weather in . . . ?* 4; **Quel temps fait-il?** *What's the weather like?* 4
le tennis *tennis,* 4; **jouer au tennis** *to play tennis,* 4
la tenue *outfit;* une tenue de gymnastique *gym suit,* 3
la terminale *final year of French high school, usually spent preparing for the* **bac**, 2
termine (terminer) *to finish,* 2
terrible *terrible, awful;* **Pas terrible.** *Not so great.* 1
le territoire d'outre-mer *overseas territory,* 12
tes *your,* 7
le théâtre *theater,* 6; **faire du théâtre** *to do drama,* 4
théorique *theoretical,* 12
le thon *tuna,* 5
Tiens! *Hey!* 3
tient (tenir) *to hold,* 12
le tilleul *lime green,* 10
le timbre *stamp,* 12
timide *shy,* 7
le tissue *cloth, fabric,* 10
toi *you,* 1; **Et toi?** *And you?* 1
le tollé *outcry,* 12
la tomate *tomato,* 8
tomber *to fall,* 10
ton *your,* 7
tondre *to mow,* 7; **tondre le gazon** *to mow the lawn,* 7
le tour *measurement;* tour de poitrine *chest size,* 10
tournez : Vous tournez... *You turn . . . ,* 12
le tournoi *tournament,* 4
tous *all,* 2
tout(e) *all,* 2; **A tout à l'heure!** *See you later!* 1; **J'ai pensé à tout.** *I've thought of everything.* 11; pas du tout *not at all,* 2; **Il/Elle ne va pas du tout avec...** *It doesn't go at all with . . . ,* 10; **C'est tout à fait ton style.** *It looks great on you!* 10; **tout de suite** *right away,* 6; **C'est tout de suite à...** *It's right there on the . . . ,* 12; **J'y vais tout de suite.** *I'll go right away.* 8; **Vous allez tout droit jusqu'à...** *You go straight ahead until you get to . . . ,* 12; tout(e) seul(e) *all alone,* 12
le train *train,* 12; **en train** *by train,* 12; **un billet de train** *train ticket,* 11
traité : être traité comme une gosse *to be treated like a kid,* 2
le trajet *route,* 12
la tranche *slice,* 8; **une tranche de** *a slice of,* 8
le travail scolaire *school work,* 2
travailler *to work,* 9; travailler la pâte *to knead the dough,* 8
les travaux pratiques (m. pl.) *lab,* 2
traverser *to cross,* 12
très *very,* 1; **Très bien.** *Very well.* 1; **Très heureux (heureuse).** *Pleased to meet you.* 7
le trésor *treasure,* 3; chasse au trésor *treasure hunt,* 3

la trompette *trumpet,* 0
trop *too (much),* 10; **Il/Elle est trop cher/chère.** *It's too expensive.* 10; **Non, pas trop.** *No, not too much.* 2
la trousse *pencil case,* 3
trouver *to find,* 9; **Comment tu trouves ça?** *What do you think of that/it?* 2; **Comment tu trouves... ?** *What do you think of . . . ?* 2; **Je le/la/les trouve...** *I think it's/they're . . . ,* 10; Tu trouves? *Do you think so?* 10
le truc *thing,* 5; **J'ai des trucs à faire.** *I have some things to do.* 5
tu *you,* 0
la Tunisie *Tunisia,* 0

un (m.) *a, an,* 3
une (f.) *a, an,* 3
l' uniforme (m.) *uniform,* 0
utiliser *to use,* 10

va : Ça va. *Fine.* 1; **(Comment) ça va?** *How's it going?* 1; **Comment est-ce qu'on y va?** *How can we get there?* 12; **Il/Elle me va?** *Does it suit me?* 10; **Il/Elle ne te/vous va pas du tout.** *It doesn't look good on you at all.* 10; **Il/Elle ne va pas du tout avec...** *It doesn't go at all with . . . ,* 10
les vacances (f. pl.) *vacation,* 1; **Bonnes vacances!** *Have a good vacation!* 11; **en colonie de vacances** *to/at a summer camp,* 11; **en vacances** *on vacation,* 4
vais : Je vais... *I'm going . . . ,* 6; *I'm going (to) . . . ,* 11; **J'y vais tout de suite.** *I'll go right away.* 8
la vaisselle *dishes,* 7; **faire la vaisselle** *to do the dishes,* 7
valable *valid,* 6
la valise *suitcase,* 11
la vanille *vanilla,* 8
vas : Qu'est-ce que tu vas faire? *What are you going to do?* 6
la vedette *celebrity,* 1
le vélo *biking,* 1; **à vélo** *by bike,* 12; **faire du vélo** *to bike,* 4
le vendeur *salesperson,* 3
la vendeuse *salesperson,* 3
vendre *to sell,* 9
vendredi *Friday,* 2; **le vendredi** *on Fridays,* 2
la vente *sales,* 6
la verdure *vegetation,* 11
véritable *real,* 11; **C'était un véritable cauchemar!** *It was a real nightmare!* 11
le verre *glass,* 6
vers *about,* 6
vert(e) *green,* 3
la veste *suit jacket, blazer,* 10
le vêtement *clothing item,* 10
veux : Je veux bien. *I'd really like to.* 6; **Tu veux... avec moi?** *Do you want . . . with me?* 6
la viande *meat,* 8
vide *empty,* 12
la vidéo *video,* 4; **faire de la vidéo** *to make videos,* 4; **des jeux vidéo** *video games,* 4
la vidéocassette *videotape,* 3
la vie scolaire *school life,* 2
viennois(e) *Viennese* (adj.), 5
viens : Tu viens? *Will you come?* 6
vietnamien(ne) *Vietnamese* (adj.), 1
vieux *old,* 4
la ville *city,* 12
le vinaigre *vinegar,* 8
la violence *violence,* 1
violet(te) *purple,* 3
la virgule *comma,* 3
visiter *to visit (a place),* 9
le visiteur *visitor,* 9
vite *fast, quickly,* 2
la vitrine *window (of a shop);* **faire les vitrines** *to window-shop,* 6
vivant *lively, living,* 7
Vive... ! *Hurray for . . . !* 3
vivre *to live,* 2
le vocabulaire *vocabulary,* 1
Voici... *Here's . . . ,* 7
Voilà. *Here.* 3; Voilà... *There's . . . ,* 7
la voile *sailing,* 11; **faire de la planche à voile** *to go wind-surfing,* 11; **faire de la voile** *to go sailing,* 11
voir *to see,* 6; **voir un film** *to see a movie,* 6; **aller voir un match** *to go see a game,* 6; **voir une pièce** *to see a play,* 6
le voisin (la voisine) *neighbor,* 1
la voiture *car,* 7; **en voiture** *by car,* 12; **laver la voiture** *to wash the car,* 7
la voix *voice,* 3
le volley(-ball) *volleyball,* 4; **jouer au volley(-ball)** *to play volleyball,* 4
volontiers *with pleasure; gladly,* 8
vos *your,* 7
votre *your,* 7
voudrais : Je voudrais... *I'd like . . .* 3
vouloir *to want,* 6; **Je n'en veux plus.** *I don't want any-more.* 8; **Je veux bien.** *I'd really like to.* 6; *Gladly.* 8; **Oui, j'en veux bien.** *Yes, I'd like some.* 8; **Oui, si tu veux.** *Yes, if you want to.* 7; **Tu veux... ?** *Do you want . . . ?* 6; **voulez : Vous voulez... ?** *Do you want . . . ?* 8
vous *you,* 1
le voyage *voyage, trip,* 0
voyager *to travel,* 1; **Bon voy-age!** *Have a good trip!* 11
vrai(e) *true,* 2
vraiment *really,* 11; **Non, pas vraiment.** *No, not really.* 11
vu (pp. of voir) *seen, saw,* 9
la vue *view,* 6

le week-end *on weekends,* 4; *weekend,* 6
le western western (movie), 0

le xylophone *xylophone,* 0

y *there,* 12; **Allons-y!** *Let's go!* 4; **Comment est-ce qu'on y va?** *How can we get there?* 12; **J'y vais tout de suite.** *I'll go right away.* 8; **On peut y aller...** *We can go there . . . ,* 12
les yaourts (m.) *yogurt,* 8
les yeux (m. pl.) *eyes,* 8
le yo-yo *yo-yo,* 0
la yole *skiff (a type of boat),* 12

le zèbre *zebra,* 0
zéro *a waste of time,* 2
le zoo *zoo,* 6
Zut! *Darn!* 3

ENGLISH-FRENCH VOCABULARY

In this vocabulary, the English definitions of all active French words in the book have been listed, followed by the French. The number after each entry refers to the chapter in which the entry is introduced. It is important to use a French word in its correct context. The use of a word can be checked easily by referring to the chapter where it appears.

French words and phrases are presented in the same way as in the French-English vocabulary.

a *un, une,* 3
able: to be able to *pouvoir,* 8
about *vers,* 6
across from *en face de,* 12
adore *adorer,* 1; **I adore . . .** *J'adore...* , 1
advise *conseiller;* **What do you advise me to do?** *Qu'est-ce que tu me conseilles?* 9
aerobics *l'aérobic* (f.), 4; **to do aerobics** *faire de l'aérobic,* 4
after *après,* 9; **And after that, . . .** *Et après ça...,* 9
afternoon *l'après-midi* (m.), 2; **afternoon off** *l'après-midi libre,* 2; **in the afternoon** *l'après-midi,* 2
afterwards *après,* 9; **Afterwards, I went out.** *Après, je suis sorti(e).* 9; **And afterwards?** *Et après?* 9
Agreed. *Entendu.* 6
algebra *l'algèbre* (f.), 2
all *tout(e)*: **Not at all.** *Pas du tout.* 4
already *déjà,* 9
also *aussi,* 1
am: I am . . . years old. *J'ai... ans.* 1
an *un, une,* 3
and *et,* 1
annoying *embêtant(e),* 7; *pénible,* 7
answer *répondre,* 9; **There's no answer.** *Ça ne répond pas.* 9
any (of it) *en,* 8; **any more: I don't want any more.** *Je n'en veux plus.* 8
anything: I didn't forget anything. *Je n'ai rien oublié.* 11
apple *la pomme,* 8
apple juice *le jus de pomme,* 5
April *avril,* 4
are: These/those are . . . *Ce sont...* , 7; **They're . . .** *Ils/Elles sont...* , 7
art class *les arts plastiques* (m. pl.), 2
at *à la, au, a l', aux,* 6; **at . . . fifteen** *à... heure(s) quinze,* 2; **at . . . forty-five** *à... heure(s) quarante-cinq,* 2; **at . . . thirty** *à... heure(s) trente,* 2; **at . . . ('s) house** *chez...* , 6; **at the record store** *chez le disquaire,* 12; **At what time?** *A quelle heure?* 6
August *août,* 4
autumn *l'automne* (m.), 4
aunt *la tante,* 7
avocado *l'avocat* (m.), 8

backpack *le sac à dos,* 3
bad *mauvais(e),* 5; **Not bad.** *Pas mal.* 1; **Oh, pas mauvais.** *Oh, not bad.* 9; **Very bad.** *Très mauvais.* 9
bag *le sac,* 3
baggy *large,* 10
bakery *la boulangerie,* 12
banana *la banane,* 8
bank *la banque,* 12
baseball *le base-ball,* 4; **to play baseball** *jouer au base-ball,* 4
basketball *le basket(-ball),* 4; **to play basketball** *jouer au basket (-ball),* 4
bathing suit *le maillot de bain,* 10
be *être,* 7
be able to, can *pouvoir,* 8; **Can you . . . ?** *Tu peux... ?* 12
beach *la plage,* 1
beans *les haricots* (m.), 8; **green beans** *les haricots verts* (m.), 8
because *parce que,* 5
beef *le bœuf,* 8
begin *commencer,* 9
behind *derrière,* 12
belt *la ceinture,* 10
better *mieux,* 9; **It's going to get better!** *Ça va aller mieux!* 9
between *entre,* 12
big *grand(e),* 10
bike *le vélo; faire du vélo,* 4; **by bike** *à vélo,* 12
biking *le vélo,* 1
binder: loose-leaf binder *le classeur,* 3
biology *la biologie,* 2
black *noir(e),* 3
blackboard *le tableau,* 0; **Go to the blackboard!** *Allez au tableau!* 0
blazer *la veste,* 10
blond *blond(e),* 7
blue *bleu(e),* 3
boat *le bateau,* 11; **by boat** *en bateau,* 12; **to go boating** *faire du bateau,* 11
book *le livre,* 0
bookstore *la librairie,* 12
boots *les bottes* (f.), 10
boring *barbant(e),* 2; **It was boring.** *C'était ennuyeux.* 11; *C'était barbant!* 11
borrow *emprunter,* 12
bottle *la bouteille,* 8; **a bottle of** *une bouteille de,* 8
box *le paquet,* 8; **a package/box of** *un paquet de,* 8
boy *le garçon,* 8
bracelet *le bracelet,* 3
bread *le pain,* 8; **long, thin loaf of bread** *la baguette,* 12
break *la récréation,* 2
breakfast *le petit déjeuner,* 8
bring *apporter,* 9; **Bring me back . . .** *Rapporte-moi...* , 8; **Please bring me . . .** *Apportez-moi...* , *s'il vous plaît.* 5; **Will you bring me . . . ?** *Tu me rapportes... ?* 8
brother *le frère,* 7
brown *marron* (inv.), 3
brunette *brun(e),* 7
bus *le bus,* 12; **by bus** *en bus,* 12; *to miss the bus* **rater le bus,** 9
busy *occupé(e),* 6; **It's busy.** *C'est occupé.* 9; **Sorry, I'm busy.** *Désolé(e), je suis occupé(e).* 6
but *mais,* 1
butter *le beurre,* 8
buy *acheter,* 9; **Buy (me) . . .** *Achète(-moi)...* , 8
Bye! *Tchao!* 1

cafeteria *la cantine,* 9; **at the school cafeteria** *à la cantine,* 9
cake *le gâteau,* 8
calculator *la calculatrice,* 3
call *téléphoner,* 9; **Call him/her/them!** *Téléphone-lui/-leur!* 9; **Can you call back later?** *Vous pouvez rappeler plus*

tard? 9; **Who's calling?** *Qui est à l'appareil?* 9
camera *l'appareil-photo* (m.), 11
camp *la colonie de vacances,* 11; **to/at a summer camp** *en colonie de vacances,* 11
camping *le camping,* 11; **to go camping** *faire du camping,* 11
can: to be able to, can *pouvoir,* 8; **Can I talk to you?** *Je peux te parler?* 9; **Can you . . . ?** *Est-ce que tu peux... ?* 12; **Can you . . . ?** *Tu peux... ?* 8; **Can I try on . . . ?** *Je peux essayer... ?* 10; **We can . . .** *On peut...* , 6; **What can I do?** *Qu'est-ce que je peux faire?* 9
can *la boîte,* 8; **a can of** *une boîte de,* 8
can't: I can't right now. *Je ne peux pas maintenant.* 8; **No, I can't.** *Non, je ne peux pas.* 12
canary *le canari,* 7
cap *la casquette,* 10
car *la voiture,* 7; **by car** *en voiture,* 12; **to wash the car** *laver la voiture,* 7
cards *les cartes* (f.), 4; **to play cards** *jouer aux cartes,* 4
carrot *la carotte,* 8
cassette tape *la cassette,* 3
cat *le chat,* 7
CD/compact disc *le disque compact/le CD,* 3
Certainly. *Bien sûr.* 9
chair *la chaise,* 0
check *l'addition* (f.), 5; **The check, please.** *L'addition, s'il vous plaît.* 5
cheese *le fromage,* 5; **toasted cheese and ham sandwich** *le croque-monsieur,* 5
chemistry *la chimie,* 2
chic *chic* (inv.), 10
chicken (animal) *la poule,* 8; **chicken meat** *le poulet,* 8
child *l'enfant* (m./f.), 7; **children** *les enfants,* 7
chocolate *le chocolat,* 1; **hot chocolate** *un chocolat,* 5
choir *la chorale,* 2
choose *choisir,* 10; **Have you chosen?** *Vous avez choisi?* 5
class *le cours,* 2; **What classes do you have . . . ?** *Tu as quels cours... ?* 2
clean: to clean house *faire le ménage,* 7
clear: to clear the table *débarrasser la table,* 7
close: Close the door! *Fermez la porte!* 0
close to *près de,* 12
clothing *les vêtements,* 10
coast *le bord,* 11; **to/on the coast** *au bord de la mer,* 11
coat *le manteau,* 10
coconut *la noix de coco,* 8
coffee *le café,* 5
cola *le coca,* 5
cold *froid,(e)* 4; **It's cold.** *Il fait froid.* 4
color *la couleur,* 3; **What color is . .?** *De quelle couleur est... ?* 3
come: Will you come? *Tu viens?* 6
compact disc/CD *le disque compact/le CD,* 3
computer *l'ordinateur* (m.), 3
computer science *l'informatique* (f.), 2
concert *le concert,* 1
continue *continuer,* 12
cool *cool,* 2; **It's cool out.** *Il fait frais.* 4; **Very cool (great).** *Très chouette.* 9
corn *le maïs,* 8
corner *le coin,* 12; **on the corner of** *au coin de,* 12
cotton (adj.) *en coton* 10
could: Could you do me a favor? *(Est-ce que) tu peux me rendre un petit service?* 12; **Could you go by . . . ?** *Tu pourrais passer à... ?* 12
countryside *la campagne,* 11; **to/in the countryside** *à la campagne,* 11
course *le cours,* 2
course: Of course. *Bien sûr.* 3
cousin *le cousin (la cousine),* 7
cross *traverser,* 12
cute *mignon(ne),* 7

D

dairy products *les produits* (m.) *laitiers,* 8
dance *danser,* 1
dance *la danse,* 2
Darn! *Zut!* 3
daughter *la fille,* 7
day *le jour,* 2
December *décembre,* 4; **in December** *en décembre,* 4
decided: Have you decided? *Vous avez choisi?* 5; **Have you decided to take . . . ?** *Vous avez décidé de prendre... ?* 10
delicious *délicieux(-euse),* 5
denim *le jean,* 10; **in denim** *en jean,* 10
deposit *déposer,* 12; **to deposit money** *déposer de l'argent,* 12
dictionary *le dictionnaire,* 3
difficult *difficile,* 2
dinner *le dîner,* 8; **to have dinner** *dîner,* 9
dishes *la vaisselle,* 7; **to do the dishes** *faire la vaisselle,* 7
dismissal (when school gets out) *la sortie,* 2
do *faire,* 4; **Do you play/do . . . ?** *Est-ce que tu fais... ?* 4; **I do.** *Moi, si.* 2; **to do homework** *faire les devoirs,* 7; **to do the dishes** *faire la vaisselle,* 7; **I don't play/do . . .** *Je ne fais pas de...* , 4; **I have errands to do.** *J'ai des courses à faire.* 5; **I play/do . . .** *Je fais...* , 4; **In your opinion, what do I do?** *A ton avis, qu'est-ce que je fais?* 9; **Sorry. I have homework to do.** *Désolé(e). J'ai des devoirs à faire.* 5; **What are you going to do . . . ?** *Qu'est-ce que tu vas faire... ?* 6; *Tu vas faire quoi... ?* 6; **What can I do?** *Qu'est-ce que je peux faire?* 9; **What did you do . . . ?** *Qu'est-ce que tu as fait... ?* 9; **What do you advise me to do?** *Qu'est-ce que tu me conseilles?* 9; **What do you do . . . ?** *Qu'est-ce que tu fais... ?* 4; **What do you do when . . . ?** *Qu'est-ce que tu fais quand... ?* 4
dog *le chien,* 7; **to walk the dog** *promener le chien,* 7
done, made *fait* (pp. of faire), 9
door *la porte,* 0
down: You go down this street to the next light. *Vous continuez jusqu'au prochain feu rouge.* 12
dozen *la douzaine,* 8; **a dozen** *une douzaine de,* 8
drama *le théâtre,* 4; **to do drama** *faire du théâtre,* 4
dress *la robe,* 10
drink *la boisson,* 5; **What do you have to drink?** *Qu'est-ce que vous avez comme boissons?* 5; **What is there to drink?** *Qu'est-ce qu'il y a à boire?* 5
drugstore *la pharmacie,* 12

E

earn *gagner,* 9
earrings *les boucles d'oreilles* (f.), 10
easy *facile,* 2
eat *manger,* 6
egg *l'œuf* (m.), 8
English (language) *l'anglais* (m.), 1
envelope *l'enveloppe* (f.), 12
eraser *la gomme,* 3
errands *les courses* (f.), 7; **I have errands to do.** *J'ai des courses à faire.* 5
especially *surtout,* 1
evening *le soir,* 4; **in the evening** *le soir,* 4
everything *tout,* 11; **I've thought of everything.** *J'ai pensé à tout.* 11

exam *l'examen* (m.), 1
excellent *excellent(e),* 5; **Yes, excellent.** *Oui, excellent.* 9
excuse: Excuse me. *Excusez-moi.* 3; **Excuse me, . . . , please?** *Pardon, ... s'il vous plaît?* 12; **Excuse me. Where is . . . , please?** *Pardon. Où est... , s'il vous plaît?* 12; **Excuse me. I'm looking for . . . , please.** *Pardon. Je cherche... , s'il vous plaît.* 12
expensive *cher (chère),* 10; **It's too expensive.** *C'est trop cher.* 10

F

fail *rater,* 9; **to fail a test** *rater un examen,* 9; **to fail a quiz** *rater une interro,* 9
fall *l'automne* (m.), 4; **in the fall** *en automne,* 4
fantastic *sensas (sensationnel),* 10
far from *loin de,* 12
fascinating *passionnant(e),* 2
fat *gros (-se),* 7
father *le père,* 7
February *février,* 4; **in February** *en février,* 4
feel: I feel like . . . *J'ai envie de... ,* 11; **I don't feel like it.** *Ça ne me dit rien.* 6
finally *enfin,* 9; *finalement,* 9
find *trouver,* 9
Fine. *Ça va.* 1; **Yes, it was fine.** *Oui, ça a été.* 9
first *d'abord,* 7; **OK, if you . . . first.** *D'accord, si tu... d'abord.* 7
fish *le poisson,* 7
flour *la farine,* 8
foot *le pied,* 12; **on foot** *à pied,* 12
football *le football américain,* 4; **to play football** *jouer au football américain,* 4
for *pour,* 3; **What do you need for . . . ?** (informal) *Qu'est qu'il te faut pour... ?* 3
forest *la forêt,* 11; **to/in the forest** *en forêt,* 11
forget *oublier,* 9; **Don't forget . . .** *N'oublie pas de... ,* 8; **Forget him/her/them!** *Oublie-le/-la/-les!* 9; **I didn't forget anything.** *Je n'ai rien oublié.* 11; **You didn't forget . . . ?** *Tu n'as pas oublié... ?* 11
franc (the French monetary unit) *le franc,* 3; **It's . . . francs.** *C'est/Ça fait...francs.* 5
French (language) *le français,* 1; **French fries** *les frites* (f.), 1
Friday *vendredi,* 2; **on Fridays** *le vendredi,* 2
friend *l'ami(e)* (m./f.), 1; **to go out with friends** *sortir avec les copains,* 1
from *de,* 0
front: in front of *devant,* 6
fruit *le fruit,* 8
fun: Did you have fun? *Tu t'es bien amusé(e)?* 11; **Have fun!** *Amuse-toi bien!* 11; **What do you do to have fun?** *Qu'est-ce que tu fais pour t'amuser?* 4
funny *amusant(e),* 7

G

gain: to gain weight *grossir,* 10
game *le match,* 6; *to play video games* **jouer à des jeux vidéo,** 4; **to watch a game (on TV)** *regarder un match,* 6; **to go see a game** *aller voir un match,* 6
geography *la géographie,* 2
geometry *la géométrie,* 2
German (language) *l'allemand* (m.), 2
get: Get . . . *Prends... ,* 8; **How can we get there?** *Comment est-ce qu'on y va?* 12
gift *le cadeau,* 11
girl *la fille,* 0
give *donner,* 5; **Please give me . . .** *Donnez-moi... , s'il vous plaît.* 5
Gladly. *Je veux bien.* 8
go *aller,* 6; **Go to the blackboard!** *Allez au tableau!* 0; **I'm going . . .** *Je vais... ,* 6; **What are you going to do . . . ?** *Tu vas faire quoi... ?* 6; **It doesn't go at all with . . .** *Il/Elle ne va pas du tout avec... ,* 10; **It goes very well with . . .** *Il/Elle va très bien avec... ,* 10; **to go out with friends** *sortir avec les copains,* 1; **I'd like . . . to go with . . .** *J'aimerais... pour aller avec... ,* 10; **Afterwards, I went out.** *Après, je suis sorti(e).* 9; **Could you go by . . . ?** *Tu pourrais passer à... ?* 12; **Did it go well?** *Ça s'est bien passé?* 11; **I'm going to have . . . , please.** *Je vais prendre... , s'il vous plaît.* 5; **What are you going to do . . . ?** *Qu'est-ce que tu vas faire... ?* 6; **I went . . .** *Je suis allé(e)... ,* 9; **I'm going to . . .** *Je vais... ,* 11; **Let's go . . .** *Allons... ,* 6; **to go for a walk** *faire une promenade,* 6; **We can go there . . .** *On peut y aller... ,* 12; **Where are you going to go . . . ?** *Où est-ce que tu vas aller... ?* 11; **Where did you go?** *Tu es allé(e) où?* 9; **You keep going until the next light.** *Vous continuez jusqu'au prochain feu rouge.* 12; **How's it going?** *(Comment) ça va?* 1
golf *le golf,* 4; **to play golf** *jouer au golf,* 4
good *bon(ne),* 5; **Have a good trip!** *Bon voyage!* 11; **Did you have a good . . . ?** *Tu as passé un bon... ?* 11; **It doesn't look good on you at all.** *Il/Elle ne te/vous va pas du tout.* 10; **It's pretty good!** *C'est pas mauvais!* 5; **not good** *pas bon,* 5; **Yes, very good.** *Oui, très bon.* 9
Goodbye! *Au revoir!* 1; *Salut!* 1
got: No, you've got to . . . *Non, tu dois... ,* 7
grandfather *le grand-père,* 7
grandmother *la grand-mère,* 7
grapes *le raisin,* 8
great *génial(e),* 2; **Great!** *Super!* 1; **It looks great on you!** *C'est tout à fait ton style!* 10; **It was great!** *C'était formidable!* 11; **Not so great.** *Pas terrible,* 1
green *vert(e),* 3
green beans *les *haricots verts* (m.), 8
grey *gris(e),* 3
grocery store (small) *l'épicerie* (f.), 12
gross *dégoûtant(e),* 5
grow *grandir,* 10
guava *la goyave,* 8
gym *le sport,* 2

H

half *demi(e),* 6; **half past** *et demie,* 6; **half past** (after *midi* and *minuit*) *et demi,* 6
ham *le jambon,* 5; **toasted cheese and ham sandwich** *le croque-monsieur,* 5
hamburger *le hamburger,* 1
hand *la main,* 0
happened: What happened? *Qu'est-ce qui s'est passé?* 9
happy *content (e),* 7
hard *difficile,* 2
hat *le chapeau,* 10
have *avoir,* 2; **At what time do you have . . . ?** *Tu as... à quelle heure?* 2; **Did you have a good weekend?** *Tu as passé un bon week-end?* 9; **Do you have . . . ?** *Vous avez... ?* 2; *Tu as... ?* 3; **Do you have that in . . . ? (size, fabric, color)** *Vous avez ça en... ?* 10; **Have . . .** *Prends/Prenez... ,* 5; **What are you having?** *Vous prenez?* 5; **I don't have . . .** *Je n'ai pas de... ,* 3; **I have some things to do.** *J'ai des trucs à faire.* 5; **I have . . .** *J'ai... ,*

2; **I'll have . . . , please.** *Je vais prendre... , s'il vous plaît.* 5; **to take or to have (food or drink)** *prendre,* 5; **We have . . .** *Nous avons...,* 2; **What classes do you have . . . ?** *Tu as quels cours... ?* 2; **What do you have . . . ?** *Tu as quoi... ?* 2; **What kind of . . . do you have?** *Qu'est-ce que vous avez comme... ?* 5; **Will you have . . . ?** *Tu prends/Vous prenez... ?* 8;

health *le cours de développement personnel et social (DPS),* 2

Hello. *Bonjour.* 1; **Hello? (on the phone)** *Allô?* 9

help: May I help you? *(Est-ce que) je peux vous aider?* 10

her *la,* 9; *son/sa/ses,* 7; **to her** *lui,* 9

Here. *Voilà.* 3; **Here's . . .** *Voici... ,* 7

Hi! *Salut!* 1

hiking *la randonnée,* 11; **to go hiking** *faire de la randonnée,* 11

him *le,* 9; **to him** *lui,* 9

his *son/sa/ses,* 7

history *l'histoire* (f.), 2

hockey *le* hockey,* 4; **to play hockey** *jouer au hockey,* 4

Hold on. *Ne quittez pas.* 9

homework *les devoirs* (m.), 2; **I've got homework to do.** *J'ai des devoirs à faire.* 5; **to do homework** *faire les devoirs,* 7

horrible *épouvantable,* 9; **It was horrible.** *C'était épouvantable.* 9

horseback riding *l'équitation* (f.), 1; **to go horseback riding** *faire de l'équitation,* 1

hose *le collant,* 10

hot chocolate *le chocolat,* 5

hot dog *le *hot-dog,* 5

hot *chaud,* 4; **It's hot.** *Il fait chaud.* 4; **not so hot** *pas super,* 2

house: at my house *chez moi,* 6; **Is this . . . 's house?** *Je suis bien chez... ?* 9; **to/at . . . 's house** *chez... ,* 6;

housework *le ménage,* 1; **to do housework** *faire le ménage,* 1

how: How old are you? *Tu as quel âge?* 1; **How about . . . ?** *On... ?* 4; **How do you like it?** *Comment tu trouves ça?* 5; **How much is . . . ?** *C'est combien... ?* 5; **How much is it?** *C'est combien?* 3; **How much is it, please? (total)** *Ça fait combien, s'il vous plaît?* 5; **How's it going?** *(Comment) ça va?* 1

how much *combien,* 3; **How much is . . . ?** *C'est combien,... ?* 3; **How much is it? (total)** *Ça fait combien, s'il vous plaît?* 5

hundred *cent,* 3; **two hundred** *deux cents,* 3

hungry: to be hungry *avoir faim,* 5; **No thanks. I'm not hungry anymore.** *Non, merci. Je n'ai plus faim.* 8

husband *le mari,* 7

I *je,* 1; **I do.** *Moi, si.* 2; **I don't.** *Moi, non.* 2

ice cream *la glace,* 1

ice-skate *faire du patin à glace,* 4

idea *l'idée (f.),* 4; **Good idea.** *Bonne idée.* 4; **I have no idea.** *Je n'en sais rien.* 11

if *si,* 7; **OK, if you . . . first.** *D'accord, si tu... d'abord...* 7

impossible *impossible,* 7; **No, that's impossible.** *Non, c'est impossible.* 7

in *dans,* 6; **in (a city or place)** *à,* 11; **in (before a feminine country)** *en,* 11; **in (before a masculine noun)** *au,* 11; **in (before a plural country)** *aux,* 11; **in front of** *devant,* 6; **in the afternoon** *l'après-midi,* 2; **in the evening** *le soir,* 4; **in the morning** *le matin,* 2

in-line skate *le roller en ligne,* 4; **to in-line skate** *faire du roller en ligne,* 4

indifference: (expression of indifference) *Bof!* 1

intend: I intend to . . . *J'ai l'intention de... ,* 11

interest: That doesn't interest me. *Ça ne me dit rien.* 4

interesting *intéressant(e),* 2

is: He is . . . *Il est... ,* 7; **It's . . .** *C'est... ,* 2; **She is . . .** *Elle est... ,* 7; **There's . . .** *Voilà... ,* 7; **This is . . .** *C'est... ; Voici... ,* 7

it *le, la,* 9

It's . . . *C'est... ,* 2; **It's . . .** *Il est...* (time), 6; **It's . . . francs.** *C'est... francs.* 5; *Ça fait... francs.* 5; **No, it's . . .** *Non, c'est... ,* 4; **Yes, it's . . .** *Oui, c'est... ,* 4

jacket *le blouson,* 10; **suit jacket** *la veste,* 10

jam *la confiture,* 8

January *janvier,* 4; **in January** *en janvier,* 4

jeans *le jean,* 3

jog *faire du jogging,* 4

jogging *le jogging,* 4

juice *le jus,* 5; **orange juice** *le jus d'orange,* 5; **apple juice** *le jus de pomme,* 5

July *juillet,* 4; **in July** *en juillet,* 4

June *juin,* 4; **in june** *en juin,* 4

kilogram *le kilo (kilogramme),* 8; **a kilogram of** *un kilo de,* 8

kind: What kind of . . . do you have? *Qu'est-ce que vous avez comme... ?* 5

know: I don't know. *Je ne sais pas.* 10

lab *les travaux pratiques* (m. pl.), 2

later: Can you call back later? *Vous pouvez rappeler plus tard?* 9; **See you later!** *A tout à l'heure!* 1

Latin (language) *le latin,* 2

lawn *le gazon,* 7; **to mow the lawn** *tondre le gazon,* 7

learn *apprendre,* 0

leather *le cuir,* 10; **in leather** *en cuir,* 10

leave *partir,* 11; **Can I leave a message?** *Je peux laisser un message?* 9; **You can't leave without . . .** *Tu ne peux pas partir sans... ,* 11

left *la gauche,* 12; **to the left** *à gauche (de),* 12

lemon *le citron,* 8

lemon soda *la limonade,* 5

lemonade *le citron pressé,* 5

let's: Let's go . . . *Allons... ,* 6; **Let's go!** *Allons-y!* 4

letter *la lettre,* 12; **to send letters** envoyer des lettres, 12

lettuce *la salade* (f.), 8

library *la bibliothèque,* 6

like *aimer,* 1; **I'd really like . . .** *Je voudrais bien... ,* 11; **Do you like . . . ?** *Tu aimes... ?* 1; **Do you like it?** *Il/Elle te (vous) plaît?* 10; **How do you like . . . ?** *Comment tu trouves... ?* 10; **How do you like it?** *Comment tu trouves ça?* 5; **I (really) like . . .** *Moi, j'aime (bien)... ,* 1; **I don't like . . .** *Je n'aime pas... ,* 1; **I like it, but it's expensive.** *Il/Elle me plaît, mais il/elle est cher (chère).* 10; **I'd like. . .** *Je voudrais... ,* 3; **I'd like . . . to go with . . .** *J'aimerais... pour aller avec... ,* 10; **I'd really like to.** *Je veux bien.* 6; **I'd like to buy . . .** *Je voudrais acheter... ,* 3; **What would you like?** *Vous désirez?* 10

like: What are they like? *Ils/Elles sont comment?* 7; **What is he like?** *Il est comment?* 7; **What is she**

like? *Elle est comment?* 7

listen *écouter,* 1; **Listen!** *Ecoutez!* 0; **I'm listening.** *Je t'écoute.* 9; **to listen to music** *écouter de la musique,* 1

liter *le litre,* 8; **a liter of** *un litre de,* 8

long *long (ue),* 10

look after: to look after . . . *garder... ,* 7

look: Look at the map! *Regardez la carte!* 0; **It doesn't look good on you at all.** *Il/Elle ne te/vous va pas du tout.* 10; **I'm looking for something for . . .** *Je cherche quelque chose pour... ,* 10; **It looks great on you!** *C'est tout à fait ton style!* 10; **Look, here's/there's/it's . . .** *Regarde, voilà... ,* 12; **No, thanks, I'm just looking.** *Non, merci, je regarde.* 10; **to look for** *chercher,* 9;

loose-leaf binder *le classeur,* 3

looks: It looks great on you! *C'est tout à fait ton style!* 10

lose *perdre,* 9; **to lose weight** *maigrir,* 10

lot: A lot. *Beaucoup.* 4

lots: I have lots of things to do. *J'ai des tas de choses à faire.* 5

lower (number) *moins,* 0

luck *la chance,* 11; **Good luck!** *Bon courage!* 2; *Bonne chance!* 11

lunch *le déjeuner,* 2; **to have lunch** *déjeuner,* 9

M

ma'am *madame (Mme),* 1

made *fait* (pp of faire), 9

magazine *le magazine,* 3

make *faire,* 4

mall *le centre commercial,* 6

mango *la mangue,* 8

map *la carte,* 0

March *mars,* 4; **in March** *en mars,* 4

market *le marché,* 8

math *les maths* (f. pl.), *les mathématiques,* 1

May *mai,* 4; **in May** *en mai,* 4

may: May I . . . ? *(Est-ce que) je peux... ?* 7; **May I help you?** *(Est-ce que) je peux vous aider?* 10

me *moi,* 2; **Me, too.** *Moi aussi.* 2; **Not me.** *Pas moi.* 2

mean *méchant(e),* 7

meat *la viande,* 8

medicine *les médicaments* (m.), 12

meet *retrouver,* 6; *rencontrer,* 9; **I'd like you to meet . . .** *Je te (vous) présente... ,* 7; **Pleased to meet you.** *Très heureux (heureuse).* 7; **OK, we'll meet . . .** *Bon, on se retrouve... ,* 6; **We'll meet. . .** *Rendez-vous... ,* 6

menu *la carte,* 5; **The menu, please.** *La carte, s'il vous plaît.* 5

message *le message,* 9; **Can I leave a message?** *Je peux laisser un message?* 9

metro *le métro,* 12; **at the . . . metro stop** *au métro... ,* 6

midnight *minuit,* 6; **It's midnight.** *Il est minuit.* 6; **It's half past midnight.** *Il est minuit et demi.* 6

milk *le lait,* 8

mineral water *l'eau minérale* (f.), 5

minute *la minute,* 9; **Do you have a minute?** *Tu as une minute?* 9

miss, Miss *mademoiselle (Mlle),* 1

miss *rater,* 9; **to miss the bus** *rater le bus,* 9

moment *le moment,* 5; **One moment, please.** *Un moment, s'il vous plaît.* 5

Monday *lundi,* 2; **on Mondays** *le lundi,* 2

money *l'argent* (m.), 11

More . . . ? *Encore de... ?* 8; **I don't want any more.** *Je n'en veux plus.* 8

morning *le matin,* 2; **in the morning** *le matin,* 2

mother *la mère,* 7

mountain *la montagne,* 11; **to/in the mountains** *à la montagne,* 11

movie *le film,* 6; **to see a movie** *voir un film,* 6

movie theater *le cinéma,* 6; **the movies** *le cinéma,* 1

mow: to mow the lawn *tondre le gazon,* 7

Mr. *monsieur (M.),* 1

Mrs. *madame (Mme),* 1

much: How much is . . . ? *C'est combien,... ?* 5; **How much is it, please?** *Ça fait combien, s'il vous plaît?* 5; **How much is it?** *C'est combien?* 3; **No, not too much.** *Non, pas trop.* 2; **Not much.** *Pas grand-chose.* 6; **Not too much.** *Pas tellement.* 4; **Not very much.** *Pas beaucoup.* 4; **Yes, very much.** *Oui, beaucoup.* 2

museum *le musée,* 6

mushroom *le champignon,* 8

music *la musique,* 2

my *mon/ma/mes,* 7

name: His/Her name is . . . *Il/Elle s'appelle... ,* 1; **My name is . . .** *Je m'appelle... ,* 0; **What is your name?** *Tu t'appelles comment?* 0

natural science *les sciences naturelles* (f.), 2

need: I need . . . *Il me faut... ,* 3; **I need . . .** *J'ai besoin de... ,* 8; **What do you need for . . . ?** (formal) *Qu'est-ce qu'il vous faut pour... ?* 3; **What do you need for . . . ?** (informal) *Qu'est-ce qu'il te faut pour... ?* 3; **What do you need?** *De quoi est-ce que tu as besoin?* 8

neither: Neither do I. *Moi non plus.* 2; **neither tall nor short** *ne... ni grand(e) ni petit(e),* 7

never *ne... jamais,* 4

next *prochain(e),* 12; **You go down this street to the next light.** *Vous continuez jusqu'au prochain feu rouge.* 12

next to *à côté de,* 12

nice *gentil (gentille),* 7; *sympa (sympathique),* 7; **It's nice weather.** *Il fait beau.* 4

nightmare *le cauchemar,* 11; **It was a real nightmare!** *C'était un véritable cauchemar!* 11

no *non,* 1

noon *midi,* 6; **It's noon.** *Il est midi.* 6; **It's half past noon.** *Il est midi et demi.* 6

not: Oh, not bad. *Oh, pas mal/mauvais.* 9; **not yet** *ne... pas encore,* 9; **Not at all.** *Pas du tout.* 4; **Not me.** *Pas moi.* 2; **Not so great.** *Pas terrible.* 1; **not very good** *pas bon,* 5; **No, not really.** *Non, pas vraiment.* 11; **No, not too much.** *Non, pas trop.* 2

notebook *le cahier,* 0, 3

nothing *rien,* 6; **Nothing special.** *Rien de spécial.* 6

novel *le roman,* 3

November *novembre,* 4; **in November** *en novembre,* 4

now *maintenant,* 2; **I can't right now.** *Je ne peux pas maintenant.* 8

o'clock *...heures,* 2; **at . . . o'clock** *à... heure(s),* 2

October *octobre,* 4; **in October** *en octobre,* 4

of *de,* 0; **of course** *bien sûr,* 3; **of it** *en,* 8; **of them** *en,* 8

often *souvent,* 4

OK. *D'accord.* 4; **Is that OK with you?** *Tu es d'accord?* 7; **Well, OK.** *Bon, d'accord.* 8; **Yes, it was OK.** *Oui, ça a été.*

okra *les gombos* (m.), 8

old: How old are you? *Tu as quel*

âge? 1; **I am . . . years old.** *J'ai... ans.* 1; **older** *âgé(e),* 7
omelette *l'omelette* (f.), 5
on: Can I try on . . . ? *Je peux essayer le/la/les... ?* 10; **on foot** *à pied,* 12; **on Fridays** *le vendredi,* 2; **on Mondays** *le lundi,* 2; **on Saturdays** *le samedi,* 2; **on Sundays** *le dimanche,* 2; **on Thursdays** *le jeudi,* 2; **on Tuesdays** *le mardi,* 2; **on Wednesdays** *le mercredi,* 2;
once: once a week *une fois par semaine,* 4
onion *l'oignon* (m.), 8
open: Open your books to page . . . *Ouvrez vos livres à la page... ,* 0
opinion *l'avis* (m.), 9; **In your opinion, what do I do?** *A ton avis, qu'est-ce que je fais?* 9
or *ou,* 1
orange (color) *orange* (inv.), 3
orange *l'orange* (f.), 8
orange juice *le jus d'orange,* 5;
our *notre/nos,* 7
out: Out of the question! *Pas question!* 7; **out of style,** *démodé(e),* 10

P

package *le paquet,* 8; **a package/box of** *un paquet de,* 8
page *la page,* 0
pancake: a very thin pancake *la crêpe,* 5
pants *le pantalon,* 10
papaya *la papaye,* 8
paper *le papier,* 0; **sheets of paper** *les feuilles de papier* (f.), 3
pardon: Pardon me. *Pardon.* 3
parent *le parent,* 7
park *le parc,* 6
party *la boum,* 6; **to go to a party** *aller à une boum,* 6
pass: You'll pass . . . *Vous passez...,* 12
passport *le passeport,* 11
pastry *la pâtisserie,* 12; **pastry shop** *la pâtisserie,* 12
peach *la pêche,* 8
pear *la poire,* 8
peas *les petits pois* (m.), 8
pen *le stylo,* 0
pencil *le crayon,* 3; **pencil case** *la trousse,* 3; **pencil sharpener** *le taille-crayon,* 3
perfect *parfait(e),* 10; **It's perfect.** *C'est parfait.* 10
phone *le téléphone,* 1; **to talk on the phone** *parler au téléphone,* 1
photography: to do photography *faire de la photo,* 4
physical education *l'éducation physique et sportive (EPS)* (f.), 2
physics *la physique,* 2
pick *choisir,* 10; **to pick up your room** *ranger ta chambre,* 7
picnic *le pique-nique,* 6; **to have a picnic** *faire un pique-nique,* 6
picture *la photo,* 4; **to take pictures** *faire des photos,* 4
pie *la tarte,* 8
piece *le morceau,* 8; **a piece of** *un morceau de,* 8
pineapple *l'ananas* (m.), 8
pink *rose,* 3
pizza *la pizza,* 1
place *l'endroit* (m.), 12
plane *l'avion* (m.), 12; **by plane** *en avion,* 12
plane ticket *le billet d'avion,* 11
plans: I don't have any plans. *Je n'ai rien de prévu.* 11
plate *l'assiette* (f.), 5
play *la pièce,* 6; **to see a play** *voir une pièce,* 6
play *jouer,* 4; *faire,* 4; **I don't play/do . . .** *Je ne fais pas de... ,* 4; **I play . . .** *Je joue... ,* 4; **I play/do. . .** *Je fais... ,* 4; **to play baseball** *jouer au base-ball,* 4; **to play basketball** *jouer au basket (-ball),* 4; **to play football** *jouer au football américain,* 4; **to play golf** *jouer au golf,* 4; **to play hockey** *jouer au hockey,* 4; **to play soccer** *jouer au foot(ball),* 4; **to play sports** *faire du sport,* 1; **to play tennis** *jouer au tennis,* 4; **to play video games** *jouer à des jeux vidéo,* 4; **to play volleyball** *jouer au volley(-ball),* 4; **What sports do you play?** *Qu'est-ce que tu fais comme sport?* 4
please *s'il te/vous plaît,* 3; **Yes, please.** *Oui, s'il te/vous plaît.* 8
pleased: Pleased to meet you. *Très heureux (euse).* 7
pleasure *le plaisir,* 8; **Yes, with pleasure.** *Oui, avec plaisir.* 8
pork *le porc,* 8
post office *la poste,* 12
poster *le poster,* 0
potato *la pomme de terre,* 8
pound *la livre,* 8; **a pound of** *une livre de,* 8
practice *répéter,* 9
prefer *préférer,* 1; **I prefer . . .** *Je préfère... ,* 1; *J'aime mieux... ,* 1
problem *le problème,* 9; **I've got a little problem.** *J'ai un petit problème.* 9
pullover (sweater) *le pull-over,* 3
purple *violet(te),* 3
put *mettre,* 10; **to put on** *mettre,* 10

Q

quarter *le quart,* 6; **quarter past** *et quart,* 6; **quarter to** *moins le quart,* 6
question: Out of the question! *Pas question!* 7
quiche *la quiche,* 5
quiz *l'interro(gation)* (f.), 9

R

radio *la radio,* 3
rain: It's raining. *Il pleut.* 4
raise: Raise your hand! *Levez la main!* 0
rarely *rarement,* 4
read *lire,* 1; **read (pp.)** *lu* (pp. of lire), 9
really *vraiment,* 11; **I (really) like . . .** *Moi, j'aime (bien)... ,* 1; **I'd really like . . .** *Je voudrais bien... ,* 11; **I'd really like to.** *Je veux bien.* 6; **No, not really.** *Non, pas vraiment.* 11
record store *le disquaire,* 12; **at the record store** *chez le disquaire,* 12
recreation center *la Maison des jeunes et de la culture (MJC),* 6
red *rouge,* 3; **redheaded** *roux (rousse),* 7
rehearse *répéter,* 9
relative *le parent,* 7
Repeat! *Répétez!* 0
restaurant *le restaurant,* 6
retro (style) *rétro* (inv.), 10
return: to return something *rendre,* 12
rice *le riz,* 8
ride: to go horseback riding *faire de l'équitation,* 1
right *la droite,* 12; **to the right** *à droite (de),* 12
right away *tout de suite,* 6; **Yes, right away.** *Oui, tout de suite.* 5; **I'll go right away.** *J'y vais tout de suite.* 8
right now *maintenant,* 8; **I can't right now.** *Je ne peux pas maintenant.* 8
right there: It's right there on the . . . *C'est tout de suite à... ,* 12
room *la chambre,* 7; **to pick up your room** *ranger ta chambre,* 7
ruler *la règle,* 3

S

sailing *la voile,* 11 **to go sailing** *faire de la voile,* 11; *faire du bateau,* 11
salad *la salade,* 8

salami *le saucisson,* 5
sandals *les sandales* (f.), 10
sandwich *un sandwich,* 5; **cheese sandwich** *un sandwich au fromage,* 5; **ham sandwich** *un sandwich au jambon,* 5; **salami sandwich** *un sandwich au saucisson,* 5; **toasted cheese and ham sandwich** *le croque-monsieur,* 5
Saturday *samedi,* 2; **on Saturdays** *le samedi,* 2
saw *vu* (pp of voir), 9
scarf *l'écharpe* (f.), 10
school *l'école* (f.), 1
science class *les sciences naturelles,* 2
scuba diving *la plongée,* 11; **to go scuba diving** *faire de la plongée,* 11
sea *la mer,* 11
second *la seconde,* 9; **One second, please.** *Une seconde, s'il vous plaît.* 9
see *voir,* 6; **See you later!** *A tout à l'heure!* 1; **See you soon.** *A bientôt.* 1; **See you tomorrow.** *A demain.* 1; **to go see a game** *aller voir un match,* 6; **to see a movie** *voir un film,* 6; **to see a play** *voir une pièce,* 6
seen *vu* (pp. of voir), 9
sell *vendre,* 9
send *envoyer,* 12; **to send letters** *envoyer des lettres,* 12
sensational *sensas,* 10
September *septembre,* 4; **in September** *en septembre,* 4
service: At your service; You're welcome. *A votre service.* 3
shall: Shall we go to the café? *On va au café?* 5
sheet *la feuille,* 0; **a sheet of paper** *une feuille de papier,* 0
shirt (man's) *la chemise,* 10; **(woman's)** *le chemisier,* 10
shoes *les chaussures* (f.), 10
shop: to go shopping *faire les magasins,* 1; **to window-shop** *faire les vitrines,* 6; **Can you do the shopping?** *Tu peux aller faire les courses?* 8
shopping *les courses* (f.), 7; **to do the shopping** *faire les courses,* 7
short (height) *petit(e),* 7; **(length)** *court(e),* 10
shorts: (pair of) shorts *le short,* 3
should: You should . . . *Tu devrais...,* 9; **You should talk to him/her/them.** *Tu devrais lui/leur parler.* 9
show *montrer,* 9
shy *timide,* 7
sing *chanter,* 9
sir *monsieur (M.),* 1
sister *la sœur,* 7
Sit down! *Asseyez-vous!* 0
size *la taille,* 10
skate: to ice-skate *faire du patin à glace,* 4; **to in-line skate** *faire du roller en ligne,* 4
ski *faire du ski,* 4; **How about skiing?** *On fait du ski?* 5; **to water-ski** *faire du ski nautique,* 4; **skiing** *le ski,* 1
skirt *la jupe,* 10
sleep *dormir,* 1
slender *mince,* 7
slice *la tranche,* 8; **a slice of** *une tranche de,* 8
small *petit(e),* 10
smart *intelligent(e),* 7
snack: afternoon snack *le goûter,* 8
snails *les escargots* (m.), 1
sneakers *les baskets* (f. pl.), 3
snow: It's snowing. *Il neige.* 4
So-so. *Comme ci, comme ça.* 1
so: not so great *pas terrible,* 5
soccer *le football,* 1; *le foot,* 4; **to play soccer** *jouer au foot(ball),* 4
socks *les chaussettes* (f.), 10
soda: lemon soda *la limonade,* 5
some *des,* 3; **some** *du, de la, de l', des,* 8; **some (of it)** *en,* 8; **Yes, I'd like some.** *Oui, j'en veux bien.* 8
something *quelque chose,* 6; **I'm looking for something for . . . ,** *Je cherche quelque chose pour... ,* 10
sometimes *quelquefois,* 4
son *le fils,* 7
soon: See you soon. *A bientôt.* 1
Sorry. *Je regrette.* 3; *Désolé(e).* 5; **Sorry, but I can't.** *Désolé(e), mais je ne peux pas.* 4; **I'm sorry, but I don't have time.** *Je regrette, mais je n'ai pas le temps.* 8; **Sorry, I'm busy.** *Désolé(e), je suis occupé(e).* 6
Spanish (language) *l'espagnol* (m.), 2
speak *parler,* 9; **Could I speak to . . . ?** *(Est-ce que) je peux parler à... ?* 9
special *spécial(e),* 6; **Nothing special.** *Rien de spécial.* 6
sports *le sport,* 1; **to play sports** *faire du sport,* 1; **What sports do you play?** *Qu'est-ce que tu fais comme sport?* 4
spring *le printemps,* 4; **in the spring** *au printemps,* 4
stadium *le stade,* 6
stamp *le timbre,* 12
stand: Stand up! *Levez-vous!* 0
start *commencer,* 9
stationery store *la papeterie,* 12
steak *le bifteck,* 8; **steak and French fries** *le steak-frites,* 5
stop: at the . . . metro stop *au métro ... ,* 6
store *le magasin,* 1
straight ahead *tout droit,* 12; **You go straight ahead until you get to . . .** *Vous allez tout droit jusqu'à... ,* 12
strawberry *la fraise,* 8; **water with strawberry syrup** *le sirop de fraises (à l'eau),* 5
street *la rue,* 12; **Take . . . Street, then cross . . . Street.** *Prenez la rue... , puis traversez la rue... ,* 12
strong *fort(e),* 7
student *l'élève* (m./f.), 2
study *étudier,* 1
study hall *l'étude* (f.), 2
style *la mode,* 10; **in style** *à la mode,* 10; **out of style** *démodé(e),* 10
subway *le métro,* 12; **by subway** *en métro,* 12
sugar *le sucre,* 7
suit jacket *la veste,* 10
suit: Does it suit me? *Il/Elle me va?* 10; **It suits you really well.** *Il/Elle te/vous va très bien.* 10
suitcase *la valise,* 11
summer *l'été* (m.), 4; **in the summer** *en été,* 4
summer camp *la colonie de vacances,* 11; **to/at a summer camp** *en colonie de vacances,* 11
Sunday *dimanche,* 2; **on Sundays** *le dimanche,* 2
sunglasses *les lunettes de soleil* (f. pl.), 10
super *super,* 2
supermarket *le supermarché,* 8
sure: I'm not sure. *J'hésite.* 10
sweater *le cardigan,* 10
sweatshirt *le sweat-shirt,* 3
swim *nager,* 1; *faire de la natation,* 4
swimming *la natation,* 4
swimming pool *la piscine,* 6
syrup: water with strawberry syrup *le sirop de fraises (à l'eau),* 5

T-shirt *le tee-shirt,* 3
table *la table,* 7; **to clear the table** *débarrasser la table,* 7
tacky *moche,* 10; **I think it's (they're) really tacky.** *Je le/la/les trouve moche(s).* 10
take or have (food or drink) *prendre,* 5; **Are you taking it/them?** *Vous le/la/les prenez?* 10; **Are you taking . . . ?** *Tu prends... ?* 11; **Have you decided to take . . . ?** *Vous avez décidé de prendre... ?* 10; **I'll take it/them.** *Je le/la/les prends.* 10; **to take a test** *passer un examen,* 9; **to take pictures**

faire des photos, 4; **We can take . . .** *On peut prendre... ,* 12; **Take . . . Street, then . . . Street.** *Prenez la rue... , puis la rue... ,* 12
take out: Take out a sheet of paper. *Prenez une feuille de papier.* 0; **to take out the trash** *sortir la poubelle,* 7
taken *pris* (pp. of prendre), 9
talk *parler,* 1; **Can I talk to you?** *Je peux te parler?* 9; **to talk on the phone** *parler au téléphone,* 1; **We talked.** *Nous avons parlé.* 9
tall *grand(e),* 7
taxi *le taxi,* 12; **by taxi** *en taxi,* 12
teacher *le professeur,* 0
telephone *le téléphone,* 0
television *la télévision,* 0
tell *dire,* 9; **Can you tell her/him that I called?** *Vous pouvez lui dire que j'ai téléphoné?* 9
tennis *le tennis,* 4; **to play tennis** *jouer au tennis,* 4
terrible *horrible,* 10
test *l'examen* (m.), 1
Thank you. *Merci.* 3; **No thanks. I'm not hungry anymore.** *Non, merci. Je n'ai plus faim.* 8
that *ce, cet, cette,* 3; **This/That is . . .** *Ça, c'est... ,* 12
theater *le théâtre,* 6
their *leur/leurs,* 7
them *les,* 9; **to them** *leur,* 9
then *ensuite,* 9
there *-là* (noun suffix), 3; **there** *il y a,* 5; **there** *y, là,* 12; **Is . . . there, please?** *(Est-ce que)... est là, s'il vous plaît?* 9; **There's . . .** *Voilà... ,* 7; **There is/There are . . .** Il y a... , 5; **What is there to drink?** *Qu'est-ce qu'il y a à boire?* 5
these *ces,* 3; **These/those are . . .** *Ce sont... ,* 7
thing *la chose,* 5; *le truc,* 5; **I have lots of things to do.** *J'ai des tas de choses à faire.* 5; **I have some things to do.** *J'ai des trucs à faire.* 5
think *penser,* 11; **I think it's/they're . . .** *Je le/la/les trouve... ,* 10; **I've thought of everything.** *J'ai pensé à tout.* 11; **What do you think of . . . ?** *Comment tu trouves... ?* 2; **What do you think of that/it?** *Comment tu trouves ça?* 2
thirsty: to be thirsty *avoir soif,* 5
this *ce, cet, cette,* 3; **This is . . .** *C'est... ,* 7; **This is . . .** *Voilà/Voici... ,* 7; **This/That is . . .** *Ça, c'est... ,* 12
those *ces,* 3; **These/Those are . . .** *Ce sont... ,* 7
Thursday *jeudi,* 4; **on Thursdays** *le jeudi,* 2
ticket *le billet,* 11; **plane ticket** *le billet d'avion,* 11; **train ticket** *le billet de train,* 11
tie *la cravate,* 10
tight *serré(e),* 10
time *le temps,* 8; **a waste of time** *zéro,* 2; **at the time of** *à l'heure de,* 1; **At what time do you have . . . ?** *Tu as... à quelle heure?* 2; **At what time?** *A quelle heure?* 6; **from time to time** *de temps en temps,* 4; **I'm sorry, but I don't have time.** *Je regrette, mais je n'ai pas le temps.* 8; *Je suis désolé(e), mais je n'ai pas le temps.* 12; **What time is it?** *Quelle heure est-il?* 6
to *à la, au, à l', aux,* 6; **to (a city or place)** *à,* 11; **to (before a feminine country)** *en,* 11; **to (before a masculine noun)** *au,* 11; **to (before a plural noun)** *aux,* 11; **to her** *lui,* 9; **to him** *lui,* 9; **to them** *leur,* 9; **five to . . .** *moins cinq,* 6
today *aujourd'hui,* 2
tomato *la tomate,* 8
tomorrow *demain,* 2; **See you tomorrow.** *A demain.* 1
tonight *ce soir,* 7; **Not tonight.** *Pas ce soir.* 7
too (much) *trop,* 10; **It's/They're too . . .** *Il/Elle est (Ils/Elles sont) trop... ,* 10; **Me too.** *Moi aussi.* 2; **No, it's too expensive.** *Non, c'est trop cher.* 10; **No, not too much.** *Non, pas trop.* 2; **Not too much.** *Pas tellement.* 4
track *l'athlétisme* (m.), 4; **to do track and field** *faire de l'athlétisme,* 4
train *le train,* 12; **by train** *en train,* 12; **train ticket** *le billet de train,* 11
trash(can) *la poubelle,* 7; **to take out the trash** *sortir la poubelle,* 7
travel *voyager,* 1
trip *le voyage,* 11; **Have a good trip!** *Bon voyage!* 11
true *vrai,* 2
try: Can I try on . . . ? *Je peux essayer... ?* 10; **Can I try it (them) on ?** *Je peux l'/les essayer?* 10
Tuesday *mardi,* 2; **on Tuesdays** *le mardi,* 2
turn *tourner,* 12; **You turn . . .** *Vous tournez... ,* 12
TV *la télé(vision),* 1; **to watch TV** *regarder la télé(vision),* 1

umbrella *le parapluie,* 11
uncle *l'oncle* (m.), 7
uncooked *cru(e),* 5
until *jusqu'à,* 12; **You go straight ahead until you get to . . .** *Vous allez tout droit jusqu'à ... ,* 12
useless *nul(le),* 2
usually *d'habitude,* 4

vacation *les vacances* (f. pl.), 1; **Have a good vacation!** *Bonnes vacances!* 11; **on vacation** *en vacances,* 4
vacuum (verb) *passer l'aspirateur,* 7
VCR (videocassette recorder) *le magnétoscope,* 0
vegetables *les légumes* (m.), 8
very *très,* 1; **Very well.** *Très bien.* 1; **Yes, very much.** *Oui, beaucoup.* 2
video *la vidéo,* 4; **to make videos** *faire de la vidéo,* 4; **video games** *des jeux vidéo,* 4
videocassette recorder, VCR *le magnétoscope,* 0
videotape *la vidéocassette,* 3
visit (a place) *visiter,* 9
volleyball *le volley(-ball),* 4; **to play volleyball** *jouer au volley(-ball),* 4

wait for *attendre,* 9
Waiter! *Monsieur!* 5
Waitress! *Madame!* 5; *Mademoiselle!* 5
walk: to go for a walk *faire une promenade,* 6; **to walk the dog** *promener le chien,* 7
wallet *le portefeuille,* 3
want *vouloir,* 6; **Do you want . . . ?** *Tu veux... ?* 6; **Do you want . . . ?** *Vous voulez... ?* 8; **I don't want any more.** *Je n'en veux plus.* 8; **Yes, if you want to.** *Oui, si tu veux.* 7
wash *laver,* 7; **to wash the car** *laver la voiture,* 7
waste: a waste of time *zéro,* 2
watch *la montre,* 3
watch *regarder,* 1; **to watch a game (on TV)** *regarder un match,* 6; **to watch TV** *regarder la télé(vision),* 1
water *l'eau* (f.), 5; **mineral water** *l'eau minérale,* 5; **water with strawberry syrup** *le sirop de fraises (à l'eau),* 5
water ski *le ski nautique,* 4; **to water ski** *faire du ski nautique,* 4
wear *mettre, porter,* 10; **I don't know what to wear for . . .** *Je ne sais pas quoi mettre pour... ,* 10;

Wear . . . *Mets...*, 10; **What shall I wear?** *Qu'est-ce que je mets?* 10; **Why don't you wear . . . ?** *Pourquoi est-ce que tu ne mets pas... ?* 10
weather *le temps*, 4; **What's the weather like?** *Quel temps fait-il?* 4
Wednesday *mercredi*, 2; **on Wednesdays** *le mercredi*, 2
week *la semaine*, 4; **once a week** *une fois par semaine*, 4
weekend *le week-end*, 6; **Did you have a good weekend?** *Tu as passé un bon week-end?* 9; **on weekends** *le week-end*, 4; **this weekend** *ce week-end*, 6
welcome: At your service; You're welcome. *A votre service.* 3
well *bien*, 1; **Did it go well?** *Ça s'est bien passé?* 11; **Very well.** *Très bien.* 1
went: Afterwards, I went out. *Après, je suis sorti(e).* 9; **I went . . .** *Je suis allé(e)...* , 9
what *comment*, 0; **What is your name?** *Tu t'appelles comment?* 0; **What do you think of. . . ?** *Comment tu trouves... ?* 2; **What do you think of that/it?** *Comment tu trouves ça?* 2; **What's his/her name?** *Il/Elle s'appelle comment?* 1
what *qu'est-ce que*, 1; **What are you going to do . . . ?** *Qu'est-ce que tu vas faire... ?* 6; **What do you do to have fun?** *Qu'est-ce que tu fais pour t'amuser?* 4; **What do you have to drink?** *Qu'est-ce que vous avez comme boissons?* 5; **What do you need for . . . ? (formal)** *Qu'est-ce qu'il vous faut pour... ?* 3; **What happened?** *Qu'est-ce qui s'est passé?* 9; **What kind of . . . do you have?** *Qu'est-ce que vous avez comme... ?* 5;
what *quoi*, 2; **I don't know what to wear for . . .** *Je ne sais pas quoi mettre pour...* , *10;* **What are you going to do . . . ?** *Tu vas faire quoi... ?* 6; **What do you have . . . ?** *Tu as quoi... ?* 2; **What do you need?** *De quoi est-ce que tu as besoin?* 5
When? *Quand (ça)?* 6
where *où*, 6; **Where?** *Où (ça)?* 6; **Where are you going to go . . . ?** *Où est-ce que tu vas aller... ?* 11; **Where did you go?** *Tu es allé(e) où?* 9
which *quel(le)*, 1
white *blanc(he)*, 3
who *qui*, 0; **Who's calling?** *Qui est à l'appareil?* 9
whom *qui*, 6; **With whom?** *Avec qui?* 6
why *pourquoi*, 0; **Why don't you . . . ?** *Pourquoi tu ne... pas?* 9; **Why not?** *Pourquoi pas?* 6
wife *la femme*, 7
win *gagner*, 9
window *la fenêtre*, 0; **to window-shop** *faire les vitrines*, 6
windsurfing *la planche à voile*, 11; **to go windsurfing** *faire de la planche à voile*, 11
winter *l'hiver* (m.), 4; **in the winter** *en hiver*, 4
with *avec*, 6; **with me** *avec moi*, 6; **With whom?** *Avec qui?* 6
withdraw *retirer*, 12; **withdraw money** *retirer de l'argent*, 12
without *sans*, 11; **You can't leave without . . .** *Tu ne peux pas partir sans...* , 11
work *travailler*, 9
worry: Don't worry! *Ne t'en fais pas!* 9
would like: I'd like to buy . . . *Je voudrais acheter...* , 3

year *l'an* (m.); **I am . . . years old.** *J'ai...ans.* 1
yellow *jaune*, 3
yes *oui*, 1; **Yes, please.** *Oui, s'il te/vous plaît.* 8
yesterday *hier*, 9
yet: not yet *ne... pas encore*, 9
yogurt *les yaourts* (m.), 8
you *tu, vous*, 0; **And you?** *Et toi?* 1
young *jeune*, 7
your *ton/ta/tes*, 7; *votre/vos*, 7

zoo *le zoo*, 6

GRAMMAR INDEX

Page numbers in boldface type refer to the **Grammaire** and **Note de grammaire** presentations. Other page numbers refer to grammar structures presented in the **Comment dit-on... ?**, **Tu te rappelles?**, **Vocabulaire**, and **A la française** sections. Page numbers beginning with **R** refer to the Grammar Summary in this Reference Section.

A

J

L

M

N

O

P

R

S

T

U

V

For permission to reprint copyrighted material, grateful acknowledgment is made to the following sources:

Agence Vu: Two photographs from "Je passe ma vie au téléphone" by Anne Vaisman, photographs by Claudine Doury, from *Phosphore,* no. 190, February 1997. Copyright © 1997 by Agence Vu.

Air France: Front of Air France boarding pass, "Carte d'accès à bord."

Bayard Presse International: From "Allez, c'est à vous de choisir," text by Florence Farcouli, illustrations by Olivier Tossan, from *Okapi,* no. 568–9, September 1995. Copyright © 1995 by Bayard Presse International. Text and illustrations from "Sondage: les lycéens ont-ils le moral?" from *Phosphore,* no. 160, September 1989. Copyright © 1989 by Bayard Presse International. From "Je passe ma vie au téléphone" by Anne Vaisman from *Phosphore,* no. 190, February 1997. Copyright © 1997 by Bayard Presse International.

C'Rock Radio, Vienne: Logo for C'Rock Radio, 89.5 MHz.

Cacharel: Four adapted photographs with captions of Cacharel products from *Rentrée très classe à prix petits: Nouvelles Galeries Lafayette.*

Caisse Nationale des Monuments Historiques et des Sites: Admission ticket, "Ministère de la Culture, C.N.M.H.S."

Canal B, Bruz: Logo for Canal B Radio, 94 MHz.

Cathédrale d'images: Advertisement, "Cathédrale d'images," from *Évasion Plus.*

Comité Français d'Éducation pour la Santé, 2, rue Auguste Comte-92170 Vanves: From "Les groupes d'aliments" from the brochure *Comment équilibrer votre alimentation,* published and edited by the Comité Français d'Éducation pour la Santé.

Éditions Leconte: Cover of brochure, *Paris Monumental.*

Éditions S.A.E.P.: Recipe and photograph for "Croissants au coco et au sésame," recipe and photograph for "Mousseline africaine de petits légumes," "Signification des symboles accompagnant les recettes," and jacket cover from *La Cuisine Africaine* by Pierrette Chalendar. Copyright © 1993 by S.A.E.P.

EF Foundation: From "Le rêve américain devient réalité, en séjour Immersion avec EF: Vivre à l'américaine," photograph, and "Vacances de Printemps" from "Les U.S.A. en cours Principal: le séjour EF idéal" from *EF Voyages Linguistiques: Hiver, Printemps, et Eté 1993.*

Femme Actuelle: Text from "En direct des refuges: Poupette, 3 ans" by Nicole Lauroy from *Femme Actuelle,* no. 414, August 31–September 6, 1992. Copyright © 1992 by Femme Actuelle. Text from "En direct des refuges: Jupiter, 7 mois" by Nicole Lauroy from *Femme Actuelle,* no. 436, February 1993. Copyright © 1993 by Femme Actuelle. Text from "En direct des refuges: Flora, 3 ans" by Nicole Lauroy from *Femme Actuelle,* no. 457, July 1993. Copyright © 1993 by Femme Actuelle. Text from "En direct des refuges: Dady, 2 ans" and from "Mayo a trouvé une famille" by Nicole Lauroy from *Femme Actuelle,* no. 466, August 30–September 5, 1993. Copyright © 1993 by Femme Actuelle. Text from "En direct des refuges: Camel, 5 ans" by Nicole Lauroy from *Femme Actuelle,* no. 472, October 11–17, 1993. Copyright © 1993 by Femme Actuelle.

France Miniature: Cover, illustration and adapted text from brochure, *Le Pays France Miniature.*

France Telecom: Front and back of the Télécarte.

Galeries Lafayette: Four adapted photographs with captions of Cacharel products and two photographs with captions of NAF NAF products from *Rentrée très classe à prix petits: Nouvelles Galeries Lafayette.*

Grands Bateaux de Provence: Advertisement, "Bateaux 'Mireio'," from *Évasion Plus.*

Grottes de Thouzon: Advertisement, "Grottes de Thouzon," photograph by M. Crotet, from *Évasion Plus,* Provence, Imprimerie Vincent, 1994.

Groupe Filipacchi: Advertisement, "Casablanca," from *7 à Paris,* no. 534, February 12–18, 1992, p. 43.

Hachette Livre (Hachette Tourisme): From "Où dormir?" and "Où manger?" from "Arles (13200)" from *Le Guide du Routard: Provence-Côte d'Azur, 1997/1998.* Copyright © 1997 by Hachette Livre (Hachette Tourisme).

L'Harmattan: Excerpts from French text and six illustrations from *Cheval de bois/Chouval bwa* by Isabelle and Henri Cadoré, illustrated by Bernadette Coléno. Copyright © 1993 by L'Harmattan.

Le Monde: From "Baccalauréat 1996. Les hauts et les bas: Taux de réussite par série" from *Le Monde de l'Éducation,* no. 240, September 1996. Copyright © 1996 by Le Monde.

Loca Center: Advertisement, "Loca Center," from *Guide des Services: La Martinique à domicile.*

Ministère de la Culture: From "Les jeunes aiment sortir" (retitled "Les loisirs préférés") from *Francoscopie: Comment vivent les Français, 1997* by Gérard Mermet.

Musée de l'Empéri: Adapted advertisement, "Musée de l'Empéri," from *Évasion Plus.*

Musée du Louvre: Admission ticket for the Louvre.

NAF NAF: Two photographs with captions of NAF NAF products from *Rentrée très classe à prix petits: Nouvelles Galeries Lafayette.*

NRJ, Paris: Adaptation of logo for NRJ Radio, 100.3 MHz.

OUÏ FM, Paris: Logo for OUÏ FM Radio, 102.3 MHz.

Parc Astérix S.A.: Cover of brochure, *Parc Astérix,* 1992. Advertisement for Parc Astérix from *Paris Vision,* 1993, p. 29.

Parc Zoologique de Paris: Cover and map from brochure, *Parc Zoologique de Paris.*

RATP: Ticket, "Section Urbaine."

RCV: La Radio Rock, Lille: Logo for RCV: La Radio Rock, 99 MHz.

Anne Vaisman: From "Je passe ma vie au téléphone" by Anne Vaisman from *Phosphore,* no. 190, February 1997. Copyright © 1997 by Bayard Presse International.

Village des Sports: Advertisement, "Village des Sports: c'est l'fun, fun, fun!," from *Région de Québec.*

PHOTOGRAPHY CREDITS

Abbreviations used: (t)top, (c) center, (b) bottom, (l) left, (r) right, (bckgd) background, (bdr) border.

CHAPTER OPENER: Background Photographs: HRW Photo by Scott Van Osdol.

TABLE OF CONTENTS: Page vii, HRW Photo/Sam Dudgeon; viii(tl), (bl), HRW Photo/Marty Granger/Edge Productions; viii(all remaining), HRW Photo/Scott Van Osdol; ix(tl), (tc), HRW Photo/Marty Granger/Edge Productions; ix(all remaining), HRW Photo/Scott Van Osdol; x(tl), (br), HRW Photo/Marty Granger/Edge Productions; x(bl), HRW Photo/Sam Dudgeon; x(all remaining), HRW Photo/Scott Van Osdol; xi(tr), (bl), HRW Photo/Marty Granger/Edge Productions; xi (bc), (br), HRW Photo/Scott Van Osdol; xi(all remaining), HRW Photo/Sam Dudgeon; xii(tl), (br), HRW Photo/Marty Granger/Edge Productions; xii(tr), (cr), (bl), HRW Photo/Sam Dudgeon; xii(all remaining), HRW Photo/Scott Van Osdol; xiii(tc),(tr), HRW Photo/Marty Granger/Edge Productions; xiii(cr), HRW Photo/Sam Dudgeon; xiii(all remaining), HRW Photo/Scott Van Osdol; xiv(tr), (bl), HRW Photo/Marty Granger/Edge Productions; xiv(all remaining), Marion Bermondy; xv(tr), HRW Photo/Louis Boireau/Edge Productions; xv (br) HRW Photo, xv(all remaining), HRW Photo; xvi(tl), (bl), HRW Photo/Marty Granger/Edge Productions; xvi(all remaining), HRW Photo/Scott Van Osdol; xvii(tc),(br), HRW Photo/Marty Granger/Edge Productions; xvii(all remaining), HRW Photo/Scott Van Osdol; xviii(tl), (br), HRW Photo/Marty Granger/Edge Productions; xviii(all remaining), HRW Photo Scott Van Osdol; xix(tr), (tl), HRW Photo/Marty Granger/Edge Productions; xix(bl), HRW Photo/Sam Dudgeon; xix(all remaining), HRW Photo/Scott Van Osdol.

PRELIMINARY CHAPTER: Page xxvi–1(tc), HRW Photo/Mark Antman; 1(bc),(tr), HRW Photo/Marty Granger/Edge Productions; 1(br), SuperStock; 2(tl), Sipa Press; 2(tr) William R. Sallaz/Duomo Photography, Inc.; 2(c), Archive Photos; 2(b), Vedat Acickalin/Sipa Press; 3(t), Gastaud/Sipa Press; 3(cl), Ron Davis/Shooting Star; 3(cr), Kathy Willens/Wide World Photos, Inc.; 3(b), Archive Photos; 4(tl), HRW Photo/Sam Dudgeon (by Victor Hugo, © Le Livre de Poche); 4(tc), Barthelemy/Sipa Press; 4(tr), Arianespace/Sipa Press; 4(cl),(c),(cr), HRW Photo/Marty Granger/Edge Productions; 4(bl), Robert Frerck/Odyssey Productions; 4(bc), David R. Frazier/David R. Frazier Photolibrary; 4(br), Derek Berwin/The Image Bank; 5(both), HRW Photo/Marty Granger/Edge Productions; 7(tl), Clay Myers/The Wildlife Collection; 7(tc), Leonard Lee Rue/FPG International, Inc.; 7(tr), (bc), Tim Laman/The Wildlife Collection; 7(bl), Jack Swenson/The Wildlife Collection; 7(br), Martin Harvey/The Wildlife Collection; 10(tl), HRW Photo/Daniel Aubry; 10(tr), HRW Photo/Ken Lax; 10(br), HRW Photo/Louis Boireau/Edge Productions; 10(bl), David Frazier PhotoLibrary; 10(all remaining), HRW Photo/Marty Granger/Edge Productions.

LOCATION: POITIERS: Page 12–13, HRW Photo/Marty Granger/Edge Productions; 14–15(bckgd), Terry Qing/FPG International, Inc.; 14(tr), Tom Craig/FPG International, Inc.; 14(cl), (br), 15 (b), Tom Craig/FPG International, 15 (all), HRW Photo/Marty Granger/Edge Productions.

Chapter One: Page 16–17(all), HRW Photo/Marty Granger/Edge Productions; 18(tcr),(tr), HRW Photo Louis Boireau/Edge Productions; 18(all remaining), 19(all), HRW Photo/Marty Granger/Edge Productions; 21(tc), HRW Photo/Sam Dudgeon; 21(br), HRW Photo/Alan Oddie; 21(all remaining), HRW Photo/Marty Granger/Edge Productions; 22(cr), HRW Photo/John Langford; 22(l), HRW Photo/Marty Granger/Edge Productions; 22(cl), HBJ Photo/Mark Antman; 22(c), HRW Photo; 22(r), IPA/The Image Works; 23–24(all), HRW Photo/Marty Granger/Edge Productions; 25(tr), Toussaint/Sipa Press; 30(all), HRW Photo/Marty Granger/Edge Productions; 34(tl), HRW Photo/Sam Dudgeon; 34(tc), HRW Photo/Marty Granger/Edge Productions; 34(tr), Robert Brenner/PhotoEdit; 34(cl), HRW Photo/David R. Frazier; 34(c), HBJ Photo/Pierre Capretz; 34(cr), Mark Antman/The Image Works; 34(bl), Lawrence Migdale/Stock Boston; 34(bc), HRW Photo/Ken Karp; 34(br), HBJ Photo/Mark Antman; 34(b), R. Lucas/The Image Works; 36(t), Frank Siteman/The Picture Cube; 36(tc), Richard Hutchings/PhotoEdit; 36(bc), David C. Bitters/The Picture Cube; 36(b), R. Lucas/The Image Works; 37(t),(b), HRW Photo/Russell Dian; 37(tc), HRW Photo/May Polycarpe; 37(bc), R. Lucas/The Image Works; 38(cl), David Young-Wolff/PhotoEdit; 38(all remaining), HRW Photo/Marty Granger/Edge Productions. **Chapter Two:** Page 42–45(all), HRW Photo/Marty Granger/Edge Productions; 56(l) HRW Photo/Louis Boireau/Edge Productions; 56(c), (r), HRW Photo/Marty Granger/Edge Productions. **Chapter Three:** Page 66–69(all), HRW Photo/Marty Granger/Edge Productions; 71(all) HRW Photo/Sam Dudgeon, 72(t), HRW Photo/Sam Dudgeon; 72 (all remaining) HRW Photo/Sam Dudgeon; 73(r) HRW Photo by Eric Beggs (l) (cl) (c) (cr) HRW Photo/Sam Dudgeon; 75(r), HRW Photo/Louis Boireau/Edge Productions; 75(l), (r), HRW Photo/Marty Granger/Edge Productions; 78(all) HRW Photo/Sam Dudgeon, 80 © European Communities; 81(all) HRW Photo/Michelle Bridwell; 84-85 HRW Photo/Sam Dudgeon; 88(all), HRW Photo/Sam Dudgeon.

LOCATION: QUEBEC: Page 90–91, J.A. Kraulis/Masterfile; 92(all), 93(ctr), (b), HRW Photo/Marty Granger/Edge Productions; 93(cl), Wolfgang Kaehler; 93(cr), Hervey Smyth, Vue de la Prise de QuÈbec, le 13 septembre 1759, Engraving, 35.9 x 47.8 cm, MusÈe du QuÈbec, 78.375, Photo by Jean-Guy KÈrouac. **Chapter Four:** Page 94–95(all), HRW Photo/Marty Granger/ Edge Productions; 96(tr), HRW Photo/Marty Granger/Edge Productions; 97(all), 99(all), HRW Photo/Marty Granger/Edge Productions; 100(tc), David Young-Wolff/PhotoEdit; 100(tr), HRW Photo/Sam Dudgeon; 100(cl), Bill Bachmann/PhotoEdit; 100(bl), David Lissy/Leo de Wys; 100(bc)HRW Photo/Marty Granger/Edge Productions, 100(br), HRW Photo; 100(all remaining), HRW Photo/Marty Granger/Edge Productions; 105(l), Robert Fried/Robert Fried Photography; 105(r), (cl), HRW Photo/Sam Dudgeon; 105(c), HBJ Photo/May Polycarpe; 105(cr), HRW Photo/Marty Granger/Edge Productions; 109(l), HRW Photo/Louis Boireau/Edge Productions; 109(r), (c), HRW Photo/Marty Granger/Edge Productions.

LOCATION: PARIS: Page 120–121, Paul Steel/The Stock Market; 122 (tr), (c), (b), HRW Photo/Marty Granger/Edge Productions; 123(bl), Peter Menzel/Stock Boston; 123 (tr), Bob Handelman/Tony Stone Images; 123(tl), (br), HRW Photo/Marty Granger/Edge Productions. **Chapter Five**: Page 124–127 (all), 134(l), (c), HRW Photo/Marty Granger/Edge Productions; 134 (r) HRW Photo/Louis Boireau/Edge Productions; 136 (tl) (tr) HRW Photos/Sam Dudgeon; 138 (cr), HRW Photo/Michelle Bridwell; 138 (all remaining) HRW Photo/Sam Dudgeon; 143 (t), (b) HRW Photo; 143 (c), Steven Mark Needham/Envision. **Chapter Six**: Page 148–149 (all), HRW Photo/Marty Granger/Edge Productions; 150 (tr), Sebastien Raymond/Sipa Press; 150–151(all remaining), HRW Photo/Marty Granger/Edge Productions; 155 (bc), David R. Frazier; 155 (tl) HRW Photo/MartyGranger, 155 (tc) (tr) (br) Marty Granger, 155 (bl) Sam Dudgeon; 156 (Row 1): (1–3), HRW Photo/Marty Granger/Edge Productions; (4), Tabuteau/The Image Works; (Row 2): (1), Jean Paul Nacivet/Leo de Wys; (2), Greg

Meadors/Stock Boston; (3–4), HRW Photo/Marty Granger/Edge Productions; (Row 3): (1), Robert Fried/Stock Boston; (2), Eva Breckmann; (3), HBJ Photo/Mark Antman; (4), R.Lucas/The Image Works; 158(l), HRW Photo/Louis Boireau/Edge Productions; 158(c),(r), HRW Photo/Marty Granger/Edge Productions; 162 (c), Ulrike Welsch/PhotoEdit; 162 (tl), HBJ Mark Antman; 162 (tr), Marty Granger/Edge Productions; 165 Marty Granger; 170 (tr), (bl), SuperStock; 170(tl), HRW Photo. **Chapter Seven**: Pages 174–175 (all), 176 (t), (cl), (cr), HRW Photo/Marty Granger/Edge Productions; 176 (b), HRW Photo/Russell Dian; 177 (b), HRW Photo/Marty Granger/Edge Productions; 177 (all remaining), HRW Photo/Edge Productions; 178, (l), (lc); HRW Photo/Russell Dian; 178 (rc), (r), HRW Photo/Edge Productions; 179 (b), HRW Photo/Russell Dian; 180 (Row 1–2(1),(2),(3)) HRW Photo/Edge Productions; 180 (Row 2), (4),(5), HRW Photo/Russel Dian; 180(Row 3): (1), HRW Photo/Edge Production; (2), HRW Photo/Marty Granger/Edge Productions; (3–5), HRW Photo/Russell Dian; 180 (Row 4): (1), Cherie Mitschke; (2), Marion Bermondy; (3), David Austen/Stock Boston; (4), John Lei/Stock Boston; 181 (l to r), HRW Photo/Daniel Aubry; David Young-Wolff/PhotoEdit; HRW Photo/May Polycarpe; Tony Freeman/PhotoEdit; HRW Photo/Sam Dudgeon; 185 (bl), Firooz Zahedi/The Kobal Collection/Paramount Studios; 185 (br), TM © 20th Century Fox Film Corp.,1992; 188 (all), HRW Photo/Marty Granger/Edge Productions; 192 (t),(b), Walter Chandoha; 192 (c), HRW Photo; 193 (t), (c), Walter Chandoha; 193 (b), Gerard Lacz/Peter Arnold, Inc.

LOCATION: ABIDJAN: Page 198–199, HRW Photo; 200 (l), John Elk III/Bruce Coleman, Inc.; 200 (tr), Nabil Zorkot/Pro Foto; 200-201 (c), Nabil Zorkot/Pro Foto; 201 (b) M.& E. Bernheim/Woodfin & Camp & Associates. **Chapter Eight:** Page 202–205 (all), HRW Photo/Louis Boireau/Edge Productions; 206 (l), HRW Photo; 206 (c), HRW Photo/Sam Dudgeon; 206 (cl), (cr), ® HRW Photo/Louis Boireau/Edge Productions; 209 Etienne Nangbo/Les images de chez nous; 211(c), HRW Photo/Louis Boireau/Edge Productions; 211(l), (r), HRW Photo/Marty Granger/Edge Productions; 216 (all), HRW Photo/Louis Boireau/Edge Productions; 217 (tl), HRW Photo/Lance Shriner; 217 (tr), HRW Photo/Louis Boireau/Edge Productions; 217 (bl), HRW Photo/Sam Dudgeon; 217 (br), HRW Photo/Eric Beggs.

LOCATION: ARLES: Page 228–229 (all), HRW Photo/Marty Granger/Edge Productions; 230 (tr), Cherie Mitschke; 230 (cr), Erich Lessing/Art Resource; 230 (bl), HRW Photo/Marty Granger/Edge Productions. Page 231 (t), W. Gontscharoff/SuperStock; 231(cl), G. Carde/ SuperStock; 231(b). **Chapter Nine**: 232–235 (all), 236 (l), (cl), (cr),HRW Photo/Marty Granger/Edge Productions; 236(r), Ermakoff/ The Image Works; 246 (all), HRW Photo/Marty Granger/Edge Productions. **Chapter Ten**: Page 256–259 (all), HRW Photo/Marty Granger/Edge Productions; 266, HRW Photo/Michelle Bridwell; 269 (l), (c), HRW Photo/Marty Granger/Edge Productions; 269 (r), HRW Photo/Louis Boireau/Edge Productions; 276 (all), 277 (l) HRW Photo/Sam Dudgeon; 277 (r), HRW Photo/Michelle Bridwell; 278 HRW Photo; 280 (l), (r), HRW Photo/Sam Dudgeon. **Chapter Eleven**: Page 282–283 (all), HRW Photo/Marty Granger/ Edge Productions; 284 (tl), HRW Photo/May Polycarpe; 284 (bcl), David Florenz/Option Photo; 284 (tr), Same Films/Edge Productions; 284(all remaining), 285–286 (all), 292 (r), HRW Photo/Marty Granger/Edge Productions; 292 (l), HRW Photo/Louis Boireau/Edge Productions; 295 (b), Pierre Jacques/FOC Photo; 297 (both), 298 (cl), HRW Photo/Marty Granger/Edge Productions; 298 (cr), Robert Fried/Stock Boston; 298 (br), J. Messerschmidt/Leo de Wys; 298 (bl), Francis De Richem/The Image Works; 298 (bc), Joachim Messer/Leo de Wys; 300 (bckgd), HRW Photo/Sam Dudgeon.

LOCATION: FORT-DE-FRANCE: Page 306–309(all), HRW Photo/Marty Granger/Edge Productions. **Chapter Twelve**: Page 310–314(all), HRW Photo/Marty Granger/Edge Productions; 315 (tl), HRW Photo; 315 (c), HBJ Photo/Pierre Capretz; 315 (cr), IPA/The Image Works; 315 (cl), HBJ Photo/Patrick Courtault; 315 (bc), Robert Fried/Stock Boston; 315 (all remaining), HRW Photo/Marty Granger/Edge Productions; 318 (tl), (br), (bc) Chris Huxley/Leo de Wys; 318 (cr), HRW Photo; 321(cl), HRW Photo/Helen Kolda; 321 (cr), HRW Photo/Sam Dudgeon (by F. Johan and N. Vogel, © CASTERMAN, Belgium); 321 (bc), HRW Photo/Russell Dian; 321(all remaining) HRW Photo/Sam Dudgeon; 322(tl), Elizabeth Zuckerman/PhotoEdit; 322(tr), Amy Etra/PhotoEdit; 322 (c), HRW Photo/Louis Boireau/Edge Productions; 322 (bc) Dean Abramson/Stock Boston; 322 (bl), Robert Rathe/Stock Boston; 322 (br) Mark Antman/The Image Works; 322 (tc), (cl), (cr), 324 (all), HRW Photo/Marty Granger/Edge Productions; 328 (tc), Chris Huxley/Leo de Wys; 328 (tl), HRW Photo/Marty Granger/Edge Productions; 330-331 (bckgd), HRW Photo/Mark Antman; 332 (l), (cl), (r), HRW Photo/Marty Granger/Edge Productions; 332 (cr), Chris Huxley/Leo de Wys.

ILLUSTRATION AND CARTOGRAPHY CREDITS

Abbreviated as follows: (t) top, (b) bottom, (l) left, (r) right, (c) center.

All art, unless otherwise noted, by Holt, Rinehart and Winston.

PRELIMINARY CHAPTER: Page i, Holly Cooper; vi, Holly Cooper; ix, Holly Cooper; xiii, Holly Cooper; xviii, Holly Cooper; xxi, GeoSystems; xxii, GeoSystems; xxiii, GeoSystems.

LOCATION: POITIERS
Chapter One: Page 6, Bruce Roberts; 9, Ellen Beier; 11, Jocelyne Bouchard; 13, GeoSystems; 22, Vincent Rio; 23, Jocelyne Bouchard; 26, Jocelyne Bouchard; 27, Yves Larvor; 28, Camille Meyer; 29, Yves Larvor; 31, Yves Larvor; 33, Vincent Rio; 40, Yves Larvor. **Chapter Two:** Page 47, Yves Larvor; 48 (t), Bruce Roberts; 48 (b), Brian Stevens; 50, Bruce Roberts; 52, Pascal Garnier; 54, Keith Petrus; 55, Guy Maestracci; 58, Brian Stevens; 64, Bruce Roberts. **Chapter Three:** Page 71, Yves Larvor; 72, Vincent Rio; 73, Michel Loppé; 74, Brian Stevens; 76, Brian Stevens; 79, Vincent Rio; 81, Michel Loppé; 82, Jean-Pierre Foissy; 83, Michel Loppé; 88, Bruce Roberts.

LOCATION: QUEBEC
Chapter Four: Page 91, GeoSystems; 101, Michel Loppé; 102, Jocelyne Bouchard; 103, Yves Larvor; 105, Jocelyne Bouchard; 106, Brian Stevens; 107, Jocelyne Bouchard; 108, Michel Loppé; 118, Jocelyne Bouchard.

LOCATION: PARIS
Chapter Five: Page 121, GeoSystems; 129, Andrew Bylo; 130, Vincent Rio; 131, Jocelyne Bouchard; 132, Vincent Rio; 133, Camille Meyer; 139, Guy Maestracci; 140, Jean-Pierre Foissy; 146, Yves Larvor. **Chapter Six:** Page 155, Jocelyne Bouchard; 157 (c), Guy Maestracci; 157 (t), Yves Larvor; 159, Jean-Pierre Foissy; 160, Brian Stevens; 161, Jean-Pierre Foissy; 163, Jean-Pierre Foissy; 164, Jocelyne Bouchard; 172 (t), Jocelyne Bouchard, 172 (b), Guy Maestracci. Chapter Seven: Page 179, Vincent Rio; 182 (cr), Guy Maestracci; 182 (b), Jocelyne Bouchard; 183, Vincent Rio; 184, Pascal Garnier; 185, Brian Stevens; 186, Jean-Pierre Foissy; 187,

Vincent Rio; 189 (br), Guy Maestracci; 189 (tr), Pascal Garnier; 190 (t), Vincent Rio; 190 (b), Pascal Garnier; 195, Guy Maestracci; 196, Pascal Garnier.

LOCATION: ABIDJAN

Chapter Eight: Page 199, GeoSystems; 207, Yves Larvor; 208, Camille Meyer; 209, George Kimani; 212, Andrew Bylo; 214, Yves Larvor; 218 (t), Michel Loppé; 218 (b), Jocelyne Bouchard; 219, Michel Loppé; 220 (bl), George Kimani; 220 (tr), Jocelyne Bouchard; 226, Yves Larvor.

LOCATION: ARLES

Chapter Nine: Page 229, GeoSystems; 237, Jean-Pierre Foissy; 238, Jean-Pierre Foissy; 239, Camille Meyer; 241, Guy Maestracci; 242, Jocelyne Bouchard; 243, Michel Loppé; 245, Andrew Bylo; 248, Brian Stevens; 254; Jocelyne Bouchard. **Chapter Ten:** Page 261, Jocelyne Bouchard; 262 (c), Michel Loppé; 262 (t), Yves Larvor; 263, Vincent Rio; 264, Jean-Pierre Foissy; 265, Jean-Pierre Foissy; 268 (t), Brian Stevens; 268 (c), Jocelyne Bouchard; 270, Jean-Pierre Foissy; 271, Michel Loppé; 272, Guy Maestracci; 274, Jean-Pierre Foissy; 280, Yves Larvor. **Chapter Eleven:** Page 287 (c), Brian Stevens; 287 (b), Russell Moore; 288, Guy Maestracci; 289, Camille Meyer; 291, Bruce Roberts; 293, Michel Loppé; 294, Yves Larvor; 296, Jean-Pierre Foissy; 304, Yves Larvor.

LOCATION: FORT-DE-FRANCE

Chapter Twelve: Page 307, GeoSystems; 317, Anne de Masson; 319, Anne de Masson; 320, Anne de Masson; 321, Jean-Pierre Foissy; 323, Brian Stevens; 325, Anne Stanley; 326, Anne de Masson; 327, Anne de Masson; 328, Anne Stanley; 332, Anne de Masson; 334, Anne de Masson.